The Selected Letters of Elia Kazan

THE
SELECTED
LETTERS OF
ELIA KAZAN

Edited by Albert J. Devlin
with Marlene J. Devlin

Alfred A. Knopf, New York 2014

THIS IS A BORZOI BOOK PUBLISHED BY ALFRED A. KNOPF

Copyright © 2014 by Frances Kazan

Introduction and annotations copyright © 2014 by Albert J. Devlin

All rights reserved. Published in the United States by Alfred A. Knopf, a division of
Random House LLC, New York, and in Canada by Random House of Canada Limited, Toronto,
Penguin Random House companies.

www.aaknopf.com

Knopf, Borzoi Books, and the colophon are registered trademarks of Random House LLC.

Library of Congress Cataloging-in-Publication Data
Kazan, Elia.
[Correspondence. Selections]
The selected letters of Elia Kazan / edited by Albert J. Devlin with Marlene J. Devlin.—
First edition.
pages cm
Includes index.
ISBN 978-0-307-26716-0 (hardcover)—ISBN 978-0-385-35041-9 (ebook)
1. Kazan, Elia—Correspondence.   2. Theatrical producers and directors—United States—
Correspondence.   3. Motion picture producers and directors—United States—
Correspondence.   I. Devlin, Albert J., editor of compilation.   II. Devlin, Marlene J.,
editor of compilation.   III. Title.
PN1998.3.K39A3 2014
791.4302'32092—dc23
[B]   2013044122

Book design by Iris Weinstein

Jacket photograph © Harry Harris/AP
Jacket design by Carol Devine Carson

Manufactured in the United States of America
First Edition

CONTENTS

INTRODUCTION

Letters are a pure form of autobiography. Those written by Elia Kazan and selected for publication begin in 1925 with an adolescent complaint of paternal authority and conclude sixty-odd years later with a father's reaffirmation of love for his five children. The intervening letters tell the story of an actor-director who trained in the Group Theatre, brought artistic rigor to Broadway, collaborated with major writers, testified as a former communist before the House Committee on Un-American Activities, inspired a generation of young actors, filmed challenging subjects in remote locations, and codirected the new Repertory Theatre of Lincoln Center. In later years he traveled widely and became a best-selling novelist. Elia often thanked correspondents for their "fine" letters and saved them all, or so it seems, including youthful scraps of correspondence from his children. He lacked the rare, extemporaneous gift for language possessed by his friend, collaborator, and frequent correspondent Tennessee Williams. But as one might expect, Kazan was diligent. Lengthy, detailed business letters were often typed on yellow paper, scrupulously edited, and retyped by a secretary, whose command of spelling and punctuation far exceeded Kazan's. Personal and family letters retain the engaging eccentricities of darting, digressive thought, convoluted syntax, rich colloquial diction, pungent humor, the occasional sharp image, and in the case of his correspondence with Molly Day Thacher, his first wife, a searing intensity of self-disclosure.

Elia Kazan was born in Constantinople in 1909, his brother Avraam nearly three years later in Berlin, where his father worked briefly for a carpet business founded by his older brother. An Anatolian Greek, George Kazanjioglou knew the fate of minority populations in wartime and wisely brought his family to the United States in 1913. Two sons (George and John) born in America completed the immediate family. George and Athena, their name shortened by convention to Kazan, settled on Riverside Drive in New York City before moving to New Rochelle in 1919. Elia's shyness, bookish inclination, and strong aversion to commerce strained father-son relations and gave rise to a conspiratorial bond with Athena, who challenged "eldest-son tradition" by arranging for Elia to enter college rather than the Kazan Carpet

Company in mid-Manhattan. Her indispensable ally was Anna Shank, Elia's former eighth-grade teacher and first known correspondent. After graduation from Williams College in 1930, Kazan enrolled in the Yale School of Fine Arts and studied under George Pierce Baker in the new drama department. His attraction to the theater was not "accidental," as he claimed at one point, but the outcome of "a great thirst for knowledge" shared by Harold Clurman and Lee Strasberg, directors of the Group Theatre, who, if they did not immediately welcome Kazan as an apprentice in 1932 or encourage his desire to act, recognized the energy and backstage skills he brought to the enterprise. Their intention to found a theater free of dramatic tricks and embroiled in contemporary American life enlisted Kazan for nearly a decade. Clurman's messianic pronouncements shaped his conception of theater as a high calling, while Strasberg's imperious control of production informed the stylized, intensely acted Broadway shows for which Kazan became famous.

No event had a more profound or enduring effect on Elia than his marriage to Molly Day Thacher in 1932. She was, as he wrote in long retrospect, "the reassuring symbol that the very heart of America, which my family had come here to find, had accepted me" (*A Life*, p. 569).

The outer shape of Kazan's career is evident in correspondence with authors, actors, agents, producers, directors, designers, and reviewers with whom he routinely interacted. Correspondence with Darryl Zanuck and Jack Warner, legendary "monsters" who ruled the studio system at Twentieth Century-Fox and Warner Bros., is especially vivid and indicative of the bicoastal fame Kazan had achieved by the end of the 1940s. The inner story of his career is more subtly distilled in *The Selected Letters*. Persistence, self-confidence, and a remarkable fund of energy drew charges of undue ambition but formed the bedrock of Kazan's determination to be "A SINCERE, CONSCIOUS, PRACTISING ARTIST." This declaration was made in a letter to Cheryl Crawford, a director of the Group Theatre, in 1935, when Kazan had few if any artistic bona fides to claim. It may seem brash, pompous, or even affected when quoted in bold relief, but no statement in letters resounds through each phase of Kazan's career with more force or integrity. One looks in vain in the correspondence for extended discussion of art, literature, politics, history, or religion—notwithstanding Kazan's love of reading and education at Williams, when a bachelor's degree in the liberal arts was still concentrated in philosophy, the classics, and study of language. Kazan's subject in correspondence is invariably the self in search of artistic fulfillment. Its realization placed the stage and film director in relation with leading artists of pre- and postwar America and with a culture whose robust economy and far-ranging international prominence in the 1950s was oddly conjoined with political and moral contraction at home.

Kazan's letter of artistic intent carried with it an equally brash, all encompassing program designed to make a director of the disappointing actor. Kazan's potential in that regard had drawn an early judgment of "no actor's emotion" by the directors and assignment to the "onerous job" of stage manager. Kazan went on to play significant roles in later Group productions, but by 1935 his stronger attraction was to stage direction. Any sense of the transition as merely expeditious is incompatible with Kazan's earnest commitment to attaining the "Raw Materials of the Director." The "production-ideas" of a director, he wrote to Cheryl Crawford, were not limited to scripts, nor did they "leap from deep and dark inspiration." Their source was "the experience of the artist—what he's felt, known, remembers—in short, experienced." Kazan would "orientate" himself to the world by frequent travel, especially to the South, a laboratory for social scientists in the 1930s, and in the meantime by amassing illustrative "'junk,'" including "photographs, clippings, notes, plans, books, etc. etc." His directorial notes—elaborate, detailed, and incisive—add to the experiential base the imperative of intensive preparation for each assignment. From this fund of experience and "conscious," that is, deliberate, planning, Kazan began the period of his major work in 1942 with Thornton Wilder's serious comedy, *The Skin of Our Teeth*. By decade's end, he had directed Fredric March, Tallulah Bankhead, Helen Hayes, Mary Martin, Jessica Tandy, Marlon Brando, and Lee J. Cobb, among others, in fourteen plays, won Tony Awards for his direction of *All My Sons* and *Death of a Salesman,* in close relationship with Arthur Miller, and helped deliver a Pulitzer Prize to Tennessee Williams for *A Streetcar Named Desire.* With the release of *Gentleman's Agreement* in 1947, Kazan won his first Oscar for direction and renegotiated a contract with Twentieth Century-Fox that gave long-term financial security. And he had founded, with Cheryl Crawford and Bobby Lewis, the influential Actors Studio.

The Anatolian who lingered in Elia Kazan was trained by heritage and a saturnine father to expect "bad news rather than good," especially following great success, and was not surprised by a summons received in late 1951 to testify before the House Committee on Un-American Activities. As both a former Communist Party member and award-winning director, Kazan was a prized target for congressmen investigating subversive activity in the motion picture industry. The first wave of hearings in late 1947 had strong political resonance in postwar America and convinced studio executives that cooperation was no longer optional. Alleged communists and fellow travelers were exposed to the enhanced power of the congressional subpoena and the industry-wide blacklist. Renewed hearings in 1951 found Kazan a vulnerable headliner. His naming of former Communist Party members of the Group Theatre in the spring of Terry Malloy. Not only was film a director's medium, but it also seemed closer than theater to the social reality that Kazan craved in the 1930s and found brilliantly expressed in John Ford's classic direction of *The Grapes of Wrath* (1940). A near majority of his own films, including *Viva Zapata!, Man on a Tightrope, On the Waterfront, Wild River,* and especially *America America,* have documentary scale and hold the daunting challenge of incorporating personal stories as intimate as the director's own family history. The films, whose subjects were not in the mainstream of popular cinema, made a bold, self-motivated director of Kazan, who arrived in Hollywood to see the end of the studio system and play a critical role in expanding both the freedom of the director and the range of film.

Elia's correspondence with Molly Day Thacher is relatively limited but the most intense and revealing in *The Selected Letters*. Molly, Elia's wife of thirty-one years, was born in 1906 and raised in a comfortable setting in South Orange, New Jersey, the daughter of a corporation attorney. She graduated from Vassar in 1928 with a devotion to the theater, if not film, and much the same artistic desire as her future husband. They produced four children of whom they were exceedingly proud. Molly's desire to write for the theater was realized in 1957 with a major Broadway production of *The Egghead,* a probing, if untimely, foray into Cold War politics, which closed after a brief run. Her critical intelligence was formidable, as correspondence and other documents held by Wesleyan University make clear. Elia married against the Anatolian grain by choosing a woman whose social antecedents and artistic inclinations bore little if any relation to the marital culture in which he was raised. Molly set aside the norms of her own society to marry "a boy without train fare, with no visible talent," whose "violence and anger" were not easily tolerated. In marriage she became Elia's "partisan," his adviser and confidant, for the next thirty years (*A Life,* p. 96). Their "profoundest differences" of moral values and temperament were reflected in Elia's infidelities, which brought the marriage twice to the point of divorce. Letters written by Elia during each crisis remove any imputation of unawareness or deceit by virtue of their immediacy and painful self-disclosure. Nothing between husband and wife is withheld or unsaid. No aspect of character or behavior dismissed. No difficulty of renewing love or achieving reconciliation underestimated.

It is only coincidental that *The Selected Letters* ends in 1988, the same year that saw the publication of *A Life,* Elia Kazan's acclaimed autobiography. The thinning of Kazan's later correspondence was the determining factor, but a final juxtaposition of letters and memoir is not without point or advantage to each. In fact they comport unusually well with each other. Only rarely in Kazan's correspondence is there evidence that events have been rearranged in

A Life for dramatic effect or altered to support a later point of view. There a mature writer—though no Prospero gentled by time—recalls the tumultuous events of six decades, determined to explain his overflowing life in stark detail and at the same time meet the formalizing needs of a far-ranging chronicle. *The Selected Letters* has a still wider range of perspective governed by the original pace of events and the fresh emotions that accompanied them. In effect, letters cut exceedingly close to the bone of experience and provide an indispensable point of departure for understanding Elia Kazan's unique contribution to mid-twentieth-century American culture.

EDITORIAL NOTE

A far-ranging search has identified some twelve hundred letters, notes, and telegrams written by Elia Kazan, from which nearly three hundred have been selected for publication.

Recipient, place of composition, and date are identified in each letter's heading. If available, postmarked envelopes (marked PM) are cited to identify place and/or date for letters lacking such authorial detail. Institutional stationery (hotels, ships, firms, etc.) used by Kazan is marked SH (stationery headed). Bracketed elements in the heading indicate an editorial intervention. A statement of provenance, using standard bibliographical abbreviations, follows each letter's annotation.

The published letters have been transcribed from photographic facsimiles, the majority preserved by Kazan, a tireless collector. Unduly long, repetitive, highly technical, or digressive elements were edited in a very limited number of cases to meet publication standards or guard the privacy of the living. The editor's deletions are identified by ellipses. To avoid confusion, Kazan's own ellipses, used rarely and only as informal punctuation, have been replaced by the long dash. Kazan's spelling errors have been silently corrected—including the persistent misspelling of "marraige." In some cases the misspelling of a given word is not consistent. In others the misspelling is highly repetitive, the great majority falling into familiar categories: doubling of consonants, ordering diphthongs, mistakes in the formation of plurals and possessives, as well as misspellings of proper nouns. Alternate and British spellings have been retained, as has Kazan's distinctive syntax, capitalization, and punctuation, including asterisks used occasionally to mark a change of subject, organization, or the passage of time. In rare cases the editor has added, in brackets, an obvious function word omitted by Kazan. A fair number of the surface errors can be attributed to hasty typing and limited skills. Salutations and closings, in some cases omitted by Kazan, are often revealing and have been preserved.

The editorial annotations following each letter are designed to locate Kazan in a specific time and place, to build context for his personal relations and professional career, and to identify references that may be unfamiliar to a contemporary reader. Film and theater projects, as well as published texts, are dated in their first appearance and thereafter, as context and clarity require. Working or provisional titles are placed within quotation marks, while the titles of performed, filmed, or published works are italicized. Particular attention has been given to cases involving censorship, the development of film and theater projects, and relations with distinguished collaborators, especially those concerning the revision of dramatic texts. To avoid editorial distraction or intrusion, annotations are placed after the letters. Insofar as possible, each annotation is designed to follow the letter's internal order of composition. Often Kazan provides all the context or explanation needed by a reader who is intent on immersion in the text. In other cases the editor has consulted a wide variety of primary sources, including letters not selected for publication, Kazan's incoming correspondence, especially Molly Kazan's astute, moving letters, directorial notes, and journal entries. Secondary material drawn from critical and scholarly sources has also contributed to the annotations. The reader who wishes to consult these sources in more detail is referred to the Key to Citations and the Key to Collections.

Two basic principles have guided the selection of letters: range and importance. As it turns out, they are inseparable. More than one hundred correspondents are represented in the letters chosen for publication, including such distinguished collaborators as Arthur Miller, Tennessee Williams, John Steinbeck, and Budd Schulberg. Kazan's early involvement in the Group Theatre also established lifelong relationships with Harold Clurman, Lee Strasberg, and Cheryl Crawford, founders of the Group, who inspired, challenged, and nurtured the future director of *Death of a Salesman* and *A Streetcar Named Desire*. Correspondence with Darryl Zanuck and Jack Warner records a second career, in film, that began formally in 1945 and placed Kazan in the forefront of cinematic innovation for the next two decades. His correspondence with Budd Schulberg adds a new dimension to the collaborative dynamics of directing *On the Waterfront* and enlisting Marlon Brando in a project that he initially rejected. Letters dealing with *America America,* the most personal of Kazan's films, provide an object lesson in determination and the pursuit of artistic independence. The later correspondence reveals a less public Kazan, whose career as a writer culminates in 1988 with the publication of a massive autobiography. Letters to his family, especially his first wife, Molly Day Thacher, add a domestic rhythm of considerable intensity to the professional career.

ABBREVIATIONS

ALS	Autograph letter signed
DFZ	Darryl F. Zanuck
EK	Elia Kazan
HRC	Harry Ransom Center
HTC	Harvard Theatre Collection
HUAC	House Committee on Un-American Activities
JLW	Jack L. Warner
JS	John Steinbeck
MDT	Molly Day Thacher
PCA	Production Code Administration
NYHT	*New York Herald Tribune*
NYT	*New York Times*
NYTBR	*New York Times Book Review*
PM	postmarked
SH	stationery headed
TL	typed letter unsigned
TLd	typed letter draft
TLS	typed letter signed
TLSx	typed letter signed copy
TLx	typed letter copy
TW	Tennessee Williams

Elia Kazan as Agate Keller in the March 1935 production of *Waiting for Lefty*

Part I

Beginnings

1925–1941

TO ANNA B. SHANK

731 Webster Ave
New Rochelle [New York]
July 17, 1925

Dear Miss Shank,

I received your card yesterday and I was very pleased to hear from you. I think you might be interested in my marks this year, although as a whole they were very poor. The only really encouraging mark I received was in Latin which I had given up as hopeless up until the week of the examination, when I made up my mind to pass it and I did although it was only 67%. The rest were but mediocre marks.

I am now working in New York in my father's office, getting a measly $12 a week which my father seems to think is enough for me. Perhaps he is right. I really don't do the work of a man yet.

You spoke of my ford in your card, a subject which is an unpleasant one for me now. I had paid eight dollars for it and after three days in my possession it was struck by a calamity. At night I kept the car in a neighboring vacant lot. One bright Sunday morning I found it in a condition hard to describe. Everything on it that was worth anything had been taken off during the night. I probably couldn't have received a dollar for it as "junk". Now it lies in the lot, just so much iron. It is true Bill Fenton and I were coming to see you in the ford but now I think it is impossible as my father won't let me buy another.

Fritz also has a ford and I am going on a trip with him the later part of the summer. Perhaps on the way back we will pass through Auburn. Anyway don't be surprised if you see us some day.

I think that is about all I can say. At present I am trying to save enough money for the trip from my salary. I will probably stop working in two weeks and rest till school.

You might be pleased to learn that I am going to Williams College. I filled out the application today. I will certainly write again.

Sincerely yours, Elia Kazan

["Mediocre marks" at New Rochelle High School, a pillaged "ford," and menial work at the Kazan Carpet Company in New York City form a litany of complaints in Elia Kazan's first known letter. Miss Anna B. Shank, Elia's former eighth-grade teacher, probably leavened many similar tales of misfortune during Elia's high school years. No doubt she was pleasantly surprised when Elia and Frederick "Fritz" Frost, a popular classmate who went on to study at Princeton, visited later in the summer. However sympathetic, she could not buffer Elia's forthcoming senior year. "Eli" joined the Dramatic Club and served on the play committee, with attention to business and tickets, but their shy classmate was "so backward

3

in coming forward" that the editors of the *Rochellean* (class of 1926) settled on his birth in Constantinople and unruly black hair as distinguishing features. Many years later Kazan annotated his yearbook portrait, "in one word, <u>frightened</u>" (Wesleyan).

Miss Shank added a poignant classroom scene to renewed correspondence with Elia in 1940: "The light from the window fell across you, seeming to touch off the head and the features and the expression that came upon your face—an unexpressed thought came to me of the great possibilities that there were in your development" (March 7, 1940, Wesleyan). Athena, Elia's mother, and Miss Shank, a co-conspirator, nurtured such promise by arranging for Elia to enter Williams College in 1926 rather than the family business. Told of the admission, George Kazan struck his wife, who arose unhurt and "triumphant," or so Elia claimed: "When you're hit this way, it's a tremendous relief; you've found that it doesn't hurt as much as you feared. And you're never again quite as afraid of that person" (*A Life,* pp. 30-31).] *ALS, 7 pp. Wesleyan*

TO LEONARD BARRON HARRIS

731 Webster Ave
New Rochelle, New York
[summer 1931]

Dear Barron:

Are you trying to establish coldness between us? Poor Theophilactos after making persevering efforts—efforts which were deserving of a kinder reward—to bring the three of us together, around a supper table at my own special request, had to report not only failure but a certain hauteur on your part which lends itself only too readily to misinterpretation from people as sensitive as I have grown to be.

At the time I was deeply mortified at your peccancy. Now, somewhat calmer I am grieved. After ten days I am able to write to you.

The year since our happier days in the Berkshires—I think them singularly loaded with joy today—has deposited a fine silt of disappointment in my heart and left my faculties unreplenished. Face to face with the serious life as it is to be lived by us all, at last, I find that temperamentally I am not

With Alan Baxter, his closest friend at Williams, 1930

fitted. I am striving this summer to retrench myself in more sober outlook, one that the world of rewards and punishments will find more to its tastes—one which will finally bring me into my own temporal possessions. It is a task of smelting, steeling and refining and then finally of pouring the finished metal, perfectly pure at length, into a mould which I could wish eternal. For six weeks I worked amid surroundings which afforded to the view neither horizon nor oasis. For the six weeks my pay came to five dollars.

Now I am at home reliving the great torture of Descartes. This is the last request I shall make for your company. It is not proud nor arrogant. Can we simply meet? Please communicate with Polyzoides of our mutual acquaintance and ask him to forward what you two arrange to your new friend—

Elia Kazan.

Jan 1932 take warning!

[Leonard Barron Harris and Theophilactos Achilles Polyzoides entered "the serious life" of law and banking after graduating from Williams College in 1930. Their classmate's ornate prose and liberal arts degree were on display a year later in a wistful reference to the "Berkshires" and the impermanence of youthful "joy." Kazan chose the Yale School of Fine Arts as "a kind of detention area" to evade the family business and decide what he wanted to do: "My goal in life was a simple one: to make a living doing something I enjoyed doing. I had no nobler ambition" (*A Life*, p. 47). Elia spent the summer of 1931 in Atlantic City organizing shows for the Toy Theatre before returning to the family in New Rochelle. There he suffered "the great torture of Descartes" and other early vivisectionists who thought animals immune to pain. Elia was relieved no doubt by a recent letter from George Pierce Baker, former director of Harvard's 47 Workshop and current head of the Yale Drama Department, stating that he had been "readmitted" for a second academic year (June 22, 1931, Wesleyan).] *TLS, 1 p., Wesleyan*

TO MOLLY DAY THACHER

[Dover Furnace, New York]
[summer 1932]

Where's Molly? that was a first name of a character in a new play which I will not send out under my name no matter. Plans and ideas are—all a-fluff. Owe money here and intentionally backward with my rent to impress on someone that I have no money. No one notices it. But it works both ways for me. Either no rent or sympathy in money matters. I don't care. I'm slowly catching on to the acting and I know how I mishandle an emotion. I do what they call 'act the result'. That is I intellectualize how I should be in the emotion (ex. head thrust forward in threatening) and despite the fact that I have the real emotion I try to enlarge it, or make it "more interesting" or more compelling by adding what I can to it by my will. What I do is simulate the result of the emotion, that I should experience and show only in the thing I'm doing without the push of the will. Its overacting, pushing. I haven't enough faith in the fact that I am projecting something without straining. Therefore the fault. Helburn up probably in the middle of August or a little after. I don't know just when. I'll have to hang around and talk with her. Later go off with her to where they're rehearsing the Guild show. I think somewhere on the road. Then there's the season in N.Y. and the regular Guild suburbs unless the Group does a show in which they need a lot of men extras, or a lot of men. In that event they'll tell me to give the Guild two weeks notice. Which I'll do. Against everybody's advice. What I think about marriage is nothing. Anybody that wants to make a fuss about it can go ahead. But I wont be party or witness to it. I don't care how many filmy night gowns you get as long as you don't wear them in bed. We can get married anywhere where we are soon. I'm not going to tell my family till after its happened. It will be their burden of adjustment then not mine. Otherwise I'd have to do a lot of arguing with them about expediency and why don't you wait, with which I'll have no truck. (Last breath of this) I wont take the ineluctable modality (J. Joyce) at anybody's valuation except my own. Neither will you. Geezuz! eh?

Clurman calls me Gadget now. Lee still nods stiffly. Crawford hardly speaks. Barber thinks I gossip too much. Sykes thinks that I'm going thru a period of self questioning. Russell Collins the great Cleveland actor suddenly popped up fairy the other night, kissed me three times on the hand, once on the brow, once on the neck. Why didn't I shrink. He's a baby. They gave him Franchot's part in the PARTY to do. He was matinee idol for nine years at the PLAYHOUSE and all the time wore a wig. (Made out of his own hair.) Franchot and I and a couple of silly girl apprentices are going out to supper tonight for a change. I think I'll go money or no money. Maybe I won't go to make an impression. If they'd take me into the Group I'd stop trying to impress them of a lot of things and be a much better guy. I may not get up to Blue etc. at all. I really can't afford it from their point of view. That should make you sore. Some week end I'll come up. I don't know when. Barber offered to lend me eighty dollars which I need to finish the summer. I don't know whether to take it or go beg them to let me off. But you see I'm trying to impress them that I'm broke. I don't want to borrow any more money from anybody, including you. The whistle for dancing. Good luck with your play.

I just read your letter with the ground plan on the envelope. I was shaken up by it. Sometimes I love you very much. Other times I'm confused and unsteady in a way I think no one can remedy or aid. Maybe you can. Life is to be taken carelessly. I love you this aft.

In a body movement class during the 1932 Group retreat at Dover Furnace.
(Kazan is second row, center.)

[Founded by Harold Clurman, Cheryl Crawford, and Lee Strasberg in 1931, the Group Theatre was a daring experiment in ensemble production that challenged the commercial tenets of Broadway for nearly a decade. Elia learned of the Group from friends and teachers at Yale and saw the inaugural production of *The House of Connelly* with Molly Day Thacher in late 1931. She continued to write and study at Yale after graduating from Vassar in 1928—an early member of Hallie Flanagan's Experimental Theatre class. Elia joined the Group as an apprentice in mid-1932 and attended the second annual retreat at Dover Furnace, New York, where he probably acquired the nickname "Gadget" for his untiring labor and backstage skills. At the same time a report of "'no actor's emotion'" cast doubt on his potential for membership. The retreat gathered some thirty actors for classes in voice, movement, and improvisational work, distilled by Harold Clurman's "fervent" lectures on the collective art of theater: "We must help one another find our common ground; we must build our house on it, arrange it as a dwelling place for the whole family of decent humanity" (Clurman, p. 30). From this ideal arose a need for acting and direction that departed from the "'petty realism'" of Broadway. It remained for Lee Strasberg to develop a unified technique designed to bring real life to the stage. The Stanislavsky system at work in productions of the Moscow Art Theatre, observed by Strasberg in 1923, provided an artistic language and became a vital, if finally controversial, guide in preparing the actor to project life experience rather than fabricate it. As an antidote to external "'indicating,'" Kazan kept a notebook of emotions derived from the "method" (Smith, p. 101).

Philip Barber, playwright, Yale professor, and associate member of the Group, recommended Kazan and Alan Baxter, Elia's closest friend at Williams, to the rather indifferent directors. Another playwright, Gerald Sykes, did not spare Kazan or the membership his penchant for offhand analysis. The disruptive behavior of Franchot Tone, whom Strasberg regarded as the company's best actor, bespoke dissatisfaction and a forthcoming decision to leave the Group Theatre for a career in film.

Apropos of marriage, Elia recalled for his daughter Judy an unpromising first impression by Molly: "I was a dish washer when I went to Yale. Your mother first saw me serving hash from a hot box and took an instant dislike to me." By late 1931 he had replaced Alan Baxter in Molly's affections. They became lovers in the spring, later in the summer Molly terminated a pregnancy, and on December 2, 1932, they married in full knowledge, if not the full presence, of each family. Kazan was denied Group membership for the time being and worked briefly as an assistant stage manager for the Theatre Guild, co-managed by Theresa Helburn and Lawrence Langner, from which the Group had evolved.

The "whistle" called Kazan to a class in dance or body movement overseen by Helen Tamiris.] *TL, 1 p., Wesleyan*

TO MOLLY DAY THACHER

PM: Warrensburg, New York, August 1, 1933

Dearest Molly:

I feel sentimental. Almost by way of apology for writing this way. We've just put on the revue which was a big hit, the best thing they've ever seen up this way. Everybody is excited and free and talking incoherently. They're all up in the canteen waiting for Luther Adler's wife, and listening to Alan explaining

Molly Day Thacher enters the family: John (Elia's youngest brother),
Elia, Athena, Molly, and George Kazan

to Cheryl what he learned from this last revue. Cheryl is very happy. More noticeably so than the other directors. She loves to put on a hit. She's telling Alan she can sure sell his skit to Max Gordon. Success Psychology is flushed on everybody. I'm standing up typing this because I've got a tired cramp in my arm. Art and Degen have retired for the night, Art a hero and Degen drooling incoherently all over him. Helen is sulking because she's not a heroine and because she flubbed a song and because she went conscious on an announcement. Gerald is calmly, intently assuring her that she was the best in a certain sketch. Bob and Margery Hyder the dancer are out walking together. Sachez Patten is lonely, jealous of Alan with Beanie. Harold is nuzzling into Helen Shay's neck, and looking around to see who's watching. Lee and Paula have gone with Walter Coy to meet Luther Adler. Joe Bromberg's wife Goldie has gone home but he is happy because Florence Gitlin a communist school teacher is up. If they suddenly found themselves with nothing to do, they'd have an affair. Ruth Nelson and Ben Challee are out dancing with the jews on the floor. Beanie is torturing Alan; Alan is droopily caressing her in public, as though he couldn't keep his hands off her, but didn't know how to caress an object such as an arm, or a shoulder. Cliff is giving some girl a break, it doesn't matter who and besides————, the Russian dancer is singing like a little bird in his heart. Julian and Eunice Stoddard are out discussing how wonderful it is that the Greek Florist's household they visited last winter treated them just as if they were in the same class.

I'm sitting on stage and feel its time to get dead serious and maybe a little grandiose. Everybody is happy, I'm uneasy. They think I'm moping about you. That was earlier in the evening. I was very rebellious suddenly and left the cafeteria. Nothing is done and there is no cue for a lot of personal sentimental indulgence. I'm tired and a little dizzy, but I'm sore as hell. The whole goddamn camp has the same sort of success psychology. They're all the same, week after week, happy, contented, wealthy, successful, proud, and the world is a whirl of shit in a pile of bombast. I've got funny ideas tonight of a totally different sort of life. I mean different as it runs from day to day. The actual content would be different. The days wouldn't be rosy and they wouldn't be sad. But something about them would be full the way nothing is full now. I don't mean I want to do what I want to do and I don't mean I want a lot of sensations. But I don't want what I'm getting now, which is doing one thing and always wishing to God that it was something else and also that I were somewhere else and always a pressing sensation that I'm being deceived, that there is something else. Its like a starving man, who's got a huge, strong meal all ready and waiting and the damn fool plays ping-pong instead of rushing into the meat course. Am I crazy or what. I asked Max why he thought Sykes hung around the Group Theatre for Chrissake, and he said its because he's timid. What am I?

Molly, I'm very susceptible. Cheryl put her arm around my shoulder tonight (and I was sort of tired); I almost cried and sex has nothing to [do] with it. Maybe if you had done it, I wouldn't have liked it. You're the only person I've ever known that I've liked that much, or that way—so that, I should always want to face reality only with you and always apologize for bull-shit or weakness in any connection with you.

I feel funny tonight. (Ha, ha) Grandiose and sort of impotent. Slightly self-pitying but better than I used to be. Determined more than angry. Scornful and not jealous of anybody in the world. I used to be jealous of a lot of successful people. It may be just an inverted defense, but I'm on the dry ground.

The night watchman's in. He's a pal, but "settin" to talk my head off. What a letter.

I was going to write you a lot about what's wrong with the Group Theatre and how they are what they are, speaking in terms of personnel and they'll damn well have to change their personnel. Also what I feel grandiose about was a sort of Theatrical heat I was in. This putting [on] Uncle Seagull, and Ten Nights, and skits by Alan Baxter is like making mud-pies and is not for me.

I could be very articulate. I'm taking up a sort of dramatic writing in a day or two, I'm going to jump into dialogue.

[Molly Kazan spent the summer of 1933 in Mexico City writing a play, while Elia toiled with the Group Theatre at Green Mansions, a resort in New York State. The third annual retreat followed a season that saw Group productions criticized for harsh treatment of American social and economic institutions. *Success Story* (John Howard Lawson) was nursed into a respectable run, while *Big Night* (Dawn Powell) closed after seven performances and left the Group penniless. Franchot Tone's departure for Hollywood added a demoralizing note to the new year. The directors briefly considered moving to Boston, or Chicago, where the competition of Broadway would be relaxed and the prospect of fund-raising improved. The allure of communism, evident at Dover Furnace, was intensified in 1933 as the Depression hardened and several Group members (not yet Kazan) joined the party. They and others became involved in New York's radical theater—as did Elia and Molly (Smith, pp. 119–27).

Kazan remained in touch with Harold Clurman and Clifford Odets through the previous season and reappeared at Green Mansions, his status with the group still uncertain and mood unstable. From a director's perch "on stage," he saw a vanity fair of personal foibles, self-indulgence, and brief sexual alliances that bore little resemblance to the Group ideal espoused by Clurman. The "success psychology" was also an ironic reversal of the preceding season, when disgruntled actors held the directors accountable for a lack of scripts, business blunders, and the failure of the Group's latest production. An elected Actors Committee was in the offing. Kazan and Alan Baxter were granted full Group membership before leaving Green Mansions in September. Kazan's elevation reportedly "annoyed" Lee Strasberg, who was not consulted by the other directors (Smith, pp. 146–47).

"Skits" by Alan Baxter and selections from *Awake and Sing!* (1935), Clifford Odets's work in progress, were traded for bed and board at Green Mansions. Nei-

Lee Strasberg, Harold Clurman, and Cheryl Crawford

ther Odets's potential as an actor nor his classic play impressed the directors at this time. An improvisation based on satirical caricatures by the German artist George Grosz was also presented by Group actors, including Kazan, Art Smith, Joe Bromberg, and Russell Collins. The improvisation was filmed by Ralph Steiner and released in 1934 as *Cafe Universal,* an antiwar film. Stills photographed by Steiner appeared in the November 1933 number of *Theatre Arts*.] *TL, 2 pp., Wesleyan*

TO CHERYL CRAWFORD AND LEE STRASBERG

[New York]
[summer 1934]

Dear Cheryl and Lee:
I'm writing you for two reasons. First I realize that there are very good reasons why I should not have a vacation and when I say <u>realize</u> I mean that these reasons have validity for me and I have considered them and they create a conflict in me at this time. And so I write you the reasons why I think I must have a vacation. Then secondly I write because I want at this time to try to relate what I have now, to what I wanted when I entered the theatre, and what I hope to do in the future, and because in this I want to enlist your help.

First, why did I enter the theatre. I've always told people it was accidental, but of course this isn't true. In a real sense it was the result of a long-continued mode of reacting to the world. I could have quit High School and gone to work. Business was thriving then. There was money, opportunity and full activity. I could have gone to work after High School. College was none too appetising a prospect. The only good college I could get into was a pompous, reactionary gentleman's school, where I would have to spend a lot of time washing dishes. It turned out to be a place where I could do what I wanted and pass with people as doing something else, something "very worthwhile". I was always thinking of quitting. After college, my father brought a lot of pressure on me to go and help him in his now fast-fading business. And when I didn't, it was hard for me to tell why. I had never been backstage in my life. Why go all of a sudden to Baker's school? It is only now that I am beginning to understand these "accidental" decisions of mine.

I always had a great thirst for knowledge. When I was younger, I actually had a fear that some kid would know more about some subject than I did. I tried to know everything about everything ~~at the same time. I didn't want to miss anything that existed~~. Under no conditions did I ever tolerate anything that shut off part of the world. I knew what I wanted and I never let anybody tell me what they thought I wanted. I early determined never to accept anybody's estimate of myself. They could fix me in place too easily, from what they saw before them. I had different ideas, of what I would be. I wanted nothing that would limit my experience of life. (Of course, everything I did limited my experience of life) I went to Yale Drama School for two reasons. First to avoid going to work at a job, that would be blinders over my eyes for ever. And secondly, I had an idea that perhaps in the theatre I could find an activity which would give play to everything I could possibly learn or experience. Of course Yale was a sour joke—perverts and aesthetes playing a game they didn't believe in. When Phil Barber told me about the Group, I immediately gave up my idea of finishing the course there and I quit.

I've been very happy in the Group up to the middle of the run of Men In White or so. I swarmed over the whole organism like Lupe Velez, and from everybody I was learning. Besides I was soon in a loop-the-loop of extra-theatrical interests and activities and studies. I found that after all the dishwashing, I hadn't learned much at college and what I had learned, I now had to largely unlearn. Everything whirred until the day Gentlewoman opened.

Don't mistake me. I don't feel I know it all now. I don't—and concretely you can see, I still go on working hard. But whereas I had always thought of our theatre as closely related to life, as in a sense an editorial force and sometimes as life itself, now things seemed different. First, while the outer world swarmed with violent and, to me, disturbing conflicts, I was at the stale business of doing what I do in M.I.W. (Again, please don't misunderstand me. I know what a theatre must come up against. I know you have to choose. I know that even when you choose, the world doesn't suddenly drop in your lap and spin slowly under your eyes.) For the first time in years, I reverted to the day-dreamy longing for what I didn't have. Each week's papers were bugles summoning me to places, where 'history' was going on. For instance, I went on a three day trip to the coal and iron district of Pennsylvania and the people I saw there excited me and absorbed me like mythical or fairytale characters fill a kid's eyes and a kid's mind as he reads of them. I had forgotten that these people existed in flesh and blood, that there was a body to the ocean of which I was the froth of the waves.

Then when I came back to town (right after GENTLEWOMAN closed), I immediately activized myself artistically, with the full bodied sense of the world's life, I had within me then. Again I was acting on the wish that the theatre be a mode of life itself, rather than something above or removed. For the first time, the slogan: "The Theatre is a weapon in the Class Struggle", found active meaning. For it found meaning in my activity. . . .

Lee asked me once why I thought it was that Art Smith hadn't developed more in the Group Theatre. I said that I thought it was because his focus was constantly kaleidoscoping and consequently was always diffuse and blunt. Beyond this there is another reason. (What follows is simply my deduction) I believe that Art feels as do some others that about one-tenth of their energies and talents are being put to use; no more. I believe this is as much Art's fault, as it is the Group's. But the fact remains that everything that he does, which is actually his own work, he finds outside Group Activities. What he does for the Group he does with one finger.

Now my case is not Art's case. I'm also restive and I also have a big appetite. But I know that the Group does not now, and will not for a long time, use me all up. I know how limited my use as an actor is, and necessarily will be until I become a good actor. And Stage Managing, after opening night, is something you do with the periphery of your mind. So what'll I do meantime? Its hightime to get some actual experience directing. You can't learn your own particular artistic problems watching others work. Now to this question, I know the answer. "Go on working, studying and when you get an idea, work it out". That is the answer. But what I cannot answer is the other problem that troubles me. What I cannot quiet is the feeling that I'm dangerously removed, for a dangerously long period of time from what's going on in the world. With shots of dead and wounded in every paper, every day; with my own eyes' witness of the class war in our city, always in my mind, I cannot be easy. I feel like an aesthete. If the theatre were an individual art, my course of action would be plain. But I found out for the first time this year what it means to belong to a collective. I wanted Men in White to close last March. For the first time in my life I had money and I wanted to take a long trip around the United States (most of which I know nothing about). But everybody had debts to pay; everybody, except myself, needed the money. Then there were the stage hands—I couldn't even make up <u>my</u> mind as to what I wanted. How do you resolve this feeling if either of you have anything like it?

About vacations, you probably see what I want to say. I don't want a vacation for my health. My health is allright, I think. I'm relaxed and easy, my digestion is perfect, and I fall asleep as I lie down. (On the other hand when I hear so much fuss made over Joe's health and Billy's health, which are supposed to be dangerously low from <u>over-work</u>, it makes me laugh. They've been living a Turkish-bath existence compared with me. If they sometimes feel a little tired, its for other reasons) Its obvious, furthermore, that if I do get a vacation I won't spend it lying on the sands at Bermuda, or under the Vermont elms, or in front of the sentimental curios of St. Augustine, Florida, or sipping Napoleon brandy on the porch of the Chateau Frontenac, or acquiring a tan at Atlantic City. I want a vacation for much more organic reasons, I mean for reasons that tie in with my whole way of life. What I have taken so much of your time with, in this letter, is to show you that this was so. I felt that if I had just mentioned it as a general kind of notion of mine, it would not have indicated that it was important to me. It is much more important to me than my health, and just as important to <u>me</u>, as their health is, to some of the other people in the Group. . . .

One last thing. It may seem exaggerated to place such reliance or faith in two weeks vacation away from the Group Theatre. Its very possible that it won't satisfy the appetite I've been describing to you. But I think it will go a long ways to appease it. I certainly wish it could be two months. I'm sure that I would have a much more productive year artistically if it could have been. . . .

Gadget.

[Actors wearied by the long run of *Men in White* (1933), a medical melodrama by Sidney Kingsley that won the Pulitzer Prize, requested a two-week paid vacation as a prelude to the annual summer retreat. The grudging approval of the Group directors was Kazan's cue to seek inclusion in the plan as well.

Far from being idealized, the years of isolation at Williams College were resented by Kazan and not forgotten but pivotal in forming "a self-reliant, tough-skinned, resolute, and determined man, five foot six." They also laid the "emotional groundwork" for his attraction to the Communist Party (*A Life*, pp. 44–47). Elia wrote several plays at Yale, acted in student productions—including *Merry-Go-Round* by Albert Maltz and George Sklar, each blacklisted in the 1940s—and directed Pirandello's *At the Gate* for the So and So Players, a theater group over which he presided. Work in the "scene shop" proved more valuable in the short and long run by instilling self-confidence and preparing the future director to meet stage designers and technicians on knowledgeable terms. Kazan later described the Yale emphasis on the pictorial, kinetic elements of theater as a corrective to

Lee Strasberg's direction, which tended to inflate the actor's personal role. Nonetheless he rejected the Yale theatrical model as "classically sterile, mannered and polite" and left in 1932 without taking a degree (*A Life*, p. 51).

John Howard Lawson's *Gentlewoman* was dismissed by critics of all persuasions as a shallow drawing-room play and closed in April 1934 after a brief run. Its effect on Kazan was to expose the Group Theatre's lack of vitality and his own separation from real life. At this critical time, he answered the "bugles" of history and joined a communist unit operating silently within the Group Theatre. He and Art Smith, co-conspirators who were given little opportunity to develop within the Group, had recently worked "outside" and contributed an antifascist sketch ("Dimitroff") to New York's radical theater. Named by Kazan in later congressional testimony, Art Smith was blacklisted in film and television and maintained a tenuous presence on Broadway through the 1950s.

In August "Comrade" Kazan, as Elia put it, began a two-week vacation in the South. His travel was designed to restore "an aesthete" to the tumultuous life of the nation. En route he met the blues musician Leadbelly, made contact with Sid Benson, a communist organizer in Tennessee, and visited New Orleans to meet other black musicians (*A Life*, pp. 109–10).

Kazan used the nickname "Gadget" or variations well into the 1970s, usually with colleagues in theater and film. Much later John Steinbeck would confront his friend and collaborator with its servile implications.] *TLS, 5 pp., Wesleyan*

TO MOLLY DAY THACHER

[Cloudland, Georgia]
[early August 1935]

Piss Pot:—

I've left the Pattens. I'm up in the mountains on the Alabama Georgia state line and I'm just fixin to lit out for Montgomery, hear?!?! And where <u>is</u> Montgomery? Its over down yon' about 2 hundred miles or so.

Dorothy backed out on driving me into the Share-croppers' land. I may not be able to get in, but I'm gonna try. Spent good part of yesterday with 2 of the Scottsboro Mothers—who live in Niggertown, Milltown, South Chattanooga. Mother Patterson had raised enough money to go see her son, Haywood, in the Birmingham jail tomorrow. Mother Williams said she wished she could go but didn't have the money. I gave her the fare. She took it, in an unconscious sort of way & we talked for a spell. Later we took a walk down the Tennessee River & saw Pat Patterson, Haywood's father—half fishing, half sleeping in the roots of a river bank tree. We didn't talk much. Mother Patterson is wonderful. Proud, erect, poised, pure in heart. A little like Mother Bloor, but no where near as smart and more simple & noble. She walks like a Tahitian negress without the baskets on her head—She'd been out selling pamphlets (to raise train fare, partly); said the best seller was Spivak's "On the Georgia Chain Gang" on account of the picture on the cover & because it told how they treated them on a chain gang—an institution in which every negro has an interest. She also said she could sell anything with pictures of the "boys" in it.

Whole movement here pre-natal almost—& stony broke. I got Patten interested & she's giving $20—Place needs Sid, though present Organizer is a very good type—an anglo-saxon mountaineer, trained at the Folk School—the kind of pure American who leads many negroes into the movement.

This place—Cloudland Park—is half small town summer resort, & half native. Last night was square dance—which is not a curiosity here but a regular thing—I shook my foot off—dancing with a worn out skinny mountain woman—I capered, jumped, dipped & did the duck walk. I dripped water on the floor—I made a new world's record for the passage of water from mouth to sweat pore. Later I went riding with some southern girls & boys.

There isn't a white Southern girl who's worth one of your discarded toe nails. This doesn't go for the negroes—some of them are spirited & beautiful & unaffected (although damn if I can make out what the hell they're talking about).

All my love
Elia Kazan

[The success of Clifford Odets's *Waiting for Lefty* and *Awake and Sing!* in 1935 delayed vacations for several weeks and angered Kazan, who denounced the "nickel-nursing, dime-adoring, squint-eyed lazeers who make up the Group Theatre" before leaving for the South once again. He wrote to Molly from Cloudland, Georgia, on pages torn from a journal and preceded by a list of genteel southern effusions—"Honey bunch," "Angel child," "Sugar Pie"—for which he substituted "Piss Pot."

Dorothy Patten, an original Group Theatre member with family roots in Tennessee, drove Kazan as far as Chattanooga, where he met the Scottsboro mothers Janie Patterson and Mamie Williams. Repeated trials and reversals inspired a wave of sympathy for nine black youths convicted in Alabama in 1931 of raping two white women on a freight train run. Seven remained under sentence of death.

Mother Ella Reeve Bloor agitated for worker rights, international peace, and justice for the Scottsboro Boys. Janie Patterson's "best seller" is a brief version of *Georgia Nigger* (1932), John L. Spivak's illustrated exposé of brutal labor practices and torture instruments used in the Georgia penal system. The pamphlet (no. 32) belongs to a series of left-wing tracts issued by the Labor Research Association and selling for five or ten cents each. The communist organizer whom Kazan met was trained at the Highlander Folk School in the mountains of southeastern Tennessee. Founded in 1932, the controversial school offered workshops in regional planning and organizing labor. Involvement in the civil rights movement led to a brief closing by the state in 1961.] ALS, 3 pp., Wesleyan

SH: Hotel Victoria, Taxco, Mexico
[August 1935]

The fucking bus company x'sed me. I left Mexico [City] for Acapulco this morning and when the bus got here I found out that it didn't go to Acapulco—in fact that you can't get from Mexico [City] to Acapulco in one day, by bus. It takes 2 days. Either the fucking bus company crossed me, or I put too much reliance on my command of the language here. Maybe the guy at the "Red Arrow" (fleche rojo, ¿verdad?) told me that the bus didn't go to Acapulco, I don't know. Anyway for 11 Bucks you can go from Acapulco to Mexico [City] by plane and that's me all over. At the moment you read this, I may be a charred remains somewhere. In that case everything I have belongs to you except my money which you give to my brothers for educational purposes. I'm getting a bug on education & students & youth—especially since I went to Chapingo.

I was so pleased at receiving your letters, that my already cavernous appetite for Mexico was sharpened & for the next 3 days I didn't have time to write you back. I was going day & night. Now that I'm in Taxco, I wish I was in Acapulco. Taxco is a pie shaped, tiny corner of the perfumed garden of forgetfulness, as far as artists go. I don't mind a little withdrawal from life—but this is a stop to somewhere else, as far as I'm concerned. I hate the pious-stinking church. I went to 3 "perfectly beautiful" private homes to see pictures and there you see time frozen alive, standing still, stultified, preserved and pickled waiting for the next art vogue—which won't be here.

I'm going to Acapulco for (1) tropics (2) seaport & fish port (3) eat & lie on Beach 2 days (4) ride thru country on bus. And I'm glad I'm flying back.

I still don't know how I'm getting back home. Airplane cost $160—I'd rather buy junk (& I am), with the money. Somebody I met, who thought my performance in Lefty was best he saw in N.Y. last year (so his advice is valuable)—advised me to go by train. I'm going to look that up when I get back to the city. I'll tell you right now tho that I'm not taking any train, air-conditioned or no air-conditioned—I can't stomach a long train ride—it makes my face all pimply & carbuncular. I don't know what to do. I'll either come backward live steerage, or I'll take a plane or maybe I'll chance the train after all—after all its air-conditioned and its only for once.

Don't you wish I'd just say something? I'd rather kid you, muchacha! (means "Baby Doll")

I had a short fruity contact with some Mexican Intellectuals—the kind the Government supports—they say, in summation, 'that poverty is not so bad in Mexico because the people are used to it.'

I bought about $7 more stuff from the guy anyway. I've bought so much junk now that I can't even remember what I have. Mostly second hand books & magazines, illustrated. I've bought an extra suitcase already and by the time I pull into N.Y. harbor you'll be able to see me from Nyack-on-Hudson. I'm thinking of coming in on the S.S. Siboney's Ducal Steerage (to distinguish it from its Regal cabin class). But I'm not sure. My flesh is tender & the bugs love it. On the other hand there are some advantages to coming by plane, I mean by steerage on the "Siboney". For example there's the feature—But why discuss this now—its stupid to waste paper & ink to send such trivia back from so stirring and inspiring an adventure as a trip to Mexico.

Speaking of thrills, I can't wait to go again to the Bull Fight. The guy from Cincinnati that I met who thought rather highly (as I told you, if I remember) of my performance in Lefty, this gentleman-student is treating me to first row seats in the shade. From there I can make eyes at the matadors & possibly I'll bring you home the most dashing one—although that would mean I'll need at least 2 porters in constant attendance and you'll be able to see me from between Nyack & Poughkeepsie on a clear day.

Anyway, although I don't quite see how it happened, I hope its what you want most and after that I hope its a little girl. With all my love, devotion, advisory capacities, I'm yours,

Gadget.

This isn't much of a letter. I'm having a better time than you think from this. I hate to get Xsed and hung up in a tourist center like this and also have a day at where I want to be, lopped off my time.

S.S. Siboney gets in 3rd about noon they say. Tell Group if they ask that I'll be there on the third even if I come by train which I won't or by plane which I doubt. For the most part I'm coming by boat—S.S. Siboney on the 3rd. If its warm I really will sleep on deck (by the life boat). Otherwise its a room with a dozen other men.

My skin has the sheen of health, baby—all I need is a little more muscle tone. Old or middle age is beginning to flax and lax my tissues and I'll have to tune up in N.Y. But I'm up on my toes, as they say in boxing. Also I talk to myself— constantly—out loud and in the mind—and I don't talk much to anyone else. I can't—my Spanish is terrible.

again yrs.

[Elia traveled to New Orleans by train and wrote to Molly of "whites [who] broke the monotony of the sabbath with a little lynching party" on the day when he "went thru." He added, "Give the negroes organization, a few fire arms & a little support from the liberals of the land, & they should be able to mobilize their own vigilantes & make this impossible." A second letter reveals Elia's ambition to direct, as well as the solidarity of husband and wife: "To you its enough to say that if I do the production, my way, with fresh, cooperative actors, it would be a landmark in the American theatre, even though the playwright . . . is a tyro" (postmarked New Orleans, August 6 and 8, 1935, Wesleyan). The play in question—*200 Were Chosen* (1936)—is based on a colonizing experiment in Alaska plagued by quarrelsome settlers and incompetent bureaucrats. Produced by the Actors Repertory Company and directed by Worthington Miner, E. P. Conkle's Broadway debut ended after thirty-five performances.

Once in Mexico City, Kazan visited nearby Chapingo, where he probably caught the education "bug" at the Autonomous University. The campus is adorned with murals by Diego Rivera depicting peasant exploitation and revolt. *The Blood of the Revolutionary Martyrs Fertilizing the Earth* (1926–27) evokes the legend of Emiliano Zapata, agrarian reformer and military leader whose life Steinbeck and Kazan would later film. A mixup stranded Kazan at Taxco, which he deplored as an effete art colony and tourist attraction, before reaching Acapulco. Its heat, he wrote to Molly, "knocks you down." Along the way Kazan satisfied a "cavernous appetite for Mexico" with illustrative "junk" added to the "Raw Materials of the Director."

"The hypothetical condition" of pregnancy "surprised and amused" Molly Kazan but later in August she reported "Nix. Nada. Nein. Rien." and advised Elia to stop "knitting."] *ALS, 6 pp., Wesleyan*

TO CHERYL CRAWFORD

[New York]
[fall 1935]

Dear Cheryl:
I'm writing this rather than talking with you about it, first because I want definite official notice taken of it and, following, definite official action; second, because the reasoning I'm going to follow carries weight only if presented carefully and in detail.

I've come back from Mexico with a clearer idea of what I want to do, of the course now necessary for me to follow than I've ever had before. Thru the five weeks of va ca tion (the damn typewriter jumps), I formula ted a program for myself and also its day to day delineation, in activity. To put the result very shortly:—stimulated by some chance remarks of Lee, I've illuminated for myself the concept of the Raw Materials of the Director. This is a notion I've never turned over before—which I've never even heard mentioned as such. The supposition generally made is that the raw materials of a director are the scripts he works from. Of course this is nonsense. The production-ideas of a director, his visualizations, dynamics, picturizations, use of rhythm, music, play with characters, objects etc. etc. etc. never leap from deep and dark inspiration. Inspiration has been segmented and lies out on the table for us to study. Scholars have traced its genesis and evolution. Everything comes from somewhere. And this <u>somewhere</u> is a definite something—the experience of the artist—what he's felt, known, remembers—in short, experienced. . . .

To tell you what I'm doing, simply, I've gone to work and started to amass these raw materials and orientate myself to the world with such a working attitude. My room is full of what somebody called "junk", though it has got a spine; full of pictures, photographs, clippings, notes, plans, books, etc. etc. I'm subscribing this year to a different class of magazine. I've even done what I've intended for five years. I've arranged to take music lessons, so that I wont have to depend upon some one else to read a simple folk song. I've already started to pick up records of the music of the people; an acquaintance with this field will certainly yield to a director. This is in short.

I've already had to curtail a number of activities I've always piddled with, to clear the way. But, as I anticipated during vacation, when I came back and slid into my position in the theatre, the one I occupied last spring, I was swamped to the eyes with obligations and with work. . . . I'm looking to see what I can cut. Besides there are other things I must do. I'm dangerously ignorant on many subjects which a director should have pat, to the minute. The list is staggering. But when I put the activities down one by one and put my self-training at the top, the list is TOP HEAVY, in my eyes. That's four-starred with me. I'm going to be lazier all around so I can do what's in my heart. I'm determined to clear the road for it. Give myself a break.

The purpose of this letter:—I ask that I be formally released from all stage-managing duties immediately, with the exception of setting up our production on the road. I except this because I'm the only actor who knows the technical end of these shows well enough to set them up fast and right. But its the only exception I make. I want no title or position for this work. I'll do it—but not as stage manager. I know you've been considering doing this, later sometime, from the talk about Irving Gordon. I ask that you do it now—giving the job to one of the actors who has very little to do in these productions and in the general Group life. . . . [B]elieve it or not, the activity of Stage Managing puts me so on edge that I'm temperamentally ready to explode. Last Saturday I called a good friend of mine down on stage from his dressing room. I called three times at intervals. He didn't deign to answer me till the third time. I didn't know if he was in the building till he later told me he was there all the time. When he finally answered, it was a superior, impatient drawl "Allright—I'll be right down!". I'm constantly getting this, and from my best friends. Every time it lands right in the pit of my stomach. I go cursing to myself and chewing my lips like it was the end of the season already. If I hadn't been so carefully impulse-broken in my youth, I'd of taken the script and done with it what would make [it] useless for ever. . . . The implication was that there were actors in the Group and then there was Gadget. If anybody else stage managed, it was just a slumming trip to give me a break. Like a true artist, such an actor would always make sure that his descent into the lower regions would be brightly labelled TEMPORARY and that such a trick of kindness should never stand in the way of his future parts.

Now I've always accepted this relation. For a long time, there were twenty odd actors in the Group and then there was me. And today I know better than before that I haven't much technique, and wherein I haven't much technique, and that maybe I have more energy than I have faith and stage kind of emotion, and further that as a type, I'm a little bit of a curio, like something you pick up in Mexico for seventeen cents American money. BUT at the same time, if I look through our press books to way back, which I did, I know that in one part and in one year as an actor, I've made more impression as an actor . . . than ten or so of the Group. I don't say I'm a better actor than these friends of mine. I'm better than a few of them, but that's not very good, and I don't mention it both for their sakes and my own. But when I encounter the adjustment from other people in the Group . . . I get sore. I will not tolerate it anymore. Its not a conscious or objective attitude so you can't batter it down. But if stage managing is an onerous job, and not for the true artist (which is baloney, in this categorical sense) I will not be accepted. And especially because in the LARGER MORE GENERAL SENSE AS A SINCERE, CONSCIOUS, PRACTISING ARTIST, I'll give place to no one in the acting company, except Cliff. There are firmer, more advanced artists among them, but none of them work harder (except maybe Cliff, and Bobby used to) and today, the way I feel this fall, I look them all in the eye.

Even if we simply consider the assigned work the Group has given me to do this fall, its clear that there are many actors who's assignments in the productions and in the Group life and activity are much lighter, less important and less inclining towards the future growth and benefit of our Theatre, and who in every respect except some slight deficiency in technical knowledge are quite capable of stage managing our shows this fall. I blurted out the above, possibly from a sense I have that I've always in the past been too aware of my deficiencies. At the same time, in a practical sense, I know what they are. I'm quite ready to forfeit a salary increase on the road, so that whoever takes over can be given a raise. At any rate please take it up officially and definitely and tell me your decision.

Gadg.

[By 1935 Harold Clurman consulted Kazan on play selection and regarded him as an ally in Group Theatre politics. His election to the Actors Committee suggests wider influence and authority, as does his release from the "onerous job" of stage manager. Featured roles also awaited Kazan in *Paradise Lost* (1935) and *Golden Boy* (1937), but condescending attitudes toward the old "Gadget" persisted as he tried to become "A SINCERE, CONSCIOUS, PRACTISING ARTIST." Sharply restricted opportunity to direct Group productions led Kazan to the Theatre of Action, known widely as a communist front, where he codirected *The Young Go First* (1935), an indictment of militarism in the Civilian Conservation Corps. Not until 1938 would he direct a Group Theatre production, and then without success. In the meanwhile he reminded Cheryl Crawford of his notable appearance in *Waiting for Lefty* (1935). Clifford Odets's strike play gave a radical edge to the Group and brought unusual attention to Kazan after the initial production in January. His character leaves the audience, mounts the stage, and exposes the company spy as his "OWN LOUSY BROTHER!!" No experience in the theater left a deeper or more lasting impression on Elia than the "approval" of the audience, which descended "like Niagara Falls" (*A Life,* pp. 114–16).

The interests of the communist unit to which Odets and Kazan belonged had not lain dormant in the production of *Lefty,* although Kazan was not at liberty to add covert political activity to the list of "obligations" presented to Cheryl Crawford.] *TLS, 3 pp., Wesleyan*

TO CLIFFORD ODETS

[Selwyn Theatre, Chicago]
[May 4, 1936]

Just arrived in Chicago and read your letter. Am typing this from the publicity office, Selwyn Theatre. Manny Eisenberg and Phil Adler are in here wrestling the telephones. We're almost clean tonight and almost sold out also for the first two weeks. We had the head start of the Guild subscription, 5000 a week guarantee. We took in 7200 in Baltimore and won the town. They're dying to have us back next season, making all kinds of offers of guarantees etc. Also won the poor lonely reviewers. The city is ugly and sterile, with no particular distinction. I had a good time—went to the races one day and went to Washington another and out in the country a third. I froze the company, so much so that Harold noticed it and asked if I was avoiding the other actors and I said yes and told him why. It brought me luck; I won at the track. Going again here.

Bud Bohnen has a baby girl and Billy Kirkland named it Budgette.

I didn't think my letter was depressing (just the facts), but yours was. I appreciate your standing on one foot ready to go nowhere. I got a chronic tick myself. I light out of here in a car as soon as this week is over and Bud Bohnen comes out. Expect to be out in H'wood at the end of the month. Going to mooch along and see the sights. Zigzag down the Mississippi valley into the hot country and then across. The way I feel today with Chicago cold and damp, when I hit the desert I'll lie out there for a week. Anyway I'm going as I please.

Don't need any dough thanks. A couple of guys are coming along and will share expenses. I still have that dough saved up from Men in White, which is enough also to pay whatever the baby will cost me. About your money problem why don't you get a robot front man who has a one-word vocabulary—No.

I don't think Harold is coming out with me. He hasn't said so but I see through him like cellophane—He claims a terrific interest in Chicago and in the whole of America, but except for theory he's still the lonely sheltered doctor's son. I love him and he exacts a tremendous loyalty from me but he's scared of the dark, can't touch an animal and thinks everything that grows out of the earth is poison ivy—somehow to be looked at through the window of a speeding train, while talking to Stella. He's a craftsman who's only material is ideas, and who's best trick is an ability to convince people of an idea that possesses him. He's got a notion now—I think its a good idea too—that the Group should be centralized. That there should be one director in charge of everything and responsible to the Group for everything—Harold Clurman. He's working this idea out and will propose it to the members this summer. Everyone in the Group is talking reorganization and readjustment. Lee doesn't want any responsibility except artistic and as for Cheryl—

Have to go down on stage now—they're setting up. Send this tomorrow with clippings. Saved them for you in Baltimore but Phil wanted them to send to a certain backer and I gave them away.

[*Awake and Sing!* won raves in Chicago on a tour made necessary by the Group's chronic insolvency and the failure of the latest production—*Case of Clyde Griffiths*, an adaptation of Dreiser's *An American Tragedy* by Erwin Piscator. The acting of the Group is "keen, searching, gifted" and Clifford Odets's Depression-era play "fired by the conviction of prophecy" (*Chicago Daily News*, May 5, 1936). Kazan served as "Gadget" in setting up the tour and played Schlosser, an immigrant janitor.

Kazan replied to Odets's "depressing" letter of May 1 with softened criticism of Harold Clurman's "awkward choked life" and identification of Stella Adler, the Group's self-appointed star and Clurman's vexing lover, as the source of the director's isolation and inertia.

Odets's initial salary as a Hollywood screenwriter—$2,500 per week—relieved the poverty of Group Theatre days but not without exposing the benefactor to needy friends and liberal causes. Elia was prepared financially for the birth of his daughter Judy on August 2, 1936, and declined Odets's offer of "dough."

Support for "centralized" governance of the Group Theatre was notable as Kazan withdrew from the Communist Party in the spring of 1936. The directors, who were doubtless aware of party activity but not members, were to be outflanked in matters of policy by democratic ploys. Kazan's reluctance to implement the strategy was cause for importing a comrade from Detroit to deal with insubordination. Kazan, the sole "transgressor," was indicted as the "foreman type" ready "to join hands with the exploiters of the working class." He soon resigned in reaction to the intolerance and "strong-arm" tactics of the party (*A Life*, pp. 128–31). In a midyear restructuring of the Group, Harold Clurman was voted managing director with full powers and final authority. Kazan acted as his reliable right hand.] *TL, 2 pp., Indiana*

TO MOLLY DAY THACHER

PM: Los Angeles, June 3, 1936

Everything is hotsy. I'm staying at Cliff's with a Pilipino butler to give me breakfast and make my bed. First couple of days I was staying at Alan's. He's in Cleveland and N.Y. on a vacation so I'm not going to see him. His place is beautiful—on a West Hollywood hill overlooking Los Angeles.

I found out that I had received a lot of bum steers in N.Y. about Movie Biz. If I had simply come out here when Case closed I could have done a couple of small parts up till now and rec'd a start. They never or almost never import character players from N.Y. as they've got a drove out here. But if you come out and are known, you can get work. As it is they want me to stay here the first few weeks in July and do a part in Winterset. Either one of the gangsters or one of the bums—anyway it would pay 350 per for two weeks. I haven't told them yet that I can't. I'm staying out here a few more days and see if I can promote myself a good screen test—so that if I ever need money I can come out here in a hurry. After that I'll be coming back—I guess it will be by train as I spent more than I thought and haven't made a cent. Cliff keeps offering me money but I don't take a cent. Everyone sponges off him. He supports half the left wing writers movements and ¾ of the Group theatre. Not me.

This is the original land of milk and honey. A swell place to die—with flowers and avocados and oranges all around in everyone's back yard and nightingales and hummingbirds in everybody's belfry. The sunshine and its not too hot. Been going to the studios and watching them shoot (Gorgeous Hussy, General Dies at Dawn, Devil Doll) and in general doing all right and having a good time.

Saw opening of Bury the Dead here. And it was a terribly sleep[y] and dull performance. Worse than N.Y. The audience is all celebrities and quasi celebs and it takes half an hour to get out of the theatre while everyone looks and tries to figure out who everybody else is.

In general, as I thought, this place is poison for an artist. Its immensely pleasurable and almost inevitable to begin believing that this toy makebelieve is the world.

Walter Coy quit the Group. He signed with Universal yesterday. The cars, girls, climate, fruit, fine liquor, beautiful sensuous life was too much for him.

Thor is here. Waiting for Alan to come back. Writing a play. He works as Alan's stand-in. $35 per. Same guy. Face neurotically wrinkled up.

Finding it hard to sell the car here for quick cash (That's the money I was going to use to fly back with) So I think Vin's going to drive it East.

Write you again soon as I know definitely when I'm coming back. Wont be long.

LOVE Baby

[Financing an extended run of *Paradise Lost,* which opened to mixed reviews in late 1935, led Clifford Odets to explore film opportunities in what he naively considered a brief excursion to Hollywood. Lewis Milestone, director of *All Quiet on the Western Front* (1930), offered him a screenwriting job soon after he arrived and arranged a lucrative contract with Paramount Pictures. Kazan visited the set of *The General Died at Dawn* (1936), Odets's first assignment, and impressed Milestone if later developments are any indication. In writing to Molly, Elia repeated Odets's warning that "the semi-tropical climate" of California instills a "fatal" complacency in the artist. No one "makes you extend yourself. You might as well be on Eugene O'Neill's island as be here" (Odets to EK, postmarked May 1, 1936, Wesleyan). Kazan's "screen test" would be delayed until 1937. Walter Coy, an original member, ended his Group association with the recent failure of the *Case of Clyde Griffiths.* Alan Baxter essentially left the Group in 1935 to begin a career playing villains in "B" films.] *TL, 1 p., Wesleyan*

TO MOLLY DAY THACHER

SH: Kazan Carpet Co., Inc.
10 West 33rd Street, New York
[c. early March 1937]

This letter is late because I wrote it two days ago and it turned out to be very confused so I tore it up. I didn't seem to know what I wanted. But things seem a little clearer now.

The root of all the trouble is the way they keep putting off starting the movie. They're still looking for a leading man, with Wanger trying to convince Milestone to take Fonda and Milly believing that will be fatal to the film. I think, sooner or later, he'll have to take him. Milly says that the reason Wanger is delaying is that he does not believe the film will make money (i.e. be popular) and that he really would like not to do it. I don't see how he can get out of it now, if even Milly is right and he would like to. He's put about $150,000 into it all ready, about half of which went to Milly himself. Anyway, the zero hour will come this week and something will have to be done.

Now, you wanted to know what I intended to do. (This where all the confusion came in last time). One thing seems clear now. Having come out here, and invested all that time and talent into the movie, the most important thing is to play in it—and play well. I was so busy writing on the script that, I had forgotten the problem of acting in it and being very good. Well that seems to be the task in hand, so I think I'll start tackling that this coming week. Now, further if the picture starts next week, the eight weeks or so of shooting will be up around May First. Milly says that if I really want to learn the business, I ought to stay a couple of weeks beyond that and be in on the whole <u>cutting</u>. I don't know about that now, i.e. whether I will stay.

All this is a hell of a long time, and even though I know I'm getting full value for my time, because I am learning a hell of a lot, about script preparation for one thing, I often wish I hadn't come out here in the first place. I needed that money and the experience, but I ask myself sometimes, did I need that money that badly, or did I NEED the money? In one way I did, in another, I could have gotten along on much less—for example, directing on the project, studying traveling—and writing one of the plays I've been thinking about for so long.

So, the earliest I'll be able to leave here is May 1st. and its possible I may stay a week or so longer—all this barring accidents.

So I hate to have you come out here and wait for me to drive back with you. You might have to wait a long time and I don't [want] to have to wait till "just before I start back" for you to come out here. Therefore I suggest that you come out here now and stay here as long as you can while I'm working and spend your time partly inspecting the studios and the general life of the place here and partly touring the whole west coast in my little Chevy. Open the atlas for a change to the states of the far west, Washington, Oregon, California, Nevada, Arizona etc. We could take week-end trips together and you could go on a longer trip up to the far north—and there are a lot of old friends of yours out here with whom you could take such a trip. There's as much to chew up there as you could possibly bite off—and all of it very new. I've been planning to take a trip up myself, but haven't had a chance. Frisco itself needs a week. And in the states above there is still the real frontier.

Anyway that's what I suggest, and I'm going out now to look for an apartment. I'm going with Thor Liljencrantz, who's three times as neurtoci (neurotic) as ever.

I guess the delay and the flagrantly insulting use of a person's time out here is what you get the big money for—but I don't think I'll do it again—unless on very very different bases. Maybe some kind of directing job next year, but only if there's nothing I'd rather do. . . .

If nothing is done by May first—I may take the script over myself and try to push the whole project—but the more I think of it, the more I believe that

Stella Adler with Clifford Odets (left) and her brother
Luther Adler, Hollywood, 1937

an excellently worked out script is necessary before you can go much further and I think that's where I have to come into it. If we don't do any shooting this spring—what I would most like to do is go to Russia for four weeks and see the theatre there before the Big War breaks. That's what I'd like most. Meantime I could work on the movie and on the play I'm planning now.

I went to the tennis matches and the concert with Milly, and his wife, who treat me great. Also the big night club, where I just sat around, got slightly plastered and day dreamed. I met a lot of people, big shots, but they don't mean a thing—not even worth writing their names. Its about like N.Y. in May here now, gets warmer in a month. Your poem was wonderful and clever. Your letters are works of art. They give a lovely sense of what a sweet girl I got. Tell me more about the beauty, please—love darling.

[Kazan and Harold Clurman arrived in California in early 1937 in the aftermath of a failed play that halted Group Theatre activities until the fall. They were joined by Cheryl Crawford and a contingent of Group actors, including Luther and Stella Adler, intent on supplementing their meager theatrical income. A dubious contract with Walter Wanger, an independent producer, would have them either "loaned" to studios or cast in his own films. The first order of business was screen testing supervised by Lewis Milestone. Much later Kazan described the clarifying effect of the camera: "One look at the test and I knew I had no future, not as an actor, in Hollywood."

A screenplay by Clifford Odets that turned out to be overlong and commercially unpromising was the main hope of the Group actors. Its shelving in early March confirmed their distrust of Hollywood, as summarized by Bud Bohnen: "'The whole spirit of the place is fake, the acting is fake, the art is synthetic'"

(Smith, pp. 297–301). The fiasco deepened the crisis facing the Group as the prospect of reorganization and planning the fall season became more urgent. Harold Clurman was "comatose," as Kazan wrote in following correspondence, while Cheryl Crawford and Lee Strasberg contemplated resignation. Kazan prospered by reason of a more constructive attitude toward filmmaking—if not Hollywood. Lewis Milestone engaged Kazan as "secretary-assistant" and gave him "a beginner's course in directing." He left the studio "every day a more confident man, determined now to become a director of films" (*A Life*, pp. 158–60).] *TL, 2 pp. Wesleyan*

TO LEE STRASBERG

[Hollywood, California]
[c. mid-March, 1937]

I believe myself entirely now when I say that I have no interest here at all. This goes, even though I know that I could and others have and can, produce distinguished films here. But such work is so hedged in by opposing circumstances, that when it does appear, it has been the combination of lucky turns—like throwing ten coins in the air and having them all come down heads. And beyond this, even under <u>ideal</u> Hollywood conditions—which by the way do not exist for anyone, even for Capra—I'm not interested. I will stay here about two or three weeks more just to see if I can make up a little bundle of cash, without killing a lot of time waiting. If I can go to work fairly soon, I'll stay. I need the money. If not, I'll be right back.

When I get back, I'm going to Russia for a couple of months—it looks like it might be a last chance before they slam the gate over there. Then I should be back in N.Y. in the late summer. And then with whatever forces can be gotten together—I will work in a Group theatre. I'm not interested in anything else and would not do anything else. I know I can work in a Group this fall—but—

The one thing I will not embark on again is an organization where the organization and relation of people was as unhealthy as it was in our Group in its last year and a half. I believe that now, in this intermediary period, many people are being motivated by a certain kind of fear. This impulse says "Let us cling to what we have, it is better than nothing—we can slowly iron out its faults as we work along—we had the best people and we had the best relation and adjustment between these people—for chrissake lets not lose what we have". I believe this attitude to be a panicky one and also extremely dangerous. I believe that if we got together this summer, the same people in the same relations etc.—the same clashes and diseases would grow up and then there would come a really terrible explosion!

Furthermore, I believe the time has come to deeply and with all the fruit of our experience, reorganize the Group. We need fresh blood; we need to take chances again with new people. If for no reason than the fact that we are losing our old people, in one form or another, to whatever varying degree. We must have new material to work with and material in whom we feel potential-ity. Loyalty is no longer enough. The struggle is too fierce. . . .

About Stella and Harold. I talked with Harold two nights ago. I told him frankly that I thought that he was in a comatose state, that he seemed to have lost his own appetite, desire and personal dynamics—that he seemed to be further embedded in his concern for Stella than he had ever been before. To this he simply answered that I was right. . . . Also, to be frank and clear, he seems to be no more determined about his relation to Cheryl and your-self. Luther says to this that we, the Board members will see that the grat-ing working parts, clear and work separately. This I believe to be mechanical and bad theatre theory. The theatre is a collective art and the working parts have to work or else. . . . For the possibility that a new basis will be evolved by time, circumstances, talks, new relations, etc. for this too, I'm willing to wait—everyone longs for the Group; all await leadership—I'm calm and full of confidence about what I want—I'm eager to go to Russia now that I have a real chance and I know I'll not miss. Then to come back and work. However I know there must be leadership—nothing will arise that's good from the will of the majority.

[The abortive film project had been "hedged in" by casting and financial concerns and shelved before Kazan wrote to Lee Strasberg in mid-March. He was not sur-prised by the reversal and answered Kazan's letter with the bitterness of a founder about to resign from a cherished institution: "Perhaps I am slighting your activ-ity but who is going to do all this work? You plan to go to Russia and when you come back you'll be ready to start work. And what about the other people who are not going and must make their plans in the meantime." Strasberg closed with a promise not to address Kazan "personally about the Group anymore" (Brenman-Gibson, p. 458). He and Cheryl Crawford resigned later in March.

Correspondence reveals that Kazan visited the South rather than Russia after returning to New York in April.] *Brenman-Gibson, pp. 456–57*

TO CLIFFORD ODETS

[New York]
[April 11, 1937]

I had a meeting with the Group members, and it was some meeting! I had made up my mind to give them a very pessimistic picture to start with and I did. I told them they should be sure of nothing. It was not sure when Harold would come back to town, we had no plays now, except the Silent Partner and . (in answer to their persistent questioning) that the people on the West Coast had no concretely worked out plan yet. I said that the main thing now was the formation or the evolution of a leadership who would in fact be the theatre, who would move things and be responsible for all decisions, for success and failure. And I said that there was only one criterion now, namely what must be done to make the Group theatre idea operative on B'way.

I further said that I thought, and that you there agreed, that the leadership of the old Group was forever destroyed and please once and for all to stop counting on it. Whatever might happen now would be something new. I described Harold's state of mind as what I believe it to be—certainly no basis of hope for them. I described the complete unconcern on the West c. about the two resignations—etc. etc.

All this to rupture once and for all their glib sentimental idealism, their reliance on FAITH and the old Holy Group idea. But some people gave it an interpretation other than I had anticipated. To Beany and Lewis Leverett all that I had said definitely proved that the real Group only lived there in the room with them. Beany said that I was not an original member, that I didn't understand the Group like they did. Also she kept heckling me, and after being saint-like about it for a while, I finally reverted to type and shut her up. After that, despite eyes which glowered like a Zealot's, she was very careful with me. The three leading advocates of the original "WORD" which was laid down six years ago and still (they say) endures were MARGARET BARKER (whose hair is snakes, whose eyes are filled with holy smoke, who fumes at the mouth, whose lips are salt-encrusted with oft-spent passion, and who was pretty drunk)——then LEWIS LEVERETT, who didn't disappear once all night——and finally ALEXANDER KIRKLAND, who is very very interested, very much for democratic rule, but to tell the truth, sane. . . .

At the end of the meeting I had everyone more or less convinced that the only thing to do was to wait a while longer—not too much—but a while and then some kind of leadership would take power, who would certainly change a lot and which they could choose to follow or not. I never, all evening, told them what some so wanted to hear, that everything was going to be great and the old Group couldn't be stopped.

And after all, to tell you the complete truth, I have a lot of affection for most of them—even some of the noble ancient ruins. I went out with some of them afterwards and once you talk practically and informally and don't pull punches everybody is heart and soul with you, full of valuable loyalty and determination, and, by God, on our side. And the next few days I received telephone calls, people stopped me on the street, came up to me at meetings all asking for the Group, or interested in forming other Group theatres, wanting classes, lessons, rehearsals, offering all their energy and time and asking for very little in return except to be in a real theatre. Maybe it was because of the contrast to what Hollywood actors think of or want, but it left a very deep impression on me. With so many allies, how can a man be afraid? With that I have a new feeling for the theatre (as against film) for the theatre folk, all of them, in all departments—and it seemed to me I knew everybody on forty-fourth street—for the medium, for the craft of it and for its peculiar force and peculiar reality and for the poetry I see and feel in it, and for what I feel again that I want to do in it. Also I think I'm a communal person and really not individualistic, although I have powers of leadership. I like and need allies and co-workers and comrades and here they all were, with hands outstretched. . . .

Cheryl I saw for a minute. She really looks like a broken woman. She gives you the impression that she's always biting her lips. Her shoulders are tenser than ever and her face more set. The impracticality of _her_ starting another Group Theatre has already appeared to her and she has changed her plans. From what I hear she's going to CHERYL CRAWFORD PRESENTS. . . . Lee, I made a date with, but at Barbetta's where we went to talk, we met Phil Loeb, Russ Collins (in the pink) and Julie. So Lee and I haven't talked yet. I'm going to try to settle him this way. That he has a years leave of absence, if he (as Tony says he will) asks for it. This will ensure us the name of the Group Theatre and not mean any actual difference in our operation. If he doesn't want it, I'm going to assume that his resignation stands and not going into the bygones for any reason. . . .

Everything is fine. Write me your frames of mind. Write me personal.

[Making the Group Theatre "operative" on Broadway would require basic changes in philosophy and practice after the failure of the last season and repudiation of the old directorate by the Actors Committee. The ideal of an ensemble sharing room and board, progressive social values, and secure company status gave way to the importation of film stars, spot casting of potential new talent, and a leaner cast of regulars paid only when performing. With the resignation of Lee Strasberg and Cheryl Crawford, "the leadership of the old Group was forever destroyed," a critical fact reinforced by Kazan when he addressed New York–based members of the company in April—including such "noble ancient ruins" as Margaret (Beany) Barker and Eunice Stoddard. From a core of influential members in California would come reorganization in the fall.

Cheryl Crawford's first independent production closed after a brief run in spite of a strong review by Brooks Atkinson. Lee Strasberg directed _All the Living_ (1938) and several Group actors played leading roles. At the same time, Harold Clurman advised Kazan to make a clean break with Strasberg rather than offer him a leave of absence: "Right now he is an unmitigated menace."] _TL, 3 pp., Indiana_

TO CLIFFORD ODETS

[New York]

[May 26, 1937]

Dearest Cliff—

I'm going to write you a long letter and tell you what I've been seeing and doing, but Bobby showed me a letter you wrote him, yesterday, and I'm so overjoyed at the news it contains about the new play you're writing for us that I want to write you this much now. Christ that will be wonderful! Please write it, swiftly and with all your heart. And we'll open the season with it. There is no better way—there is no way that at all compares for starting our new theatre. We're working hard on scripts, both here and there, but such a script by you would solve so damn many problems. What we need now, is in our first step not to lose ground. Not to seem like something new—and still of course be entirely new in many vital and life-giving respects. Your play would represent absolutely the best of the old Group, and would be done with a combination of the first fervor seen in <u>Connelly,</u> and the grim, terribly—-battling determination of <u>Lefty</u>. Now we've got to go on—and not go on in the old way, but with a fresh spirit, a greater realism, a putting aside of our old exclusiveness, and with a newly arrived at sense of exactly of what we want.

The theatre in New York is not dead. That's a silly thing to say—"its dead". The theatre in New York is dying and at the same time being reborn. I've been attending the convention and there side by side are the two periods and the two vital movements. There, the oldsters speak with sour breath, their bewilderment at what is happening and fumble for means to bring back the good old days—and then suddenly every once in a while, from the sick bed, springs a shout of new life, a thrust into the unknown. Everybody talks Group (not Group Theatre, but Group Theatre Idea) and everybody talks for the special thing in the theatre that makes it unique—that is everybody among the living. Out of the body of the old dying mother, crawls the infant. If you walked down the streets of Show Business now you won't know the faces—youth, new faces, new talents, all waiting to be brought into a bigger and greater and realer Group Theatre which will be a youth theatre, and for which the forces are now ready. The streets are fertile with talent—and they all want us and we must stop keeping them out. We must stop being exclusive and clique-loving and esoteric. The art of acting is not an esoteric one. It requires talent, training and leadership. At least one more important theatre is ready to be born in New York, and it is my hope that we will bring it out, that it will be part of the new Group. Not for selfish reasons, but because what's needed to bring it to being is leadership from experience and from knowledge, and these only we can provide. Speaking technically, we are the only bona-fide group in

N.Y.—and I know of all of them. All we need now is a start. All we need now is a first play. I think we have everything else. We have, I'm sure, what I was most worried about—a real leadership—both organic to each other, unified, bound with love, and theatrically competent. I don't need money, fame, a trip to Russia, clothes for the baby, a phonograph, an automobile—I need for the Group to have an opener—a play which will start us. I don't need to ever see Hollywood again—I need for our theatre to have a first play. And if you will please sit down and do it with devotion, and love and with all your full heart and with the great ability you have, you will be doing, with us, a service to the great history-long Theatre, that the Gods of the arts will lean from heaven, pick up your face and kiss you for.

Gadg

Love to Luise, and good fortune to her.

[*Golden Boy,* the work in progress, revived Clifford Odets and the Group Theatre after lean seasons and would give Kazan a substantial acting role.

Few "shouts" of the "living" were heard at the American Theatre Council convention attended by Kazan in late May. The presidents of Actors' Equity, the Dramatists Guild, and the League of New York Theatres spoke for officialdom in the opening session, while panels featured such establishment figures as Lawrence Langner. Burgess Meredith, an early friend of Kazan's, struck a note for rebellious youth by comparing veteran Broadway producers to "the ancient superintendents of archaic prisons" (*NYT,* May 25, 1937).

In the fall an elected council of Luther Adler, Bud Bohnen, and Kazan shared responsibility with Harold Clurman in managing a leaner, more commercial Group Theatre. Those cast in *Golden Boy* retained Group membership, while others were not formally dismissed but challenged "to prove their value elsewhere." Kazan's influence troubled the old guard, who had not forgotten the original "Gadget" (Smith, pp. 315, 325).

Clifford Odets and the German-born actress Luise Rainer were tumultuously married from 1937 to 1940.] *TLS, 2 pp., Indiana*

TO HAROLD CLURMAN

[New York]
[summer 1937]

Dear Harold

My reaction to your letter was different than Molly's or Bobby's (I didn't show it to anyone else). My reaction isn't very complicated. I guess I have a little more feeling for you than they have—and for your (what we call) personal problem. Here's what I think.

First, there's nothing that could make me happier than if you, Bud and Luther would all get on the train on July 28th., choo-choo back here, and we'd all unleash and build the theatre anew. I know then we <u>would</u> have a play to open with, and we <u>would</u> other plays. Also in ways that I hope I'll have time to write about, the situation here is full of great opportunity for us, in all ways.

But,—and I'm going by what you wrote to Molly and I—not by what Bud writes, and Luther writes about you: I'm going even more by what I know of you and your life and your present needs—I SAY STAY THERE TILL YOU REALLY WANT TO COME BACK, TILL YOU REALLY FEEL YOUTHFUL AGAIN, TILL YOU WANT TO REBUILD FOR CHRISSAKE A THEATRE AND NOT PRODUCE A PLAY OR TWO.

What makes me say this? First of all I'm not afraid. I'm not afraid of waiting. Harold, I'll wait for you. Not inactively, mind you, because with whatever help and comradeship I can get, and to the best of my talents I'm going to work in a Group Theatre this coming season. But I'd rather work with you than with anyone else—I'd rather work with you than with anyone else in the theatre—I think you and I have the motor, the energy, the fanatical desire and fanatical energy, the brains, the experience, the ruthlessness, the richness, the emotion, the appetite to build the greatest theatre ever built and I think we can do it in America, today. But we can't do it with you split up, un-resolved, hesitating, <u>un-youthful</u>.

Here's what you say in your letter. "I am therefore reluctant to go ahead at this moment, unless I am enthusiastic and sold on a script—after I have begun with something like that the mere swinging into stride <u>will no doubt urge me on to</u> further effort on all sorts of material". I say that's the attitude of a tired man, of a reclining man, of a person who's going to scuttle back to safety and security when things don't click. I don't believe you'll remain in that state, and rather than start with you in such a state, I'd rather wait. I'll wait for you to recover your "equilibrium and fortitude" (your words). Leading a Group Theatre in our U.S.A. is an almost impossible task, and only a job for fanatics, for brave zealots. Its reward is <u>only in the activity</u>—and unless you really want that activity—unless you really want to do that specific thing—I say wait till you do, because I know that time will come.

I care less than anyone in the world what Cheryl, the critics, Lee, our friends or our foes say, think, whisper or print. Fuck them all! If you don't come back right away, I say to Luther and Bud, lets start without him. It will be much less of a theatre. It wont be a continuation, really, of the Group Theatre, maybe it won't work. But for the sake of presenting the face, the semblance of the Group, I wouldn't hazard your complete <u>cure</u>—if that's what it is.

About the <u>subjective</u> element. Only one thing you said there was new to me, or significant to me. I'll type it back to you. "I shall be free in July (contractually), but . . . will it be possible for me to leave Stella alone at that time? Stella is not the kind of woman it is good to leave alone (for more reasons than one!) Later, after she has done a picture or two—her psychology will change again and her feeling about the theatre will probably change—especially if there is a play at hand for her to consider etc." . . . Its silly to slight the importance of this problem to you—or, on the other hand, for us to continue to overlook its significance, objectively, for us. In fact, in writing what you did above, you ask that I face its objective meaning for me. And here goes.

I told you when I was there that I believe that Stella's personal problem can never be solved in any Group Theatre in the USA. She'll have to wait for the USSA. And even then, I wish her luck. There's no Group Theatre possible in this country today that can meet the requirements of an actress who says "I never want to be poor again". And much as I sympathize with this wish—I think artists who insist on working in a Group Theatre, must resign themselves, at the best, to consistent, but consistently small or "modest" incomes, second hand cars, borrowed cribs for baby, necessity for loans in crises, walk-ups, and no annuities. Also, I do not see how any Group Theatre, now, can give Stella her rightful place as an actress. Its impossible. Also, to make this one of the primary problems of the theatre, I'd say, would be to very much distort the case.

I don't know how her problem can be solved. And this, I know, means your problem. On the one hand you are disinclined to leave her till she's made a picture or two, or until her "psychology" has changed—if possible thru the stimulation of a script and attractive part, if and when. On the other hand, I don't believe that her problem can be solved within a Group. In other words this too would re-inforce your adjusting to the theatre scene like an individual producer, rather than like the leader and builder of a Group Theatre. . . .

Harold, I just got back from the South, and the impression of the trip is still overwhelming—not only the misery, degradation, oppression, but more the whole sense of the two forces clutched in a death struggle, and even more, what I can't forget, the brave heroes, those ordinary good guys who work every day of their lives and sleep every night under the threat of cocked guns. I want to tell you because you weren't fortunate enough to see and experience all the little things and all the big things I did, that the world is changing, almost with the speed of thought—even as we live and breathe now. Even in the two years since the last time I was south, the whole face of the labor movement is changed. Its out on the open, working feverishly, in the sight of all—also a ready target for guns. Events and progress that used to take years of laborious effort, now happen in a few quick days. A new kind of man is springing up, and a new kind of girl. Mountain folks don't recognize their young ones. History is charging with an irresistible rush. There is no playwright in the country who is really in touch with reality. I wish to god Cliff and Irwin had come down with me. It [would] make them view their own more common environments with new eyes, and understand the events described in their papers with a new sense of truth. The greatest menace to an artist today is the compact of forces which isolate him from the real world, which pull him out of touch. Its not a matter of keeping up with the papers. Its not a matter of facts. Its experience, fundamentally a different concept than fact. Experience registers differently—and the result on the organism is another one. Experience is the other face of facts. Any college professor can coolly and pleasantly tell you of the facts of our times. But Art arises from experience, and from reaction to experience which is appetite, desire, and all the active impulses.

And I thought all the time that there was NO theatre which dealt with the real world. Except ours tried to. All the rest deal, because of their very set-up, their innermost necessity and guiding nucleus, with the world of theatre convention. You know what I mean—you were one of those who taught me to see this more clearly. The Theatre Union and such theatres deal with just as putrid, unlifelike conventions, as do the theatre of the Kaufmans' and Abbotts'.

I came back with a war of impulses. I felt maybe the best thing for me to do was to try to write plays. For Chrissake no one else was. All the playwrights were either utterly corrupt, decayed or out of the dead past OR were gradually getting that way in Hollywood. Somebody's got to set down the dramatic experience of the times. And even with less talent, it would be important that some one do such work.

Then too I felt, I've got to stand by this theatre that tried and must continue to try to vitalize on the stage the experience of our times—the real experience. . . .

LOVE. GADGET

[Harold Clurman found a niche in Hollywood as an assistant to Walter Wanger and declined to return to New York until presented with a play that merited the "heavy burdens" of production. News of Clifford Odets's work in progress provided such impetus and neatly coincided with the expiration of his contract. Clurman assured Kazan of his desire to "work again with people I love" and returned to New York in August to direct *Golden Boy* (April 23 and May 28, 1937, Wesleyan).

Clurman's readiness to "distort" the Group on Stella Adler's behalf had precedent for Kazan. Clurman proposed in 1936 that Adler and Kazan codirect *Johnny Johnson,* the failed musical (Paul Green and Kurt Weill) that had brought the company to its present impasse. Adler would assume the more challenging aspects of direction, while Kazan provided technical support. The plan did not materialize, but Kazan resented Clurman's division of labor and willingness to "sacrifice a friend's best interests in behalf of his anxiety for Stella" (*A Life,* p. 156). The offspring of a legendary acting family, Stella Adler found the Group Theatre limiting in attractive roles for women and turned to Hollywood in the late 1930s for a more lucrative and glamorous career. Only a few minor roles in unremarkable films were forthcoming. She and Harold Clurman married in 1943.

Kazan planned to spend the better part of July in Tennessee and Virginia. The "irresistible rush" of history he met in the South found no legitimate expression in the programmatic Theatre Union or the equally conventional fare of George S. Kaufman and George Abbott, veteran Broadway producers, directors, and writers. Details of Kazan's southern trip are undocumented in sources known to the editor.

Kazan added a lengthy, digressive postscript (omitted) ending with praise for Harold Clurman as "the Group Idea" and his own allegiance to its preservation: "IT'S A WAY TO LIVE A LIFE! THAT'S WHY I'VE GOT TO HAVE IT."] TLS, 7 pp., BRTC

TO IRWIN SHAW

PM: S.S. *President Harding*, June 15, 1938

Dear Irwin

Trip is long, restful, and uneventful. The sky and sea are placid, on deck—no fights, no brawls—BUT below decks everything is tension. There the battle of this century is being waged in miniature. Nazi cells fight C.P. cells. Most of the crew is made up of Germans resident in Hamburg—and although most of them seem not to be ardent pro-Hitlerites they are so much more in a very dangerous position here. Our party people on board are very staunch and seem well-led—but the fight is desperate and severe.

Kermit's ideas on Quiet City seemed very clear to me on one point— which we may not have stressed enough as such—although it was back of most of our other points. I asked him to write you a note himself—telling you what he felt in his own way and in his own words. His reaction is valuable since it approximates (we have found) the reaction of a very large part of our audience—which although it is liberal and just and progressive in its feeling, is nevertheless very commonsensical, simple & even literal minded, stubbornly realistic, the "I believe you but show me" school. Best luck.

We eagerly anticipate the "Coney-Island" play. We'll write you from London.

gadget.

[Kazan sailed with the Group Theatre for a London engagement of *Golden Boy*. Brooks Atkinson praised the original Broadway production and made special note of Kazan's "sleek racketeer" character (*NYT,* November 5, 1937). A gunman and gambler, Eddie Fuselli is attracted by the youth and beauty of Joe Bonaparte, a divided character who has given up a promising career as a violinist for the wealth and fame of a boxer. *Golden Boy* broke a string of four consecutive Group Theatre failures on Broadway and succeeded on the road as well with Kazan recast as Joe Bonaparte.

Political conflict "below decks" was set against the background of Hitler's attempt to isolate the Soviet Union through alliances with Italy and Japan. The

Sailing to London for the production of *Golden Boy*: Sanford Meisner, Kermit Bloomgarden, Kazan, and Bobby Lewis

As Joe Bonaparte in the 1938 road company of *Golden Boy*

company itself was embroiled in personal conflicts, financial worries, and disagreement over the direction of the Group. The recent failure of *Casey Jones* (1938) had taken the edge off the success of *Golden Boy* and spoiled Kazan's debut as a Broadway director. A "hostile" star (Charles Bickford) and demanding investors demonstrated the bruising politics of the commercial stage. Tighter direction, Brooks Atkinson wrote in a review, might have invigorated Robert Ardrey's homage to railroading. Once in London Kazan was consoled by a complaisant Miss Diggins and critics who praised the Group's "furious" acting (*A Life*, pp. 168–72).

Before sailing on June 8, Kazan drafted four pages of "suggestions and criticisms" for revising *Quiet City*, a play by Irwin Shaw tentatively planned for a fall production. While summarizing Group Theatre consensus, Kazan set precedent for his own advice to playwrights with stress on the "growth and development" of character, the "clarity" of their relationships, and the necessity of "combustion and direct clash" rather than "emotional projection of a difference of philosophy." In summary he urged Shaw to define the "active principle" that motivates his leading character and gives "significance" to the play (June 7, 1938, BU).] *ALS, 4 pp., BU*

TO THE CAST OF *QUIET CITY*

[New York]
[c. April 20, 1939]

If I were to select one word to describe the performance on last Sunday night I would select the word DUTIFUL—a group of conscientious boys and girls doing somebody a favor and going thru certain performances which had been in general directed for them.

You are doing no one favors when you act dutifully—you are certainly not doing the author of a play like Quiet City a favor—because the play asks of its actors anything but dutifulness—passion, indignation, guts, charged feeling of their own—but nothing of the rote.

This is an experimental production—but I believe that the only thing which is not experimental is the play. I knew what the play was and Harold knew what the play was when we started—what were its incomplete features and what were its difficulties for an audience. I can't speak for Harold but I haven't been surprised by a goddamn thing about the play. The play quiet city is not being tested—we knew what it was—the experiment is in the production.

Don't misinterpret this to mean that I don't think highly of the play—because I do—much more highly than any of you—next to Rocket to the Moon, I think it the best new play produced this season. I think Irwin is the most talented young author in the country, since Cliff has arrived—and I think and here formally predict that excluding the possibility of war, you will live to see him acclaimed at least once as the author of the year—and certainly will be one of the most popular and successful authors in the country. This play has weaknesses but it comes from a great effort, rather than from a meagre soul—it comes from an effort to say too much—more than can perhaps be said in one script—it comes from a desire to expand the bounds of the theatre, married to an inexperience with certain aspects of it. The weaknesses in other words come from the same place that the merits come—from the bursting heart of a young dramatic poet.

I assure you that I knew the play's faults and the play's weaknesses before I ever started work—and nothing has been revealed to me by any events since. For me we were not trying out a play—we have been trying out ourselves—myself, Gorelik, yourselves—we've learned I think, for example that experimental productions should have more not less time than other productions, more, not less concentration, more not less energy and effort. Max has tried out some of his ideas although severely limited by physical circumstances. I've tried out some of my ideas—although again severely inhibited by things beyond my control—and you have been confronted with problems which you have not completely solved and which it may be years before you solve.

But there was something in the dutifulness of last Sunday's performance—and I mean by dutifulness—the quality of rote that a bored but precocious child has when he recites his abc's which emphasized to me a danger in the Group which I first heard about from Lee Strasberg—and then later when he started to work more, from Harold. Very often the Group actor is a critic when he's acting, and an actor when he criticizes—put it another way—reservations he or she may have about the script or the director or the productions dilute, or completely kill a central creative impulse which is at the heart of every good performance. I emphasize a central creative impulse—because most of your performances are fundamentally clear—and as I say you go thru the motions like dutiful children, like good souls to whom blame can't be attached—but the performance Sunday did not have a glimmer of illumination from within.

Now there were and are and will be always reasons why—why it happened, why its difficult, nay impossible—but its always impossible till you do it—and reasons do not interest me or concern me. I simply am interested in reporting the truth to you.

I want to say something about the method. The method to me is not a way of acting but a way of rehearsal—in other words you can act a certain way only if scenes are rehearsed a certain way. But the core of the meaning of the method to the actor to me is not talking, or listening—both of which are essential—not the theory of action as the essence of acting—which many good actors realize instinctively and perform instinctively, not the acquaintance with spine and long distance mood—the really central and fundamental thing about the method for the actor, especially as I've experienced it in my work on stage is that the "METHOD" relates the role to the actor's own personality—it really tries to make the performance spring from something which is genuinely present and creatively operative in the personality of the actor himself. Then its really like Life. Then our stage is quick with a kind of life that we see no where else—quick of the sense of souls alive at that moment—rather than with stage business, manoeuvres and stage managers conveniences.

To me that's the central thing that was missing Sunday. It is this incandescence from within.

It may seem to you a little late to say these things. But despite the really onerous difficulties under which we have worked most of the show has been well rehearsed in the sense that you all now know what you're doing and what the real nature of what you're doing consists of—most of you have at one time or other been alive at one point or another in your parts—now you must get it back—and you must make another step to find the central creative impulse which in your soul is the part. I have never really used a spine as Harold gave it to me. I have always found not so much my phrasing of it—for what are words. I have always endeavoured to find where a part touched me—what strand of my life it related to—could be fed from—and most of you too work in one way or another from the centre—some immediately and instinctively, like Phoebe—some slowly and deliberately like Sandy.

So it is not anything in your technique which seems to be cramping your creativity—it is actually that most of you were lifeless Sunday night at the core from which the parts might spring in each of you. Now as I said there may be and there probably were reasons but reasons now do not matter. You must stop going thru the play because we scheduled, or because I'm a nice boy who should have a break or because you are members of the Group theatre and the Group theatre has theatre ethics—stop doing me and the Group or anyone else favors—do yourselves a favor.

There is only one thing I respect and like in so-called Broadway actors—and that is their competitive sense. The young alive ones in the new mould, especially the comedians are inventive and the necessity of getting, winning, holding and getting more jobs makes them work. For Christsake if despite of what I tell you or what Harold might tell you about the play, you can't believe in it—believe in yourselves—in your performances. The person with whom I've been most impressed in this production has been Norman—not because he gives the best performance in the show—for he has faults and he has difficulties, and has this bad tendency and that bad tendency—but he is the only person of whom I have consistently felt

He loves his part.

He's always thinking about his part.

He's always inventing and trying out things for his part.

He's always looking for new things in his part.

He has real use for his part and will really grow thru his work and his performance.

That doesn't mean the rest of you haven't been conscientious. I don't think Sandy has ever worked better—but whether because of weariness—or disbelief in the play—or no inspiration from the director, or too much rehearsal or spring, or marital and extra-marital difficulties /// as I said I care not about the reasons—my impression of the rest of you in general is a montage of early morning faces, ten cent container of coffees, reading newspapers during notes, everybody too too tired, and always two people—usually the council members, twenty minutes late to everybody's annoyance. . . .

Now I have purposely laid you off for nearly five days. First of all I wanted you to rest, and refresh yourself—also we needed time to discuss the play and to cut it and make the few revisions we made yesterday. I believe that the show is now in much better shape and that the response Sunday will show it. But the rest and the lay off have been worse than useless if you do not now force yourselves to actually make a fresh and full attack on the parts. . . . It is not a matter now of talking to you about the spine of the play or in speaking further about the spine of your parts—it is a matter of really relating the spine of your part, or the central thing in your part to yourself—so that when you play, an audience sees and feels thru its overt sense and thru the sixth, seventh and eighth senses, which are nameless that there breathes and lives a human soul. . . .

[Kazan inherited a makeshift cast and a script vaguely based on the misgivings of a department store executive who has given up an artistic career and feels responsible for recent labor strife. The pale dramatic effects of *Quiet City* were sharply at odds with the bold expressionism of *Bury the Dead* (1936), Irwin Shaw's earlier antiwar play. Shaw eventually fulfilled Kazan's prediction of popular success with *The Young Lions,* a World War II novel and film (1948/1958).

Kazan traced the "dutifulness" of his cast to "a danger in the Group" that arose from the systematic nature of the "METHOD" and tempted the performer to be "a critic when he's acting, and an actor when he criticizes." Presumably "reservations" about the script had caused the cast to substitute criticism for "creative impulse" in a lackluster first performance. In urging actors as gifted as Phoebe Brand and Sandy Meisner to put aside objections and find "where a part touched" them, Kazan reached the "core" of the Method and with it the vexed question of "affective memory." Lee Strasberg introduced the well-known "exercise," as it was known in the early years of the Group, to prepare the actor internally by recalling personal emotion and its unique sensory effects. Once established, such memories were "theoretically capable of working always" on stage, although Strasberg admitted that they were subject to change, erosion, and the "problem" of incorporation (Strasberg, pp. 107–14). In the contentious annals of the Group, Stella Adler confronted Strasberg in 1934 with an alternate "theory of action," as Kazan now phrased it, which relied on the "circumstances" of the play rather than the actor's personal history to create emotional stimulus and dramatic continuity (Smith, pp. 179–82). In pressing the cast to make "a fresh and full attack on the parts," Kazan sidestepped old controversies and dismissed further acting theory and terms. The goal of the company was simply to convince the next audience that

"there breathes and lives a human soul" in each part. *Quiet City* was sh
a second workshop performance on April 23 and not revived.] *TL, 4 pp.*

TO MOLLY DAY THACHER

[New
[c. early Jur

In Biloxi it was a corner room with four windows and a view of the
New Orleans its a monastic cell in the top story of the Y.M.C.A. with
of two garages, a cathedral and a statue of Gen Lee, set upon a fluted cc
Wherever you look in the South there are garages and pictures of Gei
This particular room is about the smallest I've ever slept in. I would
scrupulously clean, except that when I pulled out the first draw in the bu
there was a dead Cockroach, on its back. However it is scrupulously c
How could it be anything else, there is no circulation. Instead of another
dow they give you a fan and same is playing upon me right now. Its very m
in town. The room costs one dollar a night, and my first meal, a luncheon
me back $2.25. Both are worth exactly what I paid for them.

I spent all day yesterday in the negro section of this "most interesting
in America", and all the evening in Negro dance halls and cabarets. As a gu
I had an old negro dentist and recreation director, who is a probate offi
in the juvenile court, on the side. I must have met a hundred negroes of
varieties, many of them creole with french names and a french flavor to the
negro speech. The names are often french and spanish—Picou, Perez etc. ai
the poverty is profound. I'm leaving tomorrow morning for Texas. The fello
who's traveling with me doesn't know it, but we're either sending his wit
home or leaving her behind. She tried to stir up some unpleasantness wit!
me, and constantly comments on my ill manners, my silences and my genera
evasiveness. Of course all these are as usual present, but, when I'm with her,
unusually aggravated (I believe) by the fact that I do not like her. However
I made a very wise step when I brought this fellow along. He works for the
government, in the recreation or folk art, or some damn bureau or other, and
he gets wonderful contacts in each town which forces me into places and to
meet people that I would never happen on if left to my own ways and means.
The latest is a contact in eastern Texas (near Beaumont). This section of the
state is called the "piny woods", and we are going to visit a turpentine camp
there. I don't know how long. From there we are going on to the ranch that I
wrote you of. From there on the future is uncertain. It partly depends on how
long I stay at the ranch.

By the way I would not this summer and I will never in the future, as long as I don't need money, work in Hollywood. However if I had an offer today, I would negotiate with them, and continue negotiating until they turned me down. This keeps you actively on the market there, raises your money price in their eyes, and in general gets you talked about. This is all against the day when we go just as broke as you always fear we will. Hollywood wants only what it can't get, but they must always think they almost have you.

I'm very sorry to hear about Kermit and the ulcers; they must have gotten worse if he's carrying medicine around. I feel fine; no ulcers, no dyspepsia, no headaches, plenty of optimism riding in like a tide, plenty of pep, and appetite for life, sharpened observation and real interest in everything in the world (a thing I didn't have when I left New York). You are absolutely right about the conversation part of it, and I made a resolution about that. I try to talk to people. I attempt to converse, and I certainly don't know how. One reason I liked Little Arbeaux in Biloxi was that I could converse with him. The only trouble with my damn resolution is that there's a woman riding with us who sticks in a man's throat. I admit defeat with her. However after a year of social life and freeing talk, I will call on this sharp nosed little pullet and freely and easily exchange words, phrases, banter and observations on a series of subjects which shall be of her choosing and as such those which most flatter her ego. At the end of said afternoon, I shall feel so triumphant that I shall hit her over the head with my shoe (which by this time will sure be off) drag her body to the river and there launch it like a ship. . . . Only when the eternal ocean has disintegrated her body into its eternal parts will things return to normal in the marine world. Then everything will be hotsy once again, and I will be proclaimed as the man who can talk freely to any and every man, woman or child living. Even you will pronounce me perfect and wish secretly that you hadn't divorced me. They will tell stories of my conversations with Clurman, and especially of that one which lasted thirty eight hours, in Clurman's own apartment, with his concubine Miss Adler in the next room, and they will remark that for thirty eight hours Clurman did not get a word in. I even answered the phone when it rang. They will create apocrypha—a tale of a man that I talked to death and a woman that I talked up to an orgasm, and how my eighteenth wife punctured her eardrums in desperation, and no actor would improvise with me, and actually I would have to give up directing and all forms of work and finally I killed myself in self protection. WRITE ME DALLAS GENERAL DELIVERY WILL YOU BABE AND GIVE ME A LITTLE NEWS—NOT LIKE LAST TIME MORE! HOW ABOUT MY SON?

[The latest foray to the South began with news of unnamed traveling companions: "Man and wife, my little friend," Elia wryly informed Molly Kazan from Washington. Neither the woman's irritating ways nor the "unpleasantness" she would cause was anticipated at first.

Kazan's boycott of Hollywood soon ended with acceptance of a supporting role in *City for Conquest,* a Warner Bros. film directed by Anatole Litvak.

Kermit Bloomgarden was hired as business manager to reorganize the Group Theatre on more professional lines. His association with the Broadway producer Herman Shumlin added to the suspicion and resentment of the remaining traditionalists.

A charming rogue, Little Arbeaux Callivet represented "one of the oldest American types" in his aversion to labor and determination "to enjoy life." He appealed to Kazan as an example of his "own fundamental boyhood ambition, not to work" ("Little Arbeaux Callivet," n.d., Wesleyan).

In Dallas, Kazan "came upon the trail" of a disgruntled Clifford Odets, who "spoke many a profound utterance that sickened the stomachs of the natives. What that boy needs is a little anonymity. A good playwright, as good as he is, should be very happy to be known 100% thru his works" (to MDT, n.d., Wesleyan). In addition to marital woes, Odets was struggling with a new play and feeling neglected by the Group, notwithstanding his self-proclaimed role as its "main dynamo."

Chris, Elia's first son, was born on December 16, 1938.] *TL, 2 pp., Wesleyan*

TO HAROLD CLURMAN

SH: Schneider Hotel, Pampa, Texas
[c. June 13, 1939]

Dear Harold

I am here in Pampa for their annual Top-of-Texas Fiesta. I almost got killed yesterday out at the ranch where I was staying, so I thought I'd write you a letter. I don't know what the connection between the two is, but it seems to exist. I didn't feel much like writing any letters this trip till after this little incident happened, and now here I am writing.

I've had an extraordinary trip. For the first time in my life I've made an effort to really reach the people who live just past the barrier which is the modern motor highway—and I've been successful. Partly the effort came from a desire to really see the country—the nation and the land which we purport to render on the stage. And partly from an earnest and almost desperate effort to break thru that psychology of protective isolation which I had encircled around myself. Once I gave myself a little shove, everything came quite easily. I had to keep giving myself a little shove—for if you really want to see the country you must endure a little hardship, you must exercise more than a little patience and resolve and finally you always run the risk of disappointment. But all in all my experiences were very fruitful. I really didn't go far—once I hit New Orleans. I progressed slowly. If necessary I waited in a certain town for a man's day off—if that man had something to show me. I would travel a day—

then stay within a certain area for a week practically. I passed a week in a fishing village on the gulf of Mexico, various lengths of time around New Orleans, around Call which is a company town in a lumber centre, around Dallas and Fort Worth, and now most recently about a week in and about the panhandle of Texas. I lived with some people at the Lazy "U" ranch (that means the "U" is branded on the animals like ⊏—kind of laying over on its side). I worked with them—where I was <u>able</u> to help, and I exchanged information with them, and boozed with the boys. One of them, a young cowboy nicknamed "Cotton" is here now taking in the show with me. He and I became buddies. We drove my ford out on the range, chased Coyotes and shot what seemed to me an enormous number of jackrabbits. This fellow is a wonderful rider—but soft and delicate spoken with thick lens glasses. I visited his buddies with him, and waited for their reserve to drop a little, to discover that even when it did, their jokes were a little over my head. One of his side kicks saved my life. He shoved me out of the way when a rope broke on a rig we were using to repair a windmill, letting down what must have been half of ton of pipe and tackle. A metal block skinned past my face and bit an inch hole in a metal casing. This fellow was quick witted enough to know hell was coming down. I wasn't. My Saviour's name is "Red" and he looks like Phil Brown, but made of a much coarser grained material.

I believe that if it wasn't for yourself and the Group I'd stay down here. At least for a real length of time. Texas has about everything to appeal to me—wealth, excitement, adventure, beautiful girls and what really is a type of man I never before met. There is a convention about Texans, which has a real basis in truth. They <u>are</u> open, generous, friendly, as democratic as the plains they live on. They are also everything the man from Alabama and the old deep South is not. They are free men—free of prejudice, free of hatred, free of fear, free of legal, moral and conventional bonds. Their fundamental law is a code of their own. You can kill a man here and often get away with it—but they'll like as not shoot you for stealing a shoat or a calf. I've heard of only two killers down here incidentally. One is the sheriff of this county, Cal Gray; the other is the sheriff of the county next to Call, the lumbertown. The latter must have been a case for he killed a negro almost every Saturday night. The people around there hated him. In the deep south they'd admire him—in fact I've heard them boast in Tennessee of nigger killers. The sheriff of this county seems to be a very moral fellow. He killed three men recently for dallying when he was trying to take them in. He's in hiding now because of the fiesta here—also because one of the men he killed had two brothers. But mainly because of the fiesta—the townsfolk don't want him to put the wet blanket on their little commercial holiday.

Again about the Texans. They are very contradictory, but its the contradiction commonly found among frontier people. They are religious people, especially the women. You early learn not to make sexual references in the home, to be sure of your ground before you suggest taking a drink in mixed company, never to lay a hand on another fellow's girl or wife, and to try to eliminate swearing and rough talk. On the other hand they are awful tough people. They are fearless and lewd, when they are lewd; and life is really very cheap. Their backgrounds and customs are at war with the kind of life their environment demands they live. Seemingly at war—for there really is no conflict in this contradiction. They are polite and gracious before respectable women—virgins and wives, but when they go on a toot, you can't hold them. Their common hardships and the great distances between their ranch houses have made their hospitality an absolute necessity of life. . . . These people are the most hospitable I have ever seen. When I got to the ranch, there was no question of my eating and bunking there as long as I felt like. They kept right on riding tractor and riding fence each day, from sun-up to sun down with the wheat, and when the windmill broke, with it. I was welcome to work, or to just sit. When the cowboy saw his cattle were o.k. he had time and we'd go shooting, or I'd try to ride. There was never any other attitude but the most disarming kind of taking me for granted. Also a great intellectual curiosity about city life—especially in re night clubs. They are sold on their own lives and its the most attractive I've ever seen outside of our own, which is more of a necessity for the spirit than a way to live your life pleasurably. . . .

Something quickens in you out here. I think its the stream of life running more swiftly, crudely like the raw-stinking oil out of the earth, but also richly like the very same black gold. The timorous innuendo, the double hesitation, the refined but voracious and all-devouring ego, the sorry, sick soul, the hidden enemy, the unresolved shame, the fear of action, the fear of inaction, the fear of life, the fear of defeat either don't exist here, or I haven't looked beneath the surface. Life here seems to be bounded only by the limits of the future. Sometimes in our work and in our city, among our people, our women and the men who work with us, it begins to seem that the earth and the endeavour of man has its boundaries and frontiers with one stinking production. An artist, it seems to me, runs a great danger that he begins to bound his life from the office to the theatre and from what the director said yesterday to what the critics say tomorrow. A person like myself is liable to pay too much heed and permit himself to be too much affected, too sorely hurt by what he hears and what he thinks he hears. Achievement seems too often to narrow down to the winning of one part from another "fellow"-actor. Also and most seriously, playwriting, playacting and directing would seem to partake more of the theatre and of effectiveness, than of the people and of life itself. Its too easy to forget that you are an artist, and what the meaning of an artist is, and that an artist starts from life and works towards life—forget it because we live in an "industry", in an "enterprise", in an "investment", we live in commercial, in petty commercial competition, where, strive as you may, the real glory comes with Winchell's mentions, and not with anything more or anything less.

The problem is to keep re-relating to life. I do not of course mean by this that you have to take trips constantly or at all even. Each artist is different and works or is re-freshened differently. But an artist working in our theatre must beware his life does not become MEAN, SMALL, CONFINED by UNARTISTIC bounds. An artist must constantly refreshen in himself the sense of the LIFE from which his work naturally withdraws him. This refreshening might very well come thru deep contact with a new person, or it might come from some major event in ones personal life. But THIS CREATION AND RECREATION OF ONE'S OWN STANDARD OF LIFE, WHICH ONE'S ARTISTIC WORK SPRINGS FROM AND RELATES TO is essential. The occupational disease of the actor's spirit is insularity—spiritual insularity. And its a deathly virus. I know because I suffered from it, and from the fear and shaken confidence which accompanies its stages. Its sister disease is self-protection, and the making of the spirit unavailable to contacts and contests which might hurt it.

A great theatre must somehow put demands on its actors and working artists that send them out to life. A great theatre must have an open door thru which life flows like a stream. When that door is closed, then the theatre becomes a theatre in the Broadway sense, and that's a scurvy thing. More specifically the problem with us today consists of going on from where we are. We have in a way created one theatre. We must go on to create from it another. Our greatest assets, the machine that will drive us forward, are the free and hungry spirits of our leaders. The enemies we have surround us. Our own actors, many of them, with their protectiveness, their desire for security, both commercial and ideological, the commercial scheme in which we operate, and our own need for the comforts and riches of life. Also the fact that we are now so successful. Also the fact that we must continue to be successful.

I think it is time we went to the $2.20 top.

[Molly Kazan broke the idyll of ranch life in Texas with doubts about the "security" of her marriage and an ultimatum that "it can't be kept unless it changes." Her husband's "eccentricities" and solitary travel could be accepted only with heartfelt evidence that Elia "WANTED" her. In a following telegram she urged him to "stay" where he was and said she would be "fine" with a forthcoming break from domestic responsibility (letter and telegram, June 9, 1939, Wesleyan).

The fiesta attended by Kazan featured George "Gabby" Hayes, honored guest from Hollywood, who presided over a rodeo and other events staged to boost the oil town of Pampa, Texas. Kazan made a garbled report of a liquor enforcement raid by Sheriff Cal Rose, of Gray County, in which a constable and a bar owner died in a shootout.

Publicists and celebrities coveted "mentions" by nationally syndicated columnist and radio personality Walter Winchell. Kazan's closing paragraphs recall a spring season that had been unkind to Harold Clurman, whose leadership of the

Group Theatre was faulted at a time of relative financial stability and critical praise. Trivial plays, interloping film stars, and limited rehearsal time had succeeded all too well, some thought, in adapting the Group to Broadway.

The stimulation of "deep contact with a new person" may allude to an affair with Constance Dowling, an aspiring young actress and dancer whom Kazan met in 1937 at the Belasco Theatre in New York. He was appearing in *Golden Boy* while Dowling worked as an usher. The intermittent relationship threatened divorce in 1944.

Kazan advised a reduced "top" of $2.20 for the Group's forthcoming production of *Thunder Rock* (1939). Neither Robert Ardrey's prewar "summons to faith," as a reviewer put it, nor Kazan's second Broadway direction survived a brief run—with a standard top of $3.30.] *TL, 7 pp., Wesleyan*

Constance Dowling

TO MOLLY DAY THACHER

PM: Los Angeles, June 24, 1940

Dearest girl:

I'm sorry I haven't written you for a while. There's nothing to write in one way. I've been shooting. Its wearisome, dull work with no savour or relish, work which reduces the actor to a clever performing prop. I'll be most happy when its all over. Litvak is no director at all. He's a stock producer of entertainment, suave, self-seeking and potentially very ruthless and cruel. He forces me to do the scenes in the most obvious and what he believes to be typical-American-gangster way. I've long ago discarded the working out I had made of the part. I'm not even in a place to debate with him. When you're working on a belt line, its impossible to stop the whole works and suggest a different way to do things. Although I'm fortunate in my first part, I am not in my first director. However, as everyone here says, it will probably all come out good enough in the end. I knew what I was letting myself in for when I came out here. And still its not pleasant to be "used". Enough of this. I do not feel in a complaining mood. This is not a disaster of the first magnitude and not a disaster of any kind. I'll bring home a little money, and a sense of how fortunate we have been in the theatre, and how much I need the theatre and my own work.

The most interesting part of the experience thus far has been the studio politics. Cagney and Litvak are having a kind of subterranean feud. Cagney's ultimate aim is to nudge Litvak out of the director's seat. Litvak wants to remain where he is, unless the situation turns so that it would benefit him more to walk out. He has already beaten Cagney to the punch by offering H.B. Warner to walk out. Warner, of course, refused, as Litvak knew he would. They have taken Wexley off the picture and asked Aben Kandel to write "additional dialogue". This is a move to pacify Cagney; it will not noticeably delay matters, since Warners are very efficient and will not tolerate waste. Also times pinch today, and they have every excuse for rushing. I'm in on the thing, that is have an ear in on the thing from two or three sides—Wexley (who's a nice man), Kandel (who is not very talented) and Cagney (who is a veteran and a veteran survivor of innumerable fights with the studio and is really tough and un-sentimental). The outcome will be nothing but a rejostling of ego, some plain speaking finally, and continued work.

(By the way, if you relay any of this chatter to anyone, please use utmost discretion—I don't want Litvak to get back that I don't think he's a director etc.)

A typical way they use you is illustrated by my last three days. Litvak and Cagney saw the rushes, and disagreed about them. Cagney finally insisted on some stuff being shot over, to give him more warmth. I was called noon Thursday for retakes; making up, dressing, I spent the afternoon waiting. Finally they said tomorrow. Friday. I showed up at noon again. This time they said come back 2:30. I went to Julie's house had a swim, came back, made up, dressed. At five they moved from one sound stage to the one where our set was standing. Cagney presumably was changing into his gym clothes for the shot. At ten of six he walks in, still in the wrong costume, calls over the asst. director tells him that 'he doesn't think they'll shoot anymore that day' and walks into his Cadillac and home. He has a clause in his contract which stipulates that he never works past six, and he never gives or modifies on this rule. You certainly can't blame him. He's plenty tired at six. I had planned to go to the beach Sat. with a lot of people. Now I was called Saturday. Four oclock we shot the retake. Litvak made it warmer in a superficial, noisy and "result" way. I felt I wasn't behaving really, that I was forcing (a little); but Litvak does know what he wants and he kept pecking at me till he got it. In short, we shot the retakes after three days of waiting, in 45 minutes, and in a way that's completely antagonistic to everything that I felt or intended with the scene. By the time I went home I felt empty and fed up, nervous and restless, all in a vacuum. I had a cocktail at Frances place, dinner with Aben Kandel, wife, John Brahm at Kandel's house. We stuffed ourselves on the richest possible duck, and some final bottles of French wine. I felt the same except irritated

now in a stuffed and heavy way. Sidney Skolsky came in. He had to cover the Giant Red Cross broadcast. We listened for a while and finally I bid them all a strange adieu and went off home to bed. That's life here. Frances calls it a furnished Vacuum. If that describes it to you, bear in mind that it is furnished in the most luxurious and rich way. Everybody has everything, except what is really worth living for. Why do I bother you with this stuff?

Well here I am. Its Sunday. I just had Breakfast. The best. Alan Baxter, the pathetic, has been calling me. I don't answer. Edmund O'Brien has been calling me. I don't answer. I don't want to talk to anybody. The radio is off its top, even crazier than back east. One whirl of the dial and you want to jump out the window. All day, every day they sell GOD here, and I mean <u>sell</u> him, along with used car, soap and dainties for milady. Also Swing mixed with news of Disaster in Europe on the scale that you know. So I can't listen to the radio. I'm invited at 2 to the home of Mrs. William Wyler to a swimming party. Sounds ducky, isn't it? I'm going, mainly because Wyler is a nice intelligent sort of man and I'll play a little pool. But his house is full of refugees, most of whom, God help me, I hate. That is, most of them in Hollywood. (One of them said last week, in defense of his position that we should send armies to fight Hitler immediately "We've got to fight him sooner or later. If we go in now it may only cost fifty Millions. Later it may cost one hundred Millions". In case you're in doubt, he meant DOLLARS) So. What was I saying?

Don't let this letter depress you. I'm really in wonderful health, calm, determined and much wisened-up. Only I must find some way to live that does not involve this Paradise. I hope I will. I have some new ideas; we'll see.

Be careful of money. For lack of it you can ruin your life. Cagney, who is a millionaire, at least, says as an answer to every implied criticism of Hollywood and the industry;—"There's always Wednesday!" That is not my language. I don't even understand it out of Cagney's mouth for I rather like him.

Write me all the little news from N.Y.

Goodbye sweetheart.

[Kazan played the heavy in *Paradise Lost* and *Golden Boy* and was cast as a gangster in *City for Conquest* (1940). His character "Googi" appears as an enterprising street urchin, does a "stretch" in reform school, and thereafter darts in and out of the film, ever more dapper and well connected in the New York City rackets. He dies in a proverbial hail of gunfire defending his childhood friend Danny (played by James Cagney), a boxer blinded in a dirty title fight. Kazan's film debut produced a lifelong aversion to the "belt line" production of Hollywood and the beginning of a friendly relationship with Bosley Crowther, recently added to the staff of the *New York Times*. Crowther described Kazan's character as "a cool, calculating stick of dynamite" and "trembled," with evident hyperbole, "to think what the Warners will coax out of this magnificent talent" (*NYT*, September 28, 1940). Anatole Litvak survived "studio politics" and went on to direct several more notable films—*Sorry, Wrong Number* (1948) and *The Snake Pit* (1948). John Wexley and Aben Kandel, later dubbed the "indolent" by Kazan, shared the screenwriting credit for *Conquest*.

Kazan maintained a casual correspondence with Sidney Skolsky, a syndicated columnist based in Hollywood, who covered the Red Cross war relief benefit on June 23. John "Julie" Garfield, Frances Farmer, and Alan Baxter, "the pathetic," were former Group Theatre actors pursuing careers in Hollywood. Edmond O'Brien was beginning a prolific career in film and television. A German national who immigrated to the United States in the early 1920s, William Wyler gave refuge and professional support to wartime exiles living in Hollywood. *Wuthering Heights*, his current release, led to a second Academy nomination for best direction.

"Determined and much wisened-up" after the recent failure of *Night Music* (1940), Kazan began a prolonged search for a new "way to live" that would not "involve" Hollywood. Clifford Odets's romantic comedy had closed after twenty performances and essentially brought the experiment of the Group Theatre to an end. The failure coincided with Kazan's first leading role in a Group production, a circumstance not overlooked by Odets in accounting for the disaster.] *TL, 2 pp., Wesleyan*

TO ROBERT LEWIS

[Ojai Apartments, 1927 Whitley Ave., Hollywood]
[June 1, 1941]

Dear Bobby—
Arrived here on Thursday night. Very very glad to get your letters with all the news. Friday morning 7 a.m. off to see Steinbeck. We stayed there Friday

night and most of Saturday. Here is the exact situation. (Don't tell a soul—the guy is very jumpy about publicity. Doesn't want any) He is now writing a book, which is a scientific and philosophical description of a trip he took in the Bay of Southern California. I was as surprised as you are. It seems he is a Biologist, owns half share in a Biological Laboratory. The trip was one of investigation into the forms of invertabrae (?) life. That means they stopped all along the coast, found all the specimens of crab etc. they could and then scientifically listed same. Steinbeck kept a log, and is now writing up the journey. The book will be illustrated with coloured photography, will have a strictly scientific section written by Steinbeck's partner, and then the other half of the book from a more general, poetic, philosophic point of view. He says its his best work to date, he wont get off it for anything etc. He works upon this for four hours every morning. At night he is going to start to work with Lewis Milestone on a screen play for the RED PONY (his short story). Well we kept trying to talk theatre to him. But he said he despises the theatre considers the form artificial and constricting etc. Then we asked him about the play he had written. He perked up—asked if we would like to hear any of it. So he went and got it and read all he has written, practically. Its half done. He's stuck. He keeps losing interest in it. Then it keeps coming back into his awareness. He throws it away, then picks it up again. Well we liked it very much. Molly who will be there Tuesday morning will tell you all about it. Its a perfect play for you to direct, and you would love it. Well, Molly, especially, tried everything she could to get him to finish it. But he remained dubious. However he definitely said twice, that if he finishes it he would rather have us do it than anyone else. He wants Buzz to play a part. And Spencer Tracy to play another. We said sure. Why not? Spencer has also been begging him to finish it so that he could take it to N.Y. next season. Next step is for me to meet Tracy, socially. Above all to keep after Steinbeck. Which we will do.

I'm very disturbed about Victor. He's just a bit of a weirdy. And I hope nothing's soured him. Will feel very relieved to hear everything's allright. What is the exact status of Kondolf? How deeply is he interested? etc. write me. I'd also like very much to hear from him personally. The rent on the Adelphi is too damned high.

I haven't done anything yet here. Haven't seen Clurman. Just got back last night and am settling down at the Ojai Apartments, 1927 Whitley Ave. Hollywood, room 501.

Love

Your letters [mean] a tremendous lot to me, so whenever you're not doing much, write. And get others of the "organization" to write. Molly will tell you the other news. And I will write soon. Love to Maria.

Gadg

[The Kazans hoped to gain John Steinbeck's support for the Dollar Top Theatre, potentially a new artistic home for Elia and Molly and their friend Bobby Lewis, an original Group member. They reasoned that a "top" of one dollar would draw a popular audience and still be feasible in a sufficiently large house. Lewis Milestone eventually filmed *The Red Pony* (1949) and was probably an early link between Kazan and John Steinbeck.

Still "jumpy" from the breakup of his first marriage, Steinbeck was living in Monterey and completing *The Sea of Cortez* (1941) with Ed Ricketts, close friend, collaborator, and owner of the Pacific Biological Laboratory. The book represented "a whole new approach to thinking," Steinbeck claimed, that will "outrage the second-rate scientists who are ready to yell mysticism the moment anything gets dangerously near to careful thinking" (Steinbeck/*Letters,* pp. 214–15).

Burgess "Buzz" Meredith and Spencer Tracy, friends of Steinbeck's, would not have roles in his on-again, off-again play "God in the Pipes," nor was it submitted to the Dollar Top Theatre. Collaboration and friendship awaited Steinbeck and Kazan, but it was Molly to whom Steinbeck turned for support and understanding at this time.

Kazan remained in Hollywood to act in a second film directed by Anatole Litvak and raise money for the new theater. Bobby Lewis, codirector, and Molly, head of the playwriting department, dealt with organizational problems in New York, including Victor Wolfson, a board member and potential contributor of plays whose elusiveness "disturbed" Kazan. Negotiations with George Kondolf, a candidate for business manager, fell through.] *TLS, 2 pp., Kent State*

TO ROBERT LEWIS

[Ojai Apartments, 1927 Whitley Ave., Hollywood]
[early July 1941]

Dear Bobby

I have your very fine letter. You must forgive me if I get jumpy from time to time. Here, the most important thing in my theatrical life is taking place three thousand miles away, and I'm pissing away my energies, drop by drop, on a movie lot. My part in the picture is insignificant, but demands my being there almost every single day. When I'm not sitting around waiting to be photographed (usually B.G.A.—back ground action), I'm recording some inane tune in the music department—or trying how to fake with the clarinet. And all the time <u>my war</u> is being fought day by day on a distant front. If I didn't believe in you and trust you as I do, it would really be maddening.

You are right about not including the playwrights specifically. It would have made our work with them much more difficult. And of course you are right, the most concrete evidence that we have plays and good plays to do, will be the scripts themselves. As we get them. (Incidentally Shaw and I have still not decided whether he will rewrite LABOR for us, or do another play that he told me about, and which I think very moving, much simpler to produce and really very quick and simple for him to write. Shaw's big bugaboo is Victor Wolfson—that is the fact that we have another playwright on our board, whom, he supposes, we will give producing preference, as the Group did with Odets. Shaw is ticklish, but is really all ours)

Never fear about my utter discretion or secrecy about the theatre. The cause of 90% of my historic quarrels with Molly has been that I exclude her (she says—and quite truly) from my life-work. I can not talk or gossip about my work and never have. My bed is not a lecture platform, nor a confidence-chamber, and will never be. I treat Molly as objectively as I possibly can—no matter what her reaction has been in the past. And I expect you and know you will speak objectively about Molly to me. God knows I have experienced what you call quirks in her character, the little bandaged places in her ego. Her problem—as you say—is not serious. You find in the theatre that you have to handle EVERYONE with care, using what is good and bearing with what's simply silly and off the point. Of course your solution with the stationery is perfect. I will not discuss this matter with her further.

About the prospectuses, I suggest that you mail me a package of them. I will send some out generally to a list of professional people. Certain other people will receive theirs just before I call on them. Contacts for money will get theirs this way—so the effect of the folder, and the interest it creates will thus be immediately used. A person like Cagney is not here. There's no use sending him one—it would merely lie rotting in his mail box for a month.

Also send me a list of the people that you Victor and the others think I should contact in Hollywood. If any of these are particularly close friends of yours, like Joan Crawford, I suggest you write them and say that I will call on them—

About the theatre, I have expressed twice what I fear. You knew this consideration of "show will be lost in that house" all the time. So, I will simply leave it to you. If it looks like the New Yorker is the best we can do, and a chance comes along to take it, that we should not pass up, act as you see fit.

Fuck Lee Shubert, that fetid cadaver. He is the embodied symbol of the "Professional" theatre. Also fuck our friends on B'way, who think and feel exactly as Shubert does. (I thought someone else had long-leased the Ambassador?) . . .

*********** (time interval) **********

I just got a letter from Molly. She is very happy. Very happy to be working with you. She says: "Bobby conducts the theatre in a masterful way in faded Khaki shorts, looking like Buddha, from his tasteful Tudor City flat. (I can just

Faking the clarinet in his second Warner Bros. film,
Blues in the Night

see you)—I am having the time of my life with this theatre. Don't let me kid
you, in case sometime I don't like some little item. I am having the time of
my life."

I wrote her a letter the other day and told her to practise <u>bending</u>—said it
would do her good. . . .

E.K.

[Kazan's character in "Hot Nocturne" has dropped out of law school to play clari-
net with drifters and other ne'er-do-wells who share a passion for the "real blues."
Romantic conflicts and noir villains divide and threaten them until a violent finale
restores unity and signals a happy return to the road. His was "a cute little part,"
Kazan thought, although he considered the script a "mediocrity" and the Warner
Bros. lot "crowded and busy in the emptiest possible way" (to Lewis, n.d., Kent
State). Anatole Litvak continued to direct Kazan's second film with vague, inar-

ticulate prompts: "'More, Getch, more!'" The film was released later in 1941 as *Blues in the Night*.

Kazan praised Bobby Lewis for drafting a "brilliant" Dollar Top prospectus but soon asked for revision, including "schmaltzier" promotion of the directors and a listing of scripts to be put into production. Lewis replied that circulating such a list would deter others from writing for their new theater, as Kazan's "ticklish" relation with Irwin Shaw seemed to confirm.

Tension between Molly Kazan and Bobby Lewis flared when her name was left off the Dollar Top letterhead. Lewis assured Kazan that they were still "working together brilliantly" after Molly complained to Elia of his partner's autocratic manner. Lewis's solution was to order an ample supply of letterhead with Molly Day Thacher listed as "director of the play department." Reference to her lack of "simple human, uncritical help," as Elia put it, would arise in later correspondence during a more serious conflict.

Lee Shubert, tightfisted theater owner-producer and "fetid cadaver" of Broadway, thought the Dollar Top idea "ridiculous" and reportedly told Lewis that "'if the play is no good, no one will come to see it, and if it is good, you should get $3.30 out of it'" (Lewis, p. 129).] *TLS, 2 pp., Kent State*

TO CLIFFORD ODETS

[Ojai Apartments, 1927 Whitley Ave., Hollywood]
[mid-July 1941]

Dear Cliff—

I've resented you for a year now. Every time I would hear that you told Jed Harris, or Boris Aronson or some cafe companion at Lindy's that I ruined Night Music, I would burn up, and foolishly never say anything to you. I think everything would have been much better if you had vented your anger directly upon me, then we might have had a fight and an understanding. But the mutual distrust, tension and uneasiness which grew up, neither resolved us into opposites, nor permits us to be friends. I've discovered with other people silence and distance make for distrust, where a few quick and honest words would create connection. And I very much want connection with you! Even if you never write a play for us, I believe we <u>are</u> in the same theatre. Just as I want to stay close to Lee Strasberg—much closer than I have been. So let me say a few things to you and maybe clear the air.

What I resented about you in NIGHT MUSIC was your surly silence. Your need to pass a judgment, which had a high moral tone, handed down from a high moral position—as though I had intentionally played like a star!—regardless of direction and author's intention. I resented that you seemed [to] thrust the entire onus of the "failure" of NIGHT MUSIC upon HC and I, and take none upon yourself. But chiefly its the High Moral distance you put between yourself and the rest of pitiful mankind. A black storm of disapproval, which you stab thru occasionally with a frantic plea "Why don't people love me?" and so forth. The result is that Sandy thinks you cold and distant and superior, Bobby feels you dislike him, most of your old friends aren't comfortable with you, or speak freely in front of you, because of the wall that YOU raise. The only one of them who wouldn't know what I mean is Molly, and that is a sentimental self-deception on her part, because I've read on your face that she irks you. Now there is a great deal of defense in this attitude of yours, as well as in the need to write a journal, which I understand from the several samplers is a combination of roasting your mutual distrust, tension and uneasiness and detailed descriptions of your conquests. You have become the standard bearer of a kind of artistic absolutism which separates you from your people, and instead of contacting you with loftier souls than ourselves, brings you to Lindy's Cafe.

I think you could be the most loved guy in the theatre. You are a great artist. You have strains, thick strains of humanity, generosity. You have a desperate need for love, and the give and take of the spirit. At once one of the sweetest and saddest examples of what I mean is your relation to my kids. I think you do really like them, its possible for you to really like them. Yet its difficult for you to really connect with them. And then you go out and buy them a lot of gifts. Everytime I received a gift from you, I felt I'd prefer five minutes simple and natural contact (as much <u>my</u> fault).

I'm a tough case too. After thirty-one years I'm just beginning to realize what I'm stuck with in the way of a personality. And its tough, I mean, I'd like a lot of things differently. I've got a lot of hampering contradictions too and often I wish I were some one else. But I'm stuck with myself, so I've got to find a way of doing what I can.

Believe me, I don't want to run a DOLLAR TOP THEATRE. Its too much responsibility, too much grief, too much debate-in-an-office. I wish some one else would run it and I'd work in it. Just so long as I can function. But look at it the other way. What the hell is there for me to do? Where <u>can</u> I function? I could sit in N.Y. and wait for parts. I'd end up in three or four FIVE ALARM WALTZ, then maybe a good part in a play I like. Besides I can't abide not working. An actor is an entity (actor) only when he acts. At other times, he is a fool! usually an elegant egotist, a bore, a prey to alternating melancholia and megalomania, and a leading candidate for the nut house. I could sit in N.Y. and do radio. Horrible! I could look for plays to direct. But I don't like 92 percent of the plays that are done, and the others go to established, competent directors, like Shumlin, and great directors like McClintic. On the other hand I could come here. I could be one of Buddy DeSylva's assistant producers at Paramount. (offered) I could go to Metro and work under Pandro S. Berman. (offered) I've been offered several jobs at Warners. I've sometimes wished I

liked it here—it would solve plenty. But I don't! in fact worse than that, I
sick, I get fits, I get ugly, I begin to disappear like Leverett, drink like (
lins, walk like Margaret Barker, and talk like Grover Burgess crossed with
reverse rhapsodies of Clurman. Harold takes it better than I do. He say
himself, I'm resting my mind, and he rests. He says I'm forgetting about
Group, and reloading my spiritual batteries, and he rests. That's great.
H'wood has a violently different ~~diversely activating~~ effect on me.

So what's to do. If I'm going to have a place to function, I've got to cre
it for myself. So one day Bob and I get to talking, talking from common (
ficulties and common needs, and the idea starts; we work it out; we coll
friends to it (a process which I hope is just starting) and we go on and (
Perhaps we are a little blind about it. Certainly we are going more from desi
and intention and hope, than from sage and considered analysis. (although
did some of that last as well) But what the hell, suppose we had figured ai
figured maybe we would have decided very wisely that the idea was absolute
impossible, and September would find me in the Bette Davis picture playir
the part of a grotesque little process server ($1250 per week), or else back i
N.Y., paying my way by doing CRIME DOCTOR Sunday nights! Did you eve
hear CRIME DOCTOR?

Meantime, certain things are working out very well. Victor Wolfso
expressed a strong desire to be part of the organization. So he is. So I have
working contract (the only kind that's worth much in these swift days) with a
fine man. He's written us a new play, that Bob and Molly like very much. Irwir
is going to do us a play. Here and there we meet tremendous enthusiasm—
above all from authors, artists of all kinds—for they are the ones who are just
a little burnt and need what we need—a place to function. The very fact that
such an intention exists and is being pushed into fact, is the rallying call of a
host of artists. It gives hope to a lot of people that would give up other wise;
it holds together, for a time at least, forces that would otherwise disintegrate.
Just as Lee's classes!—I don't mean only the classes themselves, but also the
very fact that some one is teaching acting as an art.

[Kazan destroyed a "weak, complying letter" and wrote candidly to Clifford Odets
after learning of his indifference to the Dollar Top Theatre. "I will tell him the
truth, the regard I actually do have for him, and the other things I feel about him
as well. I honestly think that's the only approach to the man that will yield us ANY-
THING AT ALL" (to Lewis, n.d., Kent State).

The failure of *Night Music* occasioned a mournful entry in the author's journal.
Clifford Odets felt as though "a lovely delicate child, tender and humorous, had
been knocked down by a truck and lay dying." Harold Clurman's "bafflement"
in directing and Kazan's unreadiness to assume a romantic lead had caused the
tragic accident. Especially galling to Odets was the disparity between his unflattering reviews and Kazan's "brilliant" notices for a "clumsy, brutal, clodhopperish
performance" (Odets, pp. 41–50). Clurman was one of the known "samplers" of

the Odets journal and may have told Kazan of its existence. He and Odets worked briefly on play ideas in 1943 but without the intimacy of close friends.

The odds against the Dollar Top Theatre were longer than those faced by the Group, but the new venture addressed Kazan's urgent question: "Where can I function?" The bleak alternatives were roles in trivial Broadway fare—*Five Alarm Waltz* (1941) closed after four performances—dull studio work in Hollywood, or Sunday-night appearances on *Crime Doctor* (1940–47), a popular radio show featuring a criminal psychologist turned sleuth.] *TLd, 2 pp., Wesleyan*

TO ROMAN BOHNEN

[New York]
[September 1941]

Dear Buddy my boy—
Send me the dough for the car. I need money (oddly enough and unbelievably enough) I've thrown all my funds into a gorgeous piece of swamp and stubby hill in Connecticut, which has soaked it in without leaving a mark. So send me seventy five bucks or whatever it is you have decided to pay me for the Chevrolet. Also I still think its worth a hundred, but its too late to argue that point. If it goes over two hundred on the turn in price, don't you think you ought to give me a hundred.

About the DTT, its difficult to write. Its impossible to describe a storm when you're in the vortex. I'm buffeted and pushed and knocked around and really I can't say much except that its difficult, that we have a couple of pretty good plays, which, these days is plenty. Also N.Y.C. is wonderful, thrilling and invigorating. How is that dreary ass hole called Hollywood. If you hear anything about my picture send me that news along with the cabbage.

Your friend—gadget.

[Roman "Bud" Bohnen trained at the Goodman Theatre in Chicago and joined the Group in 1934. He and Kazan played in *Five Alarm Waltz* after the closing of the Group and searched at the same time for alternatives to conventional Broadway fare. "That dreary ass hole called Hollywood," as Kazan put it, produced the Actors Lab, which creatively engaged Bohnen until his sudden death in 1949.

Elia and Molly discovered the "gorgeous piece of swamp" on a spring drive in 1941. "Overlooking the field and the water was a farmer's home, painted white, with many windows facing west, now made golden by the setting sun. Behind the house was a saltbox barn, also white. The old sugar maples that guarded the place were beginning to show green, tinted with the red of their winged seeds" (*A Life*, p. 188). The original purchase of 115-odd acres in rural Sandy Hook, Connecticut, saw the addition of a modern house, tennis court, swimming pool, and nearby acreage.

The Dollar Top Theatre ("DTT") faced rising costs and a shortage of plays in the fall preceding Pearl Harbor. Scripts expected from Clifford Odets, John Steinbeck, and Paul Green failed to appear, while funding and theater space proved elusive. The directors postponed the first season until 1942, when they were forced to set a new ceiling of $2.10. The idea of a "People's Theatre," successor to the Group, lingered until March, when its ending was announced in the press.

"Elia Kazan burns up considerable nervous energy hopping about the screen." So wrote a *Times* reviewer, who panned the vacuous script and clumsy direction of *Blues in the Night*. Kazan later advised viewers to "skip" the film when it "comes on the late-late show" (*A Life*, p. 190).] *TLS, 1 p., BRTC*

Molly Kazan with Chris and Judy

Tallulah Bankhead, arms raised, in *The Skin of Our Teeth*: "I don't understand a word of this play."At right, Fredric March wags his finger at Montgomery Clift.

Part II

Broadway

1942–1949

[New York]
August 9 [1942]

My dearest Molly

I've read your last letters of abuse and of love several times. I'm moved two ways. Your abuse stings. You say you don't care to hurt me, still you strike at everyone of my vitals. You have for months. You say no one likes me, that I'm universally despised. You know (in your guts) that I'm so soft and good that I care a lot what everyone says about me. You know that hurts. You want to hurt me. You know its not true. Some people, many of a certain group, yes. But are they right to despise me. Is it fine that they hate me, understanding productive. Can they stand up straighter than I do. I stand straight. I stand straight because at last I've started to release myself, untie myself. Sure its hard, years later. I don't mind your calling me a shit. I never thought I was an angel. I kept telling you I wasn't an angel. It was you who had a false, exaggerated, fatuous notion of me. I didn't fall from any pedestal except the one you raised for me. And it was built of your needs, not mine.

Then you undercut me viciously and repeatedly where you know its tender and the knife slices. You say I've become artistically corrupted. (I spit at your judgment.) My prime with you was Paradise Lost. That's when I was writing that diary you have memorized sections from. And that diary is <u>half</u> of the mess. The torment, the inhibition, the confusion. The hunger, the gnawing hunger for achievement that had nothing to do with an artistic purpose, just thrusting ambition. Now I feel better. I've been thru more, I'm clearer.

You fairly scream at me in your letters to <u>be</u> confused. I am, I'm pulled and twisted. If I knew what it was, I wouldn't be, or as much. I'm sticking my neck out. You think its easy for me to hurt you and the kids. You think its easy for me to hurt you and the kids. You goddamn stupid, stiff. Scratch my eyes out! I love you, DEVOTEDLY WITH AS MUCH AS I CAN, and you you stiff necked poor, superior girl—why are you so superior. Don't you hurt? Aren't you turned. IS IT SO GODDAMN SIMPLE FOR YOU. IS EVERYTHING CLEAR FOR YOU— you sit up there LOVING ME and hating your mother. You're leaving the one guy that would help you, look after you cling to you one way or another TILL DEATH—and to your children. I'm honest. You fool. I'm honest. I'm one of the few men who sticks it out and takes it on the head with a lead pipe. My head is bleeding, I'm beat up and all you know how to say is in cool typewritten analysis that I'm motivated by self pity. So what? I take it. I'm taking it. I face the facts. I go in there and get hit again. How does your friend Steele manage it so he doesn't get hurt. How does your smug stuffy-stale friend Carnovsky manage it that he stays smooth skinned. No, no harm penetrates to Strasberg's study. He's pure and well washed and clean.

I'm a shit. That's right I went thru the shit. I did the dirty work of the Group. I built the scenery of Green Mansions. I was rejected (and correctly) for two years there. I became a stage manager. I didn't want to be a stage manager. I kept fighting, even made an actor of myself. I've directed five failures in a row, still I keep coming. I'll keep coming. I went to Hollywood, WHICH I HATED—I WENT AND CAME BACK. I tried to start a dollar top theatre. Nobody else—me. Not you, not Carnovsky, not Strasberg, not Odets, not Steele not Aronson. IT WAS IMPOSSIBLE—I TOOK THAT BEATING TOO. And you undercut that. Lewis this Lewis that. Sure you worked hard, you're a fine girl and a good worker. But simple human, uncritical help—something else. I'm not blaming you, mind you—and I'm not reviling you. I love you. I think you wonderful. But I'm sick of not answering. My pride gags. I took it, the beating ups—you call it self pity, but I took the beating ups and I call it fact. What the hell did you ever do, coupon clipper? Sit home and criticize Harold—this that—Clifford this and that. Well Harold took it too. He stuck his neck out. He plowed thru shit of all kinds and years and years of shit— and isn't it natural that some clung to the corners, under the finger nails, and perhaps a slight stench.

You keep talking about the war in a holy despairing voice. Do something about it. No you want everything. Kids must have you. I want to believe everything is fine. I know everything isn't fine. I love kids, my kids. I come from a family of kid lovers. I love my mother. I am crazy nuts, deliriously in love with my father. I'm in love with him. I feel sorry for him. Is that self pity? Analyze! He came from the otherside, a lonely boy without the American tongue and in a strange country. He went back home and picked a fine girl and got her love. She has loved him thru thick and thin for thirty years—let him have his old standards. Didn't want him to measure up to anything. I don't want to measure up to anything you have in your head. That doesn't help me. What helps me is what I have been doing. You think I care what Paula Miller thinks of my having an affair with Constance. Constance is worth thirty Paulas—in and out. I wouldn't go to bed with that slop belly, slop breasted good natured cow. How can a person who wants to be called an actress let herself go that way. Well all right, forget it, Paula is all right. What do I care what Phoebe says—well I do, Aronson, well I do, Ruth Young, what do I care, well I do. BUT I'LL LIVE MY WAY. BECAUSE I'VE GOT TO SOLVE MY PROBLEMS NOT THEIRS. I LOVE YOU NOT THEIR WOMEN AND THEIR MEN. . . .

I wish I loved Constance. I don't. She's not this and not that. I don't love her. She's this and that, I don't love her. I feel grateful to her. I'd do a lot to help her. I have done a lot to help her. You idiot. How dare you say that all I feel for other people is pity? I've done more to help some people in the theatre than anyone else. I did an awful lot for Connie. No, I don't think it sufficient reward just to give my favors. Though they are nice. I talked with her, I educated her, I told her where to go and what to do. She's a better girl due to me. I didn't loot her, or use her. . . .

You love me. After all I've done you love me. There's a reason for this. I love you. Its not easy for me. (I suppose you think that is a very superior snooty and selfish remark.) What am I going to do? How can I write you? Christ you've got me cut to little pieces that are insignificant. I was saying, I love you. You say "I would do almost anything for you. Anything that had hope for any of us. Don't know what it is. You have my love". I'll tell you what it is.

Lets unite again. We'll get another apartment. I'll be different—I want to be different, and I will be. How much, I don't know. There are no miracles, but there IS CHANGE. I think I'll be better for you. I think I will be better for you. How much I don't know. There are no miracles, but there is change. I love you, and the children. I actually and concretely want to live with you and the children. I don't want to be separated. I want to be together. . . .

And what are you concerned about my ~~being~~ becoming promiscuous (I forgot, you don't care whether I do or don't) Well if you care, my guess (as vs. your guess) is that I won't. In all my life I met one girl I loved. I loved her and married her and had two kids—the best—with her. I got married too early, but it was inevitable because I loved her. She kind of pushed me a little. But I had been going under my own steam a long time, and I wouldn't have let myself be pushed unless I wanted to. Anyway I don't regret it, and didn't. Then all the problems I had skipped came up. This hunger and that—not all about other girls, but some about that, and sometimes acute about that. Well I had plenty of chances to be promiscuous. But I never in my life slept with a whore, and I really only had one other affair. The rest never came off, one way or another. What am I telling you anything for I don't know. I know I love you. I want you. You think I'm a shit. That's where we were.

I started to say, at the beginning, that I'm also moved to simple love. I love your handwriting. I love that stuff about 35¢ meals. I love it how you look after the kids. I love the only two pictures I have of you—one the ten year old with the smile, and the other the Air-warden license, a little tense and drawn, but so good and sweet. I love you, when I wash your dishes; I like them though they're not the kind I would have picked, still I probably wouldn't have picked any. I love the dishes in the country. I love the country place, but its dust and old tin cans without you. Its classical up there. I sinned and the weeds are growing up around the weeping willow trees. But that's a morning's work to clean that out. I like it in your little study. (I took the best room didn't I; I always do, don't I?) (But isn't the whole house yours in a way. Honest and truly, I'm a mess and so on, I'm a shit, but there is something weak in me that needs that room to myself. Its too bad that I am that way. But its getting less isn't it. You need it too don't you?)

Looks to me we're losing the war. Looks terrible, doesn't it. India, Maikop, the goddamn optimism and callow tone on the radio. Horrible. Why don't I do something. I wish I could write. You will do something, I know. I have a lot of simple faith in you. It keeps coming up no matter what I have just been saying, no matter what you have just said.

I await your next poisoned missile (how in hell do you spell that. I bought a dictionary but its in the next room.)

Thank Judy for her letter (like Chris) and kiss Chris. When he gets to N.R. I'll take him out. He's my little friend and I'm already teaching him to sneak away from the party and get ice-cream. I think I got a smile like Chris. Harrity said that. Well he doesn't know me (or he wouldn't talk to me) but he does know Chris.

I'm sorry I called you any names above. I don't care about calling you any names. But I guess I'll send the letter anyway.

write me will you day?

[The Kazans separated after Paula Miller, wife of Lee Strasberg, told Molly of her husband's affair with Constance Dowling. Casting her in *The Strings, My Lord, Are False* (1942) invited gossip and was, as Elia knew, "an act of personal and professional idiocy." The "curse" of his life, he wrote much later, was the "illusion" that a "secure domestic life" and the "freedom" of a bachelor could be maintained without causing injury (*A Life*, pp. 194, 217).

Kazan "did the dirty work of the Group" for several years before playing his first important role in *Paradise Lost* (1935). His character Kewpie, a cabbie "with a dozen phony side lines," offers an illicit alternative to the son of a Depression-era family in Clifford Odets's sequel to *Awake and Sing!* (1935). The play suffered by comparison and closed after a brief run—notwithstanding an expensive advertising campaign funded by the author to save it. Elia may have been "prime" with Molly in 1935 but his notices as Kewpie were modest. The diary to which he attributed "half" of the present domestic "mess" has not been identified.

"Superior girl" and "coupon clipper" refer to Molly Day Thacher's heritage as the great-granddaughter of a Yale president and the daughter of a corporation attorney with offices on Wall Street. Elia once composed a "family motto" for the Thachers and the Days: "There's a right way and a wrong way and nothing in between." Only gradually and reluctantly did he come to admire Molly's "Yankee intransigence" (*A Life*, pp. 73–74, 423). Among the "pure and well washed" cited by Kazan are Wilbur Daniel Steele, a writer of contemporary note, and "smug stuffy-stale" Morris Carnovsky, a founding member of the Group Theatre, whom Kazan later "named" in congressional testimony.

On August 9 German forces approached the Maikop oil fields in southern Russia, a key objective of Hitler's summer offensive. Earlier in 1942 Kazan was classified III-A: married with dependents but no occupational deferment.

Judy and Chris Kazan were six and three years old respectively. Elia planned to see Chris when he visited his paternal grandparents in New Rochelle. Richard Harrity, an editor of *Yank, the Army Weekly,* was "courting Molly by wooing the whole family," or so Elia surmised (*A Life,* p. 262).] *TL, 4 pp., Wesleyan*

TO THORNTON WILDER

SH: 50 Deepwood Drive
New Haven, Connecticut
[c. October 18, 1942]

Dear Thornton—

First chance to write to you. I'm sitting in your room—party downstairs—there are a couple of things I must tell you. My own impressions at this point. These are for your ear entirely, and even now I hesitate, for I don't wish to be disloyal to Myerberg, who is, after all, our producer.

My impression of the first act is not his. He seems to think the act goes to pieces at the point of the entrance of the "Refugees". I do not feel this. There is a change here in the reaction of the audience to the performance. But I believe this change is to be expected, since there is a growing "seriousness" in the material. The comic flashes however do continue, and the tone of the act is not fundamentally changed. The response of the audience at the curtain is excellent. There is some bewilderment in the interval, but it is excitement and stimulation rather than dis-interest of any kind. IN SHORT, for me there is nothing that you need to do to the first act. If you were here we could fuss here and there, to benefit—but the first act does not worry me.

Neither the second. The "orgy" seems very skimpy at times, but this is because I'm a little short handed in the cast. I can understand Myerberg's difficulties with budget and salary list, and appreciate these—at any rate, the second act IS effective, and amusing, and does get over. Nothing fundamental to do here.

Our trouble seems to be in the third act. I have worked, and will continue to work here—but there is something about the third act that makes the audience stir a little—cough. No catarrh in Acts one and two. The rehearsal scene is hilarious. When the curtain went down after it for a moment tonight, we got an excellent hand. Then comes a gradual sobering of the mood, a slowing down of more obvious "action", and what impresses the audience (not myself, not sensitive people like John Cromwell, Phil Barry, Bob Ardrey, John O'Hara etc. etc.) as talkiness—At any rate, let me report the fact. At this point, after our second performance, the audience has both times been restless and impatient with the later half of act three. The worst spot, possibly, is after the exit of Henry with Sabina—when the Antrobus pick up the play again—the scene where they are alone together for the first time and settle down for the evening, a scene which must necessarily be quiet and subdued, seems too low for so late in the evening. At any rate they stir.

Now all this would be very simple if you were here. I feel we could fix things up in no time. But without you its DIFFICULT. Myerberg is off on his tangent about Act One, and—well if you could be here for one performance and one talk, and one short morning of cutting and trimming and slight readjusting! Can't you get two days off?, two or three? That's all that would be required, I feel. It would help your play and your cast and your producer and myself immeasurably. We are so very near to something extra-ordinarily fine here, and really I can't overstate how valuable you would be now be.

I hope you're not being worried about the reports of temperament and squabbling and Myerberg's poor etiquette, etc.,—these things are exaggerated and really neither here nor there. The important thing is that though most of the cast thoroughly dislike Michael, they still think him very astute, respect him fundamentally; the important thing is that the cast love your play and their roles, and play the show with zest and enjoyment. And finally that while some of our New Haven society "loathe" it, a lot of our good people, thought it wonderful and were thrilled watching it. I think that we have worked well and that we will go on working well. There is one thing that I, and the actors cannot do however—and that is something you can do very quickly and very easily if you were here.

I must have labored this point terribly. Of course you must wish to be here terribly—and why do I beat the point so loudly—forgive me.

I feel fine. The company really like each other and, since you keep asking, all have a wonderful time playing your play. You have certainly given them and myself great fun and deep pleasure. They are all sweetly devoted to you—even those who don't know you—very proud to be in your play.

Write me—c/o Ford's, Baltimore

Gadge

[Captain Thornton Wilder (Army Air Intelligence) was beset by a novice producer and director and quarrelsome stars while stationed in northern California. He turned to Michael Myerberg after Jed Harris, producer-director of *Our Town* (1938), rejected *The Skin of Our Teeth* with prayers that it not be given to "some foolish producer or director" in its present state. Myerberg's sole production to date—*Symphony*—was savagely reviewed by Brooks Atkinson in 1935 and closed after three performances. Robert Ardrey provided the link between Kazan and his former teacher at the University of Chicago. Wilder saw the Group production of *Thunder Rock* (1939), which opened and closed in a scant two weeks, and retained a favorable impression of Kazan's direction: "'fine comedy; superb stage management; and dry economy in emotion'" (Niven, p. 531). Fredric March and his wife Florence Eldridge played Mr. and Mrs. George Antrobus, while Tallulah

Bankhead, notorious star of *The Little Foxes* (1939), was cast as Lily Sabina, maid of all vices.

Wilder reluctantly drafted a program note to relieve the confusion of early audiences: "The Antrobuses have survived fire, flood, pestilence, the seven-year locusts, the ice age, the black pox and the double feature, a dozen wars and as many depressions. . . . They are true offspring of Adam and Eve, victims of all the ills that flesh is heir to. They have survived a thousand calamities by the skin of their teeth. Here is a tribute to their indestructibility" (Acting Edition, Samuel French, 1944).

Wilder addressed Kazan as "Gadgett, my maestro," and attributed the third act "low" to stagecraft rather than "talkiness": "Have you enough light on it? Half the audience-coughing in the world is due to an underlit scene. Always cheat lights," he advised, assuming the superior role Kazan had come to expect (October 25, 1942, Wesleyan).] *TLS, 3 pp., Beinecke*

TO MOLLY DAY THACHER

SH: The Belvedere
Charles Street at Chase
PM: Baltimore, October 21, 1942

Dear Mol—
Enclosed please find. The other notice was somewhere in between; also befuddled. I'm very discouraged about everything and everybody tonight. The atmosphere of hate between Myerberg and the cast is beginning to be felt in the performance, and it was very hard to jack the cast—feeling as they do— up to any kind of rehearsal after the notices. Bankhead is sick, March is sick, Eldridge is personally discouraged, Reed got hit on the head with the curtain, shortly following a heart attack, the cast hates M, he despises them; M. is firing three people, I am trying to dissuade him, the cast has appealed to Wilder, he answered them with evasive wires, meantime putting his backing on M., in a wire to him.

Still we do business $2500 opening night, $2600 Tuesday night after three awful notices. Baltimore is cake. The town is full of green paper money, and is show hungry. I guess the stars do it. They keep coming. We should do 20 thousand on the week, despite middling bad word of mouth, and M. will profit to the tune of a thousand dollars, or maybe two. Philadelphia should be awful however.

Its all a shame. The rehearsals were full of love and energy and enthusiasm, even from Bankhead. M. kept away. Then suddenly in New Haven, the scenery, the trick production, the sounds, the lights the animals and MYERBERG all fell in a heap upon the poor cast. I must say that they didn't distinguish themselves with either their courage or their adaptability. The Marches are too rich, and don't need the theatre with its troubles. Bankhead has been too spoiled, and resorts, first to screaming, and, when she is shouted and bulled down, to hysteria, sniveling, weeping, threatening, quitting and tears. Reed chimes in with her bombast. The scenery falls, the crew mutters threats on M.'s life. I try to keep calm, treat it like a job. I let loose just twice, to effect each time.

Then, wonder of wonders, the next day the cast comes around next morning, feeling worse than when they left the night before. It takes an hour to get them up into any kind of rehearsal spirit. I do, we start, bulldogging thru difficulties—that was New Haven.

All the intellectuals who saw the show were very enthused over it. John Cromwell, Ardrey, Freidman, John O'Hara, Philip Barry, Terry Helburn—on and on—the theatre people, the young people, the sophisticates—New Haven society "loathed" it.

I think its just a touch reactionary. Fortunately, no one knows quite what it means, I mean they don't really follow all the symbolism and notion behind notion thru, so there is no actual reactionary effect.

Here:—I'm having my troubles with M. He wants it all played more for comedy. The laughs are concrete, and plentiful. They are somehow tangible—and the first act—says he—should be "played for Laughs". I disagree. Its a dreary argument. You can't really direct unless you produce, unless you are boss, hire and fire, and I don't seem to be the type to produce.

Our big trouble to my mind is act three. Myerberg does not agree. I point to the sudden attacks of catarrh in act three. The man doesn't seem to hear them. The audience doesn't seem to want to follow Wilder's serious thought. They don't really follow the scene within the scene, other than as a stunt. Myerberg is pleased that they don't laugh here any longer—dreary, dreary debate.

Baltimore is like a box office man with a hit. You have to beg a taxi to ride you. The place is full of money, noisy, dirty. The crew of the theatre is composed exclusively of old men (the young are in the army), hard of sight and hearing and shaky of limb. It makes you feel a little idiotic to be hooked up with the thing yourself.

I wrote to Ralph tonight. First chance I've had to even sit down at anything. *** just this minute the phone rang. M. has insulted Bankhead again by refusing to see her anywhere but his room. She's sick, and worried to the point of hysteria about the scenery—the open sets, revealing the backwall of the stage house, and etc. M. says "let her come down and see me"; or "Let her put it in writing." I just refused to be middle-man again, and throw them at each other.

I have your fine long letter. There is nothing to answer directly there. Except you are right about the film job. I did feel for a moment the relief of surrendering myself to it. I'm not so enthusiastic about it all now. I don't think

I'll do anything, until I do something. And when I really and deeply feel like doing something, it will probably be right. I rant to various members of the cast about the war, the situation, our allies, the second front and the future. But how to pour this energy and feeling into work—?

I love to write. Even a letter. I could write everyday if I once got started, and settled into it.

What's the use of talking. I still have a job here for a couple of weeks. In its own way it demands courage and fortitude, and humanity. Often it feels as if I'm the only one who holds it all together—that the whole damn company, and everyone else connected are appealing to me. They tug at my arm around every corner. They ask to whisper to me, complain to me, beg me to interfere for them, in this or the other particular.

Our cast is very interesting. Full of old time has-beens. Former greats: Maude Adams understudy, the man who made the first two-reeler Movie, the wife of William G. Faversham who lists herself in the program as Mrs. William G. Faversham, the former Eva Mudge, musical comedy star, Ralph Cullinan who wrote a play that received highest praise from Eugene O'Neill, but who has given up playwriting because "there is no market for Irish plays", and on and on, all homeless, and all piquantly tragic. Many of them have little tics, physical reflexes and manners, weird little movements, nods and noises.

All these old timers get to the theatre, as they did to rehearsals, a half hour before anyone else. They have no where to go.

I live by myself. I have no close friend in the cast. No girl. I got one letter from Constance, asking me to recommend her to Clurman for the RUSSIAN PEOPLE. I told her it was a lead and he wanted someone more experienced.

The kids seemed fine Sunday. Chris had gotten broader! Judy smarter! possible? I have Judy's crayon sketch of a black cat and girl in red dress on my table. The green eyes are color contrast worthy of Aronson. Also Chris' picture in the frame.

I had a sudden letter from my mother telling me how much she loves me. Sudden, and brief; special delivery.

I sent the kids some candy. I'll try to get up there Sunday, but it depends a bit on M's plans, and what Wilder sends in the way of new Act One material.

Give Lee my regards; and Paula.

I hope your ear is all right, all better. A man is a———when he hits his wife, his former wife, or a girl he loves.

New Haven seemed deserted and empty. I guess I spent the happiest six weeks of my life there. 1932.

gadge

[Baltimore critics were either "befuddled" by *The Skin of Our Teeth* or unimpressed by its novel effects. The harshest dismissed the play for "its utter failure to generate emotion" (*Baltimore Sun*, October 20, 1942).

Tallulah Bankhead campaigned for Kazan's removal and in one notable instance cursed him before the crew, until he "let loose" a profane tirade and confirmed his authority as director. Later he admitted hating "only two people," Tallulah Bankhead and Lillian Hellman, but shortly after the opening he thanked Tallulah "for having the courage . . . [to] battle against inertia, and unconcern, and sometimes just plain dumb stubbornness" (*A Life*, pp. 212, 201; Bankhead, p. 256).

Audience reaction continued to waver in act three as George Antrobus contemplates building "new worlds" with inspiration drawn from "tattered" classics that have survived the latest war. Passages from Spinoza, Plato, Aristotle, and the Bible were laboriously chosen by Wilder and read by actors posing as crew members in a final theatrical "stunt." In late 1941, as work "bogged down" in act three, Wilder assessed the difficulty of dramatizing "ideas and books" and wondered if such allusions would be "sufficient climax for the play" (Wilder, p. 37). Kazan was doubtful and considered Wilder's sources in *The Skin of Our Teeth* "just a touch reactionary."

Kazan's early friendship with Ralph Steiner, photographer and documentary filmmaker, has left no correspondence known to the editor or to Steiner's daughter Antonia.

Molly Kazan wrote to Elia that "something just horrible's got into our relationship. I dominate, you feel beaten. No good, no fun—no good for the kids can come out of that." Her "fine long letter" also included advice regarding an apparent film offer: "You told it as if you wanted to surrender yourself, to be used, to be told what to do. And I think that's not like the best of you" (n.d., Wesleyan).

Maude Adams, chief of the "former greats," starred in the original production of J. M. Barrie's *Peter Pan* (1905). She interrupted a second career as drama instructor at Stephens College (Columbia, Missouri) to understudy in *The Skin of Our Teeth*. Montgomery Clift, a Broadway veteran in his own right at twenty-two, played Henry, a rebellious son who scorns his father's optimism and books.

Athena Kazan's "sudden letter" has not been identified, but her expression of love for "E" and Molly is pervasive in letters following the separation. "One thing I know she loves you very much her heart is broken and unhappy how long she can keep loving you and being hurt? Hope someday I write a letter of gladness to you my dear love" (to EK, June 24, 1942, Wesleyan).

No further mention of Molly's bruised ear is found in correspondence. The "happiest six weeks" refers to the spring of 1932, when Elia and Molly consummated their relationship before leaving Yale.] *TLS with enclosures, 5 pp., Wesleyan*

TO THE CAST OF *THE SKIN OF OUR TEETH*

[New York]
[c. November 18, 1942]

My dear Cast:
The next job after producing a hit is to keep it a hit. It is perfectly normal that your performances vary a little from night to night in certain respects: Mood, emotion, etc., adjustments to differing audiences, stage accidents. Such fac-

tors are not completely within our control, and, as actors, we can only do our best to make each performance our best.

But the mechanics of a performance: the matters of business, crosses, stage positions, etc., need not and must not vary. And neither must the intention we have established for each scene, or moment.

New pieces of business are often added by actors after opening night, and always with the most laudable intention of improving the show. We certainly do not want to forego anything that might help us.

But let's not have anything—no matter how slight—added to the show, or changed in the performance, unless I have been consulted and have approved the change.

Remember our experience on the road. By making what seemed like slight changes from town to town we improved the effect of the show enormously. Our show is a most delicate one. It does not need more padding with laughs, or further embroidering with business. The pace and tempo must be maintained as now.

I've asked Ben Kranz to be most scrupulous in catching any variations. I know you will all fully co-operate with him. After all these weeks you all know full well what I want.

My thanks to each of you—for your help, your loyalty and your talent. May we run forever.

Ever yours, Elia Kazan

[Reviewers accustomed to more conventional Broadway fare were buoyed by Thornton Wilder's wartime optimism and regarded *The Skin of Our Teeth* as a "splendidly sincere attempt to make some sense out of this poor old world" (*NYHT*, November 19, 1942). The play ran for a year and won the Pulitzer Prize— Wilder's second for drama.

Kazan's warning that the "mechanics" of production "must not vary" was probably aimed at Tallulah Bankhead, whose diversionary tactics especially irritated Florence Eldridge. Fredric March retaliated by gargling loudly offstage during one of Bankhead's interludes. Predictably, Tallulah dominated critical praise: "Miss Bankhead is magnificent—breezy, hard, practical by turns. She can strut and posture in broad comedy, she can be calmly serene. It is she who steps out of character to discuss the play, marvelous interludes all of them" (*NYT*, November 19, 1942).

Directing *The Skin of Our Teeth* forced Kazan to work beyond his "talent and technique," but he thought the underlying "values" of the play "conventional and finally stuffy" (*A Life*, p. 206). The director's notices were typically brief, general, and often buried in a final paragraph, but admiring nonetheless: *The Skin of Our Teeth* was "brilliantly staged" and "in the mood meant by Mr. Wilder." Burns Mantle agreed with the consensus but framed a persistent criticism of the director's tendency to excess: Kazan "permitted his troupe frequently to run away with the text, evidently in a desire to 'keep it snappy'" (*New York Daily News*, November 19, 1942).] *TLS, 1 p., BRTC*

Hotel Edison, New York City
October 11, 1943

Dear Terry and Lawrence:

I have carefully re-examined "JACOBOWSKY AND THE COLONEL" and am writing you this to make my sentiments on it clear.

This script, in my opinion, can be, in production, a great play. Its basic conception is very moving to me and can be made so to an audience. I am thrilled at the prospect of working on it.

But in its present form, I think it is not ready to go into rehearsal. And I am not ready to direct it as it is now. The task, I believe, for the authors, for yourselves and for me is one and the same. Since you seem to agree with my basic feelings about the script and about the things that must be done to make it ready for production, the next thing is for me to quickly get together with the authors and embark on a program of re-writing that will make the play what we think it should be.

It is most important, at this time, that we have no misunderstanding either between yourselves and myself, or between the authors and myself as to what I consider necessary to be done. Therefore, this letter and my convictions about the script.

1. The play is now not clear as to basic philosophic meaning. To put it baldly, an audience will not know what it all adds up to mean, and I cannot be sure, except through a series of careful discussions with the authors, whether they agree with each other as to what it means or whether I agree with them.

2. The play is now, in places, under-dramatized, as we discussed. The points are made by "eloquence" for the most part, rather than by real illustrative action, and where the action exists, it has been left in an incipient form. In the first place, the subtle triangle situation between the two men and the woman never develops, never has a progression and ends fundamentally as it begins. For instance, the character of the Colonel is a pushover. He's arrogant, pompous and, in dramatic effect, repetitive. We don't know why the girl goes for him at the end and, therefore, are not being moved by her action when she does. Then again, there is no development or growth on the part of Jacobowsky dramatically. This I also discussed with you. It is necessary to show that there is something lacking in this figure and that he, too, grows through the course of the play. And finally, the figure of Marianne and her being pulled between the two men is again implicit and never takes the form of a really dramatic scene with a body of action movement.

3. Now, since the story and the theme are subtle and delicate, it makes the

job of finding dramatizations for the story more difficult. But, before this play can become a real theatre project, this has to be done.

Finally, the situation between Odets and Werfel continues to distress me, as I think the problems over. What I would like, ideally, is to not to have to deal with any "situation" between these two men. Having worked with Odets before, I think I can best accomplish this by working with him alone, although using Mr. Werfel's conception, contributions and revisions given to me by Mr. Gassner. I think that what we need now is not a melange of nice things, but a crystal-clear and sharply-defined single point of view that will bring dramatic order and movement and thematic clarity out of "JACOBOWSKY AND THE COLONEL."

Very truly yours, Elia Kazan

[Kazan's advice to Terry Helburn and Lawrence Langner, comanagers of the Theatre Guild, bespeaks the confidence of a young director who has disarmed a formidable actress and delivered a major prize to an author with rarefied intellectual credentials. "The truth," Kazan observed, "was that I'd come to believe I was better than other (or most other) directors in New York" (*A Life*, p. 226). Discussion of a formal relationship between the Guild and Kazan commenced with the production of *Jacobowsky and the Colonel* in 1944.

A wily Jewish merchant, S. L. Jacobowsky is the perennial exile fleeing danger as German troops advance on Paris in 1940. Kazan was "reminded" of his family's precarious history as minority Greeks living under Turkish rule in Anatolia, and of his own residual anxiety: "I'm such a man. I've always felt in danger. I've never felt totally secure, even when I was most successful and every author wanted me to direct his new play" (*A Life*, pp. 71–72).

Franz Werfel, ill and at odds with Clifford Odets, based the original text of *Jacobowsky* on his flight from the Nazis in the 1930s. The critic, historian, and anthologist John Gassner directed the play department of the Theatre Guild.]
TLS, 2 pp., Beinecke

TO LAWRENCE LANGNER

SH: William Morris Agency, Inc.
202 N. Canon Drive, Beverly Hills, California
[late October 1943]

Dear Lawrence—

Thanks for your help with the draft Board. My physical condition is fine, so there is no doubt that I should be 1A. However I see no reason why they shouldn't grant me a three month deferment at your request, so that we can count on my doing J and the C.

The situation with Warners, rather the announcement, is very premature. I have signed nothing. We have had a series of conversations on a basis that is very attractive to me: to direct one picture a year in the summer months necessarily, and with a two way veto. This means that I shall not be called to direct pictures except one every summer, and that to be a picture I like. I'll keep you in touch with this as it progresses, but it in no way affects our relationship.

One of the reasons that I have been so dilatory about writing is Odets. I simply couldn't make him out when I first arrived. (please keep the following to yourself) His attitude was, to say the least, passive. He would like to see the show on, he said, but apparently with as little effort from him as possible. Well, perhaps that is being a little unfair, but certainly he had no relish for the job of rewriting, no active interest in it. And besides he was up to his neck in that comfortable, perfumed mud bath that everyone out here lies buried in. There was something inert about him. I began to hope, secretly, that I didn't have to work on the play with him. Then I discovered that he was most anxious to make a place for himself at a studio, be declared essential to the war effort (people in the industry are) and was in the process of selling two ideas of his to pictures. One was a play, half written, that he and I had worked on eight months ago in N.Y. I recommended to Jack Warner that he buy this; Warner did. It was used as one of the focal points for our conversations, Warner and I, about a deal between us.

As soon as the lunch where the deal was consummated was over, I took Odets aside and pointed out that he now could not work on Jacob. He thought a moment [and] agreed. Then I said that I wanted to bring in another author, Behrman. He thought again and agreed again. That's all there was to it. I'm very happy about the development between you and me. At the moment I am awaiting word from you about Behrman. Incidentally Odets understands that he'll have to give up some royalty.

On casting: I've been working. Its very difficult. And I'm a very careful fellow. The play has to be treated, in some respects, like a Shaw play. The speeches are a prime asset; not the plot. As you know I'm fearful of a goulash of dialects. For a day I was very hot about Franchot Tone doing the Colonel. But Franchot is far too comfortable and too settled, doesn't want to budge. Then I had an inspiration: Michael Chekhov to play Jacobowsky. How this fitted into my feeling about dialects, I refuse to discuss. Mr. Chekhov, it appears, is also too settled and too happy here. So now I've stopped with inspiration. In the next two days I'm seeing thirty possibilities, including your suggestions. Nils Asther for example, is coming in tomorrow.

I had a nice lunch with Lem Ayers, whom I know well (Harriet). He's reading the script, and we're meeting tomorrow and talking. But he would have to design the show here (as he is doing for Ernst Pascal (PEEP SHOW) and it would be executed by someone else in N.Y. I'm not enthusiastic about this kind of carrying on. I might get enthusiastic about it if Lem's ideas are brilliant. His precise situation is that he is just to start shooting on ST LOUIS (name of a picture) on which he is the PRODUCTION SUPERVISOR (brand new dandy MGM category—I imagine created especially for Mr. Ayers) and this picture will shoot 8-10 weeks says Lem. Then he has three months off. Knowing movies, I'd say, the picture will start late, shoot fourteen weeks, and Lem will be very much in evidence, when they cut, assemble, dub, preview it. However why speculate. I'll know much more tomorrow and will write you then. . . .

Werfel looks very sick. Beside his bed is an oxygen tank. Also a rewrite of his play—a fourth—new speeches mostly, much like the stuff Gassner garnered for us. Not to the point, I'm sure. My ideas now are quite concrete and I will waste no time working with Behrman.

As you see, I'm working thru Wm. Morris here. Suggest you write me there.

Yours, Gadge

[Kazan traveled to California shortly after directing *One Touch of Venus* (1943). Critics applauded the music and choreography of Kurt Weill and Agnes de Mille but saved their enthusiasm for Mary Martin's return to Broadway after a lengthy tour in Hollywood. The play ran for nearly six hundred performances and added to Kazan's stature as a director of musical comedy.

Kazan reconsidered his preference to work with Clifford Odets after learning of his commitment to studio work and lack of regard for *Jacobowsky*. Sam Behrman's interest pleased Werfel, allowed Odets to complete a screenplay for RKO, and relieved Kazan's distress—if not his cool relations with a former close friend.

Louis Calhern played the irascible Polish colonel and Oskar Karlweis the ingenious Jacobowsky. Stewart Chaney designed the production rather than Lemuel Ayers. He and Kazan had worked together in staging *Harriet* (1943) and would collaborate on a later Tennessee Williams play, *Camino Real*.

Kazan availed himself of letterhead and other conveniences of the William Morris Agency, a courtesy of Abe Lastfogel, his West Coast representative.] *TLS, 2 pp., Beinecke*

TO MOLLY DAY THACHER

SH: William Morris Agency, Inc.
202 N. Canon Drive, Beverly Hills, California
PM: Beverly Hills, California, November 16, 1943

I got your letters, darling, and the angry one about money, and I have an idea. I told it to Fitelson. He automatically takes the Venus money and puts it into my account. Well suppose I give you a lot of checks for five hundred each, predated a month apart and going into the future; then you would have a check to cash each month.

I've made no contract with a motion picture company. I don't want to come out here except with you and the children. I thought that over carefully. I'm crazy to think that way, eh? makes no damned sense. But that's how I feel.

Listen further. I'm interested, if possible in doing one picture before I go into the army for the following reasons.

For years—since Williams College, I wanted to be a director of Movies. That was my ambition. I never started on it for various reasons: too deeply involved in the theatre and so on. But one basic reason was that I didn't like this place. I hate it, in a shrieking insane way now. It resents every drop of my gristle (I'm nuts) and vice versa. Its just no good, like the grave, the tomb, the charnel pit—except its all very fancy. All very unreal.

But I want to make pictures. And pictures are made here. And the place is full of really very fine people, all in various stages of decomposition, without knowing it and with knowing it—and they all want to make pictures that are fine; but dont. Anyway I'm willing to buck the System (for that's the trouble, as the wise man said). There's the system in N.Y.C. with Myerberg, Wildberg, Miller, Crawford, and so on, Shubert, basically and the banks finally. Hell the system is all around us. I'll buck it, and keep doing what I can and soon begin to improve the situation. The important thing is to keep trying to live right, and if you can't exactly, like me now, at least try to live in the right place. That's why I never even considered a term deal.

But now they are talking to me about a picture a year, good pictures (TREE GROWS IN BROOKLYN—or Cliff Odets Soldier play, made into a movie)— much better, much realer material than I have ever touched on stage as a director, since Casey Jones. Material that I know about and feel about.

That's why I'm listening and interested and telling you about it.

My hope for life now is that I can live happily and easily and in small ways with you and my children, small ways like an ice-box together, and the god-damn problems of child psychology (I suppose you're saying: "He sure is very keen about all those problems—at a distance". But I can't and mustn't stop to guess what you're muttering and cursing at a distance. I've got to keep on the attack of saying what I hope for and think and want.)

*****

I miss you too. I rely on you. Isn't that strange. I look to you for some kind of judgment, standard, appraisal—or other days as a fine fountain—other days: My Pain—but always the real thing, the actuality.

I hope Tuck is happy. I'm very fond of him.

I keep saying and say again what happened is good because it makes towards

Molly reading *Tom Sawyer* to Chris and Judy

the fact, and our facing the fact. And in me (I mustn't talk for you) a whole jolting in to self-examination, a real questioning: what do I want. Who am I? I can have anything, what do I want. I'm giving up nothing, what do I want. And the end of the sense of being underprivileged, a mutt; the beginning of a calmness and sense of simple self-contentment.

Its very hard; but its coming.

I don't blame you anymore. At least as I'm aware of myself, my self doesn't blame you—God knows what Mittelmann might find. I've forgotten about the "criticism". Bear with you? What a question!—as Moe Jacobs would say, can you hear him—What a question! I will love you and only you all my life. Just write me occasionally and tell me what's what. I wrote my mother.

I went out with Houseman twice. He's a nice guy. A man of excellent judgment, perfect taste, in most things; curiously undeveloped in other ways. He is warmer than he seems. I think he believes I have something he lacks. He acts a tiny bit envious, with a bearish, grudging affection. I'm imagining things, I guess.

Of course the kids letters are wonderful. Judy on Chris—I'd like to have seen her sneak up on him with that kiss. Be tough on a little boy to have such a smart damned sister. Well, I'm alive, well and kicking.

P.S. my "Physical" is Wd at five thirty. On the card it says: "This examination will be of a preliminary nature, for the purpose of disclosing only obvious defects, and will not finally determine your acceptance or rejection by the armed forces." I hear that they are chiefly interested in seeing if you can walk and see and hear first.

[Elia rented a three-story house on East Ninety-second Street for his family and suggested a plan to meet Molly's concern that "large checks at long intervals" were not only "nerve wracking and hard to live by" but also demeaning when their delay forced a request for money. William Fitelson, Kazan's attorney, would administer funds derived from *One Touch of Venus*.

A press report that "Warner Bros. has set Elia Kazan to direct pictures" was soon corrected: "Elia Kazan and 20th-Fox got together on a producer-director contract with a proviso permitting Kazan to direct pictures produced by others in addition to his own. WB also thought it had Kazan but he signed 20th" (*Variety*, November 17 and December 1, 1943). The contract would remain in force until 1948 and require Kazan to direct one film per year subject to his script approval. *A Tree Grows in Brooklyn* was the first assignment.

The resumed affair with Constance Dowling caused Loretto Stevens, a family friend, to warn Elia that he was "doing two dangerous things: you are taking too much time, and you are continuing an affair that will definitely block things between you and Molly." Athena asked her son with evident sadness if there was "a hope for understanding" with Molly. If not, "we can face it get accostumed to the thought and build anew" (October 18 and November 8, 1943, Wesleyan).

Trained at the University of Prague, Bela Mittelmann came to the States in 1923 and practiced in New York with a clinical orientation toward psychoanalysis. Molly's "work" with Mittelmann led to the suggestion—or "threat," as Elia put it—that he see an analyst as a term of reconciliation.

Kazan wrote later that John Houseman "seemed to be on both sides of my street." Houseman and Constance Dowling had once spent a "weekend" together, and recently he had offered Molly a job with Voice of America, whose wartime broadcasts he supervised in New York (*A Life*, p. 214).

By late 1943 Kazan's III-A classification no longer guaranteed exemption from military service. Jack Warner offered to give Kazan a directing job and state that he was "essential" to the film industry. Kazan refused on grounds that "it would be a low act" (to MDT, October 26 [1943], Wesleyan). Through Lawrence Langner's intercession, he received a deferment until February 1, 1944, to direct *Jacobowsky*.] TL, 2 pp., Wesleyan

TO THERESA HELBURN

SH: Twentieth Century-Fox Film Corporation
Beverly Hills, California
March 24, 1944

Dear Terry:

Thank you ever so much for the notices. It was mighty thoughtful of you. I hope business is as good as everyone says it is. I think the play and our production deserve it.

I'm a little punch drunk this morning because I got my letter from the President of the United States asking me to appear for preinduction examination, which means, I suppose, if they find me physically fit I'll be in the army as soon as I finish this job. However, I'm going ahead here and learning all about this very intricate and very simple business. It's rather fascinating for a director, although, between you and me, I'd much rather be doing a play, and wouldn't swap you, my sturdy little beauty, for two Zanucks and a Selznick.

Don't forget me while I'm far away. I love hearing from you and Lawrence, if only a few words. This includes Armina.

Fond love, Gadget

[*Jacobowsky* ran for a year in spite of mixed notices and a bilious attack on the ingénue, who made one veteran reviewer "spiritually ill." Annabella, a film star of some note, retaliated by publicly offering him a bottle of castor oil. Otherwise strong acting probably saved the play from uneven writing and "drivel at the end." Kazan "is rapidly becoming a great director," declared the *Herald Tribune* (March 15, 1944).

Kazan received notification in April that he was "physically fit, acceptable by Army for general military service." Later in 1944 Lawrence Langner recommended him as "a person of unquestionable loyalty and discretion" to the Office of Strategic Services. Kazan learned from a friend in the OSS that "leftism" had probably caused an "unfavorable" review of his application (*A Life*, p. 242).] *TLS, 1 p., Beinecke*

TO MOLLY DAY THACHER

SH: Twentieth Century-Fox Film Corporation
Beverly Hills, California
PM: Los Angeles, May 11, 1944

Dearest Molly

I'm just going to keep on writing this afternoon until I get out all the thoughts and feelings I have in me. I don't care how long it takes as long as I tell you the truth one way or another. And I'm not going to read the goddamn letter, because then I'll likely not send it, like those other two letters I didn't send. This one is going, one way or another. Show it to Mittelmann. Maybe I'm nuts. But I'm sick of being nuts and confused and I'm sick of being secretive and sick of being in between and I'm sick of a hell of a lot else, which will come out in this letter. IN I DON'T CARE WHAT ORDER FOR CHRISSAKE. So I'll just throw myself and my feelings to the extent I know them on the table like a hunk of meat, and so you'll know and I'll at least stop feeling guilty. I'll meet myself and say that's me, good bad or indifferent. A thing I've wanted for years now. Let me try anyway. Bear with me and see if you can read this stuff. Here it comes. . . .

I'm going with Constance again. I enjoy it. Its not as deep as a well or as wide as a church door, but twill serve. She's tender and simple and uncomplicated. She's loving and graceful. Put it this way: she has no problem with me, except the fundamental one, whether she really has me or not. I <u>have</u> a problem with her, but its in abeyance. When it will come up, depends on what happens with me. But now its pleasant, and makes life what it should be: enjoyable and pleasurable in long enough intervals so that its PLUS not MINUS. I suppose this is awful snooty and superior to say about a girl. On the other hand, I can say more, for in some ways I'm crazy about her. She makes me feel young again. She makes me feel like a kid. That's good. Other nights I fret and its bad. Those nights I conceal it from her. How long: who knows. I don't care right now. I'm all bawled up. But there it is. I'm not ashamed of it. I'm rather proud of it. What I'm sick of and want to stop is the half way stuff. The in-between-ism. For whatever goddamn reason. If this is me, the fellow who is with Constance, that's me. If I'm passing up, if I'm destroying something much deeper and much finer, certainly I keep on destroying it, hazarding it. No matter what I say about it, in my snooty, superior way. I keep REVERTING. That's the damn point. . . . The best thing for me now is to live with Constance, and I don't care about the ulterior values. I don't care how long it will last. I don't care whether she's good enough for me, or vice versa. A lot of people here think I'm not good enough for her. Sometimes I feel I'm no good for anyone, except my mother. Other times I feel I'm the finest guy in the world and melt with pity for myself.

The mess is the children. I'm not talking about the objective mess. The hell with that for this letter. The hell with it. No one can or should or WILL sacrifice his life for anyone. The hell with generalizations. I wont. I love them I love them I love them! You don't believe it. You believe it. I don't care. You don't believe I love you. The hell with you. I love you. In what queer perverted way I don't care. There are no standard articles in love. There is no stereotype. I know I love you, because you're always somewhere in me. I carry you around. But I can't do anything with you now. Maybe I never will. I don't know. I can't plan. I don't want to know. I wont think. There's something phony about all the rules. They don't correspond to feelings with me. I'm not talking about the rest of the world. Its much more complex the way I feel it. I can't go along any other way.

I'm sick of feeling I hurt you. I'm sick of thinking of you not sleeping. I'm going to write what I think now, even if I think it only half the time. This is that half. I want to be divorced. I don't want you dependant on me. I don't want you waiting for me. I'm not in a state to be waited for. I don't want to think now about the future. The war's got something to do with it. I want to go into the war. Its crazy. But I hate myself for being out of the war all this time. I don't like my life of ease; even though I work like a dray horse. I don't want to be dead either. I want to live. I want to work. I want to sing out. I'm goddamn positive. But I hate marriage, at the moment I hate it. I wish there'd be a way for me to express to you what I feel for you, and not be called upon by the FORM to express for you what I don't feel. One thing kills me: Chris. I feel he needs me, much more than I feel Judy needs me. BUT BUT—BUT—GODDAMN IT BUT if that feeling is true. If I'm genuine—which I am, or I'll die, then if that feeling is genuine, then I'll express it. Concretely. I'll find way to express it. I'll get to Chris with it thru any and all opposition. I'll get to him and he'll be mine. I'll have my love for him fulfilled one way or the other.

I'm sick of the crap. I'm sick of the confusion. Lets stop it. You waiting there, me with my forehead wrinkling here. Three years now, that's enough. I'm no clearer, Mittelmann made me no clearer about this. I'm not going to settle down and be somebody else because of a series of conversations with Mittelmann. All M. seemed to be trying to do was to for Chrissake make me face what I am, bravely actually and simply and accept myself as Joe Schmuk, or Suskevich the great director, or Kazan the competent stage manager, or Eli the bowlegged ape, or gadget the wastrel, or Elia the student, or Eee his mother's darling. BUT I'm sick of the crap. I'm sick of you waiting on what Mittelmann is going to do for me, and me waiting on what that jolly son of a bitch is or is not going to do with me. As long as I have money you can have it. You can have my farm, you can have the eyes out of my head but I'm going to be myself. Is that peculiar how I keep screaming that: I'm going to be myself. After all these years, I keep screaming I'm going to be myself. Well you be yourself too. Just like with Chris too. If I love you, I love you, as much as I say, it will come out. I believe in my feelings. They seem to endure. They don't seem to stop. There is something staunch about them. Staunch for me. Not for you. But hungry in the same directions. Well I was saying, if they exist, and they do, they will find expression. But I beg you don't depend upon me. Divorce me. Make other friends. Lets take the stew which is spoiled and throw it out. Then anything we feel and anything we really actually want of each other, we'll have of each other. Lets stop being afraid. Lets do right. This is all crapped up. This, what we have now, has no dignity. Its not manly or womanly. Its sick. Lets stop being sick. At first it will seem less, it will seem empty. The grass will grow long at Newtown. The water pump will rust a bit. But I'm sick of the crap.

You know: since I moved out of 60 West 75th. st I've never been able to establish myself anywhere. I've never had a room of my own. Even here, I'm most of the time at the studio. The rest of the time I'm at Constance's house. Well I'm sick of that. I would like to for chrissake get a room with one arm chair that's fitted to my fat little ass, and be able to read a book. I don't think I've read a book in two and a half years. That's how long it is: two and a half years. Two years four months to be exact. Well, even if its less to be alone, I want to be somewhere. I want to be something definite. I want to do what I feel and I want to do it cleanly. I don't want to sneak anymore. If it develops that I get so that we can live together, then we can re-marry. But no more twilight sleep, or whatever it is. Lets for chrissake come out of the fog. Lets not live on a hope. . . .

I don't presume to give advice. I hope you don't hate me by now. But I'm not going to act or write from a fear that you will. I write you this way. I've gone thru two and half years of all this because I feel something very deep about you, and I don't want to lose it. But now I'll take that chance, or any other chance, for the sake of honest-to-god-ness. If my heart pumps shit and piss thru my arteries and veins that's o.k. too. I just don't want to feel any more that you disapprove of me. I don't want to feel bad. I don't want to feel except what I feel. I'm no more readier to live with you this 30th. day of April 1944 than I was two years back. Its not the solution for me. There is no solution for me. Marriage is a contrivance of law and custom where its implicit that one person is the solution for the other. I don't want you to demand that of me. I don't feel that about you. I think we should be free of each other. When I feel other wise, if, I'll say so. Let your feelings guide you. You know what you need. It must be hell for you with me. With me, without me. I think its better to be without me, than to be with me without me. Its clean and honest and factual. You can build on facts. We're building on a mess. We built all on hopes and fears, and he will change and I will get straightened out, and the children this and that, and the place in Connecticut and everything except something that is simple, direct and speechless. Maybe black night is ahead for me. But I'll get a little match and start a fire and maybe it will build enough for me to see a few feet around me. Strange. Because something in me is still tied to you, and I think always will be. That will make trouble. But I'll face it for what it is, and I will face it as it changes or develops. But no crap, or wish thinking or false solutions, or waiting. Lets be proud for chrissake. We're BOTH goddamn useful citizens, and we both can do a [little] to enjoy life and to help our fellow men and maybe just a little for future generations. We can both put in a lick or two for the Right. And we can both help the good and kick the bad— even if just a little. But for the last two years its felt as if we were crippled and wounded and the heart was out of us.

From now on lets just deal with facts and as facts are. Anyway I'm going to. Mittelmann taught me that. The fact between us is that we're not ready to live together. Its not clear yet whether we ever will be. Perhaps we will. We have ties. There are other people we like. We can't have a casual life together. We can't be married, for the simple reason that we're not. Outside the air is cold. But its clear, and there's no fog. We can meet that. I believe in you tremendously. In your capacity, your usefulness. The good you can do for your fellow man. (Fuck Kandel's play or shit like that. You're much better than crap like that, and you should work for the right someway to your full capacity.)

The kids. I'd tell them honestly. They'll face it. Its true—the other kind of in and out experience, would only rattle and mystify them.

I want to be clean. I don't want to be afraid. I don't want to cling—I want things for you too. But I'm not going to say more than I've said. My set of feelings are peculiar. But that's the way I am. I'm all mixed up, like all human beings, like every human being I've ever met. All messed up. But they all are. Pathetically. All you can hope to do is face the truth, and live truthfully, then it will be clean and whatever the situation is, whatever your needs are you can for chrissake hope to partially satisfy them. I hope I've said enough, so that you know clearly how I feel.

I still hope you like what I've said. Believe in it somehow I mean. I still want you to believe in me somehow. But if you don't, o.k., I'll face that too. I want the cobwebs out of my head. We're both too damn good, to go on living in this crippled way. If we're divorced, I don't know what will happen, but somehow or other we can start again positively, not clinging, sick and afraid.

Clear-headed. Down to bedrock. Like men.

[Molly's letters to Elia in the spring and summer of 1944 reveal plans to divorce, although questions of legal venue—Connecticut or Reno—and financial settlement seem not to have reached a definitive stage. The children were a prime concern. Telling them, especially Judy, of an impending divorce made Molly feel "like a shit" and ask, "Ever have a baby and then feed her platitudes?" Elia's emotional reserve, she thought, foretold limited contact with the children, claims of love notwithstanding. "For their sakes," she urged Elia to remove "the barrier that cuts you off from people you love." Elia's determination to reach his five-year-old son "thru any and all opposition" was tested in June when Chris refused to speak to his father and spat at the telephone. "Even though its kiddish and all, and its a kind of inverted love or jealousy or something I suppose . . . still it was painful. That happened this noon and I still don't feel very good" (to MDT, postmarked Los Angeles, June 2, 1944, Wesleyan).

Elia later faulted Bela Mittelmann's professional treatment of Molly: "Obviously I was the one who'd made all the trouble. But Mittelmann, out of a mid-European male culture, was soon all on my side and, in a way, not taking my problems seriously enough. 'If she continues as she is,' he said to me one day, 'you won't be able to live with her'" (A Life, p. 239).] TL, 6 pp., Wesleyan

SH: Twentieth Century-Fox Film Corporation
Beverly Hills, California
May 17, 1944

Terry darling:

It's so nice to have that long, newsy letter from you. I sure would love to work with you and Lawrence again, and not because I don't like working in pictures, because I do. I think my arrangement with them is just right—one a year. A guy could make one good picture a year. I'd be earning all the money I need in one year. The work is hard, however, physically strenuous, and there's always a bitter sense of disappointment five minutes after you said "Print it." You start wondering whether you couldn't have been more stubborn, more persistent, and tried harder to get something unusual. However, I'm doing a picture in which the whole point is to remain inconspicuous as a director, in which it's a virtue not to be noticed, and I've got to hide my light under that old bushel basket. . . .

About the Capehart, just hold off on that awhile. As soon as my situation in the army is settled, I'll set up a little apartment in the city and then I'll want it. So just keep your contact with that particular man a going thing. At some future date I'll ask you to exercise it.

I don't think much of the Pulitzer award one way or the other. I doubt if I would like "Searching Wind". I'm real crazy about our play and think it should have gotten all the prizes. I think "Voice of the Turtle" is really too trivial to be considered. Don't I sound snobbish? But that's what I really think. "Oklahoma!" I just love, but as you say, that doesn't merit a prize for a year but for a decade.

About "Liliom", I'm very interested in directing it and also in making some kind of institutional connection with the Theatre Guild, but I prefer waiting a little while longer and see what the army situation is. I'm not in an essential industry, I'm not a movie director, and there's something in me that draws me to the idea of going to England for the invasion. I think if I could get over somehow for a while, a few months, I'd like to do it—that is, if the army doesn't take me. If I could make a short there, or anything like that, just to really be on the ground when these great events take place, I think that I shouldn't miss the chance. So I'm really not quite settled in my mind. I think that the future of all men over 26 will depend on how bloody the invasion is. If things go badly I expect there'll be a rather general drafting of large groups of men to have replacements and new forces ready.

As for Kandel, I wrote Bill that nothing will come of the Kandel play if he's allowed to work on it alone. That is hopeless. That play needs the most strict supervision. Kandel should be gently guided with a baseball bat. He should be told just what is necessary and he should be sat over until he's written it down, otherwise he'll have nothing. Mr. Kandel is too indolent; he likes his cigars, his tenderloins and his girls, as who doesn't.

Am I having a good time? Yes, I am. I enjoy the work and, personally, am a good deal happier than I was during "Jacobowsky." You can guess why.

Break down and give Lawrence a kiss for me. Tell him I miss our eccentric conversations and I look forward to hearing from you both some time soon.

Affectionately, Gadget

[Economy and efficiency rigidly defined the studio system, as Kazan learned once filming of *A Tree Grows in Brooklyn* began in May: "The point is to get good stuff—but you are praised constantly for being on schedule. . . . One of my biggest dangers is that I can be so goddamn efficient. The stage manager before the director. Talent breaks forms, and takes time. Today I did neither. But I may be able to cause them a little trouble before I'm thru" (to MDT, postmarked Los Angeles, May 3, 1944, JKMP). As it turned out, neither Kazan's draft nor his marital status influenced the purchase of a Capehart phonograph.

The Pulitzer committee declined to name a best American play for 1944 and instead gave a special award to the Theatre Guild's massive hit *Oklahoma!* (1943). To no avail, the Guild had promoted *Jacobowsky* as an "American Play" based on Sam Behrman's adaptation of the original script. *The Searching Wind* by Lillian Hellman opened after the Pulitzer deadline and was not considered. John Van Druten's "truck with the immoralities" of a weekend affair charmed Brooks Atkinson, if not Kazan, and launched *The Voice of the Turtle* on a year's run. Rouben Mamoulian directed *Carousel,* the Rodgers and Hammerstein musical hit based on Ferenc Molnár's *Liliom* (1921).

Bill Fitelson informed Lawrence Langner that an "institutional connection" between the Theatre Guild and Kazan would be expensive. He was "now quoting to other producers $1000.00 per week with a five week minimum guaranty and two and a half percent of the gross from all companies and seven and a half percent of the gross of film price" (April 3, 1944, Beinecke).

Kazan's "army situation" was resolved in early 1945 with reclassification as II-A: key position in an essential industry. Plans for an overseas assignment were under way with the help of Abe Lastfogel.

Aben Kandel, the "indolent," was associated with Kazan in filming *City for Conquest* (1940) and perhaps as a prospective writer for the Dollar Top Theatre. "You Only Twinkle Once," his work in progress, was not produced by the Theatre Guild.] *TLS, 2 pp., Beinecke*

TO JUDY AND CHRIS KAZAN

SH: Twentieth Century-Fox Film Corporation
Beverly Hills, California
June 24, 1944

Dear Judy and Chris:

I just sent a package with your gifts off. In the meantime, till you get it, here are a few more clippings from the picture.

You'd both be surprised how often, when I'm telling the little boy and the little girl in my story what to do, I think of what I've seen you two do and say and how you've looked at me sometimes. But maybe when you see the picture you'll understand how often when I was making it I felt something about you and how important that feeling was.

Anyway, if you're in Sandy Hook now, in the lake, my heart is with you. Give my love to Nancy and Ann and Molly and especially (don't tell anybody) to Susan who, as you know, is a little bit my favorite among those four children. That doesn't mean I don't like the others, because I like Nancy very much and I'm waiting to see her next play. I hope you're both in it. And I like Ann very much. And Molly is a very sensitive little girl. But I guess I just like Susan because when she was a baby she took an instinctive liking to me, and everybody is weak enough and needs love enough to like people who like them. Am I getting too philosophic? Anyway, what do you think of this question?

One thing worries me. What about the lake up there? Did anybody ever fix the hole out of which the water was running? It was nobody's business but mine and I didn't fix it. So I'm worried whether the lake is low or not. If it is, why don't you see if Loretto can't find somebody who does that kind of work around there to plug it up, the sooner the better, before the real hot weather comes. Don't you think that's a good idea? We have a little extra money now, which I'm not spending but holding on to for just such purposes as this. It's important that the lake be high for good swimming.

Also, write me about the country, how it looks, etc. I'm sure the house must need screening for the porch windows, and maybe Loretto—or Molly, if she has time—can find somebody to do that too. Anyway, tell me all the news and I'll write you back.

Love, Daddy

[Twentieth Century-Fox acquired rights to *A Tree Grows in Brooklyn* (1943) for a reported $50,000 and lavishly rebuilt the tenement setting of Betty Smith's autobiographical first novel. Filming began on May 1 and was completed in August. Evaluation proved more intense and immediate than anything Kazan had known on Broadway: "'I suffer all the anguish of a prisoner on trial every evening when the day's rushes are shown'" (*NYT,* December 24, 1944).

Casting Peggy Ann Garner as Francie Nolan was a "miracle," Kazan thought, as well as a revelation: "The story I was making dramatized a child's struggle to hold her parents together; it spoke of the pain of separation, of a young girl caught between warring adults—a girl who reminded me, morning after morning, of my daughter, Judy." Only later did Kazan realize the extent to which the film's domestic emotion had weakened his relationship with Constance Dowling (*A Life*, pp. 257, 259).

Judy and Chris "adored" the visiting daughters of Loretto Stevens. A pet lamb that "picked on" Susan taught Judy, as she recalls, "an early lesson in the perils of being the youngest" and perhaps the favored child.] *TLS, 1 p., JKMP*

TO LESTER COWAN

SH: Twentieth Century-Fox Film Corporation
Beverly Hills, California
July 7, 1944

Dear Lester:

This is a peculiarly eccentric request, but you're probably inured to all kinds of strange requests.

I've got a great yen to meet Garbo. If you ever throw a party or tea or function of any kind where you have her, why don't you invite me. There, that's all. I think she's about the best actress pictures ever had and I'm just terribly curious to meet her and talk with her a little—nothing particular, except I'm a real "fan" of hers.

Best luck on your production. It's a swell subject and I think you've lined up a brilliant cast.

Give my love to Betty and Freddie when you see them. I'm very fond of both of them.

Yours, Elia Kazan

[Apparently Kazan was intrigued by reports that the producer Lester Cowan had signed Greta Garbo to play a Norwegian merchant marine captain in "Women of the Sea." The project, which failed to materialize, would have honored women in the service and revived Garbo's career after the misfortune of *Two-Faced Woman* in 1941. Then Archbishop Francis Spellman denounced the marital comedy and the Legion of Decency threatened condemnation before MGM agreed to eliminate the film's adulterous premise. Kazan was unaware that Garbo's legendary retirement was already under way. Many years later he wrote in admiration: "Who can plumb the mystery of Greta Garbo? She doesn't yield, she doesn't make friends; she's not after your approval, not ever" (*A Life*, p. 146).

Betty Field and "Freddie" March played leading roles in Cowan's forthcoming film *Tomorrow, the World!*] *TLS, 1 p., Herrick*

TO JUDY AND CHRIS KAZAN

SH: Twentieth Century-Fox Film Corporation
Beverly Hills, California
July 13, 1944

Dear Judy and Chris:

That was a wonderful letter from all the girls telling me the news. I'm glad the lake is still up, but I'm wondering whether the hole is in the pipe and the water is still leaking out. What kind of snake was it that Loretto killed?

I've been an awful long time on this picture and it seems like it goes on forever. The little girl who's playing Francie (her name is Peggy Ann Garner) has grown two inches taller since I started it. If I shoot another couple of months, she'll be too old for the part! Also, her hips are two inches wider around and we'll have to make new dresses for her if we don't finish the picture soon.

All that's happened to the little boy, however, is that his front teeth are getting bigger and stick out of his mouth more. He looks like a baby sea lion when he grins. Look at some of the pictures I've sent you and you'll see what I mean. I told you I call him "Pot Roast"—and sometimes "Meatball." He likes the nicknames—thinks they're terms of affection. The other night he dreamed about me. He and I were in Arabia together. We were being chased by the Turks, but we got away. He forgot how. Anyway, it was very exciting. He stood up in the middle of the floor waving an imaginary sword about his head. He's a character.

Today we had a scene where snow is falling outside the window. What do you suppose the snow is made of? Corn flakes! You can eat the snow—it's good for you for breakfast! They take corn flakes and bleach them white and they look just like snow as they fall.

We're doing a scene where the parents give the children Christmas presents and the children give their parents presents. Well, this is a very poor family, as I told you, and they have no money to waste, so they buy something "useful"—as Papoo always says. They buy both children long, itchy, white underwear. The children are terribly disappointed, of course, but they're too polite to show it. So everybody kind of laughs. Anyway, it's very funny. Outside the stage it's hot, the sun is beating down—and inside it's snowing and we're pretending it's Christmas.

I'm always thinking of you.

Daddy

[Peggy Ann Garner was twelve years old as filming of *A Tree Grows in Brooklyn* began in May. She won a special Academy Award as the outstanding child actress

The Christmas-present scene from *A Tree Grows in Brooklyn*

of 1945, but a domineering stage mother and casting by Twentieth Century-Fox in a series of trivial films damaged a promising career. Garner moved to New York, studied briefly at the Actors Studio, and worked intermittently in theater and television. Francie's younger brother Neeley, played by Ted Donaldson, earned his nicknames in novel and film by reason of a voracious appetite.

"Papoo" is George Kazan, Chris and Judy's "practical" grandfather, who dubbed Sandy Hook "the headache place" for its drain on finances.] *TLS, 1 p., JKMP*

TO JUDY AND CHRIS KAZAN

SH: Twentieth Century-Fox Film Corporation
Beverly Hills, California
July 22, 1944

Dear Judy and Chris:

My darling swimmers, champion health fiends, sun-bathed athletes, growing intellects, prize spellers, monstrous eaters, exuberant sandpile diggers, superlative mud-pie bakers, swingers from trees, eaters of fruit and ice cream, prime lollypop suckers and, in general, luscious characters—I greet you!

I'm a little dizzy this afternoon from two straight days of climbing up and down stairs. We're shooting a sequence (sequence is movie parlance for little scene in the picture) where they carry a Christmas tree up and down the stairs, singing "Holy Night." There is no Christmas tree in the history of man that has climbed up and down stairs as extensively as this one. Every step of these stairs has been swept clean with choice green balsam boughs, and as for me, I hope I never see a Christmas tree again—

There's been a slight interruption. Somebody came over to ask me to look at something to see if it was right, and so I went to look at it and it was right, and now I've come back and I've forgotten what I was saying. I guess it was some pretty silly stuff. You've got a pretty silly daddy sometimes, especially when he gets tired.

I certainly like those pictures. I think that raft that Stanley built is a beaut, and, Judy, you look very cute in your over-alls. You both look like you've grown so much. You both look so sweet and it makes me very proud. Anyway, I love you both very much.

Judy darling, I sent you today a little package which is a gift for you on your birthday. It doesn't look like I'll be there as I still have another 10 days of shooting on the picture, and after that I have to hang around a while longer while they put the picture together, and I argue and fight with a little fellow with a moustache named Mr. Zanuck, who's the boss of the whole place and can yell almost as loud as I about how the picture should be put together. Anyway, I hope you like what's in the little box and don't leave it lying around in a bureau drawer. I tried to pick it out so you could wear it all the time. It's a nice one, but it's not too nice or too precious or too costly or too delicate that you shouldn't wear it all the time, except when you go swimming. Take it off then.

With this letter goes a million kisses to you both.

[The "cruel custom" of hurling unsold trees at the poor late on Christmas Eve was one of many scenes recalled by Betty Smith from a turn-of-the-century childhood in Brooklyn. "The whole world stood still as something dark and monstrous came though the air." Francie and Neeley were "staggered" but caught the "biggest tree" of all and bore it home. Undecorated in the novel, it graces a cold front room as a mark of the family's extreme poverty. Homemade decorations and a warm family circle indicate a softening of need in the film, to which Kazan later objected.

As head of production for Twentieth Century-Fox, Darryl Zanuck supervised seven films directed by Kazan from 1945 to 1953. If any one factor strained their working relationship and pointed Kazan toward independent production, it was Zanuck's domination of the editing process.

Judy Kazan received a watch for her eighth birthday.] *TL, 1 p., JKMP*

SH: Twentieth Century-Fox Film Corporation
Beverly Hills, California
PM: Los Angeles, October 2, 1944

Dear dear Molly

You wrote me such a wonderful letter. And I love you so much. I feel much better, clearer and easier. And somehow optimistic. I'll be back in New York very very soon. So just wait a little while longer, and I'll be back, a little different, a little better-er. And I really got an awful lot out of you those two weeks. I love you. And I think I can help you now. You don't baffle me and frighten me. Neither do a lot of other people and things which did. So I'm not so scared and mean. And—oh what the hell, the sun is shining today, and I'm up in my little office alone, and I'm viewing the possibilities and I don't find them bad. When I come back I kind of feel hopeful about us. Peculiar: everytime you say you're changing etc. I feel 1/ good! my god she'll be independent as she is dependant, and that pleases me, because I'm not scared of it. She wont be competitive with me, and we can be happy together and have more children, right away. 2/ My God! you're going to lose her. (emotion of great fear) I mean 1/ Good! I'm glad that a lot of the time you're off thinking about other things. That's fine for you, and fine for me. And for me with you. It lifts some burden that I don't properly understand. 2/ And then, Marriage is some kind of inter-dependence. And further more, I want you to depend on me. And I want the kids to depend on me. And I certainly need support. And goddamn it I like to be admired. And hang it all, I want something to live up to.

Hell, the sun is shining today. And even here, its a fall day. Fall I love. Here, its a weak dilution of fall, like its a solution (medical word) of everything else. (a teaspoon in a glass of water) But this morning the sky was a cool cool blue, you know how fall is there, where its at its best. And outside my window there are some vines that AREN'T perennial, but shed their leaves, and these same plants and leaves rustled a little. And that cool blue sky and that funny little rustle made me feel pretty good. I've been feeling better month by month. Its hard to describe.

I'm glad there's no fear in you when you say "I like you!" That sounds like a real woman.

Also I look around at this pathetic spectacle here of pride, power and fear and mistrust which is Hollywood. And I certainly feel happily isolated. I'm so glad I have only a one a year deal, and don't even have to do one a year. For, as it was inevitable to happen, they're getting ever so slightly fed up with me, and in a couple of more weeks they will be ever so slightly more fed-up; and suddenly wake up to discover suddenly that they're very very fed-up; and that

I am a boy genius and a swell-head, and difficult and not a good organization man. What's happening is that I've started to turn down scripts. I've turned down six in a row—really the best pictures they plan to do in the next six months. And I find its impossible to communicate to them my reasons, my real reasons why I don't want to do these scripts. I just got a note from Zanuck, scolding me like a Dutch uncle, warning me gentle, with a steely glint here and there about balancing the needs of the organization (20th.-FOX) vs. my own needs. And he sent me a couple of more of their super duper product, which I will turn down, and then he'll be right on the verge of considering me a genius instead of a show man, and "difficult"—I knew that was bound to happen, because you can't communicate with them or him, so I'm glad that no matter what we feel personally, I still don't have to work unless I like the script, love it, feel something about it, find some feeling in it from which I can angle myself and start to work.

Just read your letter. You're so wonderful. I really love you. I mean I read it again. I'm coming east soon. And I really long to see you, and SPEND TIME with you. I have no plans for work. I feel so goddamn lazy. Its wonderful.

That was a nice bit about Lear. It does like hell make me feel uncomfortable when you talk about my possibilities. (Although, I suppose, its easier to take by a letter than face to face.) But it doesn't make me uncomfortable— These days, I feel like my whole life is ahead of me. I really have not started yet. I really haven't started living right, and working right yet, and when I do, its going to be wonderful fun. I've got terrific power in my heart, and terrific desire to really live right, and suddenly soon it will all burst loose, you wait and see. Its like I've been storing up something thru all these years, something of yearning and desire, and notions, and they're all here, inside me, waiting to burst loose. I feel suddenly I'll be somebody else, and still the same, but people will not recognize me, and I'll be happy in myself, and thru myself and the world, and not thru power or prestige or pre-eminence. Anyway I feel I'm coming thru the woods; I really do. And I love you. Not only you, but what you are. That's a tough one, figure that. What you can be with me, and what I can be with you.

TREE is being pre-viewed tomorrow night. After that it shouldn't be long. Two conferences. Finis. . . . I'm not interested in any play or any movie now. First time in a long long long time I ACTUALLY HAVE NO PROJECTS. Guess I'll take a look and a smell around. I'm enjoying the slightly mischievous joy of having everyone think I'm nuts for not doing this that or the other. They think me eccentric, what fun!

The sun is still shining. Everybody's working and the lot has a slight hum about it, like a huge electrical generator plant—you know that slight pervading hum. Its very nice. Machinery at work is nice, and even dignified. Seven lawyers just walked by. Their legal staff. Now no one. My window overlooks the great central plaza of the lot. Right beneath me is parked Zanuck's car, green and low, just big enough for one. That's him all over. The kind of man I'm not going to be.

Well. See you soon. Keep the "wire" ready.

[Visits to New York after filming *A Tree Grows in Brooklyn* ended quite differently. The first, in August, left Elia feeling "adrift" and altogether out of the current of domestic life recreated by Molly and the children (*A Life*, pp. 261–63). A second, in September, laid the groundwork for an eventual return to the family. Molly's "wonderful letter," written two weeks after Elia returned to California for previews, is alive with the possibility of change and reconciliation. New "wires" of communication freed Molly to approach her husband without "fear" or "panic." At the same time, she warned that "what's good—from here on—takes time—room—play—work—wanting—fun—WITHOUT any ultimate guarantees." While no longer "sick enough" to pursue "lost causes" or accept "cold storage," she recognized "something rare" in the marriage "to fight for" (September 24, 1944, Wesleyan).

The "mutually induced exhaustion" of Elia's last days with Constance Dowling argued against divorce and the pampered life of a "staff director" in Hollywood (*A Life*, pp. 265–68). Dowling appeared in seven films, beginning as Danny Kaye's costar in the musical comedy *Up in Arms* (1944). Cast in lesser roles after Sam Goldwyn declined to renew her option, she left the States circa 1947 for a brief career in Rome. Kazan reproached himself for ending the long relationship in absentia.

Molly raised the possibility of Elia's playing Lear one day, knowing that such "talk" made him "feel uncomfortable." To soften any hint of meddling or control, she added, "what else is being young, or thinking of you as youngkicking and growing?" (September 24, 1944). Thirty-odd years later, the possibility of directing Richard Burton in *Lear* would engage Kazan for several months of intensive preparation.

A Tree Grows in Brooklyn (1945) seemed "mushy" to Kazan, a case of "poverty *all cleaned up*," but Fox executives were "'ecstatic'" and pressured him to begin a new assignment—*Anna and the King of Siam* (*A Life*, p. 263).] *TL, 3 pp., Wesleyan*

TO MOLLY DAY THACHER

[Philippine Islands]
[c. April 1945]

Honey so much has happened that I can't tell you all. In fact, I guess I never will be able to; I can't remember what happened two days ago. Did I tell you I've made friends with a couple of Philippine Guerilla fighters? Also with a member of the Philippine House of Representatives and his daughter. The relationship between the sexes on the island by the way is exactly what it is in the "old country"—The poor G.I.'s if they want to take out a Filipino girl, have to take along the aunt, the younger sister and very often the father. It is very old fashioned. The Philippinos have opened their homes to the American boys however and they are still very friendly and very grateful. However when it comes to selling us souvenirs—they want ten pesos (five dollars U.S.) for the most minor little memento. I haven't bought anything, but have just a couple little items for Chris and Judy and a Japanese rifle and bayonet for you. We run into prisoners of the Japanese at the various hospitals. The women say they were not treated badly. However the men tell gruesome stories. I've read reports about their experiences on the "Death March" and they are substantially what we read in the states. So I go on as before talking and listening and hitchhiking around. The army is wonderful because you can talk with anyone anytime. I've had a couple of little arguments one with a good friend of mine (three days acquaintance) who made some slighting remarks about the Filipino People and the other with some little drunken prick who made remarks about New Yorkers. Did I tell you about the Navy Commander I ran into down south who said there would be another war immediately after this and that it would be between New York and the rest of the country. But most people in the army are fine. You feel very proud about most of them, and the army seems to have made better men of many of them. By the way we're deep in a very minor intrigue that has to do with how Soldier Show entertainment should be organized. Its rather silly, because either way they suggest is just all wet. I had an argument with Irving Berlin last night. He said that the only thing to do would be to bring experienced B'way producers in to do shows, follow thru on them to get them opened. This is the opposite of the tack we're taking and I told him I thought he was all wet, why—but couldn't convince him. The thing that I feel is that the army is full of talent that is just in those years (often in the middle twenties) when the development is at its greatest rate of acceleration. In other words, the boys are available in the army to do the producing and organizing work necessary, and that all they need is to be organized correctly and empowered with the necessary authority and means. Berlin said you have to do it yourself. I said trust them—naming names—they can do it. I've also discovered by now that I don't really much care (personally) about dramatics, or theatricals as such. I'm really not interested (inside) in putting shows on. I do the best job I can, work hard, see people, but my real intimate interest has nothing to do with Soldier Shows or even Theatre. I decided that Show Business is a ridiculous way for a grown man to spend his life, and at the moment the army, the movements of troops, the thoughts and feelings of the fellows their stories and their behavior is a hell of a lot more interesting. You cant help making a hand full of new friends every day, so you just sit and listen. Of course being much closer to where the fighting is (tho we're still too far behind to suit me) you hear much more interesting stories. The signs of the Japanese are all about us. The last raids were not so long ago, and outside our tents are genuine Fox holes. By the way these are difficult to install here, because once you dig down a couple of feet or so, you have a well. So often you have to sink a big metal barrel into the ground and get into that. So far nothing approaching a raid has ever happened, and I guess it wont. The animal life is Far Eastern—water buffaloes and long thin white herons. The natives wear hats that are genuinely Chinese, and the women are erect from carrying bundles on their heads. The men are most proud of the fighting roosters and train them on little wheels and by suspending them into and over a pot of water so they can just barely touch the bottom with the tips of their claws. In either case there is a powerful motion of the leg muscles developed. You ought to see these men pet and preen these birds—and the birds are very content to be spoiled that way.

Well I'll be seeing you. Our mail was sent to a place about three hours by plane north of here and has been sent for. Meantime we'll be going up that way ourselves in five or six days. We'll then meet all the big shots and I'll have to have a report drawn up by that time in which I recommend what reorganization I think necessary. I'm going to be most drastic and ask for the hundred best men in the SWP put on full time and organized by me. The army is very slow, except when they want to do something bad. Then they seem to act directly and forcibly and let the book keeping catch up if it can.

Two boys from the——General Hospital are here. I'm in the Special Service Office for this base. They've come to look over the material in the way of skits that I brought from N.Y. They're strange looking kids, but I guess they're the army's show men. One of them showed me a skit he had written yesterday that was very funny indeed. I'm taking them down to my tent.

I wonder how Chris and Judy are. Tell Chris I got him a Japanese ping pong ball with Japanese writing on it, and Judy I got here a little semi-precious stone called a "Cat's eye." I wont lose them.

Take care of your belly. Goodbye dear.

[In March the War Department ordered Kazan to prepare for "movement" overseas as a theater consultant assigned to Special Services. Abe Lastfogel, wartime president of USO Camp Shows, arranged the brief trip as therapy for a client who was "living on a ledge," as Kazan put it, and unwilling to begin a new film while his intimate relations were still raw and unsettled.

Artistic talent seen by Kazan in the ranks foretold a postwar audience "alive with a new realism" and ready to demand "grown-up" entertainment—to the peril of Broadway and Hollywood (*Theatre Arts*, October 1945). Irving Berlin's glossy revue *This Is the Army* was a case in point. Kazan saw the film version (1943) after meeting Berlin in the Philippines and deplored its "easy patriotism and corn." He was "impatient" when his own film was shown surprisingly on the island of Biak, a key staging area in General MacArthur's advance to the Philippines. Amid the "scars" of recent jungle warfare, *A Tree Grows in Brooklyn* struck the director as a "sentimental fairy tale" (*A Life,* p. 277).

The few days spent with the 32nd Infantry north of Manila exposed Kazan to the remnant of war and young soldiers under sporadic fire. "Compared to all that I was witnessing, I was ashamed of the fuss I'd made about a 'love' problem. Again I had the feeling that I didn't want to leave here, that I didn't want to go home—whatever and wherever that was." Unmentioned in letters is a dengue fever that "leveled" Kazan for several days and perhaps "determined" the rest of his life. False "acclaim" was purged, his career redirected along more personal lines, and his marriage reaffirmed with Molly's announcement that he would be "a father again" (*A Life,* pp. 290–92).

Elia returned to New York in May, purchased a brownstone on East Seventy-fourth Street, and awaited the birth of Nicholas in September. A personal statement written at Sandy Hook reveals a fragile truce with Molly: "Her stiffness is becoming unbearable. Soon I will break again, and seek PLEASURE, EASE, COMFORT, EASE, EASE, EASE elsewhere. I'm writing this June 30, 1945, as a kind of realization of what's happening while it is in process. No surprises this time, and if I break this time, it will be for good" ("Your Career and Your Wife," n.d., Wesleyan).] *TL, 2 pp., Wesleyan*

TO THERESA HELBURN

[New York]
[August 1945]

Terry darling—

Your letter made me very sad indeed. I'm very fond of you. You ought to know that by now. I hope we'll be close friends for life, and I would do nothing consciously to hurt that. I'm terribly sorry that you feel I have humiliated you, and terribly sorry that I have hurt you. My intention to you is always the opposite.

You know I did not like the Gow-d'Usseau script. I thought it very well written, but I thought it played directly into the hands of the reactionaries, who keep trying to bring the issue down to: "Would you want your sister to sleep with one." Besides this political objection, I thought that the melodramatics around the affair of the watch were extremely crude. I still think they're crude. I expressed my feelings with some violence to Molly who conveyed them to Salisbury, in more moderate tones, but with no equivocation, who then passed them on to the authors. If you are surprised at my sudden switch, imagine what Leah and Cheryl Crawford feel. I lectured them for half an hour in Cheryl's office on the insidious social effect that the play might have. If you see Cheryl soon, ask her. I'd like to have seen her face when she heard the news. And when Kermit acquired the script, the same thing happened. He approached me thru Molly. I told Molly I didn't approve of the script and she told Kermit that my answer was a flat NO. And that was that. Kermit offered the script to every director available in town, and finally was on the verge of completing arrangements with Everett Sloane to do the script.

A week ago I saw Kermit socially. I offered to advise him or help him if he ever needed advice or help. It was a sincere, but routine offer—Kermit and I are old friends. He suggested that I read the script and see whether the changes the authors had been making had helped in regard to the objections I had raised. I did, and they had somewhat. They certainly were trying to, without sacrificing what they considered to be essential. I met them and told them what I thought was wrong. I found I liked them, that they were trying to say exactly what I thought should be said, that we were at variance as to means. I also found that they were quite open minded. I began to feel a kind of admiration for them. They aroused a loyalty in me, the kind that always goes to honest bold efforts to deal with "dangerous" social issues. I told Bill F. I was getting interested. He said: Dont. I agreed with him. I told Molly I was getting interested. She said: Fine. Then I began attacking the script, throwing broadsides at her, and the play, indiscriminately. I said I wouldn't have anything to do with it. At the same time she convinced me of one thing. That if you dont bring up the sex issue, the reactionaries will surely bring it up for you, since its inevitably in the back of their minds. I saw the authors next day. I said I didn't want to do the script. Then I went into a long lecture on the way the young girl should be played. I suppose I must have been talking myself into it. At any rate I did.

That's the way it happened. I hope you haven't been bored. I guess if you must chalk the incident up to something, chalk it up to the peculiar nature of artists, or Greeks, or just me. But its really not fair to chalk it up to any lack of feeling on my part towards the Guild. Cast your mind back a few months, and remember the dogged way I stuck to the project of bringing Sam's play thru, not only for myself, but so we could all do it together. You didn't think much of my chances, I suspected, and LL told me repeatedly that he doubted whether anything could be done. But you've got it now. And remember too that I've spent ALL summer with and around Berry, while you were working on Winter's Tale and Oklahoma and Carousel and this that and the other, all of which you have a perfect right to do, and all of which bring you glory and the other more concrete rewards. And also remember that, despite the fact that I was blundering and diplomatically crude at times, I did make it my business (Bill F. told me repeatedly it wasn't) to try to bring Sam back to the Guild organizationally, because I thought he belonged there organizationally. And that now that's coming about too, I suspect.

But to hell with all that. Its crass to measure friendship by deeds misperformed, or performed. The fact remains that I feel very close to you and your

Spanish Jew. And even when you seem to forbid me Joe Mielziner (and I mutter to myself: "Hell I dont have to take this anymore from anyone") I still try to keep our relationship on a basis that will give all three of us the most fun working together. And that because I want to go on with our relationship.

Incidentally, I suppose Bill F. has told you that nothing I do with Kermit will interfere with my going into rehearsal with you on your present schedule.

And finally I was very careful to talk to Berry and tell him how I was going into the other affair, and to leave him, apparently, feeling fine about it.

Love, Gadge

P.S. And I'm certainly going to see to it that nothing I do with the other show interferes with my preparing, or completing preparing Dunnigan's Daughter. You know I've already got enough notes on that damned five-some of characters to write a book. And I most grimly mean to polish that script till it shines before we "go in".

[At issue is Kazan's "sudden switch" in agreeing to direct *Deep Are the Roots* (1945) for a rival producer after advising Terry Helburn and the Theatre Guild against its adoption. Kazan argued initially that even the unspoken love between a Negro soldier home from war and the daughter of a prominent southern family would arm "reactionaries" with an "insidious" plot. He also objected to the crude "melodramatics" of a missing heirloom watch and the false charge of theft brought against the intruder by the stock aristocrat of the play. Kermit Bloomgarden's production of the play by Arnaud d'Usseau and James Gow was critically acclaimed, as was Kazan's direction, and ran for nearly five hundred performances. Much later Kazan traced his "reversals of positions and attitudes" to "conflicting desires" and accepted the consequence of "distrust" (*A Life*, p. 219).

Dunnigan's Daughter (1945) faced casting and tryout problems and closed after thirty-eight performances on Broadway. Kazan admitted in a journal entry that he was not engaged by Sam Behrman's characters, nor could he find any evidence in the script of an underlying causality of events or motivation. "It is haphazard. It is not inevitable. It is not enough, big enough, moving enough, interesting enough" (*On Directing*, p. 23). In retrospect he was ashamed of having yielded to ill-conceived demands by the author's agent and the Theatre Guild, whose directors he privately regarded as "merchant-showmen, not artists," for whom "success" was the "final proof" of any venture (to MDT, February 19, 1945, Wesleyan).] *TLS, 2 pp., Beinecke*

TO CLIFFORD ODETS

[New York]
February 1 [1946]

Dear Cliff—

This letter in answer is late. But it wasn't easy to reply to yours, so I put it aside for a while and just now picked it up and reread it. For some reason I felt better about it, and that moved me to answer; so here goes.

The reason you dont feel "the true affection" that you once knew from me is that I dont feel it anymore. I stopped feeling in the same family with you during the period just after the opening of Night Music. And I have never felt towards you since as I did before that time.

But I must say that you're mistaken when you doubt my good wishes. We're no longer intimate—and I'll assume my share of the responsibility for that—but I really and truly, cross my heart and hope to die wish you well. I hope like hell you write plays. And I really do believe that anything you write will be creative, will be "Expression".

As for your having mixed feelings about my work, has it ever occurred to you that I might be in anything but an ecstasy of self satisfaction about it myself? Is it inconceivable to you that I might have mixed feelings about my work too? The plain fact is that I have only done one movie and one dozen productions on stage and that really doesn't amount to anything except a start, and I know it. I think of myself as a beginner. I've still got my eye on the main chance, the possibility for something real and enduring. My plans with Harold are a breather. It gives us time to look ahead, and feel out the ground, just a little bit. The only thing I didn't want is to get into anything false—and I did think the set-up Lee wrote me about was a false one, in actuality, in effect.

I'm aware that you cant change your own work without also, or even first, changing the institution and the institutional methods that we're all part of. And I dont know whether you can see it clearly, but along this line there is promise. There are better guys coming into positions of influence in the Theatre. You have to look carefully and close to see the improvement, but when you do, there they are!

Perhaps some day we'll talk about these things. But I dont think the talk will mean much more than diddling unless we're both really part of the theatre and I mean by that: have our fates tied up with it.

At any rate, I'd like to see you someday. I'd like you to come and see a run-thru of the Anderson play—I'm sure Harold would too. Also I'd like Betty and you to come up to the house. I've changed my life rather radically since I saw you last. I'm a man of property and substance now, believe it or not, with a city home and a country home and many of the other trappings of permanence. And I've even learned to enjoy them—a home for instance. And I do.

I live at 167 E. 74 and my phone is Rh 4-6892. I'm not doing a hell of a lot these days; I go to the gym, rather vaguely watch Harold rehearse, and read books around the subject of the SEA OF GRASS. I've about said it for a while. Hope I see you soon.

gadge

[The years since the failure of *Night Music* in 1940 had not been kind to Clifford Odets. *Clash by Night* (1941) starred Tallulah Bankhead and Lee J. Cobb in a gritty love story that opened shortly after Pearl Harbor to mixed reviews and a brief run. Odets's adaptation of *The Russian People* by Konstantin Simonov fared no better in 1942. Odets did not return to Broadway until the end of the decade.

Partnership with Harold Clurman went forward in spite of Molly Kazan's warning that Clurman had been "corrupted" by devotion to his wife Stella Adler and would betray Elia once again. At the same time plans to revive the Group were under discussion on both coasts and may have been stimulated by *The Fervent Years*, Clurman's informal history of the Group Theatre published in mid-1945. "Next season may see it blossom forth, but definitely not along the old lines," a columnist had recently stated. Lee Strasberg's "set-up" was probably a part of the same discussion.

There is no indication that Clifford Odets accepted Kazan's offer to attend a "run-thru" of *Truckline Cafe*—first venture of the Clurman partnership. Hostile reviews closed the play after thirteen performances, but not before Maxwell Anderson denounced his critics as a "Jukes family of journalism, who bring to the theatre nothing but their own hopelessness, recklessness and despair" (*NYHT*, March 4, 1946). Supporting roles by Marlon Brando and Karl Malden were the only bright spots in a disastrous production directed by Harold Clurman rather than Kazan.

A brief stint at "Metromill" resulted in the only film that embarrassed Kazan: *The Sea of Grass* (1947), a Western melodrama costarring Spencer Tracy and Katharine Hepburn. MGM's "organized indifference" to the role of the director reinforced Kazan's desire to do "something unique and personal" in film (*A Life*, p. 321).] *TLS, 1 p., Wesleyan*

Marlon Brando in *Truckline Cafe*

TO TENNESSEE WILLIAMS

[Beverly Hills, California]
[April 1947]

Dear Tennessee—

Thanks for your wonderful letter. As I read it I admired you and felt close to you. I'll do everything possible to do your play. I never had but one "reservation" about it, and I wasn't sure that the fault or limitation wasn't in me. You read so many mechanical plays, direct so many "well-made" plays that your (my) notion of structure begins to narrow. The first time thru it didn't quite all add up for me emotionally. After that I had that chat with you in the Fornos restaurant, and read the play again late at night with no telephone ringing to disturb me, and I began to feel it as a whole. I agree with what you say in your letter. It is like a classical tragedy in that the feeling at the end should be one of pity and terror for Blanche—even a kind of awe. Even after I broke off negotiations with Mrs. Selznick I kept on working it over and over in my mind. It stuck with me. Also it challenged me. I've got to go as good as I possibly can to live up to it. So many plays I've done, I've thought less of.

I wont rehash my trouble with Mrs. S. at any length. I'd say that the fault was nearly all mine. I was angry at Audrey for ever giving the play to Irene—a step which after all, was her business and yours. Also a "fait accompli" now. This resentment at Audrey's act, I transferred, unfairly, to Mrs. Selznick. And since you left, I've had a long talk with Audrey and understand her reasons.

There were other reasons—not so petty nor so trivial. I was determined to produce the plays I directed. I'm going to open an office. I've just broken off my partnership with Harold and Walter Fried. The experiences of Boomerang and All My Sons convinced me that I work best when I work in single collaboration with the author. I'll never go back, if I can possibly help it to working for other producers; those meetings in the Ritz Hotel of "Administrators," or production committee, and so forth. All meetings on ALL MY SONS were meetings of two people—Miller and myself and that is best.

I've talked this out with Fitelson my lawyer, and we've come to a proposal which I think Mrs. S. will find acceptable. It will depend somewhat on how badly you want me. But I dont think the main problem will be the money. Because its not my main problem. The main job will be to find some formal arrangement, some FORM between Mrs. S. and me that will include me in the production, without hurting her ego. We have a suggestion. I'm not doing this out of vanity or ego. I dont want to be partners with Irene—or anyone else. I'm insisting on it because I simply cannot separate the function of directing and the function of producing. I would require Mielziner to do one kind of set. Ty Guthrie—who by the way is a brilliant director, with what is mainly a visual gift—would need something quite different. It is the job of the Director as producer to determine the sets, the costumes, the lighting, the casting, the music etc. etc. especially in a play of this kind where all the elements of the theatre have to be made to serve one artistic purpose. In fact, much more than in a routine play the success of your play depends upon this fusion of all the capabilities of the theatre.

Again simply and bluntly: I'll be very, very happy if this works out. I sound corny but I might as well say it: I'll be honored. The play calls for me to grow, to do more than I have done, and for the American Theatre to grow, goddamn it, too. I especially agree with one thing in your letter, by the way, that sometimes the only way to communicate certain types of reality or experience is

With Arthur Miller

thru means that are "expressionistic". I've already begun to have ideas about the play, and I feel something I wasn't sure when I first read it: that I can do a good job. A wonderful thing about the play: it sticks with me. Its kind of living. The tough job is to keep it at times truthful, faithful—that is to say complex, dual no villains—not an oversimplification into the easy categories of our theatre, but rounded people. And also, wherever we move past, in our means of expression, the limits of routine realism, to still keep it REAL at basis, not fancy or superficially tricky. Tennessee, I'm really full of it, and I'm simply waiting in hopes that everything works out.

By the way I forgot to say that I had a pleasant chat of about four hours with Irene. Again I personally liked her, found her to be sensitive and very intelligent. I'm not a monster—I dont drive authors out of rehearsals. In fact I like them around every day. Miller and Gow and d'usseau were around every day. Thornton came every third day regularly on schedule. Inquire around—I have always gotten along with every producer I've ever worked with, without exception, from Mike Myerberg thru Gilbert Miller and the Theatre Guild down to Kermit Bloomgarden and Cheryl Crawford, so—I really dont think Mrs. S has anything to worry about.

What I wont do is direct this or any play unless I think its possible to do my best. I think that is possible now. The time I've spent thinking helped, as did our talk and the one I had with Irene and Audrey.

I hope you all work it out. I'll be back around the middle of May and until then I can be reached c/o 20th Century Fox Studios, Beverly Hills, Calif.

My best to you always,

[A note and the promise of a script began the collaboration of Tennessee Williams and Elia Kazan. The play "tops any direction" on Broadway, Williams wrote of *All My Sons* (1947), adding that he would send "congratulations" to Arthur Miller and a copy of his own work to Kazan. "It may not be the sort of play that interests you but I hope so." Kazan did not "rush" to read *A Streetcar Named Desire* and wondered if he and Williams "were the same kind of theatre animal—Miller seemed more my kind" (*A Life,* pp. 326–27). It remained for Molly to campaign on the home front. A contest she organized in 1938 for the Group Theatre attracted a young, unknown playwright named "Tennessee" Williams—perhaps the first recorded instance of his legendary stage name. She arranged a special prize of $100 for a series of dramatic sketches and learned only much later that Williams had subtracted three years from his age to meet the contest rules. Molly shared her discovery with Audrey Wood, a shrewd agent who brought *The Glass Menagerie* to Broadway in 1945 and oddly enough, or so it seemed to Kazan, gave *Streetcar* to Irene Selznick.

Kazan answered the playwright's "wonderful letter" after breaking off negotiations and leaving for California to begin work on *Gentleman's Agreement.* "Bitterly disappointed," Williams attempted to clarify the dramatic relationships in *Streetcar* that presumably troubled Kazan. The "tragedy" of Blanche DuBois is rooted in "the way we all see each other in life. Vanity, fear, desire, competition—all such distortions within our own egos—condition our vision of those in relation to us" (April 19, 1947, Wesleyan). With negotiations restored, Williams made a final appeal for Kazan's direction: "The cloudy dreamer type which I must admit to being needs the complementary eye of the more objective and dynamic worker. I believe you are also a dreamer. There are dreamy touches in your direction which are vastly provocative, but you have a dynamism that my work needs to be translated into exciting theatre" (n.d., Wesleyan). Kazan "gobbled up" the compliments and soon realized that Williams had provided the "key" to the production (*A Life,* p. 330).

Wealth (a divorce settlement from David O. Selznick), Hollywood connections (daughter of MGM president Louis B. Mayer), and the likelihood of deferring to the author's intention qualified Irene Selznick to produce *Streetcar* in spite of limited experience. Audrey Wood explained these and other "reasons" in a "long talk" with Kazan, but she anticipated hard terms and tough bargaining, convinced that his walkout was meant "to unnerve us, frighten us, or make him seem harder to get" (to TW, April 18, 1947, HRC). Acting as producer-director of *All My Sons,* which opened in the preceding January to strong reviews, had established a degree of autonomy that Kazan and his combative attorney Bill Fitelson intended to preserve in negotiations with Selznick.] *TL, 2 pp., Wesleyan*

TO TENNESSEE WILLIAMS

West Los Angeles,
May 5, 1947

DEAR TENNESSEE: NEVER IMAGINED I WAS SO TERRIFYING. HAVENT PUT BAYONET IN AN AUTHOR'S RIBS FOR A HECK OF A TIME. MAYBE

THATS WHATS BEEN WRONG. I HEREBY FORMALLY ACCEPT YOUR SCRIPT EXACTLY AS IS. ANY CHANGES YOU MAKE HEREAFTER ARE ON YOUR OWN RESPONSIBILITY AND BECAUSE YOU THINK SOME SUGGESTION OF MINE WOULD HELP YOUR PLAY. I HAVE A FEW IDEAS. I THINK THEY MIGHT HELP. HOWEVER NONE OF THEM ARE FUNDAMENTAL OR WHAT YOU CALL IMPORTANT. AS FOR IRENE'S JITTERS I DONT REALLY THINK SHE SHOULD BE QUITE SO FRIGHTENED. LET HER TALK TO SOME OF MY REFERENCES. THERE ARE AN AWFUL LOT OF PEOPLE IVE WORKED WITH WHOM I DIDNT TERRIFY. ANYWAY ALL THAT NERVOUSNESS OF HERS WILL DISAPPEAR AFTER ABOUT OUR SECOND CONFERENCE. THIS I KNOW FROM EXPERIENCE. LOVE ALWAYS-

Gadge.

[Tennessee Williams had endured "three-or-four-hour audiences" with Irene Selznick and shared Kazan's aversion to "the peripheral involvements, complications, arguments and discussions that go with the usual play production." Nonetheless, he urged that "a certain warmth and deference" be shown to Selznick: "I believe she visualizes herself being bodily ejected from the theatre and me writing

With Irene Selznick and Tennessee Williams on the set of *A Streetcar Named Desire*.

new scenes with a bayonet at my ribs!" Williams did not "expect to do any more <u>important</u> work" on *Streetcar* and asked Kazan if he would "accept the script as it now stands" (May 1, 1947, Wesleyan).

Irene Selznick later described Kazan as "emphatic in his demands: quite apart from Gadge's usual fee and top percentage of the gross, he must coproduce and own a chunk of the show." She was ready "to step aside" rather than "knuckle under" to such an ultimatum before a compromise was found: "Irene M. Selznick presents Elia Kazan's Production of *A Streetcar Named Desire*." Selznick gave Kazan 20 percent of the show, reducing her share accordingly, but retained executive and legal authority as producer (Selznick, pp. 299–300).]
Telegram, 1 p., HRC

TO JO MIELZINER

SH: Twentieth Century-Fox Film Corporation
Beverly Hills, California
June 10, 1947

Dear Jo:

Thanks for your ground plans. I hope I haven't been too long in giving you my reaction. I know you're waiting for it but I had to get started on the picture and kind of get that on the way before I had time to sit down and study them.

Two things concern me particularly. The first has to do with the fact that Blanche, when she enters up-left, will pass out of sight of the audience as she goes around the up-right corner of the set. I suggest that you cut off this up-right corner of the set, cut a diagonal slice off it and make sure that a person entering up-left can go all the way around and into the set proper without ever going out of sight. I know I would be giving up quite a bit in the way of stage space but it's worth it to me. I'm especially concerned about Blanche's final exit. I don't think you can hold anything on stage after she has gone off and any business that Tennessee may want or that I may cook up for Stella or Stanley will have to take place <u>as</u> she's exiting.

Maybe the thing to do is to construct the stairs on a kind of a broken angle or as if around a bay so that the lower half of the stairs faces the audience in good sight lines for the colored woman and Eunice to be sitting on them, and the other half breaks in and out of sight around the bay. At any rate, no matter how you work it out, the main thing is a clear entrance and exit for Blanche at the beginning and end of the play.

A secondary but important consideration is that Eunice and the colored woman be seen. However, I say this is secondary because I could put them down on the ground level, if necessary.

Don't worry if I lose three or four feet of stage width in the up-right corner. I can afford it.

The second thing that concerns me has to do with the scene where Stanley carries Stella to their bed. I'm still not really convinced or at ease about our concealing this piece of action with an emphasis by light on another area. The audience will be trying to peer at what's happening on the bed during the scene between Blanche and Mitch. Why can't we place a kind of sleeping porch up-left behind the stage wall of the present bathroom so that Stella and Stanley would, in effect, exit for this moment? I'd feel a lot more comfortable about it if you could devise some solution along this line.

Jo Mielziner's stage design for *A Streetcar Named Desire* (following spread)

Now here are a few minor observations:

1) "The barroom around the corner" should be indicated some way up-right, possibly by neon light that glows luringly and we could place the actual musicians way upright in that little area that's masked up there by our street drop.

2) I notice that all the props can have a slightly fantastic coloring. Tennessee seems to have a terrific visual sense or appreciation of colors all through. And the colors can have the slight fantasy of someone like Dufy, a little more colorful say than life. For example, he talks about the "red-stained meat package," etc., etc., etc. One thing that worried me a little was whether the light and airy walls that we're planning would give an impression of too uniform elegance, but I think now that elegance is excellent for us if we balance it with props and furniture that are kind of colorfully decaying. When I speak of color, Jo, I feel that all the colors here are weather-mellowed, as though the rain grayed them down.

3) Speaking of the sleeping porch off left, it might save us a foot or two in the bedroom which would compensate us for what we lose up-right if we shift that wall as I suggest.

4) I just noticed for the first time that he suggests that a lot of scenes, in their lighting, end on an iris-out on two figures or a single face or something like that. Let's take him literally. A lot of the curtains of the scenes seem terribly weak to me and I'm going to try to do something about them, but they seem much better when thought of as ending on a narrowing down of light to a couple of faces or to a single face. Scene after scene ends this way and I never took these things seriously till now.

5) As for the lamp on which Blanche puts a new shade, it should really dominate the entire bedroom. I don't know how you could do that. It shouldn't be off in one corner on one wall. Maybe it could be some kind of a fixture that comes off from the bathroom wall or from a center post at an arch and places this light bulb in a dominant position over the entire bedroom. You figure this out. All I know is that ideally, if possible, it should dominate the bedroom.

6) One final note about the sleeping porch: It would be a very valuable place for Blanche to run when the people from the institution come to get her in the last scene.

I'll write you again soon, Jo. Let me know what your reactions are to these things. I'm going over the script again this weekend and see if there's anything else.

Best, <u>Gadge</u>

cc: Irene Selznick

[Kazan returned to California to finish *Gentleman's Agreement* and consult with Irene Selznick on casting *Streetcar* from the ranks of Hollywood actors, whom she presumably knew best. Jessica Tandy signed in July to play Blanche, while John Garfield continued negotiations with Selznick as a potential Stanley. Contract discussions fell through in mid-August shortly after Kazan returned to New York. Apparently it was Bill Liebling, partner and husband of Audrey Wood, who suggested Marlon Brando to Kazan, who in turn dispatched the twenty-three-year-old actor to Provincetown. His reading elated Tennessee Williams and prompted Margo Jones, an excitable houseguest, to demand that Kazan be called "'right away!'"

Jo Mielziner's designs for *Streetcar* were "almost the best" Tennessee Williams had "ever seen." He was especially impressed by the "translucent" back wall of the set, a technique used by Mielziner in *The Glass Menagerie* to suggest the insularity of the Wingfield apartment. In *Streetcar* the innovative effect was turned outward to create "a stylized panorama . . . of the railroad yards and the city" beyond (to Jones, n.d., HRC).

Blanche remained visible through illuminated gauze as she passed along the street facing the Kowalski apartment. The stairs leading to the apartment of Steve and Eunice obscured her first entrance to the interior set and more importantly, Kazan thought, her "final exit." The spiral staircase suggested by Kazan appears in an early sketch (Mielziner, p. 143), but in annotating the present letter, Mielziner declared it "Impossible" to keep Blanche continuously in view.

Williams informed Kazan in May of "an alternative ending, physically quieter, which could be substituted if the present ending proves too difficult to stage" (May 1, 1947, Wesleyan). The present version opens with Blanche in a state of panic requiring forcible sedation with a hypodermic needle and removal in a straitjacket by a menacing doctor and one of Stanley's friends (Johns, pp. 127–30). Her symptoms were moderated in rehearsal to preserve tragic dignity and allow for more efficient departure. Smiling radiantly, Blanche is escorted past the spiral on the arm of a kindly doctor who has taken the part of "a new beau."

Mielziner used a screen to shield the lovemaking of Stella and Stanley after "the poker night" sequence. Blanche, in resumed conversation with Mitch (played by Karl Malden) on the staircase, fears to enter the apartment from which a "feeble" light issues.

The "coloring" of *Streetcar* reminded Kazan of Raoul Dufy's bold interiors. In the published stage direction, Williams related the "lurid nocturnal brilliance" of the Kowalski kitchen where the "party of apes" gathers for poker to the primary colors of van Gogh's *Night Café* (1888).] *TLS, 3 pp., BRTC*

TO ARTHUR MILLER

[Beverly Hills, California]
June 20, 1947

Dear Artie:

I was delighted to get your letter. Gee, I'm sure beginning to miss New York! I guess some people are decent human beings only when their circumstances remind them that they've got to meet other people halfway. I thought that the years alone in that hotel had rubbed most of that Belasco crap off our lady, but apparently not enough. I'm talking about Beth. I always knew there was a good, lively shit-heel in the lady. I'm only sorry that it came out at your rehearsals. That would have been a time for her to have been especially decent. It burns me up a bit that she wasn't even though you can take care of yourself. Also, she might have been nice to the replacements coming in. Apparently, she wasn't that either because I've heard indirectly from them about her attitude towards them. Somebody ought to tell her off some day. Maybe it'll be my privilege. Of course, all she'll do is walk off and go home. She's beginning to have it coming.

I'm sorry to hear about Anne and Stanislowski. They had an affair once but I thought it was all over. Isn't Stanislowski a little old for her anyway? I'm glad also that you got Bob more dough. He earned it. The main thing with Chalmers is variety. The more differently you can direct each moment, even exaggerating the differences between the moments, the better off it will be.

Chester Erskine is coming out and talking to me about "All My Sons." He's very earnest and sincere about it. He will do a very conscientious job, anyway.

This "Gentleman's Agreement" is a difficult deal, much more so than I thought. It's extremely ticklish. I'm constantly tight-rope walking—I mean, how to make our leading lady instinctively anti-Semitic, like most of the Gentile people of the Goyish upper middle class, without making her an outright louse and without making her aware of her own anti-Semitism. Zanuck, by the way, has been very helpful. His instinct, while not subtle, is true and I've enjoyed working with him. I've also got a good cast. The trouble so far has been with me. I've misdirected a couple of scenes and I've already done one over and, out of the three weeks I've shot, there are at least two more days to do over. It's all part of the game and, as a matter of fact, I'm delighted at the opportunity of a second chance. Not all studio heads would give me this.

The whole industry, by the way, is panic-stricken. Grosses have not only fallen down but are staying there. They even talk about trying to make better stories. Further, they can't go.

Irene Selznick's out here and she takes up my Sunday leisure. In one way or another, I keep occupied. By the way, I have a clause in my contract with her that I get through by Thanksgiving, and I'm looking forward to your play being ready by then. I hope you do go up to my place and let me know how it is up there. I've definitely decided that next summer no Hollywood.

Give my best to Mary. Excuse the dictation. It makes my style—and I know you're a great stickler for style—a bit formal.

Tell Norman to drop me a postcard. How is he getting along with Bloomgarden?

Take it easy. You've done your job now with Chalmers. Get the hell out of town and start on your play.

Yours,

[Arthur Miller shared honors with Kazan, who directed and coproduced *All My Sons* in partnership with Harold Clurman and Walter Fried. Brooks Atkinson found "something uncommonly exhilarating in the spectacle of a new writer bringing unusual gifts to the theatre under the sponsorship of a director with taste and enthusiasm" (*NYT,* January 30, 1947). A close friendship ensued. "We were both out of the Depression, both left-wingers, both had had problems with our fathers, considered their business worlds antihuman. We were soon exchanging every intimacy" (*A Life,* p. 319). Further collaboration lay ahead for Miller and Kazan as well as political rupture.

Miller rehearsed new members who entered the cast of *All My Sons* in June. The current level of performance, he thought, lacked the "strong and unbroken rhythm" imposed by Kazan's award-winning direction. Beth Merrill, a holdover, had lived obscurely since the 1920s, when she last starred in several David Belasco productions. Her upstaging of Ann Shepherd irritated Miller, as did Shepherd's ponderous acting (to EK, Saturday, Wesleyan). Kazan punned, "Stanislowski."

Chester Erskine produced and wrote the screenplay for *All My Sons* (1948) in association with Universal International Pictures. Irving Reis directed. Bosley Crowther wrote in his review that the original effects of a father's callous wartime capitalism were softened in the film.

"We have hit the scene too hard and too deliberately," Darryl Zanuck concluded, after seeing Kathy Lacy's "horrified" reaction to the possibility that Phil Green is Jewish. Cast as a freelance writer in *Gentleman's Agreement,* he poses as a Jew to experience anti-Semitism among "nice people" of the upper middle class. Zanuck worried lest the heavy-handed scene establish Kathy as a bigot and undermine later romance (Zanuck, pp. 131–34).

Thomas Chalmers replaced Ed Begley in *All My Sons* and would reappear as Uncle Ben in *Death of a Salesman* (1949). Arthur Miller was currently at work on *Salesman* and "Plenty Good Times," with greater emphasis on the latter. It was eventually shelved and parts incorporated into "The Hook," a screenplay Miller and Kazan planned to film independently.] *TL, 2 pp., Wesleyan*

TO CHERYL CRAWFORD

[Beverly Hills, California]
June 24, 1947

Dear Cheryl:

Thanks for your letter and enclosed is a check for Marc. I'm writing Moss today about the Lycee rehearsal room and will let you know what the deal is on it.

I saw last week a bill of One Acts at the Actors Lab. They included a monologue by Bud Bohnen, a play by Max Gorelik, and a play by a young unknown fellow about two blind soldiers. It sounds bizarre and impossible but it was by far the most interesting evening of theatre I've had at the Actors Lab. Gorelik's play was in the epic tradition, or his version of it. The actors talked at times to each other, at times to the audience. Part of it was stilted and silly, part quite well written, even eloquent in a way. Max, of course, will never be a playwright but what interested me was how easily the audience accepted this kind of going on. There was never any doubt in their mind about the "form," etc. The plays were done without scenery and much of the casting was unusual, not type, but the whole evening had an air about it of genuine novelty, people doing things they'd never done before.

During the same week I'd seen "The Skin of Our Teeth" at Jack Houseman's theatre here with a so-called All Star cast (by All Star meaning Keenan Wynn, Jane Wyatt, Hurd Hatfield, Carol Stone, etc.) The evening at the Lab was so much more stimulating and genuine than the half-baked professionalism of the stars that, as Boris Aronson would say, "I simply can't tell you."

This is the kind of evening, played to specially selected small audiences, that I think we should start after a few months with our groups. We may make gentle fools of ourselves, but only kind of in the family and for each other's sake, so to speak. I didn't mean in our last discussion that we should do plays for the general public and critics—not for years—but I think that it is so stimulating to theatre people and so enlarging to the actors working in these kind of things. A program composed solely of class work soon grows tedious.

About Lee Strasberg, I say let's get him involved right through. Consider honestly whether maybe he shouldn't give the Beginners' Class instead of me. That would be all right with me. I could help organize the kind of tiny experimental productions with new authors, directors and actors that I'm talking about. He's a wonderful man and he should be a central element in this kind of thing.

Write me again soon.

Love,

Enc.

[Bud Bohnen, Max Gorelik, and other former Group Theatre members found a congenial home at the Actors Laboratory in West Hollywood. A Stanislavsky-based acting school and theater, the Lab produced a wide variety of plays from 1941 to 1952, when charges of communist infiltration forced its closing.

Harold Clurman's announcement that he, Stella Adler, and Elia Kazan were "committed to founding a school of the theatre" seemed firm in early 1946, but within a year Kazan had withdrawn from the plan and from a partnership with Clurman and Walter Fried. The way was cleared for a second collaboration with Bobby Lewis, not a fanciful theater but an acting studio, which began to take shape in the spring of 1947 as Kazan juggled film and theater commitments. Cheryl Crawford completed the triumvirate as the perennial manager, while Lee Strasberg began teaching at the Actors Studio in 1948. Kazan stated erroneously in A Life that "it never occurred [to him] to involve Lee Strasberg" in the founding stage (p. 302).

The Actors Studio opened formally on October 5, 1947, with beginning and advanced classes taught respectively by Kazan and Lewis. The first sessions

Ralph Steiner, Bill Fitelson, and Molly at Malibu Beach

included Marlon Brando, Montgomery Clift, Julie Harris, Cloris Leachman, Karl Malden, E. G. Marshall, Maureen Stapleton, and Eli Wallach. Incorporated as a nonprofit in early 1948, the Studio was soon looking forward to an initial stage production. A quarter century later Kazan summarized its impact on the profession: "No one can appreciate what the Studio means unless he can recall what the actor was in the Broadway Theatre before the Studio existed, a part of a labor pool, his craft scoffed at—you either had it or you didn't in those days, talent was a kind of magic, mysterious, inexplicable elite. The fact that a soul could be awakened to its potential was not recognized then. Or that acting could be studied as a course of training, not only voice and make-up and stage deportment, but the actual inner technique itself" (Garfield, pp. 45–46).] *TLS with enclosure, 2 pp., Wesleyan*

TO IRENE SELZNICK

[Boston]
November 11, 1947

Dear Irene,
Not to waste time, the two intermissions will be tried tonight. I won't be there, but Tennessee will and you and he will have to discuss it. I think it is extremely dangerous to send an audience out to talk about Blanche on any solid ideas

until after the 6th scene. In other words, they should hear her story about Alan and have seen her in the 5th and 6th scene generally before they solidify any notions about her in lobby discussions. I think it very harmful to send them out after scene 3.

About the end of the 4th scene: I think the note is serious and dramatic now, despite what seems to be a coined line. However, if you think it should be more dramatic or more serious, I think you should talk to Tennessee about rewriting it. I myself am satisfied.

I also like the end of scene 9 now. Perhaps you can tell me just what you want here that is different and convince me of it. This curtain seems to be going very well and I am loathe to change it.

I have restored the Mexican Woman in scene 1 as you suggest. I have added to Stanley's part the line 'up where I come from'. I haven't placed it too well but I have asked Marlon to talk to Tennessee himself and see if Tennessee can find a better place for it. I have inserted 'Past couple of months' in speech of Blanche's as you suggest.

I am absolutely certain that there should be no music in the play before the Varsouviana in scene 1. If there is incidental music previous to the Varsouviana, it too will get over as incidental music, rather than as subjective music heard only by Blanche. I have worked and worked to get this over to the audience and I think with just the beginning of some success. Any earlier music, I feel makes an obstacle in way of our audience's understanding of the Varsouviana as subjective.

I am very anxious for more work on the trunk. I hope you'll do this. I am also anxious that the bedroom in Act. 2 be dressed up more to show Blanche's influence on the house. This room should be genuinely gay and pretty in few more details so that when she says this to Mitch we feel that it is so.

The thunder in scene 5 is indicated in Tennessee's script. It was put there by the author and I assumed to help breach the mood from the laughter and horse-play of Steve and Eunice and the scene between Blanche and her sister. I hate to cut it before we have given it a fair try as distant thunder. I don't think that an adequate thunder sound has been provided for us yet by our technical dept.

I am going to New York to see the opening of my picture and will be back here at 4 o'clock Wednesday afternoon at which time I want to have a light rehearsal with Johnny. This is just to go over the lights once more and make him as solid as possible on them before the Philadelphia opening. I am also sending a copy of this note to Tennessee.

EK

[*A Streetcar Named Desire* arrived in Boston for a two-week engagement (November 3–14) after encouraging reviews in New Haven. Tennessee Williams was no longer the unknown playwright whose first professional production (*Battle of*

Angels) was attacked by the Boston censor and ridiculed by critics in 1940. *Streetcar* was received with an awareness of the author's talent and the play's undeniable distinction. Several reviewers harbored moral reservations, and the rape of Blanche DuBois was reportedly played behind a screen at the censor's behest. Elliot Norton, dean of Boston critics, referred obliquely to the homosexuality of Blanche's husband as an "appalling defect" of character. Kazan's direction and Mielziner's lighting were acclaimed (Kolin, pp. 52–59).

Kazan feared that sending the audience to the lobby after scene three, which concludes the poker night sequence, would expose Blanche to premature judgment as a deceitful and destructive interloper. Delaying the single intermission until scene six, as *Streetcar* was played in New Haven, sent the audience to the lobby with knowledge of Blanche's tragic marriage and Stanley's threat to investigate his sister-in-law's background. Tennessee Williams viewed the scene as critical in establishing Blanche's vulnerability and gaining the compassion of the audience. As it turned out, *Streetcar* opened in New York on December 3 with brief intermissions after scenes three and six.

Kazan advised that the Varsouviana be established before any other music is introduced. Its haunting refrain was intended to evoke Blanche's corrosive memory of the evening at Moon Lake casino that ends with the suicide of her husband. Blanche's trunk, plundered by Stanley in scene two, contains the legal documentation of a lost aristocratic heritage and the trivial finery of reduced circumstances. Kazan advised "more work" on the first encounter of Stanley and Blanche.

The legendary opening of *Streetcar* was awkwardly punctuated by Tennessee Williams. Called to the stage of the Ethel Barrymore Theatre after repeated curtains, he "bowed to the actors instead of the audience."

Kazan wrote to Irene Selznick before attending the opening of *Gentleman's Agreement* in New York. The Academy nominated the film in eight fields—including Gregory Peck and Dorothy McGuire in leading roles—three winning: best picture, director, and supporting actress (Celeste Holm). It was also high on *Variety*'s annual list of top-grossing films, earning $3.9 million for Twentieth Century-Fox. In retrospect Kazan thought *Gentleman's Agreement* "patronizing" and "light-footed" in treating anti-Semitism (*A Life*, p. 333).] *TLS, 1 p., Wesleyan*

TO LAWRENCE LANGNER

[New York]
May 5, 1948

Dear Lawrence Langner:
"Within a Glass Bell" is simply not my dish of tea—aromatic tea at that. I could suggest all kinds of directors for you—just look where the lavender grows.

At 8:30 last Sunday night, I was beating my brains out through the traffic just outside of New York City. It turned out to be much heavier than we anticipated, and I was sorry that I had to miss the television show.

Yours, Gadg.

[Several managements, including the Theatre Guild, held options on "Within a Glass Bell," but William Marchant's first professional play was not produced on Broadway, at least under the present title. *To Be Continued* had a very brief run in 1952 and may be a later version. In the meanwhile, Lawrence Langner replied archly to Kazan: "I have raised my eyebrows very high on reading your letter of May fifth. Do you not know now that practically all the dramatists who write anything good come from 'where the lavender grows.'" Langner alluded to award-winning plays by Tennessee Williams (*Streetcar*) and Terence Rattigan (*The Winslow Boy*) and scolded Kazan for suggesting "directors who come from the same garden! Don't you think that lavender on lavender will be just too much?" Langner closed with a wish "for more manhood everywhere" (May 10, 1948, Beinecke).]
TLS, 1 p., Beinecke

TO DARRYL F. ZANUCK

[New York]
May 11, 1948

Dear Darryl:

I had another long, long talk with John Steinbeck yesterday. This time, as a matter of fact, he spoke of you. He is very anxious to do a picture now if the right subject and the right auspices could be found for him. He is a very faithful admirer of yours, and is very hopeful that some way can be worked out for him to work with you and myself.

He asked about THE PURITAN story and I told him that neither you nor I were keen on it, but that our attitude towards it would depend a little on how his enthusiasm rode. He said that he himself had cooled on that but had another subject now that he would propose to us. This turned out to be CHRISTOPHER COLUMBUS, on which he had done a great deal of research, but he didn't know that this was being shot in England with Freddie March.

I then proposed another subject to him, one on which I have been keen for years. This is, the life of Zapata, who was the leading figure in the Mexican revolution against the tyrant Diaz. It turned out, coincidentally, that this was John's own pet project. I explained to him that Metro owned a book called "Zapata the Invincible", and also told him that I had, on my own, made inquiries about the book and that Metro's asking price was $46,000. John said there was no need to deal with Metro; he had for years been amassing material on the subject, even down to costume plates, etc; that he had shot two films in Mexico and had encountered the legend of Zapata everywhere, among the Indians, among the film workers, among everybody.

Well, this started us going and we swopped stories and enthusiasms for a long time. He is really just as high on this subject as he possibly could be and, of course, so am I. There is nothing I'd like to do as well. Zapata himself was easily one of the greatest men who ever lived. He was a terrific fighter for the right. He was a living legend. He was a great athlete and horseman. In fact, his stunts on horseback are sung about in all the coridas which are the popular songs. He was a lover of fantastic dimensions.

The story of his life has in it more cinematic excitement than any I have ever seen. I won't tell you anything about it, but it has, I promise you, every possible element for the greatest movie of our day. The climax of it is the Judas and Christ episode, where one of his own leaders betrayed him by what amounted to the kiss of death.

I at one time started an outline on this, but as John says, nothing needs to be made up; it's all there, substantiated by fact. Furthermore, from the point of view of the ideology, his fight was against a man who was a notorious tyrant, and also, with an eye toward acceptability by the general audiences, Zapata never came into conflict with either America or, as far as I know, American interests. In other words, this is a man who fought for something that is indubitably right and we need never run into the "damn yankee gringo" business. Our record in Mexico, incidentally, is certainly nothing to be proud of, but I know these are difficult times and I would not propose to bring that up now. John asked me to keep this entirely confidential; both his interest and our conversation.

I am going to Florida on Sunday to meet Murphy and will write you of our findings there.

P.S. The perfect American actor for this, is Greg Peck, and I would bet my shirt that he would go for it, head over heels.

[John Steinbeck was pleased that "Zanuck has more than kept his word" in producing *The Grapes of Wrath* (1940). "It looks and feels like a documentary film and certainly it has a hard, truthful ring" (Steinbeck/*Letters*, p. 183).

Kazan learned in 1941 that MGM held film, if not stage, rights to *Zapata, the Unconquerable* (1941), a popular biography considered for adaptation by the Dollar Top Theatre. The project fell through, as did an offer received by Steinbeck in 1945 from Pan-American Films. It too aroused admiration for Emiliano Zapata, tempered by the reality that filming such a controversial life in Mexico would be difficult, if "made straight historically." Any "concession," Steinbeck knew, would be "a complete double cross of the things Zapata lived and died for" (Steinbeck/ *Letters*, p. 265). His personal knowledge of Mexico and extensive use of native subjects greatly exceeded Kazan's enthusiasm for the country. Filming *The Forgotten Village* (1941) on location had also taught Steinbeck to expect difficult negotiations and production delays. More the novice, Kazan prematurely dismissed "the 'damn yankee gringo' business."

Kazan and Richard Murphy were considering a Twentieth Century-Fox property ("Virgin Bar") based on the sponge-fishing industry in Tarpon Springs, Florida. Murphy's earlier collaboration with Kazan on *Boomerang* (1947) earned an Academy nomination for screenwriting.] *TL, 2 pp., Wesleyan*

TO DARRYL F. ZANUCK

[New York]
[June 1948]

Dear Darryl

. . . Needless to say I'm delighted that we're going ahead with John's story. I've never seen an author more enthusiastic about material than John is about this. If work and real feeling mean anything we should have one of the great scripts here—and a chance to make one of the really good pictures. Again I'm grateful to you for moving so cleanly and quickly. No one could have handled the whole thing as well.

About your "propaganda" & "Communism" worries, etc. Dont! John and I talked about this. We are both liberals, rather on the left side, too, but both thoroughly anti-communist. Nothing is going to scare either of us into silence or into a more "conservative" position, but, to get down to it, I would take part in a war, if we're damn fools enough to get into a war, against the Soviet Union, and I'm sure John feels the same way. I wont red bait. But I'm against their political system in every way, I'm against the intrusion of their system here, I detest their aesthetics, I gag at their philosophy. I really believe in democracy, but not what they mean by the word, but all our blunderings and mistakes much rather. I believe in government of the people, by the people and for the people, just as it says. I'm against any oligarchy, whether of class or dollar, any aristocracy except that of work, devotion and talent for good. I believe that the most valuable thing mankind has, the thing most worth fighting for is the integrity of the SINGLE HUMAN SPIRIT.

That last is John's phrase. That's what he wants to bring out, he says, in all his work, Zapata too. I go into all this, because I want you to know that both he and I realize that we are on ticklish grounds. On the one hand is retreat, on the other truth.

Perhaps John has told you that he doesn't intend to use Zapata's name except once at the end. The exciting powerful melodrama will be there in abundance—its the very essence of it. John has said again and again to me that almost no words are necessary. He does not intend to write speeches AT ALL. There will be no lachrymose pleas for tolerance and cant about social equality. The story will tell itself. These people were inarticulate and words bored them.

After GA I dont want to see another long speech. The THEME will be there only the way it is in life—to be inferred, by those who wish, from the events.

Every single idea John and I have talked about so far is on this track. I have full confidence that when you read what he writes, you will feel elated.

About Virgin Bar (do you like that title?)—there is a problem. I <u>want</u> to do it in November. I wasn't able to find a play I liked for fall production, so I am doing a musical, which is scheduled to open in N.Y. the first week in October. I will not take any more shows, because I want to do V.B. this fall, by all means.

The problem is that my wife has written a show. Its a <u>book</u> for a musical, to which the songs are now being composed. It is quite good. She has been waiting for years for this—the possibility of a production. I cant treat it lightly, or in any off hand way. I should know by Aug 15th., whether or not it is going to be done. If it is, I will push like hell for the earliest possible date. I want to be here to help her over the rough spots. If it is not going to be done, there will be no problem and I will go right into BAR. . . .

Darryl F. Zanuck

Affectionately,

[Darryl Zanuck approved *Zapata* in spite of alarming reports and the prospect of further hearings by the House Committee on Un-American Activities. Those held in late 1947 convinced studio heads that films must be scrutinized for anti-American content and the industry purged of subversives if the threat of government censorship were to be removed. From Mexico Zanuck received conflicting reports of Zapata (1879–1919) as "a great hero and martyr" and "a dirty, ruthless bandit who hung priests and nuns by their thumbs." A PCA warning of influential Mexican interests that still regarded Zapata as "an extreme agrarian radical," if not "a Communist," no doubt added to Zanuck's worry. Further in the background were "slanders" circulated during the war years by the American Legion and other conservative groups regarding Steinbeck's alleged communist sympathy and party membership (Benson, pp. 511–14).

Steinbeck informed Fox executives that he would activate his "little group of bandits in Mexico" and complete a first draft of *Zapata* by Christmas. He planned to involve Kazan in research, "not only for his direction, but for his understanding and casting" as well. The challenge of drawing Zapata's obscure personal and military history into a dramatic framework turned out to be more "ticklish" than any political concern. The breakup of Steinbeck's second marriage also intervened and substantially delayed progress on the screenplay.

Elia was set to direct *Love Life* (1948) in collaboration with Alan Jay Lerner and Kurt Weill. Molly Kazan's play, "The Queen of Sheba," suffered a temporary setback in mid-June and a final one in 1950, when the Theatre Guild declined to produce it. Lawrence Langner observed wryly to the author that "the emancipation of women from men who have several hundred wives seems . . . to be treading against windmills."

Twentieth Century-Fox released *Beneath the 12-Mile Reef* (formerly "Virgin Bar") in 1953 without the involvement of Kazan or Richard Murphy. Thirty years later Kazan returned to the Greek community of Tarpon Springs in his novel *Acts of Love*. He and Richard Murphy collaborated next on filming *Panic in the Streets* (1950).] *TLd, 2 pp., Wesleyan*

TO THE DRAMA EDITOR, *NEW YORK TIMES*

[New York]
July 25, 1948

To the Drama Editor:

May I comment on your recent report of the views and plans of Clifford Odets and Harold Clurman and the suggestion there that the Actors Studio is hankering after the mantle of the Group Theatre?

We are not. That mantle is at rest in some honorable place and, so far as we're concerned, there it can stay. Odets was perfectly right in his point. It's too early to say anything nice about the Actors Studio, except one thing: it does exist and is functioning. We haven't sought any praise for the simple reason that we haven't shown any work. The company of actors that is performing "Sundown Beach" has been together one season. I, their director, didn't know a single one of these young actors when I interviewed them last fall. We worked on "Sundown Beach" for the fun of it, which is a nice way to work. When we liked what came to be, we decided to show it. Nothing else. We do not think we are anything like as fine a company as the Group was at its best. On the other hand, we have our points.

As for the suggestion of a possible rivalry between ourselves and any studio that Messrs. Clurman and Odets might launch, let me scotch that one. There is room in New York for many studios; in fact, for many companies of actors. We will welcome them as they come to be. Any competition in the arts is always healthy. Mr. Clurman has always given the theatre a lot and Mr. Odets could be again an equally powerful force for good and growth. We are looking forward to the work they will do.

Elia Kazan

[Clifford Odets had scoffed in a recent article: "Isn't it a bit early to be handing over the mantle of the Group Theatre to Studio, Inc.?" Odets also announced that he, Harold Clurman, and "almost certainly" Stella Adler planned to organize a "studio of acting, playwriting and directing, and in the course of time hope to be producing plays on Broadway" (*NYT,* June 27, 1948). Kazan ended by alluding to Odets's long absence from the stage.

Convalescent flyers and their various love interests meet in *Sundown Beach* (1948) to drink and ruminate on the bitter experience of war. The play's setting, cast of twenty-eight, and episodic structure reminded critics of *Truckline Cafe.* Only Julie Harris and Cloris Leachman emerged from Bessie Breuer's first produced play with enhanced credentials. The show closed after seven performances with curt advice from Brooks Atkinson: "Perhaps the Actors Studio would have been wiser to keep it to themselves for trial-and-error practicing" (*NYT,* September 8, 1948).] *NYT, July 25, 1948, p. xi*

TO JO MIELZINER

SH: Twentieth Century-Fox Film Corporation
Beverly Hills, California
November 4, 1948

Dear Jo:

I received the model and I think it's going to be a wonderful set. I like the idea of the trees. Whether they're "cut out" as you've indicated them or painted on gauze as you once talked of, your judgment is best in the matter.

I thought the areas came out very well, with certain exceptions. First, I think we can use a little more room in the kitchen area and I have drawn a line on the model suggesting where this might run. It's only a foot or so more but I think it would help since more and more of our major scenes are being played in the kitchen.

The most disturbing thing in the set to me was the position of the hot water boiler, also its size. I suggest that it be made as small as realistically possible. Also, I urge you to move the landing of the stairs leading to the boy's bedroom downstage one foot and make a place behind this landing for a boiler. Thus it will be down in a natural kind of hole and will not be oppressively present as it is now. This rearrangement of the position of the boiler has the added advantage of giving us another three feet or so in the kitchen area which we can very well use and would clear the view of two very important dramatic elements—one, the steps all up and down [on] which I hope to play scenes, and the other the entrance to the living room. I hope you go for this suggestion of mine because it's the only really disturbing thing in the present layout. I also think that with the free and easy way we are treating the realistic elements no closet or wall around the hot water heater is necessary, or very little.

As far as the elevation and design is concerned, I think we can work even further in the direction of simplicity and purity. There are, perforce, so many levels, rooms, props, entrances clear and hidden that the tendency of the set might seem to be cluttered. I know when it's all done in soft material this will be perceptibly less, but I did have the reaction that what we have now might be very profitably further simplified. This, of course, is up to you. You know that for my part the more we can make the set into one simple kind of statement the more we will help to give the play a unity which it hasn't quite got and from which it will benefit.

A detail: Should the wall behind Linda's bed be solid or part of it solid or less transparent, or will lighting take care of this when Lee Cobb undresses behind this wall? Of course, he must not be seen at all and still he is playing a scene with Linda in the bedroom during which he is talking to her from what is supposed to be the bathroom.

I'm wondering if it might not be some advantage to indicate in the most skeletonic way the entrance door to the house from the outside. Is your idea here that the actor entering here should pantomime this door each time an entrance is made?

Do you think we might need some bare suggestion of kitchen props, a low ice-box or something? He does get milk and there is a little kind of casual business in the kitchen.

My reaction to the shape and pitch of the roof and gable was that it was more old-fashioned than necessary. Ditto the window in Linda's bedroom.

Since the basic idea of the house design is to reveal the structure of the house as though it were an X-ray of the house, I want to ask a question about the wings at the side. I can't quite tell from the painting on the model if your idea here is to suggest garden, trellises or some other garden structure. This seems perfectly workable to me, or is your notion to make it neutral, in which case should they be more neutral than they are? Now the ones on right stage look a little like an X-ray of the ordinary stage flat. I think it would be advantageous if we can suggest that our forestage is the backyard because I see Cobb often walking around here and sitting there as though he were seated in the backyard during other people's scenes in the kitchen.

One other thing: The most difficult problem we have still are the realistic scenes in the second act on the forestage, like Heiser's office, the hotel room. I wish there were some way to formalize these and take them out of the pattern of the dream scenes on the forestage. I haven't thought of any way to do this yet but I don't want the audience to be confused between scenes that are imagined by Willie and then dramatized on our forestage and scenes that are really going on <u>in the present </u>with Willie in them <u>in other parts of the city</u>.

The realistic scenes I guess could be back lit and we'll have to be very clever with the props and I with the business, with the music, etc., etc. Query: Will there be any way to formalize these scenes more? I don't know. I'm just fishing around the dark and expressing the worry and concern that I have.

It also worries me that we are still planning the two office scenes on the same side of the stage, or are we? If so, I don't think this is good. For instance, if Heiser's office were played on the stage left side and, after the interim scene that takes place in Willie's mind, we have Charlie's office on the stage right side, we could use what was Charlie's desk by putting a tablecloth over it as one of the tables in the restaurant.

- - - -

Next day.

I guess that's all, Jo. On looking at the model again today I felt just about the same way, especially about the hot water heater. I felt how good it would look with that out of the way.

At the risk of being very, very repetitious, only one thing still worries me— whether we will be able to sufficiently and effectively differentiate between the scenes that are in the present and take place in another part of the city and those in his mind. I just want to impress this problem on your mind and I probably have already done so to the point of boring you, so I'll work on it myself now.

Regards, <u>Gadg</u>

[As Kazan prepared to direct *Death of a Salesman,* he finalized a new contract with Twentieth Century-Fox stipulating direction of six original films in a period of ten years and six months. Fox would pay basic compensation of $1,250 per week for the full fifteen-year term of the nonexclusive contract, supplemented by $7,500 per week during periods of exclusive service. Kazan would retain the right of script submission and approval (December 18, 1947, UCLA).

Arthur Miller gave *Death of a Salesman* to Kazan *and* Jo Mielziner. The same blending of taut drama and poetic lyricism used to expose Blanche's disordered mind in *Streetcar* was required to convey, as Miller put it, the vast "discrepancy between illusion and reality" entertained by Willy Loman. Kazan staged *Salesman* on three levels to distinguish kitchen, bedroom, and loft where Biff and Happy sleep as boys. The "hot water boiler" that portends Loman's suicide from the opening scene was scaled down and removed from the kitchen to an alcove beneath the landing as Kazan requested. An "ice-box" was added to the sparsely furnished set.

Arthur Miller described the Loman house as once " 'surrounded by open country' " in Brooklyn but " 'now hemmed in with apartment houses. Trees that used to shade the house against the open sky and hot summer sun now were for the most part dead or dying.' " Jo Mielziner covered the house with projected leaf shadows to evoke the past in Willy Loman's first dream sequence (Mielziner, p. 25). Kazan later credited Mielziner with providing the "key" to his direction by envisioning the house as "the most important visual symbol" in the play. Designed "as though it were an X-ray," the house stands "like a specter behind all the scenes of the play, always present as it might be always present in Willy's mind" (*A Life,* p. 361).

Jo Mielziner's stage design for *Death of a Salesman*

Kazan differentiated the forestage scenes in *Salesman* by playing them alternately stage left and right and maintaining within each progression a rough unity and chronological order. The retrospective hotel scene in Boston and the several appearances of mythical Uncle Ben were stylized to the extent that Kazan identified them with stage space left and right respectively. The office scenes were played on opposite sides of the stage.] *TLS, 3 pp., BRTC*

TO WILLIAM LIEBLING

SH: Twentieth Century-Fox Film Corporation
Beverly Hills, California
February 26, 1949

Dear Bill:
I have talked personally and at length to John Huston, William Wyler, David Selznick and Darryl Zanuck. I'm reporting to you and Audrey on this but

please keep it in the strictest confidence. You can act on the basis of it but don't show the note to Irene or anything like that.

Wyler is the best prospect. He seemed vague but genuinely interested. He was under the impression till now that Irene wasn't really ready to talk business. I assured him the time had come and she now was. I urged him to do something about it right away, which I expect he will do. He's really stuck for material and likes the property (excuse the expression!).

Zanuck here is not interested. That's all. I cannot get him to start bidding on it. The only possibility would be if I said I wanted to do it. Even then it would be an outside chance, and if I said I wanted to do it I would have to make good on it. I will not do this picture with a Seal. There's no use going into that again or at any further length.

John Huston does not appear interested to me. He said that he kind of was but he got off the subject immediately. He's very occupied with "Quo Vadis" and nothing will happen there in my opinion—unless.

Mayer talks about it all the time. In my opinion he will distort the play's meaning but maybe this can be compromised on or bridged. The key person here is Mrs. Selznick. One of the points which you made when you gave the play to her was that she would be able to handle the movie disposition of it. Now the time has come for her to handle it.

I talked at length with David O. Selznick. He does not appear interested even though I told him that his wife would be perfect in it.

In none of these men have I run across any really pressing interest. I don't think anyone should deceive himself or herself. I asked David to help Irene, of whom he's very fond, towards whom I guess he feels guilty yet. He says he's always told her to produce it herself, that this would be the best way. I am in complete agreement with this. I think you'll wait a long time on Wyler, Huston and Company. With Kazan and Zanuck out, the thing would be for Irene to go to Metro and produce the play there. This way she could get a good price on it and the right kind of financial arrangement over a period of time—a kind of arrangement that would amount to a subsidy for Tennessee.

I can't do much more. If you can think of anything, I'll be glad to do it. I'll be here a few more days. As I say, I will do anything that I can humanly do without pretending to Zanuck that I'm going to do the picture or that I want to do the picture.

To sum up, in my opinion the most practical interest is with Mayer if Irene will produce it there. Maybe this could be done this coming summer. In the second place, Wyler may do something about it, but here are the harsh facts: Paramount Pictures has a $1,500,000 top on all budgets. Of this, $700,000 is overhead. The other $800,000 has to pay director, stars, scenery, etc., etc., etc., etc. You figure out how much they might have for story costs. Love to you and Audrey.

Best always, Gadg

[An initial fee of $650,000, depressed market conditions, and doubt that *A Streetcar Named Desire* could be filmed with PCA approval delayed sale to a major studio. Irene Selznick declined to exercise her rights, to the increasing nervousness of Tennessee Williams's agents, Bill Liebling and Audrey Wood. Before Kazan left for California, they pressed him to search for "something" that would "push forward an interest in order to make the other companies open their mouths." Spyros Skouras, president of Twentieth Century-Fox, feared that the Legion of Decency would condemn *Streetcar* and reportedly "urged" Darryl Zanuck not to acquire the property (Zanuck, p. 203).

Later in the spring Kazan offered to produce *Streetcar* in association with an independent company linked to John Garfield, who would take the role of Stanley. Kazan was ready to forgo PCA approval if necessary and to guarantee $10,000 per year for ten years against half the profits of the film. The offer was rejected, although Williams hoped "some kind of deal" could be arranged with Kazan that would provide "a few years of security" for the author and ensure that *Streetcar* was filmed "honestly" (to MDT and EK, July 12, 1949, Wesleyan).] *TLS, 2 pp., HRC*

TO JOHN MASON BROWN

SH: Twentieth Century-Fox Film Corporation
Beverly Hills, California
March 2, 1949

Dear John:
One of the nicest things that was said about "Death of a Salesman" was that it represented a challenge to the critics. It's always easier to write a witty, derisive review of a worthless or pretentious play, but to write a notice that really captures the particular worth of a play and conveys the excitement of its performance is a different thing again. I thought you did just that. Your review struck me as a kind of masterpiece and had its own special excitement as a piece of criticism. Let me say back to you, sir, congratulations!

I got a wire from New York about the television program. I just don't know if I'll be in New York by that day. I hope so, but you can never quite tell. If I am, of course I'll be overjoyed. Why don't you get Lee Cobb to appear with Art Miller, and if I'm in town I'll come and sit with you also. At any rate, I look forward to seeing you soon.

Yours, <u>Gadg</u>

[John Mason Brown wrote in his review that Kazan "captures to the full the mood and heartbreak of the script. He does this without ever surrendering to sentimentality. He manages to mingle the present and the past, the moment and the memory, so that their intertwining raises no questions and causes no confusions. His direction, so glorious in its vigor, is no less considerate of those small details which can be both mountainous and momentous in daily living." Brown was no less generous in praising Lee J. Cobb's "irresistibly touching and wonderfully unsparing" portrayal of Willy Loman in *Death of a Salesman* (*Saturday Review,* February 26, 1949).

Billed as "An Elia Kazan Production," *Salesman* won the Pulitzer Prize and Drama Critics' Circle Award and ran for nearly 750 performances. Kazan won a second Tony Award for best direction and Mielziner his first for stage design. With *Streetcar, Salesman,* and *Love Life* on the proverbial boards, Kazan was on "top" in 1949 but prepared for the inevitable reversal: "The lesson I'd learned from my father was not to expect the good to continue and, consequently, not to be crushed when it didn't" (*A Life,* p. 373).] *TLS, 1 p., Harvard*

TO CHERYL CRAWFORD

[Beverly Hills, California]
[c. May 5, 1949]

Cheryl baby, thanks for your two letters which I received very gratefully. Just a note in return. I'll be back in a week and a day or two and then we'll talk. I'm going to Europe June 4th. and be back Aug first. I'm anxious to go for the vacation part of it, but otherwise I'm not too gaga about it. I was born there and I like this country better. I'd like to bum around here more and more and do pictures about it and plays and all.

About the business association business. I'll never tie up permanently with anyone. I'm not the type as I lately found out, not a producer, not a steady fellow, not a solid citizen. I prize maneuverability and unpredictability and behave for my own amazement as well as just for fun—the only thing I'll tie to is the Studio—And am anxious to have talks about that. But I wish I were a Lieutenant there instead of a co-general, even with such a wonderful co-general as you. I'm only comfortable when I'm erratic and I guess that's about it. But I really love the studio and the kids and the idea of young people, and the whole idea of a place of NON-COMMERCIAL association where no one has an angle or an "Edge" // that to me is as near as I can come to having a home. (professionally speaking)

Oddly enough I was kind of proud that the Studio got the Peabody award—!!! You know what I think of TV.

See you soon and lets have fun. I love you and love to work with you and we'll work a lot together. I'm a little drunk.

Gadg

[Kazan wrote as filming of *Pinky* (1949) neared completion. As a favor to Darryl Zanuck, he replaced John Ford, who had resigned with a claim of illness—

doubted by Kazan in light of the film's unpromising script and cast. Pinky's light complexion, "an unfortunate trick of the genes," as Kazan put it, led to an inter-racial romance, whose only possible outcome in 1949 was reinforcement of the status quo. Novelty and controversy made *Pinky* a top-grossing film but left Kazan unimpressed by its "predictable" story line and facile technique (*A Life*, pp. 375, 382). He was not "too gaga" either about leaving for Europe to direct the London premiere of *Salesman* but followed through.

The inaugural Peabody Award for "outstanding contribution to the art of tele-vision" was much-needed salve for the Actors Studio after the fiasco of *Sundown Beach*. The Studio produced sixty-five adaptations of classic and contemporary works on ABC and CBS from 1948 to 1950. Jessica Tandy opened the first season in *Portrait of a Madonna* (1945), a one act by Tennessee Williams with strong intimations of *Streetcar*.] TLS, 1 p., BRTC

TO TENNESSEE WILLIAMS

[New York]
[summer 1949]

Tenn

I hope this letter doesn't sound presumptuous or preachy or superior or moral—but here goes anyway. Maybe I've got no call to write anybody, because I'm kind of fucked up too in my own way. But here it is, for what its worth. *** It seems to me that the very things that make it uncomfortable for you here in the states are the things that make you write. I've seen it with a lot of writers (Cliff Odets for instance) that once they had dough and the power to live in a comfortable environment (as who doesn't want to) the NECESSARY quality in their writing disappeared. It seems to me that the things that make a man want to write in the first place are those elements in his environment, personal or social, that outrage him, hurt him, make him bleed. Any artist is a misfit. What the hell would he go to all the trouble—if he could make the "adjustment" in a "normal" way. In Rome, I'd say, you felt a kind of suspension of discomfort. Things are distant, but in so far as they impinge at all, not unpleasant. You start a play about an American Dictator here in the states—I suppose in answer to things in our state of affairs that make it impossible for you to continue to be silent. You get to Rome or whatever and you can perfectly well remain silent. I dont think you'll ever turn out plays like Sidney Kingsley or Gar Kanin (to mention the best) purely out of ambition—or even in order to continue being T. Williams. You are not really Tennessee Williams in Rome. That fellow is a misfit, in his own way a rebel and a not-at-home in our Essentially Business-man's Society. Blanche was a fragile white moth beating against the unbreak-able sides of a 1000 watt bulb. But in Rome the 1000 watt bulb doesn't exist.

The moth is more or less at home—especially with the checks and the Buick and all-around what appears to be a gentle, softly-decaying civilization. ~~But your very identity is in the quality of misfit and protest and rebellion (all in personal terms, not as conventionally thought of.)~~ In Rome, in North Africa, in Mexico etc. your essential identity is lost. That's why I've always thought that, whether you like it or not, and in a way, especially since you do not, you should stay here in the States. I think you'd soon have some new plays writing that NO ONE could turn you off.

LOVE
gadg

[In Rome Elia and Molly met a dejected playwright still lamenting the failure of *Summer and Smoke*, whose direction Tennessee Williams had entrusted to his friend Margo Jones—unwisely, it turned out. The play closed on January 1, 1949, some $60,000 in debt. Travel with Paul Bowles in North Africa had been "a mistake," if not a calamity, and Rome proved more distraction than elixir. Tennessee Williams distilled these and more deeply rooted artistic fears into a letter that prompted Kazan's reply. "The simple truth is that I haven't known where to go since Streetcar. Everything that isn't an arbitrary, and consequently uninspired, experiment seems to be only an echo." Williams had put aside the "southern demagogue" play from which *Sweet Bird of Youth* would evolve, and he was little more inspired by recent work on *The Rose Tattoo*, whose outline he shared with the Kazans. The "trouble" was exhaustion. "In many ways writing is the most perilous and ephemeral of the talents, and you never know whether an impasse is only temporary or final, and the only real help lies in honesty with yourself and from others and keeping alive your interest in life itself" (to EK and MDT, July 12, 1949, Wesleyan). Writing after Williams's death, Kazan restated the "NECESSARY" discomfort of the artist: "I was to watch with an awful pain how lost Williams was as he shuttled around the bright spots of the world. The money his great success brought him allowed him to live in a way that squashed his talent. He would have been better off living in his native South, that part of the world where he was uncomfortable, even outraged, because he felt he was an outsider" (*A Life*, p. 273).

There is no indication that Williams answered, or received, Kazan's present letter—perhaps an unmailed draft.] *TLS, 1 p., Wesleyan*

TO LEE STRASBERG

[New York]
[c. fall 1949]

Dear Lee—

I thought I'd write you and tell you what Cheryl and I talked about—sort of to augment what she will report to you directly.

It all started when we went one night to see some of the work the kids had prepared: two of Williams' one acts and some scenes from Doctor Knock. I wont attempt to describe the goings-on. They were not good. Some of it was Borscht-circuit. Some of it simply half baked. The work was not representative—I'm sure you see better scenes every day in your class. But the very fact that we had been asked to come and see the scenes gave them a significance, demanded that they be taken seriously. And when you were forced in this way to look at them in dead earnest, the result for me was a terrific sense of failure. The studio—if that was to be its end product—simply wasn't worth the trouble. And the fault was that of the leadership even if it had all come about thru carelessness—or lack of supervision—or what ever. There was only one inference you could make and that was that something was wrong at the top.

The next day I met with Cheryl and said that I would be very happy to step down a couple of notches and that I thought you and she should run the studio. She had been thinking the same thing. She'll explain it to you—her reasons I mean—just as she did to me, very well. But we both finally came to something that we agreed upon. Both of us want more than ever to be part of the studio, keep it going. Both of us want you to be the artistic head of it. The meeting I hoped we could have today (Sunday) was to put this before you.

I'll speak for myself. I think it should be your place—as Stieglitz had his place. I would be very happy if I could work in it as a director who wanted to work and learn more about his work and his problems, IF you were the over-all artistic head of the enterprise. The suggestion is that you make all fundamental artistic decisions—choice of pupils, assignment of teachers, planning of the curriculum, disposition of the television. Cheryl would administrate it on a line you would set. I would function in it as I said above, as a director working with actors. I do not think I am a good teacher. I think I'm useful and have done some good things with the group you have now—but its as if I willed it but didn't really FIT when I got it going. Frankly I also think you know a hell of a lot more. Again frankly I want to work as a director, within the scheme of things at the studio, but as a director. I think that is what I am.

Here are three or four sidelights quickly thrown out. I wish you'd bring into the studio anybody you thought right for its greatest usefulness and growth. If you wanted my suggestions I would make them. I mean for example if you thought Cliff useful and right, then bring him in. I think one person, yourself, should have final say of who is a "member", and the disposition of the actors.

Another point. Legal. I think you should immediately be made a member of the board of Directors or whatever the hell its called, so that legally its also clear.

About myself and movies (Cheryl says you asked about this) I am very concerned with movies. Let me just cover the ground. My ambition is to make motion pictures on the scene. Studio shots I'd like to make in N.Y. I'm working on this. Its difficult to effect. My actual contract with Fox says that I will make six pictures in 10 and 1/2 years. But I will never go to Hollywood and unpack my bag completely. I will never leave here for more than the minimum time. I live here and my centre and focus here will be the studio. Its been my "office" for the last two years as much as I ever had an office. I dont think my movie activities will separate me from it ever in an essential way. I hope to make movies that will be representative of it—and the rest of the time I'm like to be one of the lieutenants there—not a co-general as I have been till now.

That should about clear things up. I haven't said too much in a positive way—about you and so on—But I will say one thing. The effort and work to institute and sustain the Studio will have been more than worth while if you now become its centre. I will do everything I possibly can to help. I think its a Right idea.

Gadge

One P.S. I'm sure, I'm certain that Anna S., Dorothy W. and all the students, Studio members will be overjoyed. They will feel the step to be just what it is—a real piece of integration.

[Lee Strasberg began to teach at the Actors Studio in 1948 after Bobby Lewis resigned in a dispute with Kazan that resembled the latter's appropriation of *Deep Are the Roots*. Kazan had reportedly advised Lewis to forgo directing the musical *Love Life* (1948) and soon thereafter directed the hit show himself. The once close friendship would be resumed years later. Of the several plays directed by Strasberg in the 1940s, only *The Big Knife* (1949) by Clifford Odets had a respectable run. Strasberg's rise to the directorate of the Studio in 1949, and to the role of artistic director by the 1951–52 season, coincided with Kazan's withdrawal from regular teaching prior to filming *Panic in the Streets*, *Streetcar*, and *Viva Zapata!* in rapid succession. With reference to "movies," Strasberg apparently tried to gauge Kazan's future involvement in the Studio as he contemplated his own evolving role.

Anna Sokolow, a dancer-choreographer who performed with "the urgency of the contemporary," as a reviewer put it, taught at the Studio and later assisted Kazan in staging *Camino Real* (1953). Dorothy Willard gave financial and administrative help to the Studio in the early years.] *TLS, 2 pp., Indiana*

TO CHARLES K. FELDMAN

[New York]
October 26, 1949

Dear Charlie:

I talked with Tennessee today, and here is the dope: We decided that we want to shoot the picture in New Orleans. We want to shoot it interior and exterior on location in that city. We wish you would investigate to see if there is any studio space in New Orleans. All we would need room for is enough to reproduce the interior that we would use for the bedroom and sitting-room of the Du Bois layout. It might be better for certain scenes to shoot these in a studio, but actually they take up very little room and no space would be necessary. A small studio or a place that would pass for a studio would be fine. However, Tennessee and I both agree that the best effect would be gained by shooting the picture entirely on location, and, in a way, through this and through the choice of good but unsung actors in parts other than De Havilland's, maintain an air of modesty and unpretentiousness in the external aspects of the picture. In other words, let the values of a picture come through in its contents rather than what is known in Hollywood as "PRODUCTION."

Tennessee, of course, is very glad that there is a good prospect of getting Olivia De Havilland. I said that it was almost sure which was the impression I got when I left. I suggest that you let her know, however, that we want to shoot the picture on location so there will be no surprises in store for her.

We both think it most important, in fact essential, that you sign Brando as soon as possible. It's hard for either of us to see the picture without Brando.

We talked about the censorship angle on the rape and have decided what we will try to do about this to get around, or really in effect satisfy the Catholic hierarchy. We both feel fine about the solution that we have in mind but we would rather work it out than discuss it at this time.

About the screenplay writer. Tennessee does not want the man who worked on GLASS MENAGERIE, so forget him, however, what he would like to do, and incidentally, I think it's an excellent solution, is to have someone go down to Key West where he will be living for the next few months and work with him there on the screenplay for STREETCAR. Tennessee would work with him; it would be a collaborative job, and this way it would really amount to Tennessee doing it, but wouldn't break up the work that he is in the process of doing on new plays. I like this idea, except I cannot offhand think of who would be the right person, however, we both think we will find this person—it's only a matter of looking. We would like it very much if you would send us a list of suggestions.

As you know, I will be shooting down there from December 19th through February 1st, and we hope to work it out so that Tennessee will come down there before or after I start shooting and we can spot possible locations. Tennessee who knows New Orleans very intimately, says there are many, many locations where he is sure the picture can be effectively shot.

In all these matters we are in complete agreement. Please answer this item by item, giving me your reactions. I am sending a copy of this letter to Tennessee and I hope that in this way we can continue to plan together. We both are anxious, of course, to hear that the deal with Olivia has been consummated, and we know that as soon as this has happened you will so inform us.

Cordially,

[Charles Feldman paid $350,000, roughly half the initial asking price, to produce *Streetcar* in association with Warner Bros. Kazan initially resisted Williams's plea to film *Streetcar*—"'It would be like marrying the same woman twice'"—but he was intrigued by the prospect of transforming the Broadway production into "a proper film." Only later did he realize that dramatizing offstage scenes would have diminishing returns (*A Life*, pp. 383–84).

Jessica Tandy was to be replaced by a film star of rank, notwithstanding her Tony Award nomination for originating the role of Blanche on Broadway. No actress was currently more popular or in greater demand than her intended successor. Olivia de Havilland's portrayal of madness in *The Snake Pit* (1948) probably gave an added incentive to the signing, which turned out to be less "sure" than Kazan assumed. Negotiations with de Havilland fell through, as did plans to film on location in New Orleans. Vivien Leigh put aside the burden of Scarlett O'Hara and impressed skeptical critics with a surpassing Blanche in the current London production of *Streetcar*. She and Brando were signed in the following spring.

Tennessee Williams naively assured Audrey Wood that there was "no real need to worry about censorship as rape has been handled in 'Johnny Belinda'" (1948), while the homosexuality of Blanche's husband could be solved with "the slight alteration of a few lines" (June 21, 1949, HRC).

Oscar Saul (adaptation) and Williams (screenplay) shared writing credits for *Streetcar*. Saul was an improvement, Williams initially thought, over the screenwriter hired by Feldman for *The Glass Menagerie* (1950), whose film rights he also controlled.] *TLx, 2 pp., HRC*

TO TENNESSEE WILLIAMS

[New York]
[c. mid-November 1949]

Dear Tenn—

Arrived back from New Orleans yesterday and your letter was here and today I went down and got the new pages from Audrey. I liked the stuff, especially the scene with the Baron, and, here, especially the business with the match. If you dont mind I'll keep the old scene with the Baron and merely add this on. I wont play the scene anything like the Collector scene in streetcar. Of course you can make any changes you want when you see it.

However it looks now like I wont be able to do the show till spring. I'll fool around now for a few weeks, getting it clear for myself as to style and how I should do it etc., also get the music started, and then get back to it some time after I do the New Orleans movie. I dont want to hurry myself on this as I still cant see it as a "straightforward" job.

Ford has always been my ideal, to coin a phrase. He is (really "used to be") both hard as nails, unsentimental, and still a poet, that is truly romantic. I know him, and his front is meaner and more bitter than ever, but his insides is soft Catholic mush. But Grapes of Wrath is the best American picture, no doubt. I stole a copy of the thing from Fox and I run it off every once in a while on my home machine. Among other things he's got the greatest Eye ever developed in this country. He tells pages of dialogue with one shot and he's just naturally a poet. He makes the others look like goddamn intellectuals, I mean Wyler, Huston, and Co. I'm flattered that you even think of us together.

Only one thing ever worries me about Streetcar—that we wont do it together. I know we can make something really hard and painful out of it (My lawyer, who's a sensitive guy, said after the opening here he sat in his chair and said to himself: "Why dont I stop torturing that girl"). I really and truly think that we can make something better than the play of it—I like the few ideas we talked about, the opening etc. And I like the idea of somehow making the end harder. I'll talk all this over with Saul again before he leaves for the South.

I think Saul is perfect—the premise being that you'll in effect and finally really do the screen play. I dont care when, or when we do it. I'm in no hurry about this or anything else right now. I want to do things right. This picture I do in New Orleans embarrasses me a little; it isn't so hot. But I dont quite know my business with the Camera yet and I'd like to learn a little more before I launch into something I love. So I'm kind of chalking it up to education. And in my week down there I certainly got into the inner workings of the city. I became intimate with morgue attendants, had readings for twenty policemen, five of whom are going to play speaking parts, walked on the roof of the long string of docks and also under neath—we're going to shoot both places—and met the hoodlums, some of them, thru their local Greek representative.

I've often felt the same thing about the thirties—I mean I feel an emptiness, an isolation, a cut-off ness and say to myself: 'I didn't feel that way in 1935—what's happened to me.' Other times though I feel I was sentimental in the thirties—in that very particular way—and that now I'm independent—that my thinking had become routine and codified in the thirties—in that particular "Party" way—and that now I keep getting upset on my ass. Maybe middle age is coming on me, but goddamn it I honestly feel better most of the time now, and when I feel empty and cut off and isolated and bewildered and directionless—why then I look at my old Group Associates, and the party people I know—and I'll be good goddamned if I want to go back to that stuff—the insularity and the clubbiness and the I love my co-members but no one else shit, and the intellectuality and the literal-minded-ness—Not that those are the necessary alternatives. But I do think that with me at least, one reason I felt more secure in my guts then was that I knew what to think. One of the best books I've read in ten years, and one that had a great influence on me is ESCAPE FROM FREEDOM by Erich Fromm. He wrote another too that I liked: MAN FOR HIMSELF. If you cant get them I'll be glad to send them down to you. Please ask me.

The thing that bothers me most is that thru marriage and activity, thru choice of profession and thru respectability, thru my wife, my own comfort, my possessions and my "position", thru my "responsibilities" and all that SHIT I am cut off from the mass of the human race. Actors and Theatre people bore me to Death. I except only a very few. I wont name names, but you know who and what I mean. Still ninety five percent of my time is spent with them. I have to neglect plays, hurt my wife and chance a sense

Directing Barbara Bel Geddes
and Richard Widmark in
Panic in the Streets

of bewilderment in my children to even leave home for a couple of weeks.

And then I feel that once a man has channeled his experience away from that of the mass of mankind—and I'd say WORKING mankind, too—why then he's in a tough spot. He works thru cleverness like Kanin or thru showmanship like Kingsley or good business sense like Anderson and Weill (craftsmanship— that's kinder) I'm raving.

Gadge

[Kazan spent a week in New Orleans preparing to film *Panic in the Streets* for Twentieth Century-Fox. Tennessee Williams praised him as "a man of action" and regretted being "short-circuited so much of the time" (November 11, 1949, Wesleyan). Kazan soon delayed plans to stage "Ten Blocks on the Camino Real," explaining to Audrey Wood that "scenes" at the Actors Studio "never got far enough to even think or contemplate or imagine" a production at this time.

Kazan's "worries" over censorship and artistic control of *Streetcar* prolonged negotiations with Charles Feldman and Jack Warner until the following summer, when a tenuous "understanding" allowed filming to begin. In the meanwhile, Tennessee Williams insisted to Kazan that "nothing, nothing, nothing must stand in the way" of their collaboration. "It will be the beginning of other exciting projects for us together, as I know that the screen is a good medium for us both" (December 12, 1949, Wesleyan).

A seemingly weak story line freed Kazan to explore the camera and direct *Panic in the Streets* as though it were "a 'silent,' a film that a deaf man could follow" (*A Life,* p. 378). Documentary and melodrama build suspense as a public health officer played by Richard Widmark is given forty-eight hours to track down carriers of plague while averting citywide flight. Kazan staged the climactic sequence beneath a "long string of docks," lair of Jack Palance in his menacing film debut. Richard Murphy was nominated for a second screenwriting prize, while Kazan won the International Award at the Venice Film Festival.

Tennessee Williams admired *Grapes of Wrath* and "flattered" Kazan by comparing John Ford's classic film to "something of yours." The film also led Williams to observe "how slack and flaccid we have all become since the thirties in our sense of social (moral) responsibility" (November 11, 1949). Kazan recommended *Escape from Freedom* (1941) as a corrective to Williams's nostalgia and in explanation of his own search for identity. He may have recalled a summary passage in which Erich Fromm dismissed the alternatives of a traditional order based on social and economic ties and the security promised by contemporary fascism. He held that there is "only one possible, productive solution for the relationship of individualized man with the world: his active solidarity with all men and his spontaneous activity, love and work, which unite him again with the world . . . as a free and independent individual" (Fromm, p. 36).

Kazan's final complaint looks back to the late spring, when *Pinky* was completed and the director took furlough from family and profession. At Galveston he shed the role of "a Hollywood big shot," joining his "fellow citizens, people, not stars with their plump, soft-skinned, indoor faces." The "sounds [of the harbor] were poetry, the scale enormous, the effect exotic." Kazan realized that "only the language of film" could express such emotion. "That was how this director might become a filmmaker" (*A Life,* p. 377).] *TLS, 2 pp., HRC*

In Hoboken, studying the *Waterfront* script

Part III

Filmmaker

1950–1953

TO TENNESSEE WILLIAMS

[New York]
[February 1950]

Dear Tenn—

I read the Rose Tattoo, kitchen sink version. It is a kind of a comic-grotesque Mass said in praise of the Male Force. I do not think the material is organized properly. It is, at any rate, not ready to produce, or to show. In fact I thought that you had turned, or at least squirmed around somewhere about 3/4 of the way thru in your own conception. At least I was very surprised at the ending. Its main spirit up till then seemed to be in praise of life, and its sensual, undying sensual base. Then comes the two women kneeling and gathering the ashes. That beat hell out of me. (Always bear in mind that I may not be too bright)

But let me say right here that there is something in the main story that interested me much more than it did in outline, and which I believe has a fine full length play in it. That is the UNLOCKING (the self-unlocking) of Pepina. I love her scene with the priest (You are an animal) etc. I think if you start much later in the story and present a woman who is (as they used to say in the twenties) a frozen asset—with every hint in the world of the volcanic energy boiling towards freedom within her—why then you will have real suspense to see it break forth. I'd cut out Rosario. He is much more forceful as a memory, as a legend, something she speaks of, and in name of whom she rejects all other men, not only for herself but for her daughter also. (Rose should discover this, perhaps??)

This way Pepina will have the meaning of a broader idea. All women have within them a volcanic force, and we (civilization) have done everything possible to seal it off, and tame it. Just now it is beginning to break out, and we label it immoral. Your Mass celebrates the Natural and the Immoral. I love the part attacking our "proper" system: the Strega, the RCC, and all the rest, even Mr. Hunter turns out to be proper, preferring a moral devotion to prostitutes, and really being a little uncomfortable before the natural powerful ardor of young Rose.

And there is one thing about Alvarro I like very very much. And that is represented by his three dependants. In other words, we have so organized our customs and system of approvals and morals so that his natural energy is bottled up too.

In other words I would concentrate, if I were you, on these two very "moral" people: a woman who is apparently just a neighborhood ~~spinster~~ seamstress, and a man who is devoting his life to the traditional Italian (and Greek) virtue of supporting his helpless relatives. He's afraid of good women: (You get involved, he says); and is wasting his life being right, being approved of (Why not introduce that fantastic gallery of his relatives so we see how fantastically he is wasting his life by devoting it to the support of these people)

And this woman, with her urn and the cache of dynamite below her belt, and how that dynamite is exploded, darn near against her will. It would be a comic Mass then between what man and woman are, and what they have made of themselves. And they sure as hell wouldn't be gathering ashes at the end.

I'd kind of make Mr. Hunter proper too. I think that would be a very funny sailor indeed. Make him very "Navy". And start much later: possibly with the graduation, and an introduction of Pepina as a very proper Seamstress that all the neighboring women (Strega, with the hairy legs included) look up to. Then you have somewhere to go with not only Pepina and Alvarro (hide the ram's skin painted red at first—its simple to suggest that its really there.) Let a whore just worship him, and thus suggest to Pepina what a hell of a lover the silly son of a bitch is, but he's giving it all away to the wrong people.

I like Rose—except when she gets so moral about "freedom" and "morality" in her own way.

Anyway, if you want to know more, ask me. Perhaps this whole point of view is just not what you tried to do. There is and should be something COMIC (in the biggest sense of that word: optimistic and healthy and uncontrollable) about the setting, the characters, the appertinences (I dont know how to spell that word) and the effects, the bits.

Most of the symbolic effects aren't necessary to my way of thinking—but I love the black goat and his arrogance. And I like the Rose Tattoo (title and effect too.) I thought she was at one point going to tear off the dress of the Texan woman.

Enough. I'll be waiting to hear from you. I'll show the script to no one except Molly Day Thacher. She hasn't read it yet, and it will be interesting to see what she thinks. She's a character too.

****   ****   ****

Enclosed please find.

I'd still like to open some more windows on the screen version—I mean more than I have indicated in my notes. Pictorially I know I can. But I think the subjective camera IS important. Let me know what you think of these too.

I'm leaving for H'wood tomorrow, and will meet with Feldman and Mr Jack Warner. Will probably call you from there.

Love

Gadg

[Tennessee Williams praised Kazan's "passion for organization, for seeing things in sharp focus," while claiming a broader range for his own vision: "Sometimes I can make a virtue of my disorganization by keeping closer to the cloudy outlines of life which somehow gets lost when everything is too precisely stated." Their collaboration, he knew, would "inevitably be somewhere between our two tastes in this matter" (February 24, 1950, Wesleyan). *The Rose Tattoo* was not one of those occasions, for Kazan withdrew his interest to film *Viva Zapata!*

Kazan's "enclosed" notes on *A Streetcar Named Desire* "terrified" Williams: "Why, honey, it looks like you want me to sit down and write the whole fucking thing over!!? This script is going to be the biggest patch-work quilt since the death of Aunt Dinah, and you might as well be reconciled to it." Oscar Saul's work had finally "disheartened" Williams, who was revising it "bit by bit and keeping as much of what's already done as possible" (February 24, 1950).

Williams recommended the "night-out" scene in *Streetcar* as a promising window to "open." He envisioned a "boy singing in drag and the playing of the Varsouviana" at the Wonder Club on Lake Pontchartrain. Exposing Blanche to a spectral figure of her husband in circumstances that recall the fateful evening at Moon Lake Casino would be a "bold piece of screen material and a legitimate motive for Blanche's beginning to break" (February 24, 1950). Kazan's decision to forgo such development and retain the "two small rooms" of the original production disappointed Williams but preserved the force of *Streetcar*: "Everything we'd done to 'open up' the play diluted its power" (*A Life*, p. 384). All that remains of the interior scene at the Wonder Club are a swing band and conventional dancers seen briefly as Mitch and Blanche pass through.] *TLS with enclosure, 2 pp., HRC*

TO DARRYL F. ZANUCK

[New York]
[May 1950]

Dear Darryl:—

We were delighted with your letter and the notes. We want to give you our reaction to it, paragraph by paragraph.

The first paragraph is great. Seriously, what you say about the general quality of the piece was exactly our intention, and our points of view completely meet.

It is our contention that pictures about Mexico have perhaps failed because they have not been personal pictures about individual lives, but a kind of TYPE writing and TYPE casting. In other words the "foreignness" was kept so alive and present that it was impossible for an American audience to identify themselves with the people. We hope to make Zapata immediate to the American, in fact to everyone in the world—Not a museum piece or museum figure.

It is not our intention to write or produce a historical drama. But thru this historical character and incident to highlight and perhaps explain the problems of the present day. This test is true of all surviving literature. In other words we were trying to say something about 1950 and Democracy, not about 1915 and Mexican History. We both hate historical dramas. They are almost always DULL! Our picture may be a little long, but not dull.

Incidentally it is for this very reason that we would like to keep foreignness, dialect and Spanish words OUT of the picture as much as possible. An audience which is able because of the speech to throw away the problem as foreign and past will have lost the point. By turn of phrase, intonation and rhythm we can indicate that the language spoken is Spanish, without being "cute" about it. . . .

We agree completely about the casting with more or less unknowns. There is something exciting and theatric about an unknown because you dont know exactly what he is going to do. Especially if you are asked to believe and "go with" events, you will believe in them much more without all the goddamn familiar faces. We dont think the stars are worth the money anyway, and one place we could certainly save a small fortune is in the casting. Finally, since we believe that this story is unique and original in the literature of Motion Pictures, we believe that the faces in it should be as New. We agree.

We have certainly been aware of the dangers involved in the use of the CORRIDO. And in fact until yesterday we were not quite sure of the method to be used. However now we think we have an approach and we would like to submit it to you. We think you will agree that the CORRIDO method will 1/ advance the story 2/ lay in a historical background and 3/ help with the transitions better than any other method could. Above all it is original and charming, not labored, lazy clumsy and literal.

There was a CORRIDO maker and singer with Zapata's army, named SILVA. He appears to have ridden into battle with his guitar on his back, and he is very famous thruout that country. I do not know why we did not use him from the very beginning, because he is colourful, as well being historically accurate. . . . Here's the way we have thought of it as working. At the beginning our singer is an old man, relating to younger people the experiences of his youth. In effect he is saying to Country People who are listening that this land which they live on and work was not easily won. Nor can it be easily held. . . . The next time we see the singer he is a young man. He is at the Fiesta, singing about the first thing Zapata was known as: a great horseman. . . . At the end of the picture, having performed his function of "M.C." and Historian, we see him again, AN OLD MAN, but this time hearing his own song sung by children. They are singing his melody. So he's accomplished something too. All this should be swift and very understated.

We agree with your feeling about ART or MOOD pictures whether they're by JACK FORD or anybody else. The FUGITIVE was simply a Bad Picture. But we maintain that it is quite different on the one hand to use a SINGER in place of plot, and on the other to use him to simplify and make understandable too much. Furthermore, our picture never "stops". It is all action. And finally fuck Jack Ford, who is fucking the Catholic Church and vice versa.

Your next point: Who Zapata's enemies were at the end? You are 100% right. This is not clear and a fault. We will work on this and overcome it.

In your point three, what you say about the values, we completely agree with. We thought they were clear, if indirectly stated. However if they are not, we will have to, and want to give them more emphasis. But what you state as the "message" of the picture (top of your page 7) is exactly what we want to say, except we tried to say it in terms of character and incident, rather than in terms of preachment. But, again, if it is not clear, we want to make it clear. We feel as you said at the last meeting, audiences will accept story and reject oratory. . . .

Tomorrow we will go over your small points, most of which we agree with without question. But one thing: about pages 74–81.

This scene is too long. But we had a very definite reason to include it. If we are to motivate and justify for an American audience Zapata's subsequent actions, and the actions of the people around him, WE MUST SHOW THAT HE AND HIS PEOPLE HAD NO CHOICE EXCEPT TO FIGHT. The scene in the Hacienda seemed to be the final proof to them that they could not even rely on the liberal or "moderate" to help them. In other words, we try to show here that Zapata's actions were a product of immutable tyranny which would not bend or give or SHARE. As Don Nacio says at the end of the scene—"If you do not give a little, they will have to take all." This is a damn good lesson to we who are trying to maintain a system of free enterprise. And here we see the kind of people who put up the fence and caused the trouble in the first place. . . .

On rereading this letter we think maybe we should throw out the script and shoot the letter. We mean it is pretty long itself. And perhaps that is enough for one day. We'll probably write you again tomorrow.

Yours,
John
Gadg

P.S. in re your suggestion: Joe Breen falling on his face. Is this a bad idea?

P.P.S. Besides being the most expensive, Kazan is probably the worst typist in the world.

[John Steinbeck finished a treatment of *Zapata* in late 1949 that impressed Darryl Zanuck as "the floor plan of a great and exciting motion picture." Revised and submitted in the following spring, the present draft "delighted" Zanuck as well, although it produced seventeen pages of "notes" for the collaborators to ponder (to JS and EK, May 3, 1950, Pierpont Morgan).

Steinbeck envisioned Zapata as a "strong, self-contained individual" whose stand against "collectivization" is what the "whole world needs right now" ("Introduction," April 9, 1949, Wesleyan). He and Kazan searched the annals of an ill-documented revolution for a defining gesture and settled on Zapata's abrupt departure from Mexico City in 1914. The apparent shunning of power in the moment of victory established a "relationship between abstract politics and personal character," as Kazan later claimed, which met the dramatic and political needs of the screenplay.

Zanuck worried lest singing in English with a Mexican accent suggest "an art or 'mood' picture" of the type "John Ford does when he is stuck and has run out of plot" (May 3, 1950). He probably recalled the soulful peasants and affected camerawork of *The Fugitive* (1947), Ford's highly censored version of *The Power and the Glory* (1940). The moral cleansing of Graham Greene's "whisky priest" put the director in bed with the Catholic Church, or so Kazan thought. The "CORRIDO" was soon replaced with choral singing in Spanish, which is brief, infrequent, and lacking historical narrative.

Zanuck advised cutting a lengthy scene exposing the luxury and arrogance of the *hacendados,* the landowning class of European descent whose seizure of pueblo lands inspired Zapata's revolt. It was omitted along with Don Nacio's warning to militant fellow landowners: "If you do not give a little, they will have to take all." In effect the film's political values were steered away from revolution and related to the search for a leader, a valuable idea that had been "eliminated" in the current draft. Zanuck thought it "the whole answer to the theme in the story. 'Give the people a voice and from them will come the leader.' This can be stated in the truest terms of democracy" (May 3, 1950).] *TLS, 3 pp., Pierpont Morgan*

TO CHARLES K. FELDMAN

[New York]
May 8, 1950

Dear Charlie:

I'm leaving here a week from today, and will arrive there on Wednesday morning's Super-Chief. Is it possible for me to meet with Mr. Joseph Breen immediately. I mean that same Wednesday morning, say at 11 A.M.? This is the first thing I would like to do in California. I want to clear up things finally, both for you and for me.

I don't feel at all relieved by the reports you sent me from the Breen office conference. I haven't the least intention of cutting out the scene with the young Collector. All this scene contains is the longing every woman has, in fact, every person has during moments of great loneliness and despair, for love and closeness and romance. There is nothing homosexual about the young Collector. A boy can be gentle and shy and delicate without being a fairy. On the contrary, there is something innocent and pure about him and Blanche's taste for him is not degenerate, but romantic and wistful. Every woman knows how she feels, Charlie, it's normal. The only thing unhealthy is if you think it's degenerate.

I detest the idea that everyone at the meeting hailed so eagerly. That is, that Blanche calls a lot of fellows "Alan". Once and for all, Blanche is not crazy when she comes in, she is a very, very disturbed and upset girl. She is driven crazy by the events of this play. It happens before your eyes. Also, I won't do anything to make her seem like a "heavy" or a villainous person. Some of those fellows at that meeting just don't know what it's all about. The Code is Jack Warner's problem and the problem of the other fellows who instituted it. It's not mine. It has often seemed to me hypocritical in its administration. Half the pictures that come out of Hollywood only have one point and you know what that is. I don't have to tell you. And leaving sex aside, I have seen some horrible pieces of sadistic brutality which pass Code administrators. Brutality has often been made to seem most attractive in pictures I have seen.

Frankly, Charlie, I have no intention of giving in on a damn thing that I consider essential to the honesty of this story. I want you to know this, Charlie. I say it with no bitterness or truculence. It's just a fact. I don't think you should either, but then you have a different problem and I can appreciate what that is. I still think the Breen Office can be fought on this, not fighting them by "cooperating" in the way the fellows at that meeting were cooperating.

Let me be very clear: First, neither Tennessee nor I will go for the "Alan" stuff. Neither Tennessee nor I will cut out the Collector scene. We will not specify that it was an older woman in the room with Alan when Blanche happened in. Nowhere in the present script have we said that it was a man. If there is any positive suggestion to this effect, we will iron it out so that there is no suggestion one way or another. It's not essential that the audience know it's a man.

And for the life of me, I don't see what can be done about Blanche's promiscuity. IT'S THE STORY OF THE PLAY, and for Christ's sake, she pays, and pays, and PAYS! What more do they want?

I will not have Stanley stop short of the rape. I don't believe he would have, do you? Also, the rape is his final act in destroying her. If you want a "heavy" in the piece, it's Stanley. Perhaps Blanche could never have been saved, but I certainly think it should look that way for the moment, with Mitch. The story of the latter half of this play is that Stanley doggedly hunts her down, down, down into the ground and finally makes her dirt by taking her against her will. She acts to bring it on, but he does it. He has some provocation, but the rape is the final crushing blow of a series of blows that Stanley has thrown at her.

Here is what I will do: I will try to suggest, subtly, at the end of the piece that the marriage between Stella and Stanley will never be quite the same. I am willing to urge Tennessee to do this because I honestly believe that it is true. I believe that Stella knows Stanley had Blanche even though she won't face this knowledge, but in time it will begin to chew on her insides and I believe Stella knows something much worse: namely, that Stanley gave Blanche the BIG PUSH over the edge, and this she will never forgive him. Never, even though she goes back to him at this moment. After a time there must be a hatred between them and a growing apartness and if I can by a word or two or by a look show the beginning of this estrangement, I would like to very much. In this sense, Stanley is honestly punished, and since he loves Stella the punishment is considerable. If this would satisfy the Breen Office, I would be delighted, because we would be helping the picture without tampering with its integrity.

Tell Mr. Breen that Christ didn't condemn the whore or move away from her, he said: "Let him throw the first stone, etc. etc." Mr. Williams' story is about the greatest of Christian virtues, of Charity. Some people call it compassion. I know Mr. Breen's job is difficult. He is administering a Code that he didn't write. He is subject to constant pressure. But I don't think the Code can be applied mechanically or without some imagination and to a stage masterpiece that has won every prize in the theatre world.

Charlie, let's face something that I know you have thought of, but let's face it in print. Perhaps I am not the man you need to direct your production of STREETCAR. You've been most generous and patient, and hospitable and agreeable and charming to be with. But I know you must get your production going; you have money tied up. And I know Warner has to release it with a seal that will guarantee the product for what Mr. Vizzard refers to as the "Family Audience." I'm beginning to seriously doubt that I'm the man to do this.

I'm delighted with the casting of Vivien Leigh, or at least on our deciding on her. She will be great with Brando and Malden. I will consult with you on Stella. The rest of the cast can be assembled in a day. I thoroughly disliked the art work on GLASS MENAGERIE, but then you agreed that I could bring in my own designer, and if it's not Mielziner, I'll get some one else. The script can be prepared very quickly now, Tennessee and I having agreed on the last point of difference at a meeting last week—BUT—It's a big BUT. And it's beginning to stick in my gizzard. As well as waste a lot of time for both of us. Plainly, there's only so far that I'm willing to go to meet the Breen Office. I've tried to specify in this letter. You make up your mind. Let's not waste time. If it won't work, let's knock off. I'll shake your hand and wish you luck in everything except distorting this play. If you think it's worth a fight, I'll fight like hell right down to the wire. Why don't you wire me what you think. At any rate, I'll see you next week.

My very best, Charlie

[Reconciling *Streetcar* with the Production Code tested the ingenuity of censors and producers who met before Kazan reached California. Substituting an "older woman" for Allan Grey's companion in Blanche's discovery scene would remove the problem of homosexuality, which was "absolutely forbidden" by the Code. That expedient aside, Grey's suicide must be explained "affirmatively" by a factor other than exposure as a homosexual. The film *Johnny Belinda* (1948) set precedent for treating rape, as Tennessee Williams had recently pointed out, but Stanley's rape of Blanche was dramatically "justified" by a lengthy buildup and left "unpunished." A ready solution would have Blanche "imagine" rape and call "Stanley by the name, Allan" in confirmation of her madness. Recasting Blanche as a woman "searching for romance and security" rather than "gross sex" would also relieve the film's sordid tone (PCA file, April 28, 1950, Herrick). Of all the objections, rape is probably the one that stuck in Kazan's "gizzard." The press reported on May 28 that "the last of the censorship problems" was solved and Joseph Breen had given "the go-ahead signal." In fact it was not until the near end of filming that he approved the rape scene.

Following his return to New York, Kazan announced the formation of Newtown Productions, an independent company designed to minimize problems recently encountered by merging the roles of producer and director and gaining control of script (*NYT*, June 23, 1950).] *TLS, 3 pp., Wesleyan*

TO JACK L. WARNER

[Sandy Hook, Connecticut]
[June 1950]

Dear Jack:

I've been meaning to write you for a week now and tell you how grateful I am for the generosity you have shown me. I know it would be a damned sight easier to plan this picture with me if I were living in California. And I know you must have felt this from time to time. But you have never even hinted at it. I want you to know that I am fully aware of how very very nice you have been. . . .

I know how anxious you are about the length of the script. I think I've managed to cut about a dozen pages out of the screen play since I left California. And more important, I'm getting it the way I think it should be. With all due respect to the fellows who have been working on it—including myself—we had it all a little fucked up. Now I'm down to beating the typewriter myself, which is the way Movies are made. I should be able to ship a final to you within a week.

Another problem. Leigh lives in England and I am terribly worried about her costumes. I had thought for a while that we might be able to use the clothes she wore on the stage. I had seen a couple of pictures, but when I saw the complete set that she sent me, I pretty quickly changed my mind. To put it in one word: they were "English". I mean stuffy, dull, ultra conservative and—"English". They have to be completely redesigned, in order to get the best out of Leigh. As you know I want Lucinda Ballard. All I can say about her is that she is the best. There are two things we could do, bring Leigh here early or ship Ballard over to England now. I'd like to give Leigh as much rest as possible—as you know she has been tubercular and generally not well. Nothing slows up a shooting schedule like an easily exhausted woman. And if we brought her here something like the end of July, or even the middle there would be a last minute rush.

I'd very much like to send Ballard to England right now. She could carefully work over the costumes with Leigh, so that when Leigh came to this country they would be all ready for a fitting. And Leigh would be happy with the clothes, instead of worrying about them all the time I was trying to get great scenes out of her. I know it is an added expense, but really a very small one compared with any delay or slow up in the shooting, even if it were only half a day. Ballard could go there with complete instructions from me,—after all she has already designed this show twice for me, and knows what I want, by now, better than I do. And this would allow us the couple of weeks before we start for any last minute readjustments. . . . I hope very very much that you will see this my way, Jack. I am most anxious that all these little details be right. A picture is made up of beautifully chosen details, and believe me Ballard is worth everything. I'm sure this would be the best and—in the long run—the cheapest thing to do. . . .

Please dont forget about Dave Weisbart. I really need a good cutter, since this is the one side of this business that I am still unsure about.

I'll test Roman this week. I'll test anyone else whom you think a strong possibility. I still think Baxter is our best bet—but—there's time yet on this.

Please let me hear from you as soon as possible about Ballard. I'm most anxious about this.

My very best to you, <u>Gadg</u>

P.S. One other thing about Ballard. She is from Louisiana, and has a really genuine southern accent—very very slight—really barely discernable—not one of those broad corny accents. I think it would be wonderful for Leigh to listen to her for a week or so, and model her accent on Ballard's. I understand from reports that Leigh's accent was rather heavy, and any heavy regional accent on the screen is deadly. Don't you agree?

[*Streetcar* was pared to a running time of 122 minutes, marginally within the limits of Kazan's film work to date. Presumably Tennessee Williams made "no contribution" to revising the screenplay "because of his state of mind" in the preceding spring and summer. Elia entrusted the cutting of long speeches to Molly Kazan, who "did a masterful job." Charles Feldman summarized these and other claims made by Kazan as they debated production credit for the film (to EK, November 28, 1950, Wesleyan).

Vivien Leigh played Blanche in London "as if a flame were licking at her nerves." So wrote an admiring critic when she left the cast of *Streetcar* in mid-1950. Eight months of playing a tragic figure had "tipped" the actress "over into madness," or so Leigh claimed. Ruth Roman and Anne Baxter were early candidates to play Stella.

A native of New Orleans, Lucinda Ballard designed costumes for Kazan's original production of *Streetcar* and current revival starring Uta Hagen and Anthony Quinn. She would also collaborate with Kazan on *Cat on a Hot Tin Roof* (1955), *The Dark at the Top of the Stairs* (1957), and *J.B.* (1958). A biographer reports that Leigh approved Ballard's sketches in London and that "a special understanding had grown between them."] *TLS, 2 pp., WB Archives*

TO STEPHEN B. TRILLING

1697 Broadway, New York City
July 5, 1950

Dear Steve,

I am sending you under separate cover, a couple of pictures of a young actress, Lenka Peterson, who I think has enormous talent for the screen.

She was in PANIC IN THE STREETS where I was very impressed with her, as was everybody around the picture. I think she has great possibilities for a Janet Gaynor type of role. At the time she made this picture, and later when she made the test for Fox, she was still a little plump from having a baby. As a matter of fact, when she was in New Orleans, she had to stop nursing the baby which had just come a little while before. Now she is back to normal again and you can believe me that I would not be recommending her unless she had something most original and genuine to give the screen.

You may have seen the Fox test, but don't go by that as it was made under circumstances that weren't the most fortunate for her. She is the wife of a friend of mine and she is now living in St. Louis, but it has always seemed a shame to me that she didn't continue her career and that's why the strong plug. During the time I am shooting STREETCAR, I'll be glad to make the test myself if you are interested.

Thanks for all the favors, Steve. The production seems to be in good shape except we don't seem to be able to get a "Stella." You would imagine that it would be the easiest part to cast.

Yours, Gadg—

[Steve Trilling served as casting director before taking his current post as Jack Warner's executive assistant.

Lenka Peterson studied at the Actors Studio and was favorably noticed in *Sun-*

down Beach (1948). Her character in *Panic in the Streets* (1950) plays a crucial, if minor, role in tracing the plague. Peterson's later television work was more frequent than stage or screen appearances.

Warner Bros. did not confirm the signing of Kim Hunter, who originated the role of Stella on Broadway, until August 8, a week before filming of *Streetcar* began.] *TLS, 1 p., USC*

TO JOSEPH IGNATIUS BREEN

SH: Warner Bros. Pictures, Inc.
Burbank, California
[mid-September 1950]

Dear Joe—

Just a note. I dont ever mind honest differences, but I hate misunderstandings. They're dangerous, and the quicker they're quashed the better. Jack Vizzard said that it seemed like from your side there was some possible breach of faith (or attempt at same) on ours. So, let me assure you, I wouldn't put the homosexuality back in the picture, if the Code had been revised last night and it was now permissible. I dont want it. I prefer the delicately suggested impotence theme; I prefer debility and weakness over any kind of suggestion of perversion. The revisions in the long speech came from three sources. There was a suggestion that she "despised" her husband because he couldn't hold a job, or because his poems were returned or something. Secondly after shooting four weeks I became oppressed with the feeling that the script was very very talky. Everyone has been warning me about it, and I finally began to feel it strongly myself. Gab gab gab. And most of it from Leigh. I have cut enormous hunks (in one case 2/3) out of other long speeches. And finally, I felt the punch of the speech was more diluted than it need be. I never hope to get any shock in the movie comparable to her walking into a room and finding her husband with another man. But The speech is in a strategic position in the show, and has got to do its job in that spot, OR ELSE. I didn't think it did. And I am responsible for the show, responsible to everyone. That's why the blue page. Unfortunately it took a little time and work on the actual shooting to bring me to the strong awareness necessary to sitting down and making a change. But I DONT WANT YOU TO THINK that I was trying to slip a third strike past you or anyone else. That I dont do.

I'm working on the rape thing too. I think I've got sight of a real solution, and when I have it developed a little further, I'd like to discuss it too.

Yours, Gadg <u>Kazan</u>

[As Hollywood's "official censor," Joseph Breen directed the Production Code Administration from 1934 until his retirement in the mid-1950s. He enforced a comprehensive Code, implemented in 1930 but weakly applied, in defense of his Catholic conscience and an industry threatened by external regulation and costly boycotts. "Working Principles" of the original Code were threefold: "I. No picture should lower the moral standards of those who see it. II. Law, natural or divine, must not be belittled, ridiculed, nor must a sentiment be presented against it. III. As far as possible, life should not be misrepresented, at least not in such a way as to place in the minds of youth false values on life." More specific rules governing the treatment of sex, crime, vulgarity, obscenity, costume, dancing, locations, and religion guided Breen's staff in reviewing submissions during the early script and production phase. A certificate of approval was issued on final compliance with the Code (Doherty, pp. 172–75; Martin, pp. 274–84).

Breen rejected the latest revision ("the blue page") of Blanche's "long speech" because it failed to establish "affirmatively" that "the boy's problem is something other than homosexuality" (to JLW, September 13, 1950, Herrick). Tennessee Williams placed the famous "aria" at the end of act two, where the "understanding and compassion" of the audience, as he wrote earlier to Kazan, must be given to Blanche if the play's tragedy is to be realized. Williams arrived in Burbank in answer to Charlie Feldman's plea to consider how the speech could be "cut down" without "hurting the content" and yet "meet the Breen office requirement." As filmed, no reference is made to Allan Grey's compromising situation or to Blanche's impulsive statement of "disgust." The "impotence theme" preferred by Kazan was also cut, as was Blanche's guilt for having "failed" her young husband "in some mysterious way." Immaturity and irresponsibility were emphasized instead, as Blanche states with uncharacteristic flatness: "I didn't understand why this boy who wrote poetry didn't seem able to do anything else. Lost every job."

Directing Karl Malden and Vivien Leigh in the film
version of *A Streetcar Named Desire*

Kazan's closing reference to a "real solution" of the "rape thing" put the Breen Office on full alert, as following correspondence reveals.] *TLS, 2 pp., Herrick*

TO JACK L. WARNER

SH: Warner Bros. Pictures, Inc.
Burbank, California
October 19, 1950

Dear Jack:

There are a couple of things I want to say to you now that the picture is over, and perhaps this letter is the quickest and simplest way to say them.

First, I've never had a happier experience, or been treated better than during the weeks I made STREETCAR at Warner Bros. Studios. I'm very grateful to you and to Tenny and to each of the boys who worked with me. Their cooperation was as superb as their craftsmanship, and I take leave of them all with regret. I can't imagine any director being given more than I was by every single department. I won't forget it.

There is one fellow who worked with us whose contribution will only be known by me. And since he's under contract to you and potentially very important to you, may I say something about Dave Weisbart. He helped me in so many ways that the term "<u>cutter</u>" does not cover. I consulted him with great benefit on every single shot. The final product will be chock full of his suggestions in the way of set-ups, business and everything else that generally comes under the heading of <u>Directing</u>. In short, I think you have a very fine director in this man. And having taken so much from him, I will be a little embarrassed if he is listed in the credits as <u>Film</u> <u>Editor</u>. Do you think we could list him as <u>Associate</u> <u>Producer</u>? I imagine if you and I suggested this to Charlie Feldman together, he couldn't have any possible objection. And not only would this be doing justice, but you would be taking this very real opportunity to build a man you have under contract.

One thing about the picture itself. I just saw it again and I liked it. You will have your own impression, of course, but I thought it completely clean. Whatever there is of sex and violence is truthfully done, never exploited or sensationalized. And, I think it is full of the very Christian feeling of compassion and charity.

I don't know what Mr. Joseph Breen will say but may I, before we sit down with him, recall to you the conversation we all had in your trophy room, after lunch, several months ago. That was the occasion when Joe said that the "rape" could not be in the picture—and I withdrew from the project. If you remember, Charlie Feldman asked me directly, "You mean to say that if the 'rape' is not in, you will not do the picture?" Whereupon, I said he was absolutely right and to count me out. You were there and will remember this. You will also remember that later we got together on a basis that I suggested. And this, too, was very clearly put. It consisted of (1) The rape would be in, but done by suggestion and delicacy (2) Stanley would be "punished" and that the punishment would be in terms of his loss of his wife's love. In other words, that there would be a strong indication that she would leave him.

On this understanding, I embarked on the project. And on the basis of these points, I made the picture.

At several subsequent meetings, Joe seemed to waver from this understanding, but since I had already come into the project, it was too late to bring up the <u>very basis</u> of our understanding. I never again discussed this with Joe. Charlie Feldman has known from weekly restatement how I was proceeding. So has Finlay McDermid. The picture you will see is in line with what we discussed that afternoon in your trophy room.

I do not really think we will have much trouble with Joe Breen; however, it seems to me that if he has objections that are basic, why this is an opportunity to put up a worthwhile fight. Everything is on our side. The picture is good! The stage property won every prize known in the World Theatre. We can have a perfectly clean conscience about the "sensationalism" in the picture—for absolutely none of it is for its own sake. And, I really think the picture's theme is deeply moral.

One of the very, very nice things people say about you is that when the occasion arises, you are the greatest fighter in this business. A man should carefully choose the ground on which he makes a fight. He should be on absolutely sure ground. I feel that's where we are with this picture.

And, incidentally, I'd say that we are in another unusual circumstance. Every change or deletion that Breen might ask us to make will lower the commercial value of our picture. If we come thru unscathed, I think we might have one of the really great money-makers.

I don't say this about all my pictures. I don't think it is true of the others. I think it is this time.

Yours, with gratefulness, Gadg.

[Vivien Leigh's openly stated preference for Laurence Olivier's direction of *Streetcar* caused the only tension on an otherwise harmonious set. Kazan's swift reminder that Leigh was not filming with her husband in London ended debate and apparently earned her respect: "She'd have crawled over broken glass if she thought it would help her performance. In the scenes that counted, she is excellent" (*A Life*, pp. 386–87). Marlon Brando did not clash with his British costar, as expected, but thought her perfectly cast. "In many ways she *was* Blanche. She was memorably beautiful . . . but she was also vulnerable, and her own life had been very much like that of Tennessee's wounded butterfly" (Brando, p. 152).

Kazan's "cutter" Dave Weisbart was listed in the credits as "Film Editor." He would soon be embroiled in a more serious effort to censor *Streetcar*.

The Breen Office anticipated Kazan's "real solution" and warned that any "fence-straddling" ploy allowing a "rape, or not" interpretation would probably not be "satisfactory" (PCA file, October 3, 1950, Herrick). Kazan used the occasion to remind Jack Warner of the "understanding" reached in his "trophy room" and to prompt Tennessee Williams to write in defense of the critical scene: "The rape of Blanche by Stanley is a pivotal, integral truth in the play, without which the play loses its meaning, which is the ravishment of the tender, the sensitive, the delicate by the savage and brutal forces in modern society" (to Breen, October 29, 1950, HRC).

Williams gained final PCA approval by authorizing Stanley's punishment in lines supplied to Kazan: "As Stella is crying she whispers to the baby these words of promise and reassurance. We're not going back in there. Not this time. We're never going back. Never, never back, never back again" (November 2, 1950, Herrick). Kazan met his self-imposed requirement of "suggestion and delicacy" by reducing the dramatic buildup of the rape scene and limiting Stanley's assault to a brief encounter that dissolves imagistically. As filmed, his "solution" straddled no "fence," nor was Stanley's menace or Blanche's destruction in any way diminished.] *TLS, 3 pp., WB Archives*

TO JACK L. WARNER

[New York]
December 7, 1950

Dear Jack:

I asked you before I left California whether you would consider it "none of my business" if I wrote you a little about the advertising and exploitation of A STREETCAR NAMED DESIRE. You said you would be glad to hear my views on it, so, honey-chile, you have only yourself to blame for this letter.

I am most anxious about it, most interested in it, and I will be glad to talk with anybody here, I mean specifically, Mr. Mort Blumenstock, if you think it will serve any purpose, or even half a purpose.

If you will excuse the comparison, I do hope that Warner Brothers will give STREETCAR the "Goldwyn treatment." You have really got so much to sell here. Not only the prestige and dignity of the original property—this one is really pre-sold—but the sensationalism and suggestion of drama, sex and violence with which the title is redolent (excuse my French, Maestro,) but I mean redolent. By the "Goldwyn treatment" I mean taking the Astor. If you could all think of it this way you could book it way ahead now. I mean taking the Astor and running the picture for a good long time in New York before it is shown anywhere else. I think you have got something in this picture which is comparable only to THE BEST YEARS OF OUR LIVES, as far as money-making potential goes. I am sure that the only way you will realize on this potential is by having confidence in it and gambling on it. It should be treated as something "big." That way it will turn out "big." I think you will be just throwing it away if you put it into the Strand or even into the Music Hall. I think a showman, if he has the basis for it, can generate no limit of excitement about this. I use Sam Goldwyn's name because he did it beautifully on BEST YEARS.

I saw some stuff that the New York office sent out to Alex Evelove. There was something in the copy about Vivien Leigh: "the first time since 'GONE WITH THE WIND.'" This horrified me. If there is anything that's dull it's the suggestion of a repeat. It's a mighty poor picture that has to lean on the title of another picture for its standing with the public. And this never works.

The New York office also asked for some photographic copy between Brando and Leigh that really was in the corniest of all traditions. It reminded me of some of the Ads I have seen for Argentine pictures—"Flaming Passion on the Pampas", something of that kind. In the first place, those days are gone forever, and in the second place, we have something much better to sell here and no one will take that attitude unless first you do. You and your brother Harry have to pass the word down and say: "Treat this like an important picture, dignified yet exciting, them's orders!" and then I am sure it will be done, and done right.

The greatest thing, it seems to me, to sell here is the title and the promise of a tremendous dramatic clash suggested by the linked names of Leigh and Brando.

About the art work, may I suggest the man in New York who did the work on "PINKY", which I thought was brilliant, both sexy and classy. But, Jack, I don't think you are going to have any problem about making the movie-going public aware that the picture has something to do with the relation between the sexes. It's how this is done that is important. The title tells it for one thing, and what is important is that the picture be given the stature and dignity that will make it a "must" for everybody. If your Ads are too lurid or "common" I think you will keep certain groups of the movie audiences away.

I also have no doubt that we will have some trouble with the State Censor Boards, and this, of course, is both a problem and at the same time excellent publicity. And it's what Joe Breen was talking about in my last conversation with him when he begged me to see to it, to the extent that it was within my influence, that your exploitation people kept the Ads within the bounds of good taste. I think Joe felt that he was letting us down very easy as far as the seal requirements went, and didn't want to be put further on the spot by the

Ads which might, as the "BELINDA" Ads did, be selling the rape scene. You remember, Jack, I spoke to you about this and you said of course you would do everything you could. Well, I think the first thing we have to do is to get the right kind of people working on the art work, to get it out of the run-of-the-mill. This can be done and be very exciting. It's just a matter of effort and determination. Anything I can do, Jack, to help, please feel free to call on me.

About the credits. I had a very nice letter from Charlie and will be answering him in a day or two. I will ask him to show you the letter. Best wishes for your good health and happiness.

Yours, Gadg

[Mort Blumenstock directed publicity for Warner Bros. in the East and was doubtless pleased by the enviable box office title and production history of *Streetcar*. The "original property" swept the major prizes, including the Pulitzer and Drama Critics' Circle Award, and ran for two years on Broadway. National and international road companies prepared a large audience for the film. *Streetcar* opened at the Warner Theatre in New York, rather than the Astor.

Jack Warner promised a "very discreet" advertising campaign for *Streetcar* without "any tearing of clothes" as in *Johnny Belinda* (1948). The earlier campaign exploited the rape of a young woman without speech or hearing—to the embarrassment of Joe Breen, who was increasingly subject to charges of compromising moral standards. The initial ad for *Streetcar* featured a company logo commemorating the "Silver Anniversary of Talking Pictures," with timely updating of Warner's original innovation: "Proud Anniversary Blazes to New Greatness with the Fire of 'A STREETCAR NAMED DESIRE.'" Marlon Brando, in torn shirt, executes a "dramatic clash" with Kim Hunter.

Kazan insisted on billing as stipulated by his contract: "An Elia Kazan Production." Jack Warner thought the credit line in "bad taste," but Kazan answered that he had "functioned as the producer" and was entitled to the same billing he received for the original play. Charles Feldman received a production credit and was cited as the film's copyright holder.] *TLS, 2 pp., WB Archives*

TO TENNESSEE WILLIAMS

[New York]
[January 1951]

Dear Tenn—
All the reports are wonderful! Irene and Peter Brook were genuinely enthusiastic and very very stirred. Peter is absolutely honest and an excellent judge besides. Then Cheryl came back and I saw her yesterday. She was full of pleasant statistics: eighteen curtain calls, four muffled priests who applauded vigorously and tirelessly at the end, again sixteen curtain calls, etc. Also about

the last five minutes of the play: she said you were doing something about them. You must have done some rewriting already, because this is all—Cheryl said—that needed doing. Other people have told me that there was a little more to do, and this fits in with my impression when I read it (long ago). Just take a close close look yourself, Tenn, and dont let it go. I'm very proud of you because I know that you met with some disappointments on this production and still you made all the right choices: Maureen, Danny, Boris. You've really earned this success. I just hope that you've really got the last act fixed, or will have. So that the thing will be complete. If you get a chance drop me a line and let me know how you're feeling.

I'm working with Art preparing a final version of THE HOOK. Then I'm going to California and put the music on STREETCAR and while I'm there I'll arrange for the production of the HOOK, if war and conditions permit. I'll also be working some more on ZAPATA. I know this is not right yet, but I can see a motion picture of great size in it, and I just dont seem to WANT to be discouraged about it. I wish you could also find a moment to write me your most candid opinion, and any and all suggestions you might have on it. The version you read is either the fifth or the sixth, we have lost count, and I doubt by now, if anything could dishearten me. So dont pull punches. Also, could you send me back the script.

Business in N.Y. is poor, it seems. They say it will continue this way until we settle down to the war, then it will perk up. Art's play is on the slippery verge of closing, having been budgeted much much too high. At the same time all his balcony seats are sold thru March. Something's wrong somewhere.

Love to you and best to Frank. <u>Gadg</u>

Love from Molly too.

[Notices for the Chicago tryout of *The Rose Tattoo* were mixed rather than "wonderful." Claudia Cassidy, a local ally who cheered for *The Glass Menagerie* in 1944, admired Tennessee Williams's latest work but wrote in her review that it lacked "clairvoyant direction" and "a luminous finale." Her criticism of Daniel Mann's staging bespeaks the major "disappointment" of the show: Kazan's withdrawal.

"The Hook" was victimized by pro-union, anticommunist currents of 1951 and rejected by Fox and Warner Bros. before Harry Cohn, head of Columbia Pictures, made a tentative commitment to the project. When Arthur Miller withdrew the screenplay, to Kazan's surprise and dismay, Cohn wired the author in New York: "ITS INTERESTING HOW THE MINUTE WE TRY TO MAKE THE SCRIPT PRO-AMERICAN YOU PULL OUT." Miller later described the pro-American slant as requiring that communists rather than "union crooks and their gangster protectors" be cast as "the bad guys" on the Brooklyn waterfront (Miller, p. 308).

Divorce, illness, theater projects, and a prompting to begin *East of Eden* limited Steinbeck's concentration on *Zapata* and deepened Kazan's involvement in story construction. Tennessee Williams found a "lack of sharp definition" in the present screenplay and adroitly observed that "some scripts exist only in the mind of the creator except as telegraphic flashes now and then to the reader." He had "caught" enough of those "flashes" to be enchanted by the "wonderful sweeping landscape" of Mexico: "the great clarity of space, the cloud masses, the wild mountains." With an "epic hero" of Zapata's magnitude and "Brando to play him," Williams expected "a thrillingly beautiful work" (n.d., Wesleyan).

Chinese intervention in the preceding November prolonged the Korean War until a cease-fire was signed in 1953. Arthur Miller's adaptation of *An Enemy of the People* closed on January 27 after thirty-six performances.] *TLS, 1 p., HRC*

TO JACK L. WARNER

[New York]
[March 1951]

Dear Jack:

The idea of taking me down, right then and there, to look at those spots you had doubts about was really square dealing. And I appreciate it. Thought I'd tell you.

You know I like old Charlie personally very much. (His sex life puzzled me a bit, because I never saw a woman there in the morning. But maybe he likes to sleep alone.) In fact I liked him so much that despite the fact that I disagreed with every single thing he ever said about the picture, I never raised my voice to say a harsh word to him. I simply told him in the dulcet tones of friendship that I disagreed with every fucking thing he was saying. And he would sail right along saying errant (and arrant) foolishnesses. Once he really got under my skin and I almost told him the truth which, as I see it, is: "You fucked up the Menagerie, dope, why dont you leave this one to a couple of guys who know their business?" By the way, on the Menagerie he did do exactly what he's trying to do here: bring the thing down to the taste HE THINKS the audience has. (As if any but a small percentage of our movie going populace was made up of bobby soxers, autograph waterheads and preview minded water-brains!)

The last time I met this good old fashioned type of thinking was from old L.B. Mayer who came to New Haven and tried to influence me in his best and most persuasive manner to have a happy ending tacked on to the play and make Blanche the heavy. He said it would never never go as is. (P.S. last week I got a substantial royalty check from the touring company of Streetcar which is playing some towns in the South that I never heard of. They seem to catch on to it there just as they did everywhere else. In fact they seem to like it.)

The thing that makes this piece great box office is that it has two things. 1/ It is about the three F's. 2/ It has class. No person who tries to keep in any kind of step can afford to miss it. Both are equally important. What made it a Pulitzer Prize winner—the poetry—must be kept in, untouched so that it will appeal to those who dont want to admit that they are interested in the moist seat department. (Everybody, of course, is!)

Well, Jack, one thing you got to say for me, I give a damn! The fact is that I've never been this way about a picture before. This is the only picture I ever made that I'm completely proud of.

I'll be talking to you Wednesday. Gadg

Again Thanks. I mean for everything.

[The initial showing of *Streetcar* produced laughter at Blanche's flirtation with a handsome young man in the "collector scene" and a panicky response by Charlie Feldman, one of the "preview minded water-brains." Kazan fixed the problem before returning to New York, but Feldman wired after a second West Coast preview that he had convinced Jack Warner to ship the print east for more discreet exposure. Kazan quipped to Warner that "our friend with the boyish charm still seems to be asking the ushers what they think and pressing all suggestions indiscriminately.] *TLS, 1 p., WB Archives*

TO MOLLY DAY THACHER

West Los Angeles, April 1, 1951

I ASSUME AFTER LETTER FROM GOVT MEXICO IS ALL OFF. THE CHANGES THEY WANT IN THE SCRIPT ARE COMPLETE AND REVOLUTIONARY. ENTIRE SITUATION DOWN THERE IMPOSSIBLE. LEAVING IN AN HOUR FOR SANTA FE, NEW MEXICO TO SCOUT POSSIBLE LOCATIONS THERE THEN PROCEED ALONG TEXAS, NEW MEXICO, ARIZONA, MEXICO UNITED STATES BORDER. MEANTIME THIS SEEMS LIKE THE BIGGEST MESS IN HISTORY AND I'M FIT TO BE TIED.

[Trouble with *Zapata* first appeared in mid-1950 as Steinbeck and Kazan scouted locations in Mexico and were pressured by shadowy film industry figures to treat Zapata as an insurgent with revolutionary ideals. Especially humiliating was the renunciation of power imposed by Anglos on a vibrant national hero. The government letter (unidentified) requiring "complete and revolutionary" changes in the script led Darryl Zanuck to reexamine the project. While still "keen on Zapata," he detected "a peculiar air about certain speeches" in the latest screenplay (December 1950) and worried lest Zapata's "idea" be interpreted as "Communism." Other problems included a security risk near Cuernavaca where *Zapata* was to be filmed and a PCA warning that the film must not contain material "offensive to Mexico and the Mexicans." Undeterred, Zanuck told Kazan to "take a unit manager, an art

With Marlon Brando on the set of *Viva Zapata!*

director, and a driver and go along our border with Mexico and find a location you
can use" (*A Life*, pp. 417–20).

Anthony Quinn and Jean Peters joined Marlon Brando as filming began in May
in southwest Texas. Of the three, Brando was the least experienced film actor,
although neither he nor Quinn and Peters qualified as the "unknowns" preferred
by Kazan. Lou Gilbert, Frank Silvera, and Mildred Dunnock were drawn from the
Actors Studio to play featured roles.] *Telegram, 1 p., Wesleyan*

TO JACK L. WARNER

SH: Twentieth Century-Fox Film Corporation
[Burbank, California]
May 14, 1951

Dear Jack:

I know you have been as tickled as I am with the reactions to our picture. I've
never had reactions anywhere near as good with any picture I did, including
GENTLEMAN'S AGREEMENT. Raves in Hollywood are a dime a dozen, and
I never even twitch my neck around when I hear the word "great" any more.
But this praise has a different ring. I hope to Christ they're not kidding me.
They can't be.

Of course one thing worries me, as it must you. We have one terrible hurdle
to jump yet, and that will be the last. I'm referring to the reaction of the

Legion of Decency. No one can be sure that their reaction will be a negative one. But I think that we should be prepared for a negative reaction—and when I say prepared, I'm using the word in a very practical sense.

I think there is one thing that would make them hesitate very, very much before they "condemned" the picture. That is if the picture has accumulated so many kudos by the time they get to see it that they don't dare condemn it. If we are going to use the kudos they must be used NOW — NOW — long before the picture is released, long before it is seen by any of these men. You don't know it, but I was brought up a Catholic, went to catechism school and went through all that mumbo jumbo, and I know our Catholic brethren very well. It is a practical religion. They are very interested in winning friends and influencing people. They want to make moves ONLY—that will turn out to be popular in the long run. They weigh their steps with a clear eye to the political values involved. They will hesitate a very great deal, believe me, before condemning a motion picture that leaders of thought and culture everywhere have pronounced FINE. FOREVER AMBER, which they condemned, was universally recognized as a book written to be filthy and to sell a lot of copies because it was filthy. I think they regret their move with THE MIRACLE now—witness the fact that they did nothing about it in Los Angeles—but they dared to do that only because so many prominent people in our country, people like Senator Johnson, etc., had publicly branded Rossellini as a libertine and communist.

I think we could mass behind our picture the greatest collection of "NAME" sponsors in the history of this business. There is no doubt of this in my mind after the showings we have had. I'm sure you must know this, else I would enlarge on this point.

I have another suggestion too. Bosley Crowther is himself a Catholic, but he is also a very liberal man. He took exception to Spellman himself on THE MIRACLE ruling and SAID SO in print. He is an exceptional man. I wonder if there would be a value in my writing him a confidential letter as a friend, which I am, and ask his advice. I would frankly tell him my concern about the Legion and that I think the picture is clean and even deeply Christian in its feeling. Jack, this is not a dirty picture! I feel sure if Crowther saw it he would recognize this fact. Only a sex-minded columnist like Sheilah Graham would see Dirt in it, and it's because that's what she's thinking of 90 percent of the time anyway. (I hope she's not your close friend, but if she is, my estimate and opinion still stands.) Let me know what you think; also what you think generally. I think we should and could put this picture in a position where the Catholic Hierarchy would think many many times before they gave us a "C". Of course I'll be glad to do any and everything I can personally.

Personally, I'm glad you're still in Business.

Yours,

[The "hurdle" raised by the Legion of Decency in 1934 saw 9 million Catholics pledge " 'to remain away from all motion pictures except those which do not offend decency and Christian morality.' " Renewal of the pledge was an annual rite in many dioceses, especially in the East, with a majority of theater seats. The release of *Forever Amber* in 1947 provided a notable test of the Legion's postwar influence. The adaptation of Kathleen Winsor's lusty historical romance set atten-dance records in New York before condemnation and a threat of boycott forced Darryl Zanuck to make revisions that earned a "B" rating: "morally objectionable in part for all" (Doherty, pp. 57, 182–83). It was Zanuck who foretold Joe Breen's approval of *Streetcar*, but warned Kazan, " 'What about the Catholic Church, what about the Legion of Decency?' " (*A Life*, p. 417).

New York City officials banned *The Miracle* (1948) shortly before the Legion condemned the film as a "mockery of Christian and religious truth." At issue was a simpleminded peasant (played by Anna Magnani) who believes that she has miraculously conceived by a passing stranger in the figure of St. Joseph. Open conflict was averted in Los Angeles by an agreement that Bishop McIntyre would not condemn *The Miracle* and exhibitors would refrain from showing the film. A single exception passed without incident (Walsh, p. 252). Earlier Republican sena-tor Edwin C. Johnson of Colorado assailed "the vile and unspeakable" Roberto Rossellini, who directed *The Miracle*, for his brazen affair with Ingrid Bergman. He proposed to control the "mad dogs" of Hollywood by federal licensing of film personnel and exclusion of those found guilty of "moral turpitude."

Bosley Crowther answered Cardinal Spellman's denunciation of *The Miracle* by stating that "the individual who suspects that his sensibilities may be offended by a particular picture can simply stay away. That, in the last analysis, is the best kind of censorship" (*NYT*, January 14, 1951). There is no indication in letters that Crowther was enlisted to defend *Streetcar*.

In 1952 the U.S. Supreme Court broke precedent in a suit filed on behalf of *The Miracle* and cautiously extended freedoms of the First and Fourteenth Amendments to motion pictures. The court found the charge of "sacrilege" to be "hopelessly vague," whereupon New York State officials reluctantly restored the film's license.] *TLx, 2 pp., Wesleyan*

TO STEVEN B. TRILLING

SH: Twentieth Century-Fox Film Corporation
Beverly Hills, California
July 27, 1951

Dear Steve:

I spoke to Abe Lastfogel yesterday about how disturbed I was at what was going on in New York. I mean with the Legion and the picture. I am more disturbed than I can possibly tell you. Abe thought that since I felt so upset and anxious I should communicate this to you (and through a copy to J.L.) by mail. Put it all on record as it were.

What disturbs me is the silence. The fact that SOMETHING is being done to my picture—I don't know what! And, this above all, that it is being done without consultation with me and without even informing me. I do believe you when you say that you knew nothing about Dave's mission to New York when I first asked you about it last week. I only believe you however because I know you and like you personally. If I didn't trust you as a person you can see how difficult it would be to believe that the executive of a studio, through whose office practically all company business passes, should not know about something as pressing as this. However, as I say, I do believe you.

At the same time on last Sunday I called Dave Weisbart in New York, on my own, at the Sherry Netherland hotel. He told me then that he was not in New York on STREETCAR business—although it might develop into that. He said nothing had happened so far, but something might etc. etc.—in other words the conversation was full of innuendo—and the clear implication that he had been instructed NOT TO TELL ME ANYTHING. I cannot believe that he did not know what the hell he was doing in New York or standing by for in New York—although clearly that is what he and his wife were telling me. Of course Warner Brothers Business is W.B. Business. But since I put everything I have into a picture, isn't it perfectly and completely inevitable that I should be terribly anxious when it reaches me by dribs and drabs, that some finagling is going on? To say that I got burned up is an understatement.

I called Charlie Feldman too last week. He said he knew nothing about it— that Warners were not telling him either.

Then I spoke to you yesterday. You said that the Legion had seen it once and had asked for certain deletions. You were not sure what these were, but you felt they were minor, and to quote Charlie F., "nothing to worry about." You know very well, Steve, that as far as I am concerned they are plenty to worry about. I don't want any meddling by these people into the guts of my picture, or of YOUR picture either. If the deletions really are minor, they might be o.k. with me. And they might not. What might seem minor to you and Jack, may not seem minor to me. I'd like to know. I think I should have been told.

You also said yesterday that you thought the LEGION had asked for another showing—and that "This was serious". How serious you weren't sure. You thought it might turn out, probably would, that their requests were minor— but their request for a second showing was always serious. And you stressed the thing Charlie always stresses—that I should shut up—or to put it more gently—keep a discreet and watchful silence.

This always means only one thing to me. That a fait accompli is being prepared, if you'll excuse the French. In other words, that the hope is that the cuts will be made in conformance with the LEGION, that they will then give us a B. rating and I will be so informed after the fact—And that I'll then be a good guy and let that be that. Well I may feel that way, and I may not. I want to put myself on record with you and Jack that I may be sore as hell about what the hell is done to please the LEGION and if I'm sore as hell nothing in this wide world will keep me silent. To quote an old Jewish proverb, if someone spits in my face, I will not say it's raining.

If you think I'm overboard, or if Jack does, I will listen and try to understand, because I like you all, but if I'm overboard you really have only your own silence to blame. The picture is very, very dear to me. I think it's the finest picture I've ever made, bar none. I put a hell of a lot into it—and I don't want it castrated. Let me know.

You know, Steve, I was raised a Catholic. I went to Catechism school for two years. I think Jack Vizzard is just the wrong person to have sent to New York. He was trained for the priesthood. The very fact that he was sent meant that you were all ready to do anything necessary to knuckle under to them. That they only had to name it. The Catholics are not as tough as they sound. Also to condemn FOREVER AMBER, a piece of out and out garbage, is one thing. But to condemn something that has received every prize worthy of the name, and a picture that every self-respecting, intelligent person in this land will want to see, is something else. The Catholics are like everyone else. They want to be respected and, like everyone else, they also despise no one as much as the person who licks their boots.

In closing let me say that I think it's an out and out shame that Mr. Ben Kalmenson is selling this picture. He has never to me personally said one enthusiastic word about it. How in the world can he sell it if all he feels about it is trepidation and anxiety? You and Jack know that the essence of this business is and always has been <u>enthusiasm</u>. Kalmenson just hasn't got it! Not for this picture!

Your friend, Gadg

[Kazan was finishing *Zapata* when he learned that Joseph Breen had sent Jack Vizzard, a former Jesuit seminarian, to New York to intercede with the Legion of Decency before the threat of condemnation became a public embarrassment to the PCA. Vizzard reported that lay reviewers had unanimously advised a "'C'" rating for *Streetcar*. Some who were incensed by the film's "morbid" preoccupation with sex recommended a "'D,'" to which he added, "Ouch!" The Legion's official notification of intent to condemn was Jack Warner's cue to authorize revision and send Dave Weisbart to New York. According to Vizzard, a censored print was ready for screening on July 20, shortly before Kazan called from California to interrogate his evasive cutter (Vizzard to Breen, July 5, 9, and 22, 1951, Herrick).

At the same time, Kazan urged Jack Warner to release condemned and censored versions of *Streetcar* in New York, the latter for "Catholics only." He added on a fully serious note that Catholics "are only some 20-odd percent of this country and I think that the first person or organization that treats them as a minority, with all the rights of a minority but none of the rights of a majority, will reap the rewards of righteousness" (July 20, 1951, Wesleyan). The Legion's condemnation of *Beyond the Forest* (1949) for openly treating abortion probably gave Jack Warner reason to think Kazan's defiance naive and "overboard." Theater cancellations had forced Warner and Breen to use Jack Vizzard to salvage a "B" rating (Walsh, pp. 242–44).

The present affair ended with an unsigned note accusing Kazan of having done "a bad thing to Dave—You made him lie to you!—You knew damn well why he went to New York. Jack said to Dave before he left—'Above all dont tell Kazan why you're going to New York!!'" (August 1, Wesleyan). Kazan later annotated the note: "Break the silence. They wanted me silent. I broke it."] *TLS, 2 pp., USC*

TO MARTIN J. QUIGLEY

Sandy Hook, Conn.
August 16, 1951

Dear Martin Quigley,

I am truly appreciative of the time and concern which you are giving to the—perhaps impossible—attempt to bring into harmony the conflicting codes of the Legion and of those of us who made <u>Streetcar</u>. And I am grateful for the real understanding and appreciation of the picture which you showed in our talk the other afternoon.

I enclose a list of the cuts made by Warner Brothers in order to secure a "B" rating by the Legion, together with my comments, but I anticipate that discussion and examination of the film itself with you will be more helpful than these notes.

It has taken me unexpectedly long to write this letter, for I am oppressed by the uncomfortable irony of the situation. Here am I, the director of this film, desperately asking you—who never saw it until a few weeks ago—to allow me to keep in scenes and material which I consider essential. There is something terribly humiliating about it from my side, and I imagine that you cannot be too comfortable about your stewardship or whatever. I cannot help feeling, beyond my own humiliation, that the extension of the power of the Legion of Decency into what amounts to censorship, is extremely dangerous—as is all power of one group of men over others. It seems to be leading in this instance to small scale mutilation of a few moments in a motion picture, but the practice, or principle, is much more seriously menacing. Do you or do you not agree?

I want now to state—in some cases to restate—my position, so that you will not have any false notion, even the slightest, about it.

Of course I want the film to remain just as I left it. You understand that, I am sure, from our conversation. I do not consider it objectionable, even in part, for an audience of adults or young people past their middle teens. On the contrary, I consider the picture treats difficult events with scrupulous taste and from a strong moral position. We both spoke the other day of the primacy of the moral order. I pointed out that Tennessee Williams has one morality, you another, and I a third. That is the right of each of us. That is what makes America. When you speak of the primacy of moral values, my only question is: WHOSE? And my only objection is to a situation in which, regardless of motive, the effect is the imposition of the values of one group of our population upon the rest of us. This limits one of our fundamental American rights: freedom of expression. This, to my way of thinking, is immoral.

Now I felt that you agreed with me that Streetcar is never—as many films passed by all parties are—sensational for the sake of sensationalism. It is never "sexy" for the sales value of the "sexy". Nor does it exploit sadism, with an eye to the box office, like so many films which have been passed.

I have stressed to Jack Warner, time and time again, the importance of keeping the exploitation and advertising on the level of the countrywide (indeed, worldwide) esteem in which this work of Mr. Williams is held.

To put my own position most plainly: If I were the owner as well as the director of this picture, I would much prefer accepting a "C" rating and losing the official Catholic audience. However, as you understand, I have no financial interest in the film. The financial threat is to Mr. Feldman and the Warner Brothers. Their investment is a large one and I can understand and sympathize with their present panic. I also appreciate the gamble they took in making an unroutine picture. I am, so to speak, acting now in sympathy with them, and am therefore willing to accept certain cuts in silence. However, in allowing the cuts to be made without consultation with me, the producers have done artistic damage to the picture. It is this which I hope that you and I may be able to repair thru careful consultation.

There are, for instance, several places where the cuts, from my point of view, make the film less moral instead of more so. There are other places where they have been so crudely made that there are gaping holes in the sequences and my work is shown in a very bad light. I will point instances as I go over the cuts. My objections on this score may seem "exaggerated", as you said the other day, but I can only answer that a man makes his own standards, and that I hope mine are stiff and will get stiffer. What may appear petty to you, in the exercise of your good offices towards the anxious Warner Brothers, may strike me as a kind of artistic mayhem. I cannot even imagine what Mr. Williams, Miss Leigh, Mr. Brando and Miss Hunter will feel.

I defend this picture so vehemently because I know that the intention of everyone concerned in its artistic making was completely pure. We tried, to the best of our ability, to tell the truth as we saw it.

I know of many films, and some I have made myself, which I would not rise to defend. But these cuts in Streetcar take on for me what you call "an exaggerated importance" because I am particularly proud of this film. I believe it is a most unusual and superior film. I have not thought that of most of my pictures. However, if you will look at Gentleman's Agreement, Boomerang, Pinky and A Tree Grows in Brooklyn, you will see clearly evidenced a moral attitude toward my medium and a sense of the responsibility of the films towards their audience and our nation.

I look forward to our meeting, and to showing you in the film itself the damage which I feel is being done, and of exploring with you possible ways of meeting the Legion's standards without violating the intentions and the integrity of those who made the picture. Once more, I am most grateful for the seriousness with which you approach this task and for the time which you are giving to it.

Sincerely yours,

[Martin J. Quigley published several Hollywood trade papers and worked behind the scenes as a Catholic layman to enforce the Production Code, which he and Daniel Lord, a Jesuit priest, drafted in 1929. Quigley found himself in the familiar position of reconciling the interests of a heavily invested studio to the moral standards of the Legion of Decency. "Stunned" by a first viewing of Streetcar, he declared it the "'toughest'" case ever encountered. Jack Vizzard met with Legion staff and devised a plan of revision approved by Quigley and submitted to Warner executives, who were reportedly open to change but "terribly anxious" lest they be accused of "'emasculating'" the well-known play (Vizzard to Breen, July 12 and 22, 1951, Herrick).

Kazan reluctantly accepted many of the dialogue cuts listed in the enclosure, although he resented the imputation of unsure direction caused by rough editing. He had the "most violent possible objection" to revising the "staircase scene," which is prompted by Stanley's famous call for his wife as the "poker night" sequence ends. Vizzard ruefully admitted that "we completely missed what this bastard Kazan was doing with Stella." Changing the "flavor" of the key scene would require elimination of Alex North's "carnal scoring" and substitution of "several long-shot angles to get away from the very sexy 'register' on the countenance of Stella" as she descends the stairs. "What we figure on creating here is the impression that this is more simply a devoted wife, who chooses her husband over her sister's protests, and goes back to him 'to cook his hamburgers, mend his socks, or whatever you will'" (Vizzard to Breen, July 12 and 22, 1951).

Quigley set aside claims of moral "primacy" when challenged by Kazan to defend Catholic stewardship of films in a democratic society: "'The American constitutional guarantees of freedom of expression are not a one-way street. I have the same right to say that moral considerations have a precedence over artistic considerations as you have to deny it'" (A Life, p. 435).] TL with enclosure, 6 pp., Wesleyan

Marlon Brando and Kim Hunter in the
staircase scene

TO ALEX NORTH

Box 25, Sandy Hook [Connecticut]
[c. September 1951]

Dear Alex

Warner Brothers are Warner Brothers. Can I say less!!???? They should be allowed to swim in their own shit and choke to death in it. You should never do pictures you despise—that's the long and the short of it. Anytime you want to borrow a few somethings so you can wait a few weeks or months till something good comes along, I'll loan (while I've got.) DONT TAKE YOURSELF TOO CHEAPLY. You are in the first rank of composers for films now, and everybody good will want you to do their pictures. Everybody crumby will too—but you shouldn't ever. I'm kind of glad the thing at Warners happened. Dont think cheaply of yourself. I know you were broke. But you DID have my picture and SALESMAN in the offing. (P.S. I hate Warner Brothers. I hope they drop dead—even more than I hope they go out of business.) (P.P.S. your wife wrote an excellent letter.) Who, though, were the men who came in and consulted with Sperling, President of United States Pictures, no less?)

How you coming on Z. Do you want to consult? Do you think I should come out? I want to very much if it will help the picture. If not, not. Would it help if I made a list, or a description, etc. You know what I mean. Be glad to if it would help. Write me. Box 25 Sandy Hook.

Love to Sherle & Charlie—Gadg

[After a recording session in Burbank, Milton Sperling was taken aside by unnamed advisers and forced to reconsider his enthusiasm for Alex North's composition. His face an "eerie shade of Nile green," Sperling informed North that his "corny" adventure film (*Distant Drums*) did not merit such "great" music and requested a "conventional score." North declined and left the Warner Bros. studio "relieved, happy, head held high." Sherle North's account of crass, craven producers found a willing reader in Kazan, who was seething over the censorship of *Streetcar* and preparing his own exposé of the hated Brothers.

Alex North worked with Kazan on *People of the Cumberland* (1937), a documentary filmed in the Tennessee mining country. He went on to write incidental music for stage and screen versions of *Death of a Salesman* and receive an Academy nomination for *Viva Zapata!* Kazan's imminent HUAC testimony cooled the friendship.] *TLS, 1 p., Herrick*

TO CHERYL CRAWFORD

PM: New Milford, Conn., September 4, 1951

Cheryl dear

You looked wonderful the other day. So healthy and happy and industrious for chrissake. A pleasure. Speaking of industry I feel just the opposite. I admired DESIRE very much. He was a great man, O'Neill. But with what a sense of sin and guilt! And what an awe, or FEAR of women! It would be wonderful to have it revived, so everyone could see who really started our American Theatre. But right now I dont want to do it. I feel too much IN the world. I'm too concerned about a lot of issues, and the chaos all around us. And I'd like to do something that relates to it. Or speaks of it—if only in a whisper about a remote corner. DESIRE is a piece of eternal dramatic poetry, and sometime in my life—maybe in a few months, or who knows when I'll feel like it. But I want to be engaged now. I hope it happens.

Love—Gadg.

[Cheryl Crawford was so impressed by experimental "scenes" at the Actors Studio that she proposed a revival of *Desire Under the Elms*. Brooks Atkinson may have provided additional stimulus by rebuking "an improvident theatre" for long neglect of "the finest dramatic literature we have" (*NYT*, August 19, 1951). Major revivals of *Anna Christie* and *Desire Under the Elms* were announced later in the year and produced by ANTA in 1952. The press reported that Kazan was Eugene O'Neill's choice to direct *Anna Christie,* but Harold Clurman eventually claimed the role.

The "issues" of concern to Kazan in late 1951 were varied and far reaching but commanded by the growing political power of the right and the "fates" of friends called to give testimony before the House Committee on Un-American Activities. He was all but certain that the relative safety of preparing to stage *Camino Real* in New York would be interrupted by a summons to testify (*A Life,* pp. 442–43).]
TLS, 1 p., BRTC

TO MARTIN J. QUIGLEY

1697 Broadway
September 19, 1951

Dear Martin:
One thing that still keeps disturbing me. Perhaps you can help me if you care to—perhaps you can't. I would appreciate it if you would, but you may have reasons why you might prefer not to say anything, which reasons I will respect.

You know Dave Weisbart was my cutter on STREETCAR, and also a very close friend of mine, a very valued and trusted friend as well. Warner put him in a peculiar position when he sent Dave to New York and made him promise that he wouldn't tell me what he had come to New York for, but it came to pass that I got wind of his being in New York, called him on the phone and asked him why he was in New York. Dave could not tell me the truth; in fact, he told me an untruth and I have never felt the same towards him since.

I like Dave very much and hate to feel this way about him. He told me that Father Masterson had sat in the projection room with him and had gone over many of the cuts piece by piece, bit by bit. He made it clear to me that Masterson's contacts with him were detailed and at length. Of course, this does not jibe with what you told me and I felt that Dave was not telling me the truth about this either.

I don't know what to think about this. Would you care to say anything about it? Dave didn't mention you. Only mentioned working with Masterson. Your account was that you worked with him. Perhaps it is all unimportant, except for the fact that Dave was a really good friend to me, a very fine craftsman and associate. I hate to lose either.

Martin, thank you again for your time and patience.

Sincerely,

[Confirmation that Father Patrick J. Masterson, executive secretary of the Legion of Decency, was directly involved in censoring *Streetcar* would have strengthened Kazan's forthcoming article in the *New York Times*. Martin Quigley appears to have dodged Kazan's artful request. Kazan was left to wonder along with the author and the public "how the end result differed from direct censorship by the Legion." He did not spare the anxious producers, who had urged silence while bowing to a parochial organization that represented neither the film industry nor the "great majority" of the audience. Kazan directed a final barb at the Legion's fear of publicizing objectionable films: "Meanwhile the box office is breaking records" (October 21, 1951). He speculated at the time and continued to believe that the Catholic Church, in the influential person of Cardinal Spellman, conspired with conservative politicians in his later travails (*A Life*, pp. 442–43).

Lacking some four minutes of cuts and trims, *Streetcar* received a "B" rating from the Legion, won superb notices, and claimed the New York Film Critics Award as best picture of the year. The Legion vowed to reclassify the film if the uncut version were shown in any setting, including the Venice Film Festival. Geoffrey Shurlock, Joe Breen's assistant and eventual successor, later observed that "Streetcar broke the barrier." A print was released in 1993 with the missing footage.] *TL, 1 p., Wesleyan*

TO DARRYL F. ZANUCK

[New York]
January 29, 1952

Dear Darryl:

It has occurred to me that the very best answer you could give to any one who has doubts or questions about the politics of our picture is to point to the figure of Fernando Aguirre. This personage was put in there as an embodiment of our feeling about the Communists, and two points are made. They are destructive of the very point of Communism. First, it is emphasized repeatedly that the man's chief drive is towards power. In the interests of power, he turns against his best friend and sponsor, Francisco Madero. Secondly, at a point where he sees that there is no advancement for him with Zapata, he not only leaves Zapata, but joins the palace group, who are plotting Zapata's death. The only recognizable figure at the death of Zapata is the Communist, Fernando Aguirre.

If this character is not completely destructive of the Communist as he operates in politics and in society, I don't know what is. Please remember, dear Darryl, that we put this man in with an eye towards possible attacks in the future. This picture is not only pro-democratic, but it is specifically, strongly and uncontrovertibly anti-Communist.

Just one more point. Our hero at the climax of his political career does something that no Communist would ever do. In this act, there is the whole meaning of his character and his life. I am referring to the moment when he picks up his hat and walks out of the palace, and thus walks away from power. No Communist has ever done it, nor ever will.

Love,

[Kazan's testimony before the House Committee on Un-American Activities on January 14 raised questions about the director's liability as well as the "politics" of *Viva Zapata!* The admission of a brief Communist Party membership in the 1930s came as no surprise to Fox executives, but it formed a centerpiece in resumed hearings and set the stage, as it were, for Kazan's decisive reappearance in April. The exchange of letters with Darryl Zanuck is probably related to a complaint by the Catholic War Veterans regarding "three players" in *Zapata* deemed subversive and a hero who has since been "glorified" by Mexican communists. Zanuck denied the request for a special preview, claiming that "Communists will hate our picture because it makes a strong plea for the principles of Democracy" (to Coughlin, January 24, 1952, Wesleyan). The fictional Aguirre probably did little to reassure Zanuck and was apparently lost on Spyros Skouras, who drafted a letter of "apology" in Kazan's name, including an offer to resign should the testimony cause "difficulties" in releasing *Zapata*. Kazan refused (*A Life*, p. 451).

Fernando Aguirre comes unbidden to Zapata's remote camp in the mountains as an emissary of Francisco Madero, a reformer currently in exile in the United States. He appears and disappears in early drafts of the screenplay and does not fully emerge as Zapata's influential adviser until the December 1950 text. "Stern and military" in bearing, Aguirre flourishes a small typewriter, which sets him apart from the peasant revolution, and claims to be "a friend to no one—to nothing except logic!" He decries Zapata's shunning of power after the occupation of Mexico City and joins the Federal directorate in plotting his former leader's assassination.] *TL, 1 p., Wesleyan*

TO DARRYL F. ZANUCK

[New York]
[February 1952]

dear darryl:

For the last few months we've been thinking of an idea for a comedy. It is an outgrowth of an experience that John had during the second world war. It seems to us the basis of a very funny moving picture. Naturally we've been wondering whether you'd be interested in it.

A small town boy—Jimmy Stewart type, of Ukrainian or Polish or Check descent has conceived an active dislike for the forces behind the iron curtain, which have destroyed his Mother's family. He is in love with a snobbish blonde whose eminence lies in the fact that her family has been in America two generations instead of one. The boy, suing for her hand, takes her to lunch. He tries to pay for the lunch with a ten dollar bill. The bill is a counterfeit.

Thru a series of steps that we wont go into he gets the idea of using counterfeit money as a weapon of war. It is his conviction that money dropped in great quantities from the air would set off a chain reaction in people more horrible than the atomic bomb. (This we happen to believe also).

Profoundly stirred by his conviction, he goes to Washington on his own to try to sell his idea to the powers that be. We have then a series [of] scenes dealing with the difficulty of getting to see anyone particularly if you have an idea. He meets and is instructed by the various percent boys who conduct business in the capital and eventually is able to put his weapon in the hands of proper authorities.

Their reactions are various. Some think it will work, some [*omission*] At any rate we get to a point where the idea is tried out. The experiment is conducted on the boy's own home town. The town is isolated and warned that counterfeit money is going to be dropped as an experiment and that the counterfeit money is so close that it will be almost impossible to detect it. People are warned not to pick it up or try to spend it. Then, on a day, the money is dropped by plane and we leave the results to your fruitful imagination. Chaos!

The insane scheme seems to be a success. The boy finds himself a great hero. He is suddenly even acceptable to the snooty blonde (love story incidental but present). The weapon is prepared for dropping on a test area behind the iron curtain. Ten ruble notes cleverly contrived and well aged together with messages of hope from the outside. A double edged weapon. These are to be released by the million via balloon from western Europe.

We dont go to Europe or behind the iron curtain, but from the embassies in Washington it is apparent that all hell has broken loose behind the iron curtain. Suddenly however the realization begins to creep over the official people that humans are more fissionable than plutonium. In other words we would be as much in danger from this weapon as anyone else. The scheme is quickly abandoned. And now the Jimmy Stewart character is no longer a hero. He goes back home.

This is the barest outline / The boy goes home / There are several wonderful comic characters.

John took this idea to Roosevelt during the war. F.D.R. loved it and sent it to Morgenthau. Morgenthau was so scared he blurted out: "I put counterfeiters in jail". Mr. Roosevelt's reaction was: "For the cost of one destroyer we could make enough of this weapon to immobilize a community economically for years." That's enough to give you an idea. What do you think?

LOVE

[John Steinbeck supported New Deal policies and advised the Roosevelt White House from time to time during the prewar years. A quite serious recommendation called for a propaganda office to counter Nazi influence in the Americas. A more eccentric plan targeted the German home front with a stratagem that either amused or intrigued President Roosevelt and drew an invitation to visit the White House in 1940. Joined by Melvyn Knisely, an anatomy professor from the University of Chicago who originated the idea, Steinbeck and friend set before the president a disarmingly simple plan to disrupt the German economy by scattering counterfeit paper money over the countryside. Steinbeck informed Archibald MacLeish that FDR "liked" the "deadly little plan" but "the money men didn't" (Steinbeck/*Letters,* pp. 197–98). Henry Morgenthau, Jr., was FDR's secretary of the treasury. Darryl Zanuck thought the updated film proposal "original and amusing" but vetoed it as "a 'one joke' idea" not likely to succeed.] *TL, 3 pp., Pierpont Morgan*

TO THE EDITOR, *SATURDAY REVIEW*

New York, N.Y.
April 5, 1952

Sir:

There has been an eloquent criticism of "Viva Zapata" in *The Saturday Review* by Hollis Alpert and also an eloquent defense by Laura Z. Hobson. That is as much discussion as any motion picture deserves and I do not want to add to it. However, your readers may be interested to hear how the political tensions of the present bore down on us—John Steinbeck and Darryl Zanuck and me— as we thought about and shaped a historical picture. These pressures, though nervewracking, forced us to clear our own perspectives and in this sense were useful. They also brought to me a realization of the relationship between abstract politics and personal character which I had not formulated before.

It is human character, above all, which concerns a director, writer, producer, and it was the character of Zapata which intrigued us all. He was not a man of words and what he was had to be read in what he did. Part of our interest in the beginning lay in a certain mystery about what kind of man he really was.

It was not the first and simpler part of his story which suggested an almost unique man. He had risen from nothing, illiterate, uneloquent, to overthrow the forty-year dictatorship of the "Permanent President" Diaz. He had challenged a disorganized 1910-version of the police state. He had formed and led an army. He led it with bravery, tenacity, and an astounding, untutored military skill.

Yet there were other leaders, some also brave and tenacious and effective in battle. What fascinated us about Zapata was one nakedly dramatic act. In the moment of victory, he turned his back on power. In that moment, in the capital with his ragged troops, Zapata could have made himself president, dictator, caudillo. Instead, abruptly and without explanation, he rode back to his village. There he saw to it that the people got back their farms, which had been taken from them, and there, as he must have known would happen, he was hunted down by men who had no scruple about taking power, or using it to stamp out opposition.

We felt this act of renunciation was the high point of our story and the key to Zapata himself. If we could not explain it, we did not know our man. Yet no written account gave an acceptable explanation.

We went to Morelos, Steinbeck and I, and saw the dry austere grandeur of the mountains, the poverty of the fields, the poverty and pride and almost Biblical dignity of the people. And here we walked into an attack from—call it left field.

We knew that the Communists in Mexico try to capitalize on the people's reverence for Zapata by working his figure into their propaganda—much as Communists here quote Lincoln to their purpose. We had ignored this and gone about our business, for we knew that Communists anywhere and always will try to appropriate anything to which people give allegiance—peace, prosperity, land reform, brotherhood, democracy, equality, liberty, nationalism, internationalism, free speech, or whatever. We can hardly give over these things to their claim.

So it was that, with our minds on the picture business and not on politics, we approached two men who are prominent in the Mexican film industry. We had some idea that we might want them to work with us and in any case, humbly, as foreigners writing about their national hero, we asked their opinion of our preliminary script.

They came back with an attack that left us reeling. The script was impossible! We listened. We discovered they were attacking us for including things which we knew to be historically true: that Zapata had a measure of Spanish blood and was proud of it, the very proper Spanish-Colonial style of his courtship and marriage, his vanity in the matter of dress and uniform, his abandoning of the white cotton peon costume when he could afford to, his indecision about taking up arms. But above all, they attacked with sarcastic fury our emphasis on his refusal to take power.

We digested all this on the terrace of the Hotel Marik in Cuernavaca. Four feet away, on the other side of a low wall, the Indians went by in the street. Over the houses the mountains loomed and the air was soft. John said, "I smell the Party line."

I smelled it too. Nearly two years later our guess was confirmed by a rabid attack on the picture in *The Daily Worker,* which parallels everything the two Mexicans argued, and which all but implies that John invented Zapata's renunciation of power.

No Communist, no totalitarian, ever refused power. By showing that Zapata did this, we spoiled a poster figure that the Communists have been at some pains to create. As we figured this out, we saw our man more clearly, and were readier for the attack from the opposite political pole.

It had to come. Whenever the Communists stake a claim to any concept or person that people value, the over-anxious Right plays into their hands with exasperating regularity. If they would treat the Communist claim to peace, to free speech—and to men like Zapata—with the same good sense and laughter that greets the Communist claim to the invention of the bicycle, it would make life easier for those of us who really value those things.

In any case, we were told by an organization long on vigilance but short on history that Zapata was a rebel, so he must have been a Communist. There was, of course, no such thing as a Communist Party at the time and place where Zapata fought. (*The Daily Worker* regrets it.) But there is such a thing as a Communist mentality. We created a figure of this complexion in Fernando, whom the audience indentify as "the man with the typewriter." He typifies the men who use the just grievances of the people for their own ends, who shift and twist their course, betray any friend or principle or promise to get power and keep it.

Thinking thus—not of politics but of human behavior—we saw Zapata clearly. In his moment of decision, this taciturn, untaught leader must have felt, freshly and deeply, the impact of the ancient law: power corrupts. And so he refused power.

The man who refused power was not only no Communist, he was that opposite phenomenon: a man of individual conscience.

For confirmation, we had seen the people whom he led. No weakling, no trickster, no totalitarian, leaves behind him a strong people, but the men of Morelos are respected today as the proudest and most independent in all Mexico. Their bearing is proof of the kind of man who led them out of bondage and did not betray them. I think it is also witness to the relationship of two things not usually coupled: politics and human dignity.

Elia Kazan

[Kazan timed the present letter to coincide with his appearance before the House committee on April 10: "I wrote it deliberately to put myself on record against the Communists" (Spencer Memorial Lecture, Harvard, May 14, 1952). He also sent a copy to the committee staff and cited the letter in amended testimony.

Viva Zapata! "misfired" for Hollis Alpert in spite of a "line-up of high-powered talent" and "explosive historical material." At fault were Kazan's "cliches of action" and Steinbeck's "bombastic and wooden script." Laura Hobson, author of *Gentleman's Agreement,* was "dumbfounded" by the review and queried Steinbeck, if only to relieve self-doubt. Critics, he answered, often mask disagreement with "ideas" by "attacks on the grounds of grammar or technique" (*Saturday Review,* February 9 and March 1, 1952).

The journalist Carleton Beals claimed firsthand knowledge of the revolution and dismissed the "absurd" notion that Zapata renounced power after entering Mexico City in 1914. A dangerously exposed military position explained the retreat. Rather than passively betray the revolution, Zapata continued to fight a defensive action until his assassination five years later. In reply Kazan claimed anecdotal sources for Zapata's "nakedly dramatic act" and added that he and Steinbeck had "found enormous variance" in nearly every account of their hero's public and private life (*Saturday Review,* May 24, 1952).

Beals also derided the "papier-mâché" Fernando Aguirre—played by Joseph Wiseman, a native Canadian—as "utterly devoid of Mexican savor" and "unwarranted even by box-office considerations." Aguirre proved awkward as cinema and of little political interest to reviewers, who described him as a "fanatic" or "professional" revolutionary without assigning a specific ideological role. Predictably the *Daily Worker* critic found an anticommunist subtext in Aguirre, but he was easily dismissed as a "typical movie phony" representing "nothing but another anchor to windward for Darryl Zanuck in dealing with the 'current and disquieting' subject of revolution" (March 16, 1952).

Viva Zapata! was released in the United States without difficulty but banned in Mexico, presumably because its hero had been elevated at the expense of President Francisco Madero. When Twentieth Century-Fox cut the offending material, the National Cinematographic Board relented and the film went into distribution. *Variety* accurately predicted "spotty" box office performance and limited popular appeal in the United States.] Saturday Review, *April 5, 1952, pp. 22–23*

TO HOUSE COMMITTEE ON UN-AMERICAN ACTIVITIES

New York City, N.Y.
April 9, 1952

Gentlemen:

I wish to amend the testimony which I have before you on January 14 of this year, by adding to it this letter and the accompanying sworn affidavit.

In the affidavit I answer the only question which I failed to answer at the hearing, namely, what people I knew to be members of the Communist Party between the summer of 1934, when I joined it, and the late winter or early spring of 1936, when I severed all connection with it.

I have come to the conclusion that I did wrong to withhold these names before, because secrecy serves the Communists, and is exactly what they want. The American people need the facts and all the facts about all aspects of communism in order to deal with it wisely and effectively. It is my obligation as a citizen to tell everything that I know.

Although I answered all other questions which were put to me before, the naming of these people makes it possible for me to volunteer a detailed description of my own activities and of the general activity which I witnessed. I have attempted to set these down as carefully and fully as my memory allows.

In doing so, I have necessarily repeated portions of my former testimony, but I believe that by so doing I have made a more complete picture than if I omitted it.

In the second section of the affidavit, I have tried to review comprehensively my very slight political activity in the 16 years since I left the party. Here again, I have of necessity repeated former testimony, but I wanted to make as complete an over-all picture as my fallible memory allows.

In the third section is a list of the motion pictures I have made and the plays I have chosen to direct. I call your attention to these for they constitute the entire history of my professional activity as a director.

Respectfully, Elia Kazan

[Kazan amended his executive committee testimony by naming several well-known party officials and eight former communist members of the Group Theatre. Morris Carnovsky, one of the number, had invoked the Fifth Amendment and censured his inquisitors for "unwarranted prying into the most secret and sacred areas of a man's thought" (April 1951). Clifford Odets testified later as a "friendly" witness. He confirmed Kazan's testimony, which he authorized in advance, by revealing his own party membership and naming former communist members of the Group Theatre, but suffered prodigious lapses of memory regarding past and present support of alleged front organizations (May 1952)—to the dismay and disbelief of the committee.

Kazan "emphatically" restated his initial testimony "that the Communists' attempt to take over the Group Theatre failed," as did their plan to influence Actors' Equity, a second initiative on the cultural front to which he was assigned. Still more critically, he reiterated that "no clear opposition of national interests between the United States and Russia" was known to him as a member of the Communist Party. The affidavit ends with a list of works directed to date, each annotated to meet charges of anti-American content or treatment. Kazan softened the critical tenor of *Boomerang* and *Gentleman's Agreement* by claiming that each film "shows the exact opposite of the Communist libels on America." *All My Sons* was not so easily defended in 1952 as an indictment of wartime capitalism. Kazan adroitly described the play as "a deeply moral investigation of problems of conscience and responsibility."

"Conscience and responsibility" were key terms in a brief apologia drafted by Molly Kazan in Elia's name and published in the *New York Times* to coincide with the release of the amended testimony. Only disclosure of the "facts" regarding communism can protect Americans "from a dangerous and alien conspiracy and still keep the free, open, healthy way of life that gives us self-respect." Liberals especially "must speak out," lest they be duped by a false regard for communists or suffer reprisals from those on the right who would silence their voices. Kazan's departure from the party was attributed to "a taste of the police state" that proved "bitter and unforgettable" (April 12, 1952).] *TLS, 1 p., Government Printing Office*

167 East 74th. st., New York
[c. spring 1952]

Dear Mr. Hook:

I'm writing to tell you how much your pamphlet HERESY, YES — CONSPIRACY, NO! meant to me. The very fact that there are liberals and leftists who are actively anti-communist makes some sense out of the chaos for me. (You may well ask: Where the hell have you been all this time? My answer wouldn't be satisfactory) I read your little booklet twice during some very bewildering days. It helped more than I can say. I was particularly struck with this sentence: "If the conspiratorial purposes of Communist Party teachers is glossed over by ritualistic liberals as a heresy, then all heresy comes under fire." The phrase "ritualistic liberal" was illuminating. I didn't realize until I began looking around me with this phrase in mind how hide-bound and bigoted and self-blindfolded are a great mass of New York's intellectual set. Now some of them are waking up, painfully. I appreciate their difficulty. I'm most grateful to you for helping the general process along.

Sincerely, Elia Kazan

[In *Heresy, Yes, Conspiracy, No!* (1952/1953), Sidney Hook issued a warning to liberals who were unable or unwilling to distinguish between communism as heretical idea and as a conspiracy borne in secrecy, advanced by stealth, and intent on destroying free society. His political thought was shaped by pragmatist principles—Hook studied under John Dewey at Columbia University—and informed by a youthful attraction to Marxism, which evolved into a strong anti-communist stance in the early 1940s. Long associated with New York University, Hook wrote as a professional philosopher and public intellectual, often at odds with the "'ritualistic'" liberals he encountered in academia. He was a founding member of the American Committee for Cultural Freedom, publisher of the "booklet" read by Kazan in the "bewildering" spring of 1952. The committee charter spoke of advancing "the democratic way of life in all spheres of culture" (Hook, p. 421). Kazan and Steinbeck later wrote to potential contributors in support of the organization.] *TLS, 1 p., Hoover*

Sandy Hook, Conn.
April 21, 1952

Dear Bob:

Your letter meant so much to me that I found it a little hard to answer. What can I say? You have it exactly. It was difficult and painful. No one likes to "tell". And to say that something is difficult and mean it is to face the fact that it can never come out 100% comfortable. It didn't.

I believe what I did was necessary and right. The silence of so many of the House Committee's witnesses had disgusted me. I thought what the nation needed was a sense of proportion about the problem and, for this, cold facts. Yet the first time I was called down, though I answered every question about myself and my own activities, I refused to name any other individuals. It was as if 12th. st. had kept hold of a little piece of my conscience all these years. The Communists had done violence to everything I believed in, and still somehow I stayed silent and shrugged it off and minimized and looked the other way.

Enough of that! I've been trying during these last weeks to let the air in and the light and to take a good fresh look at what's in my damned head. Painful as its been, I'm really glad it all happened.

Most gratefully yours, Gadg.

[Robert Sherwood's prewar plays—*Idiot's Delight, Abe Lincoln in Illinois, There Shall Be No Night*—blended art, commerce, and politics with uncommon distinction. Each won a Pulitzer Prize, as did *Roosevelt and Hopkins* (1948), Sherwood's massive history of an era known intimately to FDR's friend, adviser, and occasional speechwriter. Sherwood found his future collaborator's "Statement" in the *Times* "remarkably well reasoned, dignified and important." Although he never considered joining the Communist Party, he had been restrained "too often" by the "same specious reasoning" that silenced many liberals (to EK, April 15, 1952, Harvard).

The Workers School at 35 East 12th Street was New York City headquarters for V. J. Jerome, chairman of the Communist Party's Cultural Commission. He directed the Group Theatre "unit" in the 1930s and personified for Elia and Molly Kazan the dogmatism of party politics.] *TLS, 1 p., Harvard*

TO DARRYL F. ZANUCK

[New York]
May 18, 1952

Dear Darryl:

Before I get together with Bob, I want you to know what I'll be pressing for with him, and I want your o.k. to go ahead along my lines.

As I said in my previous letter, I think the love stories have now been enlarged, in Bob's outline, out of proportion. Its now a little as if the escape story had been made into a frame for the love stories. I think that the intention should be in the opposite direction. The escape story is the one that needs building up. It should always be kept central, and especially in its last half, it should be greatly enlarged. The love stories, while being improved, should be made to contribute to the escape story. The proportion of the thing was right, in other words, thru the first half of the original novelette. Bob it seems to me has started off in the wrong direction, and I think we should turn him around. . . .

I dont like at all starting with a circus performance. There has been so damned much of this; it is the most conventional possible way of starting a circus story. I liked the way the original started—right on the chase. The two men arrive in a town. We feel reticence and fear and silence from the people in the square. The two secret police do not wear leather coats. They do not walk in unison. The essence of the Russian tyranny is that they pretend to be humans. They are a "People's Government." . . .

Then the two men come to the circus. The circus is seen at rest. Some of the freaks are asleep. The elephants are being washed. Some one is practising a little: perhaps a knife thrower (a plant). There is cooking and eating among the freaks, who look more freakish than ever revealed in the sunlight, and deshabbile. A third rate little European circus is at rest. The secret police walk thru it, and they find Barova. Here, as in the novelette, we quickly sketch Zama's character and their rather simple if highly emotional relationship. Then off go the secret police with their victim. We haven't told too much. What we have shown has original character. We have shown behind the Iron Curtain and behind the big top. Its not the old stuff about shadows on a circus tent and the performance going on over intrigue behind the scenes. . . .

As for the circus, I think we should stay away from the front of it as much as possible. We should shoot everything from backstage. From backstage we should get glimpses of what is happening in front of the audience, but not much more. The foreground action for the Camera should be the back stage action of the circus. . . .

To jump to the end, I did not like the finish with Zama dying heroically. I thought this not the point. I think we must end on something that dramatises the arrival of the circus into freedom. I do not like centering on any personal story at the end. And I dont care that much for the love story between Barova and Zama. Its not that good a story inherently. For instance I do not go at all for the "iron curtain between us" material. This is so much malarkey! Their situation would be the same in America or wherever! The Russians and the Commies are always blaming the "system" for everything. Why should we go in for the same foolishness? Zama is just a hungry young woman, a little on the thrill-crazy side. She finds a lack of vigor in her husband, and a lack of courage. He does not conform to her standards of sex appeal, which have something to do with the promise of violence. That is her problem. I dont think the story should be talked to death, or labelled, even. It should be shown. Its not an important love story (whatever that means). It can be interesting and it certainly can be "sexy". But why make her a heroic character at the end dying in a heroic attitude in a piece of living statuary with an elephant?

I think an ending must be found which dramatises the arrival of the circus into the Free World—and what this means! I'm repeating but it is important. The ending should concern our main story which is not a love story and not a personal story, but the story of an escape of a group of individualists.

I was disappointed in Bob's outline when I read it two weeks ago. Then I thought: well I'll wait and see what he does when he sits down to write. . . . But the more I worked with the outline and with the conference notes, the less I liked the set-up of the story and the more fundamental I thought the trouble. Just beginning, but still! And these days in our business are too tough for anybody to kid anybody else. I know it would be wrong for me to take one step with Bob in a direction you might not like, without clearing it first with you. In fact, without your whole hearted support.

This is a story above all others, that should not be conventionalized. We're dealing with something red hot, something that will be seen and judged by the rest of the civilized world, and judged by very serious standards because it deals, in miniature, with the central issue of our day. It must have about it the stamp of complete truth. That is why I was so disappointed that it couldn't be shot in Europe. I realize now that this is probably necessary, but I think that the picture has lost something important, and I think that this puts a much greater burden on the fellows doing the job. Bob and I should go and see some of these little circuses, and then go to some place like Munich and talk to some of the people in the International Rescue Committee office who have just come thru the Iron Curtain. We should really get down and dig like we were young fellows again, making our first major picture. You know what I mean. This is a major picture. It should not and cannot be reduced to conventional "effective" movie terms. Showmanship in this case has to be found anew in the truth of the situations—I mean the actual living situation. "Color" must not be made up of the memory (unconscious or otherwise) of other circus pictures.

I still haven't sent Bob the letter I wrote him. I dont think I will. You can show him this, if you like. Its tough, but so is Bob, and he knows how much I admire him.

At any rate, I wont move now until I hear from you, so cable.

Affectionately,

[Darryl Zanuck urged Kazan to direct *Man on a Tightrope*, if only to disarm critics who questioned the sincerity of his congressional testimony. The editors of *Counterattack,* an anticommunist newsletter widely distributed in Hollywood, speculated that Kazan's "friendly" testimony had been motivated by money and career and wondered why no later confirming action or statement was forthcoming. Collaboration with Robert Sherwood, an award-winning screenwriter (*The Best Years of Our Lives*) with a strong anticommunist bias, was intended to enhance the project artistically and discourage political attacks. Neil Paterson's account of an escape by the Brumbach Circus from East Germany provided the basic plot and a sharp indictment of Cold War communism. Paterson shifted the escape to Czechoslovakia and renamed the circus after the beleaguered manager Jan Cernik (*Man on the Tightrope,* 1952). Casting Adolphe Menjou as a communist official was one of Kazan's "private jokes." His congressional testimony in 1947 earned the enmity of the left and became a benchmark of militant Americanism. Kazan balanced Menjou's turnabout by casting Fredric March, a liberal often accused of sympathy with subversive causes, as a victim of communist state control.

Many of Kazan's suggested revisions prevailed. The film establishes the repressive nature of communism with an opening convoy of downtrodden political prisoners. Secret police are seen next coldly observing a performance of Cernik (formerly Barova) as clown. Zama's alienation from her husband, one of the digressive love stories, was stripped of any "iron curtain" analogy, but a political rationale leads to reconciliation, as Cernik finds the courage to flee the police state. His role as a shrewd tactician who refuses a prominent place in the finale reprised the leadership theme of *Zapata* and prepared for his death, rather than Zama's, while disarming a spy who threatens the escape. *Man on a Tightrope* ends with a balancing long shot of the Cirkus Cernik in parade after a harrowing pass through the frontier into free Austria.

Sherwood and Kazan did in fact "dig" together for cultural background, and the film was shot on location in Europe and released in 1953.] *TL, 3 pp., Wesleyan*

TO BUDD SCHULBERG

[New York]
[spring 1952]

Dear Budd:
Thought I wrote you. Guess I misaddressed it. Or maybe I decided at the last minute not to send the letter since my plans were so liquid that I couldn't say

when I'd be in New York. Anyway I did get your letter and I got your recent one too. It was a fine letter, and I was grateful for it. The part about the friends is true: I mean you cant please them all, as I found out, and I guess, as you suggest, it isn't the real point. I believe I did the right thing, and I would do it again, only quicker. Strangely, one thing I learned is that what you plan to do in a detached mood, is not what you finally do when you really face a situation, and especially when you are forced to take a stand, officially and for keeps. For keeps, I have no tolerance of the Communists in this country, and right from the knuckles, I think its wrong as hell to contribute to their conspiracy, or secrecy. I took the stand of not naming anyone, and I was in contempt, technically, for a couple of months, and I didn't feel good about it at all. The reason I didn't tell you in January that I had received a subpoena is that they had said to me: "You dont tell anyone, we wont tell anyone." So I didn't. Of course their side leaked like hell. Well, that was a little of a shock. But even that piece of political intrigue, for so it turned out to be, was not the point. The point was that events were slowly forcing me to take a position by which I would be measured. So I did. The Commies of course are screaming "Informer", as I figured they would, and some of my friends have not communicated with me, showing their disapproval that way. O.K. It really isn't the point. I knew it wasn't a situation out of which you could emerge one hundred percent intact and comfortable. It was really a difficult situation, and exactly that.

I've been a little depressed now and then, but everytime I go over things, I feel I did right, so there is nothing to do but go on and do my work.

I was very glad that you have something you are excited about. Let's talk. I'll be at 167 East 74 this coming Wednesday and Thursday night. Either is o.k. Let me know which. Come to supper. Or after. Or before, during the day. You name it.

Yrs., Gadg

[At Molly's suggestion, the Kazans visited Budd and Vicki Schulberg in January, shortly after Elia was subpoenaed, and nearly a year after Schulberg revealed his own communist affiliation in the late 1930s and named those with whom he met or conferred. Richard Collins, the screenwriter who named Schulberg and forced his congressional testimony, had also hastened Schulberg's defection by attempting to direct the writing of *What Makes Sammy Run?* (1941) along party lines.

A committee member "leaked" Kazan's confidential testimony to the *Hollywood Reporter* before the Academy Awards ceremony in March: "'Elia Kazan, subpoenaed for the Un-American Activities session, confirmed Commie membership but refused to supply any new evidence on his old pals from the Group Theatre days, among them, John Garfield'" (qtd. in Neve, pp. 64–65). *Streetcar* was heavily favored to win the Oscar but *An American in Paris* prevailed instead. The evening was "a hideous ordeal," as Tennessee Williams recalled: "Gadg and Marlon and I were obviously screwed out of the Academy awards," presumably because of Kazan's "situation" (to Crawford, April 5, 1952, BRTC).

Kazan reacted variously to harsh criticism and silent snubs, from the left and right, from colleagues in theater and film, after testifying in April. Harold Clurman and Arthur Miller were among the silent, while the communist press screamed " 'Informer' ": "Others have betrayed their country when the fascist whip cracked. It remained for Kazan to run a paid advertisement in the press announcing his loss of manhood. Not even in Hitler days did renegade intellectuals sink so low" (*Daily Worker*, April 17, 1952).

A project based on a racial story seemed less exciting to Kazan and Schulberg than the troubled ports of New York and New Jersey. Kazan's plan to film "The Hook" in collaboration with Arthur Miller ended in early 1951, when Miller withdrew the screenplay from studio consideration and shelved it. At the same time Budd Schulberg was completing a final draft of "Crime on the Waterfront" (April 14, 1951, Wesleyan), a screenplay written in association with Monticello Films, an independent producer, and based on Malcolm Johnson's influential series of articles published in *The Sun* (1948). Later in 1951 Schulberg reportedly acquired production rights to the Johnson property, but the screenplay was also shelved after drawing familiar charges of anti-unionism and communist influence. Precisely when Kazan learned of its existence or joined Schulberg in collaboration is unclear, but by the summer of 1952 they were exchanging letters about script, casting, and production. The son of a major studio production head, Budd Schulberg had few illusions about the difficulty the project would entail.] *TLS, 1 p., Dartmouth*

TO CHERYL CRAWFORD

[New York]
[late May 1952]

Darling—
Be back in 2½ to 3 weeks. Lets hold off the final auditions at the studio till then. An awful lot to discuss and not all of it can wait so I'll write you this ragtail letter and try to cover a little.

CAMINO REAL. Tenn says it is as ready as it ever will be. He's alternated between enthusiasm and confusion, but on the whole I think he is pleased with it. I've told him and Audrey both 1/ that I think, know we need an experienced producer (a way of shouldering Bill L. out) and 2/ You are my choice. I advise you however to contact Tenn immediately. And you know what. I haven't read the script yet, so I have no opinion about that. Perhaps it will not be ready. Certainly it will be original and certainly the other stories outside of Kilroy have been expanded and improved. He'll be sending me a script to Europe (I'll be centered at 20th Century Fox, London. Molly will know other addresses). Its possible that I'll stay over there long enough (till the 16th.) to see Tenn upon his arrival. Write me what you think of the script when you read it.

If we go ahead I think I ought to make clear that I really am committed to Jo Mielziner. I know this is unfortunate from your point of view, but that is why I'm putting it down so clearly. If both you and Tenn feel very very strongly against him, exert pressure, but he worked a lot gratis on the show and also knows that he was on the wrong track. Its not fair for anyone to blame him (Liebling has been a little) for "poor" sketches. The wrong direction he went off in was in the direction that I pointed. A director is finally responsible for the scenery, and I was responsible finally for the sketches that Tenn didn't like.

I've got an ENTIRELY different idea now of how the show should be done—not only scenery wise, but direction and acting too. And I think Jo can do almost anything he is helped towards. I still would prefer him to anybody. The basic thing is that I have to solve the problem first. It is up to me. His job is to execute a conception I give him. That is for the record.

About the Studio, I've alternated and wavered. Some days I've felt like withdrawing finally and completely. But that has been seldom and only when I felt most sensitive to the rejection and bitterness growing out of my "stand" and reaching me in rumbles and rumors.

I dont want to do anything destructive. I want to do something good. On the other hand I cant—no one could—work with unfriendly people. There are some. How many I dont know. How it will go from now on, no one can guess. I dont feel anymore like working there this minute, than I did all spring when I stayed away. However one must count on the future with confidence rather than vengeance, and I know, irrespective of how active I am, the studio is tremendously important. And as an expression of what is best and priceless in Lee, I couldn't do anything but help it. . . . I think the best thing we can do with the studio is to start to turn it slowly into something like an English Club Theatre, or OLD VIC. Lets do it. That would be exciting. Lee is very excited about it.

Personally, I'm o.k. But I can use a rest and a change. The attacks haven't let up yet—The commies are very organized people. I remember. The only defense they have is to destroy my public face. And they have set themselves that task. Some fun for me?! Molly has been wonderful. Tenn is a great man. Cliff has been wonderful, so have countless other people. On other fronts I definitely have a job of personal reconstruction to do. (Lee has been very nice too. He's a fine fine man)—well, you'll be hearing all about it from almost everyone. I'm a man that doesn't like to see his name even in a good notice or a flattering comment. I've been blushing some.

So. Love. See you soon. gadge

[Tennessee Williams met the "The Terrible Turk" in Paris and informed his agent that Kazan "has manifested, so far, only the lamb-like side of his nature." He seemed "very favorably impressed" by *Camino Real* and spoke of beginning rehearsals in late October. Kazan's return voyage to New York gave ample time for drafting a nine-page letter of revisions, with a disclaimer that Williams should "ignore them" if he wished (n.d., Columbia).

Bill Liebling and Audrey Wood had long campaigned to produce as well as represent Tennessee Williams on Broadway. Liebling's inexperience provided cover for a lack of trust shared by director and playwright. Cheryl Crawford, eventual producer of *Camino Real,* was renowned for economy and reluctant to pay Jo Mielziner's typical hefty fee. Williams also rejected Mielziner's initial "sketches" of a bear pit or labyrinth as incompatible with the play's "intensely romantic" feeling. Needed instead was "the haunting loveliness of one of those lonely-looking plazas and colonnades in a Chirico" (to Mielziner, n.d., BRTC).

An earlier meeting at the Actors Studio to consider a "public stand" on Kazan's congressional testimony produced a policy of neutrality, although reactions of the membership were strongly negative and in several cases grounds for withdrawing from the workshop. One actor who wrote anonymously to Kazan claimed that "many, many people" at the Studio and on Broadway were "thoroughly sickened" by his testimony (*A Life,* pp. 467–68).

John Steinbeck was among the "countless" others who defended Kazan after his testimony and "Statement" in the *Times* became widely known. He judged him "a good and honest man" and hoped that "the second raters don't cut him to pieces now." Through it all, Tennessee Williams was Kazan's "most loyal and understanding friend" (Steinbeck/*Letters,* p. 415; *A Life,* p. 495).] *TLS, 2 pp., BRTC*

TO STEVEN B. TRILLING

SH: Twentieth Century-Fox Productions, LTD.
31 Soho Square, London, W. 1.
May 31, 1952

Dear Steve,
I am over here in London now, talking with Sherwood on my Fox picture. Tell Jack Warner I'll be at the Lancaster in Paris next week when he arrives there and to give me a ring. I want to have a short talk with him.

Two things have happened with the Williams script. First, I think we have the Breen Office problems solved, which means that Warner Bros. can and should go ahead and make their commitment to us and ours to them a definite one. There is no reason for a delay any longer on either side. However, the date is another matter. Neither Williams or I think the script is as good as it can and will be. He especially wants to keep it with him [this] summer and work on it. The outline of the action is now substantially correct and there is the framework for a tremendous climax, but Williams is not satisfied with it and I am not satisfied with it, and since we have a large interest in the profits of this venture we really don't want to start until the script is as good as it can be.

Tennessee, for the first time, is really beginning to show a very eager interest in the project. Up to now, it's rather been something that he's been doing "for me". I think from here on in he may be going to do the best writing he's done on it. That's my hope and I certainly have no intention of going ahead with this project until we have something really wonderful—it's too important for me. So I will go ahead with Sherwood this summer and sometime during my first California week I will drive out and see you and David.

Meantime, I have asked Audrey Wood to send Jack a copy of the script as it is now. It will be plainly seen that the large Breen Office problems are solved and I have told Abe Lastfogel that the contracts should now be signed so that we all know where we stand. This is especially important to Williams who, up to now, has been writing on what amounts to "spec". When you read this script, and when David reads it, I urge you both to write Williams a letter—you can get his address from Audrey—and both encourage him: tell him how much better it can be, that it has the makings of something really stupendous. Very often, the better the writer is, the more encouragement he needs—Tennessee for instance.

So. Steve, give this message to David, along with my affectionate greetings. I'll see you all in about a month's time and I think we are much better off with this programme, allowing Williams to work three or four months at his own tempo on the story.

I would very much like to have David's notes on the script and I will see that they are forwarded to Williams, or Dave can send them to Williams direct. Also, of course, Dave should call off Harry Stradling and Dick Day, for the time being. If he saw Marilyn Erskine I would like to have his impression of her. I certainly think that he should start long-range casting now. The only one set in my mind is Mildred Dunnock for Aunt Rose.

When I come out, I am bringing my tennis racket with me—that's a warning!

Love and kisses,

["HELP! HELP! SEND ME A WRITER!" So began Tennessee Williams's plea after beginning work on *Baby Doll* in early 1952. The published one acts Williams was trying to stitch together into a screenplay had been nudged aside by "new work," probably *Camino Real* (to EK, January 21, 1952, HTC). Set in the Mississippi Delta, the initial script featured arson, revenge, adultery, sadism, and murder. Censorship problems were far from being "solved," as Joseph Breen reported in August with reference to the film's "sordid tone" and the absence of any figure representing "decency and sanity" (to JLW, August 1, 1952, Herrick). Several working titles, including "Hide and Seek," were used in the slow march of *Baby Doll* to filming in late 1955.] *TLx, 2 pp., USC*

[Munich]

[August 1952]

Dear Gerd.

Please have this note translated and a copy sent to each of the Technical people working on the show, especially Hans and Fraulein Mays. I think to Friedl too.

Dear _____

Perhaps I can describe a little more clearly by a note, than by my terrible German and sign language the impression our circus should create, above all in our first two views of it, and in its dash across the border. What I am about to say goes both for the physical side of the circus, its equipment, tent, seats, decorations etc. and for the costumes that the people wear. Of course it will bear strongly upon the way the circus is photographed.

The Cernik Circus was once a Medium sized but a very fine circus. It is probably the oldest standing touring circus in Czechoslovakia. It has been in the Cernik family for three generations. Mme Cernik herself and her wagon and her costume are all evidences of this. The Cerniks were once Circus Royalty.

But a circus can go to pieces very quickly indeed if it is not kept up. From 1939 on the circus has been under tremendous difficulties, one following upon another. And of course there was never any new equipment to be had, except an odd bit here, and an odd bit there. Worn out tents, seats, motors, costumes, wigs etc. were not replaced. Mostly they were patched up. They were made to serve. Gradually the circus got more and more shabby and more and more run down. And it got smaller. When equipment broke down and couldn't be replaced it had to be abandoned. When Costumes wore out and could not be replaced, they had to be patched and improvised. When these wore out, they had to be simply thrown away.

By now there are remnants of the original grandeur. At the same time the circus has shrunk and is patched together. It is very poor. It is very improvised. The impression should be that it is held together by sheer will power. And this is the fact. It is maintained by the spirit, the bravery and the fortitude of its owner, Cernik, who would not give up. And by the image of old Mme Cernik, who stood among them all as the living embodiment of the Tradition of the Circus Eternal.

Of course when the Communists took over they had money and energy for war supplies and stock piling. But they had nothing for this little circus.

So that by the time we see it there must be something heart rending about the very appearance of the tent and the sound and appearance of the wretched little five piece band. The once gaudy signs, colors, decorations, spangles and glitter have faded out. The canvas is patched. The trucks are held together by wire and string and metal straps. The costumes have a worn, faded and improvised glory.

But also there must be ALWAYS something supremely valiant about the attempts of Cernik and his troupe to give a show under such circumstances.

And as we watch their acts, we must feel despite the shabbiness and the poverty that the circus is succeeding in giving a good show. In fact we forget the patches and the shabbiness and the worn out equipment. We feel only the brave spirit of the people of the circus.

E. K.

[*Man on a Tightrope* was the first of five Twentieth Century-Fox postwar films made in Germany using a local crew. Studio space was rented in Geiselgasteig, a suburb of Munich, for much of the interior work, with location filming staged in the foothills of the Bavarian Alps. Kazan depended heavily on his associate producer Gerd Oswald, whose idea it was to hire the original Brumbach Circus.] *TLS, 1 p., Wesleyan*

TO MOLLY DAY THACHER

SH: Twentieth Century-Fox Film Corporation
Bavaria Filmkunst, Munich-Geiselgasteig, Germany
[August 15, 1952]

Darling—
Today is the first terrible day. I mean I'm real lonely, not just longing, but bad. Its on account of its being a big Munchen (religious) holiday and the studio is closed down. My source of dope (work) taken away. Also no letter from Sandy Hook, or from anyone else today. . . . So I thought about how nice Sandy Hook was and how dear and everything good you are, and I thought about each child and I began to cry. But that wasn't bad because I relaxed. But up till today I've been so busy and so embattled that there was no time to feel anything fully. I wont say anything about the sense or non-sense of making this film. Here I am, and here we are, and I'm going to make the film. Besides, AS I HAVE TO KEEP REMINDING MYELF, it sure seemed necessary at the time. And it was.

Chambers book had a tremendous effect upon me. More so than any book I've read in years. I believe the last thing I read, or tend to, as some one pointed out, but I sure believe this guy, and Hiss sounds like a terrible liar. And a smoothie. I got a tremendous scene out of the scene when Chambers went on the Radio quiz program and they took him apart; then later when

Gloria Grahame amid "remnants of the original grandeur" of the circus in
Man on a Tightrope

they drove home, his son and he, the kid asked: why do they all hate you so?
That made me cry too. Hiss reminds me of so many of our friends, so many of
them. I'll never in my life forget one conversation I had with Lillian Hellman,
just before I testified. We were in the Plaza Hotel. She was telling me how
much she liked Zapata. But she also had serious fault to find with it. She said
that dramatically it was not realized and rather lame, in spots. She said it was
impossible to tell the whole truth today, and that therefore in her opinion it
was better to avoid the so called controversial or contemporary subjects and
stick to historical pieces and costume pieces etc. I could only help feeling that
I would only respect her if she said what she thought exactly. If it was true for
her that's what she should say. Especially if she was going to live up to her own
evaluation of herself and her own vision of the world and its course. But no,
she preferred the more comfortable position of being too good, of being separated and superior to the present. Why dont they first tell the truth I thought
about Hiss. He was so much part of the conspiracy that he didn't even know
he was in it. He took it for granted that it was right, and that he was part of an
elite that could do anything it wanted to because its end was good. But what
gets me is that I was part of it. Without knowing anything about Chambers I
would say in conversation that he looked like a fag to me. Or a psychotic (but

a fag too). I was part of the pack of wolves, the mob. So its a little hard for me to feel anything but the need for patience and waiting with anyone else. Although I do not expect it all "to come out ok" someday. I do not. I dont think there's any "road back" from this. But its hard for me to feel anger. Its just too goddamn bad, and whoever is wrong, I guess will pay some kind of price, but it will not be judged as some kind of verdict. Its just all too fucking bad. But I'm really proud of what I've done. You know you always told me that I should be, but I never would answer that I was. Because I wasn't until I read Chambers. God knows he's fruity, but he saw his duty and he done it. Its funny I've got a kind of affection for the man: his ugliness, his bad teeth, his fatness, his corny purple passages (thought much of his writing superb though—the reporting parts), his damned dirt farm, his self justifications (in an odd way he's a little like Clurman—I mean he's always telling how history has after all proved him right)—and his suits, and his sensitivity, and his talking to himself etc. etc. I felt very close to him. What he described about the pain of public appearance, and of being in the public eye was perfect. The cracks the liberal journalists made at him, sure struck home with me. I felt better that this amorphously plump man had ridden it out. It made me feel that I would too (He says "with God's help" I say "with Molly's help"). And I will too. It wont be the same, but why is that bad? Christ I had enough of those people. Really they and I were dullened to each other. We were dead for each other (all except A!M!). Another thing that struck me close was when Chambers was making up his mind to take the last step and testify about the espionage. What made him do it (one thing) was the thought of the people who lived around him in the country. How would they look at him if he hadn't told all that threatened them? Remember you always said this, and this is one thing I always felt to the same degree that you did. And this is one thing I positively enjoyed after I had testified. The fellows in the country all being extra nice and very friendly to me in a kind of reserved and Yankee way. Gee that was real nice. So—old Chambers made me feel a lot better all around.

Speaking about the country how about a letter. . . . I wonder how the hell you all are. I guess Freddie will tell me. He'll be here middle next week, and he and I will then go up and join the Brumbach circus. I have a strange feeling there is a big job of reconstruction to do on that guy. And I'm just the boy to do it too. I'll really baby him so that he wont need Florence (she threatened to come up here), and give a tremendous show too. Fortunately I feel a great deal of affection for Freddie. We should make a good combo.

Dont mind the blues and the tears described above. I feel better now. Although the letter was rambling and lousy, it helps me, so bear thru it. I feel fine mostly and bloody strong too. Nice part is the crew is nice. And the art directors. I cant bear the Studio casting department or Zanuck on casting. I hate their attitude to Freddie March. Did I tell you that I wrote him that I hoped that he did pay March more than Columbia. Zanuck wont though. He's not what you call a bighearted man. He's mostly sheer competition in a size 30 waist band.

Gerd is really an expert. I sure like a thorough professional character. He is one. Honestly Molly, dear, I'm just rambling on because I have nothing to do. I'll take a nap I guess. By the time I wake up I'll go meet Tenn's train.

Yrs., with the tenderest feelings of love and admiration and wish you were here—Kiss all the children for me.

[Preparations to film *Man on a Tightrope* came to a standstill on the Feast of the Assumption (August 15), a widely observed holy day in Roman Catholic Bavaria.

Whittaker Chambers's break with communism forms the dense personal narrative of *Witness* (1952). After leaving the party in 1938, Chambers spent the following "tranquil years" as a senior editor for *Time* magazine. Circumstances changed dramatically in 1948, when he appeared before the House Committee on Un-American Activities and identified Alger Hiss, a former State Department aide, as a communist with whom he had conspired in the 1930s. Hiss denied the allegation but was eventually convicted of perjury and sentenced to prison. Chambers's defense of informing no doubt resonated with Kazan: "If the ex-Communist truly believes that Communism is evil, if he truly means to struggle against it as an evil, and as the price of his once having accepted it, he must decide to become an informer. In that war which Communism insists on waging, and which therefore he cannot evade, he has one specific contribution to make—his special knowledge of the enemy" (Chambers, p. 455). A serialized version of *Witness* appeared in the *Saturday Evening Post* (February 9–April 12, 1952) as Kazan reconsidered his initial House testimony.

Lillian Hellman described "a strange half-hour" with Kazan in the Plaza Oak Room before she excused herself, called her producer Kermit Bloomgarden, and learned that Kazan's "fumbling" manner bespoke his intention to name former communist members of the Group Theatre. Hellman's account continues with Kazan's claim that further work in Hollywood, as Spyros Skouras warned, would require testimony as a friendly witness. The meeting ended with Kazan's statement that "'it's O.K. for you to do what you want, I guess. You've probably spent whatever you've earned'" (Hellman, pp. 66–67). Hellman's refusal to name "innocent people" in later congressional testimony (May 1952) formed a sharp, invidious, oft-noted contrast with Kazan's informing. At the time John Steinbeck observed that Kazan's stand might have taken "more courage. It is very easy to be brave and very hard to be right." Of the lost friendships, only Arthur Miller's "(A!M!)" seemed to weigh on Kazan.

Allegations that Fredric March and his wife Florence Eldridge were communists or sympathizers routinely appeared in FBI reports and caused substantial damage to their film careers. In 1948 they sued *Counterattack* and forced a retraction of similar charges. Kazan's "job of reconstruction" included casting March as a victim of communism and pampering him with "the real old fashioned Hollywood style works."] *TL, 2 pp., Wesleyan*

TO MOLLY DAY THACHER

SH: Twentieth Century-Fox Film Corporation
Bavaria Filmkunst, Munich-Geiselgasteig, Germany
PM: Munich, August 30, 1952

Darling—

I just got another letter. I guess I'll never be able to convey to you how much I love you. Your letters have a very strong effect on me. As I read them I seem to swell up, my heart seems to get tumescent with pride and love. That's the way I feel now. You should be here, for chrissake, to take advantage of it. All your letters make me feel that way. Its very strange, and very wonderful. I know I will always be your man. Sometimes your worries make me amazed. I have got the habit of secrecy or withdrawal. Its too deeply imbedded in me, and has been operating for too many years for me to lose it quickly. But I am making great progress. I certainly am so much less of fearful than I used to be that there are all kinds of bases for hope and future. I even tell you about my work now. But not entirely there either. But with more encouragement and more love from you and a little more time, and patience, I will get even better and better.

I was much much more frank with Tennessee, for instance, about his play. I told him it was unproducible as was. That Cheryl and Jo's reactions were justified. I think my frankness with him (I didn't tell him that it was phony, because I dont think it is. Its just that his world is so different from yours) made it possible for him to finally get on the right track. I think the goddamn play is now going to work. I am cautiously optimistic. But I am optimistic—but cautious. The man has too much honesty in him, and too much goodness to go down. I believe you are exaggerating the degree of danger he is in. You seem to be obsessed with it, darling. He is an outcast because of his peculiar sex. He is terribly alone. When we got thru worknights, he used to go "cruising". Geezuz, what kind of life is that? Its tough. But he is so completely frank with me now. He tells me absolutely everything. And I think that now for the first time that fellow really and completely trusts me. That had to grow within him, as well as between us. But I am very very proud that he signs his letters to me love, and that he trusts me. By the way did you notice that he included you in the list of people whose regard he wants. That is unusual, in that he has grown to a point where he wants, to a degree at least, the regard of someone who, he knows, has criticisms of him. He senses that and he imagines more. He has a memory of your writing him once that you didn't like the way he lives. That's the way he remembers it, at any rate. But when he writes your name in that list, that means growth within him. Also now, he is not in quite so much pain. Most often, when I went down to his room, he'd be laughing and kidding, and relaxed. Its hard to relax when you are "Queer". But somehow he is getting to it. And I really think the play will finally show you. At any rate you will see for yourself very very soon. It will be in New York, in an approximation of its final form, in about ten days. He's just putting the final touches to it. He knows there is more work, but I believe that the form it will be in is more or less RIGHT! Anyway I am dying to get your opinion. You seem peculiarly obsessed with the problem of Tenn. I dont quite understand it.

Early tomorrow morning we leave for Lenngries. I'll be there in the mountains for two weeks. Wish me luck. . . . I think it is going to be a good picture. How good depends upon me. I know that. If I can stick to feeling, and photograph feeling and honesty and the real goods we'll be o.k. If I can only make them believe this one is happening. The best damn thing I have on my side is Gerd Oswald. He understands and he gets me everything I want, and more too. His idea was hiring the whole Brumbach circus, and they are so real. They are on the road to the location now, in their slow torturous movement. Its inconceivable when you see them that they could get over a border. But they did. This very circus did. And Herr Brumbach led them. And his old mother who is 89 went with, and is walking around with a long black dress and black aviator shoes right now. She refuses to leave her trailer or give it up to us. But she is willing to be a Schauspieler, and so I have her playing the part of Freddie March's mother. And everytime he goes or comes back he kisses her good bye or hello. She's a right fierce old lady. And she reminds me of you know who. I like old ladies and old men. They make me feel something very strong. Esp. my grandmother. How is she. I never expect to hear from my mother or father. They haven't even written me that she broke her hip yet. I know they will never tell me that she has died. I will either be told when I get back to the States, or I will get a letter saying that she is already in the ground a couple of weeks, and that I was spared since I had so much on my mind.

So. I start Tuesday. Tomorrow very early we hit for the mountains. I enclose another picture. This shows the actual town where we shoot. This is the Bavarian side. In quotes. It looks like Border country doesn't it? So it is. But between Austria and Bavaria. By the way I went to a cocktail party and tea given by the General and his wife. I asked him if there was any danger from the Commies, and that you were worried. He said NONE. so relax. . . .

Give Judy my love. She is beautiful. Give Chris my love and tell him I miss him. And I look forward to meeting him and talking with him. And maybe take a trip with him to the mountains in the late fall. Give Nick my love and tell him I no longer look on him as frail. Give Katie my love and tell her I looked very carefully at her drawings and they are probably the best drawings for a child her age that we have had in our family. I may be wrong on this point. Its only a snap judgment, but it is nevertheless my opinion.

I will write you more and more seriously too. But I just feel pretty good this morning. I had a lot of sleep and Zanuck was helpful and most charmingly human and I got a wonderful letter from you and my chauffeur is so shy and the maid is so silly, and all in all I'm nervous but in a pleasant way. So maybe the picture will stink, but I'll learn a lot about the habits of elephants. I love you so much.

Freddie just came in for rehearsal. He feels badly. He drank too much. I hardly drink at all, when I see these other guys put it away. I guess I'm just not a desperate man.

CHILDREN I LOVE YOU ALL AND MISS YOU EACH ONE AND YOUR MOTHER I MISS TOO! GOODBYE FOR NOW!

D!

[Tennessee Williams wired his agent on August 20—"In Munich with Terrible Turk"—to report a hasty return to Rome after a depressing visit. The details were reserved for his journal: "Quelle misère. This place is no good. Not even worth talking about. Doubt that anything can be accomplished with Gadg. Too discouraged to do good work." Williams resented Jo Mielziner's recent criticism of *Camino Real* and a new outline devised by Kazan. "I have fallen off remarkably in the esteem of my coworkers when they start dictating my work to me." An invitation to dine with Kazan on the last evening in Munich was politely refused: "Said excuse me but I think I'll go cruising now" (Williams/*Notebooks*, p. 557).

"I have Tenn on my mind," Molly Kazan wrote earlier in August. "The trouble is, he thinks he's terribly special, whereas he's only a little bit more special than everyone else." She hesitated to approach Williams directly, aware that earlier criticism had made him "faintly antagonistic," but was certain that his "atmosphere" and "associates" had changed after the success of *Streetcar* in ways destructive to an artist. She thought Elia could "help" but feared he would be "dragged" into the playwright's "own swamp" in directing *Camino Real*. More solicitous thoughts were not long in coming: "He is completely winning. I don't think he knows that. If he did—I suppose he wouldn't be. But part of his despair comes of his sense of isolation and difference—and if he only knew, the human race is ready to take him into its arms" (Wesleyan). Elia reminded Molly that Williams had recently included her in a short list of friends who still might take him "seriously as a writer."

Lenggries was the primary staging area for *Tightrope*. An area farther south of Munich was used for the escape sequence and Terry Moore's game attempt to swim the icy rapids of the Isar in a romantic scene with Cameron Mitchell. The Isar River also served as a fictional boundary between communist Czechoslovakia and free Austria.

Herr Brumbach's mother played a silent role as "the living embodiment of the Tradition of the Circus Eternal." The Kazan children ranged in age from four (Katie) to sixteen (Judy).] *TLS, 3 pp., Wesleyan*

TO ABE LASTFOGEL

SH: Twentieth Century-Fox Film Corporation and H. William Fitelson
Bavaria Filmkunst Munich-Geiselgasteig, Germany
[September 1952]

Dear Abe and Bill:

I am sending this letter to Bill and asking him to send a copy to Abe, and also to Molly. I have no carbons here. I'm sitting in the back seat of car, with the typewriter on my lap. Its raining. Its been raining for twelve days almost without letup. But we've worked everyday. We haven't worked as fast as we might have in dry weather. But we haven't ever stopped. The car is parked in a little encampment our circus has made near the big outdoor set we are going to use for the climax of our picture. The rain has forced us indoors, but since there is no sound stage here, we have one tiny set set up in a barn, and another set up under a circus tent. There is another tent, the one used for stabling the horses that we actually show in the picture for what it is. There is a short delay right at this time while we wait for the generator to be brought up. So I'm sitting in the car, which is parked next to a big pile of horse manure. You know me well enough to guess that I dont find the smell of fresh rain on fresh horse manure repellent. Its all the way I like it. I dont mind the rain. My spirits are excellent. I haven't done anything to utterly fuck up the picture so far, and I still have good hopes it will turn out good. So.

The biggest conviction I have come to on this my third all location picture is that sound stages are useful, but not at all inevitable. I've known this all along. But now we have shot under conditions that would make a Hollywood crew and any member of ASC (Cameramen) throw up his copy of the Hollywood Reporter and hide behind it. Still this cameraman has shot everyday, at least half the time in rain, usually a drizzle, but often more so. Of course he is dying to please me, and will do anything I tell him. I tell him shoot. He shoots. The stuff looks rough and ready. When the cameraman, who has no English, likes the rushes, he says they look very Kazan. I take this to mean that it looks like an artistic newsreel. That's what I want, and it is also what I usually want. It seems to be my nature.

That's the good side of the picture. The bad side is my painful separation from home. On this picture I came into it with my eyes open. And Molly's eyes were open. We thought the picture necessary to do, at almost any cost. I still feel that way. But I feel the cost everynight. I dont mind for this one. But I'm thinking about the future. And I want to write you about the future.

I dont intend to go to Hollywood anymore. I intend to hold onto and honor my contract with Zanuck. But the pictures I will do must be done on location. I will do, as Abe suggested, look for stories near to home locationwise. And it will be up to me to find stories that can be done in such a way, in such a place and at a time when my family is not broken up. I know the nature of this problem, and I will work on it.

But there is something beyond that. I think now I know enough about the picture business, finally, to be on my own. I want to start my own little company. I dont mind being a subsidiary of a big releasing company. But I want to start making pictures autonomously. I've been afraid of it up till now. I've always felt I didn't know enough. I haven't. But the picture in Bavaria is being made by a fellow named Gerd Oswald, who is an absolutely first class business man and manager, and myself. There is no "producer" on the picture. The equipment is only what we could rent here. There are no sound stages, only barns, and tents. Everything is done by local labor, most of which is not movie trained. The process of making a picture has been suddenly revealed to me as terribly simple. And the smoke screen thrown up in favor of the advantages of big studio facilities etc. terribly overblown.

There is a man here in Europe who is the closest thing to what I want to be. His name is Marcel Pagnol. He shoots his pictures in Monte Carlo. He lives in Monte Carlo. He writes about the people of the north coast of the Mediterranean. Those are the people whom he knows, and in whom he is interested. I am similar. I hope so anyway, because I have a terrific admiration of this man. I dont mean I want to confine myself to shooting Brooklyn. But ninety five percent of the subjects I have done and will do have the character of reality versus glamor, inner emotion versus showmanship, intimacy versus spectacle, humanity versus Theatricalism. . . .

Lets draw up a plan. Lets say I have an office, and I'm in the business of producing films. I will dig up the stories myself. I'm not bad at that. There's plenty of room for improvement, but I can operate that way. Now I will organize the stories and that end of it. Now we need something simple. Finance and Release. Facilities, office space, advice from producers, being met at the station, suites at the Beverly Hills, mimeograph service, casting departments all that shit is a nuisance, and a very costly one.

I say lets think first now very selfishly of setting me up in an ideal operation for me. Lets offer it, on exactly my terms to Skouras and Zanuck. If they wont go for it on exactly my terms, lets offer it to Nick Schenk, then to Jack Warner, then to Bill Goetz. But lets not compromise. I find my own stories, I develop them, I produce them, I cut them. Let the Fox contract stand. But lets get going on this other. My stories, developed by me, as Zapata was, as the Williams story is, as the Schulberg story is going to be. Then I produce them. I now rate that. I know my business now. If I dont, I never will. Then I want to cut them as I want to cut them. Zanuck wont give me this, Schenk wont give me this? Then lets work with the King Brothers, Republic, Lopert, I dont care who. Until I'm proved wrong I think I can work with anyone, essentially and purely because I now know enough to work alone. You've never heard me talk this way before about pictures, because I've never felt I rated the confidence. I still have plenty to learn. But by God, this goddamn picture is being produced by me and this man Oswald. No one checked anything, except Zanuck the script. And Darryl had agreed to a story outline, when Hathaway was going to direct the picture, which was shameful.

And I know you understand now, that Geography IS important to me. I hate to leave home, but that isn't the only reason. I find the atmosphere of Hollywood, foreign, in fact, hostile, and all in all unacceptable. I dont need and I dont appreciate either their scale of operation, their conveniences and the "help" they give me. I positively dont want their help even when it is highly skilled. I am very fond of Darryl, and I will make the pictures I have contracted to make with him. But at the same time I want to start organizing myself to make my pictures in my way. . . .

I also think I can make much much more money this way. I am now sure enough of myself to want to gamble on every goddamn picture I make. I dont want my "salary" anymore. I want a big piece of the profit. I dont care if I dont get fifty thousand guaranteed. I'll take thirty, I'll take twenty five. Or I'll even take nothing. I dont care so much about the guarantees now. I'm ready to gamble. What I do care about is a favorable release, good terms, fair shake, supervision or a good square look at the book keeping etc. You all know what I mean better than I can explain it. I really think I can make better pictures this way, and more profitable pictures and live a happier life. . . .

I never wanted to have Joe Mank or Josh Logan or anyone else have the least say over what I did. You understand that, Abe, dont you. I agree with what you say about artists not being tied in together. And I'm a supremely independent fellow, especially these last five years. My recent trouble has made me more independent and more ornery, it seems. Not less so. I dont feel like clinging to anything. For instance if Warner is not ready to commit himself unequivocally to the Williams project, I'd like to do that with my own company. I dont understand how the mechanics of it would work. You can work that out. But I dont need Warner brothers to do the Williams picture. I can borrow Stradling from Goldwyn. And the rest of it is all my work. . . .

Strangely, for the first time on this picture, I feel just as confident on the movies as I do on the stage. And I think the time has come for me to be independent. Not in a big 1930-ish, David Selznick, Sam Goldwyn fashion. But more on the European style, modestly, like I am myself, "cheap" Bill Fitelson calls me. After all a picture is finally one person, the man that makes it. The rest is trimming.

Write me both of you. Send me your reaction, and send me the news. Dont forget me here in Bavaria. Thanks Bill for the piece about Arthur Miller. I hope his play is a success. He is a fine guy—with faults like we all have—but deserving a constant hearing, and an assured place. If, as you feel, he is completely wrong now, he is honest enough to find it out.

My love to both of you. I feel fortunate to be associated with you both. Take this letter most seriously.

gadge.

[Kazan wrote to his agent and attorney while enduring cold, rain, mud, cloudy skies, and a delinquent elephant in the foothills of the Alps. Ten days were required to film the climactic escape sequence in *Tightrope*.

Kazan's "all location" films to date were less profitable than earlier studio-based productions. *Viva Zapata!* failed to repay "half of the negative cost" and *Man on a Tightrope* was the "lowest grosser in the history of 20th Century-Fox"—dismal returns cited by Darryl Zanuck in later correspondence with Kazan.

Marcel Pagnol wrote, directed, and produced films with the autonomy Kazan hoped to derive from his "own little company." Later he recommended Pagnol's disarmingly simple films of village life in Provence to Tennessee Williams as a model for *Baby Doll*.

The director who began filming *Tightrope* without "the vaguest idea about how to direct an action movie" was reassured by a seasoned associate producer and "the rough comradeship" of a German crew. Arduous location shooting completed the transformation and led Kazan to declare that for the "first time" he felt equally confident directing theater and film. Jack Warner had not yet made a commitment to finance *Baby Doll*, in part because censorship problems and script delays hindered the project. In looking ahead to the "Schulberg story," Kazan anticipated difficult negotiations with Darryl Zanuck. Nonetheless he returned to New York in the fall possessed of "a new degree of energy" that would send him "spinning through ten years of unremitting work" (*A Life*, pp. 480–84). More specific plans to implement Newtown Productions were revealed in 1954, when Kazan laid before his agent and attorney an organizational scheme and instructed Bill Fitelson to examine several properties for acquisition, including *Desire Under the Elms*.

Fitelson probably enclosed a *New York Times* report that the "Damon and Pythias collaboration" has been severed and Kazan would not direct *The Crucible*. Noncommittal at the time, Arthur Miller wrote later that Kazan's congressional testimony had caused "a silence," an "invisible wash of dulled vibrations," through which the friends "could not hear or speak anymore" (Miller, pp. 332–35). Jed Harris directed *The Crucible* in 1953, to Miller's dismay.] *TLS, 3 pp., Wesleyan*

TO BUDD SCHULBERG

[New York]
[early November 1952]

Dear Budd

About the Clemente arrest. It is <u>something</u>. We cant go ahead as if it had not taken place. In a way it could serve as one of our climaxes. A climax.

I've been disturbed by Martin Gabel's attitude at Moss Hart's dinner party. What a place to discuss the waterfront! Martin said he was surprised at my naivete. When I say I was disturbed, its another way of saying that I thought: IS HE RIGHT? AM I NAIVE? AM I BECOME WHAT THEY USED TO CALL AN APOLOGIST?

Of course the important thing now is that whether we make a statement directly, or not, the movie will contain our view point. Perhaps I can think aloud here and try to formulate what it might be—in dramatic terms, of course.

I think it should be the attitude of some one—probably Terry—that you cant ever clean it up. Martin Gabel quoted Lincoln Steffens on the nature of corruption in a democracy. The gangsters have simpler ways of putting it, but the idea is always the same: there's always going to be somebody taking.

Terry's viewpoint should be that they'll never DO ANYTHING about it all. He remembers the Seabury investigation. He voices the popular (in fact, universal) cynicism. Everybody's always known it, and known it perfectly. Nothing new is being revealed to anyone. What do they mean revelations?! Sure they'll get a couple of hoodlums. There will be a couple of sacrifices. But take a guy like Clemente? Will they ever touch him? (Cf. O'D's challenge from Mexico: why dont they prosecute Anastasia?) Not that the Clemente arrest is a great landmark. But it is something.

How does a democracy work in these things? Martin Gabel said that the SHAPE would never go. This is so much shit of course. Does it reflect Martin's great knowledge of social affairs? No—I think it only shows the tremendous pervasion of the influence of the Stalinists—Democracies are doomed—they cannot cure themselves—they are necessarily corrupt etc. Well if this is so, brother, we're in a tough tough spot.

And—to the degree of this immense cynicism among a certain group of intellectuals (Art Miller, for instance would completely agree, "nothing will ever be really be done" etc.) to that degree the Stalinists have a great hold on our intellectual life. Do you think I'm nuts?

Anyway, the point is: what the hell do we want to say. We cannot pretend something ISN'T happening. If its only happening because of public pressure, so much the more so. Its late—too bad! The Democratic political brotherhood is thoroughly corrupt? Eisenhower is in. That's bad too? Lets build Stevenson. Stevenson has faith in Democracy eventually working. So do I.

I think we should show a little of that working now. Maybe—by showing it—we can do something to stop the SHAPE. What do fellows like Martie do (no attack on M.G.—I like him) but do nothing? The Shape exists only in N.Y. San Francisco has no shape, and New Orleans has no shape. Murray Kempton says the Communists are responsible for most of the real gains in unionism in this country. I leave this unchallenged, here. But even if this were so, then its the job of the liberals to do the job the Commies have done.

Budd Schulberg

Write me on this. I think the arrest of Clemente is a part of our climax. It shows that Terry's pain was worth while and it shows that IF IT WANTS TO Democracy can work. And its a spur, or should be, to go on.

And it makes us face another problem, which is the one that Martin G. very rightly brought up. Not who murdered my brother. Not even who ordered the killing of my brother. But who countenances it? Who looks the other way? Who is finally responsible? Is this part of our system inevitably part of our system?

I dont think, of course that we have to answer THESE questions. But I think we must work as if these questions did exist. They are in the air. The waterfront thing is part of the whole big hanging question. Have we got a chance. I think we have. Part of this thinking is wishful. But on the other hand I saw segregation in the army go in seven years—and I saw it go with my own eyes. And I think the Clemente arrest must mean something. And how much it will mean depends on how much it actually means to us. And how much it means depends partly on people like ourselves noting it.

In terms of simple dramatic structure, I think it extremely valuable, that there be tangible results, dramatised results from Terry's painful act of informing.

Ask yourself: do you think the waterfront will ever be quite the same again after this inquiry? Granted its late, granted its not talking about the shipowners probably preferring it this way, preferring the shape to Bridges etc., still our waterfront probably will never be the same again. I think you also have to give Bridges credit. If he's not a good national risk on a critical waterfront, that's another matter. But he did do a job. Union men do not vote out of sentiment. He brought them gains. Meantime, is the alternate to Bridges, Bridges?

I've also been thinking about our picture being "good" for a long long time. It can be, if its final "thinking" is not about the waterfront but about the operation of a democracy. About how a democracy moves, and how a democracy grows, and what a democracy must learn and do etc. The worth of our picture will depend finally on the size of its moral view point.

Write me immediately. Lets think like hell this week. Lets turn these crime commission hearings into an advantage.

g.

P.S. There is a final terror. Terry says nothing will ever happen. Hell there'll always be "taking", piecing off, and crooks, even murder. BUT he, <u>Terry</u>, did the murder. Isn't that something? When he fingered Edie's brother, he also fingered his own. It isn't, in other words, "Ah, somebody will always be murdering somebody else. Its much more: "I've got to stop murdering my brother. Not <u>they</u>'ve got to stop. <u>I</u>'ve got to stop!!!!!"

That is the essence of it. That is the essential and final answer to Martin's attitude.

In other words, if this thing still exists now it is ALL OUR FAULTS. We murdered Pete Panto, because, while we did not finger him we did just as bad, or worse, we countenanced it. This is for Father Kerry to say.

[Official investigation of harbor crime reached critical mass in November as Budd Schulberg drafted an early treatment of *On the Waterfront*. Among those arrested was Mike Clemente, business agent of Local 856 of the International Longshoremen's Association (ILA) and reputed "overlord" of the East River docks. He was eventually convicted of tax evasion and perjury and sentenced to prison. Johnny Friendly, the fictional boss whose character is based in part on Clemente, does not yet appear in the screenplay.

Actor and producer Martin Gabel could have quoted any number of passages by the journalist Lincoln Steffens, who tersely summarized the corruption of American politics: "Democracy is the party of 'capital.'" Terry Malloy, a rough-hewn former boxer with loose ties to the mob, expresses the same cynicism in Schulberg's evolving screenplay, albeit with diminishing conviction.

Reformers traced much of the corruption to the daily "shape-up," a hiring practice that involved a group of longshoremen and a powerful union boss who distributed a brass check to favored workers. With the support of Joe Ryan, ILA president for life, the shape-up lingered until late 1953 and provided a key scene in *On the Waterfront*. The "hiring hall" rather than the "shape" was used on the West Coast by Harry Bridges, who presided over an unaffiliated union (ILWU) with a reputation of harboring communists.

Pete Panto was lured from his home in 1939 and murdered for leading a reform movement in the Red Hook section of Brooklyn. Officials found his lime-encrusted body in the proverbial shallow grave in northern New Jersey. The unsolved case—Albert Anastasia, head of "Murder, Inc.," escaped prosecution after the death of a key witness—remained a vivid memory for insurgent longshoremen, as well as a dramatic framework for Budd Schulberg's screenplay.

The name and role of Father Kerry would change in later drafts. His character was played by Karl Malden and based on John M. Corridan, SJ, the "waterfront priest."] *TLS, 3 pp., Wesleyan*

TO LEMUEL AYERS

[New York]
December 3 [1952]

Dear Lem:

Here are some notes on the setting for CAMINO. We will have talked about most of them, but perhaps it maybe valuable to set them down, in case you might want to remember what it was that I had felt.

The place where the play takes place is a port of departure. (Gutman says: This is a port of arrival and departure and we have no permanent guests). It is further a port of departure into the unknown.

Obviously the play is completely unrealistic—a fantasy, it is called. But beyond this there is one other factor that makes a real problem that other fantasies do not have. That is that the play is directed by the author to be played largely in a Theatrical or presentational side. Generally, therefore, while the back areas of the stage are illusionistic, the front areas should be presentational, and the actors should have at least as much contact with the audience as do revue or even burlesque performers. This fascinating going from a fairy land, remote, eerie and forbidding, to the closest and most direct contact with the audience is one of the main problems as it is one of the main virtues of the play. It is also absolutely brand new stylistically speaking, and gives both you and I a problem that neither we nor anyone else has ever faced before.

The only Theatre I know where this kind of combination of supposedly opposite stylistic elements exists is in the Japanese Theatre, but I believe that they work too formally for the illusionistic parts of this play. I think, in other words, that we are doing something brand brand new.

This is a place where people arrive without knowing how they got there. The author describes it once most beautifully as "this far moonlit end of the Camino Real." It is the end, then of a series of converging roads. They come in, it would seem to me, from more or less one direction. In the opposite direction there is space, terror, mystery, the unknown, death. This is a jumping off place.

I've always felt that the set should sweep from the known—which is the direction of the audience, up and up and then away in back to the unknown which is seen thru the Arch (which can either be the arch of death or the arch of triumph) and beyond the arch towards space that is so unknown that it is limitless and unknowable.

In other words I think the entrances to the place should be generally from the direction of the audience. That doesn't mean thru the audience, though this should be continued too. It does mean that people enter more or less from the direction of the audience. The players move between the audience which is known and the back of the stage which is mysterious and unknown. Kilroy identifies the members of the audience as his friends. Most often he talks directly to them. He consults with them and again and again asks for their sympathy and understanding the way one should be able to go to a close friend in a crisis. He asks for their pity, explains to them his feelings, and generally shares his experience with them. Generally too the audience gets their understanding and feeling of and for the play thru Kilroy. In the opposite direction when Kilroy disappears into apotheosis as a legend, he goes up and away into the mystery beyond the arch. . . .

Of course the feeling should be a lyric one. That is it should be allusive and suggestive rather than heavy or explicit, even where it has to be handled by actors. The "feel" of the set should be one of evanescence. It should constantly seem to change. The lighting is absolutely all important. It should never be "nailed Down" into one mood.

Everything takes place in the plaza except the long scene between Esmeralda and Kilroy. This takes place in the back room of the Gypsy's. Tenn has always thought of a set on a truck being rolled out from one side of the stage. I have always withdrawn from this idea, without having a better one of my own. I do think I have an idea now that certainly I would much much prefer.

I'm suggesting that the scene between Esmeralda and Kilroy, the possession of the virgin by the chosen hero be done and set up as the final ceremony or ritual of the night of the new moon. This sounds a bit fruity. What I mean is that once the chosen hero has been chosen the revellers withdraw in part, and another part draws some curtains, which can be typically and characteristically decorated across the stage. A bed is brought on in back of the second curtain. The crystal ball and the gypsy's paraphernalia comes out of her doorway entrance which is downstage on one side. . . . The love scene in effect takes place against the ghostly background of the plaza—the way a town sometimes feels at night to lovers when no one else is awake or even in the world. The effect can be truly magical and can be on the right scale. The set can be set up and struck by the revellers, later hotel attendants (or someone else). . . . The basic idea is that the love scene is the true climax of the Fiesta, which it most certainly is. . . .

The first look at the entire set can be just a tiny bit realistic. Perhaps those square pieces of cloth on a frame and mounted on a single pole that one sees in Mexican markets can be used to advantage here. They soon disappear for good as the climate (spiritual) becomes threatening. After this opening suggestion of a poetic type of realism, there is only increasing fantasy and increasing theatricality. At the end a canopy of gauze can descend upon the roof of the Gypsy's over Esmeralda's cot. This descent can be beautiful. I would otherwise avoid all and every mechanics.

Probably this is enough in the way of generalization for the present. I will show it to Tenn. I have many detailed ideas, but I'm not a bit rigid about them, and certainly think its presumptuous to thrust them at you until you have a chance to go into the problem for yourself. I'm hoping in this note only to set the basis for an agreement on fundamentals.

I think the problem of costume on this show quite as important as setting. These too I have notions about, and they too can wait.

yrs., e.k.

[Lemuel Ayers replaced Jo Mielziner, who withdrew from *Camino Real* with a claim of pressing work. Ayers was known to Kazan as a former collaborator (*Harriet*, 1943) and to Tennessee Williams as a graduate student at the University of Iowa. His extensive credits for stage design included *Oklahoma!* (1943) and *Kiss Me, Kate* (1948).

A "dream-like" journey by rail from Mexico City to Guadalajara in 1945 gave Williams the seminal figures of *Camino Real*. An American tourist with a "worn but classically beautiful face" and a racking cough evoked Marguerite Gautier, the consumptive heroine of Alexandre Dumas's romance *Camille* (1848). "KILROY WAS HERE" appeared on "a low wall" of the station and led Williams to adopt the universal graffito of World War II as "the poor man's Don Quixote" ("Foreword," May 1946, HRC). They were joined on the Camino Real by other arch-romantics who had reached the terminal place of terror: the original Don Quixote and Sancho Panza, Jacques Casanova, Proust's obsessive homosexual, the Baron de Charlus, and Lord Byron, as well as the sadistic Gutman, proprietor of the Siete Mares Hotel, which dominates the luxurious side of the plaza.

Kazan's direction that the set "be allusive and suggestive" pertained especially to the love scene between Esmeralda and Kilroy, which evolved from a sketch Tennessee Williams began in Guadalajara after seeing the horrific painting of a werewolf. Behind the image lay the story of a king whose perverse relations with the creature produced a daughter and a curse upon the land. With each full moon, she takes "the form of a beautiful virgin" and descends from the hills to choose a lover soon to be "devoured by wolves." If the virgin were to "laugh or weep from her heart," the curse would be lifted but at the cost of her life (Cabeza de Lobo, n.d., HRC). Esmeralda plays the restored virgin in Williams's adaptation, while the Gypsy, her mother and pimp, mocks Kilroy, the "chosen hero," and dismisses a redemptive tear shed by her daughter: "You have been watching television too much." A perplexed Kazan would later question Williams as to his "idea" regarding the "sardonic" tone of the love scene and the apparent failure of the fiesta to produce the traditional restoration of the fertility rite.] *TLS, 3 pp., Wesleyan*

TO TENNESSEE WILLIAMS

SH: Twentieth Century-Fox Film Corporation
Beverly Hills, California
December 10, 1952

Dear Tenn:

You said at a recent historic meeting that Cheryl and I had not been frank and severe with you. I've never needed more invitation.

Will you please sit down and read the first act. Just once, as a single piece. Not in bits and tid-bits and gems and effects. I mean invite Frankie to leave your apartment for an hour, put the phone in a pail of lukewarm water and read act one thru as if it was someone else's play. Just do that.

I took all the versions from A to infinity on the train with me. I sat down one morning and ripped the covers off and went thru every page. By nightfall I was blind. (I recovered my sight just a few hours ago, in time to write this). The floor of my compartment was a foot and a half deep with your crumpled efforts. On the table in front of me was a little damp-seeming raft of the script gleanings I had torn out. I've saved them and will produce on request. The point is that I got those goddamn versions out of my life. They're gone. Then yesterday I sat down and read the play. You can forget the second act till rehearsal. But do not forget the first.

I've been slightly singed. I'm not going to make any concrete suggestions to you. Or, maybe I'll sneak in a few later. Probably. And incidentally I think you're quite right to do everything in your way ONLY. And if you can't find your way not at all. If you were a tenth of the talent you are, I'd still give you that. My mother brought me up right.

But do you think the first act is ready to go into rehearsal? I don't. Probably there isn't an awful lot of work, mechanically speaking, pressing on typewriter keys and all that. I just think you've got to sit down and see that goddamn act thru. I mean see your way thru it, make some kind of one piece of it. It can be a bloody peculiar piece, but one piece it should be. It should have a sequence an audience can and will follow. And above all I think it should come to a climax—a real "internal" one, a climax of story and a climax of "meaning," and one that calls for act two. A few "ole's," a light change and a flurry of movement is not an act curtain. You can bring the rag down, but you still won't have an act curtain. You'll have a disaster.

There is a simple and obviously "right" story for act one. You introduce a place of terror. You bring an innocent into it. He senses the danger. He begins to catch on where he is. He makes inquiries, he slowly discovers that he is in a very malignant place. And he begins to make efforts to get out. In this effort to get out, he becomes part of the (excuse the expression) community effort to get out. We meet the "community." Thru them and their panic and terror, Kilroy sees more and more what he is up against. He finds a bond of sympathy within him especially for Jacques. His panic to escape is climaxed in an attempt to stowaway on the FUGITIVO. When he finds himself left behind in the disaster-struck place, he draws closer to Jacques. Jacques' humiliation and abandonment by Marguerite makes him even closer still to Kilroy. Finally there they sit, alone and face to face, crowned with the headdress of humiliation. Jacques has been on the Camino longer than anyone. Kilroy is the most recent arrival at this terminal end. Jacques knows what the boy must come to face: that you can't get out alive, and that the job is to know HOW to go. How to go with Honor and Gallantry and as yourself. Integrity they call it.

I'm sure you'll say: "Yes, fine, but why make it so bloody clear?" But I'm not asking you to make this as a statement or "message" or anything literal. I'm only asking you to tell the story that is there, clearly and clearly as story. And I do have a dread of all those thousand-odd people leaving their seats for the intermission not knowing what the hell we brought them to the theatre for in the first place. To see that you're talented or brilliant? To see that I have facility and violence? Christ, we're supposed to be grown up.

And now another thing. It's all very well for you to sit in Cheryl's office and say: "Why stick to a conventional length?" Everybody there is a free soul like you, and we all sit there and nod and stay silent. And you must have something like scorn in your heart for us because you know in your heart that this play is twenty to thirty minutes too long. All right, leave it at twenty. It took two hours and forty minutes to read, and nobody got up and interrupted the reading to do the dances. Not that I saw anyway.

This play is at least twenty minutes too long by any standard and by any measure, including the only valid one: its own nature. It hasn't enough development of theme or plot to take on the jumbo length. This doesn't make it less. Not at all. This is finally and essentially a piece of theatre poetry, a lyric piece. It is more beautiful and more affecting, more touching when it is simple and not overloaded. As I say, I don't think I'm telling you something you don't in your heart know. Well, do something about it now. The actors and I can generate terror from now till next year this time, but this play is still too long.

Tennessee, everybody loves you, so that when you get outraged and pop off, everyone says: "He doesn't really mean that." At the same time, (you're right) everybody is not quite as frank and "brutal" as they might be with a lesser talent. It's the "price you pay," to quote.

But there really isn't time for all that gush now. I'm about to go into the long dark tunnel of rehearsal and lose all perspective, and I'll also begin to defend things just because I had fun staging them and then we'll be lost in the goulash of scenery, costumes, temperaments and opinions.

Be tough with yourself and for yourself and for me. Shape this act! . . . There is only one place where you have to do some real writing and be good, too. You have to write an end to the act in terms of Kilroy. You haven't solved the end of the act at all. You know that. You're good at construction. You must know that the writing of this end supersedes all other problems. You can't have a form or a sequence to an act unless you know where or towards what you're driving the sequence. And in what knot of meaning and action the act ends. The steps have significance in terms of what they lead to.

You've got the form latent in the act. It's buried and not shaped. But mainly the trouble is that you have not made up your mind what the end is. I think the end of act one is Kilroy's realization that there is no escape, and Jacques' statement that the problem is not: can you get out alive. It's: how do you go with honor. That, said out of the common bond of sympathy and pain, is the meaning the audience will take with them. It would shed a light over what they've just been watching. And it's a first statement of a theme that will be treated and resolved in Act Two.

I don't expect the act to be pulled together into any "single line." I do expect it to be pulled into one meaning and one bond of sympathy and a single FATE by the end of Act One, and above that, into a single theme: your meaning stated in your terms.

As of now the effect, as far as construction goes, is one story interrupted and replaced and finally thrown away in favor of another story, then a little hustle—bustle, CURTAIN! What the hell is that?

Read the act thru as one piece. It may dishearten you a little. It shouldn't really. I hope it makes you feel as urgently as I feel the need for solving the end of the act with a real "meaning" and a real "story" climax (Whether or not it's the one I detail). And then, by the light shed by this climax, making the act one piece. Certainly you will agree that the first simple step in this process is tying together the two stories before the intermission story-wise, sympathy-wise, meaning-wise, mechanics-wise. You took one step in that direction when you had the two men facing each other crowned with their headgear of humiliation and rejection.

I guess that does it. It won't hurt to remind you again, in light of the fact that she told me she's writing you a letter, that Molly speaks for Molly and I speak for myself. Goodbye for now. I'll be back around Wednesday. And much, much love.

Gadg

P.S. Cheryl wired me that you've done fine work on Kilroy. I'm glad. I got her wire after I wrote this letter—But I sent letter anyway.

P.P.S. Please ask Lem not to "harden" his ideas till I get back. Again, Love G.

["Versions from A to infinity" bespeak Tennessee Williams's habitual rewriting and the unfamiliar materials attacked in *Camino Real*. Kazan's own excess took the form of suggested revisions that were often diffuse, misleading, and overwhelming in number. Feeling "slightly singed" by recent encounters with Williams, Kazan gradually trimmed his criticism of *Camino Real* and focused it more sharply.

Kazan reassured Williams in mid-November of his "unwavering" love for *Camino Real* and urged that Kilroy, the "plain and simple representative" of the legendary romantics unearthed by Williams, be placed at the center of the play. This would require a first-act curtain focused on Kilroy and thereafter his incorporation into the "great middle section" of the play from which he is "excluded" (November 17, 1952, HRC). Kazan dismissed act two issues in present correspondence and advised Williams to develop "a sequence" in the first act that "an audience can and will follow." Tightening the "bond of sympathy" between Kilroy and Casanova held promise for reconciling the "two stories" of *Camino Real:* the fact that "you can't get out alive" and "how to go with Honor and Gallantry." The "real 'internal'" climax that Kazan envisioned for Kilroy would be discovery of this fatality.

Molly Kazan wrote to Williams, as Elia warned, and repeated her husband's advice "to identify with an audience," cut "45 minutes," and "create a first act climax with a carryover for Kilroy." She also rebuked Williams for demanding "total allegiance" to *Camino Real:* "You exercise, thru the intensity of your feeling, a sort of psychological weapon against your friends and colleagues. . . . They have not said so but I feel an unspoken fear, a submission finally before your desperate and intransigent identification with the play" (December 9, 1952, HRC). Williams described Molly as his "bête-noir" in related correspondence and suspected her of trying to "talk Gadge out of the play."] *TLS, 5 pp., HRC*

TO JOHN STEINBECK

SH: Twentieth Century-Fox Film Corporation
Beverly Hills, California
December 10, 1952

Dear John:

Yesterday I had a long hassle with Darryl. It literally took an hour and a half. He's evidently very stung about the loss of EAST OF EDEN. During the course of the thing, I took the position of no guilt whatsoever. The going got "extremely frank" and I told him that if there was fault in this thing, it was on the side of 20th Century-Fox. I explained to him fully that we had given him every chance to show interest in the book. Furthermore, that I could never be considered at any time more than a friend intervening with you on his behalf. I did not, in other words, "represent you" in any way, and never pretended to. I said to him that you were kind enough to hold the book six months away from any competitive consideration. That you had submitted to them both the advance galleys and an advance copy of the book, and that you had never done this before.

I further felt compelled to tell him that you were and are quite annoyed by the fact that you had never received acknowledgment of any kind from the company or from him. In fact, not even notification of receipt of either the galleys or the advance copy. I said that I, myself, felt absolutely no guilt in the matter since I had made every effort I could, and possibly more efforts than I should, to give him every opportunity to consider the book for production here. I saw no reason to not lay everything on the line with him. I don't know why we should pussy-foot or conceal our actual feelings. I hope you do not think I took too many liberties with him.

This morning he sent me a copy of a letter to you. I don't think he even knows how biased it is in his own favor. I like Darryl very much, but he's got a genius for self-hypnosis. In fact, there is sometimes a self-bewitched intensity about him that is hard to penetrate with facts.

He seems to have forgotten, for instance, that in our last conversation in Munich, I told him that I had no time to write down my ideas about the book, and further, they were not ideas—plural—but simply one notion which was, in general, to use the first third and the last third of the book. I said that was all there was in my mind and that was the extent of the "thinking" I had done about the book. Some thinking! I told him to tell this to Nunnally when he got back, and that was it. The clear purport of my conversation was to not have him wait on anything from me. The dear boy actually never showed any strong interest in the book and of course the fact is that he's not read it. He would never dissemble this—he's not a dissembler, and on the whole, I think he's a very fine man. It's just that he sees the world through Zanuck-colored glasses. And I'm sure this will never change. Why should it? It's very pleasant for him, and I suppose in his position there's nothing else he could do.

There's only one thing I'm upset about in this whole boring hassle: Annie Laurie Williams did say to me twice—once in front of William Fitelson—that Fox had turned the picture down. Not that we owe an explanation to anybody living, but I just like these relations to be clear. Especially with Darryl, who, with all his faults, is a pretty straight guy. Both Zanuck and Moskowitz are under the impression that she did not say this to me. I wish, rather impassionately, that this much were clear and then I'd forget the whole thing.

I had a couple of hours with Jack Warner yesterday and immediately following, a meeting with the Breen office. My relationship with this last group, after STREETCAR NAMED DESIRE, is very good, and they seemed rather eager to give us more leeway with the picture than we might have expected. I assured them that we had no interest in anatomising and detailing a whorehouse, but that who their mother was is a crucial piece of dramatic structure in the novel and will be, too, in the screenplay. They were most, most eager to help, believe it or not, and will let me know next week what their thoughts are.

Jack was, as ever, extremely cordial, efficient and just the least bit scatter-brained—what a character.

The weirdest part of the Zanuck business is that he <u>still</u> does not say that he has any <u>real</u> enthusiasm for EAST OF EDEN. He just doesn't want to miss anything that you and I might do. Am I wrong in thinking it peculiar that he thinks <u>we</u> should have enthusiasm for doing it with <u>him</u> under these circumstances? All very strange. See you soon. Love to Elaine.

Best, Gadg

[Darryl Zanuck insisted (in a letter of apology to Steinbeck) that *East of Eden* (1952) had not been "rejected" by Fox and attributed his delay in acknowledging receipt of the novel to Kazan's negligence in drafting a preliminary treatment. Backdoor negotiations were under way by midsummer, Zanuck later claimed, and in October Annie Laurie Williams, Steinbeck's agent, reported Jack Warner's interest to Kazan's attorney. In the meanwhile the massive novel reached the top of the *Times* best-seller list, where it remained through the spring.

The present "hassle" with Darryl Zanuck was preceded by another that Kazan apparently did not share with Steinbeck. Upon reaching California in early December, Kazan learned that "radical editing" of *Man on a Tightrope* had been completed by Zanuck, who defended the unilateral action as necessary to prevent a commercial failure (*A Life*, pp. 490–91). Kazan's return to New York was punctuated by a tart rejoinder: "Well, my dear friend, one finally ends up in the cutting room not face-to-face with Nunnally Johnson or Bobby Jacks or the cutter—but with you." Johnson and Jacks were Fox producers, the latter nominally involved in filming *Tightrope*. Jack Warner eventually coproduced *East of Eden* (1955) with an understanding that gave Kazan greater control of the editing process.

Joseph Breen recalled meeting and reassuring Kazan that he would permit Adam Trask's wife to be identified as "a prostitute" in order "to bring about the climactic tragedy" of *East of Eden*. He also "endeavored to make it clear" that the Production Code forbade "scenes dealing with any of the mechanics of prostitution," including those "laid in or around brothels" (to JLW, December 2, 1953, WB Archives).] *TLS, 3 pp., Columbia*

TO WALTER KERR

[New York]
[c. late December 1952]

Dear Walter,

That's a hell of a good piece! And is it true that the magazine has folded up? What a damned shame if it has. I liked the piece on McCarthy, too. I call "integrity" "Truth", and it is the number one standard in my scale. I believe

STREETCAR is a very moral piece and really speaks for the mixed up and the psychic unfortunates, really asks for compassion and understanding—that is why I fought so damned hard for it with the Legion and before that with Warner Brothers. It is telling no secret to write you that Warners would have done anything and everything that the Legion might have asked for. They had agreed to throw out the whole scene with the "collector" when I drove on the lot one morning. This will give you a rough idea. And all this butchery was being done on the grounds of "morality" by Jack Warner, a man who literally has none. (except that which concerns itself with the dollar and business practise—best to get the dollar) I thought your point about VOICE OF THE TURTLE excellently taken. I agree completely. It was a fancy little fib, for exactly the reasons you stated—it showed none of the complications, involvements and pain resultant from the over night stunt. *** What confuses me about the whole Catholic business in my field is how the Vatican paper in Rome can praise the MIRACLE, how the Vatican itself can give Rossellini its blessing to produce a film on St. Francis. And then look what happens out of 50th st. and Madison Ave. Is Spellman a deviationist? Is policy here one thing and policy in Europe ("people are more sophisticated morally in Europe") something quite different? Was there an official reaction, for example to your piece? Were you asked to <u>correct</u> it? Or am I thinking of the Commies?? You dont have to answer all these questions. But they are in the minds of a lot of people. And others too.

At any rate, God speed and more energy to you. If the magazine is dead, I hope you and those like you will revive it, and if you do, count on me for a small but definite contribution. Best to Jean.

Yours, <u>Gadg</u>

P.S. I've just been delighted at the way you have been winning the critics over. That bow, bouquet in hand, from Dick Watts was IT.

[In "Catholics and Hollywood" (*Commonweal*, December 19, 1952), Walter Kerr rejected the underlying premise of sectarian film criticism, which tended to equate "artistic merit" with "hoeing of the Catholic row." He went on to link this "inverted esthetic" with the acquired taste of the American Catholic moviegoer for "purity-with-popcorn." The "moral" ending imposed on *Streetcar* by the Production Code, "written under Catholic influence," seemed no more righteous to Kerr than to Kazan. "Is it actually the Catholic position that a wife must leave her husband for infidelity?" Kerr asked. "And what, in this eye-for-an-eye, tooth-for-a-tooth world, has become of the virtue of charity?" The "economic weapon" wielded by the Legion of Decency had the summary effect of curtailing innovation in Hollywood and suspending the intellectual principle of "free assent."

Kerr concluded that "we have as Catholics made it difficult for the most distinguished—and the most influential—Catholic creative voices of our time to gain access to this particular medium." *Commonweal* continues to offer "a fresh perspective in Catholic thought" as a biweekly review.] *TLS, 1 p., WHS*

TO DARRYL F. ZANUCK

[Sandy Hook, Connecticut]
December 30, 1952

Dear Darryl,

. . . Budd takes pride in his work and was a little hesitant about rushing something to you that was still going through the creative mill, but I have assured him that you have had a little experience reading treatments, synopses, outlines, step sheets and what not, and that you will be able to see from what we have how the meat can be put on the bones. I think all the essential material is here, and aside from the fact that the presentation may be a little hurried, the only thing I could wish is a somewhat different emphasis on certain story points. I think there is too much emphasis on the first part, for instance, and not nearly enough on the last half where the dramatic elements of the story really take hold. In a talk I had with Budd a little while ago we went a long way toward getting the story in proper focus, but unfortunately it would delay us several days to work all this into the outline I am airmailing you.

I think we have a very good and very human story. The waterfront crime background has been in the headlines for weeks, of course, but what appeals to me about this is that basically we have a strong and interesting love story— what happens on the waterfront changes the lives of two people in love. They are the two central characters and I think the general public will be interested in their development and their fate. A young Irish girl fresh out of a convent comes to New York's West Side to attend the funeral of her twin brother, a dock worker who stood up to the mob and wound up on the bottom of the river. At the wake she is shocked to find that no one knows who killed her brother, and even more shocked to discover that everyone, even her father, feels it is safer not to try and find out. She loved her brother very much and feels driven to find out who killed him. In the course of her search she meets a tough, young longshoreman who knew her brother. He's an ex-boxer, a forceful, physical type and, to put it bluntly, this becomes her first experience with sex. As it would for any sheltered girl, the experience is an overwhelming one for her. She inevitably tries to enlist his help, but his reaction is shifty and elusive. We are considering strengthening this situation by making his older brother part of the mob. Actually the boy is caught in a painful vise. A tough waterfront product, cynical, self-protective, he finds himself in love with a new kind of girl he isn't used to handling. At the same time the girl has enlisted the aid of a West Side priest, and this good man, modeled on the actual Father Corridan who has received a great deal of favorable publicity here lately, is uncovering too much of the truth for the comfort of the hoodlums who dominate large areas of the waterfront. The priest and the girl are warned off and finally threatened. The climax, for the priest, comes when the boy appears at the church to confess to him that he knows who killed his lover's brother. In fact he himself is somewhat implicated, although he did not know he was luring the brother to his death. He begs advice from the priest.

Meanwhile a waterfront investigation like the present one gets underway. The boy is on the spot, with the priest, with the girl, and with his own conscience. He didn't even know he had a conscience until he met this girl but her search for the truth has rubbed some of the callous off him. When he tells the girl this secret that is eating him inside, she too is faced with a moral dilemma. If the boy tells what he knows, perhaps putting the finger on his own brother, he faces the vengeance of the mob that is always turned against an informer. The girl suddenly finds herself selling out her soul to satisfy her heart. She begs him to keep quiet. They can run away—But he can't. Under the influence of the priest and what the girl has been saying until now, he feels it his duty as a citizen—though he puts this in rough waterfront lingo—to tell what he knows. Only that way, the priest has told him, will others like the girl's brother be saved. . . .

In secret session, he gives the Crime Commission the information they are looking for. As he comes out he is observed by a tail for the mob but he is not aware of it. That evening he is called to the phone by a couple of longshore pals. He goes out to join them without telling the girl where he is going. As he is on his way out, the girl suddenly recognises the circumstances: they are exactly the same as in the disappearance of her brother. In her nightgown she runs out into the street screaming for the boy. He hears her and stops. She screams her fears to him and he tells her not to worry, these are his friends. But as he looks around to indicate them, they have vanished.

Now they realize how imminent his danger is. They hurry to the priest to say goodbye. The priest doesn't tell the boy to stay. On the contrary he wishes them both good luck in their new life. He isn't blaming the boy but his run-out is going to make it more difficult for others to talk. . . . The boy and girl walk down the steps of the church but suddenly the boy can go no further. Something the girl herself has started has involved him to the end. He tells the girl he has to stick it out. He puts the best possible face on it—nobody would dare knock him off while the investigation is in progress. . . . To deepen the pathos we are considering adding several children in the boy's household, either his own children by a wife who died, or his younger brother and sisters. To protect them, the girl takes them to a bus-line, on their way to join a relative who has a little farm in Jersey. When she returns to the waterfront flat, she hears the news. A loading sling "slipped." Another one of those waterfront "accidents." The boy is killed.

The priest and the girl are together at the end. The battle of the waterfront goes on. The Crime Commission has begun to name names and heads are rolling. The FBI is moving in. Maybe not today or tomorrow but in good time the longshoremen will live a free and decent life like other American workingmen. As in war, a life has been given that others may live. So in spite of the boy's death the ending should be far from down-beat. And the tragedy is somewhat qualified by the fact that the audience should feel that the boy, crude, rough and tainted by the mob, was never the right man for girl; that she will go on to a sounder union. . . .

I want to say I have a strong conviction as to the way I want to do the picture. I would like to shoot the whole thing here on "live location"—either on one of the abandoned New York piers, or in Newark, Jersey City, Hoboken, Baltimore, etc. And I want to do with the cutting as we did on TIGHT-ROPE—I want to get a first and second cutting here, and then send it out to you. I would then come out to discuss it with you, see what you want to do and go on from there collaboratively. I think you will agree it worked out well on TIGHTROPE, with a minimum expenditure of time and effort.

As you can see, I have a great deal of what they call "faith" in this story. I think it can make one hell of a picture. Budd Schulberg is very close to the Father (Corridan) and through him I know we will have the priest's whole-hearted cooperation. . . . He is a vivid personality, unlike any priest that has ever been put on the screen. We would of course have to make a sizable contribution to the St. Xavier School to which Corridan belongs. I think Corridan, whose waterfront activities are of course backed by the Archdiocese, would also make an invaluable technical director, if he would agree to serve in this capacity. As Budd says in his article, the Father is a one-man encyclopaedia of waterfront crime.

I have had a meeting with Roy Brewer about the story. He approves whole-heartedly of our angle and has cooperated already to the extent of recommending someone in N.Y. for us to talk to. Brewer and I have had a friendly exchange of letters since. He was, by the way, a big obstacle in the Arthur Miller version. However, on this new story not only is he with us but a great deal has happened since those days to justify this kind of story. In view of the headlines every day, the disclosures about Anastasia and Murder Inc. etc., NO RESPONSIBLE PUBLIC FIGURE COULD AFFORD TO BE AGAINST THIS PICTURE TODAY. The Governor of New York, of New Jersey, the D.A., the Crime Commission and every responsible element in the community is taking the strongest possible stand against just such conditions as we will show in this picture. And the picture will have a strongly pro-American, anti-Communist theme, for these conditions will be cleaned up by loyal, religious longshore-men under the guidance of a priest—which happens to be the truth. The moral, in other words, will be somewhat as Father Corridan has stated it in many public interviews—one of the most effective ways of rooting out Communism is to take back from them the genuine grievances they exploit for their own purposes. In other words, see to it that decent, law-abiding Americans do the clean-up jobs that need to be done. I think Budd's article in the Times expresses this point of view very well.

Although both Budd and Father Corridan have had letters and wires from several different studios, I have urged him—and he has gladly agreed—to give you first refusal on this story. This is not only because you and I have had a fine relationship in the past. It is also because, as I explained to Budd, you had more guts than anyone else out there. Budd feels sincerely as I do that this is your kind of picture. . . . I wouldn't stress the time pressure so much if I didn't feel sure we had something really hot here, a story that is on top of the news, so to speak, and yet that has none of the rushed, slap-dash quality of a picture racing the headlines. I hope and am really confident that you will share my enthusiasm. Could you call me after you have read it. I'll be at Newtown Connecticut 348 W 1. Until Sunday noon my time. I do hope you will have been able to give consideration to our project before that.

With New Year's good wishes and best always,

[Kazan described *On the Waterfront* with keen awareness of problems encountered by "The Hook" in 1951. He also mended fences with Darryl Zanuck in hopes of contracting the film on a more lucrative and independent basis. Two elements, Kazan claimed, would save the enclosed treatment from any hint of a message film with political repercussions: "a strong and interesting love story" and the fact, confirmed by daily "headlines," that "NO RESPONSIBLE PUBLIC FIGURE COULD AFFORD TO BE AGAINST THIS PICTURE TODAY." The love story of Terry Malloy, initially "cynical" and "self-protective," and Edie Doyle, a convent girl who returns to investigate the murder of her crusading brother, is closely related to the investigation of waterfront crime by Terry's discovery of a conscience and halting cooperation with the Crime Commission. Describing the testimony in democratic terms—"duty as a citizen"—did not, however, relieve Zanuck's fear of offending labor or arming communists with criticism of American institutions as the Korean War dragged on. Nor was Zanuck pleased by Edie's continuing investigation of her brother's murder, a basic feature of Budd Schulberg's original script, where the probing of corruption reaches the highest levels. A revised treatment submitted in the new year would further emphasize the duties of citizenship and eliminate Terry Malloy's premature death. Kazan gave "first refusal" to Darryl Zanuck in spite of his high-handed editing of *Tightrope* and Kazan's clear resentment. The process had not "worked out well," if the later description in *A Life* is to be believed.

John M. Corridan, SJ, taught at one of several adult schools founded by the Jesuits to counteract Marxist influence on labor by instilling a Catholic "philosophy of social action" and offering practical instruction in labor law, collective bargaining, and parliamentary procedure (Fisher, pp. 72–73). He dismissed scare tactics by union officials and stated in Budd Schulberg's enclosed article that " 'the men down here, almost without exception, are loyal, God-fearing Americans. The way to fight Communism in the labor movement is to find out what the men really need in order to live healthy, happy, dignified lives and then fight for it' " (*NYT*, December 28, 1952).

Roy M. Brewer led the powerful Alliance of Theatrical Stage Employees and was often consulted by studio officials on labor issues. His present cooperation differs from an earlier attempt to obstruct filming of "The Hook." Parenthetically, Miller's account of the affair differs from Kazan's insofar as Miller claims not to have met Brewer in California and to have learned of his objections only after returning to New York (*A Life*, pp. 410–12; Miller, pp. 303–08). Brewer recalled meeting Kazan *and* Miller in Harry Cohn's office. In addition to exposing communists, Brewer was a leading "clearance man" who restored the livelihood of those who repented of political sins.] *TL with enclosures, 5 pp., Wesleyan*

TO DARRYL F. ZANUCK

[Sandy Hook, Connecticut]
[January 15, 1953]

My dear little chum:

. . . Budd Schulberg and I have retreated to my country estate and are here working on the final outline. We've done a lot of work last week, and the more we work on the thing the more human and personal it becomes. It's no longer about the specific union issue but about citizenship—about the obligation of a citizen to testify against something when he finds it to be evil. The theme is very broad and big and I feel confident you'll be very happy when you read this final outline. I know the love story has been greatly improved, and it goes right through the picture now, and all the external events are seen through the eyes of the lovers. Everyone who has heard the story agrees that we are on our way to a picture of large and universal theme and with sure-fire popular elements.

As I told you on the phone, we called Meany and he could not see us for several weeks. He is busy getting his reorganization underway, preparing for the forthcoming AFL convention, etc. But the more Budd and I thought about it, the clearer it became that while he may lend his encouragement and support, or at least not stand in our way, he would hardly give an endorsement to a script that was not written, which is what Spyros asked for. As far as I know the AFL has never actually endorsed any picture. Our story, as you could see from the outline, does not attack Ryan or unionism as such. It simply states that mobsters have muscled in on the docks, which is now not only a matter of common knowledge but a condition about which there is a great deal of public opinion, as witness the fact that every paper in the city has expressed itself strongly on the subject. . . . As I said before, we are no longer a controversial picture, first because our theme is a broader one, citizenship and its obligations, and secondly because everyone (ironically even Joe Ryan) has come out for a cleanup of gangsterism on the docks. We enclose two clips from this morning's Times that are typical. For some reason the Times has lagged behind the Journal, Mirror and News in advocating strong measures against pilferage and hoodlumism on the docks. The editorial speaks for itself. Tobey smells good publicity for himself on a SAFE ISSUE. If it weren't safe he wouldn't go near it. . . .

Furthermore Meany himself has publicly deplored the New York port conditions. The Daily News quoted him as saying, "This is a case of gangsterism taking over a union." But while we know from this that he is with us in spirit and is on record as opposed to gangsters muscling into unions, we think it is unrealistic to wait for his "endorsement." He seems to be playing a cat and mouse game with Ryan and this may make him cautious about public statements. But we KNOW that he will never do anything to impede this picture being made, or ever take a public position against it—anymore than he impedes his own labor officials, Beck, Hall and others, when they speak out strongly against the corruption of unionism in the port. Just as no newspaper can afford to support the status quo in the harbor, Meany can't afford to either. . . .

I'm not going to be delayed by anything. This is your kind of picture and I want very much to make it with you. Unless unusual pressure is brought to bear, there seems little chance to see Meany for many weeks and I think we should face the fact that a specific endorsement may not be forthcoming—or at least would hold us up too long. Unless you consider his public statement about the blight of gangsterism on the piers an endorsement. In a very definite way it endorses the action against the rackets that we dramatize in our picture. Budd and I are going ahead working every moment, but we also want to make a firm deal pretty quickly. The studios who approached the waterfront priest didn't check first to see if the idea was acceptable to organized labor. They must have assumed that this was so since the priest was on the side of organized labor. I think we should do the same thing. I think we should take the same stand that Bill Hearst Jr and the others are taking—the terrorizing of working men is wrong, its Un-American, and it must be rooted out, both by federal action and by the unions themselves.

I think if you were here, if you could read the daily press and feel the unanimity of opinion on this subject you would agree with us that while this would have been a controversial picture two years ago, it cannot possibly be thought of as such today. In other words I'm urging you to go ahead. I want to make money from this enterprise as well as enjoy the satisfaction of making a fine picture and I would never urge this if I really thought there was a real danger of labor opposition.

Let's hear from you as soon as possible as the hearings begin again Monday, interest will be at high pitch, and we're raring to go.

[Terry Malloy acquired a teenage son in the "final outline" of *On the Waterfront,* although later he became a "kid nephew" linked with Terry through the Golden Warriors, a rooftop club he informally leads. Big Joe Friendly appears as a powerful hiring boss, while Terry's older brother Charley is cast as an influential member of the mob. His death, presumably an execution, is reported in the press rather than dramatized but has a decisive effect: "What Edie started Terry has to finish." In speech that "must be faltering and awkward but moving and convincing," Terry explains "citizenship and its obligations" to Jimmy, who has scorned his father's informing: "There comes a time when a man must speak out, no matter how painful it may be to him, if he wants to stop something he knows to be evil." Terry survives the ordeal and is last seen walking on the street with Edie and Jimmy, unafraid and unashamed of having broken the "conspiracy of silence" ("The Golden Warriors," n.d., Wesleyan).

Hearings of the New York State Crime Commission resumed on January 19 with a consensus that the International Longshoremen's Association, an affiliate of the American Federation of Labor, must sever ties with organized crime and end the "shape-up." George Meany, president of the AFL, dispensed with any "cat and mouse game" in ordering the ILA "to clean house by April 30 or face expulsion from the federation." Charles Tobey, chair of the U.S. Senate Interstate Commerce Committee, predictably welcomed televised hearings of his own investigation, as noted in the *Times* enclosure cited by Kazan (January 15, 1953).

Negotiations with Twentieth Century-Fox were difficult from start to finish, beginning with the president's request that George Meany endorse the *Waterfront* project on the basis of a partial script. Darryl Zanuck remained enthusiastic but still worried about offending labor and encouraging communists to "capitalize" on the film's social criticism. He also regarded Edie's activism and Terry's son as threats to the central love story. Nor could he "visualize" Marlon Brando, his choice to play Terry, as the father of "a 13- or 14-year-old son." Lacking a complete first draft or the commitment of a major star, Zanuck parried Kazan's request for a profit-sharing arrangement with strategic delay (to EK and Schulberg, February 4 and 12, 1953, Wesleyan).] *TL with enclosures, 2 pp., Wesleyan*

TO JOSHUA LOGAN

Sandy Hook
Friday [April 10, 1953]

Dear Josh:
Been meaning to write to you ever since I saw PICNIC last Monday night. I liked it very much and especially admired your handling of the second act. This was brilliant. I know you will win the prize. I'm rooting like mad for you. Not only for you, but against your competition. Frankness between friends is a virtue. CAMINO is building. Whether enough or solidly enough is a question. We'll do over twenty this week. Five of that is Guild. Cheryl is scared of

what will happen when this stops next week. What will happen is simply that it will stop. But I got a hunch we're in for a short juicy run, and I'm going to work on the show with Williams and see if we cant make the beginning a little better. Meantime I'm working hard on movie projects. I'm going to try to do better, I've got to do better. Esp. on story. Leland was so sweet; he bawled hell out of me, said I was hasty and careless on story and always impatient, and always going somewhere etc. ALL TRUE, and I took it all in the kishkas where I deserved to have it laid into me. Give my love to Sam B., I mean love, not any of your gross affection or such, and to Nedda and again congratulations on PICNIC. Odets went with me and he enjoyed it enormously too. So. I'll be seeing you soon I hope.

ever, gadge

[*Picnic* (1953) won the major prizes, including a Pulitzer for William Inge and a Tony Award for Josh Logan, who directed the long-running Broadway hit. *The Crucible* finished a distant runner-up to *Picnic* in balloting for the Drama Critics' Circle Award. *Camino Real* received two votes.

As predicted by Kazan, *Camino* had a "short juicy run" of sixty-odd performances. Reviewers attacked the play as "an enormous jumble of five-cent philosophy," while a small band of admirers, including John Steinbeck, found "clarity and beauty" in the production and urged critics to be more tolerant "when a play of courage, imagination and invention comes along" (Steinbeck/*Letters*, p. 441). Kazan was spared harsh criticism and wryly praised for having made "the entire cast behave as if they knew what they were saying." Much later he assumed responsibility for miscasting and misdirecting the show and for accepting a stage design ill-suited to Tennessee Williams's lyricism.

Lapses of continuity in *Zapata* and *Man on a Tightrope* invited Leland Hayward's friendly criticism, as well as Kazan's resolve "to do better."] *TLS, 1 p., Library of Congress*

With Tennessee Williams

[New York]
May 18, 1953

Dear John:

It must seem strange me writing you. Doing it because I've got something tough to say and its not easy to say it. On the other hand I want to put it exactly as I feel it, no more, no less.

I spent the last three days in the country going over and over our outline. I tried to look at it as a producer. It says in the contract that I'm a producer. Beyond that, as I've told you many times, I feel a tremendous responsibility doing EDEN especially under the compensation partly by profit arrangement. And beyond that I just got to do you real proud this time. I'll be in my own private dog house for years if I dont bring this one off completely.

I blame myself for what happened to Zapata. I'm supposed to be the movie-maker of the combine. And the movie-making is what was wrong with Zapata. It ended up in the "It sure has wonderful things in it" category. The attack we took on it was just not right. And the mistake we made was made right at this stage of the work. Nothing we did (or could have done) subsequently helped, once we made the basic mistake in planning.

As you know I've been terribly concerned that I might make the same kind of mistake here. I'm a damned good director on the set. At the planning stage, I think I could still use a year or two of class "A" ball. I made the same kind of mistake on Tightrope, for instance. And again right at this point. I let get by two no good love stories that didn't tie in. I figured I could somehow cover everything with a big sauce of direction. Well I poured it on. I swam in mountain ice-cold streams, and I gave out songs and I held kisses longer than necessary for all practical purposes—and still the bloody scenes stank on film. My fault. I was responsible.

Now. I think absolutely every choice we've made thus far on EDEN right. But I dont think we're home yet planning wise or in this outline stage.

Even when you were up in Connecticut ten days ago I felt something was wrong with our outline. Remember the morning you left I suggested that we start with Cal, and stick with him all thru. This was to pitch the audience immediately into our story on the main track. Now I think Cal should be centralized even more.

The more I studied it during these last days, the more serious I felt the work we still had to do. I still think we're diffuse. Zapata was diffuse. I know we've chosen the right part of your material to work with. I know we've made excellent and even daring eliminations—but, to use and use an old and honorable word, we need a much better <u>continuity</u> before we write a line of dialogue.

So this led to the next step in my thinking. I think we ought to get you a better and more experienced movie constructionist than Gadge Kazan. Put it another way, Kazan the producer would not hire Kazan the writer to work with you on this job.

I have no false modesty. I'm a fertile director. But stress <u>director</u>. The ideas I have are basically director's ideas. I'm not a first rate constructionist—I know that. And a first rate novelist and a first rate novel should have a first rate screen technician. I dont want to take any goddamn chances with this one. Its no time for self favoring. There is too much at stake.

What I'd like to do is bring in a really first class screen artisan or craftsman. I'd like this man to take our line up of material and develop it into a first draft screen play. His job would be basically simplification and unification and continuity—singleness! He would work in consultation with you and he would work in consultation with me.

Thinking of someone like a couple of guys you've met Bob Ardrey or Paul Osborn. These guys aren't up to your ankles as writers or artists. They're not. But they are specialists. Screen writing is a special field. It is not your forte and it is not mine. The book deserves the best.

I think we've done a fine job till now. I think we'll completely take over, and work together and alone at a later stage. But right now we need someone who is not a blood relation. That's my professional opinion. This man would write a first draft, a rough one, but one that would embody his ideas on unity and simplification and singleness. Then as I see it he would bring it to us, and you could rewrite every line of dialogue, and we could make any changes we wanted to. But I have a strong hunch that if we get the right guy we'll find ourselves with a much improved continuity.

And while this person was working, you could see your musical thru, which I know you badly want to do and do right, and I could do my other work. Once we had this draft we would find ourselves with plenty of time before our Warner Brother deadline. We'd have real objectivity. We'd be "outside". And then we could move in and be real tough. And good.

Its tough for me to bring this up. There's no one I enjoy working with as much as I do you. But I'd be a poor producer and a poor friend, if I didn't tell you what I believe. We dont have to do what I suggest. I'll be back from California in ten days and we could sit down and do it ourselves as we plan. But I think the plan I outline the best one for us, and for our project.

Eden is the toughest job of dramatization I've ever seen—and for one reason: Its so rich! there's so much of it! Even when you take only the last fourth, there's much too much.

Nothing I have said is motivated by the necessities of my schedule. I dont hurry anything anymore. I only want to do real good ones. And I've already put in more time on EDEN than everything else put together. It calls for more thought. Its bigger and tougher and richer and its got to be much better to live up to its promise. It sets its own measure and standard.

Anyway give it a real good think. I've also told Annie Laurie about it. I trust her. She's a hard headed and thoroughly honest person. And she's really all for us.

Love always,

[Kazan's earliest "angle" was "to use the first third and the last third" of *East of Eden* and "throw away the middle" (to DFZ, December 11, 1952). The opening sequences were narrowed to the immediate past of Adam and Cathy Trask (later Kate) in Connecticut and California. Formerly a prostitute, she is beaten by her benefactor and rescued by Adam, whom she reluctantly marries and accompanies to the West. With the birth of twins in 1900—Aron and Cal—she abandons the family and returns to prostitution in Salinas. Kazan completed a ten-part outline in early April and conveyed his "idea" to John Steinbeck that each unit "should be projected from the point of view of a different character," whose basic motivation is "to wrestle with the problem of good and evil." Soon he further reduced the scope of the project: "Game up. Decided to do only last 3rd of Book. Begin when boys are 16. Damned good decision. That way the story has a unity, clarity, a leading man, one single leading man and no narration whatsoever." Outlines drafted by the collaborators in late April were lengthy and diffuse and apparently convinced Kazan that outside help was needed. He knew that Paul Osborn, friend and nearby neighbor in Connecticut, would do "a better job, much, than John & I. John is shaky. In a way I am too. I have my mind on too damned many things. I'll soon be working full time w Schulberg. So I dont want to be thinking of Steinbeck Tenn. Wms Robert Anderson" (notebook, Wesleyan).] *TL, 2 pp., Wesleyan*

TO JOHN STEINBECK

[Sandy Hook, Connecticut]
[c. early June 1953]

Dear John:
Just hung up from talking to you. If there ever was a half a buck well spent, it was that phone call. Made me feel real fine. You know, dont you, one: Anything I do in re our project I do because it seems to be the objectively best thing to do. Objectivity is terribly hard between friends. And even harder in re my own work (the two outlines). Secondly: I'm not, even in my own most secret opinion, infallible. I usually err on the side of being too easy to sway.

Except when it comes to craft problems. Third: Cancel one and two out! You know damned right you can have it anyway you want. I'd love to do the screen play with you, and Paul is nothing to me except a pleasant friend. My opinion had nothing to do with him. I felt Eden needed someone who was far from it to turn it into dramatic shape and length and singleness. I think Paul can help us. Underline think. How can you be sure? I never talked to him about the book, casually or any other way until after I had studied our second outline. I felt I had failed not you. I was supposed to be the objective one. How could you be? I went to Paul most likely because he lived up here and because he owed me a favor. I had done two weeks work on Point of No Return for him gratis. He always said he hoped he would have a chance to "pay me back". I wanted another professional opinion to check against my instinct that we weren't yet on the right track. Then we began to talk and very quickly worked out those things we told you. I might as well have gone to Robert Ardrey, who is a closer friend of mine and is also an expert in this particular field of editing, narrowing, aligning, slimming and gathering into unity some one else's creative work. Interestingly neither Bob nor Paul are a bit happy about their proficiency. Their ultimate hope for self esteem is that they will do something creative themselves. They try, but somehow the spring is drying up, or the old something isn't there with them, and before they know it they are once more working on the creative work of another author. Everytime they take on a job they feel they are pushing further away their hope to do something themselves. Well they're both nice guys but that's the grief that keeps them awake. So if Paul acts funny sometimes I remember that he's jealous as hell of anyone creative even while deeply admiring them. He's a sweet guy, sweet and sour, like that Chinese dish. I didn't want to propose anything to you vague. And I wasn't sure myself. It took time and thought and was one of the most difficult things I've ever done. Like all judgments in this field, its not a hundred percent, and there's no way of measuring it, and it cant be guaranteed. Its a judgment I made; its nothing more. As I say, I was supposed to be the objective one, and I felt it my failure. I was also kind of jumpy about Zapata which I had rerun a few days earlier and thought how much better that would have been if I had driven for greater unity. Paul, in his first conversation, showed an immense drive towards simplification. That's why I went on talking to him and then brought him to you. But, as I say, it might have been another fellow, there are others in this field while there are very few creative guys. And it might have been that you had said: Gadg, relax, you're jumping too fast, and I would have gone with that too. I had a long long deal with Tennessee Williams about unifying his play CAMINO REAL, and here again didn't quite act on my conviction and it was finally Tennessee who suffered most because I wasn't strong enough at the right time. That may have contributed to my feeling, in an oblique way, on EDEN. I also knew and talked to Annie Laurie about the possibility of hurting your feelings. In fact I talked to Annie Laurie every damned step of the way. Then I thought I'd be a poor friend if I worried about anything except telling you, right or wrong, exactly what I felt. So: that letter.

So I was worried, I'm trying to say, and I sure was glad to talk to you. I dont like it on the phone either, or anyway except face to face. That's easy and quick and accurate. And human.

Molly is going to call Elaine. I told her you wanted to travel in the middle of the week, so she'll talk about it that way. You can have my study and write your same hours. I'm out of doors all the time.

Love, g.

[Working with "hordes of consultants" in Hollywood for a "stipulated time" no longer satisfied Paul Osborn, who preferred to "finish successfully no matter how long it takes—and finish here in Conn." Such an independent "set-up" entailed risk, as he informed Leland Hayward in later correspondence: "I have to be careful in saying 'yes' to anything until I am sure that I can lick it. It may sometimes be a big gamble and waste for me; on the other hand, it's the way I like and, believe me, it's the way I do my best writing" (June 21, 1954, WHS). By late July Osborn had come to terms with Warner Bros. and drafted thirty pages of the *Eden* screenplay. The novel had been reduced to a fraction of the original, but Steinbeck's ambition was still a warning to the screenwriter: "There is nothing beyond this book—nothing follows it. It must contain all in the world I know and it must have everything in it of which I am capable—all styles, all techniques, all poetry" (Steinbeck/*Journal*, p. 8).

Apparently Kazan's worry about offending John Steinbeck was ungrounded. Steinbeck may have questioned the choice of Paul Osborn, but he was struggling to write the book for a musical set on Cannery Row and seems to have welcomed a professional screenwriter.] *TLS, 2 pp., Columbia*

TO JUDY KAZAN

PM: New York 21, NY, July 17, 1953

Judy dear

We got and enjoyed both your letters very very much. You sound like you're having a most educational summer. You'll probably not realize till years from now how much you're learning. I was a waiter too all thru college—four years, and I was a dish washer when I went to Yale. Your mother first saw me serving hash from a hot box and took an instant dislike to me (and the damned hash). Glad to hear you dont like drunks, but its interesting to try to figure out why people drink and what it means to them and what it does for them. It answers some kind of need in a lot of people and its not strictly an American habit either. I like it myself, but its one of the things I'm rather moderate about. Anyway you're meeting all different types, and I know you're seeing and noticing much more than you're writing or can write or are even aware of. We're having a good time too. I'm working as usual. I've got the play all cast and I think its a good cast, and I'm finding a cast and locations for the movie. Dick Day is working with me again, even though he can only give me part time because he's all wrapped up in T.V. But its fun, I drive around in the mighty and go up and down stairs (I'm looking for roof tops.) and go out on piers and all over ships and into saloons. Its fun. The characters I'm with this time are kind of tough and I may even have a body guard when I shoot the picture. What fun! Last week end John and Elaine were up and John and Chris got to be great fishing buddies. My god they spent hours out there on the lake and came home with a lot of Pickerel, all of which Chris caught. John rowed the boat. Chris was the "star". John took all the fish home and is going to smoke them in an outdoor oven he has. They're a darned nice couple. This week end we're going to sit home and see if the mumps hit or dont. Mommie has some kind of an idea to take Chris and have him tested in New Haven. In case he proves immune, then she may come to Blue after all. She wants very much to see you, and Granny wrote her a rather pathetic letter, and in her old age, (their) maybe these two characters will get real friendly. It took me a few years to get real friendly with my pop, and I guess they will make it too. Generally children and parents end up with some little tensions, that take years to wear off. Kids think parents are designed to make it impossible for them (the kids) to have a good time. But when you get back I'm even going to teach you how to drive the car. All kidding aside I hope Mommie comes up and see you. She's feeling pretty good and she's finally finishing her play, and deserves some fun. I'll get up in the Mighty, in that case, and take Chris and the Pontiac and go to Canada. (This is all based on the assumption that Chris does not get the mumps. Anyhow, we'll see.) This letter is just to encourage you to write more. And I'll try to too. I've got another new office where I'm temporarily parking (424 Madison, c/o Horizon American Films.—a kind of fly-by-night outfit. But I'm apparently too disastrous and unprofitable a diet for the substantial firms.)

Why cant you follow the Dodgers? Where the hell is your radio?

LOVE, daddy

[A few weeks shy of seventeen, Judy Kazan spent an "educational summer" at a resort on Blue Mountain Lake in New York State, where the Thachers owned a cabin occasionally used by Molly as a retreat for writing.

"The darned thing is an enormous hit," Kazan wrote in mild surprise shortly after Deborah Kerr, a film veteran, and Robert Anderson, a novice playwright, made their Broadway debut in *Tea and Sympathy* (1953). Reviewers admired Kazan's direction, although one raised the familiar complaint of a "tendency to go in for blacks and whites." Kazan credited the play with reviving him "profession-ally" after four consecutive failures on stage and screen (*A Life*, p. 506).

Simplified logistics recommended Hoboken, New Jersey, as a suitable location for *On the Waterfront*. Kazan's office address indicates rejection of the project by major Hollywood studios, including Twentieth Century-Fox. Darryl Zanuck "stunned" the collaborators in late May by citing unpopular subject matter, dra-matic limitations of the script, and especially the advent of CinemaScope, which favored large-scale productions in Technicolor (*A Life*, p. 508). By happenstance Kazan and Schulberg soon reached a profit-sharing agreement with Horizon-American, a subsidiary of Horizon Pictures, the "fly-by-night" founded by Sam Spiegel and John Huston in 1947, to film *Waterfront* in association with Columbia Pictures.

Kazan anticipated a possible trip to "Blue" in his "Mighty" Morris Minor. In the meanwhile he questioned Judy's loyalty to the Brooklyn Dodgers. Apropos of the Dodgers, Judy has recalled a visit by John and Elaine Steinbeck, nearby neighbors in Manhattan: "One night while I was doing high school homework in my room, Day called upstairs and asked me to come down. The Steinbecks were in the front hall, talking with my parents. They had just been to a Dodger game, been invited into the clubhouse afterwards, and given a real Dodger cap. They'd brought it as a present for me. There were few gifts, my whole life long, as surprising, right, and thrilling."] *TLS, 1 p., JKMP*

TO BUDD SCHULBERG

SH: Horizon-American Inc.
424 Madison Ave., New York 17, N.Y.
July 20, 1953

Dear Budd:

Just got thru looking at unknowns for TERRY. Can't get over the feeling that Brando is WRONG. But that leaves us nowhere unless I can come up with someone who is right. I'd say the second choice (after Brando, the first choice by default as it were) is Ralph Meeker. That's not a cause for enthusiasm, Ralph Meeker, is it?

I've got two candidates. Please reserve 10:30 to midnight Thursday night. The two unknowns are doing scenes for us. I think they are both excellent possibilities. If I can get Darren McGavin to do a scene that same night I'll try that. He's also a possibility. Then we'd have three unknowns trying out, and to tell you the truth I don't want Marlon Brando being surly and introverted thru this goddam picture unless I feel absolutely stymied on the unknown department.

As I've been interviewing people for the leads, I've been—I hope—getting clearer on the part. Casting does have that use. Whenever I cast an interesting thing happens. The key scenes in the part begin to come into the foreground with their demands. Their own demands. Certain scenes begin to be, rightly or wrongly, measures of the role. This has happened with several scenes of TERRY. And in one case I'm not sure the standard should be rigidly maintained.

The requirements of the last sequence of the movie is that Terry, in one way or another, be able to beat up three goons and Mr. Friendly. I found myself rejecting people because they were only middleweights (160 lbs.) and I also found myself looking for heavyweights, almost exclusively. This made it tough.

I also got thinking about the whole sequence. I went over and over and over it. How can one man beat up three goons and a head hood. "It's happened!" But has it? Well, say it has. The circumstances must have been special and the accidents all fortunate. So it becomes my job as a director to find special and fortunate circumstances whereunder Terry can beat all these guys up. So I began to cook and to cook up. I contrived and contrived. I thought: maybe a couple of the goons fall down a man hole. Maybe they are inactivated by glares of longshoremen, honest longshoremen. Maybe two of the goons begin an argument between themselves and etc., etc., and etc. You see Budd, we left it to the director, much as they did in the old Doug Fairbanks features, except that those were in costume and were supposed to have happened long ago when heroes were heroes and villains were incompetent. The thing is I found myself contriving from disbelief.

I love the final sequence thru the store window scene ("Your own friends won't know you") and thru Edie finally urging him on and thru the sudden entrance into Friendly's office. I believe his emotion and her emotion and I believe his recognition of the absolute necessity of walking in on Friendly at no matter what cost. I love what he says to Friendly, especially the "I'm fucking glad I did it" bit. But the disarming of the hoods needs some directorial contriving and the triumph of Terry over the three goons and Friendly is strictly movies.

That's the sad conclusion to which I've come brother, and like other sad conclusions I've come to on this bit or the other bit it doesn't worry me at all. We're working on a living organism that's sound and heals and grows, and I know this needs discussion and real facing, but from that, between us, we'll solve it. So now I'll spitball.

There's something very heroic about this guy needing to confront Friendly face to face and to tell him in front of the whole listening waterfront that he is glad he did what he did, that he is not ashamed and is not going to be shamed and he is not going to be driven off the waterfront and he has no intention of leaving town and that he's not going to cross the street when he sees him and that he's not going to pretend anything friendly. And above all that he knows that Friendly is no good, and that now he's his ENEMY not his VASSAL. So once Terry does this he has relieved his soul. He's o.k. He's said it, and he's no longer afraid.

BUT NOW! Let's be as honest as possible. What would happen? Would Terry want to set on Friendly and take his head off because he killed Charlie? Would he want to take just one good solid poke at Friendly in public to seal the understanding? What would happen? One thing certainly would not happen. He wouldn't be able to beat up Friendly and the three goons, no matter how I contrived it.

On the other hand, there is something to be said for HIS being beat up. (Then I could cast it any weight). Sooner or later and essentially that is what would happen. Perhaps Terry knows in his guts that its better for that inevitable beating to happen in daylight and in public. They can't go all the way in public and in daylight. If he's murdered later, everyone will have seen the incident in daylight and in public and this would practically convict Friendly. (Now we're getting practical).

The fact is that the most terrifying dramatic thing that could happen at this moment of the script is for HIM TO BE BEAT UP. (Then I could cast him at 158 lbs, or 145 lbs. even.) If such a massacre were photographed in longshots, off the fight, as it were, it could take on the aspect of a self crucifixion. Here would be the poetic spectacle of a kid walking up and taking his lumps in order to break off from a corrupt past and in order to smash a corrupt image of himself in the eyes of the other people of his world. It's a necessary thing to do no matter what. As I say, it's a kind of crucifixion. He chances dying (in quotes) so that the other longshoremen can live (in quotes too). If he gets beat up in public for what he did he will have 1/ told Friendly off. 2/ Freed himself from tension and fear. 3/ Let everyone see who he is, and let everyone see where he stands. 4/ And let everyone know that Friendly is a murderer.

And then how full heartedly the men would offer him a job! How admiring and loyal and even worshipful they would be!

Somewhere around this thinking of mine there is an ending that is really deep and unusual and un-movie-ish and one that BOTH would happen AND would have real overtones. Our ending now starts to have size and then comes this dixie finish and the director is cooking and cooking and starting to look to run old Doug Fairbanks pictures (This actually did occur to me).

ek:hb

Your unrelenting amigo.

(But this is important.)

Love
Gadg

[Passing doubts aside, Kazan's later claim that he "always preferred Brando" as Terry Malloy is consistent with a note written to Budd Schulberg in September

1952: Brando "is a superb idea! He & Julie Harris would be great! Feel free to talk to either or both. Brando is quite different from his public face" (n.d., Dartmouth). The "surly" behavior resented by Kazan was the "face" Brando turned to Hollywood in the early 1950s.

Ralph Meeker played a supporting role in *Mister Roberts* (1948) and replaced Marlon Brando in the resident company of *Streetcar* in 1949. He returned to Broadway after a brief, unpromising career in films and won solid reviews as a handsome young drifter in *Picnic*.

Budd Schulberg's enthusiasm as a boxing writer and fan exceeded Kazan's ability to contrive a "dixie finish" for *On the Waterfront*. In the April draft Terry disarms his "cousin" Mickey Friendly and three "goons," throws their guns into the river, and dares them to fight "strictly on the muscle." He also has no remorse for his testimony: "I'm glad what I done today, see?" Thereafter Terry fights "like a madman" and delivers "a bone-crushing uppercut that almost lifts Mickey off his feet." Schulberg dispatched Friendly in June. Terry lifts Mickey and "slugs him again," whereupon he "topples" into the water, bobbing up "among the garbage, his face streaked with oil, and contorted with rage" ("The Golden Warriors," April 1 and June 1, 1953, Wesleyan).] *TLS, 4 pp., Dartmouth*

TO BUDD SCHULBERG

SH: Horizon-American Inc.
424 Madison Ave., New York 17, N.Y.
[late July 1953]

Dear Budd:

One more note before I blow town. I'll have to leave the responsibility for the Brando thing with you. These next ten days I dont want to think about the picture much, and with Sam away til Sunday (I'm told) you're not only holding the fort, you are the fort, you and Brownie.

I'm not insane about Brando for this. In fact in my opinion he is quite wrong. But he's a fine actor and if he's really excited about it and will work like a beginner trying to get a start, he can be fine. He's got to be hungry and anxious. The power to be that disappears with your picture on an ad. On the other hand I promised Sam that I would take him if he wanted to make the picture and I think commercially it will no doubt help us.

At any rate he arrives in town Sunday the second of August and leaves on the fifth, and it is imperative repeat imperative that he read the script and give us his yes or no. He cannot take the script to Europe with him. Our time is beginning to run short and we cannot wait for his majesty to get comfy in Paris and send us an answer when he feels it. . . .

If we dont get Brando, and I think it most likely we wont, I'm for Paul Newman. This boy will definitely be a film star. I have absolutely no doubt.

He's just as good looking as Brando, and his masculinity which is strong is also more actual. He's not as good an actor as Brando yet, and probably will never be. But he's a darn good actor with plenty of power, plenty of insides, plenty of sex. He and Malden are working on two scenes to show to Sam and yourself. I'm for him without seeing more.

We'd have to change the set-up just a little with Paul (or even with Marlon for that matter). I think it should be stressed that he is, or rather HAS BEEN a favored one, the white haired boy, the glamor boy, awarded a sinecure for his past service to the mob and not quite a longshoreman. This is another respect in which he has allowed himself to grow a little soft. This whole idea fits in perfectly with our theme.

I'm typing a separate memo to Sam about our Hoboken location. I'm convinced now that this is IT too, and have definitely decided for it. I was over there this morning watching the shape, and there are great great possibilities over there. Dick Day is immensely enthusiastic too.

I think I will, just for the hell of it, go over once more, the rewriting notes. I hope you can do them all before Brando reads it. But I think you should by all means fix the two that concern the end and the Catholic inside-church opposition to Father Barry.

I agree with your idea that the final fight starts promisingly for TERRY. And then the goons really get the sign from Friendly and really get over the initial surprise and get down to work. The wraps come off. They begin to punch hell out of him. What would inevitably happen, happens. The fight can swirl around the end of the HOBOKEN YACHT CLUB and out of sight. CUT. A goon who's not yet involved goes around the other side of the HYC and we know that Terry is going to be trapped between two goons out of sight of the camera. CUT. On the pier, on the dock, on the tied up ship, men are watching. They are watching one of their own being beaten up for something he did for them. They feel a little ashamed. Some one is being killed and they cant go to help. They are ashamed. We hear over the shots of these onlookers, the silence of a fight punctuated by the dull thud of blows. The silence is frightening. We cut back to the HYC. We see nothing. Except the sounds of the fight are closer. We feel and know that Terry is getting his lumps. Then there's a crash. CUT. The onlookers. Their heads drop in shame. They are embarrassed in front of each other. HYC. Around the corner of the little house come the goons, wiping themselves like dogs after a fight. The longshoremen look at the goons, the goons look at the longshoremen. Then some of them led by POP go and get Terry. It looks like its going to be a free for all. NOW in some way the men are put on the spot and show their loyalty to Terry, finally by making sure that he works. If we play this whole scene absolutely really, UN-MOVIE-ish why then we'll have something terrific. No heroics. Nothing that would not happen. I dont think the men can NOT show their appreciation and loyalty to TERRY under these circumstances. In fact Terry crucified himself for them. If Tony Mike went down to the Holland American line and had a fight before Pier Five, the longshoremen would absolutely absolutely come out for him. There would be a goddamn revolution on the pier. I dont know how far we can go. I'll have to leave this up to you. But feel it thru from life. I believe it now. We've got a guy, not Errol Flynn or Kirk Douglas in a DIXIE FINISH.

What I am especially anxious to show is that his act of sacrifice (Both the Testifying and the fight) HAS A VALUE. It does benefit the men there because it takes the fear out of their hearts. This will give a genuine lift to the picture. We'll know then the future course, without anticipating. Terry accomplishes one thing: the men are no longer afraid, and to an extent they have even committed themselves to taking sides. . . .

Opposition within the Catholic church. Terribly important to me. Two brief shots of this are enough. And I thought the place you suggested good till I thought of the idea of the men TALKING as we come into the meeting, and clamming up at the sight of Terry. Leave to you! . . .

CUTS. CRUCIAL. The fight, the hold sc., etc. etc. are going to stretch greatly. I urge you to find the cuts yourself. If you dont they wont be done as organically. Its NOT a matter of a blue pencil. I tried that. Its a matter of a simpler way of telling the story, so that its told more briefly. Its a matter I FERVENTLY HOPE of the first fifty pages. Just abstractly and technically that's where we're long. We're long getting into the main line which is WILL HE SHOULD HE TESTIFY????? Start thinking drastic thoughts in re the first fifty pages. For instance going from the wake to the shape up scene. Something like that will work and just needs a little really creative work. What is ruinous BUDD is cutting film. That's not only a waste of our money, but much worse artistically bad. We cut film in MAN ON A TIGHTROPE and that is the main reason the picture seems so jumpy and there seem to be things left out in the first half. We had the same problem (and its tougher in our picture) of a story that didn't get started till page fifty or so, and we did not solve it at this stage. There we were just pissing Fox's money away. Here its our own. And this picture MUST BE GOOD. And clear.

****

I enclose, for you only, a rough draft of a letter to BRANDO. Its the only letter I could write under the circumstances. Its as good as I can do, to see it from the point of view of Sam. Please judge for me whether or not it has value to show Brando. I leave it up to you. If you, as my friend, dont think its good, put it in your drawer till I get back. If you think its a good letter, make any use of it you wish.

I just spoke to Jay Kantor on the phone. He will expect the script in his office in MCA on Monday morning August 3rd. He has formally promised me that Brando would read the script and give us his yes or no before he leaves on the 5th. of August. I have also cabled Sam to be here on the third and fourth so that he and you can see Brando together.

Dont show my letter to Sam unless you think there's a value. I have written him another one.

Love, gadge

[Paul Newman studied at the Actors Studio and made his Broadway debut in *Picnic* to modest acclaim. His role as a socially privileged, sexually diffident suitor bore little if any relation to Terry Malloy's character. Newman and Joanne Woodward, a prospective Edie, prepared a scene for Sam Spiegel's consideration but negotiations with Frank Sinatra intervened. Spiegel made a verbal agreement with the Hoboken native after Brando rejected Terry's role and left for Europe. His recruitment coincided with the release of *From Here to Eternity* (1953) in which Sinatra played an award-winning role. Later correspondence reveals that his limited availability alarmed Kazan.

Kazan's version of the fight appeared in the September draft of "Waterfront," current working title, and was filmed with little change. Rejection by fellow long-shoremen after Terry turns informer prompts the long-delayed confrontation with Friendly: "I ain't taking this. I'm going to walk in." He fights "impossible odds" with "a sense of exhilaration" now that his defiance "is in the open, for all to see." A "vicious punch drives him back around the corner of the office," out of sight, where the "goons" apply a "methodical pasting." The "unseen blows" embarrass the longshoremen, who are "powerfully affected by Terry's martyrdom." Pop Doyle, father of Edie and the slain Joey, pushes Friendly into the water, "scummy with oil slick and typical river-edge debris," as the sequence ends ("Waterfront," September 30, 1953, Wesleyan).

A former hiring boss, Anthony "Tony Mike" De Vincenzo gave testimony to the New York State Crime Commission regarding links between business and the underworld. He also gave valuable advice to Kazan and Schulberg and influenced the shaping of Terry Malloy's character.

"Opposition within the Catholic church" is present although not emphatic in the September draft of *Waterfront*. Father Vincent, a "thin-faced rather ascetic looking priest," observes "disapprovingly" but makes no comment as Father Barry opens the meeting of longshoremen in the church basement. Kazan's claim of archdiocesan support for Father Corridan's activism was either uninformed or overstated in earlier correspondence with Darryl Zanuck. In 1951 Corridan was summoned to the chancery office to answer charges brought by a fellow priest that he worked frequently on the docks, often as a longshoreman, without clerical garb, and had "engaged in fisticuffs." Corridan was also accused of having instigated the current labor strike. The charges were denied, although Corridan declined to reveal the nature or outcome of his interview with Cardinal Spellman. Later he declined to give testimony to the Crime Commission by reason of the confidential nature of his sources and information. He also knew that church superiors would not have approved (Raymond, pp. 154–57, 195–96).

By September Budd Schulberg had pared fifty-odd pages from the script, including early sequences devoted to Joey Doyle's death and Edie's sleuthing. Kazan originally described Edie as "a prism of conscience and of love" and advised Schulberg to "hew much more tightly" to her search for Joey's killer. A year later he urged Schulberg to "stick with" Terry. "His guilt is the beginning of the story and the problem of this picture. It is not about Edie. Be firm on this" ("Rewrite Notes," June 14, 1953, Wesleyan).] *TLS, 4 pp., Dartmouth*

TO MARLON BRANDO

[New York]
[late July 1953]

Dear Marlon:
I cant pretend that its easy or simple to write you. Ultimately, in our little world, everyone hears everything. I will always feel most warmly and devotedly for you, but this does not blot out the things unsaid between us. I will for the time leave them unsaid. I will write you here professionally, and you can behave as you wish from whatever criteria you wish to act from. That's your business and even your problem. I'm sending you the script of a movie in a state of preparation. I'm very very hopeful of the script. I've worked very hard on it, and I'm going to do a lot more work on it. But you're a sensitive person and you will realize its not finished, you will sense its intention and the hope involved in it. Its not yet realized, though its a great deal closer than what you read before. Its meant very seriously. It is taken from living people, though distilled and compacted. The problem which it mirrors still exists and the moral problem it treats—the social responsibility of a citizen as it comes into conflict with his personal allegiances—is one of the oldest and most universal of all problems a man can face. My own point of view towards this problem and Budd's too, is clearly set forth. But the script is more of an involvement in the problem than an exhortation of any kind. Make no mistake about it, there is a parallel inference to be drawn to the Inquiries into Communist Activities. This parallelism is not the main value of the script. This is the story of a human in torment, and in danger. The first thing I would do if you did become interested would be to take you over [to] HOBOKEN and introduce you to Tony Mike De Vincenzo who went thru exactly what our TERRY goes thru. This is a confrontation which would put flesh and blood on the issue on which our script is built. I've spent three evenings with him and its like being in the presence of a denizen of Dante's <u>Purgatorio</u>. And finally with him and with the whole waterfront of New York Harbor, the issue is not decided, and will probably be in the process of being decided as we shoot the picture.

I dont want to say more about the picture's theme. Just one word about the part. By the common measure which producers and directors use for casting, you are not right for this part. But then you weren't right for the Williams Play either and you weren't right for Zapata. This boy is a former fighter, half pure, half hoodlum. He is a boy who has lost his sense of inner dignity or self-worth. At the beginning of our story he doesn't know when he lost it or how. He only discovers that he is behaving like a hoodlum and he has been a contributor to a murder. Slowly thru the unfolding of the incidents of the story and thru his relationship with a girl he discovers the shameful estate to which he has sunken. The body of the story has to do with his effort to find his own dignity and self esteem once more. He's a boy who suffers at the slightest introspection or self examination. He goes thru hell. Finally he acts to make himself respect himself, first putting his life in danger and secondly even going out to meet a violent end, so that he will re-establish himself in the sight of his own inner eye. With this "inside", there is a jaunty exterior which is the pathetic remnant of a career where he was once the white haired boy of the neighborhood, and etc. There's much more to say, but you can go on from here, if you care to. I think its a giant of a part and a tremendous challenge.

I read your statements—I always think statements are misquoted, but I think these were probably inaccurate in detail but the larger sentiments I had heard you make before—I was saying: I read your statements on the state of American Films. You expressed a disgust with the state of our films—and the man quoted you as saying that the only pictures you ever felt like making, the only pictures of worth, were those being made in Europe, and that pictures of that mettle could not, be, and were not being made in this country. I could not disagree with the generalization. But the important thing in any field: music, verse, painting, novel are the exceptions. As you suggest, it is important that an effort, an increasing effort be made in this country to raise the level of our pictures so that they will be an art and not a buck-trap. And I do think that most directors or/and producers who are able to exercise some choice over their material have not dared or even tried. However this is an attempt and a strong and determined one. You will see that for yourself. I'm not going to say more; you still talk to yourself.

As before, gadge

[Kazan's congressional testimony dismayed and angered Marlon Brando, who initially told Sam Spiegel, or so it was reported to Kazan, that he would not work again with his former director. Brando claimed later that he accepted the role of Terry Malloy without knowing that the script "was really a metaphorical argument by Gadg and Budd Schulberg . . . to justify finking on their friends" (Brando, p. 195). In the unlikely event that Budd Schulberg circulated Kazan's unfriendly "draft" letter, Brando either forgot, overlooked, failed to comprehend, or suppressed the clear statement that Crime Commission hearings and HUAC investigation of "Communist Activities" were interrelated.

Photographs in a *Life* magazine profile (January 5, 1953) show Tony Mike De Vincenzo under police guard and taking precautions with his family after testifying for the Crime Commission. Ever litigious, he sued Hoboken city officials later in

1953 for assigning a twenty-four-hour-a-day uniformed guard in apparent retaliation for his testimony. He testified in superior court that he had never feared for his life and had not requested protection. A jury found against De Vincenzo. After release of *On the Waterfront* in 1954, he brought a damage suit against Columbia Pictures and Sam Spiegel for violating his privacy as a former waterfront hiring boss. De Vincenzo was reportedly given a small settlement. Kazan made no reference to the lawsuits in *A Life* and continued to link his own "torment" with Tony Mike's alleged "Purgatorio."

Brando was conventionally unsuited by age for his role in *Streetcar* and by ethnicity for *Zapata*. Kazan also claimed he was "not right" for Terry Malloy by reason of his sensitivity and introspection.] *TLSd, 2 pp., Dartmouth*

TO MARLON BRANDO

[New York]
November 2nd. [1953]

Dear Marlon:
Perhaps it will be more useful if put down what I think of Terry. Rather than just talking about it. Then you can have it to look at. Then, too, we can talk about it all after you've had a chance to think it all over. What the guy is, how he behaves, how he thinks, what he wants is much more important here than usual because I really hope to be photographing the kid's insides as much as exterior events. The story of this kid's regaining his dignity or self esteem—in one word, the regeneration—happens inside the man and has to be done by you so I can photograph it. Its also a more complex or DIVIDED character than Stanley, and the inner conflict is going on all the time—in even the smallest episodes—and it is not resolved til the end.

At any rate let me list, in the order that they come to me, the elements that are important for you to think about.

Crucial is the fact that he is an orphan. As a kid he felt homeless, unwanted, even scorned, inferior to the rest of mankind. Perhaps he remembers couples looking for kids to adopt passing him by. Why is Friendly his idol. Because Friendly did pick him up, made a fighter of him, lavished concern and aid and friendship on him. Only Mickey "adopted" him and brought him to the point where he was desired and even "famous".

Fighting was his move for recognition. It was his bid for a place in the sun against a world from which he had been shut out from birth. It was his revenge on a world that had rejected him. When he fought he was "someone", not an orphan. Mickey gave him this.

At the beginning of our story he had not been able to face the fact that Mickey "took" him. He cannot give up his idol. If he turns against Mickey he would be giving up the only friend he ever really had. Deprived of this one loyalty, he would have nothing. He knows in his heart that Mickey did him dirt. He just cannot look at it, he cannot face it. It would destroy too much in his inner structure. And to tell the truth Mickey still gives him a little gratitude and flattery. He's still enjoying a tiny part of the favor that he used to have one hundred percent when he was Mickey's PET.

When he looks at Mickey his eyes change from adoration to resentment, from a betrayed look to a worshipping look. He's like a rejected lover who after years still hasn't quite given up. There is no health and strength for him til he kills Mickey completely—which he symbolically does in the last sequence of the picture. It is crucial that this idolatry of Mickey be built up so that the final payoff can mean what it should. The orphan re-orphanized. The lover betrayed, but still not giving up.

The next important thing is that Terry is terribly and fundamentally lonely. Consider he lives alone in one small room with one small window. There is something of the ascetic about him. Consider: he has no girl. His best friend is the boy Jimmy and the other Golden Warriors. (They still idolize him) He cannot consider Mickey really his friend. His best friends are the pigeons. . . . His experience with girls has been an occasional whore—the girls from Mickey's entourage. He never could trust himself to them. He might have felt always that the girls were out to take him, and that, in turn, they were legitimate prey. Never before Edie has he had a chance to be close to a girl with gentleness and tenderness.

I suppose, along with everything else, there must be something of the narcissist in most fighters. Boxing is Terry's armor, and his defense. I thought that his greatest solace in times of stress or pain or confusion might be shadow boxing. I thought of him shadow boxing, when he's confused, with tears in his eyes.

Incidentally, do you see how completely different this is from Kowalski. Stanley is undivided. He is confident. He is on top. He has no self doubts. He has no sex problem. He is not conceivably lonely. He is brash, gregarious, necessarily convivial.

Terry seems to swagger and sometimes affects a jauntiness. But his eyes betray him. The swagger is a cover. When he is not being watched, or living up to the pictures on the fight cards in the ticket brokers offices—why then he is terribly gentle and withdrawing. You will find most fighters are this way, especially the young ones. Jimmy the kid seems tougher, more aggressive, more dominant than he is. Jimmy seems like HIS supreme commander. Jimmy is undivided and is confirmed in his values. Terry cannot seem sure because he is divided, and in inner conflict.

Marlon, this part is much closer to you and to myself too. It is a complex part. Not a strong color without the next moment the opposite coming up. He says cynical, arrogant things to the girl. But the next moment we should see that he's not that cynical or confident or sure—and that in his eyes there is a questioning. Kowalski had no self doubt. Even at the end he leaves Stella in the yard and returns to his poker game.

The great thing about this part is that it has an inner story. He starts one way. He ends up another. He does something at the beginning that drives home to him that he has become a bum. He meets a girl who for the first time [omission] on the side of the good in him. Thru the events and thru [omission] he finds that he has lost his self esteem and inner dignity. He finds out that he doesn't think much of himself. He finds that he hasn't faced the fact that Mickey and Charley have used him and degraded him. That he was afraid to face this. And now that he does he must agree that he has become a bum. Then he, with the unspoken encouragement of the girl, thru the felt antagonism of the priest (the Priest never gets to like him in the story) he goes out to REGAIN his Dignity and self esteem and he does—the HARD way. That is the personal story. A Bum becomes a man. That's it. . . .

I think his angers are deeper and more animal like, more superstitious, more unanswerable than Stanley's. Stanley flared and struck. Terry's angers are kept in, nursed, grow to a point where they cannot be satisfied except with murder. Terry is truly dangerous. Stanley just fights a lot. Stanley is secure in his group. He is the centre of his world. He is never challenged in the ultimate sense, because he is king of his dung heap beyond challenge. Terry is lonely, by himself, turned in, mysterious, a prey to violent emotions which were born in his early rejection. (The orphan.) Kowalski is unself questioning, beyond self doubting. Terry is full of doubt, suspicion. Suspicion is very very important. He is suspicious of all girls, of all idealism. He doesn't want to be taken or fooled. Perhaps there is a history of a girl having taken him. (cf. Joe diMag.) Kowalski has complete confidence in his cock as the leveller, the equalizer. Terry is not a confident lover.

Marlon, at the moment they seem to me like entirely different characters. I would never have compared them had you not brought Stanley up. But I can see now where there might be externals similar when both talk cynically. But Terry is well meaning. He is the opposite of destructive. He wants approval of his idol, Mickey. He misses having it. That's why he leads Joey to a beating up at the beginning.

Women? He's conquered women, but never loved one. (cf. Joe diMag.) Also, while he trusts the men of his gang he is practically brought up not to trust the women in that world. They're either dogs or they're out to make a fool of you and cheat on you, or talk about you behind your back and say you're a bust as a lay. It was far more desirable pleasurable and comfortable when he was fighting to be wanted and desired and admired by a lot of men and never obligate himself to one, never put himself in the hands of any one. So when he says: I think we're in love with each other he is a little frightened and a little confused. Its a complication he has always fought off. Its more secure and more pleasurable to be desired by 100 girls than to meet one on an equal basis. To be in love is traditionally an admission of weakness among adolescents. To lay girls is fine because you are conquering and getting something for nothing. You are in effect getting the better of the girls.

[Sam Spiegel reached an agreement with Marlon Brando shortly before filming of *Waterfront* began in mid-November. At the same time, he dismissed Frank Sinatra, who "never quite forgave [his] welshing" and demanded compensation (Fraser-Cavassoni, pp. 160–61). Budd Schulberg assumed that Spiegel had replaced Sinatra with a more established star to shift the project from United Artists to Columbia Pictures and increase his production budget—as occurred.

The rooftops of the Hoboken waterfront were a second home to Tommy Hanley, a "rough-and-ready" fourteen-year-old who was hired to care for the pigeons, an avocation shared by Budd Schulberg and Terry Malloy, and later given the role of Jimmy at a weekly salary of $250 (*Jersey Journal*, November 21, 1953). Hanley worked as a longshoreman in later life—as had his father, who disappeared in 1939, perhaps a victim of pier justice.

Apparently Brando associated the "externals" of Stanley Kowalski and Terry Malloy to a degree that concerned Kazan and required sharper definition. Brando needed no such help in distinguishing himself from the famous role: "'Why, he's the antithesis of me. He is intolerant and selfish. Kowalski is a man without any sensitivity, without any kind of morality except his own mewling, whimpering insistence on his own way. I can't think—I can't believe—that we are here for one terrible, gnashing, stomping moment and that's all'" (*Time,* October 11, 1954).

Kazan's intimacy with Marilyn Monroe, soon to be addressed in correspondence, coincided with her courtship by Joe DiMaggio in 1952 (*A Life,* pp. 454–55).] *TL, 4 pp., Wesleyan*

TO ABE LASTFOGEL

[New York]
November 2, 1953

Dear Abe:

I'm sorry I did not get to see you that night at Lindy's. I wanted to talk to you very much. But we didn't leave Sam's room till about a quarter to three, and then we stopped more from exhaustion than anything else. That was the night for the final script-go-over before it went to the Mimeograph, and we were all anxious to get it as close to final as possible.

But I was sorry that I did not speak to you and tell you my feelings about the Sinatra-Brando-Speagle affair. My feelings were not exactly like yours, and

I want you to understand how I feel. So forgive me if I take some of your time up now. Its important to me.

Obviously from my point of view the decision to go ahead with Frank was a severe compromise. Not on artistic grounds. I was quite happy that way. Frank would have been fine in the part. Brando was my first choice, but since I could not have him and had completely abandoned hope of having him, Frank was a happy choice for me. . . . The alternate to Frank was an unknown boy in the cast of PICNIC. His release was a dubious matter. Even with Frank, UA was holding Sam down to a very small budget. I frankly didn't know the details. I only felt I would start and trust to improvisation and luck. I didn't feel happy. I fully faced the fact that we would be in trouble. But my problem now is not to make pictures. My problem, as I've told you many times, is to make the pictures I want to make. Sam was making this possible, in this instance, where no one else would or could. In that sense he was fully my partner. Dont under-estimate my stubbornness. I dont take no for an answer. My only regret with Sinatra was that I would have to hurry. I hate to hurry. But there I thought: Christ if I behave sensibly the goddamn thing would never be made. The common sense thing to do would have been to abandon the project. I couldn't do that.

Then, after Frank was all set, Brando walked in one day, to my complete surprise and said he wanted to go ahead. I wanted him. Not just Sam. I wanted him. Not that I was unhappy with Frank. But with Brando there would be no time pressure. My guess is that this picture will take 42 days, and even possibly a few more. We now have a decent budget. . . . I dont like to get hurt and I hate to hurt any one. Nor do I feel that the thing was well handled by Sam. Sam says that's the only way he could have done it. I'm not at all sure it was. I'm, on the other hand, not sure it wasn't. One thing sure: the change was necessary. We had done something desperate in accepting Frank with 27 days, desperate and foolish. Its terrible and regrettable that Frank had to be hurt. But couldn't the hurt be partially assuaged by having Frank announce that he withdrew because the schedule did not permit. And couldn't another part of his hurt be softened by my writing him and assuring him that the basis of the change WITH ME was time. I had gotten myself into a foolish and desperate (But by me, necessary) spot, and I had to get out of it when I saw a way out. I'm not callous to Frank's feelings. But say this much for us: when we went into it with Frank we went in on complete good faith. In fact our demands were craven. We begged him to get us a few more days. He was unable to, so I got us three more on the phone with Lew. We did not ask him to give up the Fox musical or anything like that. We were beggars. And we begged. But too much work and pain and time from Budd and myself are riding on this thing—to do anything else than what we allowed Sam to do. I wish Sam had done it differently but Abe I want you to know I'm glad right now that we have Marlon. And make no mistake about that.

That afternoon after you and Sam had screamed at each other, and after you went out, the first one who spoke was Budd. He reminded me of an afternoon in Joe Moskowitz office in Beverly Hills where we were meeting with Lew and Joe and Ann Rosenthal about the settlement. Budd, recalling this, remarked that it seemed to him that we had been treated a lot more shabbily than Frank. We had shaken hands with Skouras in New York in your presence, we had toasted the picture in Skouras little bar. Budd had made a special trip out there to consult with Zanuck, first having refused to make the trip unless it were absolutely certain that Zanuck was going to make the picture. Then weeks later Budd and I went out three days on that goddamn train only to be told by Zanuck that he was withdrawing from the picture. And there we were humiliated beyond anything Frank has just gone thru. Our picture had been announced again and again by Fox. Budd had made two trips to Hollywood, and I one. Budd had had three long long sessions with Zanuck and had rewritten to meet Zanuck's requirements. etc. etc. I had not received one fucking cent and neither had Budd. And so on. You remember.

And the other afternoon, Budd in recalling this, said: I dont remember Abe getting so angry on our behalf. And since a friend owes a friend the truth, let me say that the exact same thought was in my mind. Ever since that incident Budd and I have been burning. But the most humiliating part of it all was the settlement we made in that room that afternoon. I made it because I have such trust in you and because I wanted the screen play free of the lawsuits that seemed to be threatened. I never have understood why you took that whole incident so lightly. Its been rankling within me ever since. I think our settlement of forty thousand dollars returnable is shameful, and only reflects, it seems to me, the low esteem you have always placed upon this project. Correct me please, dear Abe, if I'm wrong. I would never have brought this whole thing up, in fact I had never discussed it with Budd except in terms of cussing FOX.

But when Budd saw how you tore into Sam, he could only wish you had torn into Fox the same way ON OUR BEHALF. We both feel humiliated by Fox. A lot of the things you said about "human beings" "humiliation" "playing with a person's feelings" seemed to both of us as we listened to be much much more true of Budd and I sitting that afternoon in Moskowitz office and having the financial and legal shit kicked out of us without a real protest from you. I never told you that Bill Fitelson was on the phone from New York several times begging me not to take the settlement as offered—that it was humiliating etc. I simply went along with you. But ever since I've gotten more and more sore at FOX. I have never been back to see Skouras—although he has repeatedly asked me. I will never feel the same towards Zanuck.

One thing I remember your saying was that Fox's behavior could only be explained since business was so bad. But here is Speagle, without any dough to speak of, doing a picture which I, your friend, and your client want to have done when NOBODY else in the whole goddamn industry will do it. I've got to hand it to him for his determination and tenacity. His job has not been an easy one. Perhaps he could have behaved better. I think so. But I was sure glad to get out of the 27 schedule and I sure thought it was necessary to get out of it.

And I must admit every time I go over the Fox business and think of the months I spent working with them, the pictures I've made for them, the money I've made them, the friendships, the talent I brought them, the assurances I had from you and Skouras and Zanuck and Bill Fitelson that I was justified in behaving as if they were going to make the waterfront picture—and then, lap dissolve—I'm sitting in Zanuck's office and he says: "Of course we feel that we owe Budd something, but you Gadge you're too rich!" And I told you this Abe, and I dont remember you're getting sore. How the hell can you compare the kicking around and the screwing Fox gave Budd and I with the week of bad time Speagle gave Frank. Frank will get over it. I'll never feel the same towards the fellows at Fox. . . .

You know Abe, I think the world of you. I always have. I always will. I dont think all a human's actions have to be consistent. I'm not asking you for an explanation. I'm not that presumptuous, nor do I treat friends that way. Perhaps you feel sorrier for Frank with all his troubles. I must say I felt terrible when I read that crap in the Journal American about Ava and him. Perhaps you feel—as I suspect you do, and I dont say this isn't your right—that this whole goddamn project has been taking up too much of my time and that its no good anyway. That's your privilege. Molly feels that way. She's smart and for me. Its o.k. I just make up my own mind what to do, and I do them. I dont quit and I dont goof. I dont want to make the Robe. And Mogambo. I rather make this picture. I dont have to tell you. I've felt from the beginning that you've been against this whole project, and I dont resent it. I felt after the meeting at Fox that you should have been angrier for me, and you weren't because you rather hoped that the damn thing were finally dead. You, in fact, said as much, indirectly. You asked me calmly the afternoon that I left what I was going to turn to now. The assumption being that Fox's rejection had killed the project. You have a complete right and you should fight for what is good for me. I want you to. But I thought I'd tell you what I felt on my side. Martie Jurrow told Speagle, Speagle says that you assumed, when I didn't show at Lindy's that I agreed with you. That is not accurate. What I felt is above.

Always, Gadg

[Abe Lastfogel represented Frank Sinatra, as well as Kazan, and was infuriated by Sam Spiegel's rough handling of Sinatra's promising film career. As it turned out, Kazan accurately estimated the shooting schedule of *Waterfront*, which exceeded Sinatra's availability by two weeks, and also welcomed the prospect of a "decent budget." He reportedly wrote to Sinatra, who accepted the gesture of friendship and wished the project well. Such conciliation eluded Kazan. Shame and anger were fresh thirty-five years later when he recorded the equally rough handling of *Waterfront* in his autobiography. Placing the silent, unruffled Abe Lastfogel in Darryl Zanuck's office for the bruising rejection scene has created an inconsistency with the present letter. Whether faulty memory or dramatic license was at work is unclear, but Kazan's feeling of betrayal remained intact. The "settlement" of $40,000 for unreimbursed work on the screenplay was not only inadequate but also "returnable," based presumably on a threshold of the film's profit. Lastfogel became president of the William Morris Agency in 1952 after the forced retirement of its "namesake" for political activity deemed unwise. From an agent's point of view, Kazan needed a clear success after the failure of *Zapata* and *Tightrope*, without the risk of unpopular subject matter or political repercussions occasioned by criticism of labor and American institutions (*A Life*, pp. 508–12; Rose, pp. 173–75).] *TLS, 4 pp., Wesleyan*

TO SAM SPIEGEL

[New York]
[November 1953]

Dear Sam:

Every once in a while you may get a letter from me. Its a more exact way to communicate,—when I want to be exact.

You know, Sam, I dont give a damn whether you like Brownie or not. Your likes and dislikes in our present circumstances are not to the point. Its even possible that I may see a good deal less of Brownie once this picture is over. But in the present tense, I need him. I have carefully kept out of choosing my staff. You have brought together what appears to be a good one, and I have o.k.'ed them without exception as you presented them to me. But I think there is some misunderstanding about Brownie. He is not a hanger-on, he is not a drunk, he is not a fad of mine, he is not a whim of mine. He's the man I want to be my Technical man on the picture. I want him under salary as Technical man. I dont want any favors, and its not a matter of offering him a job as a favor because an eccentric director and author seem to be amused by him. He is an excellent technical man and I want him on my staff as such, so designated and so paid. I have not discussed his salary with him. But he did tell me that he quit because you offered him $100 per week, and I must say my sympathies were all with him. That is not the salary for the function I want him to fulfill for me and the one he has fulfilled till now. I am not going into his achievements either—He has done an awful lot already for this film, and several times earned the salary you have paid him till now. I only want to write you this so that you make no mistake and so that Brownie's function with me doesn't get confused in a cloud of laughter and kidding and personal distaste. This is a professional request from director to producer. And I need him immediately.

That's one. The other has to do with Marrotta. I made you a speech about Marrotta the other day and your reaction was essentially an annoyed one—in effect you asked me why did I spy on your handling of affairs and why didn't I just leave it to you, and that you would have it done.

Then Marrotta called me today (Sunday) and said that you had come to his house and you still hadn't talked money to him, and that he was not at all contented. That is what he said to me. Now I dont care what you said or did not say, what you intend in the future, what you might have hinted or intimated or anything else. I can only tell you that I would like to have Marrotta on our payroll. That doesn't mean that he should get so much per week etc. Your objections to that are well taken. I understand them. But what I do mean is that he know what he's going to get at whatever time he can get it, that he be perfectly clear about it and perfectly contented about it. I simply cannot work in Hoboken without this being the case. There is nothing personal in this, as I assure you there is nothing personal in my request for Brownie. I need these men. They are part of my tools, my professional equipment. I am not going to go into a long song and dance about the Hoboken situation. You know something about it. I simply ask you to arrive at a clear understanding today with Marrotta so that he will be solid and permanent in my camp. I dont have to suggest, I hope, that there are very likely days coming when we will be under fierce pressure from unfriendly forces. This could happen. A lot could happen.

There is a unique triangle which is the key to making this picture in Hoboken. Corridan, Browne and Marrotta. We need them all. Whatever you think of them or whatever they may be worth in other jobs, they are essential here, and have highly specific and essential functions to discharge here. Its not a laughing matter, and its not a place to squeeze on the budget. Brownie was perfectly right to quit when you offered him a hundred dollars. I would have done the same and my sympathies are all with him.

Perhaps its better that we have an exact understanding about the girl. Budd told me that you called him and pushed him hard to push me about Judy Braun. You had spoken to me a few moments before or a few moments after and never mentioned Judy Braun. I was surprised to hear about her again. I had worked very hard to get her "into" the part and after three days real work I came away with the impression that while she is talented, she is not for this picture. I also dont think Marjorie Barrett is for this picture. I worked with her, tho not nearly as hard as I did with Judy.

I mentioned on the phone to you my reluctance to start on Tuesday without the girl OR Charlie set. What it will mean is that we'll get started and then under the threat of the schedule we will be at the mercy of "the best we can

With Budd Schulberg and Father John Corridan on the
Hoboken waterfront

do" with relation to the girl. This is n.g., Sam. This story is utterly dependant upon the love story. Utterly. It is the girl, what exists between them, what is there in the way of sex and charm and longing and, again, sex which finally moves the boy to testify. Or if you dont like the word sex, call it love. Its her force on him, the image of her towards which he aspires which makes this story move—even start. I dont want to start and then be in a position where, in order to keep going, I will have to take what is unsigned and available. I dont care about destroying the morale—tho that is important. I dont think our picture will "WORK", will be worth a good god damn unless we get a girl that's good. I would rather take Janice and let her play, or make extraordinary efforts to take Janice or bargain or pay to get her or whatever. I just think we should get her. Then we'll be "professional".

The fact is I dont see how in the hell we can start Tuesday anyway. What about her wardrobe? What should she wear? After all these weeks and weeks of work why go carelessly and sloppily and stupidly into one of the handful of really, finally, important aspects of production. Dont tell me: it will work out! or GOD is over us! I think we should get Janice and take a couple of days to dress her right, present her properly—then we will have what your work and Budd's and mine merit.

I'm sorry I have felt it necessary to write you this way, or to write you at all. I know you're tired, and I myself, after a day's steady work, am tired. I could have used the time better too. But I think you better be very clear about my attitude on the points above. They're all three too important to be fuzzy about.

g.

["Movement," Kazan realized, was "the essence" of Sam Spiegel's flamboyant career. Born in Western Galicia in 1901, Spiegel lived as a settler in Palestine in the 1920s, dodged the Nazis in the 1930s, was jailed twice for fraud and ejected from three countries, including the United States, which he may have reentered illegally in 1939. "S.P. Eagle," alias and professional nom de guerre, spawned jokes and origination stories as various as the scrapes that marked Spiegel's career (Fraser-Cavassoni). A chance meeting with Kazan and Schulberg shortly after Darryl Zanuck rejected *On the Waterfront* brought Spiegel his most enduring success and the first of three Academy Awards. A pariah in Hollywood, albeit a charming one who entertained lavishly, Spiegel created a "mythological country," as Kazan put it, where chiseling and chicanery prevailed. So too did adroit casting and incisive story construction (*A Life*, pp. 513–17).

The "triangle" of Corridan, Browne, and Marotta was no luxury, Kazan argued, in penetrating the closed society of the docks and protecting cast and crew from dangerous observers. A "disciple" of Father Corridan, Arthur Browne was a self-described "insoigent," who gave the collaborators a crash course in waterfront politics and drew them into productive relationships with other rebellious long-shoremen. Brownie's feisty manner was portrayed in the character of "Kayo" Dugan, played by Pat Henning. Joe Marotta, brother of Hoboken's chief of police, carried a gun and provided security on the set.

Kazan proposed to no avail that Janice Rule play Edie's role while remaining in the cast of *Picnic* if necessary. Joanne Woodward was also considered for the part, while offers were reportedly made to Jennifer Jones and Grace Kelly. Signed in late November, Eva Marie Saint made her film debut in *Waterfront* and won the Oscar for best supporting actress. Her featured role in Horton Foote's play *Trip to Bountiful* provided a timely showcase.] *TLS, 2 pp., Wesleyan*

TO TENNESSEE WILLIAMS

SH: Mrs. Alfred B. Thacher
486 Scotland Road, South Orange, New Jersey
[late December 1953]

Dear Tenn:
Out here at Molly's mother for Xmas and this morning there was the big deal with the unwrapping of the gifts and all. Now things are comparatively quiet, the family is playing Scrabble which is a new Intelligent Kill Time game and little Katie, who is not of an age yet for intellectual pursuits is making up her face with a gift Cosmetics set. She looks like a word that is not yet said in the Breen Code, lips smeared, smears of rouge and jumping around on a pogo

Working with Brando in Hoboken

stick all the time. I'm pooped, the picture being physically very tough and no where near over. I have to face not only the elements, the racket guys, the long-shoremen and an uncut script but also the consternation, daily re-inforced, of a rapidly-becoming-bankrupt Producer. The whole thing is taking almost twice as long as he planned, what with my stubbornness and the five hours of photographable-daylight. I'm between feeling sorry for him and cautioning myself almost hysterically not to feel sorry for him and to stick to making the picture good. The several times I've been motivated by anything but getting half way decent film, the day's work stank. And so—I'm tired. The actors have been wonderful however, wonderful. Brando looks older and a little heavier, but is better than ever. He has new "manly" qualities of Tenderness and dignity and relaxation and humor. I mean relaxed humor, not eccentric humor. He's a most unusually honest artist and has saved me many times from doing things that are phony. I'm very fond of him, really love him, yet there is no way to express it to him. Malden and Lee Cobb are both magnificent, and a new girl, Eva Saint, makes a rather foolish part believable (I hope)—lets say: playable. Anyway, the actors act like comrades and colleagues and are loyal and endure cold and penny-pinching equally well. I'm very heartened by them. My God they're wonderful. All of the new generation (Actors' Studio, Neighborhood Playhouse, Stella Adler, and from the Big Parent: Group Theatre) There are a few old school small parts and about five former boxing "Greats" who lend just a touch of fantasy to the whole proceedings. The Racket Mob send their people to observe from the fringes, and they listen and smile a little foolishly at the erratically flung off bits of dialogue. Its weird. Well I'll be another few weeks, and then I'll rest. I'd like to come south for a couple of weeks, but hate to leave my children.

Agreed in your letter about the discrepancy in style between the original and "mixed-up" tone of the love scene and the body of what you wrote till now and the ending which is "straight" dramatic. I'm glad that you're searching for some way of achieving unity in tone. The more I work, the more crucial I think the unities are. Please continue not to pay too much attention to my "rewriting ideas". They may have something of value in them, but I nearly always find out later that they dont relate to the writer, but only to what I think abstractly dramatic, or pictorial and all that shit. You're the only one who can write this end right so I'm glad you raised the problem of the end as we "laid it out". You're right in challenging it.

I hope you're well. I hope you're not lonely. I think about you more often than you know and wish for you. I had a terrible sad gift this a.m. from Josh Logan. A picture of the Street Car n Desire. At the bottom an inscription: And change for the Cemeteries. Josh is back north now, and living in New Canaan. He suddenly showed up on my movie set one day, talking just 10% off the beam. And he did not look well. He's terribly touching. He's going to a different Head Man now, and his close friends feel hopeful. I dont think he ever quite got over not doing Streetcar. He chews on himself and his face, his looks, his problems, his career, and what people think of him, all people, and "it comes out here". And his sex life, whenever he goes off, the sex life is revealed in confusion and shame and frustration. He has a lot more than he's ever shown of talent and goodness. He has a kind of shamelessness that all artists have to have, and a running over tank of enthusiasm. (Dont mention about the Streetcar picture)

I haven't been to the Theatre, or been close to the news and gossip for a few months now. Jane B's play I hear was good for two acts, and Judith A, not "right". No really strong play has come out this year and the best playwrights are silent. Odets is having tremendous trouble finishing Noah. I hear Miller is onto a new play. Many people, many people ask about you and how you're doing. Brando would be perfect for our movie.

Give Grandfather my love. His flight from St Louis is next to Don Quixote the greatest. Best to Frank and if you have chance and feel like it write me.

Oh yes, thank Christ, Cheryl seems to have a big hit. At last, and well deserved and big too.

Love. g

For the new years: may you write a play and may I direct it.

[Mrs. Alfred B. Thacher continued to occupy the family home in South Orange, New Jersey, long after her husband's death in 1928.

Filming of On the Waterfront ended in mid-January 1954 with all the sequences save one—the "crucifixion sermon" delivered by Father Barry (Karl Malden)— shot on location in Hoboken. Cast as Johnny Friendly, Lee J. Cobb fought his accuser on a tethered barge, which Kazan and Schulberg found many years later in a nostalgic return to Hoboken. The casting of Cobb, a former Group Theatre actor, reversed the role of informer that he played for the House Committee on Un-American Activities shortly before filming began. Stagehands rocked the "shell" of an old taxicab to suggest movement as Brando and Rod Steiger (Charley "the Gent") played the most famous scene in the film. The venetian blind covering the cab's back window has indelibly inscribed the thrift of Sam Spiegel, who failed to supply rear-projection equipment needed to simulate traffic in motion. Envisioned as a symbol of transcendence, the New York City skyline was often covered with mist during the hours of "photographable-daylight" available to Kazan. He raged at the "elements" before declaring obscurity a "truer value" of the film. Longshoremen cast as extras added rough texture, as did several former boxing "'Greats'" who played the goons. Through it all, Sam Spiegel harangued Charlie Maguire, assistant director, to "keep Kazan to the schedule" (*A Life,* pp. 519–29).

Nearly two years of halfhearted labor by Tennessee Williams had not produced a satisfactory ending for *Baby Doll*. The present "heavy" ending lacked tonal coherence with earlier sequences and became a contentious issue that briefly divided the collaborators.

Irene Selznick turned with apparent relief to Josh Logan after Kazan withdrew from *Streetcar* negotiations in 1947. His grief upon learning of Kazan's return and acceptance caused a "drop" far deeper than any Logan could recall. His unsteady presence on the *Waterfront* set revealed the effects of a bipolar disorder that required periodic hospitalization. Tennessee Williams found Logan's situation "touching" and familiar: "Of course a lot of us have to live that way, temporizing desperately with tensions we can never solve, just playing for time, and hoping to 'con' our way through a while longer" (to EK, January 6, 1954, Wesleyan).

Closing theater "gossip" includes the failure of Jane Bowles's play *In the Summer House* (1953), starring Judith Anderson; Clifford Odets's revision of *The Flowering Peach;* Arthur Miller's untitled work in progress, described in the press as "a serious play"; and Cheryl Crawford's long-delayed hit *Oh, Men! Oh, Women!* (1953).] *TLS, 2 pp., HRC*

Kazan invited Brando to the *East of Eden* set to enjoy the hero worship of James Dean. And of Julie Harris.

Part IV

Independence

1954–1957

[NewYork]
[c. January 4, 1954]

Dear Steve:

I wrote you a letter yesterday in the country from Paul Osborn's house. I've had some added thoughts. So this is a second letter which, as in the other case, you are free to show to Jeff and Jack.

The main point was that I do not want to make the brothel attractive. The place in From Here to Eternity was full of dancing and music and had one very very pretty girl, Donna Reed, and plenty of other that no one in the audience would ever pass by. I think it would be really "moral" and uplifting if we were to show one of these dumps as they really are, drab, evil and dull. Of course we would not label it as such, nor in other ways show it to be a brothel except to an experienced eye. On the other hand I dont like to label it a "club" or any such.

Now the next point is that we would not show any of its operation. We would rewrite the Anne scene to hinge on her "entertaining" Cal. On the other hand here too I hope to do it so that an adult would feel terribly sorry for the girl and terribly tragic about her being in such a place and position. Of course we would not show other customers doing anything except lounging, sleeping, reading. No drinking. A whore house is an incredibly dull place. No slamming of doors in this picture. No towels, no negro maids, no cuteness, no humor.

The boys have had an experience with me on a delicate issue. I'm speaking of Streetcar. I would make this picture so that my daughter 17 and my daughter 6 could both go to it and benefit. Neither would quite understand what was transpiring, but they would not be DRAWN or ATTRACTED to what's going on. They would NOT get an effect of gayety. Ask the boys to trust me again. Let me as in STREETCAR do it as I wish, and if they dont like the result, we will get together afterwards and make revisions.

As I said in the other letter Paul and I agree completely about the Sheriff condoning the vice. This character and his attitude is completely and almost precisely out of John's book. We agree, and John agrees now, to change it. We will also identify the neighborhood as a bad one.

Anyway, Steve, I've always had the feeling with Jeff and Jack that they would allow a person who's intent was "honest" to attempt things that they would not allow when the intent was obviously sensationalistic.

I'll await their reaction. You are free to show them my letters if you think them advantageous. The first was kind of dictated to Paul on his machine. This is from the horse's mouth itself, that is me. A brothel is a brothel is a brothel. I know where of I speak. Zinnemann did not portray one honestly. It was social, gay and pleasurable. Zinnemann no doubt did what he had to do. I couldn't do that in an honest venture. Kate is evil and her place is evil and must be shown that way.

Happy New Year to all you hard working Sunshine boys. See you not too soon, which means when I'm rested. Signed

Gadg

[Jack Vizzard spoke for the Breen Office in rejecting Kazan's plan to treat the brothel in *East of Eden* as "drab, evil and dull." It was a "plausible" approach for a novel or play but not "the movies" (PCA file, February 16, 1954, Herrick). Kazan in turn rejected the compromise adopted by Fred Zinnemann in filming *From Here to Eternity* (1953). The original brothel in James Jones's gritty World War II novel was converted into a festive "members only" club with the merest hint of prostitution. Kazan proved more adroit. Later negotiation led to a division of evils that met the Code ban on scenes "laid in or around brothels," as Joe Breen had indelicately put it, and preserved the aura of corruption. Kate's brothel would be set in an outlying part of town and only its weatherworn exterior photographed in long shots. The prohibited interior scenes were shifted to a nearby saloon, which also served as Kate's residence. In the first of four simulated brothel scenes, Kate is identified as "the town madam" and her son Cal warned away from the distant "house" by a bouncer who tells him he is "too young." Scenes of dancing, drinking, and gambling, including Cal's brief exchange with Anne, a serving girl played by Lois Smith, are not detailed or extended, nor are they explicitly linked to Kate's primary business, but the association of bar and brothel is reinforced by propinquity and a common lewdness of behavior.

The sheriff's defense of prostitution in *East of Eden*—" 'The people want those houses' "—also drew an objection from the Breen Office and was cut with John Steinbeck's approval. "We are still getting away with murder," Kazan told the "Sunshine boys" at Warner Bros.] *TLS, 1 p., Herrick*

TO JOHN STEINBECK

[Sandy Hook, Connecticut]
[March 1954]

Dear John:

Give our love to Elaine first of all. We had a hell of a time down there. A lot of new stuff like goggle swimming and all kinds of fishing esp. bone fishing. And esp real hot weather. I liked that. That was very welcome.

Now I'm back, feeling very different. I'm up in the country and Paul and I worked all day yesterday and today on the second draft. Yesterday was bewildering, but today was the day. Today we got somewhere.

We're reconstructing the first forty five odd pages pretty thoroughly. We feel it goes pretty well after that, but the first forty five were very bad. We're finally on a line for Aron. I hope you dont mind: we made him a Wilson (Woodrow, that is) enthusiast. We took out the two historical montages. We had Europe in the war at the beginning. And Aron convinced that we'd never get in, that Wilson would keep us out. Then, the night of the birthday party, Wilson lets him down. And a lot more. The script we had, it turns out, was simply what it was, a first draft. I kept saying that, but it was nevertheless a bit of a shock when it turned out to be what I had been saying: a first draft. We'll be working all this week up here, and then a couple of days in New York. Then I'll go to Salinas and look at your back streets (The ones you told me about). Then I'll go down to Burbank FUCK IT and make the film. I hate to leave N.Y.C. And maybe this will be the last picture I make in Cal. But this one belongs out there, so.

I looked thru a lot of kids before settling on this Jimmy Dean. He hasn't Brando's stature, but he's a good deal younger and is very interesting, has balls and eccentricity and a "real problem" somewhere in his guts, I dont know what or where. He's a little bit of a bum, but he's a real good actor and I think he's the best of a poor field. Most kids who become actors at nineteen or twenty or twenty-one are very callow and strictly from N.Y. Professional school. Dean has got a real mean streak and a real sweet streak.

I had an awful time with the girl. Terrible. The young girls are worse than the young boys. My god, they are nothing. Nothing has happened to them or else they're bums. Abra is a great part. I hope you dont die now. I want to use Julie Harris. Do you think I'm nuts? The screen play depends so on her last scene with Adam and on her strength, that I had to have a real real actress. I couldn't find one aged twenty. They're nothing. Proms, dresses, beaus and all that, but nothing for my last scene. Finally I made a photographic test of Julie and she looks twenty when her face is in movement, I think. I'll just have to keep her face in movement. She's a marvelous actress. She is not Abra the way we saw her, but jeezuz I was stuck.

One pro thing. She and Jimmy Dean look fine together. They look like People, not actors. I'm real pleased with that part of it. Two people. Dean has the advantage of never having been seen on the screen. Harris, practically.

Meantime WB? Jack esp. are dying. They hoped for stars. But they didn't come up with any names. And I haven't. I know you must be a little shocked with this casting. And I know its a hell of a gamble and all on my shoulders. But I'm delighted to take it. Its the kind of gamble I like. Write me. c/o Warner Bros. Burbank Cal.

I think R&H did fair on the lead casting. And I think Clurman is one of the three or four best directors in the world today. R&H will do the musical part of it. Lots of love to you and to Elaine. Have a BALL!

"They look like People, not actors":
Julie Harris and James Dean

[Before sailing to Nassau with Molly, Elia reminded Sam Spiegel that "the complete and final dubbing, scoring, editing and cutting" of *Waterfront* was subject to the director's "approval." He added, "I know this is clear with you and me, Sam" (February 23, 1954, Wesleyan).

Julie Harris and James Dean were twenty-eight and twenty-three respectively when they signed to play costarring roles in *East of Eden*. Both studied at the Actors Studio, Dean infrequently and unhappily, Harris more productively in the late 1940s, when she appeared in *Sundown Beach* and several televised Studio dramas. Her stage credits to date included *The Member of the Wedding* (1950) and *I Am a Camera* (1951), for which she won a Tony Award as best actress. An Academy nomination marked Harris's film debut as Frankie Addams, the forlorn member of the wedding in Stanley Kramer's 1952 production. Bit parts in film and television and two minor roles on Broadway preceded Dean's appearance in *East of Eden*.

Kazan offered wry advice to Jack Warner, who had given his director a free hand in casting newcomers such as James Dean: "Impress on him again when he arrives out there, the great importance of living an outdoor life, sunshine exercise food and fucking. Just all the healthy things, and lots of sleep. He's an odd kid and I think we should make him as handsome as possible."

Rodgers and Hammerstein ("R&H") produced and did "the musical part" of *Pipe Dream* (1955), with Helen Traubel cast in a principal role. The moderately successful play was set on Cannery Row in Monterey County and based on John Steinbeck's novel *Sweet Thursday* (1954). The Steinbecks were to have "a BALL" in Europe.] *TL, 1 p., Wesleyan*

TO AUDREY WOOD

SH: Warner Bros. Pictures, Inc.
Burbank, California
April 9, 1954

Dear Audrey:

I talked with Brando here about his doing the Tennessee Williams movie. He is very interested and I would very much like to have him. He is perfect for it and I think would be invaluable.

I think the best way to proceed is to have Tennessee himself, as soon as he gets to New York, meet with Marlon and give him the latest script. This suggestion poses three problems, which I know you are genius enough to solve. One is getting ahold of Brando—two is getting ahold of Williams—and three is compiling a finished script. But I do think all these three improbable conditions should be brought to the stage of realization. These days Marlon has to be talked to long in advance and I think the best person to do it and to give him the script is Tenn himself. They are really very fond of each other—the rest is up to you.

On the ending of the script, I'll leave that up to Tennessee. I am not satisfied with it yet, but I think it is so wonderful up 'til the very end that Brando should see it right now.

Love and kisses
Gadg

EK:JP

[Kazan thought Marlon Brando "perfect" as Silva Vacarro, an outsider of Sicilian descent who plots the seduction of Baby Doll to avenge her husband's burning of the rival Syndicate cotton gin. Marlon Brando and Tennessee Williams were troubled and elusive at this time. Brando had recently walked off the set of *The Egyptian* and returned to New York for psychiatric treatment. Williams worked haphazardly on *Baby Doll* and complained to Kazan in May that Brando had not returned the latest draft. "He should, humanly, humanely, be the one to keep us in touch with each other," the playwright wrote from distant Tangier.] *TLS, 1 p., HRC*

[Burbank, California]
April 20, 1954

Dear Paul:

Just got your letter. I think your objection is very well taken. I'm working very hard now on the story, kind of feeling the line through for myself, and I think I'll be able, by the time I get to New York, to have something really good to recommend to you.

I'm sorry I dashed into print as impulsively as I did. If I could only stop myself from writing until the next day or the next week I'd do much better. However, I really do believe that I'm on the trail of something good in the way of an idea.

First, I think we're fine up to page 77. Then I don't think the progression of scenes is quite right through the German tailor scene and the scenes that follow. Furthermore, I don't think what I recommended to you in my first letter is quite right, either. It seems to me that in our present script we've gone too far off the main story, which is: the boy who is rejected by his father, kills his brother because he is rejected by his father. And we've gone too much on a story that we should keep subsidiary: the triangle love story. It seems essential, as thinking, to me, that Cal is so absorbed in the problem with his father that he can't really have a girl in any way except for half an hour. In other words, his problem with Adam is all-absorbing. It's also our story, and when we lose Adam for as long as I recommended in my previous letter, we are way off base.

Anyway, Paul, I don't think I've figured this out yet, but I'm working very hard on it. If I'm any clearer tomorrow or the next day, I'll write you so you can think about it while I'm on the train. But I don't think I'll write unless I'm at least fairly clear.

My program is as follows: I'll leave here Thursday night by train to go up to a spot about 150 miles north of San Francisco where I'll shoot for a week and then I'll come down here on Sunday, spend Monday here and likely take the train out of here Monday night.

Reactions to the script here are that it is much better for the first half, and still definitely not right in the second. I think we're not far off, but I do think we have a good week's work. Save it for me.

I'm amassing a very good staff and should have it all set by the time I leave. I will wire you the minute I know for sure when I am leaving.

Sincerely,

EK:rb

[To the "profound and perplexing" story of Cain and Abel, John Steinbeck added a triangular love story that lacked biblical authority but provided a dramatic framework for *East of Eden*. Unity in the novel was achieved, if at all, by an accumulation of generational narratives no longer available to the screenwriter. Nor was the differentiation of "main" and "subsidiary" stories that concerned Kazan pertinent to a novel from which nothing had been excluded. Losing Adam midway through *East of Eden* did not concern Steinbeck, who rationalized his absence as a "thwarted" lover's preoccupation with the image of the woman "he invented" (Steinbeck/*Journal,* p. 112). Osborn and Kazan had no such leeway and tried to counterbalance the triangular romance of Cal, Abra, and Aron by spotting Adam in scenes with the lovers in a variety of social and ethical registers. The central birthday scene recreates the biblical father's refusal of a gift deemed unworthy—a large sum of money earned by Cal from wartime speculation in beans—and the lethal rage of the rejected son. Integrating Cal's "all-absorbing" father problem, his new intimacy with Abra, and the symbolic death of Aron after being exposed to his mother's corruption is the challenge posed by the closing scene that follows Adam's paralyzing stroke. With this in mind, Kazan had cast Julie Harris for her "strength" as an actor.] *TL, 2 pp., Wesleyan*

TO JACK L. WARNER

SH: Warner Bros. Pictures, Inc.
Burbank, California
April 22, 1954

Dear Jack:

Saw some excellent stuff from A STAR IS BORN. I think you were right in using Cinemascope there. The stuff on the sound stage and the production number I saw gain immensely from the wide screen treatment.

I am still against it for EDEN. We are going to have to depend entirely for our effect upon how much human drama and emotion we can get on the screen. This to me means only one thing: Close-ups, penetration through people's eyes into their feelings. Cukor, even in the dressing room scene, which is beautifully played, had to rely upon a close two shot. I feel he directed the scene and Garland played the scene beautifully. But I felt still that photographically the old way offers much greater opportunity to get the very most in effect out of human drama. And that is <u>all</u> we have.

In STAR IS BORN it was worth giving up a little here and there in the human scenes for what you got in the colorful mass scenes and numbers. We have no numbers. George resorted to some very clever methods to get emotion out of scenes in new ways. (Judy Garland's foot over the top of the sofa behind which lie Mason and Garland, for instance.) But I think we would suffer and possibly lose a <u>lot</u>—a crucial amount, even—with Cinemascope. Also our drama is a drama of interplay between characters. One person feels something and then the drama is in the reaction of the other person. Again I don't see how to really get this over except in Close Up.

I wish there were a wide screen process which was about two to one. I guess the best thing for me to do is to mat down to 1.85 to one, as I did on the picture I just finished. This would give us the wide screen as well as the "Academy" size projection possibility.

By the way, I was very impressed with the Tuschinsky process. He worked on about ten minutes of the WATERFRONT picture. His is 2 to 1. You should see it.

E.K.

[George Cukor directed Judy Garland and James Mason in a lavish remake of *A Star Is Born* (1954). Kazan's preference for a system with a compression ratio of 2:1 became available in Superscope, a process developed by the Tushinsky brothers and adopted by RKO in 1954. Its variable ratio of 2:1—the anamorphic lens reduces or "squeezes" into the frame an image 100 percent wider than a conventional lens—produced a somewhat more intimate effect than CinemaScope's ratio of 2.55:1. A critic as unfriendly as Andrew Sarris wrote that Kazan mastered the wide-screen technique in *East of Eden* to the point where "old canards about the static, noncinematic qualities of Cinemascope would have to be revised" (*Film Culture*, May–June 1955).] *TLS, 1 p., WB Archives*

TO STEPHEN B. TRILLING

SH: Warner Bros. Pictures, Inc.
Burbank, California
July 3, 1954

Dear Steve:

I said I wouldn't send a note, but let me just say this: I will stand corrected and ask my staff, Mr. Rosenman, to check scrupulously with the Music Department on all his moves. On the other hand, I think Ray Heindorf should be told that his function in regard to me is to get the music the way I want it. If you will excuse the egotism, I repeat, the way I want it.

So far I have seen no evidence on either this picture or on STREETCAR of any intention or desire on his part to either find out how I want things or to help me get them. He went through a long and neurotic piece of behavior resenting Alex North's entry into the STREETCAR picture and now he is doing the same thing with Rosenman, who is just as talented as North and, if anything, a better technician.

I don't know what impulses lie behind Ray's behavior, but it seems to me very irrelevant to the job of getting the right score for the picture.

I love you, too. You've always been fair and understanding and decent. May I be allowed to observe, however that what makes the production of fine pictures difficult in a major studio is the over-weaning pressure of highly organized departments. The worst example is at Metro where the Art Department is so thoroughly organized that it exerts a kind of terror over a director. At Metro you simply can't get the sets you want, no matter what you do. It doesn't seem to me that Gibbie is doing a service to his studio. He is only jealously holding on to the power that he has enjoyed for so many years.

Ray is a hell of a nice guy and a very pleasant companion. But you will have to admit that the score of STREETCAR is much better than it would have been without my introduction of the foreign Alex North.

And you will also have to admit, and so will he, that we've gotten Lennie damn cheap.

Love and kisses. E.K.

[James Dean introduced Leonard Rosenman, friend and former piano teacher, to Kazan, who hired the composer "damn cheap" to score *East of Eden*—his first film assignment. He went on to compose original music for *Rebel Without a Cause* (1955), Dean's next film, and to work in cinema and television for the next forty-odd years. A serious composer with formal training, Rosenman incorporated modernist and expressionistic elements into the score of *Eden*. The Academy recognized his later adaptations for *Barry Lyndon* (1975) and *Bound for Glory* (1976) with Oscars.

Ray Heindorf directed music for Warner Bros. from 1948 to 1965, with numerous Academy nominations, three winning, including *The Music Man* in 1962. Cedric Gibbons's legendary tenure as director of art for MGM extended from 1924 to 1956. Among his innumerable credits is *The Sea of Grass* (1947), the only film that shamed Kazan.] *TLS, 1 p. USC*

TO MOLLY DAY THACHER

[Beverly Hills, California]
Monday a.m. [July 5, 1954]

Yesterday I slept till a quarter to twelve. Then I went over to Jack's and played tennis. Came back with a lot of cigars. Jack's gotten terribly effusive with me. It takes the form of cigars. Then I went to see Kind Hearts and Coronets with my companion Thomajan. I was on my back by nine thirty. The week-end weariness has come over me. Next week end, the last I hope without you, I will try to find a place at the Beach. A friend. A silent friend. A neglectful host.

With James Dean

Someone who will give me a room. We have both Sunday and Monday off. And then starts the toughest part of the picture. Night work, and then pumping emotion, or the semblance or the suggestion or the external evidences into Raymond Massey.

You made me very envious with Jo. It sounds so marvelous there. It was still drizzling here. And inside was Jo Van Fleet. Her make-up involving arthritic hands takes till eleven thirty a.m. I think she just stays in makeup to avoid facing the trial of actually being photographed, instead of talking about it brilliantly (which she does). Being photographed is tougher. You have to do it, not just talk a good game. I finally took to shouting at her, over the backs of the crew. At one point I hollered at her that she had no balls. She began to be silent and submissive. I guess the rain had affected me. Also we were falling behind again, on account of her fucking make-up.

Jimmy is inventive and true. You're going to be surprised with him. I think. Amazingly he takes to movies like it was HIS medium. Like he owned it. None of the others do. Not Julie, not Jo, not even Ray Massey who's made a million. This kid acts for movies. He is like Jim Cagney or Spencer Tracey, except twenty three. He'll be a big star. . . .

Isn't Al Van Dekker's ass pretty in the picture? About Julie Harris looking too much like a heroine,—God I hope so. She looked so much older than the boys during the first tests that I was dismayed. And got a little desperate. So far in the scenes we've had we've gotten away with it, but everybody's watching it like a hawk. She's not firm under the chin and she's got bags under her eyes, and she has discoloration under one eye, and My God I didn't expect a standard beauty, but I dont think I took a real close look at her before I cast her. Of course all her disfigurations dissolve when she smiles. She then looks twelve. But that's not 19 either. Some of her tests she looked thirty eight. Her hair, long that way is useful in that it hides part of her neck which is not exactly as it was at nineteen either. Jimmy Dean looks much older sometimes. But sometimes he is such a kid, and when he looks older he looks like a kid who's gotten older feeling before his time because of worry and neurotics and so forth. The crew all think Dick Davalos is fine. I think he functions. I cant say more. I think I made a mistake, not so much in casting him from among the people I found available, but more from the point of view of I should have looked more and more extensively. Ray is o.k. He functions, and has a quality. The thing with him is how do you get some feeling? Its all the semblance without the material. However.

I see by the paper that Alex North is coming out here to write the music for a piece of cheese called UNTAMED or UNCHAINED or something too bad.

LOVE LOVE LOVE g.

With James Dean on the set of
East of Eden

[Jo Van Fleet's "brothel" scenes required extensive makeup for a character coping with age and unaccustomed threats to her authority. Kazan's hectoring aside, Van Fleet won the Oscar for best supporting actress. Elia wrote earlier to Molly as Adam's experiment with refrigeration and Cal's speculation in beans were being filmed in the Salinas Valley. "Ray Massey is by far the weakest in the cast," while "Jimmy & Jo VF are the best." Dean is "almost always rude in front of other people, and very gentle when he's alone. I'm glad, all in all, that I cast him." Precociously mature and self-reliant in the novel, Abra was recast as an ingénue with conventional innocence and suppressed desire. Age worked against the conception and led Kazan to order that Julie Harris be filmed looking "Right" in close-ups to hide her "un-19-ish neck and chin" (June 4 and 8, 1954, Wesleyan). Richard Davalos made his film debut as Aron in *East of Eden,* while Raymond Massey, who played the biblical father, was a veteran of theater and film and would rejoin Kazan in *J.B.* (1958).

The "piece of cheese" noted by Kazan is the prison film *Unchained* (1955). Alex North won the Oscar for best music and original song ("Unchained Melody").]
TLS, 1 p., Wesleyan

TO JACK L. WARNER

SH: Warner Bros. Pictures, Inc.
Burbank, California
July 21, 1954

Dear Jack:

I just got a letter from John Steinbeck, who is living in Paris this summer. I had written John and voiced the fear that Mort Blumenstock expressed to me, namely, that some people might very justifiably be disappointed in not finding most of John's book in our film.

John suggested that we frankly say that we are only doing the last episode from the book. I don't know how this could be worded, but he certainly could and would find a way for us to word it. John is well aware that it has been absolutely impossible to put the whole of the 600 page novel into one motion picture. The way it looks at the moment we are going to be over-length even with the final incidents I have chosen to dramatize. John, himself, was completely in accord with my decision to make only the last part of the novel.

In my letter to John I also suggested to him that another movie might very well be made using the material in the first two-thirds of his book. I made this suggestion in dead earnest and I make it to you. Now, in utter seriousness, there is tremendously exciting story material there, more lurid and more melodramatic than the material I have chosen. I have no doubt that Darryl Zanuck, for example, would have chosen the first part of the book to do rather than making the choice I did. I earnestly recommend that you consider making another movie out of the first half. I, myself, wouldn't be interested in working further on this material because I have just about given everything I have to the theme during these last couple of months, but I am sure any one of a dozen first-class movie makers would find it of interest to them.

If you like, I'll make more concrete suggestions along this line. For example, I think the leading parts would be ideal for Jean Simmons and Bill Holden and another man in the Holden category.

I'm sorry about having taken so many 'takes' the other night. I just seemed to find it impossible to get anything like what I wanted and I finally dropped the scene with a sense of having partially failed on it. The cut stuff, however, is beginning to look promising.

E.K.

[John Steinbeck approached the fourth and final part of *Eden* as though it were "an entirely new book," one that "amounts to a whole novel in subject matter." With "the opening of the century," Cal and Adam were set to emerge as "powerful new people" and Abra as "the strong female principle of good as opposed to Cathy." The first three books were loose and leisurely, but the fourth, as Steinbeck knew, would require "tightness" and "speed," to the advantage of the screenwriter (Steinbeck/*Journal*, pp. 145–48).

Steinbeck and his editor Pat Covici discussed "a second volume dealing with the second 30 years," if only to relieve the author's mounting fear that he as well as *East of Eden* would soon "be finished" (Steinbeck/*Journal*, p. 164). Kazan advised filming the early books to exploit their violence and romance and perhaps capture several colorful figures excluded from the screenplay. Neither plan materialized, nor did the film carry the explanation suggested by Steinbeck.] *TLS, 1 p., WB Archives*

TO PAUL OSBORN

[Burbank, California]
[late July 1954]

Dear Paul:

Past the two thirds point. And I think its going to be pretty good. I've been discouraged about it, and then felt better. Jimmy and Dick are inexperienced and variable. Jimmy is talented though and on his good days, he's good. I think you'll love some of his scenes and you'll feel your judgment was right. Dick is not talented really. On the other hand he kind of serves. I've written you all this before. No matter what it will be an unusual picture, and original. Certainly there was never such a hero before. Warner now is worried about my being far over-length, and its true all the material has stretched and stretched. This is due not to you, but to me, my little embroideries and conceits and "corrections" and additions. Sometimes I do them and then two days later find them rather boring. Sometimes they're o.k. One thing that has happened is that the picture has much more scope than it seemed to have. I thought of it as rather an "intimate" business. It is. It also has scope.

Molly is lying out on the terrace taking a sunbath. Here you hurry to take a sunbath before it gets too hot. She has this mild case of Mononucleitisis or something. Its tiring, for her I mean. I just keep plugging heartlessly away trying to get the picture done in good style so I can go back east. Funville turned out pretty good. We shot the Ferris wheel scene up high on the Ferris wheel which was the innovation of the year. Such an innovation, in fact, that they immediately did a big picture-taking routine of the picture taking. Now Albrecht. He's a ham, but he'll be o.k. They'll all be o.k. You wont finally think of anything except the central story anyway.

I'm doing a little innovation of my own. The guy is already writing the music. He started last week on reel one which is mostly the walk, the one thru Kate's community. That's going to be practically silent. Joe, too, while a wonderful wonderful type is a little disappointing. I've cut away from him a bit.

The girl who plays Anne was a hit and is being signed to play the leading part in Mervyn LeRoy's picture. I mean the second female lead to Greer Garson. You see, you just never know. Van Fleet who is really good has had no offers. The scene where Cal brings his brother to his mother turned out o.k. Van Fleet is killing in it.

Its hot and dreary. The lines of the introduction of the geography are o.k. Thank you. Write me some news of my east coast friends. How is Josh? Give him my love, also give Millicent my love. And write me some dope.

e.k.

[Andrew Sarris saw James Dean as an instance of "the Kazan-Strasberg, Actor's Lab, East of Hollywood trend in motion pictures." "New standards," he wrote, might be needed to judge his performance in *East of Eden*. "Kazan has called upon him for a physical performance of rare intensity and Dean has delivered in a role that completely lacks distinctive dialogue" (*Film Culture*, May–June 1955).

Molly Kazan preferred the "decompression chamber" of a leisurely trip by rail as she planned to join Elia in California: "What's the use of dropping out of the clouds in those improbable machines. No woman would have invented them. Purely male & troublemaking toys" (to EK, n.d., Wesleyan). Her slow recovery from mononucleosis led Elia to quip in later correspondence that the disease "hangs on and on until you are able to spell it."

The "Funville" sequence in *East of Eden* is preceded by a public display of patriotism that narrows to the Ferris wheel scene above the small-town plane of wartime bravado, pageantry, and profiteering. The first intimacy of Cal and Abra dissolves as suddenly as it begins and the scope of the film widens to encompass mob hysteria directed at Albrecht, played by Harold Gordon, the hitherto respected German tailor.

Leonard Rosenman was scoring Kate's walk to the bank with brothel receipts in the "practically silent" opening sequence of *Eden*. Kate is observed for the first time by Cal, who follows his mother's return to the outskirts of town and is intercepted by "Joe," a colorful character whose development in the novel far exceeded his present role as Kate's bouncer. Kazan was reportedly so frustrated by Timothy Carey's antics on the set that he physically attacked the lanky actor. Lois Smith studied at the Actors Studio and played a featured role in Mervyn LeRoy's forthcoming film *Strange Lady in Town*.] *TLS, 1 p., WHS*

TO MOSS HART

[New York]
[c. early September 1954]

Dear Moss:

Saw Kitty last night at Joan Fontaine's and heard that you were in the Hospital. I guess I haven't been reading the papers because it took me completely by surprise. Kitty said you were o.k. now, that it was something about your back and that you had determined to take it easier from now on. Lets take it easy together. I'm in a condition where the sound of the word Hospital suggests only sheer luxury. Kitty says they don't allow you to take phone calls. All I could think, frankly was HOW LUCKY! How lucky he is! Enjoy it, friend. Stretch it out. Kitty says you're fine. Scotch this ugly rumor immediately. Just consider how long it is since you've seen an agent! I imagine there might be some "improvements" in ANNIVERSARY WALTZ that you DONT have to go back and take out. How I envy you. I'm going on the Liberte for five days. No telephone. I'm going Tourist class. Aside from being cheap, its also no dress suit. (Of course I cant pretend with you that I've spent many hours of many days getting in and out of a dress suit. But you know what I'm driving at)

Well its not all as bad as that. Its just that I've been working too long and too steadily, without intermission, and I'm beginning to feel it, not yet in the back, but in what has to pass as my mind. So I guess I'll just quit for a time. And write letters and articles to the Times and letters to friends, and take my kids to college, and take walks with old friends. When are you getting out?

I may go to Europe for a while with my kid Chris, now almost sixteen, and take in a few sights. That would be just for sleeping and getting to have a Holiday with my kid. And then I'm going to put in one or two more weeks editing E of E for Warner Bros, and then I'm thru. For the first time I've got nothing ahead on my schedule. No commitments no nothing.

I saw STAR IS BORN, and I thought Geo Cukor had directed it without a sense of proportion. Everything had been blown up or glamorized. Numbers which were supposed to be the essence of informality, were informal on such a huge scale! I also thought he had put too much self pity into the feelings of the two leads. On the other hand there is some magnificent work in it, and Judy has superb moments. The previews went off fabulously (to use Jack Warner's word), and no one seems to have the least doubt of a great success ahead for it. I think it is a little swamped in its "show" aspects. On the other hand it is a most colorful and lively show, with some especially good scenes. As was everyone, I was particularly moved by the scene Judy plays in her dressing room. I thought this simple little quiet "theatre" scene the best thing in the picture.

Jack himself I found nice to work with, and a very agreeable man who suddenly gets very nervous whenever his wife or his brothers come into town. He seems happy except when the people "dearest" to him are alongside. I watched Judy shoot some. My god she really comes and goes as she wishes. I greatly admired Geo. Cukes patience. That really is fabulous!

The thing that looked best to me when I came back was the countryside. Our place is so beautiful and so simple I wondered again why I ever left it. Molly isn't too well unfortunately. Some thing sinister called Mononucleosis.

This is a lingering type debilitation that hangs on and on until you are able to spell it. This takes months, and I'm still unsure.

A separate page for this message: love. Get out soon. If you have a chance get word to me when you're coming out. I'll get Molly to add something.

g.

Dear Moss—

He's said it all—ENJOY YOURSELF—It sounds heaven! And we love you—

Molly—

[Hospitalization for a back ailment saved Moss Hart from supervising *Anniversary Waltz,* a long-running Broadway hit that opened in the spring under his direction. His screenplay for *A Star Is Born,* soon to be released by Warner Bros., was nominated for honors by the Writers Guild of America. Elia remembered Hart for his "rare courage" in defending *Gentleman's Agreement* from studio-induced compromises. Kazan also envied his friend's enforced break from work and was reluctant to leave Sandy Hook to finish *East of Eden* later in September.] *TLS, 2 pp., WHS*

TO SAM SPIEGEL

[New York]
September 9, 1954

Dear Sam:

Glad to hear (thru Rheiner) that the London opening went well. And of course I'll be glad to get details about Venice. I felt badly about losing, since with this picture nothing will content me except first.

I also received thru Sam Rheiner your other message in re the billing, and it seems to me that you miss the point of what I was objecting to. The message came from Rheiner: "Tell Gadge, dont I deserve it?!" I did not ever say that you didn't deserve credit. You deserve a lot, and of course there is enough in this picture for everybody. My beef with you has two horns. First I think that Budd S is getting a disgustingly shabby deal on the publicity. Why he is not madder than he is, I dont know. No one can read his name on any of the copy without chancing eye-strain. After all, he is a well known novelist. People stop him in bars and ask him if he had anything to do with the picture. You remember, Budd started the whole goddamn thing. He needed plenty of help on the script, but I've never seen a movie writer who didn't, and that does not lessen the size of his contribution. And he wrote on it for years and he wrote innumerable versions and now he is being treated shabbily. And apparently due to an act of mine. And that is point two. When you asked me to reduce my name in one place to 25% because you (said and) thought there was too much copy on the "Paper" I was not at all given to understand that it was your intention to reduce everyone's name, in this spot, except your own. To put it differently it was at no time my understanding that by agreeing (mistakenly as it turned out) to reduce my name in my second credit to 25% I would either have to look at your name bigger than mine here, or, and this is the important point, that I would be instrumental and responsible for REDUCING BUDD'S NAME SMALLER THAN YOURS. The thought is simple even though the previous sentence is complicated and I'm sure you understand me, without further elaboration. The result I think shameful and I want it rectified immediately, Sam. It is already too late. But still I want it fixed.

And now I have another beef. This is more serious. I know you have been busy in Europe. And my guess would be that you have been doing a fine job. The fact that we did not win in Venice I'm sure is not due to any thing undone by you. And I imagine you have done an excellent job on the translations and dubbing scripts.

But I think that, after an initial pretty good start, an inadequate job is being done here. I've so written Lazarus and Jack Cohn, and I have asked them for a meeting. Schulberg and I will go to this, but it is not our job to do this. First let me explain what I think is sadly missing here.

This picture is the dream of a good publicity man. Sam Goldwyn would positively have had it built up as the greatest picture of the last decade by now. You, in effect, sit by while Columbia climbs all over us with that mediocrity CAINE. We've been nowhere but in the shadow of that picture, and this has got to stop. Even the quotes they use for Caine are better than ours. Whereas our press reception was immeasurably better, and our response from influential people much much better and more, and our public response not to be compared. There have never been comments in my memory to compare with those being made about our picture. People literally stop me on the street and thank me. This is not an exaggeration. But nowhere in the handling of the picture is THIS particular kind of excitement reflected. A whole field was open for LARGE publicity. It has been allowed to go unused, unexploited. I say large publicity.

For instance: At last we are outdoing the Europeans. For instance: At last a picture that faces up to a taboo issue///or any issue. At last a picture that deals honestly with American life, a hitherto unlooked at piece of American life. But the PICTURE, Sam, the PICTURE. They are handling the damned thing as if ALL THEY HAVE TO GO ON IS BRANDO'S PERFORMANCE. I cant see a hell of a lot of difference between these ads and those for the WILD ONE where in fact all they did have to go on was Brando's performance.

THE PICTURE! It needs someone who will really fight for it. And not from a yacht in N.Y. Harbor, but from a hotel room, with newspapermen and opinion makers. Goldwyn, who, you must admit, is a really great showman would have made it the DUTY of everyone to see it. And take their kids. He wraps a picture in an imperative and he writes the wording of the imperative himself. He insists that people see his picture, even when there isn't much there.

It happens we have the type of picture that this can be done with. Sam G. would have made it a lesson in citizenship or something. Christ knows what. His ads would have been different. Our ads are the same every week. Paul finally did a good job on the ads, a good initial job, but we're still back there with that good initial job. What the hell happens now???

Lets face it, our picture for Columbia is part of the year's program and that is all. And the picture here has been just left in their hands. And that's the way they handle it. I dont think for one goddamn minute that the Venice festival was important enough to let happen here what has happened. The big thing is CAINE. All around Caine is a shadow and in one piece of that shadow sit we. Somebody is standing with a big pistol in the back of Lazarus and the whole N.Y. office and saying: PLUG CAINE. Where the hell is your pistol? Its time for a scene or two.

I think we can sweep a lot of the prizes, but the way we're going now we'll get nothing. The public guts of this picture are leaking out. It seems to me it is your imperative duty now to all of us, including yourself to come back here and fight like hell for it. . . . We're not going to make many pictures as good as this. Neither you nor I nor Budd. I will do everything I can to help on Publicity. I may have to be pushed a little, but finally I will do a lot. I did see Archer Winston on my own. I took Crowther for a drink on my own. I will see Otis G. when he comes back to town. I talked to Lennie Lyons.

Now this next is not too important, but I think you should know about it. You've engaged, they tell me, two girls here and I know you have Blowitz on the coast, and it is the impression of everyone (everyone) that they are doing nothing but plugging you. And of course you're plugging your own horn. John Steinbeck wrote me in a letter that he did not know that you had also directed the picture. A newspaperman here who spoke to you kidded me. He was flabbergasted at how often you had "saved" the picture. And much more like this. Well o.k. you're vain I'm vain everybody's vain. Its unimportant. Except in the face of the fact that a terrific opportunity is being missed to BUILD THE PICTURE BIG. Budd and I look at it from here. We read the column in the Reporter about what a great man you are and we say the details are all wrong, but Sam did make a big contribution and all that, BUT WHERE THE HELL IS SOMETHING ABOUT THE PICTURE?? ANYWHERE?? Why doesn't Blowitz get some prominent guys to write something about the picture. There were a million anecdotes about the PICTURE. Where the hell are they? Why isn't stuff fed to TIME about the PICTURE? Columbia is just a routine organization with orders to plug a rival picture. They are following the orders of the people that pay the checks. They are letting the picture slip down into a notch labelled: EXCITING MELODRAMA. That's not it. That isn't going to get us anywhere. I'M FURIOUS!!!

That's enough. You get the idea.

g/

[Sam Spiegel's last-minute intervention persuaded officials of the Venice Film Festival to add *On the Waterfront* to the list of American entries. *The Caine Mutiny* (1954), a favorite to win the grand prize, was outpaced by *Waterfront*, which finished second and claimed a Silver Lion—the only American film to win a major award. Kazan later reflected on the rigors of transatlantic competition in declining to represent *East of Eden* at Cannes: "After my experience with ON THE WATERFRONT I just couldn't take another pushing around. I have the impression that those European fellows are very clever. They want us over there so that they can have somebody on their team beat our brains in" (to JLW, April 8, 1955, WB Archives).

Ads large and bold hailed the release of *Waterfront* in July as "a magnificent contribution to the world of drama." Kazan appears in directorial pose, with camera, while a hypersensitive likeness of Marlon Brando borders the adjacent copy: "The phrase 'directed by Elia Kazan' is the hallmark of all that's best in entertainment." Brando's "towering performance" took precedence in later ads as the director receded to smaller type. Credit for Budd Schulberg's screenplay and Leonard Bernstein's score was buried in still-smaller type at the foot of each ad. A reduced ad for *Waterfront* ran intermittently during August and early September—smaller and less prominently displayed than ads for *The Caine Mutiny*.

On the Waterfront dominated the Academy Awards, winning eight Oscars in all, including best actor, director, picture, and writing. Both Columbia releases were highly profitable, but *The Caine Mutiny*, based on a popular novel by Herman Wouk and starring Humphrey Bogart, doubled the first-year gross of *Waterfront*.] *TLS, 3 pp., Wesleyan*

TO TENNESSEE WILLIAMS

[New York]
[mid-September 1954]

Dear Tenn:

Spoke to Audrey yesterday about the Joe Mank situation. and etc. I felt very bad I hadn't answered your letter. The plain fact is that for the first time in my life I'm quite exhausted. Out of gas (petrol) No gissum left. Also rather discouraged. I dont think the last picture I made turned out too well. Perhaps its all because I've been working almost continuously without a breather or a break or a refresher. Its also—and more likely—a state of personal depression. I used to be more given to these. That's the best I can say, I used to have them more often. Anyway all this is to explain why I didn't write you. I liked the rewrite of BATTLE. Its partly rewrite, and its partly new. I still thought it needed work. (God that's an old one; it limps) But anyway I still thought it needed work. I thought the boy esp. I also thought it could be a superb piece in the Theatre. I thought the end around the boy could be wonderful. Anyway, Tenn, if Joe is hot about it, which I can imagine he is, and if you like Joe and his ideas, which I imagine you must because he's a very fine and brilliant man—why then I cant stand in the way, and I wont. I'm not in shape right now to do anything, or even to start anything. I've got to go out to California to finish EAST OF EDEN. I'll be there from the 18th Sep. to the first week of October and then I think I'll probably be just as weary and just as disgusted with everything. I ought to leave this part of the world, or the world, for a while and see if I can kind of find a new impulse. I found myself repeating myself in EAST OF E. which I suppose a person always does when he does too much too near together. Repeating effects. I found myself saying shit and knowing it, and having not much else to say to actors. And I also found myself dreading to go to work, which has never happened to me before. And other stuff I cant put into a letter. I've told all this stuff to nobody, and certainly not to Audrey, to whom I spoke in a circumspect and business like manner. I said to her: I'd rather wait for one of the new plays, if Tenn wants me to do one of them. And that is true of course, but it omits the fact that I'm jealous to do everything you write. I also had the sense from the way Audrey put the question to me that you were saying, in effect, if Gadg wants a lot of work done, I dont think it needs a lot of work, and I dont want to do a lot of work, and I have done all the work it needs ESSENTIALLY and Joe is enthusiastic about it as it is. etc. etc. You know. I said to Audrey that I read this into what she was saying to me in your behalf and she said that was likely right. And I said in that case I could only say that if I could get it up enough to say what I thought it needed, I probably would have quite a lot to say—that I do not think, for instance, that it is ready for an early rehearsal etc. But, frankly to you, I dont know how much of that is due to my state of feeling. Audrey was sweet and kind as always and sent me off with a copy of your new short stories which I was very glad to have.

Love, always. g.

[Tennessee Williams hoped to stage *Orpheus Descending* before *Cat on a Hot Tin Roof* and turned to Kazan for his direction. He came away from an earlier meeting with Joe Mankiewicz feeling that his "ideas" for directing such a poetic play were "a bit too literal or realistic." Filming *East of Eden* had discouraged Kazan and added to the burden of the preceding thirty-odd months—the direction of three Broadway shows, including two failures, and four screen projects in various stages of development. Kazan characterized the present impasse as prelude to a "terrible personal drama" that engaged the main contradictions of his professional and personal life: "I wanted to be in with the big shots of the entertainment world, but I also wanted to lead a quiet, reflective life." "I loved Molly, my smart, immaculate, completely honest and trustworthy wife, but I also wanted adventures and to be, every so often, irresponsible and out of control" (*A Life,* p. 533).

Tennessee Williams moderated his disappointment when Kazan returned *Orpheus Descending* and graciously placed him on the "threshold" of his "richest creative period" (to EK, September 16, 1954, Wesleyan). "One of the new plays" for which Kazan decided to wait was *Cat on a Hot Tin Roof.*] TLS, 1 p., HRC

TO CLIFFORD ODETS

[Burbank, California]
[c. late September 1954]

My dear, dear Cliff:
Thanks for your letter which was full of concern and friendship and a wise thought. It meant a lot to me to even tell you about how I've been feeling, and your letter meant a lot to me. I cant talk about it to anyone else, including Molly now, which is too bad. But the pain part of it I've experienced before, and I think I'm tough somewhere in my kernel and will endure. I'll do something about it, something and it wont solve anything, but I dont think in terms of solution anyway. And I do believe that I will be forced ONLY by misery and want to find out more who I'm like I am and do work that is more like me. I think its partly growing pains and partly loneliness that only a certain kind of connection can solve, one that I haven't got now. Its lonely out here, but that isn't to say that I wish I weren't here. Here I am and its better to be lonely here than congenial. I did my retakes and I'll start the real editing right off and maybe I'll be back in a couple of weeks. I wish I did have more thoughts on the play. But there was only one large lack I felt in it and I spoke to you about that. However I'd like very much to have a copy, if and when you get it mimeographed. . . .

LOVE. Gadg

[A recent meeting in New York and exchange of letters are the first overt signs of a restored friendship. The groundwork may have been laid in 1952, when Clifford Odets authorized Kazan's naming of his former party membership and in effect confirmed their mutual dilemma. Odets now advised Kazan not to "worry" or underestimate the search for identity. "I will be callow and say that men like Beethoven and Cezanne, high and great, died trying to find their identities. Why should we be more or better? . . . Perhaps this process of uncovering, of moving in closer and deeper to one's center (which of course remains elusive because it is fluid and growing, BECOMING) is the very dynamic of the creative man!" (September 18, 1954, Wesleyan). Finishing *East of Eden* would not relieve, much less "solve," Kazan's problem of finding work "more like me."

Odets was completing *The Flowering Peach,* a dramatic retelling of the Noah story forthcoming in December.] *TLS, 1 p., Indiana*

TO MOLLY DAY THACHER

PM: Burbank, California, September 30, 1954

Same day as the other letter, later in the afternoon. Well I've given up on EofE. In my heart I have. The plain fact which I'm really looking at for the first time is that the picture is no good. No use softening it. And I guess that's what I've really been so depressed by.

Its strange. You know I just ran the picture again. Just now. Then I went out and got a hamburger and I'm going to take a short nap on the sofa here and I'm running tonight again with Rosenman to work on the score. And just now when I ran: THERE were all the improvements, improvement after improvement, and still the picture had not improved one damned bit. This has happened to me before. Everything I've done has made the picture smoother, tighter, clearer and more dramatic, and still its absolutely dead at its core and has no feeling. TERRIBLE fact. But there it is. When something fundamental is wrong, you cant help the thing.

And I think something much more fundamental is wrong here than I thought. For instance the story A (This boy finds out that his mother is a madam, is she or isn't she?, and since she is he thinks he is doomed and discovers he has freedom of choice) HAS ABSOLUTELY NO RELATION TO STORY B (A boy is denied his father's love. He feels rejected. Therefore gets vengeful and ugly. He tries to regain his father's love, and suffers a Big rejection. From the pain of this he kills his brother and???) AND STORY A AND STORY B HAVE NOTHING TO DO WITH STORY C (A kid dwells under the cloud of a priggish and puritanical and smug and self righteous father and brother. His brother's girl finally discovers that with all his small faults he is at bottom better than his brother and she becomes his girl. When his brother turns on him, he proves to his brother that he has no real basis for his "PURITY".)

They just dont really relate. You would choose different material to dramatise each of them. One starts, then there is a shift to another, then another, then back and then kind of in between and etc. etc. NOTHING GETS GOING. No emotion can start to build. There is no empathy, nor is there concern, or "rooting". No unity. Unclarity.

It is very deep. As I say I just this last hour faced the fact that it cant be fixed. I loused it up. Tomorrow I have a conference with the Publicity department to plan its sale, tomorrow I run it again, Saturday I run for Warner after working with the cutter all day. Then I think I just might as well come home and write it off. No use. Am I just depressed? I dont think so. I think what I say is true and I might as well look at it.

Some fun!!

[Elia softened his criticism after further editing but finished *East of Eden* without joy or inspiration. "I'm still operating on something which is mechanical," he wrote to Molly on the following day. "I'm finishing the picture. That's the size of it. I'm going thru the movements as intelligently as I can. I'm being thorough and careful and professional and all the other virtues" (October 1, 1954, Wesleyan). Not coincidentally, as Kazan went through the final motions in Burbank, he instructed his agent and attorney "to activate" his production company and outlined the steps necessary to gain "complete artistic and operational control": "My desire is only to make the pictures I want to make, just as I want to make them and without any other personalities to 'deal with.'" The "entire operation" would be based in New York City to facilitate making "medium or modest budget" films with "strong subjects" and "fresh personalities." Script control would be vested in Kazan to eliminate the "Zanuck situation" (memorandum to Lastfogel and Fitelson, September 25, 1954, Wesleyan).] *TL, 1 p., Wesleyan*

TO TENNESSEE WILLIAMS

[New York]
20th. [October 1954]

Dear Tenn:

On the positive side, I am left at the end of Act two with an intense concern with Big Daddy's fate—not his physical fate—and I want to see how he comes out, so to speak. I wouldn't even mind him just sitting on stage for a moment or two at the beginning of act three. It would interest me more than what you have there now.

You have aroused my interest and concern with Big Daddy. You cant get me all hot and bothered and then walk away and say lets look at the view—the view of How Big Mama takes what we already know in a perfectly predictable way, the view of Rev Tooker's Hypocrisy, of which I dont need further convincing, the view of Mae and Margaret Bitching, a little of which goes a long long ways and which belongs in Act one, as a preparation rather than in act three as a climax, the view of Gooper defending himself and warning his enemies, which definitely belongs in Act One as a basic condition for the drama that follows, and not in act three as a climax. Is that clearer?

Its like I told you at our very first conversation, you've got the wrong third act. Once again around. There is no further need for illustrations of mendacity. Its too late anyway. Big Daddy and Brick have already had their scenes against it. There is no further need for illustrations of meanness and smallness no matter how truly or vividly or originally written. This has been already granted by the audience.

There is no need to sit and watch how Big Mama takes the news. In the first place we know the news and there is no surprise in what is revealed to her. We know what is going to be said to her. And in the second place her reaction is basically predictable.

And Mae and Margaret's cat fight—how much of that can you take? A little of it in Act One is o.k. But now we are supposed to be in the guts of the play and its not a play about these two queens cutting each other. And if its to illustrate what Big Daddy and Brick have ALREADY talked about—why its too late isn't it? The Hypocrisy of Tooker and the inhumanity of the Dr.? we've had it. . . .

In other words, I think the wrong material is in the first twenty pages of Act Three. Its not what you have aroused our appetite, our concern for.

You have, it seems to me, a most powerful basis for a third act. What does Big Daddy do when he hears that he has very little time left??? You got a little start on this with the notion of the gun and the Belvedere. Not so much in the geography and the prop, but more in the idea that he wants to be by himself to die, because he doesn't want to die surrounded with falseness. And he doesn't want to whimper.

And the second basis that you have for a real third act is what do Gooper and Mae do when they face the fact that there is very very little time left and they have gotten nowhere. What does Margaret do? (This last you have and its the only genuine third act element you have now)

For instance: there seems to me to be a need for a real scene between Goober and Big Daddy. Does Big Daddy tell everyone the truth, at long last, Big Mama, for instance. I'll bet there's some deeper realism. I'll bet if you just sit and dig thru yourself. Get away from me and my suggestions and Audrey telling you that you should have something on this season and Cheryl saying when do I read it, and Irene with her innuendos and Brooks and Anna M. and Burt L. and Hal W. and the whole goddamn kit and kaboodle of us friends, you'll feel your way thru to a real and true and powerful third act.

This play should be done when its ready. Not until. If its ready next month, we should begin. I want to do it badly. But I'm scared to death of getting locked into a schedule with a third act that I KNOW is wrong. You'll suffer if I do that. It takes a lot out of you. Remember Camino.

I love you and I dont want you to be less than you are in point of achievement. You have never written better than the second act of this play. In fact its the most mature and powerful thing you have written. What you have now is essentially a brilliant first draft.

What is the creative road to solving problems of form. You have a problem of form, of UNITY. You cant scorn that problem. You cant turn away from that problem in the name of organic writing. I have no good suggestions. You're out of my league. I dont think anyone else is going to help you however. You're in a game where only you know the rules.

I had one thought, which I will tell you and then throw it away. I thought that the material in the present third act that belongs in Act one should be put there. Then the play should be in two long acts—like Death of a S.—and you continue past the point where you leave Act Two, with the action uninterrupted and our view of Big Daddy never obscured right to a climax. Act one—the mendacity Act Two—How to live and die in the midst of the mendacity. I had a little more thinking—if it is that—along this line but a hint is enough, if there's anything in it.

There's a drag wind of activity in the Theatre. The season is slipping is part of it. And lets compete the other. Two big guys never gave in to it. O'Neill never let a play of his be done till HE was really satisfied. Are you REALLY satisfied with this third act? Just think that. The hell with me and Audrey and the season. The other guy is Thornton Wilder. He never let Jed or me rush him. He finished his plays and they are both monuments. I think you've got the best play here potentially in years and years. Why throw that away because this wind of <u>lets get going</u> is pushing you?

I'm not going anywhere. I want to do the play badly. I dont get but one play I really want to do every three years or so. I sure want to do this one.

Love

g

[Tennessee Williams originally drafted *Cat on a Hot Tin Roof* as "a short-long play" consisting of three scenes—Brick and Maggie, Brick and Big Daddy, the family conference—and ending with "a terrifyingly strong final curtain." Audrey Wood compared it favorably to *Streetcar* but was "troubled" by the play's brevity and assured Williams that it has "sufficient conflict to make it a solid piece of theater for a full evening." He was not immune to such commercial advice, nor did he overlook the inconvenient fact that a reconstituted second act would have "the highest degree of dramatic tension." It must "be compensated," he warned Kazan, not by "a trick or distortion" but by fidelity to "the sheer truth of the material" (n.d., HTC).

In working notes, Williams described "the geography and the prop" for Big Daddy's evolving role in act three. After learning of his impending death, Big Daddy climbs to the belvedere, gun in hand, where he delivers the curtain line of act two: "Lying! Dying! Liars!" Williams planned to keep Big Daddy "dimly visible" on the belvedere, "a white-fenced square at the center of the roof," through act three, rising from a bench when the pain of cancer strikes to mutter to the sky, "'A pig squeals: a man keeps a tight mouth about it.'" He included a note, presumably for Kazan's benefit, that Big Daddy "can have a final cathartic scene, perhaps with Brick, perhaps with Big Mama, perhaps with Margaret." None of these early directions remain in the production script, nor was Williams prepared at this time to have Big Daddy reenter the family setting as Kazan would strongly advise (n.d., HRC). The director's preference for a two-act structure was not influential in further revision of *Cat*—provisionally entitled "A Place of Stone."

Kazan read *Cat on a Hot Tin Roof* shortly after finishing *East of Eden* and reportedly made a verbal commitment in October to begin rehearsals in February. Later he informed Darryl Zanuck that he was keeping himself "open for the period from December to June" and had not yet "signed to do Tennessee Williams' play."] *TLS, 2 pp., Wesleyan*

TO AUDREY WOOD

[Burbank, California]
November 29, 1954

Dear Audrey:

Just arrived and got your telegram. My Warner Bros. arrangement doesn't affect my availability since I won't be starting on anything for them until next August. There is a situation with Fox but I have gone along on the assumption that I will be able to work that out. I think I probably will.

I did receive Tenn's new stuff and there is a lot of improvement in the part of Margaret and I think the Big Daddy scene in Act III moving. I do not like Brick as yet and I have written another of my annoying memos on this subject. I will call him in a few minutes now and will see him this afternoon and give him the paper.

I don't want any mistake between us, Audrey. You know that this is an extremely difficult play to put over. It has to come over perfectly and there must be a positive feeling in it, otherwise its subject matter, which is a man dying of cancer, his son impotent with memory and his son's wife ready to crawl for money, will frighten the audience off and we'll get the all-familiar "very nice things in it" type of notice.

I am not worried about myself. This sounds like one of those old corny lines, but you know it's true. But I am really deeply worried about another severe wound to Tenn's self-esteem, public standing, etc., etc. There is no darn need for it because this play can be solved and the thing to do is not to hurry it, to keep working along until we, I say we, but you know for myself, I mean I, think it's right. Tenn has made a lot of progress from criticisms I made. I am making this afternoon another very strong criticism which, if he will really face and accept, he might have a good chance to get the thing right and I mean right on its own terms.

And I am hoping like hell that it works out. I think it will. But this pressure of hurry and get the season or get in a few weeks earlier, etc., etc., makes me feel damned uncomfortable. There is only one important thing—to get it right. So I am working along and we'll see.

Write me, will you dear. I'm here at Warner Bros. and I'd love to hear from you what your thoughts are.

Tenn says you're hurrying him; you say he's hurrying you; I'm hurrying nobody.

Love,

EK:r

[Kazan reassured a skeptical Audrey Wood that his "arrangement" to produce a " 'series of important pictures' " for Jack Warner (*NYT*, November 24, 1954) would not delay plans to stage *Cat on a Hot Tin Roof* in the spring. Nor would his languishing contract with Twentieth Century-Fox.

Tennessee Williams solved the Big Daddy problem, at least as Kazan saw it, by returning the dying patriarch to the family conference in act three and providing a "cathartic scene" in which Maggie the Cat optimistically proclaims "a child is coming, sired by Brick," while kneeling before Big Daddy. The objection to Brick's passivity was not so easily met, as Williams wrote in his journal after meeting Kazan in Los Angeles and digesting his latest "annoying" memo (unidentified): "I do get his point but I'm afraid he doesn't quite get mine. Things are not always explained. Situations are not always resolved. Characters don't always 'progress'. But I shall, of course, try to arrive at another compromise with him" (Williams/ *Notebooks,* p. 663).

By way of compromise, Williams added dialogue to meet Kazan's request that Brick's paralysis, especially his obsessive drinking, be explained in a way that will " 'hold water.' " The new lines in act two begin with Brick's selective retelling of the Skipper story and Big Daddy's exposure of the lie that has "disgusted" his son: "You dug the grave of your friend and kicked him in it because you couldn't face the truth about something?" Williams traced the evasion to an instability, "homosexual with a heterosexual adjustment," that made Brick's type fearful of exposure. If the "mask is ripped off, suddenly, roughly," as Big Daddy does in act two, "that's quite enough to blast the whole Mechanism, the whole adjustment, knock the world out from under their feet, and leave them no alternative but—owning up to the truth or retreat into something like liquor." He asked Kazan, "Don't you feel this does it? There's your plain and simple and believable reason," but added that while the new dialogue might suggest "progress" for Brick, he did not "really think so." Brick was "doomed by the falsities and cruel prejudices of the world he comes out of, belongs to" (to EK, November 31, 1954, Wesleyan). Kazan replied in later correspondence that Big Daddy's truth had been "slighted or skimmed over" in act three.] *TL, 2 pp., Wesleyan*

PM: Burbank, California, December 7, 1954

Judy honey:

I've lived by now forty five years and how many really intimate friends do you think I have: Not very many. Very very few really intimate ones. There are people I like and am "warm" to, but as for really wanting their company or closeness or their opinions even—that's another matter. You're just discovering the facts of life, so called. And its really better that way. I like it that you dont make close friends easily, that you dont wear your heart on your sleeves. Most people are so eager to be liked (especially by the opposite sex) that they quickly and easily do anything that they think is required of them to gain and hold this esteem. In other words, they give up their own personality and integrity. And you dont. Dont worry. You'll find people you really like. Really. And you'll fall in love too. But you wont really like many people. Its a kind of contradiction in terms. And you wont fall in love many times—perhaps only once. This business of giving of yourself quickly and easily is only the mark of a shallow nature. Perhaps good, and friendly and kind and everything else—but not very deep. Also—just quite simply—a real friendship is based upon more than "I like you because you like me". Most people are searching for people who like them. Well the thing is: set your own terms. Want what you want. Its all a matter of character and the more you have the more there is to give and the more there is to give, the longer it takes to get there, to get all of it. Most friendships operate on a most casual level. People eat together or drink together or sleep together and nothing really happens. The best friendships I have had, except your mother, have been with people I've worked with. That is because we are meeting, when we work, that is, on a level of really profound involvement. The meaningless word of all time is "nice" as in "he's a nice guy". It seems that's all we presently ask of our fellow man—that he be a "nice guy" whatever the hell that is.

love
Daddy

[Judy Kazan's recent card about "running the lights on Hamlet, and how she enjoyed listening [to] the play over and over" was welcome first-semester news from Swarthmore. Whether advice on friendship and love was solicited or not is unclear. In any case, Elia declared Judy his "favorite girl in the world under twenty and over ten," as he wrote to Molly in early December.] TLS, 1 p., JKMP

TO DARRYL F. ZANUCK

[New York]
December 14, 1954

Dear Darryl:

As I wired you yesterday, I'm reading POMPEY'S HEAD again, but feel dubious about it. The fellow got hold of a pretty good theme, but treats it vaguely. Then he's got this personal story which never connects except thematically (which doesn't mean anything) with the professional story. I'm very leery, since MAN ON A TIGHTROPE of two stories that don't really connect, or tie together. I have to be very careful with you, and with everyone else, I guess. A director is blamed for absolutely everything (I guess at those prices he should be). And, despite the fact that I had nothing to do with the choice or treatment of TIGHTROPE, nor with the structure of the script, the failure of that picture has always been laid at my door. (You have told me five times if you've told me once that its the lowest grosser in Fox History.) At any rate, I don't want to get into something with you now that I don't think structurally sound. Story and structure are everything. At our level, all trouble is story trouble. That divided story business—divided story tied together only by a vague theme—spells trouble to me.

About your letter to me marked confidential and personal, I must confess that I showed it to my agent. I can appreciate very well that you work for a corporation and that the ultimate power to dispose of contracts, change understandings, etc., is not in your hands. I can't resist the temptation to remind you, Darryl, that when the current was flowing the other way, and I came into your office and offered to take considerably less than my salary for ZAPATA, it did not need a meeting of the Board to agree to accept this. And you were, as you say, very kind to me on MAN ON A TIGHTROPE (as I was providential on PINKY), but still on that one too the move to readjust my salary downward was done very simply without the gentlemen of the Board even hearing about it.

As I say I showed your letter to Abe Lastfogel, who is my agent and Bill Fitelson who is my lawyer. Since it was a letter about a contract, they know about that. I fully appreciate that with the enormous number of contracts that your company must have you cannot be familiar with every detail of mine. But nevertheless I must tell you that you're misinformed about the final operation of our machinery of choice of subject. The formula you refer to is the formula of the first contract I had with your company which was torn up a number of years ago. The essence of our standing agreement is that I finally cannot be forced to do any subject that I think I would not enjoy doing. The wording of our present agreement carries out this understanding.

I also must tell you that I have not signed to do Tennessee Williams' play. I have kept myself open for the period from December to June, and I am open now. Nor, of course, am I contemplating doing anything for Warners during this period.

I hate to discuss things on a contractual basis with you. But your letter did forcibly remind me that you're an officer of a corporation carrying out the instruments of that corporation. You're obligated to it. I'm obligated to myself. I want to do good work. I have found, the last two years that I do good work when I am unsupervised. I tried to explain this to you in your office, but I am stumbling in face to face conversations. It seems to me that the whole nature and merit (too) of your operation is that you, IN EFFECT, produce every picture on your lot and, especially when there are difficulties, you construct the stories too. I think the only reason WATERFRONT was a success is that we had a good script. To get that script, there was never a consideration of time. We went over and over and over it. We started again, several times, and we never gave up. No one was really on salary, and no one was pushing for a production date. There were no quick solutions, and no afternoon-long conferences that solved "everything". On EAST OF EDEN too I worked here, and without a time limit or a production date, or being pushed or supervised. All the solutions were mine and for better or worse the picture is my picture. No one had a hand in the editing and I have the ultimate satisfaction of knowing that its the way I really want it. I took a long time editing it and changing it around and scored it myself and dubbed it myself and for better or worse, I have the only important satisfaction: its my own.

I know you understand and I know that you sympathize in your heart— your personal heart, not your corporate heart. You're a creative man and I know that you must have had many a strong impulse to just do a couple of pictures that you really devote yourself to, instead of program of stuff, most of which you can't really like. I surmise a lot about you, but that's another subject for another day. I'm now answering your personal and confidential letter about my contract.

This last is unimportant really. You submitted to me, not two, but three stories. I read VIOLENT SATURDAY (have I got the title right?) and discussed with you my reasons for not liking it for myself. And there was MANY SPLEN-DORED THING and now POMPEY'S HEAD. It doesn't make much difference. If you want to submit another, go ahead.

I'll be getting back to you in another day or two about <u>Pompey</u>. Sorry it couldn't be quicker, but you know the reason.

With affection

ek:mf

[Darryl Zanuck was fighting a war of attrition with two stars, well known to each other and unhappy with their contracts. He suspended Marilyn Monroe and threatened to "assassinate" her in the press for declining "The Girl in Pink Tights."

Her demand for greater independence and artistic control was much the same battle waged by Kazan in negotiating a contract for *On the Waterfront*. In retrospect he felt that the film "would have been a piece of shit if [Darryl Zanuck] had done it" (to MDT, n.d., Wesleyan). Correspondence in the new year reveals no softening of Zanuck's position that Kazan fulfill the terms of his contract, to which he replied: "Once you taste independence and a piece of a picture, it is very hard to go back to salary and supervision. You know exactly what I'm talking about because you work as your own boss and thoroughly enjoy it" (January 16, 1955, UCLA). Kazan rejected Zanuck's final proposal, "Pompey's Head," and made the first of three film recommendations allowed by contract: *The Flowering Peach* by Clifford Odets. Predictably, Zanuck turned this down.

Kazan's "surmise" was accurate. Frustrated by the decline of the studio system and apparently tired of following his "corporate heart," Darryl Zanuck left Twentieth Century-Fox in 1956 to become an independent producer. Kazan put aside old differences in writing *A Life* and paid homage to Zanuck as one of the "tycoons" of Hollywood for whom "film was everything."] *TL, 3 pp., Wesleyan*

TO ERIC BENTLEY

[New York]
December 28, 1954

Dear Eric:

Just got a call from Tennessee Williams. He and Arthur Miller have been burning because you infer (in THE DRAMATIC EVENT) some co-authorship from my part as part of my production of STREETCAR and SALESMAN. They are sending you a letter which they also intend to make public thru the pages of several magazines. They note that I wrote you once saying that I had not authored a line of either play. And they note that you say I changed the very idea of their central characters and that thus, without recourse to new dialogue, I became a sort of co-author. They resent what you have to say, since it casts a slurring shadow on their best work and are writing you in very strong language. Tenn read me their letter over the telephone, and asked me if I cared to sign it. I said I did not; however that I would write you again myself and make as clear as I could my personal views.

I think Williams and Miller are right here. You say in one of your "afterthoughts": "I take it Mr. Kazan includes under the heading of authorship only the dialogue." Of course this is not so. I know as well as the next fellow that "dialogue is only one of a playwrights means of communication." But on these two plays, I did not "add", I did not "slant", I did not reangle. And I certainly disagree that I changed the "idea" of Blanche, or of Willy from what the author contained in the original script.

In fact, Eric, dont you think you glamorize me a bit? In the Theatre I work like this: to the best of my ability, by divination and communication, by direct questioning and by intuition I try to find out what the author had in mind. And then I—the French have the best word for it—I tried to _realize_ it on stage.

I have always been on the most candid and harmonious terms with Tennessee. At the time of Salesman I was on truly intimate terms with Miller. There were no differences, spoken or unspoken. We were uniquely in tune. Especially with Miller, everything was talked out. When the plays opened, both men saw what they had written and what we had discussed realized on stage. Both expressed themselves as completely satisfied. Neither thought I had changed their intentions. Both thought I had revealed their truest intentions.

No director worthy of his calling puts the words of the author on stage merely mouthed by appropriate physical types. In fact it is a poor director indeed who, having studied the author himself as well as his play, does not reveal something of the author to the author. One of the handicaps an author has when he becomes his own director is that his knowledge of himself is limited to his knowledge of himself. And nearly always he will respect his words and his conscious mind to the negligence of his passions which he tries to make right and reasonable, his contradictions, which he will not face, his inner-conflicts, which he prefers not to admit, his confusions which may embarrass him, his flesh and blood which he may regard as his least noble aspect. In short he will tend to present himself (his play) only as he wishes he were, or as his favorite public image demands.

Both Streetcar and Salesman are contemporary masterpieces. They are the product of memory and experience and emotion, not of cogitation and manipulation. Their values are deeply human, because they are profoundly mixed, not black and white. I think the actors and myself were able to realize the author's intentions, even to an extent to reveal certain of the author's realest intentions to himself as well as to the audience. We would not be true collaborators if we did not.

But you are most mistaken when you say we changed the author's central character, whether it be Blanche or Willy. To the extent we were successful we did the true job of the interpretive craftsman.

In the production of living new plays that capture something of today's experience because they capture something of the author's deepest experience, it is the single obligation of the director to put the author's experience on stage—the author's not his own. I've done Tea and Sympathy like Anderson, Death of a Salesman like Miller, Skin of Our Teeth like Wilder, Jacobowsky and the Colonel like Behrman and so on—to the extent I was successful I captured the author's nature in the stage life. I did not try to add my own, or correct the author, or criticize him, or strain him thru myself. Some of that inevitably happens. But as far as I humanly could I tried [to] put each different fellow on stage as I saw him and his experience.

In Europe the tradition and the practise are different. When new plays are written, usually their intention is not expressive (am I wrong?) but only theatric. Much of the repertoire, the large staples, is classic. The tradition is one of successive interpretations thru the years of classics. The interest is in how So and So does Hamlet, or Sophocles, or Moliere or whatever.

In the Motion Pictures, the central artist is the Picture-maker, usually the director, often, even ideally, the writer-director. The content is his. It all passes thru him. The writer-proper is one of his means. His main means is the moving picture.

But when I'm dealing with men of the stature of Williams or Miller in the Theatre (and even when I am not) I try to essentially seek out who they are and put them, not myself on the stage. That is all I tried to do in STREETCAR and SALESMAN.

May I say again how much I enjoyed reading your book. Even when I thoroughly disagreed with you as in the instance above I found you really stimulating and what you said a contribution and arousing. And, besides, I plain enjoyed the book. And more.

In the matter of Miller's dropping of me, I thought you treated an otherwhere's taboo subject with fresh candor, and cut thru a lot of shit. I especially appreciated your making public the strictures put upon you by the NR editor who led you to gather that, though you could have criticized my attitude, you must not criticize Mr. Miller's. (It was in fact this "bit" that got me writing you my first congratulatory note.) And I also was delighted with your pinpointing on the all-innocent "liberal" hero. In fact I enjoyed an awful lot of your book, Eric.

["We are told that Kazan was virtually coauthor of *Streetcar* and *Salesman* even to the extent of changing the character of the leading persons." The well-hedged statement appeared in Eric Bentley's review of *Camino Real* (*New Republic*, March 30, 1953) and had apparently eluded Tennessee Williams at the time, although not Kazan, who denied writing "one line either of *Streetcar* or *Salesman*." The original review and disclaimer were reprinted in *The Dramatic Event* (1954), along with Bentley's assumption that Kazan "includes under the heading of authorship only the dialogue." Kazan dismissed the artful logic but not before Bentley had consolidated his original claim: "It seems to me that if a director helps to create the very idea of a character—changing it from what it was in the author's original script—he is co-author—even though the creating and changing has been done without recourse to new dialogue" (Bentley, pp. 274–75). Williams learned of the reprinted material in *The Dramatic Event* and instructed his attorney to begin "proceedings" if "outstanding copies" were not recalled and the libelous statement "deleted." The controversy seems to have ended with the publisher's offer to tip an explanatory note into any future printing.

Bentley's review of *The Crucible* in 1953 led inevitably to a reconsideration of Arthur Miller's "dropping" of Kazan and its harmful effect on the playwright's latest production. At issue for Bentley was the "innocence" of Miller, "the playwright of American liberal folklore" whose characters typically lack shading. John Proctor falls short of tragedy in *The Crucible* because his innocence is "total" and therefore "unreal." Where Miller and his new director Jed Harris "joined forces to dissociate themselves and their hero from evil," Kazan would have intensified the play with his own "sense of guilt" (Bentley, pp. 92-94).] *TLd, 2 pp., Wesleyan*

TO CLIFFORD ODETS

[New York]
[January 23, 1955]

Your letter meant a lot to me. There's nothing more I can really say about it. I was most grateful and happy with it.

I'm leaving today for Mississippi. I guess I'm going as much for some quiet as anything else. Its also a kind of restimulus. Here life is spent in an office and I, for one, forget what the hell it is I'm supposed to be "imitating" on stage. I always get something crucial from the real thing. Dont think I'm a shit-kicker. I'm worried about this play. Its very naked. Almost honest, terribly painful and quite pessimistic. I think Tenn's mind (so to speak) is much more negative than the living organism, the functioning person that he is. I think he feels all the rejections and isolation any sensitive person does plus the big one of his sex. And he's spoken out pretty plainly, not quite so, but a step towards a really embarrassing nakedness. I dont want to sentimentalize him. On the other hand, the play could really come out to be something about three despicable people.

I'm doing it on a skeleton stage, with lights. No furniture. I'm trying something different. Its the right way for the play, but I dont know how its going to turn out. (Is that bad??!!)

Be happy. You're a rare one. My whole love. Will write more. Now I'm going down stairs and meet Spiegel (triumphant Spiegel last night was crowned by the N.Y. Critics as Producer of the Year). He's coming to see our New House. He's such a complex fake. He doesn't know when he's lying anymore. He's gotten to the point where he lies almost with every sentence, and still completely convinces himself. Its just a habit. He believes what he says. And I dont believe he has the least Idea that everyone feels the connivance in every other word. The calculation in each piece of deviousness. And still he's terribly fascinating specimen. Well not that fascinating, but intriguing, well not exactly intriguing, but—I guess he's just full of shit, lets face it. . . .

Jo Mielziner's stage design for *Cat on a Hot Tin Roof*

Brando IS a hell of a guy. If you ever worked with him—almost the only bond a person can make with him, real bond that is—you'd be as enamored of him as the silliest B-soxer. He's got the real magnetism. The real thing. James Dean and the others are not in the same league. This fellow has innate poetry, with the pain and everything else, there is the lifting, free thing, poetry. And humor, and delicacy. And sensitivity in each bit of him. He's really the best actor I've ever worked with and by now I'm a battered old jockey.

Again, thanks and love. Molly and I were both very moved by your letter and are eternally your friends. You know that.

g

[Kazan planned to join Tennessee Williams in Greenville and together tour the Mississippi Delta. No doubt he traveled with a host of clamoring problems, including three potentially "despicable" characters and their nervous author, who would be shocked by the "skeleton stage" he and Jo Mielziner were planning for *Cat on a Hot Tin Roof*. Williams based an early design on sources as varied as the paintings of an unnamed southern artist and the Teatro La Fenice in Venice. Properties included "a great canopied bed" and a multitude of decorative artifacts collected by Big Mama and Big Daddy on their "ritual tour" of Europe. To these imports he added "a great console phonograph-radio-TV set" that supports Brick's well-stocked bar (n.d., HRC). Kazan stripped the stage of atmospheric effects and retained only minimum furniture—double bed, wicker chair, couch, and console—scaled down and positioned on a raked platform. "This brought the play down to its essentials" and ensured a "theatrical" production (*A Life*, pp. 542–43). "Another blow" was struck when Tennessee Williams arrived in Philadelphia for tryouts and found the set "a meaningless piece of chi chi—no atmosphere, no relation to the play" (Williams/*Notebooks,* p. 667).

The New York Film Critics honored Sam Spiegel and Kazan and voted *On the Waterfront* "most distinguished picture of the year." A three-picture deal with Columbia would give Spiegel "triumphant" long-sought financial means and independence. His invitation to visit the Kazans' new home on East Seventy-second Street was probably made at Sardi's, where the Film Critics reception was held on January 22.] *TLS, 1 p., Indiana*

TO TENNESSEE WILLIAMS

[New York]
February 3, 1955

Dear Tenn:

Just a note to get down on paper the only important thing I still feel to be wrong with the script.

I think you have a serious unity problem in the third act, which, unless it is corrected may hurt the reception of the play even on your terms. I feel this strongly enough to write about it, and right now I dont want to think about the script anymore—just directing.

What follows sounds gigantic and serious. It is serious, but I'm well aware that very important changes can be gained by what are—in actuality—small changes.

The first two acts are one play. Most of Act III is another. This cannot be fixed by cutting in rehearsal. Act I and II are about Brick. The main questions posed are: What happened to him? Why is he alcoholic? Why is he punishing Maggie? Why doesn't he care about living?

And then finally, at the end of Act Two, Brick is shown that he has been blaming Maggie for a defection in loyalty of his own. He has been blaming her for killing his friend Skipper. Big Daddy shows him that he killed Skipper.

At the end of Act II it seems to me that both men should stand on stage before the audience holding the truth of their situations. Both have been mortally hit. That dual self confrontation seems to me to be the climax.

Now Act two ends with Big Daddy facing the fact that he has cancer. This is not about a man who learns that he has cancer. Its not even a play about Big Daddy, important as Big Daddy is in the play. I'm talking technically in terms of Unity. Those damn abstractions like "unity" can suddenly become terribly critical and living in front of an audience. I think the act two curtain is one sided, wrong.

In the first two acts the other story—the fight over the land and the inheritance is there, but in its proper proportion and in a decidedly subsidiary position. This is correct because you are not writing a problem play a la Lillian Hellman which is designed to show how ugly mankind becomes when it fights for money. The other characters in the first two acts are there, but scaled with reference to their relation to the mainline and their contributions to the development of the Brick Maggie story.

Up to the end of Act II the construction of the play is unconventional but since an essential unity is hued to, the construction is sound. There is both leeway for poetry, feeling, thought, beauty and at the same time a necessary rigidity, both spine and configuration.

Then comes Act III where we suddenly have a play about who's going to get the bucks. There is another play, in other words. Perhaps its more accurate to say that the emphasis has shifted, possibly only a little, but I think importantly in the wrong direction.

As I said above the trouble really starts in the last couple of moments of Act II. If what Brick is confronted with (You, not Maggie, killed Skipper)—if this confrontation means anything—it simply cannot leave Brick unshaken or the same. If it leaves him unshaken, as now, then the confrontation has no real moment—has only been rhetoric and verbal fireworks. I think Brick is laid low at the end of Act Two. I think he should behave in Act three accordingly.

In your beautifully written stage direction (snare, bird etc.) you have written your answer to parts of my other letters. I cannot escape the imputation, delicate and friendly though it is, that I would prefer an easier pat solution. I wont debate this. I have faced the fact that perhaps I tend that way more. In any case I can only here and now continue to write you what I feel to be true. In the case of a problem as serious as this one, where the success of our enterprise is affected, you'll have to excuse me for speaking with force and even with over-simplification.

Brick gives me a pain in the well-known part in Act III, the first seven eights of it. He seems to be exactly the same as he was at the beginning of Act One. I say the <u>Beginning</u> of Act One. Its as if nothing happened to him. Did you ask a thousand people to come to the Theatre to see nothing happen to Brick? Dont answer yes, because a hell of a lot does happen to him in Act one, including trying to brain his wife, and a hell of a lot happens to him in Act two including practically killing his father.

All this despite the fact that when Big Daddy says to him "You dug the grave of your friend and kicked him into it!" Brick has no answer and has no answer because he realizes it is true.

I think this climax within Brick is slighted or skimmed over, in the first place. This might be remedied by some kind of admission, indirect as you like that what Big D said was true. Let us see him face the fact that he has been unfair and cruel and inhuman to Maggie, and not facing any truth about his situation, but hiding behind a transfer of guilt.

Act III is another problem. Bear in mind little changes make big differences. I dont think Brick can say too much in this act as presently constructed. But what he now says seems absolutely wrong to me.

I know as a director I keep wondering: How can I keep Brick centre stage more—how can I keep his thinking and feeling—his experience continuously before the audience.????? How can I prevent the effect now in the script that absolutely nothing happened to him in Act Two, that it was all just rhetoric.

Its only fair to put you on notice that I'll be striving—I cant do different—to keep Brick and his thinking, his development, smack in the audience's eye all thru Act Three so they will never feel that they have stopped watching him and are watching, suddenly, a different play. I mean I have to direct Brick in Act Three to show what happened in Act two and that a lot happened in Act two. I have to work to show that there has been a progression within him, no matter how deeply concealed.

Without my usual boring apologies for clumsiness let me give you examples of what I mean. On p 3-20 Brick says: "Hey Big Mama? You gotta hold of my drinking arm. Please release it." This is the same elegant nihilism as in Act One. Suppose Brick were to say something that had this kind of meaning: "There's nothing to envy about me Maggie." Now I know that's not right. But how does he right now feel when he hears all that shit about envying him?? He says a few lines later: "Yeah let Brick go. Dont make nervous people more nervous." Right back in Act One. Mightn't this be a good spot for him to say to Gooper and Mae that they can have the fucking plantation—thus making Maggie's job harder. Or maybe that isn't right. Probably not. I'm really not suggesting replacement lines here. I just want to somehow point out to you, if I can, that Brick is written wrong in most of Act Three.

Couldn't everything about him in Act Three, the said and the UNSAID be pointed to what he does at the end. As though that storm were—as it surely is—building up within him all through the Act???

Awful lot of words to say something simple.

Love. g.

[Kazan repeated his objection to Brick's lack of development and put Tennessee Williams "on notice" that he planned to direct the character along dramatic lines whenever possible. The author's reply appears as a stage direction in act two, preceding the confrontation of Brick and Big Daddy: *The bird that I hope to catch in the net of this play is not the solution of one man's psychological problem. I'm trying to catch the true quality of experience in a group of people, that cloudy, flickering, evanescent—fiercely charged!—interplay of live human beings in the thundercloud of a common crisis. Some mystery should be left in the revelation of character in a play, just as a great deal of mystery is always left in the revelation of character in life, even in one's own character to himself."] TLS, 2 pp., Wesleyan*

TO JOSHUA LOGAN

1545 Broadway, New York City
February 7, 1955

Dear Josh:

I just want to keep you up to date on what's been going on. We bought the building. It's the church that the Theatre Wing had. We bought it for $60,000 and are now raising the money to pay for it. Aint it the truth that things always happen in reverse? Anyway, we've got half the dough. The biggest kick out of the whole thing was that the first $10,000 was raised by the members themselves, many of whom borrowed to raise it, all of whom pledged $100. I've kicked in $5,000, Roger Stevens has kicked in $5,000, and Gene Kelly the other day called Cheryl and said he wanted to contribute $10,000. As sure as hell we are going to get the building.

No crap about this. I'm not asking you for money in any subtle or indirect

Seated with Molly at the premiere party for *East of Eden*,
with (standing) John and Elaine Steinbeck, Jack Warner,
and an unidentified man

way. You've been generous enough already. What I wish you would do in your most brutal and direct fashion is to hit up Harry. Tell him that "Waterfront" is filled with Studio people. Tell him that a rich man could easier get through a needle than stay out of hell. Tell him he's pig rich, stinking rich, disgusting rich, overdoing the privilege of being rich, and the quicker he gets rid of some of it the better it will be for his soul or why don't you make up your own dialogue—you're so good at it. Anyway there's no reason on earth why this man shouldn't give us a lot of money. Tell him in turn I'll introduce him to all my women and give him a good recommendation besides. Lower the boom on him. Jack Warner gave us the proceeds from the "East of Eden" opening night and the least he can do is to give us the "Long Grey Line." Don't let him dare say no. Tell him to sell his horses—they're too slow, sell his house—it's too big, etc., etc. I've run out of inspiration.

I hear "Roberts" went over great in San Francisco. I was so glad. Dictate me a few jokes, some idle gossip, some worthless rumours, something. I am surrounded by the earnest and the venal, a worried wife and dog that pees on the rug and makes her more worried. Love to Nedda

Gadg

[After a vagabond existence, the Actors Studio found permanent quarters in a former Presbyterian church on West Forty-fourth Street in Manhattan. Kazan used the occasion to recall the "'staggering'" number of actors and directors who had worked at the Studio since 1947 and to anticipate a still greater unleashing of talent that Broadway often failed to accommodate. Lee Strasberg foresaw increased membership and a wider range of activities, including workshops for musical theater and playwrights. The new quarters also signaled a transition from individual to "'project work,'" with the hope of creating "'a repertory of a dozen good plays in two or three years'" (NYT, February 20, 1955). Prospects for theatrical production arose periodically at the Studio and were usually met by the directors with indecision, opposition, or delay.

The premiere of *East of Eden* on March 9 filled the Astor Theatre with notables escorted by "usherettes" as varied as Marilyn Monroe and Margaret Truman. The after-theater party featured entertainment by Carol Channing, Julie Stein, and Harold Arlen, with radio and television coverage. A delicate contractual issue prevented Josh Logan from lowering "the boom" on Harry Cohn. There is no indication that the "stinking rich" president of Columbia Pictures followed the lead of Jack Warner by donating opening-night proceeds from *The Long Gray Line* (1955) to the Studio. The irrepressible showman in Kazan assured potential donors that this "will be one of the most extraordinarily exciting openings in years."] *TLS, 1 p., Library of Congress*

TO CLIFFORD ODETS

[New York]
[February 26, 1955]

Baby—

Your notes were <u>fine</u> & the painful thing is that I agree with you on everything salient and still wont be able to do much about it. I asked Tenn to read
your letter, since I thought it brilliant, but this aroused some panic in him.
He feels that something most essential is open to painful criticism. He's in a
woeful condition really, much more nervous than I've ever seen him. What is
the middle-age of a person with his living pattern? He still cruises—in other
words, courts the stimulus of danger—without the dash & aplomb of youth to
"carry it off". Sometimes with a new young "Conquest" he looks like the fag
version of the sugar daddy. His eyes are often bathed in a fluid that is not quite
tears and he looks on the edge of some critical exhaustion—

Still he is <u>terribly</u> quick. His perception rushes ahead of my words to one
conclusion or another—like an army falling back in panic to various defense
positions—abandoning each before it has been tried.

At any rate, last night we had our first run thru and it went rather well
considering. And I hope today we can start to make some cuts & changes.
I've enjoyed working on it thus far. I've staged it as I imagine Shakespeare's
plays must have been put on—what the text-books call presentational. It's
interesting.

About your notes—I have tried to do some of the things you talk about
thru staging. For instance I have made the old man the moral centre. And I
believe I have made the play cohere—conceptually—a good deal more than it
does on paper. I have also inserted thru the body of the piece a (rather rickety)
framework of causation—one event causing another—

I'll write you again. Molly Kazan is seeing it tonight and I dread that. She
lacks "give"!

Fuck 'em all, big & small! Otherwise? Otherwise the same.

Love. g.

[The "notes" (unidentified) written by Clifford Odets apparently deepened a
panic in Tennessee Williams that Kazan traced to advancing "middle-age" and a
lack of youthful "aplomb." Williams made a similar assessment after the failure of
Camino Real in 1953. "Causes of defeat: first, age," he wrote, recalling youthful
days when he could "work off tensions in free physical exercise" and "spontane-
ity" lifted him over "obstructions." Now his body was "bankrupt" and "mind, too."
"Under these conditions," he wondered, "how does one continue?" Candor led
Williams to reflect on the incapacitating success of *Streetcar:* "What fearful admission do I have to make, that after 'Streetcar' I haven't been able to write anymore
except by a terrible wrenching of the brain and nerves?" (Williams/*Notebooks,*

p. 583). As Williams approached his forty-fourth birthday, the opening of *Cat* on March 24 could not have been more critical in light of his post-*Streetcar* record on Broadway: the failure of *Summer and Smoke* (1948) and *Camino Real* (1953) buffered by the modest success of *The Rose Tattoo* (1951).] *ALS, 4 pp., Indiana*

TO HELEN BOWER

[New York]
March 22, 1955

Dear Miss Bower:

Thank you for your letter. The allegation about Dean was not concerted but was made in some rather disturbing places by people whom I felt know better.

Dean actually has a talent all his own and a sizeable one. He doesn't need to imitate anyone and was not imitating anyone. He admires Brando, as do practically all young actors today. In this respect I would say that he had excellent taste. Brando has no doubt influenced Dean to some extent but he has also influenced 100 others, just as Barrymore did 30 years ago, just as Cagney and Spence Tracy did 20 years ago. The thing about my grafting a Brando-like personality and set of mannerisms on Dean is really too ridiculous to answer. I supposed it was a way of speaking rather than a remark meant literally. I actually don't think he's much like Brando. He's considerably more introverted, more drawn, more naked. Whatever he is, though, he's not an imitation of anybody. He's too proud to try to imitate anyone. He has too much difficulty—as does any decent worker in our craft—thinking about anything except playing the part as written. Critics who say he's imitating Brando just reveal a naivete about acting, direction, and production.

I would love to see your review of the picture. I gather you liked it. It meant a lot to me and I was rather upset by Crowther's reaction in New York. The other critics here, however, liked it very much indeed and the picture is doing well.

Sincerely

ek:mf

[Bosley Crowther differed sharply from Helen Bower, who thought James Dean "the sensation of a production in which all the acting is sensationally good" (*Detroit Free Press*, March 11, 1955). Crowther wrote in his review that Kazan should "be spanked" for tolerating Dean's "sophomoric" posing in *East of Eden*: "He scuffs his feet, he whirls, he pouts, he sputters, he leans against walls, he rolls his eyes, he swallows his words, he ambles slack-kneed—all like Marlon Brando used to do. Never have we seen a performer so clearly follow another's style" (*NYT*, March 10, 1955). Sam Spiegel foresaw such criticism after previewing *Eden* and traced Kazan's seeming permissiveness to diminished involvement in the film: "Had you been as deeply soaked in this picture as you were in 'Waterfront', you would have prevented him from being as precocious as he is" (to EK, February 4, 1955, Wesleyan). Kazan rejected the notion of a "concerted" attack on Dean, or himself, and later emphasized the uniqueness of Dean's performance: "Jimmy was always a bit of a mystery to me. That he was very talented no one could doubt. I think he revealed more of himself in EAST OF EDEN than he ever did in any conversation or to any interviewer. Everything you saw in EAST OF EDEN is part of his autobiography" (to Pfc. Rick Kelty, August 29, 1972, Wesleyan).

A strong property—nearly forty weeks on the *Times* best-seller list—*East of Eden* outperformed *Waterfront* at the box office and won honors at Cannes as well as Academy nominations for Dean, Kazan, and Osborn, and an Oscar for Jo Van Fleet. By year's end it had earned a place on *Variety's* list of "All-Time Top Money Films."] *TL, 1 p., Wesleyan*

TO CHRISTOPHER ISHERWOOD

[New York]
April 8, 1955

Dear Chris:

Thanks to you and to Don for your nice message. I never wrote you to thank you for your frankness and directness on CAT. Both were very much appreciated. I feel I have a good friend in you, Chris, and that I can always rely on you for the precise truth as you see it. I knew you were a good friend when you told me that you didn't like what I had done with CAT and I didn't feel any resentment or rancor at all. A lot of people I wouldn't take it from.

I don't know when I'm coming out but will look you up when I do. Good luck with the Metro movie. I feel for you. That's a tough machine to beat.

Yours
Gadg
mf

ek:mf

[Christopher Isherwood and Tennessee Williams met in California in 1943, became lifelong friends, occasional lovers, and admirers of each other's writing. In late 1954 Williams turned to Isherwood for advice and support in tense negotiations with Kazan regarding the development of *Cat*. No "friend" of the director—who was, he thought, not "a very pleasant character"—Isherwood found little to approve when he attended the Philadelphia tryout in March. The principal actors were "wrong," the "arty expressionistic" set at odds with the realism of the play, while Burl Ives, "just a gifted amateur," addressed the house "as if he were M.C. at a stag party" (Isherwood, p. 479).] *TL, 1 p., Huntington*

[New York]
June 8, 1955

Dear Tenn:

Things just got too hectic to write. I was moving around so fast, saw so damn much, all of it so evocative and affecting and even disturbing. I went way back in Asia Minor to where my old man was born and where my mother's people came from. My mother's ancestors seem to have lived in caves literally. So, just as you thought, I'm not so far from la vie de la goat. In fact, an American goat is pretty well off. Boy, life is rough in Asia Minor.

God, I've got a lot to tell you. I saw CAT first of all, and I thought it was in remarkable shape, including Ben. Ben, after all, was only trying to do what I had, in a mistaken [*omission*] of consciousness, asked him to "work on" while I was away. Of course, unguided, no actor can work on anything and Ben's version of a soft-spoken, gentle-spoken, Southern boy must have been horrible. I can just imagine, but apparently he has straightened himself out. You know, Tenn, I have never agreed with you about Ben's character. I think he is an exceptionally forthright and honest kid. He's not subtle or not a lot of other things, but I don't think he would be in the play at all if he hadn't wanted to do it and I certainly don't think he is trying to make himself undesirable around the Morosco. As a matter of fact, the opposite is happening. We now have to replace him by the first of September. Cliff Robertson is away in Kansas somewhere and I don't know when he will be back. I'm not secure about Cliff anyway. I wish to God Ben would stay on, but he won't and that's that and we are looking around right now for a new Brick. In short, Ben looks better every minute.

Millie Dunnock is going to leave in September too. Her understudy is passable but not much better and we'll have to look around for someone to take her part.

I have urged Victor most strongly to try to make some kind of deal with Burl so he will stay on with the show through June. In other words, as long as Barbara stays with it. I think a deal can be made although, of course, Burl will hold us up, no reason why he shouldn't. Anyway, I think the show will run until a year from now and as far as the box office goes it's only really dependent on Barbara and Burl. Barbara herself is in wonderful shape and Burl has kept up quite well too. The understudies seem to be, on reviewing them the day before yesterday, a mediocre lot and I'll try to do something to improve them. I rehearsed them some and will rehearse them again a little bit on Wednesday. We are also going to engage a young director to keep his eye on the show twice a week so that there is a constant sense backstage that they are being held up to standard. . . .

About ORPHEUS. I think Brando to direct is an excellent idea. He will make, in fact he is going to make, a fine director. He, believe it or not, is unusually organized as a director, clear thinking. How substantial his interest is in working in the theatre is another matter, but I think he may find that he can work in the theatre as a director without what must be to him the awful danger of a long run in a role that gets increasingly onerous. I certainly think though that if he will do ORPHEUS, I would take that chance. He is one of the most naturally-gifted theatre people in every phase that I have ever met, with a fine sense of character, extraordinary sense of reality, unfailing inventiveness, quite surprisingly precise, and all in all capable of becoming really first class.

About our project. I'm still planning to do it this fall and as early as possible. I would like to get Brando for it. I will carefully, but really carefully, consider Marilyn. Maybe she can do it. It's not impossible, but the main thing now is the script. Please send me what you have immediately. There really isn't a lot of time to waste if we are going to do it. There will be some back and forth on the script I know, and, if necessary, I can come to Europe for a visit at the end of the summer, but I will judge that when I get your material and see where we are.

I would rather read the old script with the new material in it but I did do a lot of work on the boat, sort of along the line of thinking through, or starting to, and I did work out a scheme for the end, at least as I see it. I am not send-ing it to you because I'm a little inhibited now by all the Bentley business and also by certain remarks your lawyer made to my lawyer which I thought rather foolish, but which did also disturb me a bit. At any rate, I do have thoughts about the end: in scenes, in dialogue, not writing, but kind of a concept of it. How it should be left, how it should wind-up, but I think I've got to be asked a bit before I'll send them (the ideas that is). Are you happy with what you figured out? A movie is so much more a collaborative business than a play and so much more is done pictorially. Anyway, you know all that. God, I always feel when we talk together everything is clear in a matter of ten seconds. In fact, we have never had to talk much longer than that about any work problem because we always seem to be in immediate rapport. Even when we disagree we get each other's point so quickly. . . .

About Greece. The most beautiful island that I saw is one called Hydra. Piraeus, I only stayed in an hour and it seemed more ordinary, but I only saw a bit of it near the dock. . . . Athens itself is good for a stay. It is an extraordi-nary city. I have no idea what the hunting will be like there, but everything that I did get in touch with, the air, the food, the sites, the light, the liquor, the museums, the music, I found most congenial and all of it was tied together by an extraordinary independence and dignity of just about every Greek you meet. . . . Istanbul is full of every kind of vice and pleasure. Full of poverty and license, has the veiled life and the most brutal daily life of the streets. You immediately feel that you are in Asia even though the city itself is mostly in Europe. Bosporus itself is unforgettable and there are beautiful places to stay just out of Istanbul, twenty minutes out, and that too, I think, will interest you very much. I was going it respectable for two months but there were broad hints every day of the freer life and I know you have a quick gift for finding it.

Stop talking about your "last chance to feather the nest." We can have a very successful movie that could make you more than any play if we just really produce on the script, on the direction, and on the casting of HIDE AND SEEK. I don't think we should be held to any time. On the other hand, I will work on it now. I like the little things you tell me you have done. They all seem to strengthen the main line and don't seem to be in the direction of a diffusion.

This is enough for now. Give my love to Frank. I'll type you a letter myself. It will be a little less rigid and I'll do it the first chance I get.

I still can taste those prizes. They sure tasted good. There was a horrible story about Inge having been told that he was sure to get the Pulitzer Prize, of his having prepared a party, food, invitations sent out, much liquor, Inge all dressed up, etc. The end was what you can imagine. Poor Bill.

Love

ek:mf

[Travel to Greece and Turkey in the spring was the first of several preparatory trips to film *America America* (1963). Elia interviewed relatives in Istanbul who had not taken the "gamble" and visited the ruins of Greek neighborhoods in the interior, where his ancestors had lived "outnumbered and powerless" before minority populations were expelled by the Turks in the early 1920s. He returned to New York in June with a deeper understanding of his father's courage and a commitment to speak for his "people." The following months saw a renewed drive for independent production and creative expression, with attempts to prod Tennessee Williams into activity on *Baby Doll* and begin a second collaboration with Budd Schulberg on terms of artistic equality. Further off was the seminal story of his family's coming to America, which only Kazan could tell (*A Life*, pp. 559–60).

Tennessee Williams revisited *Cat* in May and was appalled by Ben Gazzara's performance. He also resented Gazzara's early departure to rehearse *A Hatful of Rain* for an opening in November. Jack Lord briefly assumed the role of Brick, while the other principals—Barbara Bel Geddes, Burl Ives, and Mildred Dunnock, who agreed to continue as Big Mama through the fall—remained in place. An advance sale of twenty-four months caused "sell-out tantrums" at the box office.

The prospect of Marlon Brando directing *Orpheus Descending* and costarring with Marilyn Monroe in *Baby Doll* delighted Tennessee Williams, but these and other prospects dimmed as the summer wore on and he made little progress on the screenplay. "Inhibited" by the "Bentley business," Kazan withheld his thoughts about how *Baby Doll* "should wind-up."

Williams visited Greece and Turkey later in June with the hope that "some startling new place or people" would prove inspiring. He found "no trace of Hellenistic glory" in the "modern Greeks" of Athens and thought Istanbul "the ugliest, dullest city in the world" (Williams/*Notebooks,* pp. 671–75).

Cat ran for nearly 700 performances and won a second Pulitzer Prize for Tennessee Williams. He wrote that prizes "do disturb one a little as they have so little, or so fantastically remote, a connection with the period and circumstances of work." Nonetheless, "to have them gives you a deep down, slow-burning satisfaction. As if God had given a sign of being with you" (to EK, May 3, 1955, Wesleyan).] *TL, 4 pp., Wesleyan*

TO BEN ASLAN

[New York]
6/6 [1955]

Dear Ben:
I read the contract clause (16, I think) that you called to my attention, and really couldn't make head or tails of it. Perhaps if I tell you my viewpoint in detail you can see that this provision in the contract protects me.

I am not interested in what TW's lawyer says to you about what TW thinks. He has had some embarrassing moments with people giving me credit for "writing" part of STREETCAR and saying I saved CAT ON A HOT TIN ROOF etc. etc. That stuff is unfair to him and I regret it and I can understand his discomfort. But—Now we are making a contract to do a picture together. I will positively not agree to certain things, and you can call off the deal right now, if not sooner, if we cannot come to an agreement. This I mean. I also think its a considerable likelihood.

Call to the attention of Williams representatives that in The Theatre I have no say whatsoever as to what is included or what is cut in a script. I could not "write" anything. I could not change a word except thru him. I can only suggest. He can veto absolutely all of my suggestions. He can also "fire" me at any time. The rights of a director in the Theatre are very shaky. Perhaps this is as it should be. The Theatre is the playwright's medium. Dialogue is essential. Spectacle "added". The director is the playwright's helper, his servant even. I have never objected to this—with Williams above all. But I treated Bob Anderson, who had never had a play produced, with the same precise consideration and professional courtesy. Williams would tell you this himself.

However in films there are several differences. In the first place the medium is largely a visual one. In the second place work on a motion picture is much much longer and has to do with a hell of a lot that is not the WORDS. Picking location, picking each day's frames (set-ups), the long and laborious process of editing and the most important business of adding music, etc. etc.

While the Theatre is a Playwright's medium, films are a director's medium. For one thing the playwright is THERE every moment of the creative period of a play. He is not there in the production days of a picture. These start several months before shooting and endure several months after the close of shooting. Will Williams stay with me thru the entire process? Will he absolutely promise to be there every moment I'm working on the film?

Of course not. But even if he did, I will not agree that I cant make changes, deletions etc. as I'm making the film. What am I supposed to do when I see that a picture, a composition is telling the story and the words, or all the words aren't necessary? Call up Williams in Rome or Ceylon or New York or Key West? The hell with that!

Ben, he simply has to trust me! I do respect him. I will work with him intimately on the script. But in a way it will be a collaboration. The picture here is at least as important as the word. It is for me, at any rate. If this is unsatisfactory he should not work with me, and I'm quite ready, between us, to face that fact. He should direct his own films, or get some reverential fool to do them.

I want you to be very firm with the lawyer. Come to an impasse right away and let Audrey call me up about it. We're not in the position of beggars here. Warners is not high on the script, and Brando has turned it down, rather scornfully and insultingly. Williams knows he needs me. The thing is to preserve my artistic rights. I'll give away money, but I dont like to give away my artistic power.

I will contractually promise not to start until he and I agree on the script. I promise to stick in all essence and in every important particular to the script. But I will not promise NOT to adjust on the set as it seems necessary to me.

If he and I do not agree on the end I dont want to do the picture. I dont want to pay him any money, furthermore until and unless we agree on the end. I do not like the present end. And since he is out to restrict me I will agree to a restriction in general only if we agree on <u>essentials in general</u>.

After all he is not selling me a novel, only some one act plays. There is no ending that [is] inherent in the material. We have not yet agreed, between us in conversation, on any ending. I have one to suggest now that he might agree to in essence. But I have no intention of paying out any of Warners easily earned dough to Wms. unless we are in agreement as to what the ending should be.

Stress to his lawyer that I'm not in the business of photographing plays. Making a Motion Picture is quite a different matter. A lot of what must be articulated on the stage, can be told thru the medium of photograph in a film. I dont want my hands tied in any way.

******

There is finally and basically always an area of trust in all contracts that have to do with artistic work. When that no longer exists, it is finally impossible to

really make a contract. All the possible areas of friction can never be fully anticipated. Its impossible. Williams should, by now, trust me. If he doesn't he shouldn't do pictures with me. There are plenty of other directors; and writers.
******

All the above is only for your information. It is not to [be] told to his lawyer by you. I only want you to be clear as to what my attitude is and to formulate from it OUR clause 16. The general remarks and so on I will make to Miss Wood and/or to Williams.

[Ben Aslan was managing the *Baby Doll* contract and negotiating with Tennessee Williams's representatives. The present letter reflects the divisive aftermath of *Cat on a Hot Tin Roof*—its awards and financial success notwithstanding. Williams summarized his discontent in correspondence with Audrey Wood, insisting that Kazan had "cheapened" the play and vowing not to work again with him "on a basis in which he will tell me what to do and I will be so intimidated, and so anxious to please him, that I will be gutlessly willing to go against my own taste and convictions" (July 28, 1955, HRC). Apparently clause "16" was inserted by Williams's attorney to assuage a client's anger and prevent undue tampering with the forthcoming screenplay. Precisely how the legal issue was resolved is unclear. Agreement on the elusive ending of *Baby Doll* was not forthcoming until the end of principal filming. Kazan marked the present letter Not sent.] *TL, 2 pp., Wesleyan*

TO JOHN STEINBECK

[Sandy Hook, Connecticut]
[c. July 1955]

Thanks that was a hell of a letter. I'm anxious to talk to you about the money piece. Are you coming up this week end to the Rodgers'? And Monday here? Or when? If you aren't coming up this week-end, we might get out your way the week-end after this coming one. I cant be quite sure about that, but it looks like it could happen. I want to. Life has become unbearably, intolerably complicated, with visiting nieces and nephews, shifting of maids, two gangs of men working on the place and Budd Schulberg next door (2 1/2 miles act.). Budd and I are going to make a movie out of a short story of his about TV, a kind of a Godfrey, Winchell, Will Rogers character. My lawyers have advised me never to put this in writing, so throw this letter into the sound somewhere.

It seems to me about money that people want the symbol, what it means, more than anything it buys after a certain point. It gives an "end" to most living and if this end were taken away there would be a large general unhinging of everyone's psyche and thousands and thousands of people would tend to go to pieces. A lot of things also go under the disguise of "earning a living" such as sadism, such as power, such as sex self-decoration, such as all forms of competitiveness—all as you say rationalized some way as the worthy occupation of "earning a living". And I agree that money is the most sensitive instrument, also the most sensitive indicator (uncovers a man's real motives), also its, for us, the best way to open up this present day society for a real look. What's terrible today is that the goals of life have become the instead-ofs. I mean it used to be money was sought, pre-eminence was sought, success was sought, accomplishment was sought for the things they brought: land, peace, food, tools, the prettiest girls, the prettiest boats, the prettiest horses. But in our "most developed" communities, there doesn't seem to be a hell of lot anyone wants anymore. And the symbol has replaced the real thing. And if suddenly everyone could have everything, why then we'd have men sitting around with piles of dough and a vacant idiotic stare. They'd be saved by this by the quick depreciation in the value of money—in the circumstances of your play. Then there'd be another psyche crisis, and people would be going nuts because the symbol of accomplishment would have disappeared. What the hell would they be fighting for. And again I think the whole community would go nuts. It isn't only the economic system of that community that would collapse—do I read you right!?—its the soul of the community, the very humanity of a community that would be destroyed, unhinged. So the destruction of the value, and thereby the symbol, of money would destroy a community from the inside out, and it would be the most deadly weapon because it would strike at our most profound and fundamental weakness. We'd really go back to a kind of middle-ages limbo and have to start over.

If all this could be done simply and from the point of view of comedy, with a developing plot somehow we might have a marvelous piece. What concerns me is that we dont have just a series of illustrative incidents, but that one thing lead to another, and so on in an ever deepening sequence until finally the Experimenters see, and we see, that the whole community has been unhinged and is going or gone nuts and they step in to save the people—too late in many cases. (some of them are never "brought back")

What you say about the morality of evil is so terribly true that its sickening. Its also pathetic and saddening. Its another mark of the true fragility and uncertainty of man. If only man were strong enough to be a little wrong and just say hell I'm a little selfish, or venal, or cowardly. I dont say this about other men. I say it about myself. I've slowed up a lot—only having a little conversation now and then with Schulberg and an occasional look at CAT—so I have time to see what the hell I'm doing and then time to see why I think I'm doing what I'm doing and also why I'm really doing what I do. Two different things. I'm astonished at a lot of things—different things different days. And instead of getting "clearer" I'm just getting more and more confused. I now wonder if

I'm really living at all the way I want. Whether I shouldn't just go off by myself and go to China and Russia and all the places on earth that I've got maybe fifteen twenty years to look at. Whether I'm just not succumbing to family and habit. Whether I haven't had this theatre-movie business, and whether I'm not in it just out of habit and fear. Whether Molly and I aren't just habit, or fear, though I admire her and everything else, and love her, but still. And so much precious time goes by and it seems to me I get so little out of it, bull shit conversations and some drink and food and a few admiring looks at my son Chris and putting a wall down on the lake front and so on. I ask myself is this it? Is this why? Is this what I wanted to do? Is this why I accumulated what dough I have. I feel like a highly publicized meal ticket, some of the time, doing what the hell my wife and family and society expects of me and not at all—since I dont think originally enough—what I'd like to do. I can imagine great excitement to life again. But something prevents my going after it. Except occasionally in little forays into this and that. You know what. And those mean nothing. So one day if I disappear, you can go next door and hold Molly's hand and tell her I wasn't a bad guy. But I guess that's a temporary dream too. Other days I wake and look at the particular green of my place, the trees everyone of which I know, the fields, each of which I've cut now many times so that I know each rock and wild cherry stump over which I have to raise my tractor blade, and I feel so close and familiar to them, and they mean so much to me that I feel I could never leave them.

When I was but a kid starting out I felt that the hold a man had on the meaning of life was thru intercourse with his fellow man, thru actual closeness, thru practical consanguinity, thru being one of a mass (proletariat in those days). I felt that the thing was not to allow oneself to be separated or isolated from the whole body of man. And I'm still happiest now when I'm with a movie crew and we have the same end, or when I suddenly feel close to some unidentified stranger and he opens up and I get reminded of how present and desperate the struggle is. One terrible terrible thing about success and money and security and love and family and friends and 72nd. st. and Broadway is the isolation, the cutting off from the really meaningful sections of life, where it runs quickest, where the nerves are closest to the surface. I think this is what has happened to every artist who has made a "success". His success has cut him off from the sources of his success. The people I like best in the Theatre are the down and outers and the beginners. They've still got the salt and they still talk without fear of consequence and they still are living. I detest Sardi's and the Hunting room of the Astor and the rest of the Hunting Rooms, the King Cole room of the St Regis and the fucking Oak room because its all a lot of shit. Nothing is born there. They're a fence not keeping the world out, but a fence we build around ourselves keeping ourselves in a kind of $3.25 for a Hamburger STIR. *** A man I used to know once told me that a person ought to risk his life once every six months, should find himself in mortal fear and danger once every six months or else something dies in him. Well its a thought isn't it. Love.

[Collaboration with Budd Schulberg on *A Face in the Crowd* (1957) would soon require fieldwork in New York and Arkansas. In the meanwhile Steinbeck and Kazan toyed with the idea of a "play" that resembled their proposal to destabilize a communist country with counterfeit money. Its successor was based on a darker premise that a sudden excess of wealth would "unhinge" a typical modern community. Steinbeck foresaw dishonesty prevailing and even the most virtuous forced to devise a "complete set of reasons" for greed. He also foresaw a series of ironies in which real money becomes the "symbol for things," which in turn become "so plentiful" that they lose material value and give wealth a singular function: to pay "the price of peace or simplicity or rest or even death." For Steinbeck—and for Kazan, who would describe a similar "arrangement" of society—this was "the great purchase which we all make—we need the money to pay the black mail demanded of us so that we can have peace, the black mail of children and wives and friends and even enemies all of whom lie in wait for us, who must be paid off before we can be allowed to rest" (to EK, July 5, 1955, Wesleyan). Both friends wrote from beloved retreats—Sag Harbor, on Long Island, where John and Elaine owned a summer home, and Sandy Hook—that were often "complicated" by the presence of those who required "the great purchase." The present letter was not mailed, nor did the project materialize.] *TL, 2 pp., Wesleyan*

TO TENNESSEE WILLIAMS

[Sandy Hook, Connecticut]
July 29, 1955

Baby got your letter and if I thought we were really far apart in intention I would say "write it off". But we're not. I keep saying Pagnol and he produced grotesque folk comedies of the Provence country of southern France. You must have seen Bakers Wife and Well Diggers Daughter. The heroes are not only human, they are all eccentrics. And that crack you made about my trying to fit the role to accommodate D. Kerr or Grace Kelly is just so much of the well known commodity. I'm far more daring in my casting than anyone, and— well the hell with it. I wish I had never used the word fulfillment. You're right, that is one of those words. But I'm sending you the script I put together and you will see what I meant by the word. It isn't any more than what you had really. Abstract arguments are always dangerous. Semantics ugh. Anyway I'll say again, just for the hell of it, that I dont want to smooth it out and all that. When you read the script I put together you'll see that. NOW about that script. As you say we understand each other without a lot of talk. So I dont have to go into a long long deal about the dialogue I stuck in being dummy lines and so on. Its so obvious. What I was trying to do was put together a script that had unity, some sense of proportion, and inter-proportion and with an end. I dont think the end, basically, is out of style. Nor is it the most important, or the least important. It just seems to me to be the right end. I feel that the more I say that, the more your back goes up. But I cant help that. I do always tell you what I think. And you do me. And that's another crock about me wanting a yes man. I dont. But look at it from my point of view. Its tough waiting here and getting odd scraps thru Audrey, some of which are headed INSERT SOME-WHERE and others of which contradict previous bits that you sent me. Well you know. Also I hoped to get it this fall. Maybe there's an outside chance. Maybe there isn't. I'm not even thinking of that now. First things first. Lets see if we can get a script. No complaints. Just its tough working this way and finally its implicit in the way you've worked on this that you expect me to put the stuff together some way. And there wouldn't be a fucking bit of use if I just was dutiful and too respectful and like other directors and JUST STUCK EVERYTHING IN BECAUSE TW wrote it. I think the script I'm sending you is structurally on the right path. I think it has unity. There's violence implicit in every bit of your story, and in a FOLK piece grotesque comedy and violence are not mutually exclusive. Its like a pig slaughtering. Or all the other "rough" events of every day country life. Things are just coarser and there's humor in absolutely everything, and life is lived on some kind of tough terms, or what-ever the word is—BUT I REALLY DONT WANT to discuss theoretically. You read the goddamn thing and give me your reaction. I see Burl Ives playing Archie Lee. I cant see anyone but Burl Ives playing Archie Lee. We've got to find some young piece of tail for Baby Doll etc. But the hell with that too. Generalizations equal misunderstanding. (Incidentally I cribbed lines for this from three scripts and also from the original one act.) . . .

LOVE. g

[Kazan's new outline "chilled and dampened" rather than revived Tennessee Wil-liams's "weary" spirit. It was "folly," Williams insisted, to turn Baby Doll into "a starring role for Grace Kelly or Deborah Kerr." She is "touchingly comic, a gro-tesquely witless creature, about as deep as kitty-cat's pee. Who the fuck gives a shit if she is, was, or ever will be 'FULFILLED AS A WOMAN?'" The climactic frog-gigging scene, which placed Silva and Archie Lee Meighan, Baby Doll's jeal-ous husband, in mortal combat, was also incompatible with the prevailing note of folk-comedy: "You are talking about HEAVY DRAMA!—that winds up with . . . death for one man, prison for the other" (n.d., Wesleyan).

Kazan's outline was delayed for several weeks in reaching Williams, who had moved from Rome to Barcelona in a summer of discontent. In the meanwhile Kazan assembled a working script as a "test" of "where we are" and predicted Wil-liams would "like it" when he read "it all together" (July 27, 1955, HRC).] *TLS, 1 p., Wesleyan*

TO TENNESSEE WILLIAMS

Awfully glad you liked a good part of the thing I sent you. Especially glad that you liked the end. I agree with you that we have the makings of a picture. About my doing it: I certainly didn't put all the work in as an exercise in dramatic structure, nor have I been asking you to do all I have asked you to do just to keep you out of trouble. As for doing it this fall. That's another problem. I'd like to very much. I have kept the fall clear. I dont start with Schulberg till next March. I have every desire to do it in the fall, but it wont be one bit easy. I told Audrey a month ago that it was already too late to do it this fall. At the same time I've kept going as if this were not so. I'll keep on doing that.

The first thing I want to do is send a script to Brando. He "goes" with TEAHOUSE next January. He could do a picture in late October, November, December. If he was crazy about it. Despite his previous reaction I cannot quite give up on him. He would be just the person. Right now I haven't a script I can send Brando. I cant send him, under the circumstances that he read a previous incomplete script and didn't like it—I say I cant under those circumstances send him the thing I sent you with part my totally inadequate dialogue, partly script, partly outline, partly description.

If we are as close as you feel we are I cannot for the life of me see why you couldn't put in a week now and put in the pecan tree bit, which I love, the ten commandment bit which I like very much, and any other bits you like. . . . Fix it the way you think it should go. About Aunt Rose and Baby Doll singing hymns—o.k. they're foolish. Actually I dont think that. I think its a bizarre note. I remember how outraged you first were when you first heard the kids' birthday song in the second act of CAT. In time you liked it—in rather short time. Generally speaking I'll bet many of the things I do staging wise wouldn't sound so hot described in words. But to hell with it. You cant insult me as a writer, because I genuinely have no ambitions in that direction. I only did what I did to really get us moving and it seems to have accomplished that end. Its 90% your stuff and I wish to Christ you'd make it 100%. In fact that's what I'm asking you to do before I send it to Brando.

In the second place I cant go on the basis of an incomplete script. Its not a matter of whether or not I "still like taking chances." (let that pass.) I cant give an incomplete script to a business manager and say 'make me a budget it goes something like this here and more or less like this there.' And I cant give it to an art director and say the same type dialogue. And Brando or any other star male or female is the same problem. But mainly finance and production departments both must have a complete script and even before that one I have to, we must make a determined pass at Brando with a complete script—especially since you feel we're so close. . . .

I'll also start immediately on casting Baby Doll. I dont think there is a star to play this, but perhaps there is. The part has changed (and I like the change) since this business of her being twenty years old and a virgin bride. Certainly Marilyn Monroe cant play it. Or Jean Simmons. Have you any ideas? I'll look right away. I've sent a script to Jack Warner. I did this because I'm sure he'll like it, because I want his help and co-operation, and even his approval even though contractually I don't need any of them. I'll alert his department and also certain other agents and friends out there and here and see if I can find us a new Baby Doll girl, which is what I'd prefer. Archie Lee I can only see as Burl at the moment, but there must be others to play this part, and I will make a look. I'll get this activity going monday. The first step, though is Brando. We'd be silly to go past him without taking our best possible shot at him! . . .

The big question is where to shoot it. I dont want to shoot in anywhere except Mississippi. But I dont think we can do the Bayou sequence at the end anywhere except in a big sound stage. I'll get the art director's advice on that one, and will let you know. Everything else I must do in Mississippi. We could shoot this in So. Cal, where there are cotton fields (or is it Arkansas? or Arizona? some place there are cotton fields that operate different months.) But there are no old houses for their house and the main streets look different, and everything fundamental in the air is different.

Well, baby, I'll keep in touch, as they say in the TV world. You ought to get another script in a few days after this and, if I can remember, I will mark the changed parts. I'll also alert Brando that we're going to be sending him something.

Is he going to do Orpheus? With Magnani? That's real showboat! And exciting. Spiegel talked to me about it. By the way, one of his techniques is to feel around for resentments people have against other people. Very gently and delicately and sympathetically he puts his lips against the hole and sucks out the resentment. Then he goes to the other person and tells the resentment. He does this most sympathetically to both sides, suggesting that there is a little temporary rift, of no consequence which, with his good offices, will very soon be healed. The go-between spiritual nurse in the person of SS is needed, and will, if relied upon, very soon make everything o.k. In this spirit he told me that you were fed up with my asking for changes changes changes and never telling you what changes I wanted. I told him that in the first place I had been very long windedly explicit and in the second place our relationship was a frank one and you were quite able to tell me just how you felt towards anything I did.

Sometimes I think I'm an artist in spite of myself too. In fact I'm sure of it. I dont think its my brains or my experience that makes me an artist, when

I am one. Its rather something extra-mental isn't it that makes us all what we are, irrational, non rational, extra-rational. In the second place, baby I will never never win any medals for my knowledge of the south. The only thing is: I really do balk when people tell me "she wouldn't do that!" The very meaning of originality is <u>people wouldn't do that</u>.

But anyway what I've done, for better or worse has given us both confidence in the practical sense of that word—so lets go ahead. I'll be working on the casting tomorrow and as soon as you send me a complete script I will send it to Brando. And on that cruel, harsh, uncompromising note may I close with love.

g.

["Let me say right off, you're a better man than I am, Gunga Din!" Tennessee Williams saluted the "great, great, great, great THEATRE!" of Kazan's revised script, especially the frog-gigging episode—its violence notwithstanding (n.d., Wesleyan). The epic battle ends with Archie Lee "shouting to the men on the bank" of the bayou that he burned the Syndicate gin: "I did it. I did it." One of the silent witnesses, goaded by Vacarro to acknowledge the forced confession, kills the outsider with a rifle shot ("Hide and Seek," July 29, 1955, HTC).

Marlon Brando had "rather scornfully and insultingly" rejected a previous *Baby Doll* script, but Kazan could not "quite give up on him," although he still lacked a finished product to submit. As it turned out, Brando's immediate passage from *Guys and Dolls* (1955) to *Teahouse of the August Moon* (1956) ruled out *Baby Doll*. Presumably the evolution of Baby Doll's character into a twenty-year-old "virgin bride" also eliminated Marilyn Monroe, nearly thirty, from consideration. Later developments would confirm her talent for disruption on the Kazan and Miller home fronts and Elia's prudence in not casting her. Karl Malden proved an able alternative to Burl Ives, while Carroll Baker, a twenty-four-year-old drawn from the Actors Studio, played Baby Doll and received an Academy nomination.] *TLS, 3 pp., HRC*

TO MOLLY DAY THACHER

PM: Piggott, Arkansas, September 27, 1955

We had a great day today. I'm getting to know a lot of people here too. Its too much, but necessary—here. This morning we watched a drum majorette rehearsal. The Piggott High School. Then we went to the Farm Loan office and sat a while talking to the Chief Clerk. I dont know what the hell that had to do with anything, but it was instructive. Then we drove over to another town: Paragould (what towns! Paragould, Pocahontas, Piggott) And we met the owner and operator of the local Radio station. A very very small radio station with a very very local program. We talked with him a very long time and got an awful lot from him. We're going over Wednesday and spend the morning with him, watching the operation. About this time I became convinced that Jackie Gleason wasn't it. Yesterday I spent a couple of hours in the town square. In the big town square sits the Court House. It sits in the middle of a square park. Around the park is a square lining of the stores in the town. Just about every store including the dentist office is in a four sided layout around the town square. On the grass is a band stand, a world war no 1. monument, a brace of tables for the checker players who sit there most of every day playing checkers, and a couple of benches for the two whittlers. I sat with the wittlers for two hours. I got friendly with them. They do a lot of whittling (I'll finally find how to spell that goddamn word) most of it of nothing in particular. They also do a lot of knife buying and knife swapping. I bought a knife. A Case (the brand) Three bladed. One of the brands is hollow ground and is marked: "for flesh only". Its used for castrating pigs and cats and dogs. No sooner had I bought the knife than a fellow came up to me and wanted to talk swapping with his knife, which was also a good knife. I sat there and some one gave me one of five little lengths of cedar he had in his pocket. I whittled. They told stories. Very strong type stories. I got friendly with a guy named Uncle Bob who had two knives a two blader and a three blader. He didn't want to swap. He gave me something he had whittled: a finger tip belt balancer. Tell Nick I'll bring it home and give it to him. Anyway talking to these fellows made Jackie Gleason seem synthetic. I began to cool on Jackie Gleason. This afternoon I cooled more. Its always both stimulating and disturbing to visit the scene. You feel how superficial you really are. From the moment we had "settled" on Gleason we had done nothing, but adapt and adjust and justify. Finally we had him left behind by a small broken down Carnival. And that, you will agree, is strictly Zanuck or worse. Anyway for the birds and not what we started out to do. So tomorrow (tues.) we are going to spend all day right here, which is kind of tough because its so damned fascinating everywhere else. But we got to because Wednesday we're going back to Paragould and spend the day at the Radio station. Then we're going to leave Thursday, I driving to Memphis with the boys. Then I'll come to N.Y. I imagine I'll get there Saturday, and take Nick to the World Series. Its been fascinating here. It took longer than I thought, but I wish I could stay here another couple of weeks. We got a hell of a lot out of it. For instance at the end of the afternoon today we drove over to Arkansas State College and had a half hour with a Daniel Minx who is an instructor in the Music Department there, coaches the college band and in the summer school runs a "CLINIC" (their word) for Drum Majors and Drum Majorettes. By the way at Ark State they get Credit for their courses in Baton twirling. Now I never knew any such information. For instance last night I talked for an hour with the town undertaker, mortician he says. I never knew all that thinking went on. I'm fascinated. My education is barely started it seems. Meantime I put all the damned weight on again with those Bloody Marys and beer and such. I'm going to have to start with the eggs again. Tonight we're going out with the County Welfare worker. etc. etc. It goes on and on. I could stay here a month. I like Ark. All virgin territory. We had beers with a guy age 56 and tough who elaborately explained to us why they had to hang three niggers once. Have you ever heard this elaborately and heavily explained? But even down here they dont think those two fellows should have killed that fourteen year old.

I'm well. love. g.

[Plans for *A Face in the Crowd* began with midsummer meetings in Connecticut and research trips to New York to study, as Budd Schulberg put it, "the two-headed god of public persuasion, television and advertising." Larry "Lonesome" Rhodes, offspring of the "god," appears first as a "*git*-tar"-strumming vagabond in Schulberg's story "Your Arkansas Traveler" (1953). With "limitless confidence in his own charm," he moves rapidly from a small radio station in Fox, Wyoming, to the media center of New York City. He revolutionizes advertising, beguiles a national audience, and is exploited in turn by sinister corporate and political figures, until he demonstrates "the dynamic-mercurial quality of TV success" with a precipitous fall (Schulberg to EK, n.d., Dartmouth).

The opening scenes in the screenplay were shifted from Wyoming to the fictional town of Pickett, Arkansas, where Marcia Jeffries, a Sarah Lawrence girl, operates a small country radio station visited by Lonesome Rhodes. Local color scenes filmed in Piggott in 1956 feature whittlers and checker players in the town square, while the "drum majorette rehearsal" has evolved into a baton-twirling contest ogled by old-timers and judged by Rhodes in a return to the scene of his initial success. Warner Bros. provided financing and release for Kazan's second production under the Newtown label.

Emmett Till was murdered on August 28, 1955, for allegedly flirting with a white woman in Money, Mississippi. The murderers of the fourteen-year-old African American from Chicago were tried and acquitted by an all-white jury and later confessed their act in a controversial interview with William Bradford Huie (*Look*, January 1956). Unknown to Kazan at the time was the role that the murder would take in defining the civil rights movement and establishing a friendship with James Baldwin.] *TLS, 2 pp., Wesleyan*

TO BUDD SCHULBERG

[New York]
October 6, 1955

Dear Budd:

Went to see Jackie yesterday on the exact date that I promised to get back to him. He really took it great. I left with that same feeling of admiration that you must remember very well. I explained to him our thinking and expressed our very real regret. I also told him how much we admired him. I told him that the time might come when we would come back to him and ask how he was situated, but I made it very clear that at the moment it was cold between us. He said he understood and that, in fact, he agreed with us. He said if we wanted to make it a boy from Arkansas or the middle of the country anywhere, he knew as well as we that Gleason was not the right choice for it. He said he appreciated my coming in and laying it on the line to him and he wanted to work with us very much and that he was sure the time would come when we would, etc. The main thing was that his spirit was really friendly and I felt he really understood.

Feeling that his mood was good, I also told him that we would probably want to use ideas that he had given to us and he said go ahead and help yourself to everything and anything, that we were free and clear to do whatever we wished with what we had gotten from him. I really fell for the guy all over again, but this time as I watched him I felt we were really right in not casting him as Rhodes. So did he. The three of us, I assure you, are at this moment on the friendliest possible terms. He urged me to come back to him when we had a script if he could prove of any use. I'm sure that this will not all turn sour at some later date. This fat boy is quite a man.

I have thought it over and I don't think I should send you what I have on sections 4 and 5. I think the creative thing about our relationship is that we build between us as we talk and after all there is no immediate rush and we have got about half a picture very thoroughly and very satisfactorily outlined. I'm very happy with it, as you are I know, and what's the use of going off into a script conference via air mail. I think it is much better if we just let it lie. I have a lot of scattered notes on things—memos and all that junk—but I think we will do much better later when we are together. Let me know if you think I'm right about this.

I've thought of you and I know you must be having a wonderful time. Give my love to Vickie.

Always

ek:mf

[Kazan began "to cool" on casting Jackie Gleason as Lonesome Rhodes while absorbing the folkways of rural northeastern Arkansas. Budd Schulberg reluctantly agreed: "Yes the bastard has something. I feel it strongly—so much so that I weaken now and then and think maybe he can do anything, especially in your hands." Finally, though, he could not see Gleason, a Brooklyn native, "as a true Arkansawyan hobo," adding that he probably "can't get farther west than maybe Jersey City" (to EK, October 20, 1955, Wesleyan). No less telling than geography was Gleason's "synthetic" quality as a TV star associated with distinctive character roles and memorable catchphrases. High ratings for a Saturday-night variety show from 1952 to 1956 approximate the five-year span Schulberg allotted to stars in the "man-eating" cycles of early television.

"What It Was, Was Football," a humorous monologue recorded by "Deacon" Andy Griffith in 1953, sold nearly a million copies and established a folksy southern persona for the native of Mount Airy, North Carolina. Griffith made his film debut as Rhodes after receiving a Tony Award nomination for his role as an affable, bemused draftee from the South in *No Time for Sergeants* (1955).] *TL, 2 pp., Wesleyan*

TO WILLIAM BRADFORD HUIE

[New York]
October 11, 1955

Dear Bill:
I got your letter and your memo. I don't know what made you think my interest is temporary. I'm very interested actually in the TVA project. As a matter of fact, to be absolutely frank and plain, it seemed to me that what you wrote in the way of a memo, benefited in some small respect from our conversation about this subject. I am still very interested in it, but I really can't do it the way you have got it laid out. I completely agree with you about the potential here for a fine picture, but it is considerably more difficult than it sounds.

I have always spoken frankly to you, Bill, and I always will. I told you last time we talked, I would want to get the benefit of all your ideas, but I would not want you to write the screen play. That should be the job of a talent which is specifically that of a dramatist. You do your own kind of reportage—I don't know a better word for it—and in your field I think you are absolutely tops, but the talent of a dramatization is a very special one and is rather opposite to the talent of a novelist or a journalist. I won't go on boring you with an aesthetic lecture about it, but I will put this positively. If we can make a reasonable deal, U. A. and I, for the book and your notes, I would be interested in going ahead with the project, but only on those conditions. In other words, I would want to be free to make my own screen play with whatever help I saw fit to use.

Let me know your progress with this and your reaction to my letter.

Cordially

ek:mf
cc: Max Youngstein

[William Bradford Huie reported on the South with candor and sympathy in a career that spanned the years of the Depression and the civil rights movement. His autobiographical novel *Mud on the Stars* (1942) apparently stirred Kazan's interest in the Tennessee Valley Authority of the 1930s and the prospect of a location film with documentary scale and a strong personal story. The author's enclosed memo summarizes the history of "<u>one</u>, old, chauvinistic family" living on Garth's Island during "'the Roosevelt Revolution.'" The taming of the Tennessee River and the resulting loss of traditional culture provide a dramatic framework for the marriage of former ideological "enemies," who begin life anew in a region lifted from poverty and isolation by progressive social planning—proof that "the American Way can fulfill spiritual as well as material yearnings." Kazan may have detected a stiff, tendentious reading of social history in Huie's treatment and was encouraged to look elsewhere for a screenwriter. Nonetheless he and a host of later writers followed the basic dramatic structure outlined in Huie's memo ("<u>Tennessee Valley</u>: A Memorandum," n.d., Wesleyan). Twentieth Century-Fox, rather than United Artists, acquired film rights without Huie's further involvement and released *Wild River* in 1960.] *TL with enclosure, 1 p., Wesleyan*

TO JACK L. WARNER AND FINLAY MCDERMOTT

SH: Hotel Greenville
PM: Greenville, Mississippi
November 15, 1955

Dear Jack
Dear Finlay:
Excuse this letter being so late. As you can imagine I've been rushed. I'm located down here now and the crew has begun to come in. The actors will follow shortly. I've been rushed.

I will do everything the Shurlock office wants, except one thing. I cannot do that. As I wrote Jack Warner last week if I did that I'd have to throw away the whole picture. I have eliminated everything except the points I note below.

Assure Shurlock and Vizzard once more that both Williams and I specifically do not want there to have been a "sex-affair" (their phrase) between our two people. I have eliminated the lines about her skin breaking out entirely. I have eliminated the stage direction about her hurt expression when Silva says that nothing happened between them.

But this film is about one thing and only one thing. Its about a middle aged man who is held at arm's length by his young wife. Its a false marriage, falsely made and its bound to collapse because the basis of it is false. Everyone in this country knows that false marriages like other mistakes of mortal man should be broken up—everyone except the Catholics. Actually we dont show her going with another man.

Inform Shurlock and Vizzard that at the end of the picture Silva is going to walk away from her. Having forced justice on a reluctant community, he has what he wants. He doesn't really want Baby Doll. She is terribly attracted to him. He is not to her. He uses his sex appeal as a weapon. He wants one thing only: to avenge the burning of his gin. He wants to put Archie so incontrovertibly on the guilty spot that even friendship cant save him, the friendship of the local authorities, that is.

I think Silva's dropping her at the end of the film will make the adultery issue quite clear. There wasn't any, and actually while Silva has aroused her, he isn't particularly interested in her, once Archie Lee has been taken away. Tell the boys that the hero of this film, for me, is Archie Lee. He is a pathetic misguided, confused, desperate man. Sin and violence and so forth come out of fear and desperation. Archie Lee should be pathetic. And will be. And amusingly so!

I cannot reduce the element of Archie Lee's sex frustration. I dont know how you want to handle this. I will, you can be sure, handle it delicately and in good taste. And since it will all be done comical and amusingly, the sordid side of it will be eliminated. There will be nothing sordid about it. Archie Lee will be pathetically amusing. The boys know that when I say something, I make good on it. The audience will only feel how absurd his awkward and misarranged passion is. How funny! How sad! Jack and Steve and Geoff and I all being firmly bogged down in middle years will understand this.

In line with this thinking tell the boys that I cannot eliminate Archie's going into the bathroom after his wife, I cannot eliminate the dialogue on pages 9, 10 about Archie's sex frustration, I cannot change the doctor scene and furthermore assert unequivocally that it has nothing to do with sex frustration, since every middle aged man is familiar with the sudden slump of ALL his powers that comes (dismayingly) in his late forties. Furthermore I must make the scene of Archie Lee trying to make love to his wife deeply tender and loving. I do not direct vulgar sex scenes. The request they make that I eliminate Archie slugging his wife is pure bull. I wont pay any attention to that point. I above all cannot eliminate the dialogue on p 77 starting "How long did he have to wait?" etc. This is the whole nub of the story, and if I eliminate this passage or curtail it the audience wont have the vaguest idea what the hell the film is about. This is the very essence of the plot. And there is nothing wrong with it except that it violates the dictates—not of the American public—but of the Catholic church ONLY.

Furthermore Baby Doll does grow up in the story, but I will make it clear that her growing up has nothing to do with her having had her first vaginal orgasm. The lines on p 113 they want eliminated are essential to the story, and I have no intention of eliminating them. But I will cut out Baby Doll's hurt expression when Silva tells Archie Lee (truthfully) that nothing has happened between them. . . .

In general, Jack, it seems to me that with fewer and fewer people leaving their TV sets and their homes after supper, we must, we MUST strike out for exceptional subject matters and really unusual treatments of these subject matters. In one sentence we are now obliged, AS A MATTER OF SELF PRESERVATION, to put on the screen of Motion Picture Theatres ONLY what they cannot and will never see on their TV screens at home. Our industry now is in a desperate situation, and we must be bold and fight for our lives. TV is improving fast, and getting bolder every day. The wide screen gimmick cannot keep our head above the water much longer. We've got to break our own taboos and strike out for increasingly unusual and daring material. Either that or just quit and sign up with the TV guys.

There is now nothing indecent about this subject. It is a comic portrait of middle aged ardor. It has grotesque and even tragic elements, but essentially the view point is comic and affectionate. It will certainly not be sordid. That they'll have to take my word for. But where I think we must fight and fight hard is the admissibility of the grown up subject at the core of this script. I repeat again if we cannot treat Archie Lee's sex frustration, we might as well sign off right now. If we can and do, why then we may well have a picture that will really interest everyone and which people will leave their homes to see.

Finlay will you please have a copy of this letter made and send it back to me. I just moved in here and have no carbon paper.

Jack, I'll wait to hear from you on this whole issue. Send me a box of mild fine long cigars too. Its lonely here. Love to Steve. And lets hear from you

gadge

[Filming *Baby Doll* began in November with location work centered in Benoit, Mississippi, in the upper Delta, where cotton was historically grown with a minimum of aristocratic flair. The vacant ruins of the Burrus House, a Greek Revival grace note of the 1850s, gave Kazan a ready-made image of the South in decline. Objections raised by the Production Code staff would not be satisfied. "Archie Lee's sex frustration," the consequence of a dying father's decree that his daughter remain virginal in marriage until her twentieth birthday, was not negotiable. The film's opening sequence, deemed "very questionable" by Jeff Shurlock, finds Archie shortly before the epochal event poking a hole through a crumbling wall to savor Baby Doll as she sleeps in a crib—uncovered and sucking her thumb. Possessing her requires Archie to meet his part of the farcical "agreement" by providing a full set of furniture for his reluctant bride, who is primed for sex, although not with her middle-aged husband. Vacarro's rival cotton gin threatens to beggar Archie and leads to arson. The most "serious Code violations" cited by Shurlock were the "unconsummated marriage" and the dramatically "justified adultery" occasioned by Vacarro's plot of revenge, which is designed to force Baby Doll into revealing her husband's guilt (Shurlock to JLW, October 24, 1955, Herrick). Ever agile in dealing with the Production Code staff, Kazan filmed each of the objectionable scenes, including Archie's cuffing of Baby Doll when she enters his ramshackle gin in the presence of black hands.

Filming began without a suitable ending in hand. Earlier, in 1953, Tennessee

Filming Eli Wallach and Carroll Baker at the Burrus House, near
Benoit, Mississippi. Boris Kaufman is seated at Kazan's right.

Williams identified the "major problem" as one of "reconciling, artistically, the
hilarious comedy which is the keynote of the film, and the very heavy 'punishment
for sins' ending demanded by the censors, but maybe that can be cheated a little
the way we did the 'moral ending' in Streetcar" (to Wood, December 23, 1953,
HRC). The frog-gigging epsiode was finally cut in favor of a "hide and seek" farce
that still entitled the shooting script. Drunk and enraged by his wife's apparent
seduction, Archie Lee goes "berserk" with a shotgun while Vacarro and Baby Doll
crouch safely in a pecan tree. He is arrested and led away.

In a personal note dated December 6, 1956, Kazan described Williams's brief
visit to Greenville and failure to supply a suitable ending for *Baby Doll*. Feeling isolated and scorned by locals, Williams left abruptly with Kazan "holding
an incompleted script." Later he received "scattered pages" from Williams with
various endings that "didn't have much relation" to the film proper ("The Human
Race," Wesleyan). Precisely who devised the ending as filmed is unclear. Kazan
did credit Williams with the "lovely fade-out line" spoken by Carroll Baker to
Milly Dunnock (Aunt Rose) after Vacarro and Meighan have departed: "We got
nothing to do but wait for tomorrow and see if we're remembered or forgotten"
(*A Life*, p. 562).

Jack Warner needed no reminder that weekly movie attendance had declined
by 50 percent since 1946, nor that households with television sets increased from
four to thirty million between 1950 and 1955. He was already allied with TV, hav-

ing agreed to provide ABC with programming for the current season.] *TLS, 4 pp., WB Archives*

TO LEE STRASBERG

[Greenville, Mississippi]
November 16 [1955]

Dear Lee:

I met with Bob Anderson. He showed me a list he had drawn up. I either knew the playwrights or had heard of them with a few exceptions. I thought it a good list and said O.K. Then after he left, I did some thinking about the problem in general.

First I would say that the Actors' Studio should interest itself in only a limited number of playwrights. It should not run "a course for playwrights". It should not interest itself in all playwrights, or even in every "good" playwright. The playwrights should be chosen by the same unarticulated measures by which we choose actors or directors. We do not interest ourselves in all talented actors. Our taste—who we are—functions here, and it must finally function with play- wrights. They should be representative of the same impulse in Art which makes us select over and over again the same actors and the same kind of actors.

Obviously these playwrights should be attached, not to Bob Anderson, or to any "instructor" but to the Studio. I told Bob that I would like to work with him when I come back in January. He was delighted. I should say that my job should be first of all to make them more Theatre people, less literary people. And secondly to make them feel, to the best of my abilities, the impulse in art, and Theatre art, to which the Studio belongs. . . . Finally it is important that the equivalent be found for the playwright to the way we have worked with actors. This work with themselves and thru themselves is the big contribution we can make to playwrighting. In my own way I've tried some of this work. And actually I am eager to work further with playwrights, because I'm eager to work in that field myself (not stage; screen plays) I'd very much like to hear from you on this subject. I know you've thought a lot about it. . . .

Now another matter entirely. I was distressed the night of the auditions to find you attacking me a couple of times. This hasn't happened for a long time between us. I didn't say anything, but then I never do at the time. However, on thought, I better speak.

You hit at me about never being in New York or at the Studio. There seemed to be, in your manner, some resentment of me. Incidentally I've often felt it in the manner you used with Cheryl. I always thought I understood why. But the degree of your waspishness surprised me.

When I was included, the other night, I was just a little shocked. Then I thought that perhaps there is some unspoken misunderstanding. (the worst kind) And perhaps, if that is the case, perhaps I should speak my understanding and my intentions and (if you care to) you, yours.

Really from the time the Studio started I've thought of it as your place. Bob Lewis and I didn't agree on this. Cheryl and I did. Its not as though this conclusion was the result of analysis or forethinking on my part. Its simply a fact. You have already become the central influence in a generation of Theatre Workers. That has already happened. It seemed to me both just and necessary that you should have a "place". Since the day you started at the studio, that place has been, in my eyes, your place. As I say, it was nothing I had to decide. It was patently so. My teaching immediately seemed like an interim affair, keeping the store going till the boss came back.

I have done everything possible since you first came to the studio to put reluctant you in the centre of it. But it became difficult for you to resist long, not because my urging had any potency, but because in a sense the actors allowed you no choice. You were "called" to it, as they say in church circles.

You know I have very large self doubts, especially on an intellectual level. I can carry very well thru a production, play or film because of some conviction, emotional usually, that I have about each piece of material. I hold onto some personal vein of experience, and with that charge, I can push on thru.

But as a teacher I never was much. I am not learned that way. Nor does it seem to be my natural activity, even with my children. I have influenced certain people. Certain actors are devoted to me. I have given them something. I'm proud of the way they feel for me. But intellectually, in this field at least, I am literally obsessed with doubts. This reaches a point where sometimes I cannot speak at all. Especially, it appears happens after you (Harold too, used to be) have spoken. I'm o.k. in a "strange" group. I can talk like hell in California. Somewhere my self doubts have their roots in the kind of admiration I used to feel for you and for Harold in the 1930's.

I say what I have just said with regret, and even some embarrassment. I wish it were not so. I think the work of teaching is a truly noble calling. I know I, especially, could get a great deal by truly working at the Studio. And perhaps I will be able to. Probably. I am stubborn and determined.

At the present moment, though, I have a passionate yearning in another direction: films. This takes another word of explanation. In the Theatre I have felt essentially an interpreter, even a servant of the playwright. In films I have suddenly found that I can initiate projects, contribute to them, write on them, determine their fate and meaning. I initiated Viva Zapata and did most of the structure on the script, which was lousy. I initiated WATERFRONT and contributed the main events to that one too. And EofE, and this one, and the next. And I feel that at last I have found a channel of self-expression. For better or worse, I have found a way of putting something of myself in my work, and the satisfaction that comes from that. CAT is Tenn's. These movies are me. Along that path, I can grow. And I hope do better work, because more personal work.

As for the Theatre, I wait and if a script "comes along" either ready or like Lou Peterson's, full of a potential I like—I then take part. But actually there is only one thing in the Theatre to which I feel a complete or even a real loyalty. And that is the Studio. I almost wrote your Actors' Studio. I didn't because you say you dont want the responsibility.

I have it seems to me, continuously contributed something to the Actors' Studio. Clearly by your remarks and your tone the other night, you are disappointed in my contribution. I'm sorry you are. But I cannot say it will be more in the immediate future. I want to be clear about that. I will do what I said about the playwrights. I want to work with them. But my comings and goings will still finally be determined (at least for these next couple of years) by my film activities. I would have felt it needless to say this, except for your saying: Gadg is never here.

But wherever I have been, I have, with Cheryl, kept the studio's physical side functioning. This year, while she was occupied with Reuben Reuben, I organized the coming benefit. This took time and the kind of effort and activity I hate. But I did talk to the ladies' committees, and the co-chairman I wrestled down and tied up, I met with Paramount and with Wallis-Hazen, and I pleaded with the "character" who runs the Sheraton-Astor by phone from two coasts. This, as I say, I will continue to do, stuff like that.

But it seemed plain the other night that you expected more of me, and were disappointed. And I wish I had done more, and in that regard I, too, am disappointed. But main impulses sort of take hold of me, and I become blind to anything else. But what occurred to me was that just possibly you might feel better if you were backed up with a different organization for the artistic functioning of the place. So I want to say now that I will organize around you any functioning group you want. I will never leave or resign. I will always be there, even though, at this moment, "there" is not what you would like it to be (or I, entirely) and as far away as Mississippi, or wherever. . . .

To be frank, absolutely so, it also occurred to me that your tone towards me might have a more indirect source or meaning. Whatever it is or isn't I wish you would clarify it. I've often felt that if I were Cheryl, I would demand of you an explanation of your manner towards her.

I'll be here till Jan. 1. If I'm here much after that I'll have serious budget problems, loss of rights etc., so that shouldn't happen! I'll be in New York from Jan to June. I have every hope of participating more in our activity then. I have no play. All I'll be doing is editing this film, and helping Budd with his script. There, I am personally committed to Budd's writing a first draft without me. (He thinks I "helped" too much on Waterfront, just as Tennessee thinks I "helped" too damned much on Cat.)

You know I'm deeply devoted to you.

gadg

[A new Playwrights Unit directed by Robert Anderson failed to incorporate writers into the full "activity" of the Actors Studio, as Kazan hoped it would. His maintenance of the Studio's "physical side" included plans for a benefit performance of *The Rose Tattoo* on December 12. Abe Burrows served as master of ceremonies while Kazan filmed on location in Mississippi. Marilyn Monroe reprised her role as a celebrity usherette.

Before answering Lee Strasberg, Kazan drafted a personal memo to "stop the burning" and analyze the recent attack. It "must never be forgotten" in dealing with Strasberg that his "disappointment is deep and bitter" for having "utterly utterly failed [to become] a great functioning American director." The departure of "every mature grown up" from the Studio, especially Julie Harris, Marlon Brando, and Karl Malden, also rankled, Kazan thought, and led Strasberg to censure defections "with the authority of a rabbi speaking and interpreting the unchallengeable law." He also assumed that Strasberg resented his "mistreatment" of Marilyn Monroe and failure to cast her in *Baby Doll*, as Strasberg had "urged." He is "close to her. He may even have had an 'affair' with her, if you could call it that. She is weird enough to do that. She has that much uncertainty, that much need for reassurance especially in re her work." Finally, Kazan inferred that Strasberg felt "safe" in attacking him publicly because he held in reserve "the threat of resigning from the Actors' Studio" (November 12, 1955, Wesleyan).]
TLSx, 4 pp., Wesleyan

TO MOLLY DAY THACHER

PM: Greenville, Mississippi, November 29, 1955

Dearest Molly:

I was pooped at nine o'clock this evening. I worked hard all day and it was a lot of fun. Then I had a big goddamn steak and some Italian steak and a beer, and some chocolate ice-cream and a big goddamn cigar and felt like a successful contractor's foreman, and very sleepy so I lay in bed and took a nap and woke up. Because today I felt like writing you. I got your letter about the money. I felt ashamed, like I've been mistreating you. Hell we've got lots of money and you never should worry about that. Tell Marie to write you a check for a thousand or any amount you want and send it down to me and I will sign it and send it to you. I sent you (thru MF) the check for the mirrors, and the two hundred dollars and a lot of other items. But hell dont worry about money. I'll tell you when and if you have to worry about money. . . .

The reason I cant write you about what I'm ashamed of is because I'm ashamed of it. I'm ashamed I hurt you ever. On the other hand I resent being made to feel guilty and low and <u>less</u>. This harks back to the worst times I ever had when I felt low and less and all that. I dont feel that way any more ostensibly. But you never stop feeling the same about important things, or at best you make progress slowly. I just want you to know that its not a philosophy of mine or a callous piece of habitual aggression. And its not like the earlier episode because I dont feel vengeful, hardly at all if at all. I guess its absolutely accurate to say: not at all.

In one sense its true to say that it meant nothing. On the other hand it was a human experience, and it started, if that is of any significance, in a most human way. She had just had a loss. Her boy friend, or "keeper" (if you want to be mean about it) had just died. His family had not allowed her to see the body, or allowed her into the house, where she had been living after the death. She had sneaked in one night and been thrown out. I met her on Harmon Jones set when I went over to visit Harmon. Harmon thought her a ridiculous person and was fashionably scornful of her. I found her, when I was introduced in tears. I took her to dinner because she seemed like such a touching pathetic waif. She sobbed all thru dinner. I wasn't interested in her (in quotes); that came later. But I did feel terribly touched by her and did think she had a lot of talent. [omission] also is "soiled", is also talented and, except for having found and been found by [omission], and her powerful love for [omission], would be lost and adrift. I got to know her in time and introduced her to Arthur Miller, who also was very taken by her. You couldn't help being touched. She was talented, funny, vulnerable, helpless in awful pain, with no hope, and some worth and not a liar, not vicious, not catty, and with a history of orphanism that was killing to hear. She was like all Charlie Chaplin's heroines in one. I'm not ashamed at all, not a damn bit of having been attracted to her. She is nothing like what she appears to be now, or even appears to have turned into now. I dont know what she is like now, except I notice Lee Strasberg has the same reaction to her that I did. She was a little stray cat when I knew her, total possession a few clothes, and one piano. I got a lot out of her just as you do from any human experience where anyone is revealed to you and you affect anyone in any way. I guess I gave her a lot of hope, and Arthur gave her a lot of hope. She had a crush on Art, not me. I was more interested in her, especially humanly than he was. She is not a big sex pot as advertised. At least not in my experience. I dont know if there are such as "advertised" big sex pots. I didn't have anything to do with her when I went out during the testifying. She was sleeping with DiMaggio. She told me a lot about him and her, his Catholicism, and his viciousness (he struck her often, and beat her up several times) I was touched and fascinated. It was the type of experience that I do not understand and I enjoyed (not the right word) hearing about it. I certainly recommended her to Tennessee's attention. And he was very taken by her. I'm not sorry about it. I dont think a man can go thru a life without lesions, faults, slips and all that. I have no will towards same, and I have no desire to harm you. I love you and only want to help you. Everything I do, however does not have that result, or even that aim. I do not hold myself to as absolute a standard as you do. I have no terrible guilt about this. I'm awful sorry I hurt you. But in one sense it meant nothing. It was no threat to the way I felt about you. And it did not take anything away from me. I do not feel less for it. I do not feel sunk in sin. I'm sorry I hurt you. I do not look for anything like this. I do not want anything like this. I am human though. It might happen again. I hope not, and I have resisted quite some other opportunities. No loss. I got a lot out of this one, cant say I didn't. I think I helped her. I dont know the answer to all this. If you dont like what I say and feel it necessary for your own sense of honor and cleanliness to divorce me, divorce me. I want you to realize yourself, whatever is best for you. I do not take your pain lightly. But I cannot take as vital and critical things that are not to me critical, or vital. I dont think I should not be married or anything like that. If you divorce me, I'll tell you plainly I will in time get married again and have more children. I feel I'm a family man and I want a family, and am a damned good one. I dont care what your judgment is on that. I think I see the world around me (us) a hell of a lot more clearly than you do or anyone else does for that matter. I've had intimate revelations from too many men, seen their intimate lives stripped down too often not to see my self in scale and posed against the perspective of others. I'm not afraid to be alone, because I dont feel alone. I know you love me. And I know I love you. We are not the ideal couple, but we are a good and fruitful couple. Rotten marriages do not produce first class children. And ours are the best. I cant tell you anything more and will not go into anything more. I'm forty six now, and I'm thoroughly grown. I'm not going to stew about what I dont feel dishonest about. I would only feel guilty and rotten if I stayed married to you WHEN I DIDN'T LOVE YOU for money or convenience or what. But I do love you, and do love you more than any other person in the world. I'd rather be married to you than any other person in the world. But I'll be real cruel and really honest and inform you that its perfectly natural that you be more hurt and upset by this than I am. I had forgotten about it. Let me repeat: I had nothing to do with her getting into the Actors' Studio, or Lee Strasberg's classes. Nor am I coaching her, advising her, seeing her or cuddling her. I'm really weary of the whole subject just as you are. . . .

I also dont think you'll ever really be divorced from me, nor I from you. I dont have much respect for artificial and legal relationships. We have a real one. Its full of contrast and conflict, but its quite a relationship, partly because of the c and c.

Oh shit, I'm sick of this. I'm sorry. I'm sorry about the ache in your belly. But get over it, or bounce me, or hit me or shoot me. Or get yourself the kind of husband you can "trust" (YOUR quotes) and will feel secure with and will feel at peace with. (I'm not sneering) Save yourself, if I'm killing you, save yourself. I haven't too much more to live and if its only thirty years, I want them very active and lively and increasingly fruitful thirty years. I'm not going to fuck around in a goddamn stew much longer.

And you can show this letter to B Mittelmann.

The first day shooting I got Malden coming across the Mississippi in a one car ferry whose only other passengers were a large mule and three negroes. The ferry was being pushed by a flat nose row boat service by a 25 horse power outboard and Malden was pushing the driver on to greater speed. Later Malden drives a mud splattered buick up a hill and runs into a road block of cattle. It was a lot of fun. No fucking dialogue. The crew is young. Ditto the cast. Ditto the Director.

Love ALWAYS. g

[Marilyn Monroe became Kazan's "girl" and Arthur Miller's temptation in 1951, when the collaborators tried unsuccessfully to interest Hollywood in filming "The Hook." Kazan's intimacy with Monroe was briefly revived, and apparently ended, in March 1952, when the nominated director returned to California in anticipation of an Oscar for *Streetcar*. Later in the summer, on location in Germany, Elia learned that Molly had not been deceived, that his secrecy "doesn't work," and that his attraction to "this little dizzy character" was "ugly" for her. "It's not explanations I want," she wrote at the time, "it's a relationship where I can respect myself and you" (n.d., Wesleyan). Serious doubts reappeared in late 1955 against the background of Monroe's separation from Joe DiMaggio, residence in New York, and conspicuous presence at the Actors Studio. Arthur Miller's separation from wife and children in the fall was further evidence of Monroe's allure.

Molly delayed joining Elia in Mississippi after attending the premiere of *A Hatful of Rain* on November 9 and suffering an "emotional hangover" from the humiliating experience. "To go to the circus with the band playing and be sheltered from seeing the chief freak. How many, how explicitly, were occupied in this charitable enterprise?" she asked Elia (n.d., Wesleyan). The "freak," no doubt, was Marilyn Monroe, whose close friend and confidant Shelley Winters starred in the production developed at the Actors Studio and cast from its ranks.

Molly (and children) joined Elia on the set of *Baby Doll* in early December and continued to work on her play *The Egghead*. In early January she answered Elia that divorce is "not that simple. I'd feel cleaner but I'd also feel emptier." She doubted that he yet knew in his "bones" that "the 'experience' of a variety of girls prohibits the experience of a happy marriage . . . and freedom from stress." The letter ends with a bold declaration of love: "If I didn't, you couldn't upset one hair" (n.d., Wesleyan).

Of the scenes described by Kazan in closing, only Karl Malden's "ferry" passage remained in the final print of *Baby Doll*.] *TLS, 4 pp., Wesleyan*

[Greenville, Mississippi]
January 10 [1956]

Dear Eric

Sure—on the New Dramatist Notes.

I like Art Miller personally despite all the bitterness. But we didn't "burst into tears". Fast is more or less right about Art's intentions. It seems that his creative process has to have in it the element of killing something he loves. In All My Sons the boy wept when he struck his father. You remember Death of a Salesman—again the symbol of authority bankrupt, loveable, colorful, tragic, dead wrong & dead. Miller had to kill him. Now I've been elected. Art's fairer than Lillian in that he admits, to an extent, the contradiction. She's simply & purely ugly. Art did say he wept. Lillian goes around telling the Big Lie about me & poisoning people.

I'm far away from it all, and, as I say, feeling no pain. I like pictures, at the moment, better than stage. They're still comparatively new to me. I liked Waterfront. Sorry you didn't. I understand what you say about Karl M's role. But that doesn't seem central.

I'm too involved and too tired nights to really read Sol's play. Should be back in N.Y. Jan 20.

Best to you—Lets have an evening when I get back—I can't buy the NR down here. Send me your letter—.

Gadg.

["Notes" made by Kazan, probably in association with the New Dramatists Committee, were of interest to Eric Bentley. The committee supported aspiring young playwrights with craft forums, manuscript review and placement, and residential services.

The opening of A View from the Bridge in the preceding fall revived "bitterness" surrounding Kazan's congressional testimony and estrangement from Arthur Miller. Howard Fast did not cite Kazan in his Daily Worker review, but the arch informer cast a long shadow over the politics of the play. A prolific writer soon to leave the Communist Party, Fast proposed Miller as "the American dramatist of our time" and chided mainstream reviewers for not realizing that this "is a play about an informer, and all else is secondary to that fact" (November 8, 1955).

More damaging was Murray Kempton's publication of "theater gossip" alleging that Miller had sent his "new waterfront play" to Kazan, who returned it with "an enthusiastic assumption" that he would direct. Miller then withdrew the alleged offer with a statement that he had wished to underscore Kazan's betrayal. Resenting the "slur" on his integrity, Miller publicly stated that he had "never offered" the work to Kazan, adding with foresight that he would avail himself of the director's "talent" when he had an appropriate play. Molly Kazan's correspondence suggests that legal action was considered. An influential columnist who wrote on the left, Kempton did not include Kazan in a published apology offered to Miller (*New York Post,* January 3 and 13, 1956).

In *Scoundrel Time* (1976), the final installment of her controversial memoir, Lillian Hellman embellished the "Big Lie" that Kazan had testified for mercenary, career-saving motives with incriminating staging and dialogue. Before the book's publication, Eric Bentley, ever the provocateur, offered to share the present unflattering letter with Hellman: "I have a letter from Kazan from that time, when I was rather friendly with him, and he speaks of you: can show you this sometime" (October 6, 1975, HRC).] *ALS, 2 pp., HRC*

TO CLIFFORD ODETS

[New York]
[February 9, 1956]

Baby:

I've been meaning to write you, but been up to my sling in Miss. mud and problems. The producing yrself is actually a hell of a lot easier than having a villain behind your back "handling" you, and cheating all the small ones. That was Spiegel. Its nicer this way. No worry except the real ones. As to that, I dont know whether the whole thing means much, but the parts have quality, and I just have to trust to an earlier judgment and a lot of luck that it will all go together. Anyway I'm out here in Brooklyn at the old WB studio there, finishing the thing, another week or two to go, and getting a little tired. After which I will put it together, but at leisure, and no one to satisfy on that either except myself. Then the score and then I come out there. Will let you know when that is. I'd sure like to see you. I enjoyed seeing you so much last time. I'm sorry you're there, but you had to I know. I gather the JOSEPH piece has undergone changes of all kinds and Columbia and Wald have shifted and jockeyed and so on. Its a rough place. Actually I feel that it doesn't mean a damn whom you're with if only you have a script (I suppose for you: a subject) that you like. All the goddamn companies are interchangeable, and that includes the independent producers and all of them. The only thing is to get on your own and be your own boss and be accountable only on budget and fuck em all. So—well— what the hell. The other business, the woman and the home is actually much much more important. Its like the songs say, and despite the fact my wife and I are incompatible and impossible and in conflict and all that and all that in quotes, still I'm very very glad we stuck together. The disgusted feeling is less frequent. And there are large moments of peace and work, peace and work and children. Anyway—glad you're sending me the records and I'll get a small new phonograph to celebrate, one of those things that Columbia puts out with two speakers and I'll play the stuff. I made myself a new dark room, and I'll finally learn a little something about photography, which is supposed to be my craft. This summer I'll take the kids to Greece for six weeks. Want to come. June 12–Aug 1? Then I'll start on another project. Slowing up. Not doing two things at a time anymore. And no more Theatre. At least not for a while. I like Tenn. Wms new play, but he's bound and determined to cast Magnani in it. I think she's an extraordinary talent, but I cant see her in this play. Its also time Wms and I took a short rest from each other. The best play I read this season was Paddy Chayefsky's play MIDDLE OF THE NIGHT. I haven't seen it yet, going tonight, but its a beautiful play and he's the best new guy since Art Miller came along. Read the play when it comes out. It has humanity. I didn't like Art Miller's new play, which I did see. And Anne Frank is conventional and full of "lovable comic types". And I didn't move to it at all.

My movie is a comedy. A friend of mine was asking Molly on her return from Miss. how it was going and so on. She told him what she thought and concluded with "you know its a comedy." There was a long pause. Then the friend said—short and dry—"we'll see."

Any errands I can run you in N.Y. Anything you need. I'm yr friend. Love.

g

[Kazan filmed interiors on a replica of the Burrus House at the Vitagraph Studios in Brooklyn. The modestly budgeted black-and-white film was cast with principal players from the Actors Studio, including Eli Wallach, who made his feature film debut in *Baby Doll* as Silva Vacarro.

Harry Cohn shelved "Joseph and His Brethren" after Clifford Odets wrote a massive screenplay, elaborate sets were built, and several directors withdrew from the project—at a reported loss to Columbia Pictures of $1.7 million. Living precariously in Beverly Hills, Odets assumed responsibility for his children after his former wife's death in 1954. A search for "the proper woman" to mend his "broken" life was mentioned in earlier correspondence and may have led Kazan to reflect on his own "impossible," enduring marriage.

No evidence of a Kazan family trip to Greece has been found. Finishing *Baby Doll*, casting *A Face in the Crowd*, and planning *Wild River* probably filled the summer months beyond expectation.

Tennessee Williams bowed to Anna Magnani's demand for a hefty fee and a limited Broadway run in *Orpheus Descending*. Maureen Stapleton was cast after Magnani learned of Marlon Brando's unavailability and withdrew her interest. Kazan and Jo Mielziner traveled to Florida in May for "a sneak try-out," as Williams put it, of his work in progress—*Sweet Bird of Youth*, which Kazan directed in 1959 after sufficient "rest" from the playwright.

Middle of the Night (1956) ran for nearly 500 performances with Edward G. Robinson in the starring role. Paddy Chayefsky's story of a widower's late-middle-age romance with a woman half his age has much the same reverence for the "average" as the author's award-winning screenplay *Marty* (1955). Kazan "didn't like" either Arthur Miller's "new play," *A View from the Bridge,* or *The Diary of Anne Frank.*] TLS, 2 pp., Indiana

TO BORIS KAUFMAN

Dear Boris:

Ever since I started editing BABY DOLL, I've been going over, in my mind, our experience together. The film goes thru my hands and under my eyes, and I remember my problems and the solutions we reached. What we did and what we failed to do. Frankly I'm just a little disappointed in much of my own work. In instance after instance I think I could have done better. I do not blame you for my own insufficiencies. Not at all. But again and again when I see film that is so so, I remember that I was not really relaxed or really "with it" during the filming of those scenes. I was not using my best judgment either in directing the action or in viewing and judging my work as it was performed and in selecting the "prints". I think that part of the trouble was due to the new pressures on me of the double duty of director and producer. I also think, however, that a good part of the trouble was that I never succeeded in drawing from you an uninterrupted run of "takes". This constant "correcting" and fussing, "improving" reached its peak, for me, on the last day. We were making the rather simple dolly shot on Malden and the Doctor over the Checker game. We did eight takes and between everyone of the eight takes you and/or Vin took over right after I said "cut" and the continuity of my work was shattered into eight pieces. I spoke to you about this grave nuisance several times in Greenville and most earnestly. Nothing happened about it except for one night. By the time I arrived in New York, I had given up. I was suffering it.

As to your famous "slowness", I think you are doing your abundant intelligence a grave injustice if you prevent it from recognizing this as a fact. The fact, dear Boris, is that you are slow. And that it costs. It costs financially. I stand open now to a five percent penalty on my share of the profits of BABY DOLL. Part of this is due to the added material I introduced at the film's end, which was more than Johnny had calculated on. But that is far far from the whole story. I began to find myself lucky if I got four set-ups a night. Ecstatic if I got six or seven a day. We worked long hours with lots of overtime and this type of prospect is not a promising one. And this led to a more serious disturbance. I found myself giving up on close-ups in my mind—when I KNEW I needed them—close-ups that, now in the cutting room, I badly need.

I write you these few and partial words of explanation because I do esteem you and hope some day—if I can ever reasonably foresee a more equitable way of functioning with you—to work with you again. I admire your work. I feel many fundamental harmonies with you. I only feel antagonistic when I feel that your good work is obtained at the cost of my own chance for really good work. I feel that was the case here. The centre of the production operation, the goal of all the work and the purpose of all the functioning is the unhampered director working at his best. He, the director, is central—isn't he? Well, hell, I often could not get close enough to the lens to really read the scenes right. It is a trivial, but I think highly revelatory and even symbolic that hardly ever was there an effort made—a chair, a stepping aside—so that I could see my scene more squarely. And I got so I thought of the word "cut" as the signal for an avalanche of electricians—or one rather talented wiry one—descending on the scene and drowning out what I was struggling to find to convey to the actors. I know that you dont remember this, are not, probably, even aware of it. And that is just the point. But I can tell you now, as I told you twice most earnestly in Greenville, that I felt jostled and, in effect, pushed out of the way. And as for any hope of the opposite—true concern and consideration for my proper functioning—that I soon stopped hoping for.

The alternative—to use my energy and voice to bully everyone quiet—is not for me. A martinet is not a creative man. I have other uses for my energy. This, also, is not the first picture I've made. I know that this condition need not be.

So I have decided not to offer you A FACE IN THE CROWD. I will try to solve my requirements thru the help of another cameraman.

I write this to you with regret. We had something good on WATERFRONT. Perhaps we will again some time. I hope so.

Yours,
Elia Kazan

[Before writing, Kazan summarized his discontent in a private note entitled "WHAT I HAVE AGAINST KAUFMANN." He felt displaced from "the centre of the operation" by a cameraman who waged a "war" of attrition with "the typical psychology of a refugee who thinks of himself as surviving by his wits the barbarism of the American savages." In addition to costing "two hundred thousand dollars over budget," Boris Kaufman's "'slowness'" in photographing *Baby Doll* tended to produce effects quite different from the stark, comically grotesque stylization preferred by Kazan. Kaufman had "essentially gone 'Hollywood.'" His photography was academic in mood and technique, a tedious search for the "striking effect of beauty" with an incessant "fussing over trifles." Repeatedly Kazan was forced "to loosen scenes up, break marks, free constricted movements." Analysis of Kaufman's divisive effect on the crew was no less severe (n.d., Wesleyan). Kazan softened his attitude toward "the great cameraman Boris Kaufman" in writing *A Life*.

Boris Kaufman won an Oscar for *On the Waterfront* and was nominated by the Academy for *Baby Doll*. He and Kazan were reunited, under duress, for their final collaboration on *Splendor in the Grass* (1961).] *TL, 2 pp., Wesleyan*

[New York]
May 16, 1956

Gentlemen:

I am now preparing to start on another production—Budd Schulberg's A
FACE IN THE CROWD. It is my present intention to photograph this screenplay half on location in Arkansas, and one-half on a sound stage in New York
City. I would very much like you gentlemen to consider my request to have
Harry Stradling as Director of Photography. My reason for this is that this is
an unusually large and difficult production, on a daring subject. I have a very
tight schedule and a very tight budget. I have worked with Stradling twice
before, most recently on A STREETCAR NAMED DESIRE. I know the way he
works; I know that he will be able to help me meet the schedule and come in
within the budget.

Please be advised this is no reflection on any of your members, many of
whom I know. I will be very happy to work again in future productions with
members of your local. I am planning many future productions which I hope
to base in New York City and the opportunity to work with the craftsmen of
Local 644 will present itself again, I hope, very often. Furthermore, my feeling
towards you men is now and always has been most cordial. It is my sincerest
intention and my deep desire to keep what feature production there now is
in the East here and even to enlarge upon it. It is a dream of mine to make
New York City one of the greatest production centers of the world. I propose
to become increasingly acquainted with the members of your local and I know
that our relations will continue to be based on mutual help and a real understanding of each other's problems.

Of course, it goes without saying that I intend to live-up to absolutely every
rule and regulation of your local. Everyone who has ever worked with me
takes this for granted. I believe that I have earned and deserved the respect
of all the members of the locals that have worked with me on feature productions. I will not in this instance, or in the future, resort to any territorial dodge.
I am now, and hope to be, a good friend of you boys. I make this request to you
now without desire to set up a precedent, but because the special conditions
of this one production, in my opinion, demand it.

Sincerely yours

ek:mf

[Kazan's request to use a California-based photographer was indeed a "reflection"
on Boris Kaufman, as the board of Local 644 knew all too well. Harry Stradling

received permission to join a New York crew and share credit with Jay Rescher in a compromise that nominally protected union rights and encouraged Kazan to remain in the East. Before filming *A Face in the Crowd*, Stradling directed photography for *The Sea of Grass* (1947) and *A Streetcar Named Desire* (1951). Among his many nominations and awards were Oscars for *The Picture of Dorian Gray* (1945) and *My Fair Lady* (1964).] *TL, 1 p., Wesleyan*

TO LEE STRASBERG

[New York]
May 22, 1956

Dear Lee:

Contrary to what has been in the theatrical columns, here is precisely what has been done with Mrs. Eugene O'Neill.

I have told her that I would like to direct O'Neill's play at the Studio, under our conditions, with a cast that we would mutually approve; the play to be rehearsed over a longer rehearsal period, of course, than the Broadway rehearsal term. When the play is ready it will be shown at the Studio, a maximum of five times, this in case we think there is a point in showing the work. The production then could be taken, if she so wishes, and made into a reading. Explicitly expressed was my hope that when the play was mounted and shown, she would then feel that it should be shown not as a reading but as a performance. I have expressed it strongly to the producers—who are Jo Mielziner, Millie Dunnock, and Karl Malden—that I do not approve of the whole reading business, nor do I approve of the implicit spanking of the American theatre suggested by this kind of procedure. I would like, on the other hand, for the play to be done at the Studio under conditions that seem fruitful to me and be shown to a few audiences chosen by us and by her. The audience, of course, to be non-paying. They are taking it up with her and I have told her I would be glad to talk it over with her. I don't know what she will say, but we will know by Thursday. I couldn't bring myself to go for the reading thing for three reasons.

One, the play was written to be performed and I am a <u>theater</u> director. Secondly, the whole thing is sort of a kind of "punishment" for the way, says Mrs. O'Neill, the American theatre treated her husband. And thirdly, a sort of admission that our theatre is inferior to that of Sweden, England, and just about everywhere else in the world.

ek:mf

[Eugene O'Neill stipulated that *Long Day's Journey into Night* not be published until twenty-five years after his death and "'never produced as a play.'" Carlotta Monterey, widow and heir following her husband's death in 1953, dismissed criticism and arranged for the autobiographical work to be published by Random House and performed in Stockholm in early 1956—presumably as a rebuke of the American theater for long neglect of its founder (Gelb, pp. 10–17).

Kazan praised O'Neill's "courage" in facing "the truth about himself and his family" and in April proposed to John Wharton, counsel for the Playwrights' Company, a jointly sponsored production with the Actors Studio. Soon thereafter Carlotta announced that *Long Day's Journey* would tour American colleges in a series of "concert readings" sponsored by Jo Mielziner, Mildred Dunnock, and Karl Malden. The halfway measure fell through, as did Kazan's subsequent plan for a limited Studio production and transfer to Broadway under his direction. Carlotta bypassed the Theatre Guild, O'Neill's former producer, as well as the Actors Studio, and gave the play to José Quintero, director of the original Circle in the Square, a flourishing off-Broadway company. His current staging of *The Iceman Cometh* impressed Brooks Atkinson as "a major production of a major theatre work" and doubtless influenced Carlotta's decision. *Long Day's Journey* opened in November to superb reviews, ran for nearly four hundred performances at the Helen Hayes Theatre, and claimed the major awards.] *TL, 2 pp., Wesleyan*

TO JO MIELZINER

[New York]
June 18, 1956

Dear Mr. Mielziner:
We both shrink from committees and we are fairly impervious to appeals, but the American Committee for Cultural Freedom has gotten under our skins.

It's the only outfit we know that's doing a hard-hitting anti-Communist job and doing it from a liberal point of view. Some of the brightest people we know are active in it. They're civilized, they're hardworking, they're effective. You'll see their statements time and again in the papers, puncturing the latest Soviet false front. You'll also see them taking on neglected civil liberties cases. Last year, for example, they saved two lives by preventing the deportation of two anti-Communists who were up for treason trials in their homelands. The enclosed brochure tells more.

If you take seriously the encroachments of the Communists—and of their opposite numbers on the right—then you agree that somebody has to do these jobs and that they had better be done in a civilized fashion.

We, like you, are busy doing other things. The government says that what we give the Committee is tax deductible, but we don't see it as charity. It's more like insurance.

We're asking you to make the largest contribution that you can.

Sincerely,

Elia Kazan

John Steinbeck

[The American Committee for Cultural Freedom was founded in 1951 "to conduct and promulgate activities designed to further the democratic way of life in all spheres of culture" (bylaws). Lectures, forums, and publications such as Sidney Hook's pamphlet *Heresy, Yes,—Conspiracy, No!* were supported by members as politically diverse as Arthur Schlesinger, Jr., Irving Kristol, and Norman Thomas. Dispelling liberal illusions about communism went hand in hand with defending free thought and rational discourse. Shortly after the release of *Baby Doll* in 1956, the committee publicly criticized "efforts" by the Legion of Decency to suppress distribution and prevent non-Catholics from seeing the film. Senator Joseph McCarthy's zeal in exposing alleged communists was one of the more controversial issues debated by the membership before chronic financial problems ended operations in 1957. Long-standing rumors of CIA funding were confirmed in the 1960s (Hook, pp. 420–31).

James T. Farrell, Thornton Wilder, and Elia Kazan were cited in a recent *Times* editorial as illustrious committee members, who had advanced the "struggle against Communist efforts to woo the world's intellectuals" (March 25, 1955).]
TLS, 1 p., BRTC

TO JOHN D. ROCKEFELLER III

[New York]

June 20, 1956

Dear Mr. Rockefeller:

I was going to write you at length as I promised. However, my own experience with long letters is unfortunate. For the writers, I mean: I don't read them. Some of what I might have said was in Walter Kerr's Sunday piece in the Herald Tribune.

Currently, I will only say that we are prepared to take over a season of six months at the new Lincoln Square project. The effort of the Actors' Studio there would be administered by Cheryl Crawford, Lee Strasberg and myself. The players will be chosen from the pool of talent whom we have trained and prepared. Their names have been listed so often that I won't waste your time with them here.

Our repertoire will be based on our own dramatic American literature, but would also include, in a minor role, plays from world dramatic literature. But our fundamental intention would be to make our people and the world aware and proud of the work and importance of the American Theatre—its plays, its craftsmen, their techniques and their talents.

In direct functional relationship to the theatre operation would be a training program. This would be an enlargement of the program we now run. It would include work with young directors and playwrights as well as actors, but would not be a dramatic school. There are enough dramatic schools, good and bad. Our work will be only with talented young professionals and the work with them will lead directly to work before an audience on-stage. The studio room will be connected by direct corridor with the stage.

There are more factors, many details to discuss, but the above essentializes our proposal. I'd appreciate it if we could hear soon on the degree of your interest. If it is concrete and substantial, we will get together and talk everything out to the last item. I believe we could be of great help, for instance, in planning the design and layout of the building itself. We will wait to hear from you.

Sincerely yours

ek:mf
cc: Crawford

[Launched by Robert Moses, New York State's official master builder, the "Lincoln Square project" quickly found critics who condemned the displacement of minority residents and ridiculed the vast scale of the proposed arts center. In retrospect Lincoln Kirstein understated neither the cultural value of the enterprise nor the underlying motive of the "originators," which "was, and remains, the control of real property" (Kirstein, p. 8). For the Metropolitan Opera and the New York Philharmonic, original "constituents" of the center, slum clearance in a seventeen-block area of the Upper West Side met a pressing need for new quarters in Manhattan. Kirstein, an originator himself, founded the New York City Ballet in collaboration with George Balanchine and helped to design its new stage at Lincoln Center. On June 22, 1956, papers of incorporation were filed and a board of directors elected John D. Rockefeller president of the "Lincoln Center for the Performing Arts." A fund-raising drive with a goal of $75 million was unrolled in 1957, while New York City sold acreage marked for urban renewal at subsidized prices.

Kazan wrote on behalf of the Actors Studio after an exploratory committee recommended adding "units" in ballet, drama, and voice to the original membership. On cue Walter Kerr praised the Studio for having "literally given birth to the clearest, most carefully defined, most virile approach to the player's craft that the American theater has produced." The ability of Kazan and his colleagues "to set new playwrights in motion," a strategic nod at theatrical production, had established the Studio as a "creative force that breathes the air of the living moment

and that somehow stamps on its members a character that is peculiarly American"
(*NYHT,* June 17, 1956). Kazan sidestepped the Studio's lack of a resident company
and uneven production history by envisioning a "direct corridor" from training to
performance "on-stage." Whether he recalled Arthur Miller's description of the
Studio as "a reservoir with no pipe leading out of it" is unclear (*NYT,* August 21,
1955).] *TLx, 2 pp., BRTC*

TO JACK L. WARNER

SH: Newtown Productions, Inc.
1545 Broadway, New York 36, N.Y.
July 25, 1956

Dear Jack:

I talked to Ben Kalmenson and after congratulating him properly on his new
rise to fame, fortune, and headaches, I sprung the idea of the big sign on him
and his enthusiasm was very moderate. However, I kept at it and he said I
could have anything I wanted—if it wasn't too expensive, that is. He is terribly
friendly to me and I to him, but I really hate to have anything done on the basis
of friendship, Old Boy, despite my English blood and my high-tone upbring-
ing. I'm telling you so-and-so's that this is the greatest idea since the days
of Barnum. That half-sleeping, day-dreaming, thumb-sucking, long-legged
chick, astride one-block long with only Warner Bros. (small type, of course),
Tennessee Williams and yours truly's names on the sign, and a big arrow pointing down to the Victoria Theatre will be the talk not only of Broadway, but of
the show world, of cafe society, of the literati, of the lowbrows, and of everybody else. I really don't see how anybody could avoid going to the picture if we
put that sign up there. What's wrong with show business is that its balls have
been cut off and it is no longer show business. No one showboats anymore.
There is no flash in it. It is too damn much like television. That's why I don't
want to start taking out "niggers" and "wops" and every other damn thing that
will tame the script down. I tame nothing down, Jack. It is hard enough to get
them into the bloody theatres when something is wild and strong and unusual.
I have put a big motto up in my office. It says simply, "You can't see it on TV".
Television doesn't allow "nigger" and "wop" and all kinds of sexual murmurs,
etc. Now that we have the new era at Warner Bros., let's be bold. I repeat: let's
be bold. Let's judiciously spend a lot of money in a few places that are the right
places. I'm talking again about the sign. I would rather have this sign than an
ad in "Life" and "Look". I think "Life" would publish a little news story on it,
maybe. I do think it will be one big, bold, irresistible come-on.

"The greatest idea since the days of Barnum": Baby Doll rests above
the Victoria Theater on Broadway

Trust my instinct. I'm known as the Greek Barnum and I care like a son of a bitch.

Love and kisses
Gadg.

ek:mf

P.S. When I got through dictating this letter to my secretary, who is a helluva bright girl, she said, "Gee, that's a wonderful idea!" Everybody else I have mentioned it to likes it. It's old fashioned show business, man. You remember. Remember when you were in vaudeville, Jack, and people weren't afraid to say: you gotta see this show. Pictures sort of slink in now, if you know what I mean.

[With some hesitation Tennessee Williams approved "Baby Doll" as the film's provocative title. "Mississippi Woman" ran a far second in Kazan's estimation. Ben Kalmenson, recently appointed executive vice president of Warner Bros., disliked the new title and proposed exploitation, although Kazan trusted that he and Jack Warner would respect his intention "to take a personal and creative part" in publicizing the film (to JLW, December 21, 1955, Wesleyan).

"Baby Doll, with seventy-five foot legs and eight-foot eyebrows, is emerging in brave color, day by day, on a block-long billboard on the west side of Times Square." So wrote a *Times* reporter several months before the film's premiere on

December 18. He added that when Baby Doll "is finished she will be one of the biggest girls ever done in true proportion anywhere on earth—135 feet long from toes to loose-flung red-blond locks, and sixty feet high" (*NYT*, October 22, 1956). Kazan's "pictorialist" was no random choice. He designed the towering likeness of Marilyn Monroe, fifty-two feet high with skirt famously uplifted, for the opening of *The Seven Year Itch* in 1955.

Kazan retained "nigger" and "wop" in editing *Baby Doll* despite enhanced prohibition of offensive "appellations" in the revised Production Code. Jack Warner did stand "bold" in approving Kazan's exploitation of *Baby Doll* and in a forthcoming conflict with the Legion of Decency.] *TLS, 2 pp., WB Archives*

TO H. WILLIAM FITELSON

[New York]
September 10, 1956

Dear Bill:

About my using Godfrey's name in the scene. Originally, the line was different and had Herb Shriner's name in it. The line read: "Get Herb Shriner or somebody to fill in tomorrow. Counting on you to hold the fort." Shriner, who has been doing a lot of fill-ins, apparently didn't like the idea of being identified as a fill-in and didn't like the "or somebody". He refused to give permission to have this line used.

Filming Andy Griffith and Lee Remick in *A Face in the Crowd*

Godfrey has already given us clearance to use his name in one mention. This new phrasing is as follows: "See if you can get Arthur Godfrey to fill in for me. Tell him I'll do the same for him some day." This puts Lonesome on the same basis as Godfrey and also makes clear that Lonesome is not Godfrey. Is my legal brain okay or am I off? I can't see how Godfrey can object. He does exist and is a public figure, does work in the TV business and there is no derogatory reference in the phrase.

Let me know what Floria thinks and give me your opinion/opinions on this.

ek:mf

[The questionable line was used in *A Face in the Crowd,* as were distinctive features of Arthur Godfrey's radio and television career in shaping the character of Lonesome Rhodes. Both relied on a folksy manner to attract large audiences, and both were master salesmen who ridiculed standard advertising copy while substituting their own unimpeachable testimony. Godfrey's association with corporate and military figures was also reflected in the political ambition of Lonesome Rhodes. The on-air firing of Julius La Rosa, one of the "Little Godfreys" who sang on the weekly variety show, caused a backlash in 1953 from which Arthur Godfrey never entirely recovered (Singer). He knew far better than his fictional counterpart the risk of failure: "That little screen is merciless and if you aren't constantly more interesting and intriguing, they—the public—will drop you, ruthlessly."] *TL,* 1 *p., Wesleyan*

TO PHILIP K. SCHEUER

SH: Newtown Productions, Inc.
1545 Broadway, New York 36, N.Y.
December 12, 1956

Dear Phil:

I was shocked to see in a piece by you in the "Times" that you thought BABY DOLL immoral. I knew you had certain reservations and in your first review you said something about there being a suggestion of abnormal sexual practice, or something of the kind. I know you couldn't be more specific in your review, but would you mind dropping me a note and letting me know why you think the picture is immoral. You are the only reviewer so far, except Louella Parsons, who said this and I know you too well to confuse you with her. I take your opinion seriously and I'm really curious. I'm not trying to chide you or anything, believe me, I just want to know what you mean.

Sincerely
Gadg.

ek:mf

[*Baby Doll* "is immoral, with unmistakable overtones of sex deviation." Carroll Baker's "unconscious" sexuality set her apart from the voluptuous "Marilyn Monroes of today" and apparently unnerved Philip Scheuer with a strong hint of infantile sexuality. The sadistic revenge plot launched by Silva Vacarro, complete with whip, was also disturbing. Before the controversy broke, Scheuer foresaw that nothing in recent memory could prepare audiences for the "strange" emotions released by the film (*Los Angeles Times,* November 25, 1956).

Francis Cardinal Spellman denounced *Baby Doll* from the pulpit of St. Patrick's Cathedral before the film opened in mid-December. The "'revolting theme'" and "'brazen advertising'" posed a grave threat to Catholics, who were forbidden to see the film "'under pain of sin.'" To forestall criticism of Catholic censorship, Monsignor Thomas F. Little stated that in condemning *Baby Doll*, the Legion had "no discussions whatsoever" with Warner Bros. or Kazan (*NYT*, December 30, 1956). Nor was there any sign of back-door negotiation with Martin Quigley or the Production Code Administration, which had approved *Baby Doll* in the preceding September. The film was a solid, if unspectacular, performer in New York but faltered as bans, picketing, and boycotts of theaters limited distribution and attendance. To Spellman, who also impugned the patriotism of the film's producers, Kazan answered that in America "'judgments on matters of thought and taste are not handed down ironclad by an unchallengeable authority'" (*NYT*, December 17, 1956). Tennessee Williams declined "'to reply aggressively to a beloved dignitary of a great church'" when asked to comment on Spellman's criticism (Williams/ *Conversations*, p. 57).] *TLS, 1 p., Herrick*

TO ROBERT ARDREY

[New York]
March 6, 1957

Dear Bob:

I just came back from California. There was no smog, but all the other features were there. You are not missing anything; it's the same. A few more cracks in the plaster, considerably more nervousness at Metro, and the TV people cockier than ever. Marilyn Monroe, the "front", has been replaced by Vikki Dougan, the "back". This girl was at an award party where she made a presentation for the Foreign Press of Hollywood. She wore a dress that was cut so low in the back that you could see the cleavage. This caused a sensation. Only a few people thought it was in bad taste, the rest of them measured it correctly as a successful publicity thrust. Miss Dougan's back was as good as a headline in the Hollywood Reporter. She told me later that she designed the dress herself and knew just what she was doing. It's a remarkable place.

I haven't written to you about the TVA story because I have had an awful lot of trouble with A FACE IN THE CROWD. In the first place, it has been very hard to cut and in the second place, when it was put together, two large holes were apparent in the continuity. I had to do some added scenes (at my salary level retakes are called added scenes) and I think I have the thing lined up right now. And I think it's pretty good. We're still working hard on the score and the final editing, but I found time to go to California and start something on the TVA project.

I don't know whether I ever told you this, but there was a point in my work on A FACE IN THE CROWD where Fox could have stopped me. It was the time in my old Fox contract agreement for me to do a picture for them. And I had three more pictures to go. But under the gentler regime of Buddy Adler, they were generous and I made a settlement with them in which I promised to make my next one for them at my old salary figure and wash up the old contract entirely. I'm anxious to terminate the contract with them and I think I'm lucky to get away with just one picture.

Anyway, to get to the point, the next picture I'm going to do is the TVA and I'm going to do it for them. This changes everything I have talked to you about in regards to becoming involved as a partner and sharing in profits. I won't share in any profits myself. I'll just get a flat fee and the writer that works with me will have to make an arrangement directly with Fox. This is not the way I talked to you about it, I know, but I can't help what happened. Fox had me pretty well tied up.

The other change has to do with another thing that we talked about. When the project was at some distance, it seemed conceivable to me that we could do some research here together and that you could then write it in Europe. But when I got right down to it, I was not too keen on this plan. In the first place, I feel now that I want to be equally involved with the author in the evolution of the story line. I have done this now with the last four and the results may have been critically mixed, but personally they were satisfying. I not only like to do it, I think the only way I will get better at it is to keep on doing it. What worries me about our being apart is the fear that it may put a time limit on this collaborative aspect. I don't want to write a line of dialogue, but I do want to be creatively involved in the choice, shape, and telling of any stories I do from now on in. This sounds formidable in print, but I feel sure that in practice you would like it. I have done it with Steinbeck, Williams, and Schulberg and we had no problem. In other words, as a producer, I would function the way a producer does and should in films.

The third thing that has happened that is different is that there is one kernel of the story idea—the island in the river—which comes from the Huie book and to which I'm strongly committed in my mind. Aside from that, the screenplay would be a completely new creation. This can't be done in a hurry and it should be done, it seems to me, after very thorough contact with the people and environment down there. To put it in a phrase, I think we will find our story down there.

I have no plans after the opening of A FACE IN THE CROWD (on May 30). I will start slowly, taking trips down there, talking to people here in New York, Washington, Knoxville, and on the scene itself and gradually get an idea of what seems to me like "the story". One of the first things I want to do is milk Huie for everything he remembers. Another first thing I want to do is to go to Knoxville and talk to the old timers who were around the project in the mid-thirties and get their memories and reminiscences. And I want to ride the area thoroughly in my jeep.

I'm giving you all this, Bob, so that you will know how I'm thinking now. I don't know what you have been doing (except the Reporter articles, which I enjoyed enormously). I don't know what you are thinking now or how you will react to all of this, so write me and tell me.

I wouldn't want to minimize, and I hope I haven't, how collaborative I think the preparation of a film script should be, and I'm sorry this Fox situation changed the profit possibilities of this project for a writer, but I just couldn't help that. As for the time you should spend with me—well, I don't think either of us can make up anything as exciting and original as what we'll dig up on the scene. This I feel from recent experience.

I thought to start work some time around the first of May. Work being the field trips. I realize in a sense I'm presenting you with a different project and I can understand your not wanting to go into this. I hope you will though. At any rate, write me about it and we'll discuss it by mail.

My love to Helen, to Ross and to Dan.

Best

ek:mf

[*Casey Jones* (1938) and *Thunder Rock* (1939), each directed by Kazan, closed after brief runs without fulfilling the early promise of Robert Ardrey's dramatic career. Thereafter Ardrey became proficient in the "editorial arts," as Kazan put it, and worked primarily in film and television. Collaboration with Kazan on *Wild River* promised to relieve Ardrey's familiar complaint that "no one yet has evolved a system for making films which does not leave the author-writer in a constrained position" (to EK, November 27, 1955, Wesleyan). Ardrey was "disappointed" to learn of the "Fox situation," which precluded plans for an independent production.

Vikki Dougan parlayed daring attire into a minor film career, including a part in *The Great Man* (1956), an exposé of the radio industry released shortly before *A Face in the Crowd*.

Kazan met Barbara Loden at a recording studio in New York while finishing *A Face in the Crowd*. An aspiring young actress from North Carolina, "she observed none of the conventional middle-class boundaries" and was not "in awe" of Kazan's reputation. Their ensuing affair was intense, intermittent, and often divisive but a timely stimulus for Kazan—forty-seven and subject to recurring self-doubt (*A Life*, pp. 571–73).

Buddy Adler administered a far less uniform studio system as Darryl Zanuck's successor at Twentieth Century-Fox. Kazan made no secret of his displeasure with Fox, nor was the financial return of his last three films a strong incentive for Adler to enforce the present contract.] *TL, 3 pp., Wesleyan*

TO JOHN D. ROCKEFELLER III

[New York]
March 14, 1957

Dear Mr. Rockefeller:

Let me start by putting it this way. We are ready to assume the responsibility of creating a Theatre in one of the Lincoln Square Theatre buildings. The artists would come from the people we have trained at the ACTORS' STUDIO. Its repertoire would be largely based on the American classics; its leadership and responsibility would be solely ours.

I first state this fact—our willingness and readiness to assume this responsibility—because you must realize, as we do, that it is not only a most sobering responsibility, but an enormous job of work. I asked Jean-Louis Barrault when he was here how long they took to rehearse the repertoire they played here on their recent visit—how many weeks. His answer was: twenty years.

We will not require twenty years, but this is the reason why when one of you said at our last get together that the Theatre Building would not be ready until 1960, none of us was dismayed. We could well use three years of preparation. A part of the work: the creation and training of a fine group of Actors has already been largely accomplished. But the planning and preparation of six productions of the kind we want to create—this would take a real piece of time.

And the reason for this is the simplest possible. We are only interested in the whole project if we can truly aim for the BEST. There have been attempts to create companies playing repertoire in recent years. They have all had on them the stamp of an intolerable mediocrity. To speak plainly, the impression was that actors who could not get good jobs elsewhere had been banded together at cut salaries to play "worthy" but dusty plays in literal and pedestrian productions.

We have neither the time nor the patience to be "worthy" or "arty." We are, each of the three of us, very busy on our own projects and enterprises. And we are all deeply interested in what we are doing. We would only give up what we are doing now and assume so heavy a responsibility for the opportunity to create something superlative. Anything short of this absolute goal is not worth the years, and the effort.

We would have and in fact do now have sources of financing. We have had a preliminary talk with several of our people and they have evinced the strongest possible interest. But in each case we stressed to them that our budget would not be a "modest" one. For instance we have no intention (in the words of an earlier repertory Theatre project) of making up for the lack of scenery by the art of suggestion. We want the scenery, elaborate or simple, whichever is right for each particular production to be doing its full job as part of the whole. By nature no one of us is extravagant. But our sights would be set only towards the most perfect goal on the stage—not on a housewifely budget. We have access to and would obtain the best acting talent in this country. As producers and directors we would work long and hard to produce a Theatre of which our Nation can be justly proud. Everything would take its scale from this.

I have stressed in previous letters to you the importance of a patriotic element in our impulse to do this job. We have all eaten a little too much crow in our overseas visits. But while we have often resented the supercilious superiority of some Europeans towards our culture, there were, nevertheless, certain facts we had to face. It was true and is true that while we are the richest country in the world, we still have no repertory Theatre. While we are the richest country in the world we have no single up to date Theatre building, in fact stopped building theatres twenty years ago. While we are the richest country in the world the back stage equipment at our best professional Theatres is disgracefully short of what is available in the best European Theatres. Poor democracies who live on the Marshall plan are often better equipped in this respect than we are. For instance, there is still no professional Theatre in this country that has an electronic Switchboard. We cannot "afford" it.

And, much more serious, we have allowed our Theatre Classics to sit on the shelves of our libraries and gather dust. Until a couple of years ago you had to travel to the Scandinavian peninsula or to Athens to see a play by Eugene O'Neill on the stage. Here a play opens, and no matter what its importance and meaningfulness, it plays its course and is forgotten. Actually we have, as I asserted in earlier letters to you, a body of contemporary dramatic literature that deserves the name of classic. I am not a scholar and have no interest in comparing it with the Elizabethan drama or the Greek plays of the 5th century B.C. The importance that our American plays of the last forty years have, that interests me, is the importance for us. They are our dramatic tradition, a source of inspiration for future playwrights, a source of understanding for our people of their own lives and times. They comprise a truly popular Theatre. They are part of our National Resources. The best of them should be kept alive, seen every few years for the sake of the meaning they have for us. The O'Neill plays, "Death of a Salesman," "Skin of Our Teeth," "Our Town," "The Glass Menagerie," "Streetcar Named Desire," "Awake and Sing," "Golden Boy," "Abe Lincoln in Illinois," "Mister Roberts," "Pal Joey"—I could go on and on, but these plays come immediately to mind, they are our culture, our tradition, who we are, what we have to say, what we are anxious about and what we are proud of; our understanding of ourselves and of each other expressed in the terms of the Art of the Theatre. They should be continuously on view in our Theatre Capital and on tour—much as we can from time to time hear the great works for the Symphony orchestra.

You may ask why, since I feel so strongly about all this, have we made no effort until now to mount and run such an institution. I will briefly try to answer this.

No real step forward can be taken until the way has been prepared. The wish is not enough. Nor is an act of will enough. For years Lee Strasberg, Cheryl Crawford and I knew that the real goal of the Actors' Studio could only be the kind of Theatre I am describing. But, at the same time, and out of the same knowledge, no one knew as well as we did what the difficulties were.

The conditions that must exist for the creation of a Theatre are very special and severely demanding. First of all there must exist a leadership, people who are both experienced and devoted, at the same time both artists and administrators. They must have the poise, confidence, and power that comes only from years of experience and still possess the devotion and enthusiasm, the idealism which is usually associated only with young people.

Secondly, the artistic and craft level of the people who will work in the Theatre must be high, in fact the highest. An audience must not be asked to come to the Theatre to support a "worthy cause." The product ON STAGE must be unique. It must be superlatively exciting. We have all seen too many Theatre groups founder and collapse because the Theatre product was well intentioned but mediocre. Nor are idealistic pronouncements enough.

Thirdly, there has to be in existence a large group of trained Theatre artists— actors pre-eminently—of the first calibre. And they have to be devoted and committed. The heart of the Theatre is its ensemble, its corps of actors who make up its body. They cannot be willed into existence. A manager, no matter how well intentioned or eloquent, going about with a sheaf of yearly contracts in hand cannot find them. We have all hoped that one day there would exist in America a Great acting company to rival any in the world, but wishing cannot do it.

Fourthly, such a Theatre if it is to be truly sound must be a Popular Theatre, in the same sense that Shakespeare's theatre was a popular Theatre. (In fact all great theatres have been popular Theatres. They give dramatic utterance to the spirits and preoccupations of the people of their day; are truly "meaningful.") The artist, in other words, had to be not only highly trained and highly responsible, but also had to be OUT OF the fabric of their life and times. Without trying, as it were, the artists had to Speak to the audience. The converse is an animated library.

And the fifth essential for the creation of a true Theatre must be the right kind of physical plant, the actual Theatre building necessary to house this type of operation. Only the existence of such a Theatre building would make the planning of a Theatre like this a practical activity.

These five requirements are rigid and not easily met. And each of us would not be ready to assume the leadership responsibility of such an enterprise if we did not believe, that for the first time in our Theatre history, all these requirements can be met and satisfied.

First of all we believe that the proper leadership for such an enterprise is now in existence. The fact that the theatre and film world has recognized the work of Lee Strasberg would not suffice for us if we did not see the work and recognize its quality. He has proved his right to the position of leadership. His work with actors is widely acknowledged as the best in the world today. Cheryl Crawford has had more experience and actually knows more about the administration of a real Theatre than anyone in this country. She was one of the co-founders of the Group Theatre, the boldest as well as the soundest theatre endeavor we have ever had in this country. Elia Kazan is completely a product of this kind of Theatre movement and this fact taken with his broad general experience make him fitted to assume the other third of the leadership responsibility.

No Theatre has ever or can ever endure without a strong and unified leadership. Nor can a Theatre be governed by committee. Nor can there be a workable distinction between its chief artists and its administrators. If the triumvirate of leadership, as I have described it, did not exist, it could not be created or willed into existence. The fact that they have a harmony of taste and understanding which has been proven over the years is unique, as is also their particular combination of artistic and administrative abilities.

Behind these three people there are not only people of talent but people of large talent. The gush of talent that has come out of the Actors' Studio in the last few years has actually amazed the world. And here again this could not have been willed into existence. It came about through work and time. It's as though, in the back of the minds of the people who started and worked in the Studio, the goal of a Theatre was always intended.

A glance at the list of Studio members which is appended to this letter will reveal many names already recognized as the finest young actors in the country. Another look, a few years hence, will reveal many more names that you will then recognize. And since talent and nothing else makes Theatre—our talent promises the finest theatre in our history.

Behind these top talents are a hundred or so finely trained young actors who will be the force from which our ensemble will be drawn. They all are trained to work together. (And the method of training has too amply proven itself in results and broad recognition to need defense.) But despite the recognition of so many individual performers the Studio has never yet been seen as a UNIFIED EFFORT. We have still to show to the theatre public the extent and the solidarity of our work. . . .

Now as to the "Popular" nature of our Theatre. We could not be anything but an American Theatre. It is the tradition of the Group Theatre from which we came. It is the tradition of work of the three directors. It can be seen in the kind of plays we have produced and directed and in our films too. It is with an eye to what is most alive in contemporary life that we have chosen our young actors for membership in the Studio. Our aspiration is to a live theatre—a Theatre which says in dramatic terms things that are meaningful and "alive" to a contemporary audience. The Old Vic should and does do English plays, the Comedie Francaise, the French classics, and an American Theatre should put before our people and keep available to them American plays with real meaning for them.

The core of our repertoire would be the Contemporary American classics, those plays of the last forty years which illuminate the contemporary experience. But we would not confine ourselves to these works. Perhaps it would be the production of an older play, or the production of a play from another land which will be significant or meaningful to us today. We would be free and in fact charged to do such a production. And hopefully we would look for new plays of this calibre.

And now to my final requisite: the Physical plant. A Theatre such as the one I've been sketching cannot operate in a Broadway house. This is not a spiritual observation. It is concretely so. There is not enough rehearsal space. There is not enough storage space. Above all there is not the plastic elasticity backstage and in the stage mechanics to make any production except the standard type (or some narrow variation) possible.

Now for the first time, men of responsibility and conscience are preparing to build new theatre buildings. If your group and ours can get together on the operation of one of them, our very first request would be to consult on the physical plant that you would build. Space requirements, mechanical and equipment requirements, the light units and their control devices should all be chosen carefully with an eye to this particular type of enterprise. If correctly chosen all these physical elements would help make this Theatre more exciting, more unusual, more unique.

To sum up briefly for a moment, we think we now have in hand or at ready the very special and severe requirements necessary for the creation in this country of the best in Theatre, the forces, the experience, the knowledge, the talent, the spirit in the air, the physical plant in plan, the existing repertoire, the desire and the desire in the right people.

Now it comes to more particular planning. Here rhetoric and generalizations are not enough. We have asked Miss Crawford to provisionally put down some plans in more concrete form.

[A committee charged with defining criteria for new units reported that in addition to setting "artistic standards of the highest quality," each must have "an institutional framework designed to assure continuity and financial stability" (Young, pp. 56–57). Neither ANTA (American National Theatre and Academy) nor the Actors Studio, rival contenders for the drama sponsorship, could approach the establishment or equity of the Metropolitan Opera, the Philharmonic, or the Juilliard School of Music, recently admitted to Lincoln Center. In representing the Studio, Kazan overstated its financial resources and organizational coherence, while glossing over the perennial workshop-theater debate that hampered production. With reference to artistic "results" that need no "defense," he also underestimated resistance to the Studio's controversial training of actors in the Stanislavsky system. Lee Strasberg's indecision and tortuous syntax are evident in remarks concluding the Studio's tenth season: "'Certainly while the vista intrigues us, the responsibility slightly, not exactly frightens us, but nonetheless appalls us. We're not easily frightened. We bear up. But it is not a light goal or task to undertake. So I frankly do not quite know what is to happen'" (Garfield, p. 127).] *TL, 6 pp., Houston*

TO TENNESSEE WILLIAMS

[New York]
March 27, 1957

Dear Tenn:
I called you this morning before I left town. The answering service got it and said that you were working and I was over-whelmed with admiration at your new efficiency. I feel strongly that I should say something to you and not dissolve into silence. I owe it to you and even though what I have to say isn't too pleasant, I will try to say it exactly the way I feel.

First of all, I think more work should have been done on the script. I know you will say to this that you did an enormous amount of work and that it says exactly what you want, but I still stand by what I just said. I think you should have gotten more of a fight from somebody; a tougher, a keener, or possibly more unpleasant collaborator, telling you more objectively what was wrong with the script, where it was unclear, where it was too sudden, where it appeared unmotivated and abrupt. In fact, you needed someone to take the chance that I took in CAT. To take the chance that you would be resentful later and feel that you had been too strongly influenced. A perfect script doesn't need a strong director. "Orpheus", which is full of brilliance, full of real feeling, full of true observations and full of real poetry, did need a stronger collaboration with a tougher guy, whether producer or director, in the preparatory stages. You might have written another preface saying, "I didn't really mean that, that version you saw on the Broadway stage", but still I think all in all you would have been happier now.

At the risk of appearing invidious, I must say too that I think an ordinary job was done by the director. I didn't like the setting at all. I thought it cluttered and often tasteless. I thought a lot of the acting was "theatric" in the bad sense of the word, and I thought the costumes were too heavily colored. Of course, the older I get, the narrower my vision seems to get. I can only see things one way—the way I would do them—and I suppose I'm developing into an opinionated egotist. I take the chance that you'll say that when I write you this way, but I know that I have got to tell you what I think really and truly and I trust that you will realize that this letter is only for you and not for anyone elses eyes. Please don't think that I mean that I would have done it better. I may have, but it is just that the more difficult things we attempt, the tougher and sterner we have to be with ourselves and with each other.

I think Maureen Stapleton is a brilliant actress, for instance, a really wonderful talent. Absolutely true and honest, but I think she was miscast for the play. She had the wrong personality in that spot. She strongly gives you the impression that she is competent to take care of herself, that she has combated it and at the bottom healthy. She didn't appear to me like "Lady". Cliff I thought was very good. Lois I thought wonderful for the part, but indulgent as an actress and untethered so that she was often tasteless, even self-favoring, narcissistic, etc.

One last negative impression. I thought you were a little too tough on Southern people in general. I know they can be cruel and violent, but like everyone else they always have a reason for it and I thought too often your "heavies" behaved liked stage "heavies" and not as fellows who have their own type, their rationale and self-esteem.

Right about in here I thought "should I send this to Tennessee. He has 'tsouras' as it is", but I really would be a lousy friend if I didn't send it and I am really a loving and true friend and always will be no matter what.

ek:mf

[Kazan shared the critical consensus that for all its "beauty" and "compassion," *Orpheus Descending* lacked "a satisfying singleness of purpose." The much revised play opened on March 21 and closed after sixty-eight performances, barely outlasting *Camino Real*. Notices for Harold Clurman's direction were respectful, while Maureen Stapleton's portrayal of Lady Torrance was widely praised. Cliff Robertson played the male lead and Lois Smith a featured role, to Kazan's greater satisfaction. Tennessee Williams addressed his reluctant savior once it was clear *Orpheus* would close: "I think your appreciation of its basic truth would have inspired me to lift it above its theatricalism. . . . You could have staged the ending so it would play and score. You would have found the 'key' in which the play is written, not just intellectually but with an artist's and a poet's vision" (to EK, April 3, 1957, Wesleyan).

The "original" and "Broadway" versions of act three appeared in the first edition of *Cat on a Hot Tin Roof* (New Directions, 1955) with an authorial "preface" that Kazan considered misleading and subtly vindictive. Williams noted the "dangers" of working with "a powerful and highly imaginative director," before claiming that he and Kazan had "avoided" the risk because of their "deepest mutual respect."

Nonetheless a stark listing of Kazan's "suggestions" for revising act three, combined with the author's preference for the original and fear of losing the director's "interest," added fuel to the third act controversy and hurt Kazan professionally—feelings he reserved for later correspondence.] *TL, 2 pp., Wesleyan*

TO JUDY KAZAN

PM: New York, NY, May 5, 1957

Dear Judy:

No wonder you think we're once in a while completely dead. Especially me. I dont write you at all. I think about you a lot and I love you a lot. But I dont write you at all. You know part of the reason. I'm Chris' father and he's inherited some of my compulsive solitude or whatever the hell it is. Another reason is that I get awful intense about these movies I do. I become, in fact, obsessed with them. Right now I literally cannot think of much else. I'm on this thing all the time. I keep making small changes and readjustments and cuts and reinterpretations until my film editor is beginning to go nuts. Anatole France once said that a work of art is never finished, its abandoned. You can say even worse about me. They will have to take the negative away from me. And, as a matter of fact, they are on the verge of doing that. But I am very aware that I make it now and it exists for the rest of my life and people judge me, and I judge myself from it. So I really bend over it and do my damnedest. I think its a good deal improved since you saw it. But, probably not from your point of view. I mean its as mean spirited as ever. Bitter, they say. Well its hard to talk about TV and TV's commercial side, and the big agencies and the Commercials etc. etc. without getting a little nasty, if not more so. A few people have seen it and they come out of it as though they had suddenly contracted a very severe headache. They rush out of the room looking for air and comfort and quiet. A lot of people say too loud and too oppressive and too long. Its discouraging a little. But I didn't compromise while making it and have no one to blame but myself, so now, if it comes to that, I've got to stand still and take my medicine. Anyway I can work on it maybe two more weeks, maybe, and that will be that. We're going to preview it next week in South Orange New Jersey. Which gives me a chance to study Granny's reaction! Now why the hell it should be arranged that I show this thing to that poor woman, I dont know. I imagine this would be the most complete mismating in history. And the touching thing is that after she sees one of these horrors that I make, which rock her sense of taste and value and what a polite son in law should provide as entertainment for a well bred mother in law—well she's so polite and sweet and just faintly puzzled, but determined not to inflict her bewilderment on me as a burden. Oh well—One important piece of news has to do with Sandy Hook. They passed the bill to go ahead and tar the road between our land and the Foster's—there was some move to stop this, but it failed, and they are going ahead with a "state" type road. In fact they've already been there and put stakes on our land, straightening everything out into some mediocre pattern. So Molly and I are going up Sunday and see if we can do anything in the way of obstructionism. You'll hear how it turns out—Everything else is o.k. I mean, spring is here and May is beautiful and I've taken to the backyard, and the food is good, and Nick K is growing up in a fashion that still surprises me—after watching it with you and Chris, twice before, still surprising. Molly is a new woman, the centre of a fascinating commotion, being consulted, her approval and favor sought, dates made to her convenience, pointed to as being that mysterious figure: the "author", and rejecting and half approving, and asking for another reading and in general being the source of employment and possible good things for actors. She looks better and feels better and its really quite a phenomenon, coming comparatively late in her life as it has. Very noble. Very noble. Anyway, this sudden burst of communication is because you sqwacked (misspelled) ever so gently, which should teach you a lesson ITS GOOD TO SQUACK. If you're right, yell hard.

Love, from Daddy

[Kazan's tinkering with *A Face in the Crowd* would take a serious turn with news that the Legion of Decency planned to condemn the film. "Granny," Elia's mother-in-law, lived in South Orange and presumably attended the local preview.

Plans to stage *The Egghead* accounted for the "commotion" surrounding Molly Kazan, the "mysterious" author. Principal casting was complete and rehearsals set to begin on August 19 with direction by Hume Cronyn.] *TLS, 1 p., JKMP*

TO BEN KALMENSON

[New York]
May 20, 1957

Dear Ben:

Budd and I met yesterday and had a good talk about our problem with the Legion of Decency. Before suggesting concretely what we'd be willing to do in the way of deletions, I'd like to call a couple of things to your attention— just for the record. I think the plainer we are with each other, at all times, the better our relationship.

First place, make no mistake about it, I am very appreciative of Warner Brothers and the way they have dealt with me. I was always given complete freedom within my contract, and I was always treated with real generosity and understanding. And, I do understand your problem now. I mean your problem with exhibitors and your problem in relation to cost.

But I don't want to disguise certain other developments. First, no matter how disguised by polite palaver, I am being asked not only to get a seal from MPAA, but I am also being required to get the approval of the Legion of Decency for my picture. This is not our contractual arrangement.

In the second place, no matter whether you meant it entirely seriously or only partly seriously, you did say that if I did not get the approval of the Legion of Decency, you would not release the picture. This puts us in the peculiar position, Budd and I, of having worked two years on a film, meeting every contractual obligation, only to see the film not released. Neither of us can afford this, to put it mildly. We'd have to sue you if you did any such thing, and we would. Plainly, it is a breach of contract.

Another point. Plainly we do not want to make any changes. We did everything the Seal of the MPAA requires and MORE. We are convinced that this picture will not offend the theatre-goer, except for a very, very special group. The fact is that despite Martin's soft voice and polite manner, Budd and I were sitting there being threatened. We were threatened with Boycott and Picketing if we did not alter our film. This is an extremely humiliating position to be in, and we resent it like hell.

Frankly, too, we do not know how much he is bargaining and how much he means. We do not even know that if we comply with his requests which were broad and vague, what would prevent the Legion (which Martin stated was not at all committed by him) from coming forward with more requests. Their technique, Martin's and the Legion's, is a very effective one. In effect, we feel we might finally be asked to do almost anything they see fit to ask. You yourself said that if your contract with me was other than what it is you would "do anything". You'd jump cut, you'd harm story elements, etc., in short, you'd somehow or other get the Legion approval.

Let me say for us, now, that we will do nothing, but nothing that will hurt our story. We put too much into it and our pride is at stake. We will, however, make some changes in emphasis. In other words, we will under-emphasize a couple of the points that Martin objected to. We do this only because we would give up a little to get a passable rating, and because we appreciate your position.

But we will go no further than we state below. I really think it is your turn now, not to fight with us, but to fight with them. They, not we, are the menaces to your corporation. And if you give them more rein, they will feel their increased power over you and next time go further.

Here's what we will and will not do. We will not touch the scene in the hall where the suitcase appears. Mel's appearance here, his knocking on the door of the girl he's falling in love with and then his seeing LR's suitcase outside the door, is an essential part of the story and cannot go out.

However, once we go into the room with Joey De Palma we will eliminate as many as possible, closeups of Marcia peeking thru the bathroom door. Perhaps we can eliminate them all. But, bear in mind, that if we do eliminate them all she will still be seen in the long shot of the action and this cannot be eliminated by anyone who has a conscience. I hope this satisfies Martin on this point.

As for the montage, we will eliminate the girl in bed's second line ("I'll be waiting for you when you do") which does have a clearly sexual connotation. We will substitute a line from an announcer here ("She's talking about the large economy size"). From there on we will make the montage very short. In other words, we will eliminate the last third almost entirely. We feel here that possibly it's the rubbing in of the point that upsets Martin and that if it's treated more lightly he might not have the same impression.

We cannot change the scene in the advertising office where LR chases the girls. After all the films where Harpo Marx chased girls, it's a little late to come up with this now.

Budd and I went over the scene in her bedroom and we gave it careful consideration. We feel that we cannot change this scene. It is the climax of our story, it is completely but completely moral in its attitude, and it is above all absolutely essential to the telling of our story.

I don't think we should go ahead and make these changes unless we receive assurance from Martin (who cannot speak for the Legion but can speak for himself) that if we make these changes he will be our advocate with Father Little. The people who run the Film Industry had better do something about all this. Hidden power, secretly manipulated is very dangerous.

Let me say, finally, that it is my conviction that neither Quigley nor the Legion want to make damn fools of themselves by giving a "C" to this film. There is so little sex in it, it is clearly so deeply moral in conception and execution, it is done with such complete good taste and finally they have given "B" ratings to films so very much worse that I hardly think they can afford to be in a public position of condemning it. I say this to you because I want to tell you what you must already know, that you too are in a good bargaining position.

Let me also say that no matter what gives now, both Budd and I are extremely aware of your difficult position and that of Warner Brothers and extremely fond of you personally.

With affection

ek:mf

[Ben Kalmenson endorsed Martin Quigley's latest attempt to avert the Legion's condemnation of a film financed by Warner Bros. and certified by the Production

Code Administration (a unit of the Motion Picture Association of America). The fiasco of *Baby Doll* would not be repeated.

Revision of *A Face in the Crowd* followed Kazan's listing of what "will and will not" be done to meet Quigley's objections. Retained was the suggestive "suitcase" dropped and left overnight in the hallway by Lonesome Rhodes when Marcia Jeffries, his original benefactor and hesitant lover (played by Patricia Neal), draws him into her hotel room in Memphis. Two brief long shots replaced close-ups of her peeking through the bathroom door when visitors arrive the next morning. Kazan also toned down a montage of commercials promoting a harmless pep pill ("Vitajex") as a romantic elixir. A sultry blonde in bed, a Monroe look-alike, delivers a replacement line only slightly less risqué than the original: "I bought my boyfriend a ten year's supply." Kazan retained the farcical chase scene in the advertising office, as well as the final bedroom encounter of Marcia and Rhodes. Strong physical desire is evident before she withdraws, determined to expose his cynicism and end a dangerous political career. Kazan later identified a secondary or "'hidden'" story line reflecting "the emotional life" of the screenwriter and director: "It is the story of women as conscience" (*A Life*, p. 568).

Hesitancy to air claims of rectitude or denounce censorship apparently marked negotiations. While the Legion of Decency had limited the financial return of *Baby Doll*, the broad imposition of Roman Catholic values caused a backlash against parochial censorship and coincided with an emphasis on the promotion of morally responsible films rather than bans and pickets. Not wishing to be known as a salacious producer, Kazan agreed to cuts of eight minutes and refrained from exposing the "hidden power" of the Legion as he had in the case of *Streetcar*. He was "glad" to inform Geoffrey Shurlock on May 22 that *A Face in the Crowd* has "a B rating from the Legion."] *TL, 3 pp., Wesleyan*

TO BUDD SCHULBERG

[New York]
June 3, 1957

Dear Budd:

More bad news. This is the day for it: Black Monday. I have just been over to Warner Bros. and I read the out-of-town reviews. They are really excellent. The last reviews I read were from Boston and they were uniformly enthusiastic. Then I saw the Warner Bros. sheet on the box-office receipts. In five days, in two theaters in Boston, we did $8700. This is, as you realize, disastrously bad. It is not just bad, it is a bad side rejection. There is no other way to look at it I'm afraid. We should have done that much business in one theatre in one day.

Something just about as bad, happened in Chicago. L.A. is a little better. Not much. The business in New York is poor. Not disastrous, but poor. On Sunday, "O.K. Corral" did $9,000; we did $3500. This is despite a very good Sunday press. There is something fundamental going on here. I don't know what, but I feel too depressed about it all at the moment to analyze it or try to analyze it.

Jack Warner just won my heart. I don't know why people have to keep winning your heart, but apparently they do. But I have liked Jack a long time. After I had read the notices and seen the figure sheets, I went up to Jack's office to call on him (he's in town). He was so genuinely and warmly cordial that I was filled with admiration for him. Benny was what might look like cool, except that I know him well and it is just that he was in a very low phase. Even a statement like "the end of the cycle and pre-sold novel, etc., etc." did not have the old sting in them. They have already given-up on the picture, however. That is clear. I have not, although the figures disturb me terribly.

We are changing the ads. We're trying to give them more a sense of the scenes in the picture and we are also trying to appeal to the characteristic movie-going audience more. Kids, that is, and everyone except the taxi-riding intellectual that has been coming to the Globe. Joe is working like hell. We are screening today in Washington for Walter Lippmann. I have put a man on in Washington out of my own pocket to try to get some stir in the national columns. I'm not asking Warners to pay for this because they certainly won't go for added expense at this point. I'm having more lunches and cocktails with TV columnists, etc.

Sorry to write you so depressing a letter, but I'm giving it to you the way I got the story. All the intellectuals around here are grinding out their rationalizations for the poor business but in a morbid sort of way it's enjoyable. Drop me a line.

Love

ek:mf

P. S. I still think the boys at Warners who did work awfully hard on promotion and publicity, would greatly appreciate copies of the book with your signature.

[Kazan wrote earlier on "Black Monday" to inform Budd Schulberg of "really bad" business in New York, Chicago, and Los Angeles. Ben Kalmenson was "down in an atom bomb cellar of despair," while Kazan held out hope that a sunny weekend had driven potential customers from the cities (Dartmouth). "More bad news" convinced him that "something" beyond weather was at work. Released to exploit the Memorial Day weekend, *A Face in the Crowd* met stiff competition from *The Ten Commandments* and *Around the World in Eighty Days*, holdovers from 1956, and *Gunfight at the O.K. Corral,* a current release. The first wave of reviews in *Life, Time,* and *Newsweek* warned the "characteristic movie-going audience" that *A Face in the Crowd* is "much too long for its own good" (126 minutes), and its satire on television has "gone haywire." The same popular audience was already looking ahead to a romantic extravaganza filmed on Barbados in CinemaScope and due for release on June 12. *Island in the Sun* was "uniformly sock," as *Variety* put it, and would gross $500,000 in the first week. It was Darryl Zanuck's first independent production.

A Face in the Crowd was published in 1957 with a preface by Kazan recounting the progress of the screenwriter from humiliating origins in Hollywood to the creative independence of Budd Schulberg.] *TL, 2 pp., Wesleyan*

TO CLIFFORD ODETS

[New York]
[July 1, 1957]

Dear Cliff:

Been up in the country and just got your card. I think I'll be out there about the 15th. of July. And I'll write you or call you before I come out so we can have long times together. There's something working out or developing here that I want to tell you about. Molly has improved her play a lot. I just wish that it were coming out in 1954 or 55. Otherwise its the best play she ever did and I'm just delighted she's going to get a viewing. She's earned it. Never saw anyone work as hard. Up morning after morning at 4:30 so that she could get a day's work in before the children came home from school. Hell she's really got material in her. They've cast it well with Karl Malden, Phyllis Love, Biff McGuire, Ed Franz and some newcomers. Hume Cronyn is directing. Molly's tougher than he is. He's used to women assuming their rightful place (under him I assume.) He's a cute little guy, but naively autocratic. There may be some comic by-play. ** I was very disappointed in the outcome of Face in the Crowd. Both in the mistakes Budd and I made and in the reception. But I'm living and on the whole feeling pretty good. I worked a year and a half on that film. Slighting nothing. I did the goddamn sound recording myself. Even! ** I haven't seen your film yet. (half yours? less?) I thought Lancaster looked absurd in the ads. I was glad to see some of the papers talk about your dialogue as unmistakable. But that's so little to what you should be getting (in the way of recognition) or doing. And time is so short. I used to think I would live for ever. Now I have only days when I feel so fine that I know I'm immortal. But that feeling grows because of the events of the day. I dont wake up that way anymore. And now I know there is just so many more plays and or movies I am going to do. I've been trying to push Lee Strasberg and the Actors' Studio into some institutional activity that I'll tell you about. With him it is a last chance, baldly. He has done a very very good job, though with his classes both at the studio and privately. ** Judy is at Grenoble, France taking a summer course there—with a girl friend. Chris is in Europe too, I dont know where. He is independent as hell. All I know is three kids from Harvard, of which he is one, are in Volks Wagen driving around somewhere. Chris is capable though and I think he's an artist. He is tough, keeps his own counsel, and lives only on his experience. He does not "adjust".

I'll let you know when I'm coming out. I long to see you.

Love, Gadg

Best place to address letters is to my office 1545 Bway

[The "something working out" probably refers to Lincoln Center and Kazan's hope to enlist Clifford Odets as a contributing playwright.

Karl Malden played a "softheaded" liberal professor who defends a former Negro student accused of communism, only to learn that he is an active party member. Maxwell Anderson shared Kazan's concern over timing and had rejected *The Egghead* when it was submitted to the Playwrights' Company in the preceding fall. The play, he thought, "would have been timely in the year when Gadge recanted publicly and named names," but "the temper of the argument has cooled" and it "doesn't have a chance" (Anderson, p. 284). Molly Kazan's warning to liberals was judged "lamentably untheatrical" and closed after twenty-odd performances.

In "private notes" dated January 4, 1958, Kazan attributed the failure of *A Face in the Crowd* to unbalanced story construction. He and Budd Schulberg had "left out" the known "complexity" of their subject in urgently warning the American people of forces akin to fascism in their politics and media. "Above all we were out to show what a son of a bitch LR was—where we should have been showing that LR was us" (Ciment, p. 112). The failure so rankled that years later Kazan and Schulberg seriously considered a remake of the film.

Odets shared screenwriting credit with Ernest Lehman for *Sweet Smell of Success* (1957). Burt Lancaster played a cynical Broadway columnist who uses an unsavory press agent (Tony Curtis) in plotting the destruction of a young musician.

Odets replied to Kazan's reflection on time passing with vintage dialogue: "Peace, it is wonderful how life does go on! All credit and honor to Life! It hurts often but it is wonderful to live!! The other night I said to a girl, 'It is actually a privilege to suffer,' but I doubt if she understood me" (July 3, 1957, Wesleyan).]
TLS, 1 p., Wesleyan

Surveying the construction of the Vivian Beaumont Theater
at Lincoln Center with Robert Whitehead

Part V

Theater and Film

1957–1961

[Beverly Hills, California]
[c. July 20, 1957]

Dear Bob:

It was awful good to hear from you. And it was especially good to hear from Molly that on the whole you liked the Inge play very much. I hadn't entirely expected you would, but again I underrated you. Molly told me some of the critical remarks you made and they certainly are cogent. But mainly I was glad to hear that the balance of your opinion was on the favorable side. Not many people seem to like the play. Fitelson says its the worst play Bill ever wrote. Fitelson's partner Mayer who's a very acute business man (made over two million dollars in the stock market the last couple of years) said he wouldn't advise anyone to invest in it except for the fact that I was doing it. Harry Mayer the idiot that runs the play department of Warner Brothers here in New York told his people that he wouldn't advise them to invest in the play even considering the fact that I was doing it. Saint Subber's step brother just wouldn't invest in it at all, and since he is the money source for Saint—well that leaves us all in a strange position. But you and Molly like it and I'm going ahead cheerfully. Well not quite cheerfully. I wish there was one more person who liked it. Oh yes, Bill Inge likes it and that is three. Or maybe I shouldn't count him. Oh, I've got it! Bill's analyst likes it. Or maybe I shouldn't count him either. After all Bill pays him to improve his (Bill's) work and he'd seem to be robbing poor old Inge if he didn't notice an improvement. Oh everything is so difficult, Bob! Whom can you trust. Now Tennessee Williams says he likes the play. But he's so involved psychologically. I mean he's a little sick, dont you think? I mean he might have all kinds of double jointed reasons for saying he likes it. For one thing he might have simply the impulse to be generous. That can cause a lot of trouble right there. Or else he might feel he's a bigger man if he can like some one else's work—I mean at least one other person's. Actually Tennessee is generous. Oh I dont know. I get all confused trying to attribute motives. But the thing is <u>have I enough to go on</u>??? If I just had three solid ones! Oh gosh! Is that too much to ask? But I haven't I just have you and Molly—though god knows that you're both very solid and wouldn't kid me along. But I keep coming back to the idea that I ought to have three. I dont dare take the word of an actor. Karl liked it but he's in Molly's play and he's awful good but very naive. Then Jo Mielziner didn't like it. You see a man begins to get confused. Still to just plunge into things like I have in the past. I dont know! If I have another catastrophe (I'm referring, rather obliquely sir, to A FACE IN THE CROWD) I mean they'd start cutting my salary again, like they did once before. So I dont know what to do. Oh! You could do me one favor. Write me and tell me why you liked it, and how, and what the things were that you liked so much. Write me a couple, three pages. That may set me on fire. It might just do the trick. Molly just says: its good and that I shouldn't ask a lot of questions. She acts like I haven't much of a mind, and if once I would admit and accept (yes, even embrace) that fact I'd get along a whole lot better. She just wants me to go ahead and direct it and take her goddamn word its good. But that doesn't leave me very much pride does it? What should I do, Bob? I wish you were here. I even wish Spiegel were here. He's a comfort. Spiegel! Well, anyway, I hope you do write me. Love, as ever and we do miss you.

Gadg

P.S. I know one reason you like it! It's a love story! Right???

[Robert Anderson remained active in theater, film, and television during a long career, although he would not repeat the early success of *Tea and Sympathy* (1953), whose chances Kazan had "underrated." Mock confusion and dubious advice are layered with an unusually playful touch as Elia debates the wisdom of directing *The Dark at the Top of the Stairs*. Reference to Sam Spiegel underscores the humor with a hint of the producer's friendly menace. Much later Elia disavowed the "'poor, sensitive soul'" plays of William Inge and characterized his agreement to direct the forthcoming hit as a gesture of "professional respect" for Molly, their "strongest bond" at the time (*A Life*, pp. 572–73). The present letter is marked "Not sent—might hurt Bob's feelings."] *TLS, 1 p., Wesleyan*

TO WILLIAM INGE

[New York]
November 1, 1957

Dear Bill:

Just a note to sum up what I tried to say. I always have a feeling that I stumble when I talk generally and haven't quite made my point. Perhaps I have, but in case I didn't I thought I'd write it out and get it to you.

At the beginning of Act 2 Cora is ready to break up her marriage because she considers it a failure. No matter that she says "I have failed". She blames Reuben. Reuben doesn't help raise the kids right, he cheats, he isn't her image (the image created by her father, her mother and the ethic of their social group) of what a husband and father should be. And, he hit her. The point is, she blames Reuben.

Lottie says in essence: I wish I had married a man like that. And much more cogently she says to Cora: He saved you from the condition in which our parents left us. He rescued you. I was not rescued. My life was blighted. You fight, but you have a marriage. So far so good. But Cora doesn't rush to the phone to call Reuben only because it has been pointed out to her by Lottie that she is having sex with Reuben and Lottie doesn't have it with Morris. She has always known that. In fact, she even took it for granted.

It seems to me that Cora needs to be knocked down much more fundamentally at the end of Act 2 and I think Lottie is the girl to do it. Lottie's emotion would come from older-sisterly resentment and out of her own jealousy and frustration. But she cannot tolerate Cora's stand: that it is Reuben's fault, and she is perfectly familiar both from Cora and her parents with the old family stand, we are right—everybody else is wrong. In other words, she makes Cora look at the fact that it is her fault, at least in part, not just Reuben's. What has gone wrong with the kids, what has gone wrong with Reuben, have their reason somewhere in Cora's character and training.

I do not think Cora should defend Reuben. Lottie, in her way and with her emotional reasons does. (That's the kind of man I should have married). The trouble now is that at the end of the "big" scene between Cora and Lottie in Act 2, our eyes are on Lottie, her tragedy, her pain, but Lottie's pain is another play. Our play is about Cora. Somewhere we should be looking at Cora, feel for her as she is flattened and humbled, aware that something basic in her has been challenged and torn apart. Then she would run to the phone for fundamental reasons that have to do with a sudden violent revelation to her that she has been wrong.

Something should happen to Cora at the end of Act 2 that leaves her changed for the rest of the play. That is dramatic. Lottie's tragedy is a most touching vignette, but not on the line.

What I say is already in the play. The rewriting is not extensive. I don't think the large body of the Cora-Lottie scene need be changed. But what happens to Cora at the end of the scene with Lottie is muffled and veiled. It is not thrust through into the open. It is not dramatized.

And, parenthetically, I wish somewhere at the end of this scene with Lottie, Cora could have one short violent outburst of pain and self-defense which Lottie also knocks down. Sort of the last outburst: (It is his fault).

Having dictated this I am not much surer it is any clearer than what I said to you, but at least it's the gist of what I can see at the moment. I am not concerned with the criticism that we are losing Cora all through Act 2. I think I can help this by direction and Teresa can help it by a little different playing. The moment that does seem wrong to me is the moment just at Lottie's exit. Perhaps I have misdirected this, but I feel somehow Cora should be shattered and stripped of her defenses and brought face to face with her own "sin".

Love,

EK:nm

[Kazan warned Bill Inge midway through rehearsals that *The Dark at the Top of the Stairs* would not "mean a hell of a lot, is in fact going to be scattered and intermittent in its effects, unless you and your audience latch on to Cora. Cora has to be made the emotional centre of the play. You must feel for her. You must make the audience feel for her. In fact she is the play" (notebook, Wesleyan). Act two unfolds as Cora and Lottie probe their intimate sexual histories and break through a long-reserved sisterhood. Lottie's self-examination is the deeper and more affecting, while Cora hesitates to move beyond the parental legacy of respectability that has driven her husband, a traveling salesman prone to infidelity, to leave his family in a storm of discontent. The son of a pioneer family, Reuben (later Rubin) sells harness in Oklahoma in the dawning age of the automobile, which threatens his livelihood and masculinity. As staged by Kazan, act two ends with a "muffled" rather than "violent revelation" of Cora's complicity in the faltering marriage.

William Inge's fourth consecutive hit opened on December 5, 1957, ran for a year on Broadway, and was nominated for several major awards. All admired Kazan's staging, while Teresa Wright was judged "eminently right" as Cora. She and Robert Anderson married in 1959.] *TL, 2 pp., Wesleyan*

TO CLIFFORD ODETS

[New York]
February 24, 1958

Dear Cliff:

As always I was very happy to hear from you. I plainly wish you were here and participating in what we were trying to do and to some extent doing. But there is time. The Rockefeller thing took a disappointing turn. Rockefeller and his committee of Presbyterians decided to choose Rob't Whitehead to be their "Advisor" on repertory. What the hell the word in quotes means, I dont know. But they did not choose us. That much is clear and damned plain. I hope I'm not falling into the Clurman-Strasberg pattern of rationalizing everything, but I do feel that we're better off this way. Rockefeller's Theatre for the "Dramatic Arts" (which we hoped to occupy) will not be built and completed for five years. In other words the whole thing of Waiting for Rockefeller was only another edition of "Someday we will etc. etc." and I've had enough of that for a life time. The "Ideal" as some realistic poets have pointed out, can be a very wasting thing. I was annoyed with John R. the 3rd. because I had already done a lot of advising, attending many meetings with him and his group and writing several prospecti. But in the end consanguinity told. And the air is cleared. Now another prospect is up. And this one more immediate. We have been approached by a go between from the state department to send three plays in rep. played by a company to Europe the summer after this. And this we are planning to do. Of course we want to send one of your plays. We are especially anxious to show off, not only our modern American Dramatic classics (plays like yrs. O'Neill, Wilder, Williams etc.) but also our resources in actors and personnel, and our production skills. We are going to try to put together a "fabulous" company and tour three plays that permit really startling casting. We have approached M. Brando for one and gotten the: "I'd like to if time permits" answer. I really believe he'd like to very much, and we'd very much like to have him. But when one has a company on a Major lot, time never does seem to permit. However there are other actors and more coming. If it were Brando we'd like to do GOLDEN BOY. What plays we choose will depend partly on the actors and the parts they can play. I'm thinking, right now, of doing DESIRE UNDER THE ELMS. It may be another play though. Have you ideas? . . .

As for myself, I'm nowhere, right now. I've been working on the same screen play for three months or is it six. And my work has not been rewarded (Lee Cobb's word. He always said "rewarding".) My work has not been rewarding or rewarded or even good. But I'm an unnaturally tenacious beast and I'm going to give it another spin, a month or two more. People look at me with some concern and say: "The truly brave thing to do is give up." And they smile. What the hell. I dont see why I shouldn't see it thru. I make about 900$/week out of Inge's play and that pays the household expenses and I dont need more. So I might as well see it and thru and to the end. You learn only that way. Meantime I have a couple of play expectations for fall, four to be exact, and maybe one of them will come thru interestingly. The Spring of this coming year will go to the preparation of the European tour. At least I've laid the time aside in my mind for that. The STUDIO is much busier and is for the first time rather peppy. My children are basically o.k. all with various interesting problems and crises, one after another. Nick Kazan spent four dollars on a date the other day, and that's something of a landmark. Concretely I wont know what I'm going to do this Spring until I get thru with my next go thru on the script. But I have space reserved on the Olympia (a greek Boat, N.Y. to Athens) and I look forward to taking the whole family to Greece. Last chance probably. The last summer of Chris and Judy being kids. My health is good. My spirits are o.k. I'm interested in the world around me. And no one is pushing me, only me myself. As always.

Love
Gadg

[Neither ANTA nor the Actors Studio, contenders for the drama sponsorship, met the institutional criteria set by Lincoln Center. A new repertory theater would be formed instead with Robert Whitehead, director of The Producers Theatre, serving as chief adviser and presumptive leader of the company. Kazan and Cheryl Crawford were appointed to a steering committee from which Lee Strasberg was excluded. Architectural planning for a theater seating twelve hundred began in September under the supervision of Eero Saarinen and Jo Mielziner. Once assured that drama would be an "integral part" of Lincoln Center, hitherto dominated by music, Mrs. Vivian Beaumont Allen pledged $3 million toward construction of a building scheduled to open in 1963.

The prospect of an overseas tour sponsored by the State Department and the Actors Studio proved no more substantial than Marlon Brando's agreement to join the company "on principle." Kazan extracted the vague promise during "a long evening" in various Japanese clubs, which gave him "a terrible hangover the next morning." Elia reported the meeting to Cheryl Crawford, whose "peppy" plan to produce a series of plays "by arrangement" with the Actors Studio would fare little better. Controversy marked each stage of the first production (a revival of *The Shadow of a Gunman* by Sean O'Casey) and confirmed Lee Strasberg's fear of ventures lacking the full imprimatur of the directorate.] *TLS, 2 pp., Indiana*

TO TENNESSEE WILLIAMS

PM: New York, NY, February 26, 1958

Dear Tenn:

Thanks for reading it. And your words were kind. I always thought you the kindest of men. The "pedant" observation is certainly true. That's the trouble with the mind of a director. He's trained to organize material. And sometimes, perhaps usually this is important in directing some one else's play or film script. Even then there is a danger that you have to be on guard about: that you might "straighten it out" too much. But on a more or less original story— well it comes out as you said, pedantic. Anyway I'm going to take one more stab at it. I really do enjoy this new experience. And I want to give it another spin. Dont duck. I wont ask you to read this one. That would be too much. And I dont think I'll continue on this writing jag. One of my ambitions is to some day do a couple of films, even a "series" about my family, how they came to this country and how they fucked it up here, one way and another. I feel full of affection for them and I dont know how to begin to transmit this to a "writer". So there, in that case, I'd be much better off if I could do it myself. That's really why I'm trying now and here to learn something about it, and get some practise. I'm also disposed to do this script, if its at all possible, to sort of complete the experience. You were much kinder than anyone except John Steinbeck. He liked it. But Inge thought all the characters unbelievable and Paul Osborn thought I'd gone about the whole thing all wrong. Molly Kazan?!! Well you know that one!

Anyway, baby, thanks. Your kind words (I dont mean I thought them insincere in the least, but they did seem kind) meant a lot to me. Just think: aren't you glad you aren't a director! Suppose I asked you: would you like to direct this? Jeezuz! And so as the sun sets behind the FBI building, we take another drink of scotch and bring this letter to an end.

I'm going to stay in the country next week. Sandy Hook. Box 25. I'll be back March 10.

Love, gadg

[Kazan's "direct and simple" writing produced a "feeling of reality," but Tennessee Williams wondered if the Tennessee Valley Authority was "still a topical, live issue, with which a mass audience will identify." The documentary basis of the screenplay reminded him of "the WPA theatre project of the late thirties" and risked a "connotation of the pedantic" (to EK, February 26, 1958, Wesleyan). Kazan completed a third draft of *Wild River* in April before turning the project over to Paul Osborn, who was "very indifferent" to his friend's writing. Generally, Molly Kazan doubted the wisdom of Elia's turn to screenwriting.] *TLS, 1 p., Columbia*

TO ARCHIBALD MACLEISH

[New York]
[late spring 1958]

Dear Mr. MacLeish:

First, a few general remarks. My enthusiasm for your play has not only survived several readings, but has grown with time and thought.

Let me immediately say once more that you may quite understandably not be interested in the detailed suggestions that follow. After all, your play has not only found acceptance, but most enthusiastic recognition from our leading dramatic critic. And there is no way that I can be sure that what I am suggesting in this letter will change the views of those whose enthusiasm was qualified.

At any rate, in what follows, I haven't inhibited myself. It is best in these circumstances that you know my full thoughts candidly expressed. You may think me presumptuous but you need have no fear that I have left unsaid any "thoughts I am saving for another day".

I have tried, in the time I've had, to think up the production scheme that I would follow, and the textual rearrangements that I suggest derive from this scheme. I do not suggest any rewriting. I do not think any serious rewriting is necessary. There always are slight changes that become necessary when passages are rearranged. I do not go into these changes.

Let me first say that there is something basically underdramatic to me about staging which alternates between action and comment on action. The marvelous thing about your play to me is that in time Zuss and Nickles become emotionally involved in what's happening and become partisan. I would try to involve Nickles particularly <u>from the very beginning</u>.

In general, my idea would be to produce the play in two acts of completely continuous action. I think there should be no sense of hiatus or of "Breaks" and that the scene designations you make should be treated in the same way that those of Shakespeare or Moliere were: That is, they designate a change of attention or a new movement of thought and action, rather than in any way referring to a formal break in time or place or an <u>interruption</u> in stage life.

In fact, I believe that the staging should be basically "Shakespearian". It should acknowledge the presence of the audience and by this the relevance of what's being said to the audience's <u>present</u> concerns. Further, it should, in its sweep, envelop the audience. I do not think of your play as a religio-moralistic fairy tale in a picture frame setting. I think that might result in its being "holy" and sententious. The thing I like so much about your play is that it is about our state of soul and feeling, our Fates as presently felt by us all, our Future. In other words, it is not a play about Job, it's a play about the midcentury American, and midcentury America. The question you ask is: Will America be able to take it when it comes? I think the play should be staged so it says: Will you, the audience, be able to take it? . . .

Cordially, Elia Kazan

[Strong reviews brought *J.B.* to the attention of the Actors Studio after a brief run at the Yale School of Drama in April. Archibald MacLeish's reworking of the Job story appealed to Studio directors as a profitable venture and a chance to broaden their dramatic interests. Alfred de Liagre prevailed instead and recruited Kazan, who probably had not seen the original production.

The new production would be staged in a "frank theatric manner," as Kazan outlined in five pages of particulars following "general remarks" selected for publication. With the cutting and rearrangement of lines in act one, he stressed the "intermingling" of story and frame: J.B. and his family, anonymous players who reenact the Old Testament Book of Job on the side stage of a traveling circus; and Mr. Zuss and Nickles, originally conceived as aged vendors of balloons and popcorn, who take the overarching roles of God and Satan. Kazan's rejection of *J.B.* as "a religio-moralistic fairy tale" required that Nickles be "emotionally involved" in his dissident counsel to man "<u>from the very beginning</u>." His disdain for J.B.'s wealth and complacency and for God's authorship of the latest calamity, a war that ends in utter destruction, would also help to establish the play's historicity and pertinence to "midcentury America." Kazan advised in a later note that "we suggest very economically and swiftly New York City as Hiroshima," to which MacLeish replied in a marginal notation, "Generalized 'a' war hullaballoo."

Kazan's closing remarks include no apology for "editorial impudence" and end with a statement that "directors are traditionally this bold only with the dead." Nonetheless Kazan would be "disappointed" if MacLeish were to answer "bluntly, 'Hands off, thank you.'" Their rapport allowed for timely revision of *J.B.* during a difficult tryout in November (*A Life*, pp. 582–84).] *TLS, 8 pp., Beinecke*

PM: New York, NY, May 20, 1958

Dear Tennessee:

Well, here they are—my main points. Everything of any importance. The rest are all details and can wait easily.

First, I want to say that CHANCE has the potential of being a character as memorable as any you have written. That's saying a lot. Maybe it is going too far. I don't think so. He is a sort of grotesque mid-twentieth century Hamlet. I agree with you. All the sickness of our time is contained in him. His anxiety about keeping up with the parade, his pathetic, desperate measures to achieve recognition, his clumsy blackmail, his bizarre bigshot behavior, are all heartbreaking and tragic and meaningful. He is also a great _stage_ figure. I mean that the audience will watch him with a combination of recognition and concern and identification, the way they do other great stage figures.

You see, I am in a complimentary mood, but I do mean it. The potential is there for something really wonderful.

I also think you have for the first time since STREETCAR the set up for a genuine tragedy. I won't go into a lot of theory about it. But I do mean this and I do mean it in the most classic sense. CHANCE has a tragic flaw in the same way that BLANCHE did, in the same way that OEDIPUS did, in the same way that WILLY LOMAN did. And he dies as a result of this tragic flaw. I think you are dead wrong to have the same ending to this play that you did to ORPHEUS, for that is what you do have, Tennessee, no matter how skillfully you try to disguise it by underwriting the stage direction. I see thru your stage direction. I see that some shadowy, underlit villains will come out and take the boy out into the wings, presumably to castrate him. I didn't believe it in ORPHEUS and I don't believe it as I read it in this script.

Let me tell you a story. I had a friend in the 30's. A man named Manny Eisenberg, who was half artist, half homosexual. He did publicity for the Group Theatre. He was full of pretensions, yet I liked him very much. Indeed, I was touched by his pretensions. He was talented in many ways, but in every field the degree of his talent was very small. He was a writer, a photographer, a producer, a wit, a poet—all just a little bit. But he aspired. He wanted to be big, and recognized. And of course the city didn't. It looked scornfully at him. Manny Eisenberg was doomed from the day I met him. One day he came to recognize that everybody was laughing behind his back and that he was a figure of ridicule. He was losing his hair by then, getting fat, and was losing jobs because he had begun to drink too much. I began to be oppressed by a feeling that within the near future this man was going to kill himself. Here's how he did it. He chartered a small airplane and instructed the pilot to fly over the

Broadway theatrical district, and to fly rather low. The pilot did this, circling several times. At a certain point Manny stepped out of the plane and dived out on the city that had scorned him. He reminds me of your character. I thought from the very beginning CHANCE was doomed. In fact, CHANCE smells of doom. It comes out of him like sweat, or like a radiation. When you showed me in the first act that he had a pistol, I thought, "this man will kill himself". Early in Act 2 he says to the Princess, either I will make a good thing of it, or else! I think he should kill himself. It seems dead right for him. How he does it I have no suggestion for, and if I had it would be no damn good. But all thru the play I felt CHANCE was bringing on his own end.

And he dies because of what he is and because of what society has made him and because of the way he has twisted himself to fit what he thinks society demands of him. He dies for profound and inner reasons, not because there are a few monsters in a certain part of this country. Tennessee, I don't believe people in the South are any more cruel than the people in the North. I think you are unfair to the South. In many ways the people I met down there are more human than the people on Broadway, or in Hollywood, or on Madison Avenue, or in New England, or in the Bible belt of the Midwest. You pick on the South, son, because your own personal nightmares are set there. Southern bullies frightened you once, or something. I don't know. But it seems to me that it's possible for you now to take a more "balanced" view of it. I was embarrassed by the villains at the end of ORPHEUS, although I did think Harold staged that scene miserably. But the story of CHANCE is completely All-American. There is a little guy around me named Guy Thomajan. I feel he is quite possibly going to kill himself. There are CHANCES all over the place—all phenomena of this particular time, this particular society. All of them doomed because of their own natures and because they have gone with the false ideals of our society. CHANCE is significant because he is trying to go with the system, succeed by its standards, which are false standards. Somehow making him a victim, not of his own nature and not of a broad social ideal, but of a "heavy", makes your play much smaller than it really is.

Remember my old joke with you that whenever you were in difficulties you got lyrical and whenever I was in difficulties I got loud? When I see you getting lyrical at the end of a play and trying to make an ending around HEAVENLY, when all the audience should be feeling, and will be feeling, is WHAT HAPPENS TO CHANCE?—then I know that something unsatisfactory is going on with you and that in your heart you know it. I think the end of the play has to do with CHANCE and you must really conclude his story. I thought the lyricism about HEAVENLY becoming a nun, although much, much better in the rewriting, and I believe an excellent end for her, should not have the emphasis it has now.

Anyway, I am going on and on about the same thing. You, by now, have my feeling on this point. On to the next. In general, I feel there is a little too much of the Grand Guignol in your play. It's as though you didn't trust your own material and felt obliged by the particular anxiety a playwright feels to hop it up with a lot of sensational bits. For example, I think it is marvelous that the Princess is losing her memory. That in fact she has none when she wakes on this particular morning. Further, I think the new stuff you have written on why she smokes hash is wonderful and will make the audience feel themselves into the Princess. But the oxygen mask business seems over gruesome, as though it were an end in itself. And I felt the same way about the line, "Make love to her with your knife". And a number of other things. We get it all without having it rubbed in our faces. Again I say it's as if you don't trust your own legitimate dramatic powers and resorted to these external shockers to jazz up the audience. It's as though Shakespeare had decided to be the author of THE DUCHESS OF MALFI—Webster, I believe. . . .

Now here is the suggestion that you are going to hate. I hope you don't. I suggest that in the cocktail lounge there be a big TV set. If the show is produced and directed, as it should be, larger than life, this TV set could be larger than life too. In fact, at a point in the action of the last scene of the present Second Act, it could become even bigger, opening up at the corners as you sometimes see screens doing in motion picture theatres. The rally should be presented filmically on this enlarged television screen. We could show a real Southern audience in a real Southern hall with believable supernumeraries going into believable events in a believable environment. At a certain moment all our audience should see on the stage is an enormous screen with this grotesque rally going on, the camera cutting from enormous close-ups of the Boss' face to shots of the audience, to shots of the heckler, to shots of Heavenly. . . . This, Tennessee, would be entirely in style and would be really NEW THEATRE. What you have now seems old-fashioned to me and I think it is terribly true as a theatre image to have this enormous image of BOSS FINLEY bellowing away while some hoodlums are beating up a heckler, and CHANCE is watching, frightened to death, a witness to a preview of his own fate. . . .

I think the style of the play is an advance of what you did on CAT. I think the arias are wonderfully done and will be most effective and are an advance on CAT and can be staged more frankly even than we did those in CAT. I think your writing is as good as it ever was. I think the psychoanalysis has done you good and you should go back. The only thing that disturbs me from this point of view is your insistence on what I call Grand Guignol. You don't need it, my dear, dear friend. So cut it out. Let up on us.

I have some other notes, but they are all detailed. I am not going into them. I have been awfully rough on you, but please put it down to the fact that I like the play a lot, and its author, and I feel that utter candor is the least I can give you. I haven't held anything back. I have said just what I think. I would like to do the play, if after reading this letter you still want me to. There is a practical problem, which I talked to Audrey about. I cannot do anything till after the first of the year. I am already committed for the Fall and was when I first read your play. But if you want to wait for me I'll be your boy. As I say, if you still want me after reading this letter. Incidentally, there is now going on the worst jam for theatres that there has been within my memory. According to Roger Stevens there are no theatres available till February. Write me.

Love, Gadg

EK:nm

[Tennessee Williams mailed *Sweet Bird of Youth* to Kazan on May 12 with a letter emphasizing both the currency of the play—it "puts its finger precisely on the sickness of our time"—and its roots in the racial violence and political extremity of the South. The random "emasculation" of a young Negro in Alabama had caused "quite a stir" and led Williams to conclude that Chance Wayne, the "mid-twentieth century Hamlet," as Kazan put it, "ought to suffer the same symbolic fate" (May 12, 1958, Wesleyan). Williams wired acceptance of "nearly all" Kazan's ideas for staging *Sweet Bird of Youth* and thought a projection of the rally scene a "truly brilliant idea," if "technically possible." He agreed in follow-up correspondence with Kazan that castration was "too much like the end of *Orpheus*" but rejected the "actual, physical suicide" of Chance Wayne as a "theatrical cliché" (May 22, 1958)—unaware that Kazan had marked the inconclusive ending of the April 1958 draft "a cheat," adding in blue pencil that "Chance should shoot himself." Parenthetically, Emanuel "Manny" Eisenberg's spectacular leap occurred on March 14, 1940, but not as Kazan has described it. The surviving pilot testified that Eisenberg attacked him while they were flying over Brooklyn, seized the controls, and caused the small training plane to crash into the Upper Bay near Staten Island, where Eisenberg's body was recovered. Guy Thomajan served as Kazan's stage manager for *Camino Real* and *Sweet Bird of Youth* and died in 2005 at the age of eighty-seven.

As a "quick, off the cuff, idea," Williams proposed in the letter of May 22 that Chance retreat "into the shadows of the palm garden as the sad silver trumpets blow for him." The alternatives of castration or suicide would be set aside in favor of symbolic retribution and dramatic space cleared for Heavenly's prayer of dedication to the Blessed Virgin after Chance has been rejected. Neither his uncertain fate nor the misplaced presence of Heavenly in the final scene would answer Kazan's pivotal question: "WHAT HAPPENS TO CHANCE?" Does he indecisively leave St. Cloud with the Princess, whose car horns beckon, or remain to atone for his defilement of Heavenly?

Williams retained the "gruesome" oxygen mask used to revive the Princess, an aging film star who flees Hollywood and picks up Chance Wayne after the presumed failure of a comeback attempt. Their arrival in St. Cloud, "somewhere along the Gulf Coast," is conditioned by the Princess's desire for oblivion and Chance's search for youth, love, and fame.] *TLS, 6 pp., Columbia*

TO WILLIAM K. ZINSSER

Dear Bill

This is a sort of good-by letter. I wasn't happy to read that you were no longer reviewing movies for the *Trib*. The announcement said you were pleased to be moving over to the editorial page, where you would have more scope. Well, you certainly will have.

But it did occur to me that there might be sounder measures of a man's worth to a newspaper than his scope. And I must admit that the very first question that came to my mind was: "Why *are* they moving him?" After all, anyone could see that your reviews were growing in perception and candor and strength. Well, that's between the *Trib* and you. I simply say that as one reader I am damn sorry to see you go.

Most people think of criticism as a big bite out of someone's back. But the single piece of criticism I remember best is an appreciation. It is the essay that G.B.S. wrote comparing the acting styles of Duse and Bernhardt, with admiration for each. What he said about them was "criticism," but when I finished reading the piece I liked them both, I had more insight into the particular talent of each, and more appreciation of the art of acting. And, most important of all, I felt a renewed desire to work in the theater, a revived sense of its possibilities and promise.

In other words, the critic can be, and on occasion he has been, a creative factor in an art. Just speaking for myself, I have taken some pretty good poundings from members of your fraternity, and I have been angry. But even anger is a stimulant. It energizes, it does not debilitate. And in time I have faced around from the harsh words and taken a harder, closer look at myself and what I'd been doing.

My colleagues in Hollywood have the protection of the "trade papers," a number of small sheets which are the favorite breakfast reading of the colony there. But a few weeks' sampling of their reviews will make even the most praise-hungry fellow doubt whether much comfort can be derived from a vocabulary where the superlative has lost its meaning from over-use. Not that the Hollywood press is venal or bought. But as you read it you do feel part of a frantic conspiracy by a whole community of people to hide the facts from each other.

At least once a week, to believe these little papers, a true masterpiece is revealed to an eagerly awaiting world audience. Almost every morning brings glad tidings of another "Academy Award" performance, though the statuette is given out only once a year and there is only one in each category. Triumphs are recorded even before they are accomplished. "Reports from the first pre-production reading of 'Spring Comes To Emily' say that there is *no* way for the 'cleavage' *not* to get an Academy Award on this one."

Of course, all this lard goes up in brown smoke when the films reach New York. A scale of values is reasserted. Order is restored. We've come to rely on a few of you fellows here for that.

But the fellows in California read the unbrotherly pieces from New York and cry: "Murder!" They don't want criticism, they want comfort. After all, the motion picture industry is spending its last days in the mouth of its voracious stepchild, the television industry, and always the question quickly comes down to: "Whose side are you on? We are fighting for our lives."

As I write this I know I sound unsympathetic. I am not. A man like Skouras is a giant, and there is something truly gallant in the fight he has been putting up. The decline of power and authority is always an awesome spectacle, especially if one has seen, as I have, the Great Days. Consider what men like Skouras, Warner, and the others once had.

This spring my wife and I were in Ireland. We were taking a walk at about eleven o'clock one night through the city of Cork. It was a fine evening and we were enjoying the streets, even though to New Yorkers they seemed deserted. Suddenly something dramatic happened. A movie theater adjourned, all the doors flinging open at once, the people coming out and out and out. I felt the old surprise that a theater could hold that many people. But what made it meaningful, beside the fact that I hadn't seen anything like it in our country for a long time, was that the movie being shown that night was a mediocrity that had been scorned off our screens. The people of Cork had not gone to a movie. They were still going to The Movies. The institution.

Is it any wonder that the giants who built this institution, with its "inevitable profit" and "consumer devotion," might expect in the present crisis that critical values be let down? War is a time for total loyalty.

But by the nature of change, a crisis is also an opportunity, and in any crisis, as you watch the downward curve, you see another rising. And that is now going on. The few really good films are drawing bigger crowds than ever. Within the profession itself the innovators and creators are more prized than ever. The tide is running their way. Creative writers, directors, producers, and actors are taking charge increasingly, as they should.

And as this is going on, more than ever there is a need for the fellows who speak not in the vocabulary of compliance, not in false words to quiet the terror, but say rather: "You're not being good enough! Consider! You've just started in this medium! You've only begun to realize its potential! And stories? You've barely touched America and the stories of its people! You've only begun to make films about your fellow humans."

Now more than ever do we need the really good critics, the men who can praise with authority and with reason, rip the cover off fraud, recognize accomplishments, make standards, then define and preserve them, throw a light of welcome on hitherto hidden promise, inspire, goad, champion—in short, work creatively in the art of the motion picture.

This is a peculiar way to say good-by to you, Bill. After all, you've already moved to a post where what I'm saying doesn't relate. But I hate to see a good man go. And perhaps this letter will make you hold a thought for us wherever you go and perhaps, one day, come back.

In friendship
Elia Kazan

[Kazan's letter served as an introduction to William Zinsser's memoir *Seen Any Good Movies Lately*. Its reprinting follows the Doubleday text published in 1958.

Eleonora Duse enjoyed the advantage in George Bernard Shaw's criticism when she and Sarah Bernhardt shared the London stage in June 1895. Divine Sarah's art in *Heimat* was a case of "'cajoling'" the audience and exploiting their "'weaknesses.'" Several days later Duse repeated the role and claimed the "'moral high notes'" by reason of her fertile "'dramatic imagination'" (West).

Zinsser claimed that Kazan was "a different kind of director" in reviewing *East of Eden* and *Baby Doll* for the *Herald Tribune*. "The people in his films are complex, and he wants to be very sure that you get to know and understand them. He takes his time. He lets his characters unfold slowly, and when they finally erupt into anger or violence, you know exactly why. This is the secret of 'East of Eden,' Kazan's unbelievably sensitive movie." Kazan also "refuses to be rushed" in *Baby Doll*, "at least when leisure is important." The seduction "unfolds insidiously, over the course of a whole steamy afternoon, this chess game of move and response that is the heart of the movie." Zinsser was no less firm in dismissing "the last twenty minutes" of *A Face in the Crowd:* "The writing and direction are trite, the acting is frantic and corny, and there is a fair share of moralizing."]

TO ARCHIBALD MACLEISH

[Athens]
[c. July 22, 1958]

Dear Archie:

Just got back from another island (and another eye-opening experience). I have to explain this—and I have to no one else. But its due you. And I know you must be wondering what the hell is that maniac doing there. Well—its involved. But I'll just tell you in a couple of sentences. I've reached some sort of stage now—within myself that is—where I'm more than I was curious as to what I am and where I came from and what the hell made me like I am and why and so on. Not that I haven't always been interested—but actually not as interested as most. And I've been always in a mad rush of work and ambition-hunger. Well a lot of that last has subsided and even some disappeared and I've become a lot quieter (from what I was, i.e.) Well about a year ago I began asking my parents questions—for the first time, can you imagine?—about their past, and the situation into which I was born and thru which I spent my first years. And I sort of took a long look at them. And I became interested in what they were—well I said I'd keep this short—and what they were and what made them what they were and what I was and what besides the genes and America made me the particular way I am. And in the midst of this I began to feel very Anatolian-Greek. Which is a very special thing. That I wont go into either, though I'm full of it right now. Anyway I've just been to Lesbos, which is the island of Greece closest to Turkey and full of Greeks that were run out of Asia Minor by the Turks in 1912 and again in 1922. And I met and talked with a lot of these Those-who-were-chased-out people. In Turkish. And as I say—well it was a revelation. Someday when the play is on and we have leisure to talk of many things, perhaps this can be one of them. But the whole thing is obsessive with me, right now. And I wont talk about it again. In a week I'll just put it away and forget it for a while.

I also think J.B. is a play that will live for long time. And you know I'll do everything within my powers to make you proud of it. I dont want you ever however to do one thing that you dont feel entirely all right about. And I'm very flattered when you say "my play". But for me its only one thing: its MacLeish speaking. And I'll try to be your voice. You'll see I'm a good speaker for other people. And while I'll always tell you what I think, it will not be me speaking, and if it ever is, you think, tell me so and we'll turn things right. But I'm glad that you feel the way you do about the potential of this play. Because you should. Its true. Its what's kept you going so long on it.

I was terribly worried for a long time that I had been too blunt on the ending. But its better to be (not blunt) but candid. The hardest thing in the world to obtain in our field from a co-worker is candour. Its the friendliest thing to give as long as people are working together and for each other and in good spirit. I hate fudging. And you saw how moved I was by your first act. And while I haven't studied your second as closely as I should have by now (I've been unsettled and unable to settle to a single thought) I know that's good. And (this is what worried me) I dont want you to think you're far from the end. But I dont think you are there yet. And I'm not one damn bit worried about it so dont you. I'm doing the worrying for two now (paraphrasing what they say about pregnant women).

About the curtain. I'd say it will be a CURTAIN of some kind. This need not be a piece of cloth hung on a batten and dropped between the players and the audience. It can also be a fade out of lights. And during this fade out we can have the barest briefest suggestion that Sarah and J.B. were going on. Such a CURTAIN could also be a black out, suddenly. Or it could be the standard cloth. Nothing is final about what Aronson and I talked about until you and I meet and talk things over. But—and this is my point—Sarah and J.B.'s exiting is wrong. And I believe meeting this purely mechanical requirement gave you difficulty. They cannot exit into the "wings" if the point we are making is that they are starting to rebuild a family in a home etc. What the hell are the wings? What do they represent? I'm at fault for ever allowing anyone else to talk with you about such points of drama—I asked Boris to describe the setting we had talked about, but this, this requirement for the ending gets really into playwriting. And, as I say, if they are to begin again and if there is to be in time, another family, another home, another Thanksgiving there might be the briefest barest hint of all this—perhaps AS THE lights are dimming. It shouldn't take any time. But we should make the point we want to make—and they cannot by exiting.

Well now having stated that about five times, I'll drop it. I certainly do overwrite my notes dont I?

One other note about the end. I thought J.B.'s reconciliation with Sarah was duplex—he did it twice—which I think wrong. And I thought it was a mite too easy. And despite the fact that J.B.'s starting again is dramatised in his reconciliation with Sarah he does have a score to settle that's tougher than is now felt (by me). In a sense he has to answer the D.V. He does this with an act, yes. But somehow J.B. should be answering the basic, terrible unanswerable questions that the D.V. put to him. And answering the questions within himself that Nickles put to him.

I didn't mean to get into any of this. But now that its down, I'll let it stand. The great danger and the only serious criticism I heard seriously about your play was that the ending was not quite on the scale of the rest. Or, to put it facetiously, that there might be a hint of Love Conquers All, all difficulties, all questions no matter how big.

These are just questions I raise. We'll talk when I get back. Today I'm thinking of coming home a little sooner, a few days earlier. But haven't decided yet. At any rate I'll call you within the hour of my arrival. And we'll have abundant time.

Love to you and Ada. g.

[Kazan recalls flying to Athens alone "to break the bind of meaningless escapades and a somnolent marriage." He would also shun "prestige and flattery," specifically the Lincoln Center project into which he felt himself "slipping," by moving "back in time as well as in geography" to his origin as an Anatolian Greek. Only in part are the details of travel accurate. Elia and family sailed from New York on June 21 and stayed at the Hotel Grande Bretagne in Athens. He gave the children lessons in Greek, conferred with Boris Aronson on staging J.B., and reluctantly kept abreast of casting and script revision in New York. Regional flare-ups caused

Molly and the children to return to the United States prematurely. Elia's solitary tour of the Greek islands prompted timely questions—"'Why do you direct plays you don't really like?'"—and a realization that the "middle-class American boy" was still "a stranger" to his family history. "I wasn't ready, if I ever would be, to conceive and write screenplays for my own films, especially on a subject in which I had no experience" (*A Life,* pp. 579–81).

Kazan advised author and producer in related correspondence not to rush plans for *J.B.* and definitely not to cast Fredric March and his wife Florence Eldridge in leading roles. They were far too old to play a couple in their mid-thirties, and they also lacked the "man woman thing" needed to make the intimacy of J.B. and Sarah plausible, if not moving. Pat Hingle and Nan Martin were cast later in the summer. Kazan staged the ending without an exit into meaningless space or a traditional curtain, which was removed from the ANTA Playhouse at his request. Amid the "rubble" of the circus ring, a grim remainder of war, love is restored and the desire to begin anew sealed when J.B. "touches Sarah's cheek with his hand." A gauze curtain drops and the lights fade out.

The Distant Voice ("D.V.") of God heard in the Old Testament narrative rebuking Job's pride is quoted verbatim in act two. Kazan's concern with answering the D.V.'s "terrible unanswerable questions" would remain unsolved for the moment and arise in later correspondence with MacLeish.

Kazan returned to New York in August to resume the "mad rush" of directing *J.B.*, developing scripts for *Sweet Bird of Youth* and *Wild River,* and planning his third independent film production, *Splendor in the Grass.*] TLS, 2 pp., Beinecke

TO TENNESSEE WILLIAMS

[New York]
August 28, 1958

Dear Tennessee:
Molly woke up this morning and said, "You better write Tennessee. God knows what they're telling him." I was going to anyway. Then I got your cable this morning and I just now dictated an answer and here's the letter.

There is a hassle, as you probably know (although they told me three days ago that they hadn't been able to get in touch with you. Apparently now they have.) But I don't really make deals with agents. I know that the agents and lawyers have to get into it and sometimes there are sore points, but the only one who can call a deal off between you and me would be you. You can call it off if you like, or I can call it off to you. But agent-talk is all bargaining and wrangling, conniving, penis competition, plumage display, flexing and unflexing of muscles, and bullying, bullying bullying! I did say to Audrey to consider me out. I also told her I wouldn't make any other arrangements until. "Until" means until I heard from you.

So, now to go back and tell you what happened. I got back from Europe and Bill Fitelson told me everything was settled but one point. This point was that he had asked for me that I have the right to put up the money for the percentage of the profits that I had coming to me as compensation. This would make it possible, Bill said, for me to treat my share of the show as a capital asset. He has been telling me for years, just as Audrey's been telling you, how impossible it actually is to make any money in our business, i.e. save any, and I have listened with a dull expression. I have enough and it doesn't make too much difference. He's awfully strong on this, but I wasn't going to make too much of a fuss about it. I was inclined to say, "Oh, forget it. What's the difference?" But then he said to me that Eddie Colton had said, "That's the deal, or else. Tennessee backs the play 100% and you not at all, and that's the deal, or else!" Well, I had the right with the Inge play to provide the backing for my piece of it, and I did. And it seemed to me that I really should have the right here, and if someone was going to deny it to me on an "or else" basis, I was going to get insistent about it.

At any rate, the next day, Bill had a meeting with Colton and he called me from the office while Colton was there. Colton had said, "That is it, or the deal is off" again. And furthermore, he said there was another director standing by. Well, there is only one thing you can say to that kind of threat. You can't be cowed by it, and you can't knuckle under to it. You can only come back with profanity. So I said I wanted it, or else. The threat about the other director standing by annoyed me.

Later, Audrey calls me up and I said to her, "There is no deal. I am out of it." And I told her about what Colton said about another director standing by, feeling a little silly because I was behaving like one of those egos. So Audrey comes back with commiseration and made that motherly "tst-tst-tst" sound of hers, and acted horrified at Colton's saying any such thing.

The only joker about this was that Paul Newman called me up in a couple of days and said that Audrey had been inquiring from him, through an opposite number in the California M.C.A., how he would take it if Jose Quintero or Peter Brook directed the play. Newman said that he would quit. I don't know whether he would or not, but that is what he said and I assume that is what was brought back to Audrey. Well, after I heard this from Newman, I kept thinking of Audrey's motherly sounds of shock and sympathetic outrage, and the mud got pretty thick and sticky by then, and the next time I was in the office my secretary tells me that Audrey had called and said she had not been able to get in touch with you yet and that they were going to meet that afternoon—they being your lawyer, your tax agents and the rest of the leeches, and by now I was in a puking mood and began to doubt that they hadn't gotten in touch with you and began to wonder about your silence—where you were and what was happening. Anyway, as I said at the beginning of this letter and in my cable, I would never walk away from a play of yours without a word from you that for one reason or another you didn't want me. We are too close and I think too much of you, as you well know, to make that kind of a decision to an agent. I don't like agents. They are in an untrustworthy line of endeavor. I suppose they can't really tell the exact truth at any time because they are dealing so many ways and all at once.

So, don't be concerned. I am sitting here and just let me know what you want to do.

There used to be a day in the theatre when you dealt with the producer and his job was to be fair to all hands. Now you deal with the author's agent and his job is squeezing the shit out of anybody except his client. Poor Cheryl feels the same way I do about the right to provide the backing for your show up to her interest in it but, of course, there is no question of her getting her right. She is not in any position of power to demand it. In other words, she can't quit. The result is that she's a sort of an errand boy. She feels a gently melancholic acceptance of her servant role. It is pretty hard to expect her to act like a producer with muscles when all her muscles are taken away from her right at this stage.

Incidentally, I have felt for a number of years that M.C.A. was pushing things too far. I told the head of the company at great length about this when I was drunk one night and got an enigmatic smile—the smile that crosses the face of rich men when they think how much money they have in the bank. M.C.A. is very prosperous. So what's the difference what anyone thinks about how they proceed.

Anyway, baby, I'm at the same address. 1545 Broadway. Write me and let me know what your wishes are. We are seeing Margaret Leighton on September 5th. I think it would be awfully nice if you were here. I also don't want to proceed on the set without your approval. I am also enclosing an ad from this week's VARIETY. The subject of the ad has become convinced that she is too young for the part. I still am not convinced. However, for the moment I have given up with her and am looking around in other directions. Much love—no matter what happens—much love,

Gadg

EK:nm
Enc.

[Tennessee Williams ended the "hassle" by accepting Kazan's terms for directing *Sweet Bird of Youth*. "I think I came to the right decision about hanging on to Gadg despite the cost," he wrote to Audrey Wood from London. "However," he added, "I am determined not to submit to being served up like a roast pig with apple in mouth for any more hungry people. A star like Newman must naturally get paid well, but he mustn't try to screw me: that I will only take from Kazan" (August 31, 1958, HRC). Paul Newman, last seen on Broadway in *The Desperate Hours* (1955), signed to play Chance Wayne in the fall. Cheryl Crawford produced *Sweet Bird* and reportedly held a 15 percent interest in the play.

In 1954 MCA (Music Corporation of America) added the small but distinguished firm of Liebling-Wood to its portfolio. Audrey Wood continued to represent her clients in plush new quarters on Madison Avenue, while her husband turned to independent production. Either Jules Stein (chairman) or Lew Wasserman (president) was the MCA "head" to whom Kazan complained of aggressive tactics.

Tennessee Williams informed Audrey Wood that Margaret Leighton "could play the pants off the Princess!" after seeing her in the London production of Terence Rattigan's *Variation on a Theme* (1958). In 1957 Geraldine Page replaced Leighton in the Broadway production of *Separate Tables,* Rattigan's earlier double bill, and apparently continued on tour. The *Variety* "ad" enclosed by Kazan implicitly addressed the question of her suitability to play the aging Princess in *Sweet Bird of Youth*. Tennessee Williams, Cheryl Crawford, and Sam Spiegel, an occasional adviser, agreed with Page herself that at thirty-three she was "too young for the part." Her "first-rate acting" in *Separate Tables* as a desperate woman of forty whose beauty is fading argued differently, or so Kazan thought. Page was cast in *Sweet Bird* to her great advantage.] *TLS with enclosure, 4 pp., Columbia*

TO BORIS ARONSON

[New York]
September 3, 1958

Dear Boris:
Here are the notes on the set that I promised you. I think your over all design brilliant and a most helpful "solution" to this play. As Archie says, it makes his play <u>possible</u>. I don't think any finer compliment has been given a designer by a writer. The set does make his play, as he meant it to be, possible. For that both of us are grateful to you.

Now I am urging you in the direction of simplification. I'll put it constructively: Let the main design speak. Anything that stands in the way of your main design statement should be simplified out, or blended into the whole.

The simplification I am urging is not in the direction of "simple" props. For example, ladders instead of stairs. It is deeper than that. It is the elimination of all unessentials. Excuse the reference to another designer, but it was the one great gift Jones had. It is like that story I told you about my wife. She wrote me she didn't have time to write me a short letter so she was writing me a long letter. Simplification is not easy to attain. It needs much work and much thought. But in your design your basic statement is so right and so strong that anything that is added decoratively, or not absolutely necessary, should be eliminated.

Above all, the tipped up pattern of the ring, and paths leading to the ring and Heaven and Home, these paths and these areas, should all be blended into one unified design with a cohesion of its own. What you have now, especially on stage right, is a collection of elements. I said this to you yesterday and I think you understood. I also suggested last night a way out of the stage right arrangement. Heaven and the Wardrobe could be connected with the Ring and thereby blended into the Ring by the Path. This unity, this making ONE of complex of paths and areas so the whole tipped up ground plan is one design, is terribly important. Last night also in the clumsy drawing I left with you, I suggested the addition of another path and I drew it for you as I see it. I have nothing to add to that except that it is essential for the staging of the play.

I also suggested that we give the whole design a sort of logic on its own terms or sense. In other words, that the stage left exit lead into other parts of J.B.'s house, used only for that. I have worked the play out so this can be. When they go off stage left up that short path past and behind your backing, it should be, and will be clear, that they are going into other rooms in J.B.'s house.

The new path I added, which enters the Ring upstage, left of center, is the path to the outside "real world". Here the Messengers come. Here J.B. and Sarah walk home from the movies. Along this path come the Comforters, etc. Now, this path also will be used only for this purpose and only with this meaning. It will be the path from the outside world to the Ring. And the same goes for the path down right, which leads to "Heaven". This will be used only by Nickles, and once by Zuss.

It's possible, of course, that in a delicate way, since each path has so specialized a meaning and significance in my mind, that when you design them you delicately give them a corresponding quality. This is not essential. You may think that in the interests of simplicity it is better not to color them, so to speak. But perhaps they should only be a color or a tint. Perhaps something in the nature of the surface or the dimension or proportion of the paths. In short, I am trying to blend my mechanics and ground plan, and my meanings, into your design.

Now we come to the problem of color. Archie said in his letter that we are all agreed that the tent should be made up of patches and pieces inherited from all the religions of history, from the witch doctors down to the Roman Catholic Church. But he stressed that these pieces have been woven into the fabric of the tent for so long that the colors have all faded. And I would add, FADED INTO ONE. Of all your sketches that I have seen, I still like the black and white best. I have never felt this about a design of yours before because you are brilliant at color. You have the subtlest palette of any designer in New York. But essentially the simplicity of this play demands a simplicity in its design. Furthermore, simply technically I don't want J.B. to be backed up by a mottled background. I want him to stand out from it. I don't want him part of it. I want him dominant in front of it. I don't want him minimized, I want him maximized. I am even concerned a little about the scale. Let us think of making this show no bigger than necessary. But I'm not nearly so much concerned about the scale as I am about the "busyness" of the colors. As we both commented yesterday, Archie has simplified the canvas of the world. There is a purity in his nature that only a man who sees life simply can have.

My only other big point has to do with what happens to the set when the atom bomb hits. This should be a design in itself. Of course, it only happens to the Ring and the parts of the Paths that are close to the Ring. It's as though the place where J.B. lives is suddenly twisted by an enormous force. If you will look at some of the pictures of Hiroshima or any city that has been hit by modern high explosives, you will see that the structural elements have been taken and twisted into designs that tell-tale the force of the explosion. This you have to do with something about the Ring, and do it so simply that two or three angles and twisted elements will "tell it all". Also, what's done has to be so simple that Nickles in his last scene in the play can go and quickly shove all pieces back into place and bring the world into order again.

These are the essential notes. The others are trifles and I won't include them. They are bound to come up in our discussions, and they are bound to be solved.

I do want, however, to continue working the way we have been on this set. This show, more than any other I've done, requires the designer and director to work hand in hand. It's almost as though the line of demarcation between your work and mine was not clearly marked at certain points.

I am also anxious, Boris, to get your reaction to the new script, which I will send to you the moment I have it. After you have read this letter please call me. I will be at home tonight. And let me know if I have made everything clear.

Best,

EK:nm

[Listed in the enclosed "notes" were the "Essentials" of Kazan's meeting with Boris Aronson in Athens: *J.B.* "is not a circus. It *looks* like a circus. . . . People represent essences, they are not individuals. . . . The play is, in a way, the dream or nightmare of an America starting from Anxiety about what our fate is to be. . . . The tent is the whole apparatus which man put up to stand over his head, protect him and shelter him, and which, in fact, stood between him and God" (Rich, p. 140). Steeped in European modernism and practiced in American stage design through association with the Group Theatre, Aronson was also conversant with vaudeville and the circus and was uniquely qualified to execute the director's plan for *J.B.* His design, Kazan claimed, "was, at all times, the most artistic thing on the stage."

An acrobat's perch used by Zuss overlooks the elevated circus ring of family space and the surrounding area in which Nickles ranges in observation of man. The stage left exit hints of unseen rooms and a once-flourishing domestic life inside J.B.'s home. Nickles cuts imaginary guy ropes of the tent in act one to

"At all times, the most artistic thing on the stage":
Boris Aronson's stage design for *J.B.*

expose J.B. to an inscrutable universe without a distracting religious presence. Observers of the run-through criticized the "'hypo-ed'" (Lillian Hellman's term) tone of the production, especially the atomic blast and its resounding aftermath. "As I understand it," MacLeish wrote to Kazan at the time, "there will be a blinding flash, a distant reverberation of some kind. Would it not be far more effective to follow that with silence," rather than "all those coughing cries after the bombing" ("Staging a Play," p. 155). The catastrophe was finally represented by a red light that "shoots up" from a trapdoor, destroying J.B.'s industrial wealth along with Ruth, the last surviving child.

Collaborators in the past, Aronson and Kazan worked together again in staging *Incident at Vichy* in 1964.] *TL with enclosure, 4 pp., Wesleyan*

TO JO MIELZINER

[New York]
September 9, 1958

Dear Jo:
I had a good weekend on SBY. I've put in a lot of time on it, and I believe, finally figured out what I want to do with it. And, therefore, at last I know how I want to proceed. I didn't the last time I met with you and I was wobbling pretty badly the time before. It is a tough play to do and could go so many ways and the important thing is to go the organic "route".

So I am rushing this letter to you. For one thing, to tell you to STOP. I know how you are. I know that in between lighting sessions you will be opening your despatch case and taking out the folder marked SBY, and the little revolving stage, and your colored pencils, and by the time you get back to New York it will all be done. Therefore this letter post haste. Please, Jo, stop! I think we are on the wrong track. We are certainly up the wrong tree, if we are up a tree. In effect, we have to start over. That doesn't mean a lot of the things we discussed aren't completely right. But basically—basically there was no basis—I never solved the play from the point of view of the director. I never told you what I needed to make the play "work" for me. I think you've solved it from the designer's point of view up to a point. Up to the point, that is, where I stopped helping you. I mean, I think it will look beautiful in the theatre and it will work quickly and well. But something about this show makes it necessary for me to have more help from the production scheme. It needs a production scheme, in other words, one that is organic and really dramatizes the play. It has to be done just right. It will only make sense if the production makes the RIGHT sense.

A lot of what is in this letter, Jo, is thinking aloud. But I can think aloud in an uninhibited fashion with an old friend, so just bear with me.

I think this is the most truly autobiographic play Williams ever wrote. Not in the way MENAGERIE was autobiographic—not a memory, softened and romanticized by time, of his youth, but Tennessee trying to describe his state of soul and state of being today and now. It is the frankest play he has written, dealing as it does with his own corruption and his wish to return to the purity he once had. It certainly deals more plainly with his world, that is, the world as he sees it. And while we again have the central romanticized figure of the boy surrounded by threatening and murderous forces, this time this central figure is not romanticized as it was in ORPHEUS, but male, partly corrupted and true. In fact, I believe it is Tennessee himself in disguise, right down to the thinning hair. CHANCE is in a trap, or he is in a pit, and he is surrounded by murderous forces that want to do away with him or castrate him. He has the choice of either leaving town and cutting himself off forever from his "pure" roots, or of staying there and being killed. He is not strong enough to fight these murderous forces. And perhaps he doesn't even want to escape. I increasingly feel that unconsciously he wants to stay there, be punished, pay for his sins, meet his deserts painful though they be, deadly though they be, cleanse himself through penance of the most awful physical and mental kind. It was as though Tennessee felt that after all he has done he should be punished or castrated. This is the strangely and unexpectedly puritanical side of Williams. He is obsessed with his own sin, and I suppose it is this sense of guilt that makes his vision so universal. We all have it to some degree or other.

Now, whatever else the director does or does not do, he absolutely must dramatize and directly put on the stage in physical form this basic situation. We have to picturize CHANCE in this trap, or pit, finally having no escape or just one degrading escape possible. Like the bull in the pit surrounded by hostile and jeering crowds who cheer at his betrayers and murderers and await his death with the pleasure of vengeance.

Gruesome? Well, when I did BABY DOLL in Greenville, Mississippi, Williams came down to visit me. He stayed at the Greenville Hotel for three days, and there, if ever I saw one, was a trapped man. He felt quite clearly that the people of the town hated him. He complained that no one called him. He smarted over snubs, real or imaginary, from people he passed in the street. He began to feel that he was trapped. In one obsessive drunken moment he said he hoped he could get out of town alive, and he began to be panic stricken. I couldn't find him a swimming pool, and this lack of physical outlet made him more panicky. After three days he disappeared without warning. He had even felt, and I have felt this, trapped in his hotel room. That in case of an emergency or of sudden danger, there was no way out of the hotel room. And, after all, there was only one way out for him. Down through the lobby full of people that knew him and, as he saw it, hated him.

You get the idea. It's all in the play. The scene in the cocktail lounge is exactly this. And, furthermore, I am only treating the matter superficially. He feels the whole world is against him as an artist and as a homosexual both. Well, you are familiar with the man and you know the situation that he thinks he is in. Sometimes I wonder how the hell he lives!

Now, that is one thing that somehow should be caught in a production scheme. Here comes the other. How does Williams get out of the trap? For on certain occasions he does. On certain occasions, for temporary short terms of time. Well, for one thing, which is like CHANCE, increasingly by drink. This makes him suddenly confident, light, fearless, social, gay. It is temporary. But he must drink. He is compelled to. I suppose he has taken dope, though I doubt if he is given to this a great deal. But still Tennessee only writes what he has been through. And then by the act of loving. Tennessee complains that as he gets older this is a decreasingly frequent escape for him. And then by the greatest of all, an act of imagination. Through the act of memory recall, for instance, and either written down or not, through the process which is the artistic process. In this way he is able every morning as he shuts himself up in his room and looks through the door at the wolves outside waiting to devour him, he is able to go into the land that John Keats describes and to be free and happy again, pure again, free again.

I don't think Tennessee could live if he were unable to function as a writer. His art is necessary for him. You recall how often in his plays the idea of flight is dwelt upon.

Now I say, Jo, that these two worlds, the threatening, hostile, murderous, real world, from which CHANCE (Tennessee) can transport himself into the imaginary world by an act of art, or by some extraordinary stimulus, that is the two worlds are the <u>alternating Environments of this play</u>. The fact that one of the traps is a hotel room and the other a cocktail lounge is important, but not central. Tennessee has gone past realism. The realistic trimmings are peripheral. The core is what has to be made to live in concrete terms of stage art.

And as these two worlds are the environments of the play, the PROCESS of the play is again and again how CHANCE passes from one world to the other. And this is done more frankly and plainly and directly than the author has ever done it before. We see CHANCE and THE PRINCESS and even THE BOSS come forward under the author's direction, and recreate for themselves and for us their wish-dreams, their romanticized pasts, their lost glory. And as this happens, the author, now confident in the capabilities of the new stage says in his stage direction "'Room changes'". "'Bar disappears'". "'They are alone in the Palm Garden'". "'He is alone with himself'". In other words, the TRAPPED ONE is transported on the wings of this spiritual experience— drink, dope, romance, sex, longing, imagination, memory, whatever—OUT OF THIS WORLD.

I am very leery these days, Jo, of highly colored words that remain words. This is Harold Clurman's great deficiency. He does not take his own eloquence seriously enough. He does not turn it into movement, scenery, costumes and behavior. I want to be very bold on this show, more probably than Tennessee may wish for. I want to physicalize this going from "reality into the world of dreams". This back and forth process. I say we have to physicalize this quite literally, in the literalness, that is, of art. We have to show the background, threatening and hostile and suddenly they are swimming in another environment, an environment which is created by their imaginations or their over-stimulated senses. And the point is that this imagined environment is realer than the so called real one. THE PRINCESS lives in her memory, like many an old actress we know. CHANCE lives in his imaginings, like many a person we know who "walks around in a fog all day". And who only comes down to earth when he is writing or loving or drinking. I see the figures of CHANCE, of THE PRINCESS, bathed in this environment, which they have created and where they feel at home and without fear. Of course, this is exactly what drink and dope and love and memory and the exercise of the artistic faculties do. Some people would add to this list religion. My point is that I want to find a theatrical form for this and this is the help I need from you. We have to create a set which changes magically the chairs and furniture and objects in hand. They have to simply disappear. Suddenly the threatening picture is gone. Suddenly the overbearing physical relationships have eased. Suddenly the people, the strange people, are in a new world of their own making. A non-specific world, a non-literal world, a world of the imagination.

Well, after I figured out what the core of this thing is, I began to figure out how this could be done. The show is peculiar. There aren't a lot of sets; three sets. But in a way you can do it so there are a lot of environments, memory environments, dream environments. If you begin to think of the scenery as subjective scenery, and if you begin to think of CHANCE's world as the world that an artist inhabits, then perhaps there are more than three sets.

For example, this scheme makes our idea of the TV picture on the big screen ABSOLUTELY in style. Of course, CHANCE sees nothing at that time in the room except the enormous, threatening, animated photograph of BOSS FINLEY. You might say as CHANCE watches the TV "he doesn't know where he is". That is all that exists for him in the world. Sometimes when you are drunk you really literally do forget where you are. You are living in a world of your own. I would like to try, Jo, to think of the scenery in this way, that is, as subjective scenery.

At the end of Act Two, as I see it, CHANCE is caught in a pit which is in the shape and with the "trim" of a cocktail lounge, and there in the proxy of THE HECKLER he is beaten up. In Act Three, CHANCE is left behind. He allows himself to be left behind in a pit which is THE PRINCESS' room, and as he lies there finally the murderous figures begin to converge on him. He is caught there for the last time. He won't walk out of that pit, or that trap, alive. In other words, both these sets have to be designed so you feel the boy is in some sort of a declivity, and at the mercy, because of the very nature of a pit or trap, of his hostile fellow humans. But all through both acts and in the first act too, he is getting out of it and the set must make this change possible and physical.

Other changes, like bringing the bed nearer or further, or shifting the furniture by means of a revolving stage MUST NOT be made. They are unimportant. The only important changes are the ones I have tried to describe above and they should be the only changes made. And these changes that are important must be made before our eyes and magically and by lights. Nothing else must shift. It confuses things to have other movement and other changes. The changes in the subjective scenery, changes, changes made by lights, are the only changes to be made. I have become convinced of this and that is why I am writing you now, not even waiting for you to return to New York to tell you to stop working on the revolving stage idea.

Now, how can all of this be done? What physical arrangement, mechanics, equipment, design, will solve this? I had to ask myself this question before I asked it of you. And to an extent, as a director, I had to solve it for myself before I could put it to you and ask you to solve it as a designer. I think I have. It is not much designwise, but I have an arrangement idea, a basic picture idea and also a mechanical idea. I have sketched out four little ground plans, which I am attaching, which you can read perfectly well. They are crudely done, so you will have questions on them, and ask me. And then there are some notes which also are attached as to how these things can work. I hope the ground plans are clear, but if they are not, pick up a phone, or let me know when you are coming to New York next and first thing is for us to get together and talk this thing out. . . .

Love, Gadg

EK:nm
Enc.

[If Tennessee Williams had written "before the technical development of translucent and transparent scenery," he would "have invented it" (Mielziner, p. 124). The "development" cited by Jo Mielziner was prompted by Williams's poetic theater and executed by Mielziner's innovative lighting of *The Glass Menagerie* and *Streetcar*. The fluid scene changes and manifestations found in the earlier plays reappear as stage directions in *Sweet Bird of Youth:* "'Room changes'". "'Bar disappears'". "'They are alone in the Palm Garden'". "'He is alone with himself'". The hostile "Environments" of hotel room and cocktail lounge open onto the shadowy palm garden, which is swept by a mournful prevailing wind from the Gulf Coast. Kazan instructed Mielziner to abandon the original "revolving stage idea" and limit set changes to those "made by lights."

In a lengthy postscript marked "Next Day!" (not included here), Kazan noted that his "poor little ground plans" include a "screen" suggested by prints used in Japanese theater. Could they, he wondered, be used as "a sort of lap dissolve," in which a scenic drop painted from the rear would be backlit to produce a "formalized 'realism'" and then transformed into "a projected non-realistic, non-literal" image. Mielziner answered "Yes" in the margin.

Tennessee Williams reviewed Mielziner's initial design for *Sweet Bird* with more concern than enthusiasm. The cocktail lounge, he thought, was "not clearly defined," while the "height" and "glaring whiteness" of platforms used as playing areas threatened to obscure the play's "visual poetry." Williams added with evident resignation that "a stage-designer always gets his best results when he is least interfered with, that is, after author and director have indicated what the stage-action requires" (to EK and Mielziner, November 11, 1958, BRTC).

Kazan wondered if the 16 mm projector used to "throw an image" in the political rally scene was adequate and asked Mielziner to schedule a test, "since we're so 'far out' with this idea" (December 20, 1958, BRTC). Mielziner later described the problem as one of "scale" rather than visibility. "The moment the filmed image of a man in motion is scaled down to the size of a living actor, it loses authenticity in the third dimension. Even the combination of the live actor's voice, heard unamplified, and the electronic-sounding voice heard on sound film creates a serious production problem. Someday this will probably be solved. But in *Sweet Bird of Youth* I was conscious only of the lack of cohesion in what was otherwise a stunning performance and a colorful production" (Mielziner, p. 202).] *TLS with enclosures, 10 pp., BRTC*

TO LUCINDA BALLARD

Dear Cindy:

I was thinking after we left the other day, Archie and I, "All that talk and nothing about the style of the show, all that character analysis, and nothing about the show itself and how it should be done. After all you cant have a set that is three quarters circus and the rest cosmic and costume the players in outfits that they can run down to the corner in for a coffee between the acts." Then Boris and I began talking about the set and the play and the rewriting and everything and I became convinced that I had left out something very vital in my conversation with you.

So I went over the thing in my mind yesterday. What style should the clothes be in. I mean they are to be clothed in an outfit that is so profoundly characteristic of a type—! Then I said TYPE that's the word.

Well the word type usually means something shallow in the Theatre. It most often signifies a lack in insight by the playwright and the actor. But I thought: there are types that are among the greatest creations in literature. For example Don Quixote—the "type" or "symbol" of Romanticism. And of course the complementary type Sancho Panza. And Uriah Heep—who EQUALS hypocritical humbleness. And Hamlet the intellectual who's unable to act. And Peter Pan: Youth, Captain Ahab: Vengeance, The Hairy Ape.

Well you can make up your own list. You will see that they are not shallow or thin creations, but memorable as among the really great reaches of man— the writer. And then there are living people who are "types," MM and BB. Emmett Kelly. Tallulah Bankhead. etc.

And then I remembered that we had said a lot of things about J.B. but one thing that stuck hard in my mind was WENDELL WILLKIE. Willkie was a whole era—liberal Capitalism—a man who was forced to break out of his mold and learn and learn because History was moving so fast. A man with the natural homely resilience and horse sense and outspokenness of the middle of this country—oh I cant describe it—but I see him in one characteristic piece.

Dolls and Puppets tend to be this: Types. They are usually built on ONE HUMAN QUALITY, often to the exclusion of all others. And I repeat they are not necessarily superficial creations.

For instance many different actors can interpret Hamlet in many different ways—but it always must remain a study in hesitation and impotence and a man confronting demands upon himself for action that are too big for him. Iago, ditto, must always remain a study in Iago-ism—no matter seen how, no matter what psychological motivation chosen.

Well then I began to think of the characters in J.B. this way. Here's a hasty, little list and you and I can do much better. But—and here's the point—IT IS A WAY OF THINKING ABOUT THESE CLOTHES THAT MAKES THEM FIT INTO THE STYLE OF THE PLAY AND THE STYLE OF THE SET

J.B. is all businessman.
Sarah is all—yankee
    she is all—mother
Nickles: the Devil as BEAT GENERATION
    the Devil as Teddy Boy.
    the Devil as Angry Young Man
    the Devil as Jimmy Dean.
Zuss: the GOD MAN CREATED in the image of his own father. The God
    man created because he was frightened
2nd Messenger. The citizen soldier who's been intimate with Death and
    cant
    forget it.
1st Messenger. The Professional soldier who's seen so much of Death that
    he thinks nothing of it.
Bildad: The Labor Leader who still thinks its 1930.
Zophar: the Catholic who's so rigidly fundamentalist that even the
    Catholics wont have him.
Eliphaz: the psychoanalyst as Society-racketeer

These aren't brilliant and are off the top of my head—but you get the idea. If you designed THOSE, you would have Stylized costumes—and costumes that fit the set. By the way the above is exactly what Daumier did. And Goya. And Giotto (?)

This is the kind of a show where all one character's clothes are one color and no other character wears that color. What is this COSTUME AS MASK? It is an exaggeration of the most characteristic aspect of a character—an exaggeration which eliminates all non-typical aspects. It is a matter of a narrow selection except that because it is Narrow it goes deep. It is a probing and finally a selection for each character of his most typical characteristic and rendering that and only that into clothes. It is a costume which provokes from an audience a smile of recognition and still a recognition that something is being revealed as fundamental—as though the costume is so well chosen and so thoroughly unified that it cuts the ESSENCE of the character and LEAVES EVERYTHING ELSE OUT.

I hope it all sounds like fun. Anyway lets call it a basis for discussion—One thing is very clear: Style has to be discussed. The costumes have to work in this play and in this set.

Love Always. Gadg

[Mr. Zuss and Nickles were initially conceived as a type of "the broken-down actor fallen on evil days." Kazan's point that defiant lines spoken by Nickles suggest youth rather than age led MacLeish to recast Satan as a beat generation type, variously identified with English Teddy boys and John Osborne's angry young man, as well as James Dean.

Zuss and Nickles wear masks designed to remove "all non-typical aspects" of their roles. Nickles adjusts his robe with a curse and bitterly surveys the mask while receiving it from Zuss: "Look at those lips. They've tasted something / Bitter as a broth of blood / And spat the sup out. Was that evil?" Scornful of beauty, "the Creator's bait," Nickles prefers to "wear this ache of loathing" and agrees to "play the part" of Satan.

Kazan informed Cheryl Crawford after the opening of *J.B.* that he would not work again with Lucinda Ballard "under any conditions." Nor did he "like dealing with the author's agent," Audrey Wood, who had recommended Ballard for *Sweet Bird of Youth*. Kazan described Ballard later as "a true artist, with a volatile temperament" (*A Life*, p. 339).] *TLSx, 3 pp., Beinecke*

TO CHRIS KAZAN

[New York]
October 15, 1958

Dear Chris:

Haven't heard back from you in ans. to my letter. I've gotten used to that. I dont like it a damn bit, but I've gotten used to it. I only hear from you when you have a bill. So shit I'll write you about the bill. I paid part of that last bill. How much do I still owe the Harv. Corp.? Let me know and I'll get it up. And while I'm at it why the hell dont you drop me a note once in a while. I dont want anything from you. I dont want to tell you how or where or with whom to live your life. I think you sometimes drink a little too much. But you're about twenty now and finally its going to be all your business and I'm sidelined watching it. I feel very friendly and loving towards you. But in time, getting little back, even in the way of a word or a slight effort, and the idea penetrates. I also think you're rude towards your mother. She takes the trouble to call you about your painting, and you sound—so she tells me—as though you resented her calling you. What the hell! Common courtesy man. I know parents traditionally take it in the belly from their kids. But I dont like it. I can be a good friend to you all your life long, and a help, and a lot of other things. But if you resent something, give me the gift of candor. I'm fed up too with hearing the most fundamental news about your daily existence from other people. Its embarrassing and a nuisance. For instance we hear that you now have your motor bike. O.K. with me. We hear you might move. etc. What is happening?

Money has no privileges, in a sense, and the money you have been given has gone to you willing, but it may not continue so. You act as though its there entirely at your whim. I've just paid a large bill for your tuition and room and board. What happens to that when you move. I work damned hard, goddamn hard to make that money. Its not just in the bank, sitting there like a number. I sweat for it. And give up years for it. I dont like to have it taken for granted. I want to know what happens to it, and I insist on feeling some sense from you that you know its worth. Not the worth of the money. But you are spending my effort, my energy. I've been feeling these things for a while. But this is the first time I've written you about them. I mean you're an adult now. And I'm sick of falling into the supine position and being kicked. That's how it feels. I'm sick of sending letters off to you and receiving no answers, or being grateful for small favors, a few brief words. Since you're an adult, act like one. If you're resentful say so. Say why. If you're not speak. A letter deserves if not an answer, an acknowledgment. I say this to you in love. I'll always feel that. You cant freeze that by neglect. But you can diminish it. I think its finally going to be your loss. Only you wont feel it for a while. I speak to you as an adult now. All behavior has its consequences. Neglect brings ~~attrition~~ stiffness and distance. You want it, you'll get it, not at all because I want to be that way to you. But its inevitable. Friendship thrives on contact. I know and appreciate that you have to find your own way. Not mine, not anyone else's. Your own. I like that. I dont minimize the problem. I like your spirit. I like and admire your independence. I know you may end up in another world from me, in another country possibly, in another environment. I'm here to help you do what you want, not what I want. I've never never never asked you to do what I want. But I dont like to be treated scornfully. My pride rebels against that. And that is what you often do. I like it even that you have no false dutifulness to me. Or false "respect", or kowtowing or whatever. You're your own man and I respect that. But the role of the football never did suit me, and that's how you often make me feel. I thought you ought to know it.

[Nearly twenty and soon to be a sophomore at Harvard, Chris Kazan had tested his father's understanding in the preceding summer by declining to join the family trip to Greece. "He sounds right, his reasons seem sound," Elia wrote at the time to Archibald MacLeish, "and of course he can only grow up away from us" (n.d., Beinecke). Elia's uneasy relationship with his older son appears in earlier correspondence as well. "One thing kills me," Elia wrote to Molly in 1944, as film work in California and the affair with Constance Dowling prolonged his absence from the family: "Chris. I feel he needs me, much more than I feel Judy needs me." When a similar concern was shared with John Steinbeck in early 1959, Steinbeck answered perhaps with a trace of his own parental guilt: "You say that you feel guilty about Chris. Don't let yourself, or call it by its name. I know there is strangeness here—as though you two were not related and were trying to make it so. . . . If you are able to build a guilt about Chris—you can be sure that there is something you don't understand or don't want to understand. Or you might be seeking to chain him to you with your guilt. Set him free! Only then can you be friends" (Steinbeck/*Letters,* p. 630). Kazan marked the present letter "Not Sent," adding "I don't <u>really</u> feel this way."] *TL, 1 p., Wesleyan*

TO ARCHIBALD MACLEISH

[Washington, D.C.]
[November 26, 1958]

Dear Archie:

Thinking thru our morning's conversation again. I think there are two things WE must do. And I believe these two things are critical to the reception and success of our play.

First we need the big scene. The big scene, the classical recognition scene now happens when I have turned J.B.'s back to the audience. We now come to the turning point of the play and then throw it away. How did we miss it? I'll try to answer that.

We played the last speech of J.B. to the D.V. MIXED. We understood each other here—that J.B. is humbled but also "ironic" about his <u>wherefore</u>. But the audience did not and never will understand US. I dont think it can all hang—this most important inner turn and development of J.B.'s on the reading of one word "Wherefore"! and the sentences, the sentence that follows.

What we must substitute for this duplex of mixed values is FIRST one value and THEN the next. We must substitute a Development for an irony. A development INSIDE J.B. that we watch and that is much more important for the clarity and the emotion of the play than the Zuss Nickles scene.

The Development? First he should be genuinely humbled. OVER-WHELMED. GENUINELY SO. The Lord has thrown the whole creation at him. And the Lord has made him aware of his insignificance.

AND THEN in the cool of thought. J.B. must think what the hell have I repented of, what has humbled me, and ABOVE ALL where does that leave me. He must realize that (YOU've put this brilliantly to me in notes and conversation and I cant say it right) insignificant yes, alone yes but also independent and with his own dignity as man.

This development inside, repeat INSIDE J.B. is the crucial moment of the WHOLE G.D. PLAY. I MEAN ITS CRUCIAL. It is the classic (Greek, Aristotelian) recognition and we have left it out. All we have done is leave out (turning the Actors' back to the audience)—the TURNING POINT OF THE PLAY

After he changes here and after we make the audience clearly realize this change, we should then watch and appreciate that he is behaving differently—He becomes a different man. We MUST MARK HIS CHANGE. We must tell the audience clearly that at this critical moment in the course of the play he has changed so that no critic can ever say that he is the same at the end as he was at the beginning. The reason one critic was able to say this is that we HAVE NOT DRAMATISED THE MOMENT OF CHANGE. So I suggest that we dramatize here a development. Perhaps Zuss should comment first on his complete humbling and then comment and be appalled at the change that is beginning to happen under his eyes. . . . What we have onstage now is dramatic "mud" and what we have succeeded in doing is ducking completely the key moment in the play. How stupid can an experienced director be?? I'M ashamed of myself.

The second point is also critically important. The audience must be put into the emotional position where they are concerned about the outcome of the Comforters scene. We have partly done this thru J.B.'s calling for help. We simply want him to get help. But how is the issue of J.B.'s enduring faith and trust in the Universe, in God's justice related to the apparently "new" dramatic concept of guilt. I can tell you the answer, yes, BUT THE AUDIENCE DOES NOT FEEL IT. Nickles and Zuss can help here by becoming partisan. I can help a lot in how I handle Pat. But we cant do too much here. It is the moment where the play drifts off into a debate—much less than it used to. But still.

Now I have a revolutionary thought. I agree about Zuss attitude. He's not very bright and rides on "the BOOK" and faith and he just "knows" that there is no comfort except in the acceptance of God's will and he scorns the comforters. But I think we're wrong with Nickles. Follow me a moment.

Nickles is surprised, or should be by the appearance of the comforters. Zuss expects them. He knows that whenever the play is played three comforters appear and he knows, has faith that the outcome will be as ever. But Nickles should be, it seems to me, thrown into the kind of panic, by their appearance, that will presage his end. For these "friends" are brilliant and powerful exponents of three philosophies that have given lots of comfort to millions. It is not impossible that they might explain J.B.'s guilt to him that will make him retain his sanity and bearing and NOT ALLOW him to curse God and die.

The comforters might ruin Nickles. So he plays each scene, in profound apprehension sort of "with" J.B., anxiously watching, hanging on every word, powerfully and deeply and emotionally involved in the outcome of each scene, elated, each time more as J.B. dismisses one after another of these men—and finally the last burst of triumph.

This would "emotionalize" the whole scene. Nickles cause should hang by a thread all thru this scene. And each time one is scorned and pushed off, he should have a powerful emotional reaction—And building to his final blast of triumph.

I'm terribly embarrassed all this is so late.

LOVE

G

[A cast headed by Pat Hingle (J.B.), Raymond Massey (Mr. Zuss), and Christopher Plummer (Nickles) opened in Washington to mixed reviews. The critic who praised the show's "theatricality" also observed that J.B. "is the same man at the end as he was in the beginning. This is noble but it is not dramatic" (*Washington Post,* November 25, 1958). Kazan soon realized that the recognition scene in act two "had been left un-*dramatized.*" It begins with the departure of the biblical comforters, who have failed to enlighten or console J.B. The Distant Voice rebukes his cry of "wrong" with lines drawn from the Old Testament source: "Where wast thou when I laid the foundations of the earth?" J.B. is humbled by God's majesty: "Wherefore I abhor myself and repent." In revision MacLeish reinforced the "moment of change" by separating J.B.'s abasement from the critical reflection and framing the discovery of human dignity in a series of "cool" reversals of the D.V.'s offstage proclamation. Kazan marked the change by deft restaging: *"J.B. lifts his face from the earth, his eyes on the audience. His voice a whisper at first in which the great words he has heard return to his mouth with the sour of mortality on them"* ("Staging a Play," p. 157).

The comforters scene in act two raised a "second point" broached earlier by Kazan. MacLeish modernized the Old Testament visitors by assigning roles of Marxist, psychoanalyst, and priest with nostrums to match. J.B. easily rejected their arguments, but it was more difficult for MacLeish to reconcile J.B.'s "enduring faith" in God's "justice" and the "'new' dramatic concept of guilt" that has lifted the penitent from abasement. MacLeish's answer, stated in an interview, circumvents the biblical imperative of submission to God's will and rests instead on human agency: "'J.B. makes the great human discovery. He is at least a man whatever else he is. He must rely on his manhood, humanity to survive'" (*Washington Post,* November 30, 1958). Kenneth Tynan noted the equivocation when *J.B.* reached New York: "[MacLeish] seems to have been determined to wound nobody, even in passing, and to keep up, at all costs, the appearance of devotion to an antique and extravagant concept of the Deity. Even at curtain fall, we do not know where he really stands" (*New Yorker,* December 20, 1958).] *TLS, 2 pp., Beinecke*

TO CLIFFORD ODETS

[New York]

[c. December 18, 1958]

Dear Cliff:

Everything o.k. here now. At the time I wrote you, I thought J.B. wouldn't earn any money. But its doing well. Utter surprise. We had very discouraging reactions at the run thrus. And Washington didn't come to the play, notices poor, no audience, people walking out etc. But we stuck with it and, as it turned out, did just the right re-writing and restaging. And then, opening night here a sort of "miracle" happened, and it suddenly seemed to surpass itself. The toughest part of it was that many of the people around the show, stage managers, press man, even the producer for a few days, the wives etc. had given up. Only MacLeish and the actors, because they are innocent and naive, and I, because I'm mean, didn't give up. I guess, in our time-fuse theatre, tenacity is the most practical and necessary virtue. So I'm financially o.k. again. I thought for a while there that I'd be out to California to do a picture ready or not. But I wont be. Relax about the dough. Dont need it now. Sorry you've had the bad weeks. And the perfidy! What can I say about that? Animals in captivity turn on each other. Two lionesses, the other day, tore a male lion to pieces, suddenly, for no "reason", in their cage. What happened to the Front Page Story? Wish I could help you. But from a distance, here is my hand and my love.

G.

[*J.B.*'s arrival in New York on December 11 coincided with a newspaper strike that restricted advertising and delayed publication of mainstream reviews. Nonetheless, the play gained momentum and Kazan withdrew a request that Clifford Odets repay a $5,000 loan needed to meet expenses for an unidentified project. The cast was lavishly praised, as was Kazan, who received no more glowing theater notices than he did for *J.B.* In parting for the holidays, he advised the actors to "enjoy" their success. "The old timers among you will know how rare it is—this good! Good bye old queens, young hams, loyal and talented actors all. Take care of yourselves and the play." *J.B.* ran for nearly a year and delivered Tony Awards to author, director, and producer, as well as a third Pulitzer to Archibald MacLeish—his first for drama.

Kazan delayed filming *Wild River* until late 1959. He regretted being unable to work with Clifford Odets, who wrote and eventually directed *The Story on Page One* (1959) for Twentieth Century-Fox. "Perfidy!" aside, Odets was upbeat about writing for Hollywood as the film entered production: "'Today a movie writer can write a screen play the way he would a play for Broadway. You can do almost anything you want in Hollywood providing you're a good writer'" (*NYT,* October 1, 1959).] *TLS, 1 p., Indiana*

TO TENNESSEE WILLIAMS

[New York]
[late December 1958]

BABY:
I got terribly depressed yesterday. Sam S. called me up and said he was going down to Miami. And I thought: Christ he's working on Suddenly Last Sum-

mer, on Orpheus, on Period of Readjustment and when the hell is he going to get time to do the last work on Sweet Bird of Youth which is the only important one because its the one which is going to come to public attention right soon, and the one that's going to hurt you most if it doesn't get the reaction you like. And then Cuba! I imagine you felt that way when I was doing three plays. And you showed it to me. Now I'm showing it to you. I dont think you've got the size of this play yet, and I dont think you're ever going to if you split yourself up and have your mind all ways between Gore Vidal, Sam Spiegel (an anthropofagos if there ever was one) Meade Roberts, Audrey Wood, Shepherd and Jurow, Jurow and Shepherd, and their agents, and then whoever the hell is the cast of characters on this new one, with heavy discussions etc. Its like directing a play written by a TRUST. You should be here now. That's the fact of it. And I'm forgetting (till this second) Summer and Smoke, which I understand is also on the phone with you. If I hear that Spiegel is in Cuba with you or Gore Vidal or anyone else from any other play (I dont care whom you fuck as long as they're not writing a screen play for you) Oh Shit I sound like a nagging wife. But I'm worried about the third act of Sweet Bird of Youth, and I FEEL LIKE I'M WORRYING ALONE. I think Act One is wonderful. And Act Two fine once its cut down. But what worries me is something about the clinching of the character of Chance. The most important thing about any character, I'm beginning to think, is the last thing he does, the last big thing he does. And the last big thing that Chance does is NOT TO LEAVE. He can leave and he doesn't. This cannot be just an accident. I think it should be dramatised as having the importance it does have. And as I wrote you, I think there should be a cold cock scene early in the act where the Princess says: what the hell is it with you: 'Are you looking for Punishment? I'm beginning to think you want to have your balls cut off? You can go. Now. With me! Come on!' And he doesn't. Its terribly significant and revelatory and BIG, OF BIG DIMENSION to me that Chance can escape and does not. That he <u>CHOOSES?</u> CHOOSES, CHOOSES to stay there and ATONE and BE PUNISHED. That that makes him feel better. That for some deep reason he prefers it. And I think the reason (search within yourself) is deeper than the speech about the clock and time etc. I think it has something to do with making up with people, of atoning, of getting back with the people, of being loved again, by all, of being like he was when he was happiest, a beloved babe, admired, coddled, cuddled. OR WHATEVER. I'm not trying to tell you what. I'm saying its the most significant piece of behavior in your whole play. The ending always is. And I'm not saying, I'M NOT! that I want it crystal clear, or simple, over-simplified or anything. I just want the third act fixed so that the piece of behaviour of STAYING is given the significance it actually has. It can be hinted at, suggested—as long as we know why he's courting death like a lover, awaiting castration like it was his due, awaiting it like it was the right thing and in fact the thing that he wants above and beyond everything else. Granted he's stoned, turned on etc. still he's behaving, therefore, from a deeper core of feeling than if he were not turned on.

And this. The end of a play is deceptive. It only occupies so many pages, usually very few. But it is much much larger than it appears in print. And suddenly this March, there'll we be stuck with it, struggling with it, there it will be the MOST IMPORTANT thing in our whole evening. And what is wrong is not the "writing" of the end. No speech about the clock and the irrevocable second hand is going to solve it. Its not a matter of writing something better—its only a matter of SETTING IT UP RIGHT. Feeling it thru right. Finding out what is contained in this eloquent piece of negative action. We both feel its dead right for him to choose to stay. This must be made to seem like 1/ a choice of his, unconscious albeit. 2/ the most profoundly characteristic and INEVITABLE THING HE COULD DO.

LOVE. Gadg

THE DANGERS OF A STRONG AND EXCITABLE DIRECTOR. JEALOUS TOO.

[Tennessee Williams excused Kazan's "forceful importunities" and declared his "total commitment" to *Sweet Bird of Youth.* "At great expense of ego," he had put aside work on *Suddenly, Last Summer* and accepted Gore Vidal's collaboration. It was also "psychologically better" for Williams to be occupied with the tryout of his "serious comedy," *Period of Adjustment,* than "to sit here fretting and stewing and palpitating" about the fate of *Sweet Bird.* There was no "disagreement" about act three either. "From the very first," Williams wrote, "Chance did make a choice . . . to stay, not escape, and suffer the fate of his sweetheart. That's never been anything in my mind but the truth of the play." Only briefly in the preceding spring did he consider a "psychological castration" of Chance and departure with the Princess on her humiliating terms. Fear of repeating Val Xavier's mutilation in *Orpheus Descending* (1957) and losing Kazan's direction were at issue. After all, he reminded Kazan, it was he who had convinced the nervous playwright that his "first instinct" to have Chance "stay and atone" was dramatically correct (December 29, 1958, HRC).

In earlier correspondence Williams reported working on the "very end" of *Sweet Bird,* hoping to find a "summation comparable to Blanche's last line in Streetcar: 'Whoever you are, I've always depended on the kindness of strangers.'" Such a "moment of dignity" would produce a "legitimate, true catharsis" for Chance (to EK and Mielziner, November 11, 1958, BRTC). Kazan replied that discovering "what is contained" in Chance's "negative action" rather than "writing something better" was needed to solve the dramatic problem. As finally staged, *Sweet Bird* ends with Chance speaking directly to the audience as enemies close in: "I don't ask for your pity, but just for your understanding—not even that—no. Just for your recognition of me in you, and the enemy, time, in us all."] *TLS, 2 pp., Wesleyan*

TO ARCHIBALD MACLEISH

[New York]
[January 19, 1959]

Dear Archie:

I believe Molly is writing you about dates but here is a word from the horse's ass. SBY opens in N.Y. March tenth. Next day, the 11th.? I should be here the next day to pick up the pieces or act modest or get angry again at the critics or whatever seems to be called for. We could leave the 12th of March? Is that too late? If it isn't, any advice about the planes?

Rehearsals are tough. I seem to have run out my best string on J.B. I think I'm tired. Too quick one upon the other, I guess. I have to "work at it". You know what I mean, it isn't flowing like it sometimes does when you've got a full head of steam and it just seems to come out and you're surprised yourself how easy it is. That's when its good, when its all there and you sort of operate automatically. But that's when you have a full head of steam.

I'm watching the play. And of course I'll go see it again. Bob sends me a card every day. And after I bawled him out last time for letting Andreas twitch-dance, Bob is much more careful I think. He just lacks stomach. But the three principals are the cream as far as consistency and devotion and conscience go. I dont think the show will ever wander far.

I'M FURIOUS AT THE NEW YORK TIMES SUNDAY SECTION. I haven't had a fist fight in a few years, quite a few, but I feel very very much like taking on a man named Lew Funke who runs the Sunday sheet. This week again he had a letter saying our play was dull. This is the second one. Presumably their policy is to balance the letters, one good one bad etc. But this bastard is wilful, petty God and I feel he is out to give me a hard time. Anyway, the first letter said I had ruined your original script, which is o.k. with me, I mean one letter on that count is, I expected some of that. But yesterday he published a letter which had no point, no style, no intelligence, nothing just saying the play was dull. And I told old Delly to take off his head and raise hell. Delly called him, but as far as I'm concerned got no real satisfaction out of it. I guess muscle has to match muscle in these things. I'm going to egg Delly on until we get some letters now on our side. The damn thing is the position of a play (yours at the top) can be slowly eaten away by unanswered little snipings. B'way is a gossip eaten, petty-whispering, eye-rolling mental ghetto and the guy at the head of a production's sale and promotion has to be a furious monster. Which I hope Delly will be, jealous of every slight, furious at the drop of the wrong adjective. Does Delly send you the reviews? Helen? Not that you should pay any attention, but this is a matter of the continued life of the show and if its to live thru the summer that is NOW BEING DECIDED. It is decided now—

prizes etc. determine it—and not in the summer itself. If you feel like spurring on Delly do so. I think even the nicest, sportiest horse needs an occasional nick of the spurs. Love to you both. Tell the fish I'm coming.

G

[Plans were under way for the Kazans to visit Ada and Archie MacLeish in Antigua after the opening of *Sweet Bird* on March 10. In the meanwhile Kazan would revisit *J.B.* and curtail the "twitch-dance" of an exuberant biblical comforter. An episode of "cardiovascular spasms" in February and a doctor's order that MacLeish rest after seeing *J.B.* through successive productions did not prevent the Kazans' visit (Donaldson, p. 459). Elia returned to New York in late March "browner and generally better."

A writer to "The Drama Mailbag" accused Kazan of undermining J.B.'s tragic stature "by substituting cowardly submission for the God-forgiving acceptance of MacLeish's play." It followed for a second writer that the overall production was "dull and disappointing" and the audience indifferent to the fate of the protagonist, whose weakness hindered sympathetic identification (*NYT,* January 4 and 18, 1959). Kazan hoped to spur the play's producer to belabor Lewis Funke, columnist and Sunday drama editor of the *New York Times.*] TLS, 1 p., Beinecke

TO TENNESSEE WILLIAMS

SH: The Warwick, Philadelphia, PA.
[February 1959]

Dear Tenn:

I was depressed last night too. Not because of the awkwardness of a transition. That can be smoothened out. Its mechanical and we can do it.

What depressed hell out of me was that the second act for the first time seemed shallow. It seemed to be transpiring in the field of external events. Occurrences in a bar! Instead of within the heart of Chance. I feel, as I've always felt that it is the Aunt Nonnie scene that sends you into the bar INSIDE Chance. And I feel still that the info about the Garden of Allah is told too early. It should be the cap on unfolding of guilt. It is the recognition of Guilt that makes Chance STAY and be castrated. Only that.

I think now that the story is being mistold. I know its not easy to do. But still I think still that we should try. Yesterday morning I read the "Original". The first script that I read. It is more moving than what we are playing now. And nearly altogether because the story is told right. The right bits in the right places.

I think now we are off on the wrong track. We are essentially settling for a flashy performance by Geraldine Page. I'd like to get a few of the actors and

Geraldine Page and Paul Newman in *Sweet Bird of Youth*

read the April version. Or have us read it aloud. And study it. Something is going very wrong. Your plays are only good when they're <u>inside</u>.

With all Paul's insufficiencies, it is never the Actor's fault. Not finally. It is always Playwriting and Direction. Much worse performances than Paul's have been hailed as the expression of genius. If the Garden of Allah story is told too early all we can do in the bar is groan and bullshit. That's all Paul can do.

The idea of sending him into the bar still struggling, still UNAWARE OF HOW ENTIRE HIS GUILT IS! is right. That's the construction of the April version and its right. And THE NONNIE STORY IS a piece of story telling—The soliloquy about guts and luck does NOT replace it. TALK TO ME.

e.k.

[Molly Kazan's uninvited "notes" on *Sweet Bird of Youth* frayed the author's "nervous-system" and further darkened the "storm-cloud" that followed the production from rehearsals in New York to a three-week engagement in Philadelphia. Tennessee Williams threatened to close the play if he was exposed to any more "visiting firemen" (to EK, n.d., HTC). Kazan's belated preference for the "April version" involved scenes either cut or presumably misplaced by Williams in revision. Cut in act two was a long narrative scene with Nonnie, Heavenly's aunt, in which Chance recounts the years of his "clean, unashamed youth" and love for Heavenly, which he is determined to restore. Kazan argued that a carryover of such naive, uninformed hope was essential to the following hotel "bar" scene, in which Chance is exposed for the first time to Heavenly's faded beauty and submission to her father's corrupt political will. Otherwise the scene is mere "occurrences" in a cocktail lounge. Still unknown to Chance at this time are the details of the "Garden of Allah" story, which lies behind Heavenly's desolation.

The off-stage story begins in the preceding summer with a call that Heavenly join Chance in California and ends at the Garden of Allah—a raffish hotel complex in West Hollywood known to Williams and Kazan—where she is drugged and gang-raped while he is in jail. Williams originally delayed Chance's knowledge of the rape, infection, and sterilizing operation until late in act three, when the former lovers meet in the palm garden. In revision he "transplanted" this climactic scene to act two, reduced it to a telephone call from Heavenly, and prematurely, Kazan thought, revealed the underlying "Allah" story to Chance. The author's intent was to make way for the Princess in her own redemptive encounter with Chance in "the last big scene of the play" (TW to Wood, May 26, 1958, private collection).

The Philadelphia critics found individual scenes "stirring" and the overall production "stunning," although the playwright's "essential purpose," as well as the motivation of characters, especially Paul Newman's Chance Wayne, seemed "vague" or "elusive." Kazan restated a long-held position that "it is never the Actor's fault" in reply to Williams's letter of criticism regarding Newman's performance: "I think we have got to draw out of Paul an approximation of a kind of subtlety and sophistication and decadence that he doesn't have in him, and that is the 'Rub'" (February 18, 1959, Wesleyan).] *TLS, 1 p., Columbia*

TO CHERYL CRAWFORD

[New York]
March 10 [1959]

Cheryl, darling:
May this be it for you. I have always hoped for you to have a big hit. A whopper. Where you refuse tickets to people, where you act aloof, where you are unavailable on the telephone, hard to reach, mysterious, difficult, pressured by lawyers, constantly recasting, changing costumes, carpets, replacing worn out equipment, and replacing worn out technicians. I hope this is it. I am not sure, but I hope so. Anyway—

My love, Gadg.

[Kazan returned from Philadelphia fearing that "we didn't really solve the problem of the play. And I'm afraid we're in for it. Maybe real bad" (to MacLeish, n.d., Beinecke). *Sweet Bird of Youth* opened on March 10 to repeated curtain calls and nearly unanimous praise. Brilliant theater poetry, astute direction, imaginative sets, and a memorable performance by Geraldine Page overrode structural defects and spelled "box-office dynamite" for Cheryl Crawford—the unlucky producer who had refused *Cat on a Hot Tin Roof* and *Death of a Salesman*. An advance sale of $390,000 and demand for tickets into 1960 assured *Sweet Bird* a run of nearly four hundred performances.

A relaxed Tennessee Williams sidestepped rumors of an author-director controversy and assured Brooks Atkinson that Kazan had been "marvelous: so patient and understanding during the whole ordeal" (March 27, 1959, BRTC). Notes written during the rehearsal of *Sweet Bird* tell a different story, one that nearly severed "the Gordian knot" of friendship with Kazan. Williams accused him of "deliberate aggression" in his "busy-busy direction" of scenes involving the Princess, especially her final encounter with Chance in act three: "You knew, you couldn't help knowing, that in the character of Ariadne Del Lago I was expressing and tragically purging my own fearful dilemma, my own obsession, my terror, of losing my power as an artist and being obliged to live out the rest of my life with liquor and drugs and whores" (n.d., HTC).] *TLS, 1 p., BRTC*

TO JOHN D. ROCKEFELLER III

[New York]
April 28, 1959

Dear John:
This letter is my resignation from the Advisory Board of the Lincoln Centre Repertory Theatre. I submit it with regret. I have come to respect your great good will and integrity as well as the enormous potential of the project.

Many months ago at your request I wrote out my recommendations for the training centre and the Rep Theatre. I did not imagine that they would be adopted in toto, perhaps not even in part. But since I was on an Advisory Board, I did assume that the content of my two papers would be deliberated in committee along with the recommendations of others.

It turned out, however, that the effective deliberations were being carried on in another meeting—not that of the Advisory Committee. I learned of the appointment of M. Saint-Denis from the mimeo of a press release. It was as much news to me as it was to the general public. I didn't even know he was being considered.

I felt I had been deluded—or had deluded myself—as to the nature of the function I had been brought in to perform. I have come to the conclusion that I was something rather like window dressing. What could be more absurd than my coming to a meeting of an "advisory" committee where the actual step being contemplated is not even broached?

I have asked myself why I wasn't given an intimation as to the person being considered. After all, it is my field. The only answer I could find is that it was anticipated that I would oppose this choice.

I do. I know M. Saint-Denis' work only at second hand. Some men whose opinions I respect have spoken well of him. Nevertheless I am profoundly troubled at his selection.

We have in this country the best and most celebrated man in the world in the field of training actors. This estimate is not merely my opinion. It is by now generally allowed. Of course I mean Lee Strasberg. He has done great service to the theatre of our country for thirty years. He has added immeasurably to the wealth of talent in this country. When he is passed over, I feel the slight as if it were to myself. That he should not be recognized and honored and sustained in his work now when the opportunity has come, is simply more than I can bear.

The fact that the Juilliard is autonomously responsible for the appointment of M. Saint-Denis does not make it more palatable. The essence of the repertory theatre idea is that the performing group of actors and those in training must be bound together in an organic relationship. The school overflows onto the stage. They cannot be separated in policy or aesthetic.

There is now growing in this country a native tradition of theatrical art. It is unlike that of other countries. It truly derives from no system. It springs from our national temperament—the nature of our people. It has been developing step by step with the plays of our dramatic literature. That a man from another country and another culture should be chosen to direct the training of actors for our theatre seems to me not only deplorable but even tragic.

Your committee must have considered the propaganda result. It will surely be said in Europe that we haven't an American whom we feel we can trust with our actors' training. If this were true, I could grin and bear it. But since we have the best man in the world, here in this city—

Feeling as I do I cannot sit on a nominal, advisory board and seem to acquiesce in this crucial decision. Precisely because The Lincoln Centre is important, its course must be taken seriously. Therefore this resignation.

Warm personal regards,

EK:nm

[The Juilliard Foundation joined Lincoln Center with an understanding that its school would provide a single unified training program in the several theater arts. Juilliard's president publicly announced the selection of Michel Saint-Denis as chief consultant in early January while Kazan was absorbed in *Sweet Bird of Youth*. His return from Antigua in late March coincided with a statement of intent by Saint-Denis that doubtless incensed Kazan: "'What we want is the actor that we have produced in London and Paris before—an actor who can act various sorts of texts; who can sing, who can mime, who can dance, so that he is provided with as many sides of acting as possible'" (*NYT*, April 5, 1959). Added to a distinguished career in repertory theater and dramatic training was an influential meeting with John D. Rockefeller in Strasbourg, where Saint-Denis had built a state-sponsored theater and school. Entrusting the preparation of American actors to a European trained in the French classical and popular English traditions would continue to resonate in Kazan's subsequent return to Lincoln Center.] *TLx, 2 pp., Wesleyan*

TO PAUL OSBORN

Dear Paul:

I'm giving you the script that Fox feels has possibilities. And I'm giving it to you as is, without some changes I've recently made and without the cuts. The script is pathetic, in some ways. But then I'm not a writer. It was just my effort to show Fox "what I had in mind". Recently I have cut 98% of "Dave's Voice". I'm embarrassed to have you read it, now, but—! Of course its preposterous.

What I want to say however in this note is that I have never succeeded at any time with this thing in getting down on paper, dramatised, the reason why I embarked on this project, what attracted me to it.

My first idea was <u>an affectionate look back on our youth</u>. I remember the days of the New Deal with a special feeling. I was in some of it, and very much enlisted in all of it. It was the period of my life when I liked my fellow American and my fellow human best. It was a time when we all felt we could do anything. We were bumptious and cocky, but we were all daring too. What we were doing in the Theatre, paralleled in spirit what was going on in Washington. I was teaching a course in Directing at 25 years old—a thing that I doubt I'd attempt presently. My class was full of older men, towards whom I had a kindly tolerant attitude. I spoke with an absolute positiveness—a tone that I've never been able to fill out since. I was ridiculous in some ways, as were all of us "world-changers"—but there was something effervescent and marvelous in the air that is sadly lacking in this sodden era. This all—and more—is what I should have captured in the character of DAVE—which I didn't.

My interest was never dams, water levels, buckets of concrete and jack hammers. I was not trying to make a "Russian-type" epic of social progress. Rather what I was trying to do and again not succeeding (though you will see traces of this effort) is to make that most elusive of all forms: a love story. A love story between two opposites. Dave is what I've hinted at above. He comes down absolutely sure of every conviction (you might say: prejudice) He meets up against some people who are from a certain point of view (his) crazy. And wrong. And worthless. He is there to act towards them for the greater good in an official capacity. He slowly begins to feel towards them an unaccustomed emotion. And he finally realizes that he is in love with them, and by this, deprived of his absolute convictions and of his ability to act. You might oversimplify the story thus: A man is assigned to kill someone. He falls in love with them. And then cant kill them. Instead he joins them.

The nearest thing to this type of story that I know of is another script you once worked on: A BELL FOR ADANO. Not as story, as <u>type</u> of story.

You'll have to stagger thru some awful rubbish of mine (I'm sorry). But I still believe and always will that there is the kernel of a marvelous picture here. And there are opportunities for wonderful comedy between Dave and Carol and between Dave and the old woman. Against this rather larger background, I see this as a play of two opposite types. Dave who knows and is sure of, absolutely sure of everything, pig headed, iron willed (he thinks) finally really prejudiced, finally really a snob (just as I once was: a "proletariat" snob) vs. a group of people who not only have tradition, but actually have reality (as vs. a DREAM). The old lady HAS what she wants. She knows what she wants concretely.

I thought of the girl between these two view points. Intellectually she knows what Dave is representing is inevitable. And in a way, she "wants" it and "believes" in it. But she also appreciates and very deeply what the old woman and that way of life represents. "All progress is at the cost of pain". Somebody has to die for things to move ahead. Dave is humanized, and at the end he is bewildered and not so clear—but perhaps better.

I DID NOT INTEND AND DO NOT INTEND NOW to make a story of How did they get that old woman off the island. I never intended to build any suspense as to will she or wont she get off the island. There's never any doubt of this. The gates of the dam at the beginning have already been closed. Its not a question of whether or not she will get off. Its another story entirely.

Well perhaps that's enough. These notes can be terribly boring. I've done some more work—the first of which was to cut the thing marked DAVE'S VOICE. And you know me well enough to believe me when I say: I'm not defensive about any of it. Not a word.

I hope you'll want to work on it. I'm not sure you will, but if you do it will be fun. And as far as I'm concerned you can have any conditions you want. I cant speak for FOX (I could for Warners on E. of E.) but I think they'll be simply overjoyed too.

E.K.

[Before turning the screenplay over to Paul Osborn, Kazan began a third and final draft of *Wild River* with an urgent need to "become Dave," herald of regional planning from Washington, whose mission is to clear Garth's Island of an "old woman" determined to resist the intrusion of the Tennessee Valley Authority. "If I could tap something in unconscious memory, so that Dave will flow out of me it would be so much truer and better," Kazan wrote in a personal memo filled with the same "affectionate" memories recalled for Osborn ("I am Dave," n.d., Wesleyan). Kazan knew that the "love story" of Dave (later Chuck) and Carol must be inherently moving and imprinted with the unique factors of time and place lest the mistakes of *Viva Zapata!* and *Man on a Tightrope* be repeated. The character of Miss Ella, matriarch of the Garths, held the related challenge of dramatizing a perspective on traditional land ownership that was personal and local rather than abstract and imposed. After Osborn accepted the commission, Kazan wrote to underscore Dave's character as an idealist who "dealt with humanity in a bold and creative way because he thought he was creating a new society" (July 25, 1959, Wesleyan).

John Hersey's World War Two novel *A Bell for Adano* (1944) resembles *Wild River* insofar as an American sergeant comes to respect the traditional values of a Sicilian village while exposing the defeated people to democracy. Twentieth Century-Fox released the film version in 1945 without screenwriting credit for Paul Osborn.] *TLS, 2 pp., Wesleyan*

TO ROBERT WHITEHEAD

SH: Twentieth Century-Fox Film Corporation
[Beverly Hills, California]
September 2, 1959

Dear Bob:

I've been meaning to write you for ten days now. Just an hour ago, we gave our script to be multilithed. It now exists as far as the departments and the budget people are concerned, so they can go to work and I can have my first breathing spell. Until this morning Osborn and I had been getting up each day at seven and working until late afternoon. We turned out a complete script these past five and a half weeks and that's going some. I think (the blindness of proximity?) that it's okay. I'll know that better in a week or two.

The point is that I'm doing the movie this fall. Immediately. For one thing I'm afraid to let my momentum, now rolling, collapse again. This is the sixth script, and it's been more difficult to "get it up" again each time. Then I'm also sick of having it sitting like the albatross of legend on my head, or wherever the albatross sat. This way I'll be completely free of entangling alliances on January 1960, finally for good and all. Which brings me to—

I'm very excited about the Lincoln Square project. I've been thinking a lot about it. And in case it's necessary to say it again, let me say again that I want to go ahead with you on it.

There is only one piece of understanding that I have to have with you before I start. Everything else I'm perfectly happy to settle as we go along and as each problem comes up. I'm assuming that our relationship is going to be the one you spoke of—fifty fifty partners. So now I'll spell out the one thing that is of great concern to me. And I'll do so by making a suggestion.

My suggestion is first that we leave the school plan as it is. Let St. Denis organize his school, with our supervisory collaboration, at the Juilliard. It has gone too far, it seems to me, to adjust or change now. And perhaps, an absolutely fresh attack from him will be interesting and stimulating. I suggest we consult with St. Denis about the school and that he consult with us and make his recommendations on every aspect of the Repertory Theatre.

But I think that we should make all decisions as to the Repertory Theatre between us. I think you and I will quickly get to an understanding. Most of it already exists between us without talk since we've both been working in the same theatre and in the same tradition. I don't think we need any formal understanding on this. Rather, I'm perfectly content to set it as simply as this: we'll consult and then we'll decide.

Now about the Actors' Studio, here is my suggestion. I say let's attach it to the Lincoln Centre Repertory Theatre. Make it a part of the functioning of the Repertory Theatre. It is NOT a school either in intent or in functioning. Let it be the STUDIO of the Lincoln Centre Repertory Theatre. That way we'd have every good actor in our Theatre, or a hell of a big percentage of them, attached to us, part of our life and activity. It can be of immeasurable value to us. But, beyond that, it is the right thing to do. It is natural. It is organic.

And just as with St. Denis—we consult with Lee Strasberg, who is the artistic head of the Actors' Studio, on all its functionings. And he consults with us on the operation of the Repertory Theatre. We hear him and consult with him and use his broad knowledge just as we listen to M. St. Denis and use his broad knowledge.

The School and the Studio need have nothing to do with each other. They will in time inevitably. But at this point let them be distinct and separate. And, as with St. Denis, Lee would not have any executive voice in the decisions concerning the Repertory Theatre. Those decisions will be yours and mine, between us, and only between us.

That's my idea. I've put it to you simply and briefly, because like all sound ideas, it is a simple one. If you agree, I would commit myself. I am sending this letter to Lee so that he will know exactly what my proposal is. I think it is the right proposal, and I think it is best if I state it baldly and let you both think it over and have your reactions.

I think the Actors' Studio should come in with all its parts: I mean the Playwrights Group and the Directors Group as well as Lee's sessions with Actors. I think it should do its work in the small two hundred seat Theatre which is being planned as part of the Rep Building. Studio productions can be done there. New plays or parts of them can be done there. The Directors' classes can be held there.

We would not give up our present building. We need more room; we can use the present building as well.

There would be financial support for the Actors' Studio provided for in the budget planning of the Lincoln Repertory. Actually we have in the works a plan for raising a sizeable amount of money for the Studio. This plan can be still carried out if we move under the Rep's roof.

I guess that's it in essence. I'll be in Newtown over this week end, and I'll be in New York Tuesday morning. Call me either place. My Newtown number is Garden 6-2298. On Tuesday afternoon I'm going to Chattanooga, Tennessee to look for location. They have telephones there and we can do a lot over the phone. I can come in from there any time too.

Yours,

EK: ah

[Discussions with Robert Whitehead were under way as Kazan informed Jo Mielziner before leaving for film work (*Wild River*) in California: "I'd like to do the thing very much. His proposal was a fifty fifty partnership in running the Theatre. I'd say that might work out. I hope so." John D. Rockefeller officially thanked Kazan in October for past "generous counsel" and for accepting "Mr. Whitehead's invitation to share in bringing the repertory theatre to reality" (*NYT*, October 22, 1959). The prestige and the prospect of comradeship with a company reminiscent of the Group Theatre were not easily denied—nor was Molly Kazan's urging.

Nominal acceptance of Michel Saint-Denis would be offset by the presence of Lee Strasberg in a role set apart from management of the Repertory Theatre and restricted to a secondary stage. Studio activities would be retained in full measure, presumably with Lincoln Center funding, but also kept "distinct and separate" from the Juilliard drama school at least initially. There is no indication that Kazan's "idea" was considered seriously at the time, much less implemented, nor did Kazan, or apparently Whitehead, act on a "suggestion" made with the near force of an ultimatum. Lee Strasberg's distrust of Lincoln Center grew with the appointment of Saint-Denis, whose remoteness from the "'indigenous American theater movement'" held little promise for its advancement (Garfield, p. 199).]
TLx, 3 pp., BRTC

TO SPYROS SKOURAS AND BUDDY ADLER

Cleveland, Tennessee
December 12, 1959

Dear Spyros:
Dear Buddy:
I'm going to be plain with you. There's only one thing you want from me. You want a very good picture. A good picture, just a good picture, won't do. There's too much invested in it now. Besides, as we all know, a picture on this theme cannot get by at the Box Office unless it is very, very good. It's got to be what they call "great". It won't have a chance otherwise.

We're about three-quarters of the way thru today as I write this. And I think we have a chance to have a very good picture. I also think that we have a chance to have a picture that everyone in the country will want to see. It's got enough romance, humor, beauty, meaning, violence, pathos, etc. It's got the popular elements. I know these elements are there. What is not there yet is Size and Punch. I'm not talking about outer size. We have some of that and we'll have more. I'm talking about inner size, the thing that "gets" people and makes them go and tell their friends they've got to go. And punch, wallop, emotion we have—but not enough—not enough to put it over the top.

I've made a lot of pictures on ticklish themes—perhaps I've made more successful ones of that type than any other director in this country. And some that were <u>almost</u> successful; in other words, failures. I think I've learned more from the failures than the successes. And here's what I've learned.

First, whatever "big" theme you choose it has to be transmuted into personal terms. It's the imprint on the individual that counts. And secondly, the more difficult and less usual the theme, the more perfect the treatment of it must be. When you're travelling off the beaten road, you cannot afford <u>Any</u> mistakes. The first requirement I think I've met. The second I have still to meet.

It is for this reason that I was terribly upset when I heard yesterday that you intended to release this picture in March, this on top of the requests from Buddy to cut the film <u>now</u> as I was shooting it. I was asked to do this because of the March first tax date, etc. But the underlying message was the same: HURRY! HURREE! HURREE!!

Gentlemen, let's be real grown up and face facts now. I could throw this picture down the drain. I could here and now accept it as another "ALMOST" and piss it down the drain. I can rush it to completion "one way or another". In that case I absolutely guarantee you a $2,250,000 bust.

Or you and I can be tough minded and tough hearted. Go with me on this faith. I think we've got the makings of really the surprise picture of the year. It might just come off as a great picture. But that will only happen if you and I, mostly I, do a complete and thorough and unrelenting job on it from here on in.

This will never happen if you fellows out of whatever reasons of worry (sometimes, frankly, it sounds more like panic) and economics start hurrying me at this late date. Up till now, you've gone on the faith that if you gave me a free hand and "let me alone" I might produce something real good for you. I think I have exceeded your expectations up till now. Frankly, I've exceeded my own in some respects, especially the performances of my leads, and the beauty of our backgrounds. But you'll never get out of me what your gamble and faith merit if you crowd me now and hurry me.

I say let's face facts. There isn't a way in the world, despite my working every day (which I fully mean to do) that this picture can be cut by March first. Frankly it won't be cut, negative and all by April first. There is one long montage section that I haven't even planned yet, no less shot. And it's crucial to the picture. And no cutter can cut this picture. I'm very apprehensive, frankly, about letting Reynolds, good as he is, cut any of it. I'm afraid I'll have to do a lot over. And I don't want him to do any of the important scenes. Only the Director and no one else knows in a film like this what <u>Emotion</u> he wants to produce.

The fact I want you to face is that you should immediately ship all the negative to New York. As well as ship all the positive we have printed up. Then Reynolds should set up and organize a cutting room there. It will take him a couple of weeks to do this. He should start NOW on this, so that when I get back around the first of the year, he is ready to knock on it. It will take him a couple of weeks to complete this shift.

I'm further asking you to face the fact now that you should be ready to pay the extra tax—UNLESS you can evade it by shipping the negative to New York. A fact that might help you legally is that none of the footage was shot in the State of California. But I don't know the legalities. And I say we should face this fact—if it comes to it, I think you should pay the tax and give me time and the opportunity to give you a very good picture. I can do it.

I don't have to go into lengthy reminders of films that you have rushed into release that have been rushed into disastrous failure. Your memory of them must be much more painful than mine. I wondered how in the hell you got BELOVED INFIDEL out so quickly, until I read the reviews. Then I understood how you were able to get it out so quickly.

On the telephone the other day, you Buddy, brought up the example of Otto Preminger and <u>Anatomy</u> of <u>Murder</u>. Let me say first that I bow to Preminger's superior energy, organization and talent. I can't do what he does. I can't. I'm too tired at night. In the second place that was a film made from a well written and well constructed best seller, a story that was in a familiar pattern, that had intense but mechanical suspense, whose elements were entirely familiar ones given little twists here and there to make them seem unfamiliar. I, here, am making this story up, more or less, as I go along. I'm finding the emotion in it. It is not on the surface of the script. I just couldn't "shoot the script". You'd have nothing then. Let's face another fact: when I get back to New York with it, I'll have to build up sequences with tiny close-ups here and there. I'll need added shots. Fortunately, Remick will be in a play there, Clift lives there and will be there until he starts his next picture in the summer, and Jo Van Fleet, whose next picture will probably be one for me, will also be living there. I can get what I need to make the film as powerful as possible.

I have been slower than you hoped. But if you have looked at any of the footage, you must realize why. And I'm not in the mood to give any explanations to anybody on this subject.

In closing I want to urge you, for the sake of your own ease of mind, to face the facts now. Prepare to pay the tax. Don't try to rush me. I simply won't be rushed. I like the picture too much. And if you ever do succeed, God forbid, in hurrying me, you'll then have only what you deserve, an "ALMOST".

Cordially,

With Jo Van Fleet on the set of *Wild River*

[Buddy Adler set the industry standard for "Punch" in reviewing an early draft of *Wild River:* The "sell-ing feature" of the film "must be the love story between Dave and Carol," but it "needs more empha-sis—it must have more violence, more build up, more scenes" (to EK, n.d., Wesleyan).

Filming *Wild River* began in October in southeastern Tennes-see and was not finished until the following January. Kazan lacked the ready-made sources and conve-nient locations of recent films and dismissed the studio's imperative to "HURRY! HURREE! HURREE!!" *Beloved Infidel,* based on Sheilah Graham's popular account of an affair with F. Scott Fitzgerald, was "rushed" to the screen by Twentieth Century-Fox with "disas-trous" results, or so Kazan thought. He bowed to "the superior energy, organiza-tion and talent" of Otto Preminger in bringing *Anatomy of a Murder,* a best-selling novel with a "familiar pattern" and "mechanical suspense," to completion in three months of overall production for Columbia Pictures. Release of *Wild River* in late May 1960 probably negated a tax advantage.

Reviewers admired Kazan's daring subject, Jo Van Fleet's portrayal of Ella Garth, and the "magical" photography of "Elly" Fredericks. The love story of cul-tural opposites was thought abrupt, ill-proportioned, and capped with a conve-nient marriage. Its prominence obscured Kazan's true interest in the "upheaval" caused by New Deal social engineering and the poignant effect on Ella Garth. Filmed "thoughtfully, compassionately and with many touches of meaningful art-istry," *Wild River* fell into the "'ALMOST'" category and quickly disappeared from *Variety*'s survey of leading films (*NYT,* May 27, 1960).

Kazan retained a strong respect for the crew and principal cast, including Mont-gomery Clift (Chuck), Lee Remick (Carol), and Jo Van Fleet (Ella Garth). An intimate relationship with Kazan underscored Barbara Loden's casting in a minor role. Born in North Carolina in 1932, Loden arrived in New York as a seventeen-year-old armed with youth, beauty, native intelligence, and a resolve (as stated in a later interview) to make "'something glamorous'" of herself. Modeling and bit parts in television and on Broadway preceded roles in *Wild River* and *Splendor in the Grass.*] TLx, 3 pp., Wesleyan

[New York]
January 20, 1960

Dear Eero:

Here are a few thoughts that keep going through our mind as a result of our last meeting:

1. The legitimate theatre takes its scale from the human face. The biggest effects are sometimes in some actress' eyes.

2. The auditorium should propel the attention of the audience inevitably towards the stage. It should "lean" towards the stage and "embrace" it.

3. The essence of Theatre is surprise. The Stage and Theatre should not look the same for every show.

4. Every play designs itself. In other words it calls for a unique and individual solution.

These last two points demand that everything about the stage be FLEX-IBLE and completely adaptable to the demands, individual in each case, of the various plays we are going to produce.

5. Great width of stage dwarfs the human figure and diffuses concentration. Great height can have the same result, unless used extremely carefully—in which case it can then have an effectiveness (the ceiling in the Frank Lloyd Wright Theatre seemed too low, however—it seemed to be pressing down upon us). Great depth makes possible powerful effects and perspective. Great width is bad for us. Great depth of stage space is necessary (it can also be poetic). Panorama is not a requirement.

6. The auditorium should at no time compete with what's happening on stage. No one comes there to see an auditorium perform. The great function of the auditorium should be to prepare the audience for the events that are about to transpire on stage.

7. There is a very important critical point (60 feet) after which facial expressions of an actor don't count. This has to be religiously observed and not trifled with. In the Theatre of "legitimate" drama, the climactic effects, etc., are often on a space, roughly eight inches by five inches—Julie Harris' face.

8. Everyone should be able to see a recumbent figure on the stage floor.

Your note (to Gadg), which has just arrived seems to make most of this letter redundant. However, we have put it on paper if only to focus our own feelings. Best wishes.

Sincerely,

Elia Kazan
Robert Whitehead

[A *Time* cover story placed Eero Saarinen at the center of America's "pre-eminence in modern architecture" for an array of designs marked by "imagination, versatility and good sense." Signature projects such as the Gateway Arch (St. Louis) and the TWA terminal (Idlewild) had been commissioned when Saarinen was chosen to design the repertory theater at Lincoln Center. His early background in auditorium and theater design was extensive and no doubt influential in the selection process. A Finnish national whose family immigrated to the States in 1923, Saarinen studied in the Yale School of Fine Arts in the early 1930s—unbeknown to Kazan. "Architecture is not just to fulfill man's need for shelter, but also to fulfill man's belief in the nobility of his existence on earth. Our architecture is too humble. It should be prouder, more aggressive, much richer and larger than we see it today" (*Time*, July 2, 1956). Kazan's belief that theater "speaks to and for people" and "should not be embarrassed to take itself seriously, very seriously," established common cause with Saarinen and ensured a productive relationship.]
TL, 2 pp., Wesleyan

TO JAY GAYNE RESCHER

[New York]
March 11, 1960

Dear Jay:
I am writing you on behalf of my company, Newtown, and through you I am addressing the Board.

I want to bring in Elly Fredericks on my production, SPLENDOUR IN THE GRASS. For various reasons that I won't go into, but all of which have to do with Elly Frederick's artistry and his personal contribution, I think he is the best man to photograph this film. For various reasons that I also won't go into and which differ with the individuals, I don't know of anyone in New York with whom I would be happy on this film. I am laying this on the line, Jay, so that you and the Board will be clear as to what my feelings are. I will not go into individual consideration of the cameramen here in New York except to say that in the case of Boris Kaufman I have the highest regard for him. I don't know of a cameraman on the West Coast—and I have worked with the very best—who is a finer artist than Boris Kaufman. I think his photography of BABY DOLL and ON THE WATERFRONT was absolutely first class. I do not, however, want to make this subject with him. I am not going to go into the reasons for this, but may I only say that these reasons have been carefully thought through, even sympathetically thought through. I am not acting on a whim or an impulse. I hope to work with Boris in the future. I also hope to become acquainted with other cameramen in the New York area, one way or another, and some day I know I'll be working with some of them. This picture is my last picture for a big Hollywood company. My contract with Fox has been concluded with the making of WILD RIVER, and my contract with Warner Bros. is now about to be concluded with the making of SPLENDOUR IN THE GRASS. How I'll operate in the future I don't know, but I do know it will be in total independence.

Very briefly, without betraying any confidences, I must say to you and the Board that the pressure on me from Warner Bros. has been onerous and constant. The pressure has been three-fold. It has been, first, to use their facilities—to make the picture on the Burbank back lot. They have shown me in detail how much cheaper I could make it there. They have offered me financial guarantees that the picture could be made more cheaply there. They have cited A FACE IN THE CROWD, a disastrous failure to the tune of $1,500,000, and BABY DOLL, also still in the red.

Secondly, Warner Bros. has applied pressure on me to make the picture on location in Kansas with a California crew and cameramen. There are great artistic advantages, by the way, in this way, and for a time I was planning to make the picture in Kansas with a California crew just as I made WILD RIVER in Tennessee with a California crew. I planned this sort of operation for over a year. For entirely personal reasons I have given it up. I want to make the picture all within the city limits of New York, or close to it. I want to use New York personnel entirely, with the exception of Ellsworth Fredericks.

Thirdly, Warner Bros. has been urging me very strongly to use a Hollywood cameraman and staff. May I just say on this that the reasons had to do with speed. As I said before, my two pictures for Newtown have both been failures. BABY DOLL should have made money, but it hasn't and when it does, it will be years from now. A FACE IN THE CROWD, the failure of which I attribute to no one except myself, lost Warner Bros. $1,500,000! That picture really didn't get back its prints and advertising costs. As I say, I blame no one but myself, but naturally, when I sit across the table from Jack Warner he is most apprehensive about the financial side of this coming feature. I am making this picture with Natalie Wood, who is not a star in the sense of being a "draw". I didn't have stars in my other movies for Warners. I can't blame Jack Warner for being worried now. Can you?

Now, Jay, I have held the line. My reasons are personal. I live in New York. My office is here. My legitimate theatre business is here. I have no desire to leave town. My kids will be home for their summer vacations. I don't see three of them throughout the school year. I would like to spend weekends with them. I could take the whole kit and kaboodle and live in a house in Kansas for three months, but the fact is I have a summer place in Connecticut that I am very fond of and I would rather live in it. But I cannot be unmindful of Warner's side in all this. They have their point. They have lost enough money on me. In the present mood of panic they are less inclined than they might ordinarily be to lose money, and they wouldn't be inclined that way ever. But I have insisted, so far, on doing the picture in New York, with a New York crew, with a New York staff, without their accountant, with a New York camera operator and a New York assistant, and so on and so on. And I will hold this line, Jay. But I would like the permission of you and your Board to bring in one person.

I know that in my last letter to you, which was over three years ago, I asked for permission to bring in Harry Stradling on A FACE IN THE CROWD and I said that this would be the last time I would ask this. I would feel much more comfortable at this moment if I weren't asking again for something I hoped never to ask for again. I would much rather there were a man in New York that I thought suited to this particular picture I am making and the correct choice to help me solve the situation I am in. But there isn't.

You know as well as I do that anyone's position in the motion picture industry today is a precarious one. I have had three financial flops in a row now in films, and, after all, it is a business, Jay. Warner Bros. has agreed to what I am suggesting to your Board. I can only hope you will.

I am enclosing a copy of a letter I have written Jack Warner asking him to use his power to employ one of the members of your local to photograph a picture on the West Coast—a sort of reciprocal arrangement. I hope Jack will do this, but I can do nothing but petition him. As you see, the petition is worded strongly, but I haven't the power to do anything but ask for help from him.

You are all experienced men and men of good heart. You have watched me making pictures in the East. I don't flatter myself unduly when I say that I brought about a revival of big feature making in the East. I want to keep my office open. I want to stay in business and I want to stay in the business of making feature pictures in the East. You have been in my office. It is a permanent office and my interest in film making is permanent. I hope we will have many films together, but I am afraid this one time with respect to one man, I must ask your indulgence and help.

Sincerely,

EK:nm
Enc.

[Local 644 of the International Photographers was "kicking like a mule" and unlikely to grant Kazan's request for territorial leeway in filming *Splendor in the Grass*. Boris Kaufman was still "too goddamn slow," while other New York camera work seemed "mediocre" by contrast (EK to JLW, March 11, 1960, WB Archives). Jay Rescher served as Kazan's initial contact, but it was Charles Austin, secretary of Local 644, who reported the board's "unanimous" denial of the petition and dismissal of the claim that only Ellsworth Fredericks was suited to film *Splendor in the Grass*. Labor rules on the West Coast prevented a "reciprocal arrangement" with a Hollywood studio. Boris Kaufman filmed *Splendor* on location in metropolitan New York and at Filmways Studio in Manhattan.] *TL, 3 pp., Wesleyan*

TO EERO SAARINEN

[New York]
March 14, 1960

Dear Eero:

You remember our visit to the Morosco Theatre where we made a very—what is for us—crucial judgment. We decided at the time that in order for the expression on Julie Harris' face to register, to have meaning and dramatic weight, we should never go back farther than 58 feet. This should apply not to the thrust only, but to the reasonable downstage areas on the permanent apron and on the downstage sections of the turntable. Once we let this figure get much above 58 feet, we pass from the realm of drama to the realm of spectacle. In other words, human experience counts for little or nothing, and the director and playwright must rely on movement, picturization and spectacle.

At the same time, it was necessary, in order to support of repertory company, to gross at least $40,000 a week, and this meant a minimum of 1000 seats.

At our meeting in Detroit with you, we had not taken into account the placement of lighting units and control areas with full sight-lines that would be necessary to light the action correctly, and especially to light the action on the thrust stage. Once we had, in our work here, placed the necessary units in the correct places, we found that we had eaten up much of the suitable seating room in the reverse balconies. In the first reverse balcony we found ourselves with a total of only 32 seats; in the second reverse balcony we found ourselves with a pitch that was too extreme for decent viewing, but even here we found ourselves with very few seats; and finally, in the third reverse balcony, we found that we needed all of the space for lights and that no seating was possible here, because the pitch was too extreme.

By the time we had placed all the vital light and control areas in the March 1st scheme, we had cut far too many seats to meet economic needs. In other words, the really remarkable dramatic effect that one got in looking at your model from the viewpoint of the stage—we mean the three tiers of viewers leaning toward the stage—was a piece of wishful thinking which did not exist when the lighting and sight-line problems were solved.

At the same time, as we said, we had to get the necessary seating somewhere, and we found ourselves going much too far back in the orchestra for the kind of plays and productions we had hoped to do. Jo has mailed you plans which you've already seen which illustrate our attempt to justify the reverse balconies. Perhaps you can find the solution. We couldn't. In an effort to find another solution we asked Jo to re-study a single-tier balcony that has about 300 seats in it and a reduced floor size where the distance would be kept within the range that we think essential, and at the same time, give our lighting and control acceptable locations. Naturally many of the balcony seats will be beyond the range of good viewing in distance, but they must at least have an angle of viewing within a reasonably good angle, ie. 20° to 25°.

I asked Jo to explain why we now are plotting two locations for follow spots and two for face lighting. He explained that since the H scheme of last spring, we all have accepted the need for an advanced thrust. The 16 odd feet of distance between the lip of the permanent stage and the lip of the extreme thrust, creates the need for the additional light locations.

We're sorry about this belated enlightenment on our part, but it only came out of very realistic consideration of the absolutely essential distance, sight-line, and technical control factors. We realize that this may mean that the reverse balconies are not feasible. We also realize that you may have a solution to the problems that we met, but much as we were fascinated by the reverse balconies, if they force us to violate our basic concept of intimacy, we feel now that they should go.

By the way, we showed our plans of March 1st to Michel Saint Denis who is a vastly experienced man and consultant, and while he was very appreciative of the factors of the fluency and flexibility on the front of the floor, his immediate, violent reaction was: "But this is a theatre for spectacle!" This was a shock to us, but it did lend another jolt to a reappraisal we've been making of the whole situation.

Best regards,

EK/pb
cc: Robert Whitehead
Jo Mielziner

[Eero Saarinen and Jo Mielziner initially resisted the theater board's preference for a dual-stage building in designing the Vivian Beaumont at Lincoln Center. The main floor, steeply pitched in a semicircle, addressed the problems of "essential distance, sight-line, and technical control factors." A playing area of ten thousand square feet, controlled by a turntable system, incorporated a variable apron-thrust and proscenium stage of unusually wide dimension. Main-floor seating varied with each configuration, but overall capacity did not fall below the minimum one thousand required by Kazan, nor was the "essential distance" more than sixty-two feet from the stage. The innovative reverse balcony with a cowled forward leaning profile gave way to a "single-tier" design seating 330 (Pelkonen, pp. 214–15).

Eero Saarinen died in 1961 after surgery for a brain tumor. Of the four theaters at Lincoln Center, only the Vivian Beaumont escaped intense architectural criticism upon completion.] *TL, 2 pp., BRTC*

[New York]
April 22, 1960

Dear Tenn:

I'm furious at the way you spoke to me on the phone. You haven't a right in the world to infer that I'm lying to you. I have never lied to you. And have I ever asked you to crawl? Has our relationship ever dealt in pity? We have a clean relationship and I did my share to keep it clean.

I don't believe you can listen now. But I want to put down a few facts and maybe they will sink in. You're right: I did promise to do your play. I did because I wanted to do it, and I wanted to do it because I think it's a beautiful play and a deep one. At that time I intended to get out of the Inge movie. I'm in psycho-analysis again and I found myself especially harassed and discouraged and weary. I still am, incidentally, but that is no concern in this now.

But when it got right down to it I couldn't get out of Bill's movie. Not because of any contractual reason. But because I had initiated the project, I had made him write it. The date on his first complete script is APRIL 1958. That means we were having conversations about it at least nine months before. How the hell can you pull out of a project that has cost a writer that much work and thought? Especially when I started the whole thing. I couldn't. I didn't.

NEXT. As to how much work it is. That again was my fault. I underestimated it. I thought I could do both. I guess I could—but at terrific cost to myself. Example. I finished shooting WILD RIVER on the 4th of January. I will finish putting the score on it May 2nd. That means I did four months work on it after I was thru shooting. Charlie Maguire estimates I will finish shooting Inge's film August 7th. I should then, by all indications, finish putting the score on this one December 5th. Furthermore, since I am producing Inge's script, as well as directing it, I will be responsible for the ad campaign, the promotion, booking of the first theatre, the exploitation, the selling, etc. In other words, I will have much more work to do on this one, than on "Wild River."

I'm not Otto Preminger. I can, but I don't glory in doing several things at once. I've done too much of it. I haven't done justice to your play at the readings I've attended. I think your play is a very fine one, but I've been half-there at the readings. I haven't yet really worked with Jo Mielziner. I should have. Generally I've felt like I was heavily overloaded and the fall especially looked like sheer hell, with my being so busy that I could neither do your play well nor do the job I should on Inge's film. If your play had been a difficult one, and if I felt that it really needed some extra-ordinary "treatment" why then I would somehow have done it and to hell with the cost to me in energy, etc. But I think it's a play that could be done very well by a lot of directors. If it's cast right with good actors, it will almost play itself. I'm not even sure that a lighter hand than mine wouldn't be better. I might over dramatize it. I'm not sure I'm just exactly right for it.

I knew you were bound to think that I didn't really like your play. I expected that. But I didn't expect the insults. Frankly it appears to me that the loyalties in our relationship have run more from me to you than the other way. I stuck onto BABY DOLL thru the thick and thin of your indifference and disappearing. (No swimming pools in Greenville). I stuck with "Sweet Bird of Youth" when you thought it was crap. I insisted on Gerry Page when you all thought she was wrong. And I have taken for four years a whole campaign of vilification in the press to the effect that I was distorting your work. You started this line with your preface on CAT. As you wrote it down, that was an honest preface. But in context and in effect it was not. It gave people generally the idea that I had forced you to rewrite CAT. I can't force you to rewrite anything, first because you are strong, secondly because you are protected by your guild. The contrary is the true fact: that I offered ten days before the New York opening to put in your original third act. You never stated that in your preface, nor did you note that I offered repeatedly to put your original third act into the road company. You made the decision not to. Since then a host of people, unleashed by your preface, have been attacking me for distorting your work. This was climaxed, as far as I was concerned, by the enclosed. I called this to Audrey's attention. She shrugged it off.

You will shrug it off. I've come to the conclusion that somehow you were willing to have me blamed for the faults in your plays, while you are praised for their virtues. Why otherwise have you never said one word in the press in my defense? Is that fair? Did I make you rewrite the second act of SWEET BIRD OF YOUTH? You know goddamn well that if the shoe was on the other foot, if you were being blamed unrelentingly for my faults, I would have spoken up long ago. What other conclusion can I come to except that consciously or unconsciously you agree with them? That you want it believed that way? It's been four years now that this horse shit has been in the press: Hewes, Atkinson, Cassidy, and all of them and YOU HAVE NEVER ONCE SAID A WORD!!

I went to Milwaukee to see SWEET BIRD OF YOUTH. I needed every day here, but Audrey and thru her, you, pleaded with me to go out. I did. And I saw the play, and took notes and gave notes. All the time I was there I felt taxed and over-worked, I felt that I was being unfair to Bill and to myself in re his movie. At the same time I went very carefully thru PERIOD OF ADJUSTMENT, planning the direction so that I knew how it would move on the stage so that I could give Jo Mielziner a ground plan before he left for Europe. I thought many times I should quit P. of A. But never seriously because I have always put you first. Then came Cassidy's piece, and I began to think. It isn't that I care what she thinks. I truly don't. And Hewes is an ass. And Atkinson is a man whose opinions I'm indifferent to. I only cared that YOU were silent. And I was forced to think that really and truly you felt the same way.

Then I thought, why does he want me to direct his plays. The Answer: because of some superstition that I bring commercial success. Which you terrifyingly want. But that is part of the same distasteful picture. Just as I can't help but think you agree with Cassidy, I also think that you think of me as the person who can make your plays "go" and that you are willing to make some sacrifice in integrity and personal values to get the commercial success which I bring you. Well, Tennessee, fuck that! That is a hell of a humiliating position, and I don't want any goddamn part of it. You should have come to my defense long ago. Ask yourself the reasons why you didn't.

And, after I came back, as I sat at the readings and [you] hadn't even come up for them, I thought the hell with this. I'm not going to break my neck, slough off Inge's movie, do a half-ass job on "Period of Adjustment" only to be told in time, again, that I had misdirected your play into a hit. And then, to wait and wait for you to say something and wait for nothing. What the hell kind of position it that for a man? It's not for me.

Anyway, baby, you really don't need me on this one. I know it will work without me (Cheryl, incidentally, agrees). Get a new boy and a new relationship. The play will work with another director. This is a beautiful, funny, human play but it's also unified and well constructed. I think a lot of it and I think a lot of you. I truly wish you all success. And I love you.

Gadg

P.S. I wrote this before lunch with Audrey Wood

[Rumors of "The Big Walk-Out" surfaced in mid-April after Tennessee Williams announced that Kazan would direct *Period of Adjustment*. The retreat was made all the more surprising by Kazan's initial request to produce the new play. A columnist interviewed both and published a revealing exchange in the *Times*. Williams doubted Kazan's official reason for withdrawing—a commitment to film *Splendor in the Grass*—nor did he expect to work again with his former director. He speculated that Kazan wished to avoid further sniping at his desire for "'success'" and the "'so-called melodramatic interpretation of my plays.'" Neither, Williams insisted, was true, nor was the more serious charge of forcing revision on a vulnerable playwright. "'The fact is, Kazan has been falsely blamed for my own desire for success,'" to which Kazan replied, "'he should have said that earlier.'" Deeply ingrained stubbornness, Williams insisted, made the idea of his domination "'ridiculous. Nobody can budge me an inch. Kazan simply tried to interpret, honestly, what I have to say'" (*NYT,* May 1, 1960).

Claudia Cassidy's review of the touring *Sweet Bird of Youth* (probably the enclosure) included gossip that Williams "rewrote" his current play "to satisfy" Kazan. Cassidy herself claimed that "both gifted men work brilliantly at their best but in antithetical manner. Williams applies pressure from within, so that its tensions are individual and characteristic. Kazan applies pressure from without. It has a way of demolishing Williams characters" (*Chicago Daily Tribune*, April 12, 1960).] *TLS with enclosure, 4 pp., Wesleyan*

TO TENNESSEE WILLIAMS

[New York]
[May 1960]

Dear Tenn:

Thanks for your letter. Who knows why a person suddenly feels weary, finds life and work tasteless, begins to look for some kind of "salvation" in a new direction? I dont know. No doubt I've been working too continuously. J.B. , Sweet Bird, Wild River and now into this one without the least pause except for five weeks off last summer. I feel like an old rubber battery. Its shocking to me because I've never felt that way before. But weariness is not physical. And the "real" reasons—? I dont entirely know them now. But something has happened to me no doubt. And is that bad? I dont think so. I'm not afraid of it, or anything. Something in me knows shock is necessary. Abrupt, jolting derailment. I'm sorry it all happened on your play. I do like your play, that's the hell of it. And I'm prepared to be totally selfish and self-interested now with anyone and everyone excluding just a tiny few, of which few you are one. I guess that's why I put it off. Then later I planned to quit Bill Inge's movie. And tried. But that would have been a monstrous piece of unfairness because I started the whole damned thing and he'd been working on it so long. So finally everything got tighter and tighter, narrower and blacker and more pinching and threatening and there we are in the N.Y. Times. I hate those pieces. They cant help but being inaccurate. I think our friendship will survive this and I think we will work together again. We're too close. I can understand why you're sore at me. After all I said repeatedly I'd do it, and I was doing it and then suddenly—. Well I anticipated how you'd feel. And I think, all considered, you behaved very well. You're also quite right in saying that its deeper than it seems. I guess psychic exhaustion is one thing, but the sense of being threatened and gobbled up, under which I'm laboring, is something more neurotic. But, while I like sympathy, pity is not necessary, since the Greek tissue is an elastic one and I'll be back, partly with new face, maybe with a partly new face, but back. In all confidence, I'd give a tit not to have to do this movie. I dread it. There's no way I can do a good job of it. But I cant stand being totally, despicably unfair. And I'd rather give the months away. About Claudia Cassidy: I didn't send the letter, either one. It will look now as if you're doing it to "get me back", as if I've got some kind of pistol in your back, or had just recently and you wrote it.

Lets forget her for now. I still believe that I was unfairly zeroed in on by the brother hood, but the one I resent most is Atkinson who never stopped with self righteous and sly innuendo. Tynan is sort of a shit isn't he, isn't he really when you get down to it, sort of an impotent, be-pimpled, nervous stutterer. Cassidy? who cares, and why waste anger on Henry Hewes? I was surprised to find that they all had gotten under my skin. But Cas's piece was just the last bit of water that flushes the bowl. If I were you I'd not do anything about it now. Its sort of beneath you to rush into print or into anything. As far as I'm concerned, relax. I send you a lot of love. I do think an awful lot of you, value you a lot, more than you know.

G

[Tennessee Williams reassured Kazan of his "friendship" and presumed that some-day the "unstated" reasons for declining *Period of Adjustment* would be revealed. In the meanwhile he would grant Kazan much the same moral latitude claimed by Blanche DuBois in *Streetcar:* "the reluctance that we ferocious old pirates still have in our hearts to hurt or betray, deliberately" (April 28, 1960, Wesleyan). Kazan agreed that his problems were "deeper" than he had admitted and described him-self as living with "the sense of being threatened and gobbled up." The period from mid-1954 to the present, framed by the reluctant filming of *East of Eden* and *Splendor in the Grass,* would provide fertile ground for a phase of personal writing already under way in *America America.* Kazan's best-selling novel (*The Arrange-ment,* 1967) waited further in the background as a study of "psychic exhaustion" in the service of others. The withdrawal from *Period of Adjustment* marks the beginning of a decade summarized by Kazan as "a time of self-confrontation." By declining the Williams play, he was, "in effect, refusing all other plays by authors of similar stature" (*A Life,* pp. 595–96). *Sweet Bird* ended the Williams-Kazan col-laboration in theater and film—if not their friendship and correspondence.

Period of Adjustment opened in November 1960 to solid reviews and modest success under the direction of George Roy Hill, a recent Tony Award nominee for *Look Homeward, Angel.*] TLS, 1 p., Columbia

TO JOHN STEINBECK

[Sandy Hook, Connecticut]
August 27, 1960

Dear John:
I've been meaning to write you. But I found it difficult. I felt a tension between us which I regretted, but didn't want to do anything about. For some reason I dont entirely understand, I felt that if I tried to do anything about it, my effort would not be true. And I'm awfully sick of something that seems to go on everywhere between people: politeness, the assumption of a harmony that in

fact doesn't exist, and surface talk to suit. Maybe I'll never be able to talk easily to anyone again. That is possible. At the moment I dont regret it, rather prefer it. On the other hand I do not want to lose you as a friend. I didn't answer your last letter—the signing off one—not because I didn't understand it or appreciate it. But it seemed to me that it asked for: no answer. Except possibly an acknowledgment which this is. I also want to say this. The letter meant a lot to me. Not because it was "friendly" or "concerned". But because it told me a real truth in a very cutting way. The truth was contained in your very first words: "Dear Gadg, nee Elia". During the last months I've come to the same conclusion. My nickname has taken on a particularly disgusting meaning for me. It marks the abdication of a true identity and the assumption of a false one. False because the mask: GADG suggests ever-ready compliance, a subservient, scattershot friendliness and an adaptability which made it possible for me to be the "necessary" thing to any man. A most successful mask! I wont go on with this except to say again that the insight from you contained in those words shocked me and so helped me. And I'm thanking you. Good luck on your trip. I hope you really get part of what you're looking for. And stay well.

E.K.

[With "'Dear Gadg, nee Elia,'" John Steinbeck confronted Kazan with the implications of his instrumental nickname. It was not the first time he had charged his friend with self-betrayal, nor was it Kazan's first "abdication of a true identity." The "mask" worn by Kazan as the director of plays and films and as the servitor of bankers and realtors at Lincoln Center would be imparted to his fictional characters, as evident in working notes for *America America*. With the completion of a first draft in 1961, he wrote of Stavros, launched on an epic journey, that his "Asia Minor mask of compliance and 'humility' hid tremendous resentment. It—the circumstances— heated up a furious hunger" (notebook, January 29, 1961, Wesleyan). Kazan moderated but did not discontinue use of his nickname in later correspondence.

Steinbeck's "signing off" letter (unidentified) preceded a cross-country tour that became the basis of *Travels with Charley* (1962). Kazan's "acknowledgment" was written shortly after the completion of *Splendor in the Grass* and marked "Not Sent" in the author's hand.] *TLS, 1 p., Wesleyan*

TO ROBERT WHITEHEAD

[New York]
September 27, 1960

Dear Bob:

A person would have to be mighty peculiar to go into this project of ours. Did you ever ask yourself: Why am I doing it? Do I really want to? Do I want to give up some of the best years of my life for it—give up producing other plays, free-wheeling, enjoying the tension and the terror of Broadway production? Did you ever look at this thing candidly? . . .

A Rep Theatre is just about impossible here. People say it's against our tradition. And they are right. It is. It's counter to every acquired taste of our audience. It's against our economic system. The rewards, if such there are, are non-negotiable. It's against our form of union organization. Every guild and union will be against us, no matter what they profess. When it comes right down to it, they will not make things easy for us. They will make them tough. And as for our artists, we're going to have the goddamnedest time acquiring new plays and in holding actors to contracts on which we have their signatures. (I can hear them: "But I'm just not happy here, Bob—")

And as for us, the work will be back-breaking. And all devouring. As I said, it's going to make a lot of things we like, impossible. We're even going to have to watch our personal behavior. Will we have to cultivate the impeccable dignity of the president of a large Rockefeller Subsidiary? Be Mr. Lincoln Centre Rep Theatre all the time? Christ, it does sound awful!

So why? Very seriously. We're neither of us do-gooders. There's no reason to do this whole bloody thing. Is there? Unless, most simply, it's exhilarating! Unless it's an adventure, unless it fills us with the sense that we're making the impossible come to be, unless the work itself is much more gratifying than work on B'way, and unless the result, in a word, is Art. It's got to be an ART THEATRE—

I don't mean by that anything like the work of the other rep theatres that we've had in this city. They aspired to mediocrity. Their leaders were decent, well-intentioned, common-sensical, worthy people—rather cautious, a little dull. This thing is not worth the effort unless it goes all the way—as they say in those articles on teenagers. I don't want to flirt with it, and diddle it, and do it just a little. I don't want any part of it if we're going to go half way.

I won't go into this in any spirit of compromise. I'm not in the mood to be cautious or polite. I'm not in the mood to be decent and common sensical. I'm not in the mood to be a good boy, quote authorities, oblige anyone, save feelings or for an instant do what I don't believe in. I am not in the mood to pretend. I'm very restive.

But at the same time I am ready to give everything I have to this. I am ready to attempt something that has never been attempted before. I am ready to lead people. I will take on, gladly, if I am leading them towards something that I believe in completely. . . .

I want to create an ART THEATRE. Most simply what I have against the B'way Theatre is that it is organized purely as a business operation. I want a place organized with one purpose: to make the best Theatre work possible. This means, since ours is a collective art, that we have to organize a collective.

I want to in time discuss who should be in this collective and how they should be organized.

And we must think of the word Theatre as having a different meaning than the one we're used to. I don't think of the Theatre as a place to go to pass an evening. I like fun. But I think of the Theatre—comedy or tragedy—as a place that speaks to and for people. I do think of it as dramatizing a message. Its concern is morality, justice, good, evil and the nature of man. I do think of it as a place of serious commitments. It has a creative role in society. I think it should cause ferment and change. I think it is part of the conscience of society. I think an Art Theatre should not be embarrassed to take itself seriously, very seriously.

I feel that artists are our only hope, today. I see this country as sick. I think Big Business has succeeded in dominating and degrading our whole scene. I think Television is mostly poison. I think the movies debase one of the finest art forms ever invented by man. Our Political leaders only want to stay in office and will do what's necessary to that end. Our only hope is the men, those few men, the artists, who tell us what we are and what we are doing and where we are heading. Only they might wake us up. Only they speak the truth or some of it. They yell when we all hurt, become furious when we are all outraged, show us our shame, awake us from our habitual indifference.

In other words, while I think the LC Rep should perform a variety of plays and styles, I don't think it should do anything just because people will pay to see it, because it can be sold. We've had enough of that. I don't want any more of that.

I think we should be a social Theatre. I don't mean this in the narrow sense of the Thirties (although I'd prefer that to our own theatre). To put it another way, it should be a thematic Theatre. It should be a Theatre of Themes. Each play, each production should say something. I want us to do comedies, musicals, fantasies, pantomimes, childrens plays, as well as tragedies and dramas—but I don't want to do anything unless something in the core of the play or the production-to-be is STIRRING to me. I want to become the centre of a Group of Contemporary American Artists: playwrights, directors, designers, actors, technicians all of whom think of the Theatre as a cause.

The English Theatre (with the exception of the people around the Royal Court and Joan Littlewood's work shop) is the Theatre Eclectic. Its leading exponents pride themselves on being able to do anything. I'm talking about the Theatre of the Peter's and Tony's. They do an American Musical, a Roumanian piece of "Style", a restoration bit, their own re-interpretation of Shakespeare and Tennessee Williams' CAT ON A HOT TIN ROOF in French in Paris. It's all very very versatile and adaptable and catholic and elastic. But the productions of the Tonys and the Peters don't have anything for me. Their entrances and exits are very lively, but when you get down to the scenes they have nothing to say. I'm sick of their empty sense of style. They steal a little from Brecht, and a little from me and a little from Vakhtangov and Reinhardt and a little from the Movies and a little from Radio, all understood and woven together cleverly and efficiently. But I don't know who they are. They have not exposed their face. I've met the lot of them at parties and I've taken note of their intelligence and their broad knowledge of many things and their great adaptability and their candor in conversation and their common sense. But I still don't know them.

I am very leery of the word "style". You close your statement with a quote from Michel's book that I utterly reject—"a contribution of the movement by which the American Theatre intent upon creating and building a dramatic tradition is consciously in search of a style."

I resented that statement and I didn't like your quoting it. In the first place we have a style. They've been imitating it over in England since Olivier did a "Streetcar Named Desire" in 1947. That was an imitation of my production. "Death of a Salesman" was the most generally imitated theatre piece of that decade. They'll all tell you how much they have derived from our Theatre. If it gets down to it, we have much more "style" than they do. . . .

There have been two genuinely creative styles in the modern Theatre. Two new styles have come forward. They were necessary. They came from content. First there was the style developed in the United States. It started from the new demands made by the plays of Eugene O'Neill on actors and directors and designers. It was developed by the Group Theatre to realize the works of Odets. In production it came from a couple of men who brought a new impulse to the theatre. Lee Strasberg and Harold Clurman. Then this style was developed further by myself in order to realize the works of Miller and Williams and the others.

This style is not a realistic one, though it is called that. The realism is so highly selected and so enlarged that, whether it reaches those heights or not, it aspires to a Theatre Poetry. The poetry was based on the materials which come from the lives of "ordinary" people. I won't go on describing it, that is another subject. But the point is this: it is a genuine style. And it was developed to realize a certain content. No one was trying to be style-ish!

The other real style that has emerged in our day is the style that is used by Brecht to play his plays. The Berliner Ensemble was organized to play Brecht and the actors were chosen by Brecht, and the mise-en-scene and physical elements were chosen by Brecht. It is personal. It is his style.

Both these styles were not evolved thru a desire to create STYLE as such. The style was a result. It was the result of a creative effort which came from the plays themselves and had no formal external result as a prime end. As in fine architecture, or fine anything else, the process was from the inside out.

And when it was all done, observers and especially Brecht himself most articulately realized: 'My God this is a new style!'

How will we get more stylized productions? Not self-consciously. Let's find the best way in our free Theatre to do the plays we want to do, and we may some day, hear someone saying: "They have developed a new style!" Then we should shrug and go on about our business. And our business will be to produce each play in a way that will realize the play and what it has to say fully. . . .

Now about new works. You said the other day you'd like to open with a new play. I'd like that too. But let me be the Devil's advocate again. Do I have to remind you how rare good new plays are? Of course I don't, but I am. You've known what it is to wait and wait. And you, as I, have done plays because they were the best available and we were determined to simply keep working in the theatre.

So then let's go after the best playwrights. Let's go after Williams and Miller of course! But let's also be realistic about Williams and Miller. I don't expect any help from Kay Brown or Audrey Wood, do you? They are there to get the most money for their authors. I think your idea to give up eighty per cent of the movie money is a good one. It will help. But no repertory can give Tennessee the dollars "Streetcar" brought him. . . .

And we have another problem, much tougher than any I have mentioned. It is a creative problem and an artistic problem. That's why it's tough. In effect we have to create for Lincoln Centre a new kind of dramatic literature. Remember that we are not going to make it, as a Theatre, unless we are daring and adventurous and new. Remember our dusty predecessors. We're either going to be creative or soon dead. And that's a fact.

I cannot imagine a Theatre of this kind in our city without Lee in it. I'd better be plain about this. And we'd better face it. I mean we'd better face that I feel so strongly about it. You've said many times that you agree. But now the time has come for concrete talk. I want Lee involved actively and centrally. . . . A vague agreement with me on this is no longer possible. I mean we're now at a point where you'd better disagree with me if you think it over and do disagree. I can't see myself working in this kind of venture with him somewhere else. Life is too short, we all have too little time left, true teachers and truly fine people are too rare. I think this is the most devoted and learned man in our Theatre and I'd like to make a prominent place for him with us.

I don't want him as part of the school. I'm sure he wouldn't be interested in that. But I do have an idea for him. I have to go a little round about to get to it. I want to open on a night in the fall of 1963 BOTH with a production in the big Theatre and a production in the experimental Theatre. I think this would be the very best way to dramatize who we are. As showmanship it is good. It is also accurate—we'll be showing our true face.

I'd like to ask Lee to be the leader of the Studio of the Lincoln Centre Repertory Theatre. And I'd like him to operate (with whatever executive help he needs) our Small Theatre. . . . I think Lee should also be preparing a production for the big Theatre. He might want to work on it a year with a small group of Actors and we might, with him, schedule it for the second year. That would depend upon what the project was, and how Lee felt about it. But I say we should make a place for him in the LC Rep. . . .

Now about the Actors' Studio. I've got to discuss my problem with you. I cannot give it up. I think it is too valuable. Still it is actually impossible for me to do both the Actors' Studio and the LC Rep. It's too much and there would be too much overlapping. I can do one of two things. I can try to bring over to the LC Rep the elements and activities of the Actors' Studio. For if I set out to organize an institutional Theatre organization at Lincoln Centre, I would only try to do again what we have done at the Actors' Studio.

First of all this means the presence of Lee. Then it means the kind of all-talent-is-welcome policy that is inclusive rather than exclusive. Then it requires the working affiliation of playwrights. (And the best person we have found to organize such a group—after trying Odets, Inge and Anderson—is Molly. So I would have to set out to involve her.) Then the young directors group—we finally got off to a fine start on that last year. And, in fact, all our projects and experimental activities—I would have to try to set up these activities around our LC Rep.

I say I can either try to bring the Actors' Studio to Lincoln Centre or I can continue Actors' Studio as now and work in the LC Rep only as a director of an occasional play. I mean this. I just can't seem to see it otherwise. It's a recognition, a little belated, of the facts of my nature and life. I cannot come over to 66th Street and start unless I come over there whole. But, also for the most practical of reasons, I think the LC Rep will only work if it is organized on the broad base and with all the various activities I have been describing. . . .

Think of a broad field of grass and turf and saplings. In the middle of it stands a great tree. The grass and turf are a hundred or a hundred and fifty actors whose artistic and spiritual life is centered in the LC Rep. They go to classes there. They work in experimental projects there. They go to lectures and talks there. They eat lunch and dinner in our private dining room. They come to special performances there. They have rights of in and out. They rightfully hope to work there some day. They will. It's their place. It's their place as much as the people—the twenty five odd—who are at that time under contract (the tree of my image). . . . The side activities, the classes and the talks, the experimental activities, the projects, the visiting artists from other countries and from other art forms, the restaurant and the informal conversation that takes place there—these are our hope for survival. They're worth much much more than twenty five contracts. I'd rather rely on them than the twenty five contracts. And this broad green field in constant growth is where our continuing artistic health lies. . . .

One last thing: You may think after reading this letter that I am laying down ultimatums. Well, the fact is, I am—a very few. Not in any hostile spirit, and of course not directed at you. But when it gets down to it, I say when it gets right down to it, I have only one face. I've tried to set down here what it is: who I am, what I want, what I will or won't do. I've tried to do this now. Beforehand. I think it is the friendliest and most constructive thing I could do. I think you must do the same thing. And then I think we must see if we do agree on these concrete, specific fundamental points of departure, the ones that mean a lot to me and those that mean a lot to you. Once we have agreed on basic points you will not find me obdurate or stubborn. But let us also face the simple fact that upon close examination we may find that we see things differently. If we decide that, I will resign as co-whatever-I am and I will be open to invitations to direct a show for you your first season.

Finally we cannot run this thing without running it completely. We must immediately take complete charge. Consider how much time and how much energy, our time and our energy, has been squandered trying to rationalize the choice of St. Denis by Rockefeller staff men. I think that within the next six months we have to become so clear in what we want, that we cannot be bumped off our line. Now THEORIES are essential. They are practical! Our tools, our defense, our compass, our motor—use any figure of speech you like, it all adds up to this: What we need now is the knowledge of our convictions; the ideas we are going to work from. Depending upon how clear we are, and how convinced, we will have the strength and the energy, the durability and the tenacity to get this job done right.

Yours, E.K.

[Kazan rejected the "style-ish" productions of Peter Hall and Tony Richardson, as well as a passage quoted by Robert Whitehead from a slim volume of lectures written by Michel Saint-Denis. He hoped that his remarks would contribute "to the movement by which the American theatre, intent upon creating and building a dramatic tradition, is consciously in search of a style" (Saint-Denis, p. 110). An earlier tour designed to familiarize Saint-Denis with American theatrical conditions left him unimpressed with the overall quality of acting.

The company of actors, directors, designers, and dramaturges gathered by Bertolt Brecht impressed Kazan as a model of organic production. He first visited the Ensemble in East Berlin in 1959, several years after Brecht's death.

Kazan approached Tennessee Williams with an offer to produce his most non-conforming plays and "put wonder back in the corpse of our Theatre." Courting Arthur Miller fell to Whitehead, who coproduced A View from the Bridge in 1955.

Kazan proposed to involve Lee Strasberg more "centrally" in the Repertory Theatre by offering him a main stage production in the second year, in addition to leadership of the small experimental theatre. Apparently Whitehead did not answer the present letter by hand, nor did Kazan's either-or ultimatum regarding the Actors Studio produce agreement or clarity in the following months. Kazan wondered in a "stock-taking" letter to Whitehead marked "Not Sent" if he had not chosen "the wrong guy" and would be more comfortable with Tony Guthrie and Saint-Denis. "By now, I am a tradition," Kazan claimed, and he could not be expected to build an "ENDURING INSTITUTION" that was not a "continuation" of the Group Theatre tradition and the Actors Studio. "What else can I be expected to do except develop from what I am" (July 4, 1961, Wesleyan). Later Whitehead specified his opposition to Lee Strasberg and the Actors Studio in terms that Kazan partially shared.] *TLS, 20 pp., Wesleyan*

TO BUDD SCHULBERG

[Sandy Hook, Connecticut]
[c. October 11, 1960]

Dear Budd:

I've been a long time answering your card. And for no good reason. Except that I just haven't been doing anything. Well, in a slow, leisurely, expensive way I have been cutting my film. That is putting it together—the cutting comes later. I'm a little more than half thru. I'm exactly at that point in the assembly when I (you) begin to worry about the advertising. Remember? Now! What am I really doing? I'm writing a film. I can hear you groan from here. Friend I can hear you groan. But that is it. And I'm enjoying it. There isn't a hell of a lot on paper yet. But its a subject I am involved in, and that is everything. I mean I'm truly enjoying it. So much so that I haven't even thought whether its any good or not. I'll show it to you,—(I was going to say: get my lumps.) But the fact is I dont feel that way about it. Its just what I'm doing and its part of a whole course I'm following which started with a return to P-analysis, giving up the Williams play, giving up the Inge play I had, probably bowing out of the Lincoln Centre—although that isn't final yet—and generally changing the course of my life. I had come to a dead end, and I knew it. So now lets see! Otherwise. As I say. Exterior evidences: nothing. My father died. He had actually died in stages over the last five years. Really longer. But we buried him three weeks ago. And it was a drama so personally important to me that I cant really describe it. I mean not that I cried and so on. But its as though, for the first time I studied him and, of course, my self. It came at a time when I had become more contemplative, and I think I understood a hell of a lot about everything from it. My mother is o.k. She lives in a small apartment that they had moved into just in time. He spent five uneasy days sitting on the edge of an arm chair in that apartment, resenting the hell out of it. Then one day his prostate became inflamed, cut off his urethra. He kept having the sensation that he had to go. The third time he tried to get up, my mother gave up and didn't help him. He fell and broke his hip. The next day he was in the hospital. He never left it except for one day in a nursing home. He had the prostate thing, the broken hip which necessitated an operation to pin it together, a massive double hernia, parkinson's disease, and advanced Arterio Sclerosis. His heart was good. My brother, who comes to a blunt point like all doctors, said: he is turning into a vegetable. He resented being moved from New Rochelle. Sort of the old woman in WILD RIVER come real. His last days in the hospital with his last strength were spent planning how he could get out and go back to New Rochelle. He thought of a hospital as a place where you die. You see. I was there all the time. He was gallant his last weeks. Arterio Sclerosis disinhibits. He was mean but honest. At the end I liked him. That's enough. I've never written anyone about him. *** At the moment I'm up in S. Hook with Katie. She's baking a cake. I'm about to make Spaghetti Sauce for Linguine. Molly is in New York. Her plays are in rehearsal three days. And the first couple of readings revealed problems—as they always do. She's at them. Today I didn't do much except look at the foliage. This is the peak day. The last warm day. The brightest day before some overbright winter day when the snow hurts your eyes. I cut a tree up. And took the screens down. All those automatic familiar tasks: put the boat away, called the plumber to drain the old house, bring in fire wood. I think Chris is [going to] Mexico. Either that or he'll be in the army. He's absolutely set on being a writer. And of course he knows its time for him to leave home. I hate to see him go. But I dont say much about it. He's very much himself, that kid, and he'll do everything his own way. Judy just quit her job with the Congressional Quarterly. She says she's going to take a job as a waitress. Some peculiar quirk of getting closer to people that way. She has a steady now—a fellow just as decent as she is. Nick is at Millbrook and was elected "Chairman" of his class. Katie is gangling, almost thirteen, in love with her daddy, who very much feels the responsibility. Bob Anderson is writing a film on Tom Dooley. T. Williams is on the road with the play I didn't do. He was sore at me for a while. But is friendly again. I think he knows now that I just couldn't. Anyway his play is a big hit, and that straightens out a lot. Inge is writing a screen play. Paul is fretting and drinking too much again. The most enjoyable play of the season, I guess, is the HOSTAGE. I say "I guess" because its the only one I've seen. But I truly did enjoy it. I've lost interest in Broadway as I became more interested in myself. Here is a leaf from here. Write me.

ever, E.

John S bought a GM 3/4 ton truck, outfitted it with a bed, a writing desk, an ice box, a heater and is working his way across the country in it. He says he's forgotten how people talk and is trying to get back in tune.

My father died of one of the things that were wrong with him. He contracted pneumonia and it killed him in 36 hours. Despite every known antibiotic and drug. His body couldn't anymore.

[Finishing *Splendor in the Grass* for Warner Bros. and writing an original screenplay immersed in family history placed servant and creator side by side as Kazan attempted to change the "course" of his life. Initially conceived as the first in a trilogy of films, *America America* engaged Kazan to a degree that no other work had approached to date. His son Chris was also implicated in the Stavros character. "This is a boy very much like Chris is now. Heavy set, determined, ruthless, scowling, gay and despairing by turns. . . . Think of Chris when he is open a little. Or you the way you were. Not to be thwarted. Not to be denied" (notebook, September 29, 1960, Wesleyan).

In *The Arrangement* Elia would realize his father's wish to return to the family home in New Rochelle, however implausible the fictional escape from the hospital may have been. Any filial reserve in correspondence was released in the novel: "He was one human and I was another. He was my brother" (p. 489).

Molly Kazan's one-act plays *The Alligators* and *Rosemary* starred Jo Van Fleet and Piper Laurie and were moderately well received in an off-Broadway production. *The Hostage,* Brendan Behan's farrago of romance and Anglo-Irish politics, won the 1961 Tony Award for best play in spite of mixed reviews and a fairly brief run on Broadway.] *TLS, 2 pp., Dartmouth*

TO MICHEL SAINT-DENIS

[New York]
January 20, 1961

Dear Michel:

I am shamefully late in writing you but I got involved this fall in writing a screen play which I am still working on. And since Bob was on the road with two new productions our process of planning for Lincoln Center was inevitably interrupted. We had no real talks.

I did start to draw up a plan for a curriculum as I promised you I would. But when I was working on it I realized that it would not, from the external evidences contained in an outline of courses, define the real differences between us. These have not to do with the appearance on a schedule of body courses, dance courses, voice and speech courses, or courses in the history of the theatre. The essential problem is one of emphasis.

And when I came down to trying to describe these differences, I found that I was only repeating what I had said to you during that rather uncomfortable evening at my home. A word in passing about that evening—I felt uncomfortable because I had become fond of you and I had only disturbing things to say to you. That was one thing that made it not the way I'd like to pass time with you. In the second place, I have a very intense feeling that generally in artistic matters people should not be brought together. I rather think people in our field should hold on very hard to whatever distinctiveness they have.

That night at my house I made two points. I am not going into them again here except most briefly. First, I felt that the teaching of new students should be based on the way we teach the Stanislavsky method here in this country. I say "we teach it" because it might not be what he did. But that's not important. This basic training must not only be extensive but very intensive. I mean it should be laid down very firmly as training over a considerable period of time before any attack on style is made. This intensive, detailed training on a realistic basis must be the groundwork for later departures into stylized production or acting. I felt that in your schedule you were starting on a much broader program initially. And this emphasis, I felt, would produce a different result in the type of theatrical artist developed by the school.

Secondly, I think that style when it is approached must be based on the specific reality of the period from which each dramatic work derives and from the nature of the author. In fact, I stiffen at the general use of the word style. I believe that each play needs originality and a stylistic solution. And that perhaps style as such should not even be taught or broached with actors. To judge by what I have seen come from France in the way of stylized work, I would say that the training that produced it is not the type of training that I would want. And the actors who engaged in it were not trained as I would like the actors around me to be trained. I am referring particularly to the work I saw by Vilar and Barrault. I thought that essentially the stage deportment of their actors was an imitation of past styles and not a unique personal solution of a director with reference to a particular work attempted.

I must say, at this point, that I am not an eclectic person. I am not a person of broad tastes. I am not culturally catholic. Perhaps I should not be one of the heads of a theatre that's going to produce many works. But I have been trying, in my own way, to open up our theatre, particularly in my work on the Williams' plays and on MacLeish's play. I do have a strong urge to go further in that direction based on my own convictions and feelings.

The one theatre I saw in Europe whose work and style I liked was the Brecht Theatre in East Berlin. I thought that this style was unique. It came from the vision of the director and was sound. I have also recently read a book by Gorchakov about the rehearsals of "Princess Turandot" as conducted by Vakhtangov. Here again I thought the work was organic and came from the particular vision of a director with reference to a particular play. It would suit no other play, could never be imitated, would not set a style, or start a school of theatre.

This does not mean that our actors are trained now to be able to give a director what he will need for a stylized production. They are not trained properly. They are not equipped technically. They are not dedicated theatrically. I do not for a minute question the absolute need for a school where actors should be trained to be able to give us what we need. And as I told you I admired the scope and breadth of your program.

I know, Michel, that this letter is not what you expected to get from me. But it is what I feel. I am embarrassed to speak to you negatively. As I say I got fond of you and I do want to work with you. I've expressed to Bob several times my hope that you would do a production at Lincoln Center. And also that other artists who see things differently than I do and whose natures are different than my own would work there. It is only when it comes down to my participation in laying down the basic spirit of a school and its essential point of attack on our theatrical problems, that I must speak from my own taste and in the direction that I hope will lead to the fulfillment of my own hopes.

Affectionately,

EK:ed

[The curriculum in European schools directed by Michel Saint-Denis began with silent improvisation to accustom students to the "very fact" of being onstage and to strengthen "inner feelings." With later interpretative training came the word. Saint-Denis insisted that the "psychological and emotional understanding of a character" be derived from the text, "not from outside it." Once the actor's "whole complex machinery is at work," Stanislavsky can help, he conceded, although "without his system, please" (Saint-Denis, pp. 68–69). Kazan doubted that Saint-Denis understood the Stanislavsky Method or that his objective type of instruction would help the actor to reach "the greatest depth of reality." Most simply put, "his approach is the IMITATION OF REALITY from exterior observations. It is a kind of mimicry" (to Whitehead, September 27, 1960, Wesleyan).

"Style," by contrast, held similar meanings for Saint-Denis and Kazan. They agreed that actors should be trained to play a variety of stylized historical roles. Saint-Denis also held, as did Kazan, that style was derived from "the country and period" of origin and was usually known in retrospect. Giraudoux was "unable to separate thinking from style" and necessarily imprinted the text with directions that govern production (Saint-Denis, p. 79). In *Sweet Bird of Youth*—on stage during Saint-Denis's tenure in New York—neither Williams nor Kazan could separate the play's emotional construction from the stylistic imperatives of the stage directions. Kazan and Saint-Denis differed mainly in timing the exposure of students to historical styles—Kazan thought much too early and deliberately in Saint-Denis's classical curriculum.

Saint-Denis returned to London in late 1961 to direct *The Cherry Orchard* for the Royal Shakespeare Company. Soon thereafter he accepted the post of artistic adviser and ended his relationship with Lincoln Center. Interim plans for an acting school were not released until March 1962.] *TL, 3 pp., Wesleyan*

TO JACK L. WARNER

[New York]
February 27, 1961

Dear Jack:

I am writing you this before I have seen your cut version. Actually, this is Monday morning and my cutter is still at Barnett trying to find your shipment. It hasn't come yet as far as we know and we have been waiting anxiously for it Saturday, Sunday and still are today.

But I have been thinking about the cuts you and Shurlock discussed all weekend. And last night I went to see a picture called "Butterfield 8" and I got terribly worked up. This is clearly a picture that sells sensationalism for its own sake and with an eye towards the boxoffice. It is vulgar. How Geoffrey Shurlock could pass it and make any objections to "Splendor in the Grass" I do not and never will understand.

Item: Elizabeth Taylor is telling about her first introduction to sex and describes a week and half she spent with her mother's lover during which "he taught her all about sin." And (says Miss Taylor boldly) "I loved every minute of it." This would be all right except for the fact that the little girl is thirteen. And if such a scene isn't an incentive for every girl of thirteen to learn about all there is to know about sin—because she will love every minute of it—I don't know what other effect it could have. I consider this immoral.

Item: Elizabeth Taylor sewn in a slip which is too small for her. With a lot of cleavage showing. Her breasts so compressed that they squash out on the sides. Puts one of her mammary glands in the face of Eddie Fisher and says with sly innuendo something like "Is there anything I can do for you?" This little scene is stolen obviously from the first reel of a stag picture. What point it serves except to make the audience hot and bothered I couldn't see.

Item: Miss Taylor and Mr. Laurence Harvey arrive at a motel where he has been a regular patron. He is greeted by the proprietress who is a loquacious woman. She goes into their room with them but won't stop talking. They are clearly eager to be alone and not to discuss the weather. In time the proprietress notices this and she observes "Oh, yes, of course a man must get his rest—regular!" This is read with particular savor by a very good actress, can mean only one thing, it is very vulgar. The audience hoots and howls. Why was this passed? It actually glamorizes infidelity. Makes it attractive, adventurous, encourages it. It makes sneaking off to a motel the greatest fun in the world. What was Geoff thinking about when he passed this? . . . I can't help feeling this morning that somehow, for some reason, I am being discriminated against. And I will not stand for it. You will have to take out these things over my dead body boys. Geoff I know is a completely honest man but for some reason—perhaps his experience with "Baby Doll" or whatever or perhaps fear of the Legion I don't know what—he is being much tougher on my absolutely clean picture than he has been on vulgar, sensational scenes like the ones I quote above.

Let me call to your attention that the character played by Natalie Wood in my picture never has sexual intercourse with anybody through the course of the film. Let me call to your attention that the whole point of my picture, which I believe Geoff missed or won't recognize—is that these two young people should have been allowed by their parents to get married since their love is a pure one and a genuine one involving both physical attraction and spiritual depth of feeling for each other. Let me call to your attention that the villains in my picture are the parents. And they are villains not only because of their lack of understanding but because they prevent these two kids from doing what they want—which is to get married and help each other in every way a husband and wife do help each other. . . .

It is my confirmed opinion that Geoff and his associates no longer know what they are looking at. Some judgment as far as intention and taste must be made. An effort which is clearly to sell sensationalism must be differentiated from an effort to tell a moral story. Simply to make judgment on the basis of the positions of a body is deeply corrupted and mechanical. And I believe that Geoff and Jack Vizzard should question themselves and look to their own consciences here. To put it simply, I think that they have dirty minds. And I say this about two men I like. And I say it because I just think they have seen too much filth and are looking for it. . . .

After seeing "Butterfield 8" last night I can't pretend to discuss this with a cool head. Let's talk about business and money. I have worked a long time on this film—over two years. My weekly salary, if we start talking about that, is a pittance if you divide the salary I receive by the actual weeks I worked on the picture. I cannot afford to have bad notices. Maybe I will get them but I cannot afford to have them because of unclarities that are not of my doing. Everything that is in this picture is necessary to tell the story. Nothing that is in this picture is sensational for its own sake. I think Geoff should recognize this. I think Geoff should make a recommendation to the Board that the picture be passed. I think Geoff should make a human judgment for he is a good human being. This picture will not corrupt youth where I believe "Butterfield 8" does and countless other pictures that have been passed recently do.

As I say, I am writing this on the morning after having my experience with "Butterfield 8". I haven't seen your cuts yet but perhaps it is better this way. I know what the cuts are. I know why those scenes are in the film. I know what damage will be done to the organic structure and to the simple story logic of "Splendor in the Grass" if these cuts are made. You apparently don't care, Jack. You say let's get it out of the way and go on to something else. This is the farthest thing from my mind. I don't want to get it out of the way. I want to preserve it. All "Splendor in the Grass" has meant to you is, I hope, a pleasant social association with me and one meeting with Geoff Shurlock. I spent over two years carefully constructing this film, directing it and photographing it with every bit of effort, skill and integrity I have. I will try—difficult as it is going to be—to consider the cuts you and Geoff have suggested objectively. But there is no use pretending I can be objective. I am not an indifferent person. If I do something, I do it because I believe in it. And for that reason alone I believe in this film.

EK:ed
cc: G. Shurlock

Conferring with Natalie Wood on
Splendor in the Grass

[Geoffrey Shurlock originally found *Splendor in the Grass* "acceptable" by Production Code standards, but he warned Kazan, apparently to no avail, that "excessive candor" in filming youthful romance had caused "severe complaints" and urged "restraint" (April 6, 1960, Herrick).

Bosley Crowther described *Butterfield 8* as a repetition of "the ancient, hackneyed story of the tinseled but tarnished prostitute who thinks she has finally discovered the silver lining for her life in Mr. Right" (*NYT*, November 17, 1960). Unfortunately he is married and his affair with Gloria Wandrous, played by Elizabeth Taylor in an Oscar-winning role, is not a singular occurrence. Kazan's itemized descriptions of *Butterfield 8* are accurate, although Shurlock probably "passed" Gloria's admission of enjoying sex as a thirteen-year-old because it occurs in a scene of remorse and regeneration.

Splendor in the Grass is William Inge's equally familiar story of a rich boy–poor girl romance blocked by insensitive parents and ending in bittersweet resolution. Natalie Wood and Warren Beatty, twenty-three and twenty-four respectively, play teenage lovers in small-town, Depression-era Kansas. The opening scene of their "necking" in a roadster against the background of tumultuous falls was especially troubling to Shurlock. The boy's hand begins to wander in forbidden lower regions and is checked by the girl's restraint, "You mustn't, Bud." Kazan reluctantly accepted a proposed cut in the scene and agreed to "re-mix" the entire sequence with less emphasis on Deanie's "heaving." He prudently summarized other negotiated "cuts" and "restorations" in a memo addressed to Jack Warner and also dated February 27, 1961. With the agreement, Shurlock issued a PCA certificate on March 8.

The present letter marked "Did not send" by Kazan is another case of second thought. It did not, however, exhaust his outrage, as following correspondence reveals.] *TL, 8 pp., Wesleyan*

TO JACK L. WARNER AND BENJAMIN KALMENSON

[New York]
May 25, 1961

Dear Jack and Ben:

Although I am writing this letter personally, it is for my company, and although I am addressing it to you personally, it is for your company.

SPLENDOR IN THE GRASS has been completed—fully cut, edited and scored. It is under two hours and five minutes long. It was produced in accordance with the Code requirements, and has secured a seal.

The picture belongs to my company. I do not wish to have it tampered with in any way. I am sure that there are pressure groups who would like to see it cut one way, and other pressure groups who would like to see it cut another way, just as I am sure that there are individuals who would like to see it cut one way or another. But I do not and will not yield to any pressure from any group.

Bill Inge and I have spent a couple of years developing, producing and finishing this picture. I probably could have earned a million dollars in salary in that time, instead of $125,000. But, I preferred the $125,000. in order to make a fine work independently and without interference. I believe that result has been accomplished. I believe I have a beautiful picture—a fine, clean, moral picture. I also hope that it will be commercial.

I want to go on record that I have heard that you may wish to have the picture cut further to meet the demands of a private group. In fact, Bill Fitelson told me that Ben told him to tell me that he, Ben Kalmenson, would cut the picture no matter what our contract provides. I hope this was a joke. I have no intention of cutting the picture any further. And I warn you not to tamper with it—not one inch of it. Our contract forbids you to. If you do, I will go to the courts, the highest courts, if necessary, for as long as it takes to stop any one from touching the picture. And I will sue for millions of dollars. And I will go to the public, to the church, to any and every one I can if such a scandalous thing happens. Believe me, I was never more serious.

Sincerely,

EK:ed

[Jack Vizzard interceded once again on behalf of Warner Bros. and the Production Code Administration after the Legion of Decency threatened to condemn *Splen-*

dor in the Grass. Kazan withdrew the threat of legal action against Warner Bros. and revised two objectionable scenes. A "considerable portion" of the "line-up" leading to the rape of Bud's alcoholic sister (played with notable energy by Barbara Loden) was cut short so that only "attempted rape" was feasible. He also agreed to reshoot a brief scene that carried the "odious suggestion" of oral sex. For Bud's command, "Get down on your knees. You'll do anything I want," Bill Inge substituted dialogue that seemed "a little more playful" to Jack Vizzard: "At my feet slave. Say you'll always be mine" (PCA file, June 26, 1961, Herrick).

With "teeth bared," Kazan had prevailed, or so he boasted to Clifford Odets, over cowardly studio executives and "the capons in black frocks," who initially demanded more extensive cuts in *Splendor* than the "inconsequential" eight feet ultimately agreed upon. He added that while "public, or semi-public coercion is hard to swallow," he did not "like S in the G well enough to make a 'cause' of it" (June 28, 1961, Wesleyan). Of Kazan's last four films, only *Wild River* had escaped the threat, or consequence, of Legion censorship. *Splendor in the Grass* received a "B" rating with the standard proviso that "no scenes will be reinserted in the picture for foreign release."] *TL, 2 pp., Wesleyan*

Barbara Loden and Warren Beatty
in the New Year's Eve scene

TO TENNESSEE WILLIAMS

[New York]
June 28, 1961

Dear Tenn:

Now they send rockets into the air to hit other rockets. This is one. I don't know where you are. But I do know that occasionally you pass thru Rome. So will this, and may it have some luck. I told Audrey to tell you what I want. I want you to give Lincoln Centre a play. Audrey asked me what sort of arrangements we were going to make with authors. I told Bob Whitehead to meet with her. Obviously you won't make as much money at LC as you would on Broadway.

But there are compensations. We can make of you a living playwright in the same sense that Brecht is a living playwright in East Berlin. Is Irene planning a revival of "Streetcar"? If we had done it at LC, I'd be breaking my neck now to capture Gerry Page for our company and, among other things, she'd play "Streetcar" there our first season. That is good medicine for battered egos. Also good for the Theatre, that vast mess. Honestly, baby, isn't it time. You're fifty now. Most everyone experiments when they're young, but the real good ones, Picasso, Michelangelo, Chaplin and Goya experiment when they have their full gift. I wish to God I had Camino now. I'd open the Theatre with it. And I could do it a lot better. I know for sure that this whole Lincoln Centre Rep idea can die the death! The death the other Repertory groups in this country died: asphyxiation in the dust of worthiness. I intend to be, if nothing else, bold and daring. We are going to do "classics" but only when some mad director has an idea that will make them contemporary. Since Bob and I aren't getting much money (so far, nothing—I'm living off "Waterfront" and he off a certain Canadian Beer) no one scares us. So I'm asking you. You must have ideas that you hesitated about because they were too far outside of out. Or too ugly, or too hateful, or too dirty, or too painful, or too tragic, or too true. I want them. I'm in a crashing mood.

We're going to have a hell of a theatre. In the first place we'll have the most wonderful Theatre building in New York, one that I can only tell you about when I see you, but it's really unique. Backstage it is unrelated to any theatre you've ever seen in this country. You can write stage directions and not pass outside the range of the concretely possible. I hope we'll have the hottest and hungriest young actors in this country. And I'll be as I once was. When I bowed out of "Period of Adjustment" I was weary and disheartened. I was dying for lack of belief. Now I believe in this. And if you and a few other playwrights and actors will be caught up somehow in the potential of this thing (as vs. its drawbacks which are too obvious to even call attention to) we can do wonders. Don't we live by our hope in ourselves? I only say all this because one day you said to me: "You're not going into that, I hope!!" Well the answer is: Yes, I am, I am in it and I think it is the only agency that can do your plays so you'll be proud of them on stage. I honestly believe that, I'm not just pitching. And I believe that you need a true theatre just as Brecht has the Berliner Ensemble, where your plays will be kept alive and revered. Instead of selling the rights to your past plays to Roger Stevens (someone told me you had been planning that) which money will be turned into more paper to sit in a vault, I think you ought to give us those rights on the condition that we keep the plays being performed, one after the other, continuously.

Baby, we're going to do this thing even if you never give us a play. But I want you to, oh my, I want you to. That's why this missile. I want you to give us a difficult one, an impossible one, a truthful one, a painful, honest, uncompromising one, all personal statement, all _inconvenience_, all _untraditional_, all _uncommercial_. We can put wonder back in the corpse of our Theatre. Write me. I'm coming to Europe mid-July, c/o Athens American Express. Where will you be in August? I hope this rocket reaches you.

con amore

cc: T. Williams
c/o Audrey Wood
MCA, N.Y.C.

[Kazan's creative "approach" to Lincoln Center "thrilled" Tennessee Williams, but he would not "have anything to offer the theatre except off-B'dway in the foreseeable future," unless there were "some release from fatigue and depression and disgust" (to EK, n.d., HTC). Kazan made a related announcement in the spring that he would leave Broadway to concentrate on films and Lincoln Center. "'The whole Broadway set-up is inimical to the theatre. . . . Producers are actually abandoning plays they know to be worthwhile, because of the high cost of running them'" (_NYT_, April 7, 1961). Williams continued to appear on Broadway in spite of his aversion to "the big money boys" who controlled the legitimate theater. _Night of the Iguana_ opened in December 1961 to strong reviews and a profitable run.

Gerry Page was surprised to learn, inaccurately, that Lincoln Center players would earn the "minimum" and be committed to five years of exclusive service. She reportedly asked Kazan during a backstage recruiting visit if he would observe the same conditions (Garfield, p. 211). _A Streetcar Named Desire_ was revived at Lincoln Center in 1973, long after Kazan and Whitehead had departed and without Page in the cast.

Edward Albee, James Baldwin, S. N. Behrman, Robert Bolt, Lillian Hellman, William Inge, and Clifford Odets were among those encouraged to write for the Repertory Theatre, in addition to Tennessee Williams and Arthur Miller. Paddy Chayefsky was "sick of hits on Broadway" and planned to offer his forthcoming play to Lincoln Center.] _TL, 2 pp., Wesleyan_

TO MOLLY DAY THACHER

PM: Athens, August 2, 1961

Had a good week end. I took a guy named Nikos Gatsos, a poet, a big lumbering man, who has a poet's appreciation of plain facts and I did the Delphi ride. I remembered some marvelous scenery just past Delphi, rocky hillsides, endless stonewalls, the barest subsistence level in agriculture. I thought it might be useful if I shoot most of this film in Greece, which seems to be likely. And

I think all around Delphi is perfect background for the journey to Ankara. I gave Gatsos the script to read and his reaction to it was extremely favorable. He says I've got the Greek family and the feeling which binds that unit together very well. Meantime I keep thinking about the inevitability of shooting some of the stuff in Istanbul. I made a list etc. and I'm going back there for a few days this week (as soon as I get Paxinou and Rondiris off my neck) Going to Istanbul from here is 55 minutes. And I'm going to try to figure out the minimum I can do there, silent, with the minimum crew and fuss, and still obtain what I so desperately need for the Hamal scenes. I'm thinking hard about my leading character. What has helped is that I decided to meet all the up and coming young actors in Greece who can speak English. Kritas, my producer friend here, sent out a call, and tomorrow morning I'm meeting thirty odd. In preparing my mind for this event (!) I realized how little definition my lead has. And, in a way, how unattractive he is. I've had thoughts that I hope will cure that. But I can now see what people meant when they omit enthusiasm about Stavros, or the script. I dont go by Logan, but his reaction to the script was quite negative. And no one has expressed any pleasure about my lead, not a word, not in re an incident. Still anyone who meets Skouras, even those who immediately feel he is FOS, all somehow feel his charm or whatever you call it, his animalism if nothing else, his power even if it is somehow crudely exerted and even if it is immediately felt to be ruthless and selfish. So by now, I've achieved distance. And I can see something is seriously wrong and I'm not only ready to fix it, but even eager to. And this is important in fact crucial before you start to do what Paul Osborn calls "fussing". In fact "fussing" is just what I dont want to do. *** Kritas, who is a wheel made after the most go-getting-yankee model has also made a date for me next week with the minister of Industry, whom he describes as "young and a good boy". He says this M of I is frantically eager to break bread with me as prelude to placing the whole of Greece at my feet. I keep talking about Yugoslavia, and they keep putting Yugoslavia down. But by now its a game. And its clear that when the time comes to make this film I will make it in Greece, centered here, with an excursion of a couple of weeks into Turkey if I can arrange it. Meantime I've had people looking up costs both here and in Yugos. And they are fantastically low. I can see why they've been making so many films abroad. And it cant last much longer. Sooner or later these countries are going to have unions, or in the case of Yugos they're going to want to share in the profits: And, of course, they should. They are being taken advantage of now.

So. Here's what my program looks like. This is Monday A.M. Today, tonight, I'm with Rondiris. He loves me. But its a little too much for my neo-yankee soul. Too much honey over everything. But I believe (I have to make everything useful) I believe I can get into a useful conversation about Greek drama, and here, on his home ground, level much more with him and try my Linc Centre Prod ideas out on him. And I will. Tomorrow is Paxinou day. She has gone nuts. But I am finally accepting lunch, dinner, the overwhelming beating your digestive tract can take only every so often at her table. Tomorrow night I'm going to her opening night: The phoenician women. Wednesday I'm going to Istanbul. First I will make a list of the minimum SILENT scenes I can get away with there, and what the problems are, esp. costume wise in photographing the bazaar and the waterfront areas for the Hamal section. I will also see what I can do in the way of collecting photographs. etc. This will keep me for the rest of the week. The main thing, of course, I'll try to get as close to the Hamals as I can. I already made one friend, and I will try to look him up and eat with him etc. If not him, some one else. I did some of that already, and I found out what I always find out that they are only human, and I can get close to them very quickly. And artistically I've got to now. A week from today I'll be back here. I will then meet with the Minister of Industry etc. and confirm the fact that I have intentions of shooting a film here and lay down the basic premises. I have to give him a rough list of what I want. I will also make an airplane hop to IOANNINA which is in the north. I thought of it as a possible sub for Kayseri. (as well as Komotini) That would mean that all my Turkish shooting will be confined to Istanbul. THEN HOME. Just about what I told you: between five and six weeks. Maybe a day in Rome to bring you the Ardrey report. I miss you now. And think of home a lot.

Love.

[Kazan scouted locations in Istanbul and the central Anatolian region of Kayseri, where oppression of Greek and Armenian minorities formed an authentic historical background for the initial journey to Ankara in *America America*. These scenes were eventually filmed in Greece, as Kazan anticipated, but the "hamal scenes" could only be filmed on Istanbul's waterfront and were necessary to complete the hardening of Stavros as a porter subject to inhuman labor. Even a sharply reduced filming schedule in Turkey would require persistent negotiation with a multilayered bureaucracy that censored freedom of expression while desiring tourism, economic development, and exposure to the West.

The poet Nikos Gatsos composed songs for *America America* and assured Kazan that his view of Greek family life was accurate. Apparently he also omitted "enthusiasm" for the character of Stavros, soon to emerge as an obstacle to funding. Parenthetically, Kazan wondered how Spyros Skouras, Greek immigrant president of Twentieth Century-Fox, could retain his "charm" while no less "ruthless" than the film's seemingly "unattractive" star, who lived in constant peril. Skouras reportedly turned down *America America* because the story was alien and atypical: "'This isn't Kazan!'" (*A Life,* p. 628).

The director Dimitris Rondiris was set to bring a Greek troupe to the United States in the fall. Katina Paxinou played an Oscar-winning role (Pilar) in *For Whom the Bell Tolls* (1943) and acted in classical Greek theater.

Barbara Loden, three months pregnant with their son Leo, accompanied Kazan and helped to chart locations in difficult terrain.] *TL, 2 pp., Wesleyan*

TO H. WILLIAM FITELSON

[New York]
September 5, 1961

Dear Bill:

I want to talk to you very soon and very seriously about the financing of my new picture. I am about to start rewriting it. I have my ideas as to what I want to do and by now it seems certain that whatever I do nothing fundamentally is going to be changed. It will be shorter and more succinct—perhaps a little punchier and so on—but it is going to be the same old chicken, making the same kind of noises.

Let's face it, Bill, as far as America is concerned, we have a subject for the art houses here that's a fact. There's nobody more liberal minded that Youngstein and certainly nobody is more anxious to get a film from me than Columbia despite that you see how they behave. We have an art subject as far as America is concerned.

And that doesn't make me one damn bit sad either. Let's stop worrying about getting me $500,000 divided over ten years. I don't want it. Not because I dislike money but because it means I would have to make a lot of sacrifices as far as content and so forth goes that I don't want to make. I don't want the $500,000 or anything. I have enough money now—if I don't waste it or spend it or take to gambling or women and so on.

I would like to produce the picture on a moderate budget. My research in Greece shows me all budgets are moderate. Costs are roughly one-third of what they are in this country. I could make this picture very inexpensively in Greece. But even if I couldn't I would want to because I don't think we are going to get a lot of money. And I don't want to make the sacrifices to my inner state of happiness that would result from my taking a lot of money. Bill, I want to make a picture for the art houses. I don't want to meet with Vizzard and Shurlock anymore. And I don't want to be frightened by the Legion of Decency and worry what Father Little is thinking about.

I am fifty-two years old and I have had it. I don't want to go into the customary profanity because I am dictating to a very nice young lady, but I have had it.

I don't want to be richer and I don't want you or Abe to set a record salary for me. You don't have to prove to me you are good by showing me how much money you can make for me—or what a marvelous deal you can make. I think we have to readjust our whole way of thinking—not only to me in general but especially to this project in particular.

Let me hear from you. I have sent a copy of this letter to Abe Lastfogel.

Best,

EK:ed
cc: a last fogel

[Kazan discarded the notion that he was "on the wrong track" as he prepared to revise *America America* in early 1961: "I began to say to myself that I had to find something of worth in the boy. That is dead wrong. You have to find life in him. LIFE. Liveliness, livingness, individuality" (notebook, February 18, 1961, Wesleyan). Later in the year Max Youngstein, production head of United Artists, described Stavros as "repellent" for stabbing a thief in the back while he prayed and for seducing an older woman on "a straight money basis." The project could not succeed with such a degraded hero, he advised, nor were the "economics" of making the picture for "over a million dollars" justifiable (to Fitelson, July 24, 1961, Wesleyan). Kazan accurately identified *America America* as a "subject for the art houses." The film also gave no reason to fear Roman Catholic censorship— quite the opposite, as it turned out.] *TL, 2 pp., Wesleyan*

TO LEE STRASBERG

SH: The Repertory Theatre at Lincoln Centre
September 18, 1961

Dear Lee:
As you know, Paula sent me a recording of your final remarks at the Studio last June. When I returned from Greece, I listened carefully to what you had said. I felt that you were trying to describe our true situation as well as to express your own feelings. It was a useful thing to do and I agreed with many of the things you said. At the same time, you stated views with which I disagreed. You now deserve from me an effort to return to you the truth as I see it.

You said that in going ahead with Lincoln Centre I had taken a step which the members and yourself had to accept as the end of any intentions I had had of someday turning the Studio into a Theatre. This is correct.

I did try for two years to arrange an organic connection—wedding or transition—between the Studio and the Repertory Company. I did not succeed. I've now given up on that.

From the moment Lincoln Centre was first mentioned to me, I tried to involve you in a fitting and worthy way. I am still trying. It must be obvious to you that if I—with my great feeling for you—couldn't manage this, no other pressure could. And certainly not the threat contained in a petition initiated by Paula and signed by any group of Actors.

It is very simple to "blame" Bob Whitehead, or to scorn him as I felt you did in your talk. He does have limitations—different ones than we do. But I believe now as I have right along, that he is the best person available for this particular job, better than Cheryl, better than Kermit, better than anyone I know in our theatre.

What was incorrect was the suggestion in what you said that, in effect, "read me out" of the Studio. This is quite inaccurate. I have told you repeatedly that I have no intention of resigning from the Actors' Studio. I started it because I thought it was necessary, in fact, vital. I think so no less today.

When we were able to bring you into the Studio I thought the movement had found its perfect leader. I still think so. I said to Cheryl at that time that I wanted to "give" the Studio to you. And I did.

At the same time I have never been far away. And I have no intention of leaving it, now or later. If anything were to happen to you, or to your connection with the Studio—and that would be a great disaster—I would make sure that the work and life there continued the best way it could. I'm sure you yourself would not want it to stop. I promise you it will not.

But I don't want to make a Theatre of it. I believe now that there are two separate and distinct needs, and they demand two separate and distinct organizations. The organization for a Studio is not the organization for a Theatre and the inner spirit of one is different than that of the other.

In other words I do not agree with the inference in what Hyams quoted you as saying: that if the Studio did not become a Theatre it would disintegrate. I don't think it should become a Theatre. And I don't believe it will disintegrate. But I do think there should be adaptations and changes now. The course of your work has made these necessary.

There was a tone in your recorded speech of some disappointment in me. I can understand why this is. But I must tell you that I too have been disappointed in one aspect of the work at the Studio over the last few years.

You will remember that at the time when Cheryl and I undertook to see to it that you were paid fittingly for your commitment and work, our expressed hope was that if we were able to bring you the money you should have, you, on your side, would give up enough of your personal classes to be able to devote real time to specifically "studio" work on 44th Street. In other words we were working to make it possible for you to function there in an enlarged and creative capacity. We hoped that from this, a new type of activity in the production of plays would come to be.

What happened was that you gave up no classes, rather took on one more class: the Directors' Group. You merely added to the burden on your time and your health. That was not what we had in mind for the Studio. Nor was it what we hoped for you personally.

I think the next step in the progress of the Studio is for you to devote all your time there to the creation of "projects". I don't think an annual urging from you to the members will accomplish this. Clearly it has not. If for a time your other work is curtailed, I'd say it was worth it. Cheryl should help organize these projects. And I will, this fall again, do another scene preparatory to a production of the "Oresteia". I got great value from the fifty-minute bit I did there last year and from the discussion which followed.

Let me know your reaction to all this. Now another point. You may feel, and quite correctly, that I won't be around enough in the next year or so to carry my share of the load. I am going ahead with the movie I've written—probably next summer in Greece—and the preparations for this and for Lincoln Centre will take up an awful lot of my time and energy. Furthermore, I will be out of the country a good bit after the first of the year.

Therefore I want to propose that I take a leave of absence as a director of the Studio, starting on December the first and going on until I have finished photographing my film. Judging from your talk last June you too feel that some sort of new phase should start in the work there. And perhaps my withdrawal from the central councils will allow you and whoever you choose to organize any new turn of work with you and for you to function more effectively. Let me assure you again that if this "leave" does take place, I will still be close by if there is any sort of crisis. Let me know your reaction to this proposal.

And now I want to make an official offer from Lincoln Centre to the Actors' Studio. As you know the small Theatre in our building will be running concurrently with the larger Theatre upstairs. Bob and I would like the Studio to do two productions there each year. The idea is Bob's and I am enthusiastic about it. It means that the Studio will have a realistic and living tie with the activity at Lincoln Centre, while, at the same time, preserving its own identity completely. Both these productions might arise from your work in the Directors' Group. I urge you and Cheryl to give this proposal favorable consideration. I'm all for it.

I know that you must have done a great deal of thinking this summer. You may still feel, as you did in June, that you have no interest whatever in what happens at Lincoln Centre. I hope this is no longer true. But if it is, do say so to me plainly again. I am hoping that you will be as enthusiastic about Bob's proposal as I am.

So I'll wait to hear from you. I'm going to Chicago, Minneapolis, Detroit, Toronto and some way stations to peddle my picture. And I'll be back in town the first of October.

E.K.

[Lee Strasberg closed the fourteenth season of the Actors Studio in 1961 with criticism of Lincoln Center and Kazan's disloyalty in accepting a codirectorship of the Repertory Theatre. Elia's research for *A Life* turned up the old recording supplied by Paula Strasberg and with it delayed sympathy: "I realized what a terrible disappointment it must have been for this man to be insufficiently supported by someone he'd trained and trusted, myself, and then to be muscled out, no matter how gently, from a plan to set up the kind of theatre he'd worked all his life training actors for. When I heard his speech, I felt for him" (*A Life*, p. 607).

In 1963 Bob Whitehead explained his opposition to Lee Strasberg and the Actors Studio: "'I feel that Strasberg is responsible for the cult that destroyed the healthy idea—the outrageous cry-out necessary to our drama in the thirties. Through Strasberg the psycho-sexual interpretation of the subtext has become a major force now. At Lincoln Center we will be anti-psychoanalytic. We want to establish a new character for our performers, as well as the theatre'" (Gray, pp. 53–54). Kazan later informed Strasberg that "the Juilliard people" who controlled the educational unit at Lincoln Center had an "unshakeable prejudice" against the Studio.

Kazan's plan to take a "leave of absence" was a mild step in light of further developments at the Studio. For his part, Strasberg reportedly declined the "official offer" of directing the Forum, the studio theater planned for Lincoln Center. The tide was running toward stronger leadership by Studio actors and a more visible, independent stage than the Forum would provide.] *TLS, 3 pp., Wesleyan*

TO RICHARD LEDERER

[New York]
October 16, 1961

Dear Dick:

I am sending copies of this letter to Joe Hyams and Phil Solomons so they will be thinking and will have some reactions to what I say by the time you get back from California. I wish you were here now, of course. You have been like a rock all through this picture and so have all of the boys working on it. I can't tell you how grateful I've been all through for your devotion, imagination and just plain interest. No picture I have ever had have the people working on it, on your side, been so devoted and creative. And, of course, business now seems to be excellent.

But, being an old worrier, I am worried that we are going to let up and just coast along. . . . It seems to me that all film advertising lapses into the routine once the picture has opened. It's as though the job had been done and that's that. At the same time this conversation about whether or not the picture has "legs", well I am worried about this too, but maybe we can help give it legs. And maybe we can be as imaginative in the post-opening advertising, even though we don't spend nearly the money, as we were in the pre-opening advertising. My ideas, as you know by now, are not the most brilliant in the world, but here are a few:

First and negative one—I'd forget about the controversy. That's a ball game we played and won two weeks ago. It's another Saturday now and we are playing on another field. I'd burn all the panels about response cards and controversy and sixteen year-olds and all that stuff. It's a dead issue.

2) I would try, in the advertising, to give the picture as much broad calibre as possible. Obviously, this picture is drawing now from the broadest kind of audience. It isn't just a teen-age picture, although the teen-agers are going. It's a picture for everyone. The word of mouth, as I hear it, is immense.

3) One kind of ad I think would be valuable is if we have a big sign saying "and not only in New York but everywhere in the United States" and then quote some bits from the notices in Boston, Detroit, Philadelphia and Los Angeles. I have seen these papers and there are quotes in them just as good as anything in Crowther, Winsten or Newsweek. In fact, they are better. There's a marvelous review in the Miami paper for instance. And, I think, the fact that this picture is now spread-eagling this country and knocking the reviewers absolutely dead everywhere should be brought to the attention of New Yorkers. I certainly prefer the space being used this way to that kiss, which many people think is Natalie Wood kissing a Negro man.

4) I think we should start pointing towards the Academy campaign. You must have seen the Skolsky column that rules out "Judgment at Nuremburg" and says that the Academy campaign would be between WEST SIDE STORY and SPLENDOR IN THE GRASS. And that he personally favors SPLENDOR IN THE GRASS because its problems will always be with us. I think Skolsky doesn't mean anything in the New York Times and Tribune but perhaps a quote like this in one of the trade papers or in the Journal and the News here would have a tremendous effect. People are interested in the Academy Awards and like to see films that are going to be leading contenders. . . .

5) I think something should be done about the lines in front of the boxoffice. On this day, Monday, the 16th, there's been absolutely nothing in the columns about the enormous lines and the enormous business we are doing. An old-timer on Broadway just called me on the phone and said he hadn't seen lines like these outside of a Broadway theatre since the old days of when Sinatra was at the Paramount.

6) I think it would be wonderful if we had a series of still portraits in the lobby of the theatre of all the minor characters. More than any film in years, this picture has been getting attention for its "so-called" supporting players. And a lot of them, I believe, will be getting Oscar consideration. . . . So many people have called me up about Pat Hingle. And there is no real evidence from the front of our theatre that there is this tremendous characterization in

Warren Beatty

our film. So many people have raved about Audrey Christie deservedly. Why not do something about it. Barbara Loden gives a performance that's one of the showiest and flashiest in years. It's an attraction in itself. Zohra has, time and time again, been mentioned to me as being "the best thing in the picture" and so on. Our lobby now is dull, conventional and dead. I always wonder what theatre managers do all day except stand out front and worry. I'd like to put a bomb under those fellows downstairs. Let's do it together. . . .

7) I also think there should be special ads just about Natalie Wood and already pointing towards an Academy Award nomination, which she's sure to get. And another one about Warren Beatty saying—"this is the young actor you have been hearing about. He's to be seen only at the Victoria Theatre" and then list some of his quotes. Even if the ads were small. I know you don't want to spend a lot of money and you shouldn't. Let's at least make them original from now on so that there's life and imagination and so that they are just not routine. I am just scared to death that we will disintegrate now into just a routine plugging of this picture. . . .

Let's keep going. I'm like an anxious father. But still I should be shouldn't I?

Best,

EK: ed

[Richard Lederer's campaign began with a breathless ad in the *New York Times:* "A CONTROVERSIAL NEW MOVIE HAS CAUSED AN EVENT UNPARALLELED IN THEATRE HISTORY." Scheduled for September 15 was a special paid preview of *Splendor in the Grass* to test audience opinion and justify "ELIA KAZAN'S BOLDEST PRODUCTION" to date (*NYT,* September 13, 1961). The results of a self-fulfilling questionnaire were published serially before the film's release on October 10. By wide margins, the audience recommended the film for sixteen-year-olds, found nothing "censorable" in the story line, and agreed that Hollywood should attempt such mature "themes" as Kazan has directed.

Archer Winsten wrote in the *New York Post* that this is "Kazan at his best. This is cinema art, perfectly matched to its subject." Reviewers for *Time, Nation,* and the *New Republic* deplored Kazan's blunt direction of an overheated teenage romance and probably helped to swell the box office beyond the expectations of Lederer, who headed publicity for Warner Bros. *Splendor* ran second to *Breakfast*

THEATER AND FILM

at Tiffany's during the New York engagement and by year's end had proven its "'legs'" with earnings of $5.5 million and a place on the *Variety* list of "All-Time Top Gross Films." After three consecutive failures, it was Kazan's most profitable film to date.

Fanny was the only Warner Bros. film nominated by the Academy in a year dominated by *West Side Story*. As Kazan foresaw, Natalie Wood received her first nomination as best actress—Sophia Loren won for *Two Women*. William Inge won the award for best writing, story, and screenplay.] *TL, 4 pp., Wesleyan*

TO WILLIAM SCHUMAN

[New York]
November 13, 1961

Dear Bill:

There has been one significant omission from the plans for Lincoln Centre: motion pictures. I believe we must have some kind of program which recognizes the importance of films as a great contemporary performing art.

In some ways it is the most important of all of the performing arts. It reaches and affects the most people. It is the medium through which we—the United States—are most graphically known in the other countries of the world. And, in the opinion of many people, it is the medium, which more than any other, is able to capture the rhythm and character of modern living.

And then it is ours. America has contributed two art forms of worth to the world. One of these is jazz music and the other is the motion picture.

Films in this country, unfortunately, have fallen into the hands of the merchants. Activity in this art form is called the Film Industry. And, of course, that is exactly what it is. It is a big, big business, which must, by its nature, please everyone and offend no one. Out of such a basic stance no art can come.

But despite that it must not be forgotten that we have produced the first great world master in this form, D. W. Griffith, as well as the man who is the greatest performing genius in our century, Charlie Chaplin. And many, many fine and artistically important films.

Significantly, there is no periodical, weekly, monthly or quarterly, that treats films seriously here in the United States. This, despite the fact that there's a surging interest in the old film masterpieces. These are being revived again and again and again in the so-called "art theatres" all over this country.

In other words, here is a function that Lincoln Centre can perform and even an obligation that it must meet. We can play a positive and significant role in the recognition of the lasting importance of films and thereby in their future potential. I think we should try to work out some kind of program for

Lincoln Centre that can make it <u>the</u> place where films are recognized on a level with the other major performing arts in this country.

I will not go into details here. I only want to bring the subject up and urge you to act on it vigorously and soon. A feasible procedure, it seems to me, would be to form a small committee that would consult on the subject and bring you and Mr. John Rockefeller specific recommendations. Of course I will be very glad to be on any committee of this kind.

Yours cordially,

EK:ed

[The producer Jerry Wald anticipated Kazan by advising that "provision" be made at Lincoln Center for "an internationally popular art form that America can claim to have made most strongly its own" (*NYT,* January 1, 1961). William Schuman, newly designated president of Lincoln Center, reversed the board's original decision to limit the repertory to "live" performance and declared in March 1962 that film was "'a cultural necessity.'" Kazan agreed to advise a steering committee, although other duties would prevent his full-scale involvement. An inaugural film festival was held in 1963, and in 1969, after surviving budget deficits, the program gained solvency and official status as the Film Society of Lincoln Center (Young, pp. 297–98).] *TL, 2 pp., Wesleyan*

TO CLIFFORD ODETS

[New York]
December 28, 1961

Dear Cliff:
I had lunch with Moss the day before he left New York. Since "Gentleman's Agreement" we've been friends. Before that I had thought of him in the most stereotype way. It's amazing to me how long that Group Theatre snobbery lasted. Also—part of the snobbery—I judged everyone only by their work. But on our film Moss behaved with rare courage. The field of battle was Zanuck's office. Time after time I found him behaving with more candor and directness than me. All through he was unwavering. I had to like him. As the level of my own snobbery went down I was able to see him for what he was—one of the fine people. Over the years we'd meet a couple of times a week for a walk or lunch—that is for a conversation. When I first thought to try writing movie scripts he was most encouraging. At our last lunch he asked me if it wasn't time for him to read what I had done. I said I'd send it to him. So—So now send it back to me when your're done with it. At our last lunch he was very

troubled. He started to say something about it but finally really didn't. We die in the midst of life.

I am very late answering your last. This is not because I didn't know my answer. I've been so involved in getting my script finished that I didn't do anything else for a month, six weeks. I'm going to do the film in Greece this summer, and it was necessary to immediately embark (script in hand) on the business of financing. That is now going on.

I have six months still to work on the script. So please do send me your reactions. Don't fear hurting me or discouraging me. I don't become discouraged and some slight hurt is the condition of my life. I mean I'm punchy to it. Furthermore I've always worked out of a hole, and if there wasn't a hole there, I'd dig it. Something can be done about everything except the basic idea, and I'm not about to change that. I also know that small changes in a script make large differences in effect. Etc. So please do write me soon.

There was a change in tone between my first and my second letters. But not because I suddenly thought less of you or because I had another script in hand. It was due to one sentence in your letter—which I haven't before me at this moment. It said that you have to stay there for a while to write "one more movie".

I understand there are reasons: Human, important, private why you have to do this. And I'm not superior about movies. I don't think Bloomgarden or Merrick and the others are superior to Wallis, Wald and Berman, and etc. In fact, there are many more good directors in California than here.

It's just that the two activities are so separated. And that it takes so long to write and/or direct that "one last movie." I've never known anyone who could do both at the same time. I've never been able to, though sometimes it's seemed that I've "gotten away with it." They're just totally different activities—writing a play out of yourself, and for yourself as vs. doing a film script from some one else's material and "for" some one else. I'm telling you! For one thing you are not really under your own command—well—you know—

Then between the two letters we felt the pressure of our own schedule. . . . We have a new play, half written. The author has asked us not to announce it so I'm not naming him. He has read us what he has done. It's on a contemporary theme. He's working on it constantly and he is working only on it, full time. We know the kind of person we need for the lead and we're thinking now specifically about casting it. And we know something about the other roles. We know the period, the style, the basic settings. We know what scene designer we are going to use. We know how it fits into our Theatre building.

Secondly, we are going to do the Oresteia of Æschylus. I'm going to England on January 2nd to talk with Bob Bolt whom we are interested in adapting it for us. I've already had one conversation with him. To my surprise he had been thinking independently about this trilogy for years. He's now completing a job for Spiegel ("Lawrence of Arabia"). But should be thru by the time I get there. I hope he'll work out. If not we'll turn elsewhere. But here too we know the characters, and I know how I'm going to do the plays. I've done two bits of them at the ACTORS' STUDIO. And presently I'm working on the first third of the Eumenides, which is by far the most difficult part of the production. But for immediate action, we know what parts have to be filled, now. . . .

Our third and fourth plays are not yet definitely chosen. But we would like the third play to be a broad, wild and irreverent farce. What play we don't know. But we feel we need it for general balance and a change of tone in our program. I'm going to direct the first two plays. We are talking to directors for the third play. It would be an adaptation too. The play here depends upon the director. We want to do an O'Neill play for the fourth and final offering. We have not agreed upon which one. But perhaps it will be "All God's Chillun." We think this play extremely good, one of his best, and never yet seen by this generation. . . .

The situation on actors differs from the Group days. Then there was no one trained "right". In fact everyone was trained "wrong". But now there is a pool of talent—thanks to Lee and the Actors' Studio and to a number of other fine teachers, Sandy, Bobby, Paul Mann, Herbert Berghof and so on. I believe we can build a company that is very broad as far as types go, that will work and work and work to prepare themselves to play classic plays, and plays in style, a company that will have real talent, a company of people of character. . . . In other words I'm going to put together and train a company that will be—I know—broader than the Group, and—I believe—more talented. We'll have about ten "leading" actors, about fifteen "character" people. And then we'll have about thirty absolutely new people whom we will train from the very beginning, the very beginning. Fifteen-odd of these will be under contract to us, from the beginning. But there probably will be shifts and changes here and we will train thirty young people so that we can end up with fifteen real good ones, the leading players of the future. . . .

Let me jump. Would you come to New York sometime this winter or spring as our guest (does that sound institutional enough?) spend some time here with us, let us show you our Theatre plans and talk everything over? As they say: no obligation. Just come, talk, go. . . . I do not believe that we are fated not to work together. I think we're fated to work together. I think you and I are more alike than Williams and I—a great deal more so. And I think when we do work together, you will be happy with me. I still believe we have a chance to do great things together. UNLESS—unless you unconsciously don't want to, or have some resistance to me that you haven't expressed or even don't know. That is possible. But failing that I believe we will work together. I certainly want to very much.

People have said to me: forget him, he's not going to write for the Theatre again. He's too anchored there. But I don't believe them. Not because you are more "idealistic" than others or anything like that. Simply because the Theatre is your natural form and the films are not. And I think—since you are one of the proudest people I've ever known, that this will some day soon make it impossible for you to continue there.

Suppose for example that we talked about your writing us a play to open our second season. You told me you have four or five plays that you have ready to write. Perhaps you could tell us something about these plays and we would select one of them that the Lincoln Repertory Theatre would option and plan on beginning right now. Suppose at the same time we planned a revival of "Waiting for Lefty" and "Camino Real"—which would make a wonderful evening. We'd set Lefty deep in the thirties—perhaps with a preamble of newsreels and finally pull out the last bit of film and allow the hot flickering arc to hit Fat square in the eye as he begins his first speech.

As I say we'd like to do your new plays—and also keep you "living" thru revivals. There is a whole new generation that has not seen Odets. "Paradise Lost" I am very anxious to revive. "Rocket to the Moon" too. And so on.

I'd like to talk to you about all this. Obviously this letter is too long already. I'm going to England and then to Greece (to make preliminary production plans there for next summer). Will be back February 1st. Anytime after that. What do you say? You see I'm a stubborn man. And I do love you.

[Moss Hart died on December 20, 1961, several weeks after he and his family moved from New York to Palm Springs. A heart attack, the second in thirteen months, was the cause of death. "The Anatolian Smile," a late draft of *America America*, is probably the script Hart offered to read.

Kazan tempered his praise for Clifford Odets in earlier correspondence—"You are the most talented American playwright living today"—with a friendly rebuke for "not producing" in accordance with his gifts. The letter seemed to offer an advance for a new play and special prominence at Lincoln Center. "Take it personally," Kazan urged, "I need you." A second letter seemed less "beguiling and seductive" to Odets and appeared to withdraw "attractive offers" now that plans for the opening season were under way. Odets suppressed a sharp reply and answered that he was "saddened" to realize that "while we will remain friends until the end, we will never work together on a mutual project" (November 8, 1961, Indiana). His need to write "one more movie" before returning to the stage had added uncertainty to Kazan's planning for the inaugural season—optimistically scheduled for September 1963. Of the plays currently under consideration, only *After the Fall*, "half written" at the time, would be performed at Lincoln Center.] *TL, 6 pp., Wesleyan*

[New York]
December 28, 1961

Dear Bob:

I'll be in London the 3rd, 4th and 5th of January. And I'll call you. Save me a lunch or dinner or a tea or an hour. If I don't get you on the phone it will be because I forgot to bring your phone number along or wrote it down wrong or—my God!—will you be in Spain with Spiegel!? Anyway, if you don't hear from me get to me. I'll be at one of those fat cat hotels that no one can afford except movie-makers whose bills are being "taken care of" by Film Companies. Warner Brothers Publicity will know which.

I didn't write you about "Man For All Seasons". I liked it very much, but I wasn't prepared to be as ecstatic about it all as were our critics here. And since unqualified praise is so rare I didn't want to cast the least shadow on it.

I think we have some differences in taste. What you call purity in Scofield seems "cool" to me and technical. He is a superb actor of his kind. But it is the kind I admire and admire only. I thought there was much more humanity in the script than came over from the stage. I thought Scofield always safe, the character I mean, as if nothing finally could happen to him worse than an heroic and graceful death as a revered martyr. In manner I thought him like a gracious host leading us, the audience, thru a journey to an end out of which all the sting had been taken. He made the difficult struggle seem easy. The fangs of pain had been pulled. No real difficulty. Why? Because no real choice? I don't really know. Also all the antagonists were so obviously crumby that the audience was made to feel that the only thing they would have done or could have done under similar circumstances was what More did. Very flattering to the audience. But I think a little dangerous. It does not prepare them for "real" crisis. Idealism has been made comfortable. I thought there was much more in your script.

On the good side I did always feel his intelligence at work and this was always pleasurable. And he does have a fine face, drawn, ascetic, reserved, not easy or available, truly inner-orientated, fine. And he is brilliant technically except for his habit of raising his eyebrows towards the audience and "thinking with them". In the old silent film days they used to call it "registering".

Do call me up despite all the above. I'm not as mean and ungenerous as I sound. And even if we differ so much in taste that we can't work together, I'd like very much to get to know you. And if we are going to work together on the Oresteia—which I want very much—it's best that I be totally candid now. Anyway it's more fun that way. I love differences and only fear simulated agreements.

Want more? I thought the relationship of husband and wife pure English pansy Theatre, cool, unreal, boring. And here I blame the casting and the direction. The daughter-father better, but not as good as it should have been, again just not tangible or immediate—cool. I didn't like the casting of Carol Goodner and I didn't get any real warmth out of the girl who played the daughter.

I like reserve in human relationships. But reserve means that there very definitely has to be something in reserve. Between Goodner and Scofield I would say there was nothing warmer than professionalism—and even that not too cordial. This kind of casting and relationship seems so prevalent to me in the English Theatre. And I suppose you think we, and I, schmaltz it up over here. I do think this has been a fault in me. But—well by the very placement you gave the scene between father and daughter at the end, I had to feel that you hoped for something more than happened on stage the night I saw it.

I thought the <u>common man</u> brilliant, in concept and brilliant in execution. It's the thing I liked best and I liked it enormously. I thought the scene between Henry VIII and More brilliant and original and true in concept. But spoiled by the casting and not helped by the direction. I thought the actor here especially inadequate and the direction fustian. I thought all the heavies underrated. Which made them occasionally just a little predictable and boring.

I thought the writing fine. I really did find it very much to my taste, hard-headed, unsentimental and—dangerous word, so loaded!—manly. So many of our contemporary authors are begging for pity or special consideration. With a man, you feel his pain, but you also feel he doesn't want a goddamn thing from you—even that you see it. You feel his difficulty is real and that he is deeply in danger and in trouble, but that you can't help him by your sympathy and that he doesn't really want it. It's something he has to settle with himself. He doesn't care if you feel sorry for him or not, or if you totally understand him—even. That's the feeling I had from you, and about you. Independence. And I thought the words were solid and firm and didn't pretend to be "more" than they were. There wasn't any phony poetry. I felt thought and I felt emotion, but you weren't sucking up to me.

More? That's enough. I liked the play. I enjoyed the evening. I'm awful tough. I don't like most evenings in the theatre. But I do love the Theatre.

I hope you will decide to go ahead with us on Aeschylus. But first you better get to know me (and VV.) I look forward very much to seeing you again. Give your wife my warm greetings.

[The Kazans flew to Europe in the new year to publicize *Splendor in the Grass*. By "prearranged code," Elia learned that Barbara Loden had given birth to their son Leo on January 2. "The singular aspect of the situation was that I took it in stride. I'd become so accustomed to a life in layers that nothing could penetrate my indifference to personal danger and disruption. I'd anesthetized myself" (*A Life,* pp. 5–6).

Robert Bolt was nominated by the Academy and shared the screenwriting credit with Michael Wilson, blacklisted and initially uncredited, for Sam Spiegel's production of *Lawrence of Arabia* (1962). Bolt's earlier play, *A Man for All Seasons,* was an immense hit in London before opening to "ecstatic" reviews in New York. The lack of "struggle" and "real choice" in the character of Sir Thomas More, played by Paul Scofield in his American debut, limited Kazan's appreciation of the play, but not that of reviewers, especially Howard Taubman of the *Times,* who praised Scofield's martyred character as one who "deepens rather than alters" (November 23, 1961).

The prologue of the Common Man establishes a "humanity" Kazan thought otherwise lacking in the Broadway production: "If a King or a Cardinal had done the prologue he'd have had the right materials. And an intellectual would have shown enough majestic meanings, colored propositions, and closely woven liturgical stuff to dress the House of Lords! But this! Is this a costume? Does this say anything? It barely covers one man's nakedness!" Thereafter the Common Man performs a variety of workmanlike chores, setting the stage for each scene and beheading Sir Thomas More.

Kazan worked on "scenes" from the *Oresteia* of Aeschylus at the Actors Studio in the early 1960s and later wrote and directed a presentational version of *Agamemnon.* Kazan advised Robert Bolt to know him "very very" well before undertaking a production (unrealized) of the *Oresteia* at Lincoln Center.] *TL, 3 pp., Wesleyan*

Part VI

Writer

1962–1969

[New York]
[February 7, 1962]

Dear Cliff:

Thank you for your letter. After I read it I wanted to hug you. I have never believed, ever, ever the people who said to me that you would not write for the Theatre, or independently again. Never. Ever. But one day soon, I'll really answer your letter. I'm full of things I want to say to you. Of course you shouldn't give us your plays unless it has real value for you, real concrete worth. I think it has. I'll tell you soon in detail. I cant now because I am rewriting my script. I think I am improving it a good deal. I know some of the dialogue is "wooden" or worse. But I believe in the essence of it, in the legend itself. I think its good, and strong and important. But I think I can improve the script, and I'm hard at work, really hard at work on it. I'm awfully committed to it. Well you can imagine! What it means to me! Remember how I was two years ago? Now listen: may I send you the rewrite when I've got it done and get your reaction, suggestions etc to <u>that</u>. You'll probably feel that it isn't too much different. I sweat and sweat and then produce a little mouse of a change. But it is tremendously exhilarating. Send the one you have back. I'll send you another one in three weeks. I have to be terribly careful that the Turkish government NO WAY get any idea of the content. I also feel that I've been unfair to them, and am busy making them more human, the individuals that is. Oddly enough I like the Turks. *** Thanks for the words about Splendor in the Grass. Very very much appreciated. Also—in re my father—that was the big problem of my life, so its appearing, so its turning out. I hope after this film to make a series on the same family, one after another. That's all I'll do in the movie line—and in Theatre only LCRep. I've got a lot to tell you, but mostly that I very much appreciated your letter, and whether you do or whether you dont, whether we work together or whether we never do or whatever, I do love you. You're a real human.

E.K.

[Elia's letter of December 28 charmed Clifford Odets more than any other. It was "open and friendly, brisk too as usual, but 'unguarded'. It also had in it a sort of sunny satisfaction that comes from good work finished and good work ahead." Odets still hoped to write for Lincoln Center but would delay commitment until the "next play or two" was ready. The latest draft of *America America* revealed "a more <u>inclusive</u> view of life, more classic, larger, less 'romantic' and violent." *Splendor in the Grass,* by contrast, was a "moving" summation of Kazan's work to date from which Odets inferred an intense concern with "son-parents relationships." His own father, he added, had almost driven him to suicide "three times" (January 15, 1962, Indiana).

Death from cancer on August 14, 1963, foreclosed the possibility of Clifford Odets writing again for the theater. He received Elia's final visit to California with a typical flourish: "'I may fool you, Gadg. I may not die.'" Kazan dismissed such bravado and warned that we live on "short leases" in a brief eulogy reserved for the company of *After the Fall*. "The tragedy of our time in the theatre is the tragedy of Clifford Odets." His legend of "forces dispersed instead of gathered," of "talents unused or used at a fraction of their worth," lingers along with his profound influence "on a generation of playwrights." Kazan urged the company to embrace the "surprising opportunity" offered by Lincoln Center at a time when his own interest was fading (*A Life*, pp. 663–65).

Lincoln Center staged an award-winning revival of *Awake and Sing!* in 2006 at the Belasco Theatre, where the play was performed in 1935. It was Odets's first appearance in the repertory after forty-odd years of production.] *TLS, 1 p., Indiana*

TO WARREN BEATTY

[New York]
February 7, 1962

Dear Warren:

I've just been with Abe Lastfogel, and he told me about his conversation with you. And we discussed the casting of STAVROS. I'm just where I was the last time we talked face to face. And although I very much appreciate your working so hard (and incidentally well) on a nose, I must tell you again that there is really only the very slightest chance for you for this film of mine. Abe was worried that you were giving up other offers on the chance that maybe someday I might change my mind. Well you know me well enough now to know that I don't change my mind, that I do have very definite notions, feelings, objectives in casting. And I just don't want to—even by indirection or silence—lead you on.

Let me put it plainly. I am going to find a latin boy, a Greek or an Italian, some sort of mediterranean for this role. It is not—at least for films—a matter of a nose, or a speech pattern. It is built in. It's a matter of temperament and the kind of behavior that a kid takes in with his mother's milk. Anything synthetic in this particular film would ruin it—perhaps in ways that would not be apparent, but in some deep instinctive way. My kid is a Greek—and I am setting out now to find him. I can't believe that he doesn't exist. I write this to you so plainly and explicitly because I don't want you to build up hopes that have no substantial basis. And also because I appreciate and am touched by your tremendous determination to play my part.

Actually you did a good job with the nose, and you showed excellent taste in the kind of nose you choose. But I'm a great believer—especially in films—of type casting, of inner type, of spiritual propinquity. And I just don't "feel" you as this boy. I want you to know that I am not only desirous of working with you again, but even eager to. I think you have real talent, real taste and great intelligence. I do believe that you need help and a really strong direction. I think when you haven't got a director who makes you mind, you are not at your best.

But, as I told Abe, I have an absolute certainty of your future in this field. I don't think the other two films you made after ours particularly helped you. But I think perhaps you have learned a lot from them. Despite the fact that I was not really comfortable with you on our last two meetings and despite a certain annoyance I felt and expressed at those meetings, I want you to know that I think a lot of you, that I am your friend, and that I am always available to you for help, advice and just simple conversation.

Affectionately,

[Cosmetic surgery aside, Kazan declined to cast Warren Beatty as Stavros in *America America*. Costarring roles in *The Roman Spring of Mrs. Stone* (1961) and *All Fall Down* (1962) followed Beatty's debut in *Splendor in the Grass* and taught him that "films are entirely a director's medium and directors you can depend upon are rare" (to EK, February 10, 1962, Wesleyan). He was "broke" at the time and apparently no more pleased with the roles than Bosley Crowther. "Hopelessly" miscast as a gigolo in *The Roman Spring*, Beatty reminded the *Times* reviewer "of a freshman trying to put on airs at a college prom." José Quintero's moody direction of the Tennessee Williams novella had not helped Beatty adjust to an implausible role. Crowther also faulted John Frankenheimer for tolerating, if not encouraging, Beatty's imitation of Marlon Brando and James Dean in *All Fall Down*.] TL, 2 pp., Wesleyan

TO LEE STRASBERG

[New York]
[March 28, 1962]

Dear Lee:
. . . Up to a certain point last year I kept you posted on everything I did at LCRep. That "point" was your final speech at the Studio. Paula sent me a recorded copy of that speech and I listened to it last August when I got back from Europe. There were also the two interviews. I couldn't possibly have any impression from these and from the speech except the one you clearly stated: that you had no further personal interest in LCRep whatever. You said this at the talk at the Studio. And both interviews were strongly so-colored.

You can therefore understand that it was the farthest thing from my mind that you would be willing to "take a class for us". And I couldn't in the least urge you to do so. Such an effort for you, except as part of a total involvement, would make no sense. And at the moment I was not able to offer you any such involvement that was worthy of you.

And I still cant. But I haven't stopped trying. Not at all. I once wrote Bob Whitehead, long ago, that I couldn't imagine the LCRep without you. This is not strictly true. I can. But more than any man in our Theatre I think you belong there, more than any man in our Theatre I personally value you. And I hope and fully intend to involve you. I still dont know how, when, in what way this will work out. But time and process is one thing I do understand. And I can tell you that this hope is always on my mind. I am constantly looking for the right way to enlist you in our effort, the right thing to offer you.

Let me, meantime, tell you a few things that we've done. I do hope that you will keep these plans to yourself alone. Though there is inevitably the liveliest gossip about our doings, what I'm about to tell you is not fully known.

One of the first things I wanted to do was to make a start on a training program. I wanted to make a start, I say, on a program of training actors that had a broad and compulsory base, that would involve actors in co-ordinated work on acting, movement, speech and voice. The first move I wanted to make in this direction (most difficult in this society now) was to start work with a group of comparative beginners. I hope they will all be under twenty-two or three. And I thought that Bobby, since he was once a dancer, since he knows music and singing, since he is well organized and since he is personally "hungry", would do an excellent job for us here. . . .

This co-ordinated three-ply work is only a start, since it will concern only a single group of youngsters, most of whom will be just starting to work. There will be other programs later, with other groups of actors, as our needs and ideas develop. At the same time there have developed certain changes at the Juilliard. Michel St Denis, as you must have heard, has withdrawn from his post there. He has accepted a position with the Royal Shakespeare Theatre where the people in charge are, professionally speaking, much more receptive to his methods and ideas. Upon this development—one which I long anticipated—the Juilliard came to Bob and to me for advice. I said then that I doubted that you would consider the job, but that to my way of thinking you were the wisest man in the Theatre, and that you would be my first choice.

The fact still is, however, that the Juilliard people have an unshakeable prejudice against the Actors' Studio. I then suggested Harold Clurman as an artistic head with an executive to do the administrative work under him. They are, presently, considering this proposal more sympathetically. But, I regret to note, that they are still considering, interviewing etc people like Ted Hoffman, Blau, Chapman, Clancy etc. That would make it impossible for Bob and I to make genuine use of the school. I have made it again clear that if the head of the school is unacceptable to me, I will again publicly turn my back on it. Meantime the opening of the Theatre has again been postponed. May '64 seems to be a realistic date at the moment. We are working hard to get new plays, talked to all our leading playwrights etc. etc. And find revivals.

Lee, it is inevitable, it seems to me that a large part of our efforts in this field will be—at first—misdirected, or even total failures. The job is a tough one anywhere. Our particular climate—Hollywood, T.V., the nature of prestige here, the lack of tradition and etc. etc.—makes it especially difficult. However I'd say I'm rather strongly inoculated vs. criticism, and can take an awful lot of it. We've already been criticized for productions we haven't even done. That's o.k. I think the only important thing is to start for the right goal. Perhaps the people we have picked are not the perfect ones. They are the ones we have picked for our first effort. The important thing is that we start in the right direction. And I believe we have. We will learn as we go along. I know we will learn.

But I'd much rather not be cut off from you. It has occurred to me several times that I should resign from the AS. There will inevitably be certain areas of conflict, opposite interests. Furthermore I cannot help feeling that your disappointment in what I have been able to do has communicated itself to some of the actors. They would wish it differently. I understand that. But nevertheless, I dont enjoy it—that somehow I have been placed in the position of the <u>heavy</u> there.

But, as I told you in the other letter, I will never resign from the Studio. I am open to suggestions for changes in the administration there. I welcome the involvement of the actors. I spoke with utter candor to them, and tried to be as helpful as I could. If you think you can administrate the AS better, at this moment, without me, I'm ready to take a LEAVE for a couple of years. But resign I will not do.

What I do not want is to be cut off from you. I do want the privilege of consulting and discussing with you the moves I make—as I once did. I think, in the larger sense, we both want the same thing. If now, our paths are separate, I persist in believing they are quite precisely parallel.

Of course I want and expect your comments to what I have set down in this letter. But more than that I'd like some expression—FOR MY EARS ALONE—of what you'd want, you would like in the present circumstances.

What do you feel? What production would you want to do, you personally? I want you to do a major production for us. Under what circumstances would you want to work on it. I think I can organize these circumstances. What general relationship do you see possible for yourself now, immediately. I will put fantastic efforts into making this come to be. What about the two productions annually in the small Theatre.

And please do help us with the formation of this young group for total training. I dont want more than 30 people in it now. I mean the work to be total, completely intensive, and I want the best youngsters in the country involved in it, not only the most talented, but particularly those youngsters whose talents can be realized not in TV, not in Hollywood, but specifically in a Theatre effort of this kind.

[Kazan was "thoroughly embarrassed" by his "craven" letter and marked it "NOT SENT" in a cover note dated March 29: "There is something very wrong with a relationship where you feel compelled to write a man this kind of letter. STOP APOLOGIZING. Strasberg is the last person to whom you apologize, constantly. That's enough. You owe him nothing. Consult Boris Aronson. You got free of him once. Now for the last time, get away from this marginal tiny foolish remnant of your father terror. If other people want to stay murked down in all that crap, that is their business. And his blaming you for his not doing more with the Actors' Studio is sick. Just plain sick. Now I dont feel any guilt about that. But I do seem to still want to rush to take care of him. ENOUGH!!!!" (Wesleyan).] *TL, 6 pp., Wesleyan*

TO WILLIAM INGE

[New York]
April 2, 1962

Dear Bill:

I have just gotten back from Europe and this is the first opportunity I have had to answer your letter of an evening with "Swifty" Lazar and the Axelrods. I am very fond of the Axelrods and I know George does very well there. I am fond of Swifty too. He's a cute little bug. But his intent toward you is so obvious I won't even go into it.

I talked to Bill Fitelson about your letter and he is sending me a memo which I will pass on to you when I get it. In the meantime, let me say a few things: First there's a tremendous difference between the part ownership of a project which permits a sale and what's known as straight income which does not. I have screen writer friends out there who are broke year after year after year whom Swifty Lazar represents. Swifty, as you know, is not broke.

The estimated gross today, which I just got from Warners on "Splendor", is over six million dollars. This is conservative in my opinion. There will be some items in the costs that we'll challenge but at this gross figure we are going to make, contrary to what the boys tell you, a profit, a substantial one.

Would you like me to feel around and see what you can get for your share? Now bear in mind again that there's a tremendous difference between straight income and the money you can keep. Agents live on their business expenses. Every meal Swifty eats is deductible. And judging from his glamourous wardrobe I imagine his suits can be considered an advertisement for himself. Ditto his cars, his chauffeur, his household, his butler, his perfume, his many trips and so on. Unfortunately, writers and directors are not always "protected" in this way. So don't lose any sleep over what you've been told. I'm sure Bill Fitelson's memo (which is attached) is more explicit.

Enclosed find a number of my notes on "Natural Affection". They will give you the rough ideas I have about it. I am anxious to talk to you about this at length for Lincoln Center. But that will wait until we met next. I think it would be a wonderful production, most startling and "new" on our stage. If you agree to the basic attack I have, I would be overjoyed to be working with you on it.

Love,

EK:es
enc.

[Bill Inge described a recent evening in Hollywood "centered almost entirely upon what fools" he and Kazan had been in dealing with "the movie companies out here." Irving "Swifty" Lazar doubted that anyone would "make another cent" from *Splendor in the Grass* and advised Inge to take his money "'up front'" rather than as a percentage. George Axelrod, a successful screenwriter, opined that Lazar would "have gotten" $250,000 for *Splendor*—currently in nomination for an Oscar. "New York lawyers" such as Bill Fitelson were "hopeless" in Hollywood, if not in collusion with studio executives. Inge found the evening "disquieting" and invited Kazan to share his "thoughts" (March 12, 1962, Wesleyan). He obliged by characterizing Lazar as "a cute little bug" intent on adding Inge to his list of famous clients. Kazan accurately predicted a "substantial" return based on estimated receipts (*Splendor* was released in October 1961) and reminded Inge, typically oblivious to business matters, of the "tremendous difference between straight income and the money you can keep." Neither his calming advice nor Fitelson's "more explicit" memo (unidentified) would end a brewing controversy.

An undercurrent of incest, nymphomania, and homosexuality released in a stark urban setting (Chicago) and culminating in murder removed *Natural Affection* (1963) from Inge's typical field of study.] *TL with enclosures, 2 pp., Wesleyan*

TO TENNESSEE WILLIAMS

[New York]
April 25, 1962

Dear Tenn:
Just got back from a rather dark part of the world, Turkey, and the city of Ankara where officials of their government are trying to rationalize a movie

that is soaked in hostility against them. Why do they want it? They want film production in Turkey, they want tourists, they want to come out of the dark they've been living in. And they are trying to take a more liberal stance in the modern world. In fact it's touching to see these men struggling to change a way of behaving they've not questioned for centuries and centuries. At first they simply said NO and YOU WRITE LIKE OUR ENEMY. Some eight hours of talk later we were drinking Raki (oozoo to you) and eating off an endless parade of appetizers and I was accepting compliments like the most traditional near-easterner on my growing command of Turkish. Now I'm back and I think, i.e. hope, that everything is finally all set for me to photograph part of my film there.

When I got back I found the column in the TIMES about your having given a play to the Actors' Studio Production Unit. I hope this isn't the play you were talking to Bob Whitehead and to me about. We really need that play, badly. And we really need your relationship, BADLY. It won't be much of a repertory-theatre-aspiring-to-be-a-National Theatre if we don't do your plays. And we just must do one the very first season, straight off, number one or number two, to go into rehearsal (we'll be rehearsing the first three at once) in the fall of 1963. And further, as I told you that night, we want to revive one of your plays, CAMINO, possibly, as soon as we can. We want to make Lincoln Center, among other things, a place where a Williams play can be seen every year, the "successes" and the most far-out things you can write, a place where these pieces live by being constantly played.

I think the Actors' Studio has earned your devotion and your gratitude. But while I have a sentimental loyalty to the actors there, what they are planning is not my idea of how a permanent theatre should be organized. I don't like the idea of a floating company of "stars" who drop in from Hollywood or from more lucrative activities, from time to time. Our people will be committed to us, and will work like the committed, constantly, without interruption. And I hope, that thru them and thru this commitment, we will create the kind of Theatre production that no one has seen before in this country. We will play the plays in our repertory, forever, as it were, disappearing only to come back again when a new audience has grown up for them. That is our hope and our goal, to do the really live new plays and to keep them alive, and at the same time, to keep alive our contemporary classics.

You are one of the handful of men who have written plays that deserve not to disappear into the libraries. It would be a stunning blow to us, to me, if we don't get some of your new plays and all of your old ones. That's what I'm asking of you. We'll do right by them.

Congratulations on the Critics' prize. "Iguana" deserved it. Simple justice.

Love

Gadg

[Kazan learned earlier in April that *America America* would need extensive revision if key scenes were to be filmed in Turkey. The Film Control Commission objected to the first part of the script—set in 1896—whose tone was inimical to modern Turkey as the oppressor of Greek and Armenian minorities. Kazan's return to Ankara produced a tentative agreement subject to further negotiation of key elements. Filming was set to begin in August with funding provided by Seven Arts, a rapidly expanding company with national and international interests in stage, screen, television, and music. Warner Bros. and Twentieth Century-Fox had declined to back the project.

A columnist reported in Kazan's absence that Tennessee Williams was "championing" the Actors Studio and had promised *The Milk Train Doesn't Stop Here Anymore* or "The Mutilated" to the new production unit. Independent producers staged the plays in 1963 and 1966 respectively without Studio, or Lincoln Center, involvement. "The Mutilated" was of current interest to Kazan.

Night of the Iguana (1961) won the New York Drama Critics' Circle award as best play of the season.] *TLS, 2 pp., Columbia*

TO MESERREF HEKIMOGLOU

[New York]
May 8, 1962

Mush dear:

I am sending you a copy of my long, final letter to the CENTRAL FILM CONTROL COMMISSION. I cannot go any further than I have in this letter on certain points. On other points I have agreed to some changes, but again I have gone as far as I can.

Nothing I say in the letter to the Commission about the pressure of time on me is overstated. It is precise. I do have locations in Greece ready. I am literally being besieged by the Yugoslavs. They have offered me financial and practical inducements. They want the film badly. And they have no censor committees. No CENTRAL FILM CONTROL COMMISSIONS.

Like any artist I do not like censors. I'm not speaking personally. I had a fine time one afternoon with a couple of the men from the Commission. They were very warm and very human over the raki. But, Mush, can a committee make a film? Can a committee paint a picture, chisel a piece of sculpture? The greatest sculptor of our day, Vigeland, offended his own country. Was Shakespeare a committee? Did someone tell Beethoven what theme to use? Or not to use a chorus at the end of the Ninth Symphony? Russia has killed its art this way. Poor Pasternak!

Your committee has taken to making suggestions to me as to how scenes should go. They are not good playwrights. I felt in our meeting in Evliyaoglou's office that Kamuran found these men a burden too. Now they want me to send a new script. And wait again for another discussion. I really can't wait again. My impression is that these men are decent and honorable, but a couple of them seem to me to be men of rather narrow views. Beware the bureaucrat in art! No wonder I kept thinking all through our meeting, no wonder the Turks have not yet produced a single film worthy of world attention! How could they with five men sitting on top of the artist's head? How can an artist create anything with five men saying all the time: Be careful! Don't do this. You can't do that! Look out you'll offend this person, or that group!! Look out, look out, look out!!

Mush, you know as well as I do that the important thing in our field is the single individual artist, his feeling, his conscience, his emotion.

By now, it's beginning to seem as if my film was about politics. It is not! It has very, very little about politics in it. I'm not interested in politics.

And suppose there is some slight thing in it that offends some Turks? So what? We do films here every day that offend Americans. So do the English, the French, the Greeks, the Indians, the Japanese. The Russians don't! Or are they just beginning to in what has been heralded as the beginning of freedom there? VIVA ZAPATA offended some Mexicans who were very vociferous. Now it's acknowledged as an international classic. ON THE WATERFRONT, an Academy Award Film, offended some sections of American opinion. "Gentleman's Agreement" offended some of the wealthy people in Hollywood but it too won an Academy Award.

Is Turkey so small, so weak that a motion picture with a few critical views of the Turkey of 1896 can hurt it??!! My GOD, Mush!! 1896!! Sixty-six years ago!

I'm really in despair. Everyone here is advising me not to go to Turkey. It's much cheaper and much more practical to make the whole film in Greece—or in Yugoslavia. But I want to come to Turkey—for three weeks, for four weeks. I must want it badly to go through all this. But I am a stubborn man. I don't even know why I want it so badly. I simply do.

But now it's the end of the road. I've got to decide next week. If you can help me, I'd be terribly appreciative. If you can't, I'll still be terribly appreciative of all your friendship and hospitality. But whatever happens, what I need more than anything else at this moment is final definite encouragement to go ahead with a completely artistic creation.

My affectionate regards to you and to Kuvet.

EK:es

[Kazan warned the Turkish Film Control Commission in a "long, final letter" that he must proceed as though a firm, workable agreement "was not going to happen." He rejected a proposal by the Historical Institute that old and new Turkey, autocratic and progressive, be distinguished in a formal prologue. Such a "political tract" would violate the "personal and individual story" Kazan hoped to tell in *America America*. Substantially changing the opening "ice incident, in which an army officer harasses Stavros and Vartan, an Armenian friend, was also out of bounds, although Kazan claimed that the officer was finally treated in a positive light. More offensive was the burning of an Armenian church with the tacit approval of the central government. Kazan refused to substitute a house for the church but offered to provide "sufficient motivation" for the assault by heightening the threat of Armenian terrorists. Discussion of other contested points ended with a hopeful flourish: "What better way is there to emphasize progressive and democratic aspirations and institutions than to not only permit but encourage the artist to work freely" (May 8, 1962, Wesleyan).

Yusuf Mardin, deputy director of Press, Broadcasting, and Tourism, assured Kazan on May 23 that an "official permit to shoot" would be issued on delivery of the original script and a formal list of agreed-upon changes. "Mush" Hekimoglou was probably a functionary in the same department.] *TL, 3 pp., Wesleyan*

TO LEE STRASBERG

[New York]
May 8, 1962

Dear Lee:

I had a conversation Thursday with Cheryl, and discussed with her what I'm writing you below. She was in agreement.

I have had to postpone the start of my film again—this time for another two months. And I still face unbelievably complicated difficulties. I hope I won't have to put it off still another time. But that could happen. If it does, I'll be running into rains and cold weather.

The earliest I can start now is the fifth of August. Suppose I do. I would be back in this country the first of December—hopefully. I would then have at least four months of intensive editing, since I am not going to do any of that overseas. And after the first rough cut exists, there come further fine editing and scoring, dubbing, much "running", all kinds of readjustments and tampering, then advertising meetings, sales meetings and God knows what all. That's leaving out censorship problems, which I hope won't be as tough on this one as they have been on my other recent films.

At the same time, thru all of this, I'll be preparing the scripts and the company for the rehearsals of the Repertory Theatre at Lincoln Center. The date for these rehearsals is now September or October of 1963. And I am absolutely committed to them. In fact, I have been minimizing this commitment and I will not continue to do so.

It seems clear to me that I cannot direct a play for the Studio Production

Unit. I thought I might when Lincoln Center was first postponed. But that was before this last series of problems on my film came down on me. I feel now that I'm gasping for time. And I don't want to think of anything except doing my film as well as I can. It means more to me than anything I've done in a long time. So the Production Committee will have to be told that I am definitely "out" as far as their plans go.

Furthermore I have now had to face something else. Up until a few months ago I could function in my place at the Studio and still work at Lincoln Center. While the Studio was a Studio and nothing else it was quite possible. But now there's a question: Is it possible to sit on the Production Committee of the Studio when I am the co-producer of the Lincoln Center Repertory?

Lately I have found I was wearing two hats. For example I had to write Tennessee Williams last week and say to him that I trusted that the play he was giving the Production Committee was not the play he had talked to Bob Whitehead and myself about. And I further felt it necessary to say that the one aspect of the plan of the Production Committee with which I was not in sympathy was the idea of the floating company. I said that Lincoln Center would have a company that was committed and "permanent".

I also had to say to Bill Inge that I wanted his play "Natural Affection". I had done considerable work on this play and felt a start when he told me that he had said to the Production Committee they could have it. I had to take a stand with him and urged him to follow my suggestions for rewriting, etc. As it happens I don't think he will follow my suggestions. He doesn't agree with them. But as I urged them on him I felt somehow uncomfortable.

In other words, I have been doing things that any producer would do. But, in the present circumstance, they somehow made me feel—well uncomfortable is the only word that I can think of.

Then something else happened. Mendy Wager came to my house the other night and said that the Production Committee wanted enough power from the directors of the Studio so that they could be confident that if they started something it would not then—at some point—be "blocked". I discussed with him what I have written to you above and said I did not know what turn to take. When Mendy asked me to give up some power to the Committee I felt, peculiarly, that I no longer actually had that power to give up. I was elsewhere doing something else. And the Studio had taken a short but decisive step in another direction.

I've thought over all these circumstances and problems. And I'd like to make the following strong recommendation to you and to Cheryl and to the Production Committee. I recommend that the Production Committee should be organized and legally incorporated separately.

They should be called something like: THE COMPANY OF THE ACTORS' STUDIO. Thus the set-up of the Actors' Studio itself would not be in any way disrupted. I could continue as I have been at the Studio. I would not be part, in any way, of the new organization called THE COMPANY OF THE ACTORS' STUDIO or whatever.

For one thing I am not eager to give anyone power at the Actors' Studio except ourselves. I think it is most important that your work carry on there as it has been, and the same with the work of the Directors' Unit and the Playwright Unit. These three activities are of crucial importance to the Theatre as a whole and I don't want them disturbed.

On the other hand, I am in sympathy with the desires and aspirations of the actors at the Studio to "do something". I'm sorry that what I said three or four weeks ago at your house has not stood up. I spoke impulsively and emotionally because I was and am emotionally enlisted by what the actors want to do. I hope they will do some fine productions. But their program is simply not what I now want to do. If I had the choice to make again, I would again select to try to create a completely committed company of actors playing repertory. I prefer this to the floating company idea. And to the prospect of sitting on any committee whatsoever. I have never been one for committees.

I have what I think is the solution that will take care of all aspects of this problem. The actors will have what they are asking for. They can create a new organization which will be suited to the task of organizing and carrying through productions. I think they should designate a part of the profits to the Actors' Studio, Inc.

At the same time the Actors' Studio itself, your work with the actors, your work with the directors, and the program with the playwrights will still continue. I believe that the Studio as it is now organized is correctly organized for this work. Of course we must give careful consideration to all the Committee's suggestions in relation to the Studio work. And, in this way, I could continue in my function at the Studio. But since I will be functioning in what is inevitably a competing organization, I will have to disassociate myself both privately and in some way publicly from the new production organization. Advice I can give but I think if I don't clear up my actual place, activity and responsibility there will be a succession of what the English call "awkward" situations.

My love always, Gadg

[A newly formed Members Committee met a severe financial crisis by recommending that a production unit be established to increase revenue and improve the image of the Actors Studio. The directors were "entirely enthusiastic," as reported in the press, although Kazan was not "eager" to share power and opposed the idea of a "floating" company with a limited commitment of five months by a succession of actors. Lee Strasberg described the overall plan as modified repertory in which selected plays would reappear from time to time. The request of Michael Wager, a member of the Production Board, led Kazan to reflect on his overlapping roles at the Studio and Lincoln Center and recommend separate legal

status for the new theatrical unit. In a final backward glance, Strasberg rebuked Lincoln Center for excluding the Actors Studio, "'the most significant internationally recognized American contribution to the theatre'" (*NYT,* May 28, 1962).]
TLS, 3 pp., Houston

TO CHERYL CRAWFORD

[New York]
May 25, 1962

Cheryl dear (and Lee dear too):
Life is tough enough without making it tougher. This morning I got up and went over your letter, Cheryl, and I could only think: Well, God bless them all, and why do any of us do anything except make things easier for each other?" Last week-end I did my best thinking on this whole issue and I put down my conclusions in a letter to you, Lee (cc to CAC) as precisely and as clearly as I could. So now you two disagree. And want to go ahead as you see fit and right. I certainly don't want to do the least thing to impede or delay. Or sit here and look disapproving. Not my role in life, is it? Or to be off in Turkey this summer—the absent dissident! The hell with that! I'll simply resign from the Board of Directors which is clean and quick, always the best way, and give you all my blessing and most fervent warm wishes. And as a member of the body of Actors' Studio, which I always will be, I am at your service. So I am sending a short announcement to the hungry press as follows:

> The time is now coming for active production at the Lincoln Center Repertory Theatre of which I am co-producer. At the same time the Actors' Studio, on whose Board of Directors I sit, has embarked upon its own program of production. While I am in general sympathy with this program, I must now recognize that it overlaps and even competes with some of the activity for which I'll be responsible at the LCRep. It seems right to me that I now resign from the Board of Directors of the Actors' Studio in order to be able to give my undivided effort to my job at the LCRep. That resignation I have effected today and I am now no longer a Director of the Actors' Studio.

Now! Isn't the air clearer? I suppose it's as important as it is difficult to recognize and accept change. And especially so and most painfully so when it concerns something of which I am as proud as I am of the Studio and as proud as I am of my relationship with the two of you.

Ever, Gadg

[The production unit would lose the Studio's tax-exempt status if Kazan's recommendation of separate legal status were adopted. Cheryl Crawford suggested a compromise, whereby Kazan would remain on the board of directors while agreeing to add two actors to its membership and establish the new unit within the legal framework of the Studio. Apparently he accepted the conditions but resigned from the board on May 26, as did Bill Fitelson. Kazan posted the following note:

> To All: I resigned as a director—only. That was necessary. But I'm still with
> you. And very much for any and all efforts you make. I'm sure that whatever
> you do will bring credit to our years of work and to Lee's teaching.
>
> The First Member

Cheryl Crawford was named executive producer of the newly minted Actors Studio Theatre and Lee Strasberg the artistic director. Gerry Page and Rip Torn were added to the board. Much later Kazan explained his resignation in organizational terms: "To make a theatre of the Studio would require a fundamental change in its purpose, its organization, and its leadership. Since I didn't believe that Lee would be a capable leader for a production theatre, I decided that a complete break would be best for both sides" (*A Life,* p. 631). A majority of the Studio membership preferred to think Kazan disloyal and did not regret his departure.]
TLS, 2 pp., BRTC

•

TO ALFRED DE LIAGRE

[New York]
July 6, 1962

Dear Delly:

We know each other too well so I shall kid you not. I couldn't read "Hamlet" if it came in now and there's no use of my holding your script. What can I do but tell you the facts. I am swamped. I am about to leave for Greece and Turkey and I truly am overwhelmed with work. Furthermore, my mind, such as it is, is all this way and that. The production of the film is three months of the kind of thing we went through those three critical days in Washington on J.B. Everyday is like that. Whether I am looking forward to it or not doesn't matter that's the way it's going to be and it has started already. You understand?

Anyway Bob Whitehead will be here all summer and he will be reading stuff. But it's probably more correct if I send the script back to you and have you send it to him. About the lunch—I'd love to have lunch but let's make it in November when I'll be back.

Have a good summer. Don't play too much tennis. You're a little old and a little soft to be knocking yourself out on the courts. Try to keep yourself relaxed. You're not a young man anymore, Delly, and it would be better if you sat more, drank less, and cultivated the powers of conversation. The trouble with handsome men like yourself is they take for granted that their effect on women is immediate and unqualifiedly successful. This cannot continue to be the case, Delly. I would start learning a few stories and jokes if I were you. What you lack in physical vigor you will have to make up some resources of entertainment that you should have. I know some particularly effective jokes that I have used myself. And something else—a very effective thing in dealing with young ladies is giving them a list of books that you think will broaden their outlook. Sometimes the best way to a girl's heart is through what passes for her mind. This will take some effort on your part, Delly, but prepare yourself it's worth it.

I seem to have wandered off the point which is THE CARMELITES. I can't read it now but don't give up on me. I will be reading plays again—that's if I come out of the next few months with any of my sanity left. Do you think that's possible?

Affectionately, Elia Kazan

["Dialogues of the Carmelites," the flamescript in question, is based on the execution of the Carmelite nuns of Compiègne during the French Revolution. A partial screenplay written by Georges Bernanos in the late 1940s and staged by his heirs in 1952 gained the interest of Alfred de Liagre, but the project did not reach Broadway under his management. The former producer of *J.B.* lived an additional twenty-five years after receiving Kazan's advice.] *TLSx, 1 p., BRTC*

TO MOLLY DAY THACHER

SH: Athena Enterprises Corp.
1545 Broadway, New York 36, N.Y.
PM: Athens, August 6, 1962

The connection to the states wasn't too bad. And I'll try again this coming week-end. My address is hard to believe, the spelling of it I mean. Loykiannoy 24. No LOYKIANOY 24. It still doesn't look quite right. But that is it. My phone is 716432. I know that's spelled correctly. I'm o.k. But everyone does have the impression that they "escaped" from Turkey. And they are all terribly glad to be out of there. It was just a little dangerous. The script girl had in her room the correct script, and also another copy of the correct script that one of the actors had brought. Meantime on the set was a plainclothesman from Istanbul police protecting, as it were, the representative of the Government from Ankara. This man had a copy of the approved script, and every time I departed from it the least bit he'd come up with his copy, in Turkish, and show me what the script said. This wasn't bad, because I didn't change a word of

America America: Scouting in the Turkish hills and, with Stathis Giallelis
on his left, filming on an Istanbul street before the escape to Athens

the dialogue. But anything you write in this business is an approximation, and you get many many more shots than you ever say. Well on all these he would come jumping up at me. Then he'd tell me that he was going to get in bad trouble if I diverged from the script the least bit and etc., that they had given him orders in Ankara to see to it that I didn't get off the absolutely fixed details of what we had agreed to. The fact was that I had told these people verbally repeatedly and had told them in writing twice that I would have to feel free on the set etc., that the script in a film is an approx. Finally I called up the minister and told him to get the censor guy off my back. Characteristically the minister said that he had not told the man to harass me. But there he was the next day. The worst of it all was the costumes. They really wanted everything spotless, "old, maybe, sometimes, maybe, but always clean". This, with all the fantastic filth around us, and the actual hamals in their cruddy clothes! For the first time I saw Johnny Johnston very discouraged and ready to quit. She told Charlie Maguire she wished she were home. So you can see it was tough. The last day a member of the secret police was there, a mean grim little man who raised strong objections against a scene I was doing, bawling out the guy from the censor. I feel sorry for them. Every decent man I talked to ended up a conversation by asking me if I could help him get out of there. Meantime the newspapers (all except the best one, the equivalent of the N.Y. Times) were attacking us. One particular paper was quite vicious. A columnist sort of like Pegler. Every morning things would start with some one or other running up with a paper, then another guy with another paper. Some fun, brother horse.

Love to you

Hello Katie! Where's my letter?!

[The "approved script" represented a "gentleman's agreement" signed by Kazan in July to revise the ice field sequence in favor of the army officer and eliminate the church burning. Yusuf Mardin advised his friend to "'agree to anything then do whatever you want,'" adding that officials were merely seeking a "'disclaimer of responsibility'" and had "'no way of checking'" once filming of *America America* began (diary, n.d., Wesleyan). Surveillance proved more thorough than expected, as Kazan would learn, but a much greater threat arose in late July when Seven Arts withdrew from the project. Warner Bros. stepped in with a budget of $1.5 million.

The cast and company "'escaped'" from Istanbul after five days of closely watched filming. Street scenes and the Blue Mosque were photographed before Kazan filmed the hamal montages on the Golden Horn, the inner harbor of Istanbul, where Stavros and his friend Garabet work as human pack animals. Charlie Maguire, Kazan's ingenious associate producer, advised the move to Athens when censorship became intolerable, if not "a little dangerous," and arranged for the exposed film to be smuggled out of Turkey. A hostile reporter reminded Kazan of Westbrook Pegler, a syndicated American columnist who espoused right-wing causes with uncommon vigor. From Athens Elia reassured his mother that "the Turkish people were extremely generous" and the hamals "especially friendly and cooperative."] *TL, 1 p., Wesleyan*

TO MOLLY DAY THACHER

SH: Athena Enterprises Corp.
1545 Broadway, New York 36, N.Y.
PM: Athens, October 22, 1962

Geezuz (I just got yur letter) I'm not that bad. I'm just normally going thru a tough job in pretty fair style. Everything is not sunny. And it is the toughest picture I've done, and I haven't as good help as I've had. But I chose the ring and the opponent, and the distance, so—No complaints. Only I wish I were a better artist. That's about all I wish. And Stathis was something more of an actor. And that it wasn't so long. The script is too long. But its my first and I'll do better next time. And it wont be so long now. I really feel pretty. Of course I despair and get blue. But creating a film is an intense process, and I've been very discouraged. Other days less so. Occasionally some optimism. I dont know. But its not a "sensible" procedure. And, as I explained to you, I'm not the innocent, confident, cocky boy of 35 that I was during Gentleman's Agreement and Boomerang. I know too much to be simply and purely happy about anything. And I always have the feeling that I'm somehow falling a little short of what I should be doing. I only had one real good moment. That isn't much. I should be doing better. But maybe I will from here on in. Next time I'll do a better script. And maybe have better actors. But I chose Stathis. And I knew it would be tough. And it is. So what. I cant sing with joy about it to you—And I'm not grim, just embattled, and determined to do better. Maybe I will in the next weeks. But pleasure, pure pleasure? Well—a few minutes here and there—maybe—anyway dont worry, I'm not dying, and I'm o.k., and I do take care of myself. Today, for instance. I went to Gk Orthodox Mass (Sunday) at 8:30 with Johnny Johnston. At 9:30 Charley and I went out looking for our last locations. At one thirty I took Charley and his asst, Burt, to dinner. At 3 I came home and slept for 45 minutes. At four rehearsal of the family stuff. At seven they went home. I had some tea and cookies. At eight I turned the ball game on, and am listening to it as I type this letter. Nine thirty BED. At five thirty up. Since I'm going to church I have to wear a suit, the suit, for the first time in this film. I go show them the set up at six, before they move in. And etc. *** Anyway all you lovely people sounded wonderful on the phone from Abe's place. Wonderful family. My God! And I'm so glad you're going to sleep at Aunt Clara's apartment. I dont like you sleeping in that big house alone. What happened to Sobie by the by?

I'm going to sleep now. I'll try to write manana. Anyway, dont worry. They always come to an end, and this one wont be long. Nov 10th. Charley says, and Charley is realistic about me and my speed. So—Goodnight, baby and Love. You sound wonderful. Take it easy. Dont think you're all all all all o.k.

Filming a shipboard scene on the Aegean

Remember how your knees felt when you first got out of bed // And if its not done today, it will be done tomorrow.

Love. You sound wonderful.

[Added to problems of cast and crew was an illustration in the *New York Times* of a church engulfed in flames and captioned with reference to Turkish "cruelty" (*NYT,* October 7, 1962). Kazan replied to an official protest from Ankara that he had promised only to consider sparing the church and decided to follow his original intention. Publication of *America America* in December led the embarrassed director of press to inform the Production Code Administration that additional material "'offending the Turkish Nation'" presumably remained in the screenplay, along with key scenes Kazan had specifically agreed to revise or eliminate (December 5, 1962, Herrick).

Stathis Giallelis answered a casting call in 1961 but lacked English or acting experience and initially declined to read for Kazan. Nonetheless, he had caught the director's eye "physically" and in later meetings would demonstrate an "unswerving" desire to play the role of Stavros. In 1962 Giallelis made his own impossible trip to New York without the guarantee of a part, took odd jobs, studied English, and was cast by the "gambler" in Kazan to play the lead in *America America (NYHT,* December 8, 1963).

Molly Kazan's drive to furnish the new "'perfect and forever'" apartment overlooking Central Park was not to be slowed by a recent hospitalization (phlebitis): "She'll inevitably try to do it all too fast because she cant stand disorder. She has no gift for chaos. She likes things Right. And she is constantly going against the current of humanity and this old world to get things the 'way they should be'" (EK to Judy Kazan Morris, October 22, 1962, JKMP).] *TL, 1 p., Wesleyan*

Stathis Giallelis (Stavros), with his arm around
Gregory Rozakis, on shipboard

TO MOLLY DAY THACHER

SH: Athena Enterprises Corp.
1545 Broadway, New York 36, N.Y.
PM: Athens, November 15, 1962

Now this really is the last letter you'll get from me. This is Thursday. I now have another week. I'll not be home for Thanksgiving, that means, but probably the day after. I'm sorry about the further extended delays, but its not anyone particular person's fault. Its mostly, I'm afraid, me. I do blame the crew and the cameraman, both of whom are second rate or worse. And I've gotten to scorn the cameraman and the American and Greek contingents of the crew. They are understandably exhausted and just plain sick of this picture. And of each other, and I imagine, me. They heartily dislike Charlie and he really hates them (the Americans, he calls them the "ugly Americans" and the cameraman). He has reason. And they have none. Charlie is fair with them and they are spoiled. But whatever the reasons, I have been further delayed, and I'm sorry. I really expected to be home the day before Thanksgiving. The main reason for the delay is my own self. The script, as I have explained, is deceptive. Its much much longer than it seems. And much longer to shoot, with constant locale moves which are the things that take the time. Most of the time in lighting is taken up with the so-called establishing shot, the introduction of the new locale. This is the traditional "longshot". And when I have the location of the action changing sometimes two or three times on each page, there's the main reason. Furthermore I know more of the possibilities of film now and therefore take longer. And finally I'm always covering for Stathis' inadequacies. Remember the days when I had real good actors. Today I'm hitting the bottom of the barrel. I have a scene of half a page with Gregory Rozakis who is Gregory Rozakis and a man whom I never saw before yesterday, a man who never acted before in his life playing the third class doctor. Furthermore this stranger was brought in the morning of shooting his first scene—a desperate and hazardous replacement for a Greek actor who had defected without explanation or excuse (the Gks have faulty senses of honor). Furthermore, I say, this stranger cannot speak English at all. He has no English. And he has two rather long paragraphs to say. So that's the characteristic kind of thing that goes on. I dont know what I'll do. Also the man is seventy and will be lucky, really, if he lives thru the day. So you see a little time will be required, and so I'll fall further behind little by little. I've decided to stop worrying about it. I've just decided that I'm going to live it out and not tear myself apart over it. And so its a matter of a few more days. For a while I was paying too much of a price in a useless restless fretting. But the hell with it. I'll be home when I get home. And dont wait for me and know that you'll see me. We almost packed the whole thing in night before last and turned to finishing it in the states. But gave the idea up as bad one, or an impossible one with so many actors to bring over etc. Also we have the big Ellis Island scene still to do with four hundred extras. Four hundred extras in USA cost minimum $15000 per day. Here two thousand dollars. So you see. I'm sorry, baby, but I'm delayed. I'll have turkey a couple of days later. I do want Turkey though. I really do. I never want to see Olive Oil again, not for a long time. Or any other kind of oil. Or butter. Or greasy meat, or grease. I'd just like plain white meat of Turkey, chestnut stuffing, cranberry sauce and white dry wine. You think you can help me out with that?

I gather from the silence that the book got bad notices. Silences are so dramatic. I cant help thinking that if the reaction in the press had been good there would have been cables etc. I suppose silence is as good a way to deal with the situation as any other. It is explicit.

Love. I'll sure be glad to get home. You can count on that. And wherever you eat Thanksgiving dinner, pass my regards around with the stuff and stuff.

[Among the many locations were shipboard scenes filmed on the Aegean in November. High seas added authentic peril to the immigration story, but little else seemed to cohere as a disgruntled crew began the fourth month of *America America*. Kazan's relations with Pete Wexler, director of photography, were tense and would lead to a candid exchange of letters. Gregory Rozakis, one of the unknowns, played a consumptive wanderer who meets Stavros on the road to Ankara, reappears coincidentally in Constantinople, and sacrifices himself aboard ship so that Stavros can enter America.

"Notices" for the publication of *America America* (1962) surpassed Kazan's expectation. The brief cinematic units and staccato dialogue formed an "electric shorthand" well suited to the brutal lessons of the road. The violence that offended early critics of the screenplay was moderated for reviewers by the aura of myth and idealism surrounding Stavros as he pursues the elusive American dream. Kazan disliked the "'anxious'" cover of Stein and Day's initial publication, but it was necessary, the publisher held, to counteract the author's nonliterary reputation as "a successful, talented, rich middle-aged beatnik" (Stein to EK, June 20, 1962, Wesleyan). Dark brooding eyes overlook a mass of blurbs by James Baldwin, Archibald MacLeish, John Steinbeck, Harold Clurman, and Robert F. Kennedy. Sale of subsidiary rights to the Reader's Digest Condensed Book Club produced a solid return before *America America* reached the bookstores.] *TL*, 2 pp., *Wesleyan*

TO HASKELL "PETE" WEXLER

[New York]
November 27, 1962

Dear Pete:

Our last conversation, the one that took place outside of the Mosque set on our final morning, floored me. You said to me: "I really didn't like the script at all." You were referring to the first time you read it, and what startled me was the absolutely cool way you described your initial reaction. Apparently you don't feel that it's odd for a cameraman to accept an assignment to photograph a script he doesn't like. I think it unethical. It's done everyday, but I think it unethical. It's beyond my understanding that one sensitive man would do that to another. There are few professional relationships as intimate as that between cameraman and director. I had to walk on my set for four months and face a cameraman who didn't like the script he was photographing and who was artistically scornful of my work in general.

Who the hell needs it? If I continued with you now under these circumstances it would be the plainest masochism. I don't go for that. I'm going to have someone else finish the job for me.

You know I think you're a good cameraman. But under these circumstances I simply can't take you. I resent you and I don't want to see you.

I wish you'd make notations in the margin of the enclosed list of shots-still-to-be-done relative to lighting, filters, etc. This is for the man who will do the rest of the work. I'm anxious that what he does fits in with what you've done.

Sincerely,

[Without referring to *America America*, Pete Wexler admitted in a later interview that not every assignment has been satisfying and claimed that "'most scripts are talk scripts, with fake camera directions. The cameraman should be able to tell the director how to make a script more visual'" (*NYT*, September 18, 1966). Wexler was thirty-six and possessed of modest credits when he reportedly told Kazan in

Istanbul that he had no "'eye.'" Kazan attributed the excess of candor to Wexler's youthful arrogance and resentment of his anticommunist testimony. Their correspondence ended on a conciliatory note, when Kazan reviewed the "dailies" and informed Wexler that with "very, very few exceptions" his work was "excellent and exactly what [he] wanted" (March 13, 1963, Wesleyan).

Wexler received Academy Awards for *Who's Afraid of Virginia Woolf?* (1966) and *Bound for Glory* (1976). The American Society of Cinematographers recognized his achievement in 1993 with a lifetime award.] *TL with enclosure, 1 p., Wesleyan*

TO ROBERT F. KENNEDY

[New York]
December 17, 1962

Dear Bob Kennedy:
I feel very unhappy about what happened between Budd and me. But he got more insulting than I will stomach and I had to ask him to leave my house.

At no time did I give Budd a basis to believe that we could consider "The Enemy Within" for our opening production. We have been committed to Arthur Miller on this for nine months.

I wasn't present at their conversations, but I gather that my partner, Bob Whitehead, did say certain things out of his enthusiasm that Budd interpreted to mean that Whitehead wanted to open our program with "The Enemy Within". Whitehead regrets this and he expressed this regret the night that he and I met with Budd. But, whatever was said, it was not what Budd called it: "part of a con act". At the very worst it was careless talk between new friends.

My own hope was to transfer to the stage a piece of work written for the screen. Clearly such a transfer is not a simple job. I knew there was always a chance that I might work many hours on such a project and in the end come to the conclusion that it could not be done. Too much of what is essential for delivering the story and documenting the theme might prove to be lost without the scope and graphic power of film. But I was ready to get down to work and see what the problems were. And I have a hunch I could have solved them. I certainly wanted to. But how could a date be set for a project that finally might not prove to be workable. Even Budd admitted, when I first told him my notion, that he didn't see how it could possibly be put on the stage. I have been around too long to confuse hope and fact, or make plans based on wishful thinking. In my line a project is either sound or it isn't. It will either work or it won't. I don't con other people and I don't con myself.

I have admired you. I have been greatly enlisted by your public acts. I believe strongly in the theme of your book. I regret that what has happened between Budd and myself cuts me off from the chance of knowing you better.

Cordially,

[At issue was Budd Schulberg's assumption that *The Enemy Within* (1960) was under serious discussion as the opening production of the Repertory Theatre. Disabused of the notion, presumably a result of "careless talk," Schulberg accused Kazan of conning the author, Attorney General Robert F. Kennedy. The book recounted his years as chief counsel (1957–59) to a U.S. Senate subcommittee investigating "improper activities" in labor-management relations. Sharp exchanges with Jimmy Hoffa, president of the Teamsters, gave unexpected drama to the televised hearings and established Kennedy as a tenacious prosecutor of organized crime. His warning that "a conspiracy of evil" threatens democratic institutions "enlisted" Kazan, who justified his congressional testimony in similar terms. "Bobby was the only politician I've ever liked," Kazan wrote in *A Life*. Later correspondence reveals that Budd Schulberg's eviction was temporary.] *TL, 2 pp., Wesleyan*

TO H. WILLIAM FITELSON

[New York]
December 19, 1962

Dear Bill:

Bob Whitehead and I met with Wharton and Bob Montgomery last night. We all felt that it was time to pin the Repertory Theatre board down to facts and program. Bob Whitehead and I can go no further in the way of signing playwrights, actors, and doing all the other many jobs we have to do until our own situation is clear and we know what our powers and privileges and what our status is. Whitehead feels that the first step towards this is a clarification of our employment arrangement. I strongly made the point that in this discussion about our arrangements certain guarantees of power, and an absolute clarification of what our position is, is just as important and really much more important than remuneration. We discussed the whole matter. And I made the following points to them:

1) That the amount of money that we were asking for was based on the theatre having a $5.00 top for subscribers. In other words, I felt that Whitehead and I were asking for a very moderate amount indeed in the way of compensation. And we were asking for a moderate amount only because we thought the whole scale of our budget, in all respects, should take its cue and measure from our fees.

2) I further made the point that if the top for subscribers got to be more

than $5.00—by some action not our own—the whole matter of what we were paid and so on would have to be reopened.

Bill, I think this is most important to me. I don't want a theatre beyond the reaches of the lower middle class person. I want an audience very much like the one at City Center. And to put it conversely I don't want an audience that depends on the expense account. We will have subscriptions at $5.00, $4.00 and $3.00. This is more than a token for me. It's a warrant of our intentions as far as the audience goes. If this is changed "from above" and we can't do anything about it, I will consider my employment contract with Lincoln Center void.

It is very important, however, that we sign on a clear understanding that there will be no interference from above. All artistic rights must be ours absolutely. What actors we sign; how much the actors get; how long their employment period; how we shift them about; what plays we do; how long we run them. I never want to go to any board and say the word please. We must have the unquestioned power to run the Repertory artistically, precisely as we wish.

I made the further point in discussing compensation that no actor, no director, no executive get more than I get.

I gave them your formula—$500 a week, fifty-two weeks a year, to start immediately—whether I work or not; whether I am there or not; no matter what else I am doing. That there be added to this the sum of $7,500 for expenses. And that I further get 2% of the royalties on each and every play I do. Bob brought up his formula—about 1% producer's royalty. He said you had objections to this. And they all want to discuss these objections with you.

We discussed a ceiling for myself of $60,000 a year and a ceiling for Bob of $50,000 a year. I would rather have Bob get $50,000 a year than $45,000. It's clearly understood that I would do no other work in the theatre. It's also clearly understood that I can do anything in films I want. I want no restraints on this whatever.

Incidentally, Wharton and Bob Montgomery have questioned the $7,500 expense item from a legal point of view and they will discuss. I know you will listen to their qualms about this.

I'll leave the compensation to you. It does seem moderate to me. But if we are running the kind of financial operation I think we will be, it's alright with me. To repeat—it's alright with me as long as we are charging a $5.00 top for subscribers, and as long as no actor gets more than I do.

Wharton and Bob Montgomery both strongly made the point that in our letter to them we make clear that we cannot proceed now unless the money necessary for the next two and one-half years operation be there for us. When we do begin to sign actors we will be signing them for two and one-half years.

Eileen is typing this up now at ten o'clock and you should have it in your office in not too long. Could you call me here at twelve noon, at my office, and

Kazan at bat for Lincoln Center's Repertory Theatre team

ask me whatever questions you might have about it. There might be simpler arrangements but you would know best. One such simple arrangement was simply to pay me $60,000 a year and Bob $50,000 a year. I don't think anyone at Lincoln Center would object to this. Rudolph Bing gets $100,000. Good luck.

Best,

EK:es

[Kazan wrote from Athens in September to summarize progress of the Repertory Theatre and distinguish its operating principles from the Actors Studio, which threatened to upstage a less agile competitor. He reserved sharpest criticism for the Studio's "preoccupation with the purely psychological side of acting" and corresponding tendency to diminish the role of the playwright. Polemics aside, the remainder of 1962 saw a formal announcement of Arthur Miller's opening contribution to Lincoln Center, although *After the Fall* was not yet identified by title or subject. Miller shared Kazan's hope that modest prices would draw "the masses" and that true repertory would "create a new atmosphere in the theater—a tribunal rather than a show shop" (*NYT*, September 23 and October 26, 1962). A revival of *Marco Millions* (1928), Eugene O'Neill's satire on materialism, and *But for Whom Charlie,* Sam Behrman's serious comedy, would fill out the first season. A sum of $500,000 had been set aside for preliminary expenses in developing the company. Later documentation indicates that Kazan was paid $1,000 per week, with the annual "ceiling" of $60,000 perhaps reached by an expense account. As it turned out, he continued to work without signing a formal contract. Eileen Shanahan was Kazan's loyal and trusted personal secretary.] *TL, 3 pp., Wesleyan*

[New York]
[winter 1962–63]

Dear Art:

I got a lot out of reading your first act. And so I began to work on the play. The first question a director asks himself is the basic one: What is the play about? I don't mean by that what lesson does it teach or what thesis does it prove. I mean what is it about?

It's always a ticklish moment, I know, when someone else tells you what he gets from your work. Perhaps just at this moment it may have some value for you. If it doesn't, put this letter back in its envelope and read it when you finish the draft of the second act. In other words, if this is coming to you at the wrong moment, don't read on.

Here it goes for whatever it is worth. A man for the first time in his life is putting the pieces of himself under a candid light and scrutinizing them. Why is he doing this at the particular moment? Because he's got to. Because in the afternoon of that day a girl is coming from Europe whom he feels he could love and who certainly loves him and clearly wants to marry him. But the man is mysteriously reluctant in his relationship with this girl. He doesn't understand why. Or why so much. The discovery of the reasons for this reluctance are the first actions of the play. And as these reasons begin to be brought to light they become the condition of the further action of the play.

Recently this man has withdrawn from his position, from his work, from other people, from further love relationships, from the world. He is also examining the reasons for these withdrawals. And for the first time he is experiencing them, at least in part, as personal failures.

So the decision whether or not to marry the girl who is arriving from Europe has come to be a symbolic act for him. It appears that he is either going to go on with his life with some confidence or if he doesn't it is a continuation of his pattern of withdrawal and further admission of his failure.

The decision he is to make will depend upon what he discovers about his past life, about his past relationships, about his past being and particularly about the real reasons for his past behavior. In other words, who is he?

So he begins to look at his past and his self. The man had a marriage with children. The marriage broke up. At the time of the dissolution he blamed his wife entirely. Now for the first time he must admit to the possibility that at least a good part of the responsibility is his.

The man had a love affair with a girl who aroused in him certain areas of experiencing that he hardly knew existed. I don't know what you intend with Maggie in the last half of act two. But you did tell me that the play in its final moments included Maggies death. Whether this is suicide or a "natural" death I don't know. But it does seem to me that somehow here, too, he must begin to feel some significant responsibility. How much shame results? How much guilt? How much doubt about himself? About his standards, convictions, defenses, habits, about his essential nature, I don't know.

The man had a relationship with his parents which still continues to disturb him profoundly. It seemed particularly significant to me, Art, that you thought Quentin felt some guilt at not defending his father when his mother was "murdering" him.

The man played a role in a drama of testimony in the early '50's and his behavior here doesn't seem to sit easy with him either. Just why I don't know. Is he not sure that he behaved with entire humanity? I don't know. But, after ten years, he still seems to be disturbed by it and by his part in it.

In the face of this scrutiny of himself and his past acts, he must now doubt aspects of himself that he at one time believed unassailable. And the result now is that he doesn't know how to continue confidently in the future. He can no longer move ahead with wholehearted belief in what he is and what he stands for.

Must he reconstruct entirely before he goes on? Should he take the symbolic affirmative step of marriage now? Will this marriage result differently? Or will it end as before because he himself is unalterably the same person he was. Are there answers to these questions? In the flow of a man's life is it possible to wait for "answers" and resolutions? Isn't the important thing the struggle itself? That and the admission to conscience of all questioning and scrutiny no matter how painful and how disruptive.

And that is as far as I got. I don't know the end of act two, which is the crucial point in any play for meaning. So I don't know what the play intoto is about. In other words, what happens? I have tried to put down what it seems to me to be dealing with as far as I read and as far as I know it.

I do think what might be of value, and more thoroughly dramatized throughout, is the series of <u>discoveries</u>. In other words, whereas in the past he saw event after event and his behavior in situation after situation <u>one way</u>, he now begins to see them, crucially, in <u>another</u> light and from another point of view. In other words, I think we should watch Quentin discover and attempt to face up to his own complicity in events, his own failures, his own mistaken postures.

And this series of "discoveries" seem highly dramatic to me. Of course I may not be right on the target. In fact, I may be well off target. But, if so, it is important that you set me straight and the sooner the better.

****

I hope the above, if you have read it, has some value for you. If you haven't read it, I'll perfectly well understand why. May I just say again to you that I think you're writing better than you ever did. And I am tickled to death to be working on this play with you. Perhaps that did not need to be said but sometimes it is better to speak even at the risk of being obvious.

E.K.

["We were together on a raft in the middle of the ocean, and there was nothing for us to do but paddle; to save my life, I had to save his" (*A Life*, p. 629). Kazan needed a strong opening by a playwright of Arthur Miller's distinction, if only to fend off critics of Lincoln Center and gain time. Miller rationalized Kazan's congressional testimony with the thought that "perhaps it was just as well not to cast too wide a net; for one thing, how many who knew by now that they had been supporting a paranoid and murderous Stalinist regime had really confronted their abetting of it?" Kazan's "talent and his invaluable experience with the Group" were not lost on Miller, who anticipated a successful return to the stage after an absence of eight years. To reject Kazan's direction of *After the Fall* was also "to reject the hope for a national theatre in this time" (Miller, pp. 529–30).

The memory of acts ranging from Quentin's betrayal of a father to the defense of a former communist reveal a mind "questing over its own surfaces and into its depths" (*After the Fall*). Maggie—based on Marilyn Monroe, Miller's wife from 1956 to 1961—releases Quentin, a middle-aged attorney, from a tedious first marriage before revealing her own insecurity and contempt for his egotism. Whether she commits suicide or dies a "'natural'" death in the play was unknown to Kazan at this time. Marilyn Monroe's death in August 1962 complicated the later development of *After the Fall* and overwhelmed the play's reception with charges that Miller had treated his deceased ex-wife unfairly. With her suicide confirmed in the production script, Maggie gives way to Holga, whose arrival from Europe impels the confessional sequences that tempt Quentin to love once again. Her character is based on Inge Morath, Miller's third wife (1962–2002), an Austrian national who met Miller on assignment to photograph the filming of *The Misfits* in 1960 and witnessed the disintegration of his marriage to Monroe. Her wartime experience lent historical range to the play and a metaphysical basis to Quentin's conception of guilt and responsibility.

Traces of the present letter appear in Kazan's record of directorial "talks" with Miller in late 1962 and early 1963 (notebook, Wesleyan). At the time Miller was preparing a draft of act two completed in the late spring or early summer.] *TLS, 4 pp., Wesleyan*

TO DARRYL F. ZANUCK

[New York]
March 6, 1963

Dear Darryl:

John Steinbeck was at my house the other night for dinner and we were talking about "Viva Zapata". The Morgan Library in New York had asked him for all his notebooks and scripts on this picture and also to ask me for what I had saved. I got out seven scripts for him that I had kept, the various stages of our work on the story, and I gave them to John along with a very thick bound notebook of his research on the picture. John said that this was the first picture the Morgan Library has ever asked for.

He also reported to me some conversations with friends in U.S.I.A. These people had seen the film and had thought it a most valuable contribution in their fight against Castroism in South America. They had urged him to do what he could towards a re-release of this picture.

I don't know whether you realize what standing "Viva Zapata" has in Europe. I don't know about the rest of the world but it's the best known and the most highly esteemed of all your films in Europe. I say this without hesitation because wherever I go in Europe, and I spent most of last year there, it is the first film of mine that I am asked about and the one that I feel has aroused the greatest enthusiasm. I have actually had kids follow me in the streets of Istanbul calling after me—Zapata, Zapata, Zapata. When I was in Athens, later in the summer, it was being run for the ninth time on a circuit there. I met many young people who had seen it six times, nine times, a dozen times, and they never miss the theme. They know what it is about and what it is saying. And they like it. It stirs them.

John's friends in the U.S.I.A. thought it was the most trenchant attack on this new turn of Communism, which Castro exemplifies, that there is. At any rate, to go back to my evening with John, we started talking about how eager we would both be to have the picture re-released. He feels, as I do, that it was treated shabbily by your promotion and publicity people and your sales force. The fact is, Darryl, that the picture was ahead of its time. And you were ahead of your time with it. The other fact is that nobody at Fox, from Spyros down to the Merchandising Department, knew what it was about or cared. Any uncertainty about a product in the sales force or in the publicity department always reflects itself. The final fact is that the picture did try to cover too much ground. And it was not clear at all times what was happening and when it was happening to whom. Sequence of time and the flow of events were here and there muddled. The picture was sold uncertainly. And it wasn't edited in a way to quite allow it to be seen at its best.

Both John and I would like to have it re-released. But before it is we would like to work on it and cut it down some and do whatever else we could to make it clearer. One thought we had was to insert a commentary that John would write and that John would also read, which would make the action absolutely clear. John is now a Nobel Prize winner and I further suggest on my own (this is not his suggestion) that the picture start with a shot of him in which he introduces the picture and says briefly what it means to him. Very briefly. And that from time to time his voice link the events and link them meaningfully.

All this would cost very little since neither of us would want a salary but only some participation in whatever success the picture might have. We think if this whole step were to be taken with a show of confidence and from the top level with real urgent feeling and a conviction that the picture had something important to say to the whole world at this moment, "Viva Zapata", for the first time, would have a life in America, in England, etc.

The first thing I think we should do is that John should go to Washington and see Ed Murrow, who is a close friend of his as well as a friend of mine. And I also think he should show the picture to the President. This can be arranged. Kennedy is a great moviegoer. Bob Kennedy is a friend of mine and I promise you I can arrange for him to see it. Then after we set it up there, and hopefully arrange that it become a project that is blessed by our own government, we could then go to work on it. Tighten it up. Make it clear. Have some new prints made which would include John's presence and his commentary and re-release it or rather release it for the first time as it should be released.

There is no need to call your attention that Brando now is not what he was at the time he made "Viva Zapata". Also he's better in "Viva Zapata" than he has ever been in anything. This is Marlon's stand-out performance. Quinn also now is a genuine attraction.

Darryl, you should do this. I am convinced you should. And so is John. We are waiting to hear from you.

Best regards,

EK:es

[Darryl Zanuck informed Kazan that *Viva Zapata!* was "locked out" by a television contract until 1972. He also regretted that some of the "best moments" had been cut "to make room for the commercials." Zanuck did not defend the original promotion of *Zapata,* nor did he remind Kazan of the film's exceptionally weak performance at home and abroad (March 13, 1963, Wesleyan).

John Steinbeck answered critics who doubted his worthiness as a Nobel laureate (1962) with an aggressive defense of literature as a vital social art, not "a game for the cloistered elect, the tinhorn mendicants of low calorie despair." USIA director Edward R. Murrow and other "friends" at the agency helped to arrange Steinbeck's participation in a cultural exchange with the Soviet Union in the fall.]
TL, 3 pp., Wesleyan

TO WARREN BEATTY

[New York]
May 22, 1963

Dear Warren:

Forgive the impertinence of a friend. I really do like you, and it disheartens me when I hear from the underground that you are giving everybody a bad time in Maryland. I know rumors are unreliable and it's not right to repeat them. But, damn it, they dishearten me. I always say: "Warren at bottom is a damn fine guy!" But there's some contradiction all through your behavior. On the one hand you say that you want to be a movie star. You've said it again and again not only to me but to lots of people. But I must tell you that becoming a first flight movie star depends, as you well know, on working with the elite directors on the real good stories. And when these director-glamour boys hear that you are being "difficult" their only reaction can be: "Who needs it?"

It seems to me that you must find a way of legitimately asserting yourself and even forcibly making your opinions and impulses felt. While, at the same time, being agreeable to work with, decent to deal with, fun to be with, and a contributor to an overall effort. It's very regrettable that so many people think of you as a special problem. You have so much: intelligence, talent, sensitivity. You are handsome, vigorous, physically able. But all this can be nullified or badly handicapped by the kind of stories—true, part true, quite false, whatever—that have been getting back to me here.

As I said, it's possibly impertinent of me to write you this way. I am not your father or your brother, only a friend. But think about what I say.

Yours,

[Kazan's letter reportedly "'upset'" Warren Beatty and led Robert Rossen, director of *Lilith* (1964), to offer to call Kazan and deny rumors of a controversy. Relations between Jean Seberg and Beatty—her character a seductive patient in a sanitarium, his a sensitive aide—have been described as tense but far milder than conflicts with Rossen, who dismissed Beatty's requests for motivation and script revision and scorned his deliberate acting. A biographer reports that Beatty's publicist was sufficiently alarmed by the controversy to revamp the original "*enfant terrible*" campaign in favor of a mature image. In time Beatty generously came to understand the effects of Rossen's illness and exhaustion while filming *Lilith* (Finstad, pp. 300–08).] *TL, 1 p., Wesleyan*

[New York]
June 7, 1963

Dear Bill:

I think you ought to take a hard look at yourself. I think you ought to really face a few facts, then take a hard look at yourself and write me again. I'm going to suggest a few questions.

Do you really mean to pretend to yourself (not to me) that you did not know about the contract and its terms before you signed it? Really Bill? Or do you think you just "forgot"? It seems to me that no matter what you now believe, you knew—at one time—all about our arrangement, clearly and thoroughly, long before contracts were signed. You had the woman I consider the best agent in the business, you had a highly experienced lawyer, and, in addition, a highly capable tax lawyer. We—at their request and after very long consultations—rearranged my company's deal with Warner Brothers to accommodate their plans for you. And so we obtained for you a more advantageous deal than you had already agreed to. Are you really able to tell yourself that throughout all this you didn't know anything about the terms of the deal till a few weeks ago? Ever? After four, what is it, five years? Bill!

Are you aware that your deal with me is better than the one I had with Tennessee on "Baby Doll" and Schulberg on "Face in the Crowd"? Are they your peers?

Can you look at the fact that I did a unique thing with you: I agreed to make a film on the basis of a conversation, on a story that you told me one day. Does anybody else do that? Answer that? There was no play, no book, no short story, no outline, nothing. Just a story that you told me. On "Baby Doll", for instance, I acquired the rights to three one-act plays, on "Face in the Crowd" a well-known short story, the title of a book; on "Gentleman's Agreement" a novel; on "Streetcar", "Streetcar"; on "East of Eden" an enormous best seller. What's the going price on conversation Bill?

Do you really think you worked harder and longer on "Splendor" than other fellows work on original screen plays? Why don't you look into this before you shoot off at me? You did work hard and well but I'd say Budd Schulberg from beginning to end put in five times the time and effort, the days and thought and persistence and follow thru on "Face in the Crowd". He started writing it two years before, did nothing else but, did endless research, took innumerable trips, accompanied me on every scouting expedition, was at every single day's shooting ready to rewrite and was with me throughout the scoring, dubbing, re-recording, advertising, censorship fights, selling. Where were you through most of this?

Do you have any recollection of the script of "Splendor" when you first gave it to me? I have it. I have examined it. Are you able to look at this whole side of our relationship on this? Let's see. What you gave me, Bill, was a dramatic narrative with dialogue. It was a good piece of work, basically well constructed with true characters and an important theme. But it was not a screen play. You said to me many times that you didn't know how to write a screen play and I said many times to you that you need not worry about that, that you should simply write the story and leave the rest to me. Do you remember that I typed through your whole script for you, cutting great hunks out here, rearranging there, pushing it into form and shape that made it good enough to get you an Academy Award? Now that is not what you call "writing" and it's only a part of what I call writing and not the important part. But we both have friends in the movie business, men at the top of their profession, well-respected men, who would have asked, in fact demanded co-authorship of the screen play for what I did. Not of the original story. But of the screen play. What I'm saying to you is that you were throughout our work protected to an extraordinary degree. And that you have totally and conveniently forgotten—every bit of that.

Have you any way, in your self indulgent mood, to compare the amount of work I put into "Splendor" and what you did? Bill, I put more time into that movie AFTER I GOT THROUGH SHOOTING than you did the entire time. I did every single step, dubbing, cutting, re-cutting, re-recutting, fighting with the Legion of Decency, fighting with Warners, scoring, re-scoring, previewing it to the Warner people, going to California to preview it there for the festival, fighting out the advertising step by step for months. Then I went to Europe and toured there ahead of the picture. The big grosses in the countries where there were big grosses came from the work I did "ahead" of our movie.

Where was the Associate Producer through all this? Do you remember asking me could your name be on the film as Associate Producer and my giving you that when and where I didn't have to, and when and where I knew you would do nothing about carrying out any such function? But you asked for it, and you got it.

Do you really think you are being underpaid for "Splendor"? I think you're getting what you deserve, a very very large sum of money indeed. Do you really think you're being underpaid? Really? Am I wrong in thinking that "Splendor" may turn out to be one of the two or three biggest assets you have ever created? Or is it the single biggest?

Another question please. Ask yourself: "What the hell am I really sore at him about?" Is it really this about your compensation for "Splendor". You've been psychoanalyzed for years. Ask yourself this question!! You know what it means? What, actually, are you sore at me about?

And who's been talking to you? If over five years you felt nothing like dissatisfaction with our deal, this now can't be your true reaction. Who's got you steamed up and behaving like a cunt? And what did they ever do for you? Did they do a first class movie from a story you told them in a conversation? Did they work their hands off for three-four years on a movie, no matter what your whim or mood was, how you felt? Through the disappearances and the reappearances? Did they make you a load of money? Did they get you an Academy Award? Did they raise your standing in the "industry" to a point where the big agents and producers—people like themselves—would think it worth their time to poison your mind?

What movie are you known for, Bill?

Who started it?

Who did it for you?

Who saw you through it?

Who gave himself in utter devotion to it, never stopped, never flagged, no matter what came up, Bill, fought, held on, saw it through, traveled from Denmark to California to sell it, and backed it up with anything and everything he had?

Did they—anyone—do anything like that for you? Could they? Really: could they?

Have they since? Anyone?

Think!

And you talk about humility!!

You talk about gratitude.

I think your letter is utter shit.

We all have some of that, me, you, our best friends. It's human. But I think you owe me an apology.

Yours with continued love,
a little less, temporarily, but still.

[A letter from Bill Inge claiming ignorance of contractual terms and accusing Kazan of deception in dividing the profits of *Splendor in the Grass* drew an unusually severe reply. Edward Colton drew the contract and insisted in a recent meeting with Inge that its terms had been explained before execution, but to no avail. Now that the "stunning truth" was known, Inge felt "a little gullible" for assuming Kazan would use his "power with some generosity" and share 50 percent of the profits on an equal basis. He was tempted to close the letter as "'Your former friend'" (June 5, 1963, Wesleyan).

Inge wrote twice on June 8 in reply to Kazan's "questions." He held that the terms of the contract were only recently made known to him and surmised that his agent Audrey Wood "perhaps purposely, let me keep myself deluded." He also claimed that no one had "worked" him up and only he was "to blame" for the present lack of understanding. Kazan's care in bringing *Splendor* to the screen was appreciated, but the "suffering" from which the story arose and the struggle of twenty-odd years to express it belonged to Inge alone. In a second letter he drew on an insight from analysis and admitted that quite often his "perspective changes on a troubling situation." Perhaps he would eventually see Kazan's position as "totally right." In the meanwhile Inge recalled the director's misguided congratulation for writing a script " 'in no time at all.' " The unnamed work "was half my life. It took me two decades of self-abuse and hard analysis to finally arrive at the point where I could write it as simply as I did" (June 8, 1963, Wesleyan).

Financial statements held by Wesleyan indicate that Bill Inge received approximately $260,000 from 1963 to 1966 for his share of *Splendor in the Grass*. Kazan's share for producing, directing, and marketing the film is unclear.] *TL, 4 pp., Wesleyan*

TO JAMES BALDWIN

[New York]
June 9, 1963

Dear old James:

You disturbed me. It wasn't so much losing your play. That did hurt like hell. That you are now talking to some one else, Lee Strasberg, Cheryl Crawford, Rip and the committee, whoever, about what I started, that I'll never get over. But perhaps what disturbed me more was what you felt about the Repertory Theatre. My fault because I never told you about it. But the FACT IS THAT I went into Lincoln Centre because 1/ I was afraid that if I didn't it might become what you think it is and 2/ I was determined that it be a "People's Theatre", that it not be "respectable", only that I respect it, that it not be an imitation of other repertory theatres around the world, that it in no way be an Academy and so still born but that it be a real part of the living of all the people in this city. And that's what its going to be with or without your play or anyone else's play. But if Bob W. and I had not gotten into it, without us, it easily could have been an institution run by moneyed patrons and so dead, dead in the way that the Metropolitan Opera is dead. Bob and I could not tolerate its being turned over to the stiffs. We had to prevent its becoming what the other theatres of this kind in this country have been, what the theatre at Stratford, Conn. now is, "worthwhile", but no ear to the ground, no least tremor in response to the vibration of everything else going on all around it. One reason we fought so hard for the temporary building, the so-called "tent", is that we could so make known to the world, with more than words, that our effort was made of living stuff, and not an institution designed to continue tradition after its time. That's why we're starting with Miller's play which is as contemporary as sweat and not with, for instance, Hamlet, which is the opening production of Olivier's National Theatre of Great Britain. And I wanted to open your play immediately after Miller's not only because I was personally so fired by it, but also because it would again be a statement thru action that this theatre is tuned to the issues of the day, would sound off loud and clear, and not live only in the area of "art". As I see our effort its what used to be called "infiltrating"—not in any secretive sense, not without LC knowing what our course and our aspiration is, but thru the power of our present prestige and with their acquiescence.

About the Actors' Studio, I really and truly and in all sympathy cant see any genuine difference between their operation and Broadway. Strange Interlude looked to me like one of those productions I did for twenty years. It had the same actors I used to use, the same kind of stage goings-on, actually, to be frank, not as well done because the director was not as tough with the actors or as persisting as I used to be, but nothing wrong with it, perfectly honourable, well-intentioned, clean. I like the Actors' Studio in their new phase. But it is the new Broadway, the next orthodoxy coming in. And a much better one. But our theatre really is going to be new. We are the challengers. We are in danger. We are breaking tradition and breaking clean of the old crap. We are (your phrase) going for broke.

Well whatever explanations I make now are late. You're with the Studio, and its their gain and our loss allright. But you can see from what I've said that its impossible for me to accept the situation as final. In fact I have to talk to you as if it didn't happen yet. So I ask you, I ask you: why do you, why the hell did you act as if the Repertory Theatre is already "written-off"? For instance why didn't you, why dont you help us get a real cadre of negro actors into our repertory company? Legitimately? Not being pushed into roles where they dont rightly belong, not by having parts "adapted" or "re-interpreted" for them, but in their rightful place, and in good numbers and in full activity? What a great thing you would do, could have done, if you gave us your play, and we had Diana Sands, Ossie Davis, James Jones, Bill Gunn and the others who have come to the point artistically where they belong in a rep company and so would not be just (your phrase) niggers in the window to show off how integrated we are. That way, in our second play, we would introduce negro artists, in goodly numbers, part of a permanent set-up, permanently enlisted, thoroughly involved, trained and being further trained, integrated! Well now you've given your play to the Actors' Studio and we will still have an "integrated" company, that is we will still have negroes in it, but its going to be much tougher, not only for us, but also for them. You can see that.

There is finally something else. A person becomes a director because he wants to direct, but he continues a director after years and years for the plays which come along that he feels passionately for. They are few. You saw me thru two where clearly I didn't. I did the best I could, worked hard, did well on one, very well, but when it came to central involvement—it wasn't there. I do feel a passion about yours. I just say that to you, simply and once. I cant elaborate. Its embarrassing to speak about myself. But whatever my gifts are, they are really engaged by your play. And I really feel that it can be a classic. And to be awfully plain with you, old friend, while I think your play will be a success no matter who does it, just <u>how</u> good it is, just where it reaches as permanent art and not as an incendiary voice of today (which is fine, but it seems to me, lower on the scale of values you should reach for) all that depends how strong, persisting and honest and unafraid of you the people who do your play are. Flattery is your danger. Look out when they tell you there is very little to do just as you should look very sharp when anyone tells you there is lots to do and ask (them) (whoever): Exactly what? and why, why, why? I have no doubt your play will be a success. Its a matter of just what company it finally keeps, what arena it chooses to compete in. And I have this apprehension: that in your perfectly natural desire to be sought after, admired, respected, thanked and adored, adored! (You are a lover) you may avoid the uncomfortable. The Theatre is a much tougher work than the essay or the novel. Well, you know what I mean. And I dont want to sound like the disappointed woman who's lost her man to a younger mistress, although that's how I must inevitably sound. But you know me well enough to realize that my instinct would be to say: Fuck you, good luck, kid, but fuck you. I'm not because I really do respect you, and I really do think I can speak to you honestly.

Now the suggestion Bob Whitehead made to you is born of desperation. It is not what we'd ideally want. Its what a loser would (in this case gladly) settle for. But it does have some very very real values for you as well as for us. And the clearest and the realest have to do with calling public attention to the immediacy of the issue and the very present danger as well as the tremendous merits of the play. For the first time in our theatre history a play is esteemed so highly that it is done in quick succession in two major productions in the theatre capital of the nation, and almost immediately afterwards in theatres from coast to coast. I think <u>we</u> should open it in Washington. Then move it to New York and play it for our subscribers. The Actors' Studio could have been playing it three months by then, and have established themselves here. We would here reserve only the audience of our subscribers, seven weeks of people at the most. After that we'd play it only occasionally, leaving the inside of the lamb shop for the Studio. In other words we will take second place. But we will want to play it the following summer (two years from now) for the world's fair crowds in our new building. I'd passionately like it to be part of the opening repertory in the building, along with whatever other plays prob-ably Arthur Miller's and the Oresteia of Aeschylus. That's the main thing for us. Now what is wrong with that suggestion? It doesn't take anything away from the Studio either in Kudos or in masses of people, or very little there, since we will only hold out seven weeks of subscribers and whatever other performances we would decide upon. We would play Washington first, which is nothing for them. After coming here and playing our subscribers we play the play in repertory as infrequently as you and they like, if it gets down to that. We'd want to play it as often as possible, but we realize that is a problem. But we must have it for the opening trio or foursome of plays and productions with which we inaugurate our new building. I want a negro's voice to be heard immediately in that building! Really, think, Jimmy, think. I am not trying to embarrass the Studio. I cant take defeat gracefully, in fact I cant take defeat period, but I'm admitting here that we're second and we're taking the leavings and doing so gladly, thinking it our privilege and our obligation to do your play and to above all have it as part of the continuing life of our theatre. Jimmy its right, really it is. And I even think the Studio people, if they think about it, will see that this is right. And should be. Write me. Love.

E.K.

[Kazan replied to surprising news that the Actors Studio Theatre would soon gain rights to *Blues for Mister Charlie*. The author, James Baldwin, was in "seclusion" finishing the third act. His association with the Studio and the likelihood of several members playing key roles were cited as decisive factors (*NYT*, June 9, 1963). The Studio's revival of *Strange Interlude* opened to strong reviews on March 13 and may have influenced the decision as well. Kazan was unimpressed by the production of O'Neill's marathon and reminded Baldwin that it was he who had suggested and nurtured the writing of a play based on the murder of Emmett Till. Later Baldwin "casually" explained his defection to Kazan. He "was too much like his father and he wanted to be on his own," and "Lincoln Center had no blacks on its board" (*A Life*, p. 703).

Baldwin's evolving role in the civil rights movement complicated the Studio production of *Blues for Mister Charlie* and led to irreconcilable differences with Frank Corsaro, the original director, who was replaced by Burgess Meredith. Diana Sands, Pat Hingle, and Rip Torn offset criticism of undue length, disorderly structure, and polemical excess when *Charlie* opened in April 1964. The play ran for several months on Broadway before a disastrous summer engagement in London. A proposed sharing arrangement with Lincoln Center did not materialize.]
TLSx, 2 pp., Wesleyan

TO WILLIAM INGE

[New York]
June 10, 1963

Dear Bill:

Thank you for writing me as you did. I suppose no one can understand how much goes into another person's script. I should know, but—I'm writing, trying to write, another one now. Yesterday I came across some notes on it that were dated 1955. Some of the characters in AA were in a play I wrote at the Yale

Drama School in 1932. I think it was callow of me to say: "Gee Bill you turned out that script in no time at all." But I've been known to be callow. When I really think, however, I <u>do</u> know what's involved (I'm also sorry Bill Fitelson made any insulting remarks directed at you. But I won't say anything to him about them—unless you'd like me to—because I just don't call anyone on second or third hand stuff any longer. There is so much mix-up in that kind of traffic now. Bill's main feeling is a protective one for me and that is why he's a good lawyer for me, thoroughly embattled loyal and concerned. Like any "wife" he has his blind spots towards other peoples' contributions. For instance in dealing with Lincoln Center now I find him tending to be unfair to Bob Whitehead etc., and not realizing that, by the nature of that effort, I cannot make any money on it. But that I intend to do it anyway, even if the salary doesn't pay my bills, etc., etc.) At any rate the only point now is that I really HOPE you know that I value you very much both as a friend and as a fellow I have worked with well. I do want to work with you again. I hope I see you from time to time. I hope you don't move permanently anywhere to where I can't see you. I truly admire you, I guess mostly because of what you've made of yourself over what was a rough road. I admire that. I know something about that from experience, that one's toughest job is with himself, and there is never any credit given there. But I've worked with lots of people and you are among the very few best and I don't draw any line, in a clinch between professional and personal. You have a lot to admire about yourself, and I sometimes wish you did more. You have a right to blow off at me, and I think it's healthy I blew back at you. You are not, incidentally, bitchy; I do not think of you that way at all. You're not.

[Bill Inge left for California in July to write several television scripts and complete a novel but not before promising Kazan his next dramatic work. The unnamed play would treat "contemporary life and the problems people have in finding their place in American society" (*NYT,* July 23, 1963). *Natural Affection* treated similar problems and closed earlier in 1963 after a brief run on Broadway. Reviewers preferred the Inge of old to the "junior-varsity Tennessee Williams," who had set up in Chicago to dispense "little dainties of depravity." Neither the unnamed work in progress, nor any play by Inge, has been staged to date at Lincoln Center.] *TL, 2 pp., Wesleyan*

TO ARTHUR MILLER

[New York]
July 1, 1963

Dear Art:

I guess the following is confidential. Why the hell I don't know. But everything that comes out of that place is whispered to me and reaches me as if through an underground. There's been a revolt in the Playwrights' Group over at the Actors' Studio. The odd beats, the faggots, seem to have taken it over. At least that's the way it is put to me. The above estimate being hearsay not my own observation.

Personally, I think Albee has talent. He's tough and ruthless, but also has a very nice side to him. And I like him. Anyway, he apparently lead putsch and kicked out everybody except twenty people, most of whom seem to be in the lavender area. A couple of the fellows that are still in came to me and in some disgust said: "Why doesn't Lincoln Center have a Playwrights' Group and maybe Art Miller would be interested in heading it up?"

Personally, I would rather you wrote than told other people how to write. But I think we ought to talk about this. In fact, I think we ought to have such a group and perhaps you and I can overlord it, plan it, and so forth. Anyway I'll be seeing you probably on Friday. I'll call you when I get up Thursday, which is now Thursday morning.

Our psouris with the city is a little bit better—is or are—in other words, although I'm grammatically lost, what I mean to say is things are looking up. This is all hearsay and estimations and so forth. I'll know myself tomorrow when I go to a Bureau of Standards meeting with Bob.

Best,

[Molly Kazan resigned leadership of the Playwrights Unit in early 1962 to follow her own dramatic interests. An ensuing plan to remove casual or ineffective members reduced the unit by two-thirds but not without controversy and recrimination along lines suggested by Kazan. A reported leader of the "putsch," Edward Albee graced the Actors Studio with a workshop production of *The Zoo Story* and in 1962 offered the Studio Theatre an opportunity to coproduce *Who's Afraid of Virginia Woolf?*—lost to indecision and delay. Albee cited the press of work and "disenchantment" with Studio leadership in resigning from the Production Board in 1964. Kazan's suggestion that Arthur Miller lead a similar group at Lincoln Center fell on deaf ears. Miller stated in his autobiography that he had "no position" other than playwright in the repertory theater and "no interest" in the "politics of its administration."

The directors met construction delays in opening the Vivian Beaumont with plans for a temporary stage on a campus site donated by New York University. Conflict with the city was resolved on July 2, when the Bureau of Standards issued a permit for a prefabricated building known fondly as the "steel tent." Designed by Jo Mielziner and Saarinen Associates in conformity with the Vivian Beaumont, the ANTA Washington Square Theatre would prove a divisive issue in Lincoln Center politics. In retrospect Kazan preferred its simplicity to the splendors of the Vivian Beaumont.

José Quintero's appointment to direct *Marco Millions* completed essential planning for the first season of repertory at Lincoln Center, definitively set for January 1964.] TL, 1 p., Wesleyan

TO JO MIELZINER

[New York]
August 5, 1963

Dear Jo:
The final pages of AFTER THE FALL make clear what the subject matter, the theme and the meaning of this play are. Miller is dramatizing the fact that man has survived, does survive and always has survived by murder. He is recognizing this in his hero and, so, in himself and in all of us. He even goes so far as to handcuff his hero and the Nazi mass murderers. At the end of the play, he, in effect, says that we live thru murder, that we have always lived through murder, and that we the SURVIVORS go on only because others die. And finally that we need and unconsciously want the death of others.

On the personal level the play is about a man who discovers that he has survived by the deaths of other people with whom he's been related, particularly those whom he has known in bonds of love. These murders came about, on his part, by a wish, by his walking away at a critical moment, or even by his accepting the death of someone else as convenient.

So you will immediately recognize that the mood of the play as Miller and I have come to feel it, is not in the set as your first sketch had it. You did very well what we asked for. But we were not clear enough or definite enough as to what we wanted.

What we have now is a beautiful arrangement of spatial elements, permitting and encouraging graceful movement and arrangements of people. But even the beauty of the set works against what we need.

The set now looks new. It should seem primordial, as old as murder itself. The set looks friendly, inviting, attractive, even elegant. It should be forbidding, mysterious and threatening. It is clean. It should seem stained with old hatreds, old bloodsheds. It is now easy to take, easy to look at. It should in fact be indigestible, difficult, turgid, oppressive.

It is simply and perfectly unified since it is all made of the same elements and all of the same materials. While, of course, every setting should be unified artistically, the unity of this set should be a difficult one. Actually it should be composed as the play is made up of fragments, the remembered pieces of his environment where the "action" took place, where the climaxes of his life were played out. Particularly the thing about each environment which affected the way the climax was played out. As the play is so should the set be.

The set should not be pleasant and inviting. It should be where murder was discovered by the murderer. And since this is basically a poetic play, where mankind has, from the beginning discovered that he has killed. That is to say his memories in his conscience.

The set should not be airy. It should be cavernous, deep and dark. It should be made up of the corners of his memory into which his mind has never penetrated before, because it never dared to. It should not have the quality of light, but rather should suggest the dark corners of his psyche into which he has never before been able to see.

Quentin's process of discovering what he has done in his past should be a frightening one. It takes place in these caverns and recesses, little corners and odd areas, shaped and decorated with what he can recall of the various arenas of his living.

Now to speak only of basic shape and arrangement, of space and mass; they i.e. what we <u>now</u> have seem formally correct for the most part. The basic shape seems right. It is designed to make it possible that during the action of the play the various personages might stay "alive", behind and above Quentin, more or less in the same place, and surrounded there by little fragments out of the environment in which Quentin remembers them. Their presence above and behind Quentin throughout the action presses down upon him, oppressively, hemming him in, not permitting him any escape without confrontation. That's what the shape and basic arrangement of the set makes possible.

But the main entrance is wrong, as we NOW see the problem (We didn't see this clearly before). The most important entrance should not be from the side, but from a cavern or hole far up center. From out of this tunnel or cavern, Quentin leads his past and his relationships up and out and to us for judgment. All the people should enter and exit only from this hole.

The Tower we feel is necessary. The last page of the script makes clear how all embracing Miller intended this symbol to be. It represents man's need to kill, his eternal practice of surviving only by the death of others. This symbol, the Tower, also should be unrealistic, highly fragmented, highly stylized, made up of the most frightening bits of these towers as they were, heightened by the imagination to make it what it seems to Miller now, using the "eyes" especially. It should sit there throughout behind and above everything, a malignant presence, squat as a toad, or the silhouette of a tank, equally deadly, ugly, massive, lumpy, old. It should have the quality of something exhumed. It has been there all through man's history.

The set should not achieve its unity by being uniform in color or shade. It should be fragmented in the way a BRAQUE is fragmented, a special arrangement in this case of Quentin's homes, beds, places of going and coming, of living and of crisis, of the memory of pain, hatred and desperation and the arenas of Quentin's agonies. Of course unity is important. But this should be a difficult unity, the unity of complexities held together by theme and meaning and the color of murder. Each place suggested is where a murder took place and where Quentin managed to survive while others did not. And the whole is the place where these people, these guilts are brought forward by Quentin in front of an audience to be recognized for what they are, measured, judged and finally disposed of.

E.K.

["Long, long" meetings with Arthur Miller were the order of the summer for the codirectors, who knew that *After the Fall* must "work" whatever its faults might be. Kazan admitted he was excessively "compliant and respectful" of Miller and probably not "much help" as he completed a first draft of the play. In effect Kazan had been "spoiled" for collaboration by the relative independence of filming *America America* (*A Life,* p. 630).

The only familiar property in Jo Mielziner's stage design was a chair placed in front of the audience to suggest exchanges between Quentin and an off-stage "Listener"—initially an analyst. Other properties associated with the "climaxes" of Quentin's life were molded from steps and platforms to convey the stark, forbidding subjectivity of the play. Kazan emphasized the "solidity" of the concentration camp tower and rejected Mielziner's advice that a projection be used instead to establish the Holocaust as ground for Quentin's meditation on the violence of history, "after the Fall, after many, many deaths." Inge Morath suffered the rigors of war near the end, as did many privileged Germans, and deepened her husband's recognition of the Holocaust.

Mielziner later observed that "the stylization of the watch tower confused and puzzled most of the audiences, and neither the author nor I felt completely happy about it" (Mielziner, p. 218). Reviewers were also confused, if their scant notice of the tower, whose " 'eyes' " glowed on cue, or of Holga, deemed "a rather cryptic German," is sufficient evidence.] *TLS, 3 pp., BRTC*

TO PAUL MANN

[New York]
August 21, 1963

Dear Paul:
We both enjoyed your letter and appreciated your feelings. But cannot agree with the essential points you make. Wish we could. We certainly would like you to be satisfied. But, much as we want this, we have a much greater responsibility, you must realize, and that is to the REPERTORY Theatre. It becomes clearer to us each and every day how difficult this is to organize and how very complex it is to manage.

There is no one who is working in this theatre who is not doing two or three men's work or who is not going to be asked to do two or three men's work. In the second place, there is no one who is engaged for the theatre who is not going into it at a great financial sacrifice. What we personally are getting out of it, for instance, is a small fraction of what we have been earning over the years. Jason is coming in at an enormous financial sacrifice, in fact is not getting enough money from us to pay his living expenses. Of course, his living expenses, due to his several wives and his many children, are heavy, but over all I think he is making a greater financial sacrifice to come along with us than anyone in the Theatre.

No one of us can judge what his salary is by comparing it to a "Broadway" salary. A Broadway salary is taken as a gamble. It's like betting on a horse. If it comes through you are hog rich, if not you are dead. In the second place, when we talk about a weekly wage we are talking also about a 52-week guarantee and, therefore, we are talking about a yearly rate. We are offering you $26,000 a year, Paul, for two and a half years, guaranteed. And that is a lot of money in the chaos in which we live. We are not offering you separate salaries for teaching and for acting. I do not get separate salaries for directing and producing and administrating and being a Press Agent, and for taking the responsibility with Bob that this thing runs in such a way to please a Board.

Again I want to say $26,000 is a lot of money especially so when it is guaranteed for two and a half years. And we think you should accept it and congratulate yourself. There are actors on our list more in demand on Broadway than you, Paul, who are getting less, and there are actors who are going to play more critically important parts than we see for you at the moment who are going to get less. We are paying you to be involved in our total effort. Our criterion is mainly usefulness to our theatre. But it is also and just as importantly what will enable an actor to get by and be comfortably happy. "To each according to his needs" is part of it. "How much will they contribute?" is another. Your salary is in the upper regions of our list.

A choice has to be made in life, Paul. One cannot have everything. If you really want more money, you won't be able to come with us. If you want a certain type of equalitarianism, I don't know where you will find it. And I don't believe in it. I believe in distinctions based on the two points I cited: what a person needs to live decently and comfortably and how much he is contributing to the Theatre. Or will. You will contribute a lot in various ways. That is why you are getting one of the highest salaries we have. But none of us are getting what we deserve. If we start paying people what they deserve where will anyone find the money, dear Paul, to pay me?? And I will contribute more than anyone except Bob who will contribute more than anyone except me; therefore, we get the most. But my salary does not pay my living expenses. Yours will. I envy you.

Your friend,

EK:es

[Paul Mann was recruited at fifty to play mature supporting roles and train younger members of the repertory company. He and Kazan played minor parts in *Johnny*

Johnson (1936), a Group Theatre production, and Mann later performed under Kazan's direction in *Flight into Egypt* (1952) and *America America*. He appeared in four plays at Lincoln Center, while continuing as director of the Paul Mann Actors Workshop in New York.

Jason Robards, Jr., thrice married to date, joined the company in April knowing full well the financial sacrifice, if not the difficulty, of repertory theatre: "'I feel I have to do it; it's not for the money, I assure you.'" He would play leading roles in *After the Fall* and *But for Whom Charlie*.] *TL, 2 pp., Wesleyan*

TO JACK L. WARNER

[New York]
October 22, 1963

Dear Jack:

Sorry I'm so late in answering your letter. Of course you can see the positive dupe of the work print when you get here in November. I'm just sorry I haven't anything better to show you. What worries me about your seeing the work print is not the quality of the photography, nor all of the red lines, fade and dissolve marks and so forth. It is that the lead boy is sixty percent incomprehensible and many of the other actors talk Turkish, Greek and gobbledegook, animal talk and so on. You won't know what the hell anyone is saying over half of the time and there will be large areas where you simply won't get the plot. I have straightened all of this out. And I'm adding the most brilliant musical score I have ever had. It's going to be a wonderful picture. And, Jack, I want you to like this picture! I know what a difference it will make in its ultimate fate. I know (and don't in the least resent) that you didn't like SPLENDOR IN THE GRASS when you first saw it. The fellows, especially Ben Kalmenson and Dick Lederer, did a brilliant job on it. But I always thought it would have had an extra push if you had liked it. I've always shown you all of my other films early. And I've always tried to benefit from your suggestions. After all you are, to say the least, a seasoned showman and fabulous producer. But this one worries the hell out of me because so much depends on your knowing or anyones knowing, <u>what's going on.</u> If you want to see my work print with the miserable incomprehensible track on it, I'll certainly show it to you. But I hope you'll wait. I won't have an answer print unfortunately until the 11th of December. Maybe a day or two before. The first thing I'll do is arrange to show it to you.

Meantime, one question, friend to friend, advise me. I have spent three years on this film, writing, producing, directing, supervising, location hunting, dubbing, rerecording, selling, God knows what. Do you think I'm a damned fool to give any film this much time for the comparatively moderate fees I get?

It's a big gamble on profits isn't it? Am I nuts? I know I am generally but on this issue am I? What should I do next time?

Affectionately, <u>Gadg</u>

[Reviews of *America America* were wide-ranging but on the whole more positive than Kazan expected or has recalled. Joan Didion concisely stated the virtue of the film and factors working against popular success: "*America America* is massively repetitive, insistently obvious, almost interminable, and, perhaps in spite of itself, immensely, miraculously moving" (*Vogue,* February 1, 1964). The film premiered at the Paris Theatre in New York on December 15 with a running time of 174 minutes. Academy nominations for best picture, direction, and screenplay were forthcoming, while *L'Osservatore Romano,* the Vatican's newspaper, called it the best American film of 1963. Overall weak returns argued against funding the sequels described by Kazan in pre-release publicity.] *TLS, 1 p., WB Archives*

MOLLY DAY THACHER KAZAN, "THANKSGIVING, 1963"

Molly Day Thacher Kazan died from a cerebral hemorrhage on December 14, 1963. "Day" was mourned by Elia and family and by more than four hundred who attended a memorial service at St. Clement's Episcopal Church in Manhattan's theatre district. Elia delivered a characteristically taut statement of "regret, love, longing, and admiration": "This immaculate girl was struck down without warning, cause or reason, lived without hope of survival for twenty hours, after which her heart stopped. She was not a member of any church. If she had a religion, it was the truth, telling it at any cost. She mothered four fine children, helped playwrights, who are here to acknowledge her support, helped me in everything I did for thirty-one years. She leaves her own monument" (*A Life,* p. 677). The Rev. Sidney Lanier, vicar of St. Clement's, conducted the requiem. Among the playwrights in attendance was his cousin, Tennessee Williams, whose inchoate talent Molly was the first in New York to recognize and encourage. Her passing was overshadowed by the assassination of President Kennedy, but with an artist's peculiar adroitness, she mourned his untimely death in a poem whose publication in the *Herald Tribune* (December 8, 1963) preceded her own by less than a week.

"Thanksgiving, 1963"

I think that what he gave us most was pride.
It felt good to have a President like that;
bright, brave and funny and good-looking.

I saw him once drive down East Seventy-second
Street in an open car, in the autumn sun
(as he drove yesterday, in Dallas).

His thatch of brown hair looked as though it had
grown extra thick the way our wood animals in Connecticut
grow extra fur for winter.
And he looked as though it was fun to be alive,
to be a politician,
to be President,
to be a Kennedy,
to be a man.

He revived our pride.
It felt good to have a President
who read his mail,
who read the papers,
who read books and played touch football.
It was a pleasure and a cause for pride
to watch him take the quizzing of the press
with cameras grinding—
take it in his stride,
with zest.
He'd parry, thrust, answer or duck,
and fire a verbal shot on target,
hitting, with the same answer,
   the segregationists in a Louisiana hamlet
   and a government in Southeast Asia.
He made you feel that he knew
   what was going on in both places.
He would come out of the quiz with an "A"
in Economics, Military Science,
   Constitutional Law, Farm Problems, and
   the moonshot program,
and still take time to appreciate Miss May Craig.

It felt good to have a President
who looked well in Vienna, Paris, Rome, Berlin,
and at the podium of the United Nations
—and who would go to Dublin,
put a wreath where it did the most good,
and leave unspoken
the satisfaction of an Irishman
en route to 10 Downing Street
as head of the U.S. Government.

Our children cried when the news came.
*   They phoned and we*
phoned and we cried and
*   we were not ashamed of crying but we were*
*   ashamed of what had happened.*
The youngest could not remember
*   any other President, not clearly.*
She felt as if the world had stopped.

We said, It is a shame, a very deep shame,
But this country will go on
more proudly
and with a clearer sense of who we are
and what we have it in us to become
because we had a President like that.
He revived our pride.
We are lucky that we had him for three years.

TO BARBARA LODEN

[New York]
[c. January 10 1964]

Bar dear:

I think you're wonderful in the part of Maggie now. I also think you can be so much better! You can do something in the part that will never be forgotten by any of us. It all depends on what we do these next two weeks. And I want you so much to be as good as you can be. I often feel, as I do now, that I have a much more secure sense of what you're worth than you have, and a much more confident sense of your potential than you do. And I want to talk very straight to you now so that you do everything in this role that I think you can do—which is a lot.

Let me repeat: you are wonderful in the part, exceeding not what I thought you could do, but certainly exceeding anything Art Miller or Bob Whitehead had any right to expect. The fact is that they are very pleased with you. You have taken your place as the second person in the cast and the place belongs to you rightfully because of the work you have done till now.

There is one area where I'm not sure you and I have ever quite come together. This has to do with the size of this girl's craving for worth. Maggie has, in the past, been able to quiet some of this craving by making men desire her sexually. But finally this has not been sufficient to satisfy her. She longs to be somebody, to be esteemed for what she is humanly. Furthermore she sees around her how much shit there is in our society, how general is the fraud. At the same time she sees that there are a few people who have ideals, who do try to tell the truth about their experience (if its only in a pop song) and that there are a very few people who have the particular size which comes from inner worth. She longs to be with this small number. Note she becomes the "girl" of a judge, an old man.

There is a word that you use frequently and to you meaningfully and that word is PERSON. She wants to be a person. I guess she felt that all the men who used to fuck her were somehow putting her down. I guess she also felt that while she was fucking them, at the same time, she didn't know just why she was, that she was doing it for some compulsive reason, some necessity, some fear. She wanted a relationship with a man whom she could desire and respect at the same time. A casual encounter with Quentin in the park gives her a glimpse of the possibility that some one that good, that smart, that idealistic, that worthy, that estimable, that classy might value her for what she is and for what she might become—and still also desire her passionately. For three years after this encounter she couldn't forget Quentin and for three years he grew in her mind till he became a sort of magic touchstone to her own worth. If he would like her, she'd be somebody, she'd be a person.

At the end of her life her disappointment with Quentin is that he didn't live up to what she believed he was. The failure with Quentin for her is a failure in idealism. She was reaching for something perfect in marriage and in Quentin and they didn't stand up. She feels betrayed. Her God let her down. He turned out not to be a God.

Speaking of idealism (another way to say it is a Dream of Perfection), consider it in reverse. Her attacks on the phony people around her, on the faults of our society, on the frauds in the "art" business, on the "so-called respectable women" are also related to her idealism and should have that color. She attacks them because they fail to measure up to her standards of the way things should be. . . . A girl like Maggie, for all her ignorance, naivete and lack of education can think straighter, sees what she sees. She sees injustice, prejudice, narrowness and fraud all around her and even in her husband she sees caution, pettiness, fearfulness and false respectability. Naturally she is an easy convert to left-wing political idealism. She is revulsed by what she sees, revolts against it. She has the truth, a truth that no one else can assert as naively and directly or as boldly either. And because she says what she thinks so directly, so boldly, so directly and so emotionally, she has, at times, a certain moral grandeur. Unexpected! Quentin says: "She had the truth, that night, I didn't." . . .

I've stressed to you that the "nervous little girl laugh" should stop mid way thru the Andy Sc. But that is only saying something negative to you which is not being really helpful. I think you and I should look into this scene from the point of view that everything she does there is to win Quentin's regard for her sensitivity, her aspiration, her desire to make contact with her past and deal with it honestly, her desire to tell the truth. She is describing things she did that she believes Quentin would approve of, and she is so seeking Quentin's approval. . . . Later, in the park scene (especially the way you and Jason have now developed it) I think her proposal to go to Washington can have more the color of a certain adventurousness. You are probably now thinking: "What the hell is Daddy talking about?" But let me point out where you have sounded just this way with me. Just after we've made love or sometimes in the very moment of love you have sometimes said: "Take me away, Daddy!" Or, much simpler, "Lets go, dad, lets go, lets go." Maggie says: "I'll go on the same train and so forth" and you do it beautifully. But it can and should have more the color of to hell with what anyone might think, lets be wild, lets be honest, lets do what we feel now that we feel it strongly, lets right now, right now, behave truly from our feelings." When you give expression to this kind of feeling with me, its thrilling and especially thrilling because it strikes up an idealistic response in me, expressing what I am reluctant to let loose: namely my own impatience with middle class morality and the standard proprieties of our society. When you talk to me that way, in love, there is a wildness about your tone, an adventurousness, that is much TRUER than common sense, so called. And when Maggie did it this way to Quentin, it stirred him to the marrow. . . .

I respected those moments because they were based on a premise that you were worthy, and therefore were not to be taken for granted, insulted, trifled with. But I truly believe in you and therefore I believe that EMERGING there is much more of this quality. And I think it should break loose in this play, in art before it does in life. It is true among artists generally that what they cannot allow to be seen in life, they can and do want to release in their work and are able to release in their work. You are an artist. You are also an emerging, developing person. You are now at a sort of midway point. I say: step over the line. Let go. I believe that at this moment of your life you are on the verge of speaking up for yourself, boldly and in the full belief that you are as good as anybody and have the rights anyone else has. Release that now in this part. Dont play it from saying "She's just one of those girls." Actually she was more. But also the part can be made into more. She is dumb, maybe, naive certainly, uneducated without a doubt. But we dont measure people that way. She wanted the truth and she aspired to being a person, on her own, by her standards, trying to find her way, and her loyalties, her values. You have to esteem her for that. Thought of this way the part becomes the story of a tragedy of a human being. Otherwise it is a case history. . . .

Now to look at it technically. I think your voice, like every voice developed from what you were psychologically, just as everything about all of us came to be that way. Your voice was made by what you were in your childhood to CONCEAL not to EXPRESS. As a kid it was necessary for you to conceal what you felt. What you felt (so you told me) was unacceptable socially or morally. You were called a "bad girl". You encountered wide disapproval. Furthermore you yourself felt that you had no "right" to feel what you felt, want what you wanted etc. Well you do. And you did then. But your voice, like my own and many many other people's was there NOT to reveal, that is to NOT reveal.

But in the theatre, especially ours down town, we want the opposite. We should not only be expressive, but largely expressive, poetically expressive, boldly expressive. Actually, when you're deeply "prepared" you do it beautifully, superbly. But I want you to speak with full vocal expressivity much much more often. Like you do in the surprise scenes, when you sing out so; like you do in the "I was married to a king" scene, which no one I know could do better. I want you to start now and be bolder with your voice thru out, be big, be expressive, to inflect, to almost sing certain lines. Thru out. You know this is necessary yourself. You took one look at the theatre and it stimulated you, encouraged you, made a demand on you. You knew immediately that you had to speak and LIVE in a certain way, and that way was in the scale of the theatre itself. Let out your expressivity. It is hard for you and for most of us to do so in life. But that's what art is for. I could never say about myself directly the things that I say about myself indirectly in AMERICA AMERICA. Most artists become artists because they need to. Here and now you should work to take what you feel and make it as bold and big and largely expressive as you possibly can. Often its just the matter of a reading or of a line having a certain inflection or melody. It is there now in small, and it is true, so you can trust to make it large and bold and expressive. Go to town! This theatre downtown makes that demand on you.

I guess all in all I'm saying to you that I believe in you, I love you and I believe you can do much more than you believe, that you can exceed yourself. Except to me it wont be exceeding yourself. I know the stuff you've got in you. I've seen it, felt it. Live up to what I know you are. You dont have to be afraid or cautious or veiled anymore. The time has come. Step out.

I love you. I also respect you.

E.K.

[Kazan followed a typical hunch and cast Barbara Loden as Maggie in spite of a lack of stage experience: "I knew her past in detail and knew Marilyn's personal history as well. They'd both been 'floaters' and come out of almost identical childhood experiences, which had left them neurotic, often desperate, and in passion difficult to control. It was obvious to everyone at the first cast reading, even to those actresses who hadn't understood why I'd given her the role, that she could be brilliant" (*A Life*, p. 668).

After the Fall opened on January 23 to mixed reviews: Arthur Miller "gets the

Repertory Theatre off to an impressive start," Quentin's search for love is "over-powering in its emotional effect," Miller seems "to discuss himself, to indulge himself, to justify himself," Marilyn Monroe "might have been permitted to rest in peace." Later reviews in the periodical press were fierce and unrelenting by comparison and crushed any hope of a welcome return to the theater. Robert Brustein, a devoted critic of Lincoln Center, found "a misogynistic strain" in Mill-er's treatment of his wives, especially the disinterment of Marilyn Monroe for purposes of "self-justification." Exposure of Miller's "political anatomy" produced one of the "murkiest moments" in the play, as Kazan's congressional testimony was revisited in the figure of Mickey, a prosperous attorney, who will name former communists in order "to live a straight-forward, open life!" (*New Republic*, Febru-ary 8, 1964). As harsh reviews continued to appear, Miller wrote to Kazan, whose direction was also under attack, that he would continue "to anger, embarrass, and finally to define" the "enemies of truthfulness," although he could "see no place" for himself on Broadway (February 16, 1964, Wesleyan).

After the Fall enjoyed the notoriety of a minor *succès de scandale* and was the only "hit" Kazan and Whitehead produced at Lincoln Center. Barbara Loden won a Tony Award as best featured actress for a performance that Brustein, in the minority, considered "shrill" and "one-dimensional." Publicly she expressed satisfaction with her position at Lincoln Center but in private moments reportedly attacked the Repertory Theatre for lacking "'idealism'" and Kazan for uninspiring direction (*A Life*, p. 725).] *TLS, 4 pp., Wesleyan*

TO S. N. BEHRMAN

[New York]
March 31, 1964

Dear Sam:
I am not a pliable man. And I have a special revulsion for the way "failure" is dealt with in our time and in our theatre. Those two statements being a pref-ace to what follows.

I saw CHARLIE Sunday night. My impressions are as follows. The audi-ence did not enjoy the first scene first act. They did enjoy the rest of the play. At the end, they had a good time. Ralph Meeker was not good in the first act, first scene. He was touching in the second scene of the first act (the proposal scene). And in the second act I thought him an excellent foil for Jason, both as type and as performance. I regretted very much that we had not put back somewhere the material about Charlie's father. And we did Ralph a disservice that way. One of the premises of casting Ralph was the background in the script about his father being killed by gangsters. I thought of Charlie as having the special desperation, and the somewhat forced high-spirits of a man operat-ing outside of his proper arena. When we took these lines away from Charlie in the panic-cutting, we exposed Ralph to a judgment that wasn't fair to him. I don't think Charlie is a "typical Behrman character", whatever that is. I don't think it can be played on just one "tone". About Jason I thought his part could be played on one tone, and it is a much easier part to play and to score in. I thought Jason was a tremendous asset and I cannot tell you how dangerous a thing it would be for the effect of the production to take him out of "Seymour". The audience eats him up and they would not react in any similar way to Joe Wiseman who's quite a different personality. In other words I believe that the switch you are urging on us would harm your play very much indeed. I don't think you know Wiseman. I do, very well having worked with him. I also think that Ralph, AFTER the first act is effective and helpful in the play. The biggest source of difficulty in the effect of your play and our production both is the text of the first scene of the play. I failed in that I was not able to help you with this sufficiently. But it is extremely undramatic and therefore seems extremely "wordy".

. . . I want to say again that I'm sorry I didn't do more for the play. But the fact remains that I don't remember having worked longer or harder on anything than I worked on the first act of your play. I did not bring it off. I don't know, now, at this moment, what I could have done more. I don't know either why the critics didn't take to the evening more warmly. I suppose that in such a situation (I know something is wrong but I don't know quite what) I should look at the one thing that is hardest for anyone to look at: myself. I think quite possibly a director with a lighter touch would have done a more successful job. I suggest that you blame me and the text of the first act.

I send you this with love, Gadg

[Sam Behrman so disliked the performance of Jason Robards, Jr., that he urged Kazan to replace him after *But for Whom Charlie* opened on March 12. Robards was cast against type as Seymour, the shy, unassuming founder of a philanthropic foundation devoted to subsidizing impecunious, and undeserving, writers. Ralph Meeker plays an opportunistic character who manages the enterprise and serves as foil to Seymour, with little more success than Robards, or so Behrman thought. Kazan warned that the basic problems of the play would not be solved by replacing Robards with Joseph Wiseman, a member of the Repertory Theatre whom he last directed in *Viva Zapata!* Reviewers were divided. One accused Kazan of producing "an intentional caricature" of a typical Behrman play by overwrought direction, while another admired the "exceptional shades of understanding" he drew from the cast. Praise for Behrman's "text" was muted at best, and the cast gave little evidence of ensemble acting as the first season of repertory came to an inauspicious close. Robards completed an abbreviated run of *Charlie* before taking an indefinite leave of absence to work in film—no more pleased with his role as Quentin in *After the Fall*. Kazan's final direction of a Behrman play ended unhappily: "Sam, understandably, blamed me and never spoke to me again. He retreated into a dark back room of his apartment on Park Avenue and rarely came out of it" (*A Life*, p. 691).] TLS, 2 pp., NYPL

[New York]
May 8, 1964

Dear G. Fraulein:

Jesus your plays made me sad. I wanted to put my arms around you and tell you I love you and value you and it's not all that bad, it's tough and mean, but it's not quite that bad. There is kindness in the world etc.—and people are— what the hell—us! Anyway I liked the MUTILATED. I thought it theatric and lively and touching and occasionally poetic. But I didn't like it as well as I do you. It needs perfect casting. The two women have to be enormous and I'm not referring to size. We don't have character women, none really, none that could do that job. But we should have, and I'm going to start thinking of who could. Julie Bavasso? Do you know her? She seems young, but she is gifted. And I'll read the play next week and get back to you in more detail if you'll let me know where the hell you are. This is strictly shooting an arrow into the air.

The G. Fraulein I like less. I thought it ran down hill a bit, and it did begin to exhaust my interest. Everything you do has talent and interest and fascination—but I don't like your thinking of yourself that way.

If this letter reaches you, let me know where you are, where to write you, how you are and so on. With love,

Yours, always

[Charles Bowden produced *The Mutilated* and *The Gnadiges Fraulein* as *Slapstick Tragedy* in 1966 after the Actors Studio Theatre failed to exercise rights granted by Tennessee Williams. In *The Mutilated* Kate Reid and Margaret Leighton play "fading tarts" living marginally in New Orleans in the 1930s. Savage notices routed the production (directed by Alan Schneider, a member of the Studio) after seven performances on Broadway and inaugurated the legend of Williams's self-destruction. Forthcoming events at Lincoln Center would overwhelm any plans Kazan may have had for *The Mutilated*.] *TL, 1 p., Wesleyan*

TO JO MIELZINER

[New York]
July 2, 1964

Dear Jo:

I wanted to write you about the Miller play so you would hear from me before you read about it in the papers. But it all moved so quickly. I didn't

In the ANTA Washington Square Theatre for *The Changeling*,
his final engagement at Lincoln Center

know the play was anywhere near finished when I had dinner with you
last week. Art read it to me Sunday. Bob and I talked over the phone and
decided to go ahead with it. Monday I wasn't in town. Tuesday we worked
on the release in the morning, and I rehearsed all afternoon. So this letter is
late.

Among the first things Art said to me was that he wanted Boris to design
this particular play. I couldn't have any objection. I admire Boris and the play
is well within his world. And of course I always wanted him to work with us.
But you know that every time you don't work with us it is a loss to me from
the point of view of simple pleasure as well as professionally. I will miss you.
Incidentally, I won't be directing Art's play—someone else (probably Harold
Clurman) will.

Yours, <u>Gadg</u>

[Boris Aronson faced the challenge of narrowing the open thrust stage of the "steel
tent" to convey the diminished expectations of suspected Jews held for interroga-
tion in occupied France. He agreed with Kazan and Bob Whitehead that the set
once installed was too bright and showy—it "looked like an Art Nouveau subway
entrance," he commented—and agreed to darken the overall impression. *Incident
at Vichy* followed *The Changeling* in the second season of repertory and opened
on December 3 to an "unexcited if respectful welcome," as Arthur Miller recalled.
He admired Harold Clurman's direction and Aronson's "almost mythic police station." Kazan welcomed signs of ensemble acting in the all-male cast.] *TLS, 1 p.,
BRTC*

[New York]
October 23, 1964

Dear Chuck and Bill:

I have to write you now in very plain and very personal language. What I will tell you, of course, is for you only. I am showing this letter to no one else except Bob Whitehead, and my friend and lawyer, Bill Fitelson.

I will simply make a series of statement of fact and opinion. They are my situation. Since the death of my wife last December, I haven't fully enjoyed one day's work. I thought this personal blow would work itself out with the passing of time. And, in one way or another, it will, but apparently, through some eventuality I haven't been able to predict or bring on—and in its own time.

Despite this fact of my life, I have continued my work for Lincoln Center without a break because I gave my word I would, and because today I think the Repertory Theater even more important than I did four years ago when I started it.

What I feel today about our work and our progress, I expressed as candidly as I could in the N.Y. Times Drama Section of August 9th. I believe that by the time this coming season is over, we will have made considerably more progress towards our goals on every front. I am not unhappy about our condition.

The premise on which I accepted my post with the Repertory Theater (one expressly understood and agreed to by all concerned) was that I could and would continue my motion picture work. This, it is now evident, was a naive plan on my part. Of course, I have not been able to. Our work at the Repertory Theater has taken all the time and energy I have. By October 29th, I will have directed three of the four productions we will have presented, and all within the time of one year. This, of course, is in addition to all my other work in the Theater. It is obvious now that if I continue in the Repertory Theater in my present capacity, after the original period, I would have to give up my motion picture work. I am not in the least prepared to do this.

We have no signed contract. We have needed none. I will live up to the letter of our spoken understanding to stay through the opening of the Vivian Beaumont Theater, as the time period was defined.

However, because I am deeply concerned, I am alerting you now, long in advance, that I will leave my present post after the opening of the Vivian Beaumont Theater, at the end of the time period we defined.

Furthermore, since I came in on the expressly understood basis that I could and certainly would continue my movie work during my time with the Repertory Theater, and also would have two five week vacations, I plan to leave some time just after the first of the year (1965) for several months to go somewhere else and write on the two films I had been planning and have had to put aside. The time I have selected to take off is not the most convenient for me, but fits in best, I think, with the needs of the Theater. Before I leave, all production plans for this season and next will have been completed. And, of course, I will get back in time to make all the essential preparations for the first season at the Vivian Beaumont Theater as well as for the HOUSE OF ATREUS, with which we plan to open that theatre and which I will direct.

I want to also say that while Bob and I have worked in harmony, I am now convinced that a two man equal-power leadership arrangement is NOT a correct one for the Repertory Theatre. It could be organized several different ways, but not successfully, in my opinion in the fifty-fifty arrangement we now have.

Finally, I want to say that it is not at all my wish to leave the Repertory Theater. It is, on the other hand, absolutely necessary, if I am to continue to work there, that a functioning relationship be found that will allow for my personal artistic needs.

I will definitely take the steps I have cited, both this coming January and after the opening of the Vivian Beaumont Theater. If we can find some way for me to function thereafter, I would certainly like that.

I also recognize that it is possible you may want to make entirely different plans.

Cordially, <u>Gadg</u>

[Kazan's claim that "ups and downs" (*NYT*, August 9, 1964) were unavoidable in developing an acting company did not deter hostile critics or satisfy the board of directors at Lincoln Center. The present letter was answered in November with a request that Kazan leave sooner than planned, indeed "very soon," on the pretext of cutting costs and keeping the theater solvent. Fresh in corporate memory no doubt was the reception of *The Changeling*, which opened the second season of repertory on a dismal note. Such a friendly critic as Walter Kerr declared that "Elia Kazan hasn't the least notion of how he means to play Middleton and Rowley's pop melodrama of the 1620's" (*NYHT*, October 30, 1964). The press reported later in December that officials were "dissatisfied" with spiraling costs and unfavorable reviews and had been "considering" replacement of the codirectors for some time. William Schuman, president of Lincoln Center, brought the controversy to a head with a clumsy back-door attempt to hire the assistant manager of the Metropolitan Opera as "undisputed" head of the theater. Robert Whitehead resigned, claiming breach of contract and "wrongful discharge." Kazan knew and later admitted that his own resignation, although handled quietly, was "a public humiliation" (*A Life*, p. 687).

The Actors Studio Theatre failed at the same time Kazan's tenure at Lincoln Center was ending in disarray. Of six productions, three were well received in varying degree, but the initial season failed to generate sufficient interest or funding to warrant continuation. The harsh treatment of *Blues for Mister Charlie* and

Three Sisters by London critics in mid-1964 dealt "a humiliating, lacerating blow to the reputation of the Actors Studio" and signaled the end of production (Crawford, p. 241).] *TLS, 2 pp., Wesleyan*

TO JUDY KAZAN MORRIS

SH: Grosvenor House, Park Lane, London
PM: London, January 29, 1965

Judy dear,

Thank you for your letter which I enjoyed enormously and which made me prouder of you than I was if that's possible. I'll certainly make the New Delhi contacts. So maybe your friend can write her parents (they seem likelier than his) that I will call them when there. I dont know how long I'll take to get there. I feel like driving around the Gk countryside a bit, and also like visiting Israel. Having accepted the designation "Ancient Sophomore" with some pride, I will proceed to behave like one. Meantime I am holed up with room service in a posh London hotel as per above and trying to turn the well, long and hard earned leisure to some purpose. I work all day and then have a bite and go to the theatre. I've seen three plays in three days. Tonight I'm going to see Sir Laurence in Othello and tomorrow I will go out all day and watch Churchill being drawn thru the streets of London on a caisson pulled by a hundred odd sailors or whatever. My diversions beside the theatre consist of buying a raincoat and a pair of water proof shoes, both of which they turn out expertly here. I am not alone, but have a pleasant companion to whom my relationship is informal but occasionally ardent. I am not as young as I was, but do enjoy the good things of life. Still. I'm glad you liked the pictures. And if you want more, for Dorothy and Charles say, write Eileen and she will send them to you, or them. I left KK and Nick fine. And I also left them to you, which is fine. I send you and Jonas and Hugh my love, and will send you bulletins from time to time. Eileen knows my exact whereabouts at all times. Other than that, and except for all of you the A.S. has disappeared into the rest of the world.

[Elia could scarcely remember 1964 when he came to write his autobiography. All that remained was a guilty presumption that his behavior had aggravated the aneurysm that ended Molly Kazan's life. That end had also removed any reason for continuing the ill-advised commitment to Lincoln Center. Relations with Barbara Loden were intermittent and lacked "zest," and those with Elia's son Leo, now three, any sign of recognition. Recovery began with the awareness that Molly's death had altered the future and released artistic emotion: "I found myself standing on a mound of years from which I could survey without shame everything that had happened, and from this vantage point of time and space I could try to understand myself" (*A Life*, p. 722). Fifty-five and in sound health, the "'Ancient Sophomore'" immersed himself in travel and relished the opportunity to resume "movie work," although his immediate writing would take the form of a long autobiographical novel. The presence of a young traveling companion—a poet— bespeaks Kazan's desire to loosen the bonds with Barbara Loden, who was reportedly unaware of the arrangement.

Winston Churchill died on January 24 and received a last farewell in London on the 30th. Judy Kazan married in 1961 and lived with her husband, Jonas Morris, and infant son, Hugh, in Washington.] *TL, 1 p., JKMP*

TO KATHARINE KAZAN

SH: Kings Hotel, Jerusalem
PM: Bombay, February 22, 1965

Well KK I'm now in India. I didn't like it the first day because of all the shocking poverty and undernourishment. People sleep on the streets at night, and there are beggars everywhere with fantastic illnesses and diseases. It is still terrible. But there is something nice about the place too. And I dont know what it is. Perhaps the simplicity and decency of the people. Perhaps I've degenerated a little in the month of my travels. I started out in Spiegel's London Posh flat and now I'm in a third class hotel. And I like this better. I dont even mind the dirt—that's what I mean by degeneration—I've become used to that, wear the same shirt three days running, and so on. And I walk around a lot looking everybody over. I certainly dont think of time as a pressure anymore. And I dont think of myself as a tourist at all. And I like the music and the food. But being a Turk, I had a head start in that. The people I like best are the Indians the very native natives, and the people I like least are the American business men (and the tourists, though they are just embarrasing (sp)). For instance right now, speaking of the Indians, on the roof of a house next to mine there is a class in twisting and so forth, that has changed to a class in Indian dancing. You see the world has become one. At the same time the women all go around in Saris which I like very much and look very pretty on the girls and even on the older beefier types. But I think its the rhythm and human bustle of the place I like best. Its slow and easy. People lie down on hired cots wherever they find themselves and take naps in the middle of the day. They sleep in the corners of public monuments and many many of the poor sleep wherever night finds them. Its awful, but so natural. Like animals. I was disgusted (at the social system) by it at first, then gradually its begun to appear natural. And I'm thinking of staying here. Well of course I wont. But I did think of how nice it might be. I dont even mind the slight dirt everywhere.

The only thing I dont like is that I'm not supposed to drink the water or eat the fruit. I dont. But oh my the fruit looks good. This is Saturday. Tuesday I'm getting on a train and going to Delhi. Its a twenty-one hour road on what must be a very slow train. But its the only way I have been able to figure out to see the interior of this part of India. The roads they say are very bad. Not useable. When I get to Delhi I will look up Judy's friends' parents and perhaps one of them will take me on a hunting week-end. Not that I would kill anything, but I would like to get into the country. Tonight I'm going to an expensive restaurant that a fellow I met last night told me about where they have Indian dancing. Tomorrow I'll write in the morning, and go to the zoo in the afternoon. And so forth. Its a nice life and I dont miss but a very very few people, you and Nick and my mother and a couple of others. Judy, of course. I hope to write her after I have seen her friends' parents. And Chris, after I have some sort of adventure. My life is so steady and even and so on that it almost appears there is nothing to write about. Here, in Bombay, for instance, I dont know a soul, and have not looked up any one. In Delhi I will look up some people, but mostly because Judy urged me to. I myself am contented quiet. And require very little. I forgot anything like Lincoln Centre ever existed. What is After the Fall? Eileen writes me regularly. At first I had her looking up people for me, making contacts and so on. But I've stopped that. And she doesn't send me clippings from the NY dramatic columns because I dont ask her for them. Its a new life. Write me, now, c/o American Express Tokyo where I'll be two weeks from today (March 8) OR if you write quick write to American Express Calcutta India. I would like that better love love love love love love love love.

[Elia wrote periodically to Katie Kazan, seventeen and a student at the George School in Bucks County, Pennsylvania, as he traveled from London to Paris, Rome, Athens, and Israel before arriving in Bombay. From Paris he wrote that *The Arrangement*, the work in progress, was "no longer a screen play," and that he had seen the Luchino Visconti production of *After the Fall*—"USA version better, no doubt of that!" Elia also asked Katie to "forgive" his fussing over her: "I have never been a mother before."] *TL, 2 pp., KKP*

TO KATHARINE KAZAN

SH: Palace Hotel, Hong Kong
PM: Hong Kong, March 7, 1965

I'll bet you think I disappeared for good into South East Asia. I haven't. I'm in Hong Kong, see above, and in two days I leave here for the final destination of my trip, Tokyo. I hope to settle in there a little more than I have anywhere else, maybe stay a month, and therefore I may try to sublease an apartment and live like the natives do. Or live in a Japanese type hotel. They call them INNS. In anticipation of this I am mastering the chop stick and the rice bowl. You hold the rice bowl up right under your lower lip and shovel in the food. Its very difficult, though, because the trick is to get the slippery finely minced food from the plate to the rice bowl. Once you've got it there you've got it made. Rice sticks and its easy to get it in with the food stuck to it. Last night I had Shark's Fin soup. Delicious. Really. Anyway I've been having a good time. I even enjoyed India with all its poverty. Bombay was terribly poor, even hopeless. I thought they ought to destroy the city. But New Delhi is much nicer and there is some sense there they will one day solve all their problems of poverty, nutrition, disease and population explosion. I guess all those problems are related and the people in New Delhi (sort of like Washington DC, an official city) I met seemed sort of hopeful. Nobody in Delhi can be very hopeful. They are just too poor, and there are just too many of them. But perhaps with all they're doing, spreading people, putting factories, new ones, out in the country and teaching people something about modern farming and so on, they will one day get out of trouble. Calcutta is full of ferment and I hung around there with that Indian Film Director who makes those fine pictures, maybe you saw them, Pather Panchali and Aparajito and the others. He was with me all day. So I saw more of the creative side of Indian life there, and less of the poverty and the disease and the fantastic beggars. Begging they tell me is a profession and a rather skilled one. I never saw an Indian, for instance, give anything to a beggar. The beggars aim strictly at us foreigners. But still the signs of disease, twisted limbs, leprosy and the rest of it all are too vivid and heart searing to deny. *** I then went to Thailand, Bangkok, which is a modern lively little place, with a lot of temples from the old days, preserved and in pretty good shape. Those Buddhist monks who have been dousing themselves with gasoline and committing suicide in Vietnam are all over the place there too. And the temples are fantastic. In one there was a reclining Buddha, honest to God one hundred and fifty feet long and seventy five feet high, lying on his side, like papoo used to do, and this temple building was built around him. He was, of course, covered with Gold paint like he was in a James Bond thriller. I miss you and think about you a lot. Write me—o.k. then write me again.

love. Daddy

[Kazan "envied" the modest scale of Satyajit Ray's film production: "He has perhaps twenty people with him, that is all. And he arranges matters with his little world, in the small studios of Calcutta, or around it, in nature." The Apu trilogy was "marvelous, wonderful," Kazan thought, and probably influential in shaping his film plans beyond *America America* (Baer, p. 99).

The bombing of North Vietnam and deployment of American troops in early March 1965 marked a decisive escalation of the war in Vietnam.

Kazan's companion returned to the United States after reaching New Delhi. Plans were under way at the same time for Barbara Loden to join Elia in Tokyo for the remainder of the trip. "The basic premise" of their meeting would not change: "No enduring relationship was to be formed." As *The Arrangement* continued to unfold, Kazan discovered that "the character of the woman who stirred up the discontent of the hero was inspired by Barbara" (*A Life*, p. 736).] *TLS, 1 p., KKP*

TO SOL STEIN

[New York]
April 5, 1965

Dear Sol:

I am hard at work on what has turned out to be a novel. Anyway, I've written about two-hundred odd pages and I'm going strong. Should have some rough draft by July.

About Bert Wolfe's book—I am simply not interested in making films of anyone else's material, at least for the time being. I love Burl Ives as a man as well as a personality but I just don't want to make any films with anybody. And that goes for Burl and Rivera.

Let's get together next week. I look forward to seeing you.

My best to Pat, <u>Gadg</u>

[The flight from oppression in *America America* had narrowed to a commercial venture governed by an "arrangement" that entitled the novel in progress and defined Kazan's surrogate hero: "'I give up a piece of my soul; you give me bread. We all, to one degree or another, pretend we like what we abhor. Usually we do it for so long that we forget we abhor it'" (*The Arrangement*, p. 471). Eddie Anderson's successful career as an advertising executive in Los Angeles and his conventionally happy marriage are disrupted by Gwen Ward, a young woman whose contempt for pretense and self-delusion launches Anderson on a series of rebellious acts culminating in arson. Joe Arness, legendary Stavros of *America America*, appears from time to time in *The Arrangement* to cast a "lupine smile" on the ironic issue of his adventure. The novel moves toward a judgment only implied by the earlier film. As Anderson sets fire to the cavernous house on Long Island Sound—probably modeled on Kazan's boyhood home in New Rochelle—he confirms the despair of his dying father, who had embraced the "American system" only to see it fail in the Great Depression: "What had he acquired here to make that migration worthwhile?" (p. 431).

Kazan declined to film Bertram Wolfe's biography of Diego Rivera—a recent publication of Stein and Day. Publisher and author shared anticommunist politics with Kazan, as well as membership in the American Committee for Cultural Freedom.] *TLS, 1 p., Columbia*

[Montauk, Long Island]
PM: New York, NY, July 8, 1965

Well after you left everything got suddenly quiet. Judy went back to Wash with Hughbabe. Chris went up to Sandy Hook where he now is, writing on his book. And Bubbles and I (I dont think she likes that name, but I dont use it often) we-all came out here, which is Montauk by the Sea. I'm sitting by me desk, and occasionally I give the sea the OO (once over to you, you square). Its a little different every day. Yesterday it was so calm that I went in twice. Today it looks too rough for me so I think I will admire it from above. Anyway here I live. I never get off the place. There is no one within reach whom I'd like to see. I'd sort of like to [see] Steinbeck, but I find it hard to take his bickering with his hausfrau Texas style. But I'll probably call him one of these days. But all I do is work. I get up early, work all day till around four, then I work outside on the place, then I have some drinks, a lot of food (B is getting to be a genius cook) and I'm so completely knockedout that I fall asleep till eleven, P.M. that is, when I suddenly wake, go out and read awhile, survey the world by night, then go back and sleep till dawn. Then the same routine again. I do this every day. Can you imagine how monotonous it must be for B? How she takes it I dont know, because I hardly speak all day. But that's the way I want it now. And I do work very hard and very productively on my book. It may not be any good, but it is sure long. And I enjoy doing it. This morning I varied by writing my two youngest letters. I figure Rita is going in today and she can mail this in N.Y. tonight and have it get to Paris in time. You better write me more often than I you. I expect a stream of beautiful postcards as well as some psychologically penetrating analyses of your wheelmates, and your leader. Well as I say there really isn't much to write about here. I dont get off the place and all I know of the outside world comes from the newspapers which B brings me, and thru an occasional phone call from Eileen to tell me that there is no news. Chris I spoke to yesterday. He said it rained an hour and a half the day before yesterday which garden-wise is news. He also says there are a lot of Zucchini, and he is feeding on same. He must have invented several new Zucchini dishes by now. He is also writing. He sits out on the back porch, he says, and does it there. Judy I haven't heard from. I rode her up to Starr's after we left you and off she went with Hugh. My plans: I'm leaving here Sunday and going to the Connecticut Valley State Hospital for the Mentally Nuts. I will not become an inmate, wise guy, only do research for two days maybe. Then I will go to Sandy Hook (Chris coming here) and write the last couple of chapters of my book there. Then come August I will either go or not go to Europe. I probably wont go. Both these places are so beautiful now that I want to enjoy them while I can. A better time for me to go is Feb, Mar, Apr. This coming winter-spring, I'll probably go to Africa, where I have never been. And then maybe end up in Japan again. Anyway I dont like it in the eastern USA during the dog days of Winter and the Uncertain days of first spring, and now everything is so beautiful here, either place. Abe and his three kids are going to use the Montauk place from Aug 1 to Aug 8, otherwise its free. On the other hand I just may surprise you by being in Athens. If not give Maria my love, and Alice, and take care of yourself.

Love from you know who.

[Elia sent "love" to Katie later in July and claimed to be "a wealthy man as Greeks count wealth: land, children and appetite for food, health. The rest of it is lawyer's stuff anyway." Included in "land" was a second retreat near the tip of Long Island, twenty-odd miles east of the Steinbecks' summer home at Sag Harbor.

Elaine Steinbeck recounted a visit at this time to Kazan's cabin overlooking the sea: "I guess he's all right. He's got himself a new girl—27—actress, who's left husband and babies for him. I <u>hope</u> he's all right. But as somebody said, the punishment fits the crime" (to Gladys Hill and John Huston, n.d., Herrick). Barbara Loden's ("Bubbles") presence at Montauk indicates a period of stability after the reunion in Tokyo. Elaine Steinbeck was apparently unaware of the mixed parentage of the "babies." The younger, Marco, was the son of Loden (thirty-two rather than twenty-seven) and her husband Laurence Joachim, a film and television producer. Leo, the older child, was Elia's.

Kazan planned to visit the Connecticut Valley Hospital in Middletown to absorb background for Eddie Anderson's commitment after setting fire to the childhood home. A brief incarceration arranged by Anderson's wife, Florence, helped to slow the momentum of a long novel with a period of introspection.

Avraam "Abe" Kazan, Elia's younger brother, and his children used "the Montauk place," as did Chris, who formerly reported for a newspaper in Little Rock and was now writing a novel. Maria Kalkanis is Elia's Greek cousin living in Athens and Alice a traveling companion of Katie.] *TL, 1 p., KKP*

TO ARCHIBALD MACLEISH

Sandy Hook, Connecticut
[September 15, 1965]

Dear Archie:
I was awfully glad to hear from you. Everything here is fine. I've sort of retired. From what? You name it. I figured I'd begin to enjoy a wider range of things, earlier rather than later. I've quit the theatre for good. I'm planning some more films, but no hurry about them. I've just about finished a first draft of guess what, a novel. Its, by my estimate, about 250000 words. That is long,

ambitious and rather arrogant. But I'm enjoying hell out of it. After that I might write a screen play. I might. What I will definitely do is go to Africa in January and spend three months there. Then I'll live for a month in the Japanese country side. I've got a friend there who has offered me his family's old country place, servants and all, for a month. Who in his right mind, could refuse that? I dont miss the theatre at all. The last thing I did with a full heart was JB. From then on I was going thru the motions. Actually from the day M. died my interest in the theatre died. I would have quit immediately if I hadn't made all those commitments to the Lincoln Centre people. And a lot of the actors were there mostly on account of me. So I did my best. But it wasn't much. You cant perform without a hard on. I'm a conscientious man and I'd whip myself, but nothing really happened. Now its far gone. I dont miss it and I dont miss films. On the other hand I enjoy a lot of other things more. Nick is twenty, today, and is a marvelous boy to be with. Katie is purely wonderful and I love her. "Love" is less an abstract word. I do more about it now. Chris is writing a novel, having quit the paper in Little Rock. I admire him enormously, he's a completely honest and most perceptive person. Judy is just rolling in it, a son, a new home, and an extra good husband. I read books, I loaf, I play tennis, I garden. I even read the papers. I didn't know what I was missing with all that drive. My thirst for pre-eminence seems to have been tied up, in some mysterious way that puzzles hell out of me, with M. It doesn't bother me anymore. I dont know just what happened. But, I dont finally care. I like this new way, whether its a phase or "it". I also have a steady girl whom I enjoy. She is quite unlike M. That's a new kind of thing too. And I enjoy it.

I think you did just right with your play. Miss Harris is an excellent actress. And Alan Schneider a very good director. If I could bestow a blessing, if I had that power, I would do it. I cant, so I wish you well. I wish for you. I think the world of Ada and you. I haven't left my place here or in Montauk (I have a three room cabin there now. I always wanted a bit of the sea) all summer long. But if I were to take a trip, it would be to see a few friends, you one of them. But I honestly dont want to go anywhere. I write every morning four or five hours. Sundays included. And its like Crackerjack. And the country is what that needs. I'm planning to give up my big apartment in New York and get me a small place, three rooms, where I can go instead of a hotel. Right now I'm just a country boy, who smells poison when he breathes the N.Y. smog.

Of course I'll read anything you send me, and I'll give it, what the advertising people call, the benefit of my very best thinking. So send it to me. And let me know your movements. I could be in N.Y. when you are.

Love. E.

[Kazan probably offered to read "Herakles," Archibald MacLeish's forthcoming play in verse. Plans for a Broadway production were abandoned after a disap-

pointing tryout at the University of Michigan in late October (Donaldson, p. 482).]
TLS, 1 p., Library of Congress

TO JO MIELZINER

[New York]
October 19, 1965

Dear Jo:

Well, as a guy that started on the theatre with you, maybe I'm the best one to congratulate you on its opening.

I don't think anybody in this whole city knows as well as I do how much work and what persistent devotion you gave to it.

I am not sorry that I am not there tomorrow night as a functioning person except for the fact that I would be completing the work that we started together. I do regret that I am not doing that.

At any rate, I am thinking of you and herewith comes my admiration and devotion.

Gadg

[Howard Taubman declared the Vivian Beaumont "a beauty in red and black" and praised the new directors—Herbert Blau and Jules Irving, former professors associated with the San Francisco Actor's Workshop—for launching their "regime" with an ambitious production of *Danton's Death* (Georg Büchner, 1835). Although seriously flawed, the inaugural performance revealed "heartening signs of a viewpoint and commitment" at Lincoln Center (*NYT,* October 22, 1965). Kazan was unimpressed by selections for the first season and surmised that "consultation" with "campus-based critics" had unduly influenced the new directors.]
TLS, 1 p., BRTC

TO JUDY KAZAN MORRIS

[New York]
November 1, 1965

Dear Judy:

Katie and I and Barbara went to Antioch College. And I must say I liked it. I was a little hesitant about it the first few hours because bohemianism is rampant there. There are a lot of girls with long hair and the idiotic folk-music-type get-up. There's also a big, old fat-assed thing with a dulcimer on the lawn. And maybe ten percent of the boys had beards. But when I got to talking to some of the students in the dining room, we ate all our meals there, I found they were bright and intelligent and really liked the place. I guess my own inspection of it was superficial, but whatever it was I ended up for it. And certainly did not try to talk Katie out of it. That would be pretty hard to do because she's out of her mind about the place. The one reservation she had was that it was full of communists. But I went to a "Stop The War In Vietnam" meeting. There were only about fifty people there and half of them were from the town itself—all good solid Bill Inge type Republicans for all you could see, but not for our policy in Vietnam. Anyway there were not many students there and those that were there seemed to cover quite a spectrum. Of course what's great about the school is the fact that you study three months then you work three months then you go back and study three months and so on. This means that in the term of five years you would have sampled quite a few different occupations and environments. And that I think is awfully good especially for Katharine.

Anyway, as I say, she is all sold on it. And now she is going to spend the next months on pins and needles waiting to see if they accept her. All I can say about that is if they don't accept her whom are they going to accept? But she doesn't see it that way. She says it's quite possible they won't, and the person that interviewed her gave her no encouragement whatsoever. I didn't give her any kind of false cheer and said she had better get another school in case they don't. But I think they will.

Thanks for the news about the book. I don't care if they buy it at a dollar or they buy it at a quarter as long as it gets around some.

About Thanksgiving—so far the group consists of Ave, Elaine and Starr, Nick, Katie, Barbara, my mother and Jonas, Hugh and you. I'm also thinking of inviting a young Japanese girl whose parents were extremely hospitable to us when we were in Japan and who is here studying.

Just as I was dictating this letter to Eileen I got your last letter saying that you are coming up three days before the weekend before Thanksgiving. That's wonderful! And that finishes that subject. I'm so glad about it. Let me know exactly what day you are showing up so I can plan a dinner.

Chris' address is the same—care of the Arkansas Gazette, Little Rock.

Love to you all, Daddy

[Katie Kazan graduated from the George School in 1966 and briefly attended Antioch College in Yellow Springs, Ohio. In 1954 the House Committee on Un-American Activities investigated complaints of communist activity in the Yellow Springs area and cited an uncooperative Antioch instructor for contempt of Congress. The free speech movement, civil rights, and opposition to the Vietnam War swept the campus in the 1960s, to the detriment of the institution—later reformers claimed.] *TLS, 2 pp., KKP*

TO KATHARINE KAZAN

SH: Bristol Hotel Kempinski, Berlin
PM: Cairo, January 23, 1966

Well you can see that I dont care where I steal writing paper and envelopes. Well they get it free anyway, in the one case from Olympic airlines, and the other from the Dresdner Bank. Now, I'm in Egypt, Cairo, reading Alan Moorehead's THE BLUE NILE which is a wonderful book, and recounts the history of this very territory. Yesterday I had a very reflective day. I went out to the Pyramids—about a ten mile ride on a bus—and sat there most of the day, waiting for the Sphinx to speak. Her expression actually is enigmatic. I mean she "gives" nothing. They've built a sort of tourist trap all around the tombs, the pyramids and the Sphinx and I drank a lot of their real bad tea. But my stomach wasn't too good, perhaps the first hints of diarrhea, so I didn't eat anything. The night before, however, I'd had a heavily spiced Egyptian style dinner. The Egyptians? I dont have much of an impression so far, other than they do put a lot of energy trying to get the better of you in minor transactions, like cab rides, and restaurant bills. This unfortunately distracts them from other more important tasks like keeping the city clean. Well, the above is not entirely accurate, they have built up the city quite a lot, skyscraper hotels by Hilton and luxury apartments etc. And it is a very beautiful setting. The Nile is a broad river, almost as wide as the Mississippi at New Orleans, and is full of very colorful traffic, sailboats and so on. (The chamber maid just bawled me out for working on Sundays. She says she doesn't except today with the national holiday on, the hotel insisted. She is Catholic—they even got here—and she objects on principle to people working on the Holy Day. She says she will not even cook on Sundays. Poor husband.) Anyway here I am, in a room overlooking the Nile, and taking it real easy. I'm going to stay here a few more days, and if B meets me here, I'll wait for her, and if she doesn't, and will only in Nairobi, I'll go on and spend a couple of days in Addis Ababa. That's Ethiopia, you ignorant girl! And then on to the Safari. It appears to be definite now that Cronyn will come along with me, or us. He seems to be making a documentary for sure, and sent me a long log book of his days. He must have got some pretty good shots, from the way he describes them. I'll stick to still cameras. I'm going to have one loaded with color at all times, and the other with tri-X for dawn, dusk, and storm. *** I think the red mill is being sold at last. As you can imagine, I'm awful glad to get it off my neck. I dont know who's buying it. I didn't even ask. Molly bought it so that we could control the neighbors we have up there. But I got so fed up with keeping up with its natural disintegration, and spending money on it, that now, at the end, I dont give a damn about anything so long as I get out of it the money I put into it, and dont have to take care of it further. Write me.

Love Daddy

[Kazan acquired "paper and envelopes" while visiting East Berlin, Vienna, Belgrade, and Athens. In Cairo he discussed plans for a sequel to *America America* with an official of the state-owned production company. Old Cairo resembled the Anatolian town of his father's birth and seemed a perfect substitute for out-of-bounds Istanbul. Alan Moorehead's account of French, Turkish, and British imperialism in *The Blue Nile* (1962) gave Kazan a passing idea for a "costume epic" dealing with Egyptian history. He also explored a project based on *The Autobiography of Malcolm X* (1965)—in an early planning stage with Alex Haley and James Baldwin.] *TLS, 1 p., KKP*

TO KATHARINE KAZAN

SH: New Stanley Hotel, Nairobi-Kenya
PM: Nairobi, February 19, 1966

Dear KK

Well we're back from the biggest part of our safari. We have about five days more in an opposite direction, so we passed thru Nairobi and had a night in the hotel and all that goes with that. I washed my hair, believe it or not. We're having a wonderful time. We've seen over a hundred lions, and all kinds of other animals, close up and in all kinds of states of mind. Its really unforgettable, and you must do it some day, not too late in life. I wish I'd done it some twenty years ago, but then I was too busy working to enjoy the world. The animals are fascinating. They're so much like human beings. At least I think so. B doesn't. She thinks they behave differently. I look at them and I see my human acquaintances and so on. One of the nicest things we saw was the affection displayed in a "pride" of lions, one for the other. They really have a family feeling. No matter how fierce and ruthless they get when they hunt, they seem extremely affectionate when they've fed and feel at ease. One remarkable thing is how they take cars for granted. And their passengers. If you're in a car, they pay no attention. You can get very close. It frightened me at first. But I've gotten used to it now. They barely look at you. In fact what they seem is disdainful. The King of Beasts. Our hunter, Tony Archer, says that the real King of beasts is the elephant. The elephant walks without challenge. No one dares challenge him. No one challenges a lion in its pride either. The big animals respect each other, and just go by each other. The worst disposition is that of the Rhino. This may be because he cant see too well. Any animal is mean when she is a female and has cubs. The last couple of days we were following some Cheetah. They are the most beautiful animals in motion of all. Their run is very fast and seemingly effortless. In fact, however, they tire after about a sprint of one hundred and fifty yards, and quit. All the big cats are sprinters. We watched the Cheetah hunt for one entire day, and though they twice tried very earnestly to get a Wildebeast calf, they failed both times. Once the mother and aunts of the calf got around it and protected it. The other time, the Cheetah couldn't get quite close enough to feel confident that their surge would carry them to the prey. That is the whole tactic—to get close enough. And the tactic of the herbivores is to make sure no predator gets that close. As long as they keep one hundred yards between them, they are safe. Over a longer distance, they can outrun the cats. Interesting, what?

Love. Love. Daddy

[Barbara Loden joined Elia (and Hume Cronyn and Jessica Tandy) in Nairobi and acquitted herself in a way that changed their relationship: "I realized I had something special in that girl. She was a lot tougher than I, and in a crisis of lions—or any other kind of animal, as three muggings on the streets of New York would later verify—she could hold her own. I was the chicken-hearted one, she the lioness-hearted." In effect "she established an equality between us, certainly in the more essential human virtues. Ours was a union confirmed in stages and consummated without our awareness" (*A Life,* pp. 743–44). They married in June 1967.

Kazan made passing reference to safari in *The Arrangement* (novel and film) and extensive use in *The Understudy* (1975), a later novel.] *TLS, 1 p., KKP*

TO SI-LAN CHEN AND JAY LEYDA

[New York]
March 16, 1966

Dear Chen and Jay:

I'm awfully glad you liked the films. And you can continue the Festival anytime you want, wherever you are. Did you see "Face In The Crowd"? Did you see "Viva Zapata"?

You should see these two next. And then "Wild River". And then "Baby Doll". You ought to see those pictures. I can arrange them to be shown to you in Paris I'm sure and possibly in London—although I'm not on the best terms with Warner Brothers at the moment. But I sure as hell will try. And if you do go to Paris, I will arrange them there. You should see them. I think you would like them too. I wish you were coming here. I'd like to see more of both of you.

What the father says in "America America" is not my opinion. I feel the same way, Chen, about that as you do. That's the only way the man can live with himself. Like many people in an oppressed minority, he has got to believe—

that is the only way he can exist. I am working on the sequel now. But first I have to get my novel out.

Do you ever go anywhere except East Berlin? Can you write me what's happening there? What happened with the big crisis in the art world there? I would like to hear. Let's keep in contact. If you write me, I'll write you. I'll also be back in East Berlin—but not before a year, probably the same time next winter. I became very fond of Felsenstein this time and would like to see him again.

I had nothing to do with the Ghana coup. But I must tell you on the way to Africa I read a book by Nkrumah—a very flattering book about him—and I was completely enlisted by him, especially by his own writing. What happened? Explain that to me. I understand the animals best. Both the herbivores and the predators. Anyway, I never got to Ghana. The day we were going was the day of the military coup and no planes were going in—so we just gave it up.

Fond greetings to you both, Gadg

[Jay Leyda studied film theory and direction with Sergei Eisenstein in Moscow and in 1936 accepted a curatorial position with the Museum of Modern Art. A notable historian of Russian and Chinese cinema, he also compiled influential life studies of Herman Melville and Emily Dickinson. Si-Lan Chen, his wife, studied dance in London and Moscow, performed internationally, and worked as a choreographer in Hollywood in the 1940s. Precisely when Leyda and Kazan met is unclear, but in 1937 they joined as director (Leyda) and assistant in filming *People of the Cumberland* (Frontier Films).

The father Isaac rationalizes his accommodation of the Turk in *America America:* "'Stavros, I have always kept my honor safe inside me. Safe inside me! And, you see, we're still living. After a time you don't feel the shame.'"

Kazan attended performances of the Komische Oper in East Berlin, the "best" in the world, he thought, and was invited by the director Walter Felsenstein to mount a production of *Carmen*. Leyda conducted film research in East Berlin in the 1960s and was conversant with the politically charged artistic scene.

President Kwame Nkrumah was deposed before Kazan could visit Ghana in search of background for the Malcolm X project. Nkrumah's Pan-Africanism had "enlisted" Malcolm X, whose visit to Ghana in 1964 was received with enthusiasm and recorded in the *Autobiography*.] *TLS, 2 pp., NYU*

TO JUDY KAZAN MORRIS

[Sandy Hook, Connecticut]
[April 1966]

Judy dear:
Well the fact is that Newtown Productions is going to own a little piece (1/6th) of the Miller Theatre. Here's how that happened. Its interesting. A corporation

(Newtown Prod Inc.) is supposed to use its money, not sit on it. If it doesn't, then after a year or two the Fed Govt goes after it and takes big size bites out of its corporate ass. This law was devised to keep the economy rolling and to keep employment up. Newtown made some money just once, on a thing called Splendor in the Grass, not one of my favorite pictures, but a modest box office success. Newtown had about two hundred thousand dollars. And as Uncle Sam's greedy hand got closer and closer, the time became shorter and shorter to do something, to make that money "go to work" (lawyers are always talking about putting money to work) Several schemes were thought of by Fitelson (I, personally, wouldn't give it a thought, had already resigned myself to losing the money) among them to buy some old G man films for TV "exposure" and etc. All the schemes fell thru. Fitelson "wouldn't let me" (another lawyer's phrase) buy the TV films unless he could, at the same time, make a deal for their sale. But he couldn't. Its also just the least bit illegal. Money, in the Capitalist bible, must be risked. Risk, that's the thing. Well then now up came this idea of the Miller. That at least is real estate. Its there. And it can depreciate in value, but not a hell of a lot. And there is always the hope that some broadcast company can take it for mounting their TV specials and etc for a ten year period, in which case we might even make money. Who knows. Ho hum. Well all I can say for it is that its better than letting the govt have the money. That's been my "thinking" (another lawyer's phrase) on this. *** Otherwise I have hardly any interest in N.Y. I've been in about a half a day a week for the last three weeks. I just stay out here, and plant my garden. And work on my book. There's still a lot of work on that. It just depends how good I want to make it, and how much patience I've got, or spiritual stickum / Anyway, to date, I'm still at it. Fitelson, meantime (is he in my life!) is still negotiating with this publisher and that. Random House wants to publish it and they have a lot more power than Stein who also wants to publish it. Fitelson showed the first draft to Dell (paper-backs) and they want to publish it too. They have the following advantage over Stein—namely they can give me a big guarantee ($100000, says the same Fitel-son) spread, which means in something like 5-20000 installments. I'd like that because it would amount to a subsidy and allow me to stay up here on the farm and continue my present way of life. On the other hand I had enough to con-tinue my present way of life anyway, even without Dell, for quite a few years. The advantages to Stein are that he published AA, and I wouldn't have a guilty feeling of having by-passed a man who had once done me good. But he can-not give an advance. What I really need is a good editor, who will be as tough with me as MDTK used to be. Stein is pretty good, and maybe excellent. But I don't know others. The editor at Random House who read it is a guy named Epstein. Did you read the N. Y. Times article on the Literary Establishment. He was designated as its "Robespierre". He agrees with me that it doesn't need an awful lot of cutting. Stein thinks it does. Fitelson thinks it should be cut in half. That's when I get tired of Fitelson when he has literary opinions contrary to my own. On the other hand, he may be right Yuk Yuk! I'm sort of enjoying it all. Don't forget June 4th. KK's grad. June 27th. I drive her to Yellow Springs Ohio (Antioch). I bought us a new VW Station wagon so we could take her baggage out. I may go on from there to see Chris. If Fitelson will let me. Love and that's to all. Glad to hear about the weight gaining. Name?

[The press reported in mid-April that Bill Fitelson was negotiating on behalf of Kazan and other investors to buy the Henry Miller Theatre on West Forty-third Street—asking price $650,000. Eventually the Nederlander family of Detroit purchased the building from Mrs. Gilbert Miller for $500,000 with the stipulation that its original name and use as a legitimate theater be maintained. From 1946 to 1980, years which encompass Kazan's productive career, the "Fed Govt" tax rate fell slowly from 91 to 70 percent for annual wage earners above $250,000.

Kazan completed a third and final draft of *The Arrangement* in September and entrusted publication once again to Stein and Day. Jason Epstein of Random House was dubbed the "Robespierre of the paperback revolution" and regarded as a presiding member of New York's intellectual society.

Judy and Jonas Morris named their second child Willa Day—born on March 17, 1966.] *TL, 1 p., KKP*

TO ELEANOR PERRY

[New York]
[c. January1967]

Dear E:

Glad you enjoyed the champagne. We'll have some together when you two get back.

I hope that film works out for you. I spent an evening with Mastroianni once. He's intelligent, very. Especially for an actor. I know Frank will enjoy working with him. He made a great comment on Miller's AFTER THE FALL. He liked the first act, but couldn't understand the second. (the one about Miller's "trouble" with MM) "All that trouble about a woman!" he marveled. It was incomprehensible to an Italian.

I'll let Barbara write or tell you about the S.S. matter herself. But Sam didn't even pay her the courtesy of "manipulating Barbara into an impossible position" and so on. He just had his secretary call her twice to tell her that he would call her in a day or two. Then there was a silence. And finally Sam had jolly Roger, the producer, call and beat about the bush for a while (B. on the phone way ahead of him) and then tell her that they were going to get someone else. That was it. They call it old world courtesy.

Yes he is invited to the party. The list was made up by Sol and looked over by me before all the above happened. But in some quiet moment before during or after, I will tell him what I think of what he did. Not that it will do the least good. His behaviour is hard concrete—and on the nose for that generation of producers, classic. Jack Warner would play it the same way. And L.B. Dont let the human interfere. And above all dont cut off one director before you have another—or writer or actress. And let your sec'y tell the lies and get a hireling to drop the axe, so that you yourself never fog your aureole of culture and gentility. Notice Spiegel calls business meetings with artists <u>chats</u>? As for Barbara, she's been around a long time and her reaction was realistic: she said she didn't expect anything different or better from Spiegel. And wont ever. No surprises for that chick. That's why when they get to be successful and therefore powerful they turn into Joan Crawford, ball breakers, and Burt Lancaster, producer-killers. [*Omission*] is road company of that. The terrible thing for the girls is that that toughness shows on their face after a little. They look "worn". The men can get away with it (Bogart), but girls lose their girlness. They aren't feminine anymore. That community out there is a community of monsters. They prong, knife, slice, double-deal, maim and kill each other all day long, meet in the restaurants or parties at night and embrace, pair off and go home to prong, knife and etc. Its been so described a thousand times and its a cliche by now, but no less true. You just have to live your life elsewhere, in your own country. One reason I started writing books. As for Barbara, I think if she hadn't been secure with me, it might have upset her a lot. Imagine hanging your life on Spiegel's favor!! Anyway it was real nice of you both to write her. Thanks.

May everything go wonderfully for you both. See you when you get back and look forward to it.

Love, E.K.

[*The Swimmer* is based on John Cheever's well-known story of an aging "voyager," who proposes to reach his home in suburban Connecticut by swimming the pools of friends and a former mistress—played initially by Barbara Loden. Eleanor and her husband Frank Perry wrote, directed, and produced the film in association with Sam Spiegel and Columbia Pictures. The Perrys found "jolly Roger" Lewis, Spiegel's producer, unsuitable for the role, while Burt Lancaster, cast as the delusional swimmer, was unimpressed by Frank Perry's direction and resented Spiegel's distant relationship with the project. Disappointed by the rough cut, Spiegel conferred with Kazan regarding dramatic shortcomings in Loden's key scene with Lancaster. His advice to find a new "'attack, a creative key,'" was overlooked and Loden dismissed. The Perrys left the project when Spiegel hired Janice Rule to film retakes under new direction. Released in 1968, *The Swimmer* failed commercially but was thought an interesting experiment (Fraser-Cavassoni, pp. 283–88). Sam Spiegel did not attend the pre-publication party for *The Arrangement* on February 6.] *TLS, 1 p., Herrick*

TO ALEX HALEY

[New York]
February 3, 1967

Dear Alex:

I checked on Palca immediately but I only checked with one person, a friend of mine who's a theatrical lawyer. His advice was stay away from him. This doesn't mean he's right. It's just one man's opinion.

But may I say something to you about all this. The least of our problems is going to be getting financing and a sponsor. We are going to get the money and we are going to get auspices. It's fun to play around with that kind of thing. And it's very flattering having someone pursuing you at this stage of the game. It's courtship. But I just want to make this point, Alex, that we will get much much better terms when we have a strong script in hand. The danger in these situations is to act too early, too hastily, too anxiously. I mean if it will be fun for you to have lunch with Mr. Palca, go ahead. If I were you, all I would say to him is the three of us are going to work on it as a play and when we get the play done we will be thinking about sponsorship, auspices, financing and so on, but, at the moment, that's ahead of us. Just relax. A word of caution about Jimmy again. Jimmy, as you know, loves to be courted and, sure as hell, Palca will be after him. He'll have to push a lot of others out of the way and that's fun for Jimmy. And I guess fun for anyone. But this kind of talk is really twaddle. Just like detailed talk about casting too early. It's usually the authors way of avoiding a genuine problem, which is making the script good. You will see with Jimmy just like all authors—he is no exception—every time you get stuck on the script he'll start talking about who should play Betty and so on and so on. The simple fact is that we only have one problem which is to get a complete manuscript that is sound and worthy of your book—and that is going to be quite a job. Jimmy is a slippery fish. I don't mean he's fishy—I mean he's slippery. He will be jumping all over the place you'll see. Fortunately you and I are persistent and have some talent for slogging as well as everything else. But I think that again and again we are going to have to turn Jimmy around and point him to the table with the typewriter on it. Incidentally, this is exactly what went wrong with "Blues For Mr. Charlie". He had two-thirds of a play. The last act was a disgraceful affair. Of course Jimmy blamed it all on the producers and directors and actors. But the simple fact was he had no last act.

As I say if you want to meet with Palca go ahead—but I'm against doing anything at all until we have three acts in hand.

Affectionately,

P.S. Barbara was thrilled with the cook book.

g.

[Kazan was advised to "stay away" from Alfred Palca, writer-producer of *The Harlem Globetrotters* (1951) and *Go Man Go* (1954). His blacklisting in 1953 precluded film production and required that *Go Man Go* be credited to a stand-in. Shortly before his death in 1998, Palca described himself as an "'old lefty'" who was "'for the underdog.'" More eligible figures would soon bargain with Alex Haley and Malcolm's widow, Betty Shabazz, for production rights to *The Autobiography of Malcolm X* (1965).

The Autobiography is based on extensive interviews and notes woven by Alex Haley into a narrative ending with Malcolm's assassination on February 21, 1965. Kazan met with Haley and Baldwin in late 1966 when Baldwin returned to the States from Istanbul, but it was not until the following spring that he finished a novel in progress and began the Malcolm play (Lemming, pp. 284–88).

Barbara Loden's gift recalls Alex Haley's early career as a mess attendant in the Coast Guard. He enlisted in 1939 and retired with Chief Journalist rating in 1959.]
TLS, 2 pp., Wesleyan

TO JAMES BALDWIN

[New York]
February 17, 1967

Dear Jimmy:

Very relieved about Brando. He sounds shook up. I heard a terrible thing yesterday from a fellow who worked with him at Fox on a picture called "Morituri". Marlon couldn't remember his lines. Jesus that's awful. I wonder what he does all day? Where he moves and why? I'm worried about him. I've been trying to defend him on some TV and radio shows here. A fellow named Bill Redfield wrote a book about him saying that he was washed up. Has it ever occurred to you that people have a need to kill each other? I don't know why Redfield would want to publicly assassinate Marlon but I thought he did. And I'm sorry to say it generally applies even to people in the theatre. They are so eager to write him off. I know he's shaky, but can you write anyone off with that much talent and that much sweetness in him?

I've gotten to know Haley very well and like him enormously. Don't hurry but we will be waiting for you when you get back. I'm sorry about your book but reading your letter it seemed to me that perhaps this was just temporary. Maybe you are just tired. I hope so. I wish I could have dinner with you tonight. Haley, Barbara and I are going to see a film taken of one of Lenny Bruce's acts and then we are going to a Jewish restaurant. Do you want us to send you anything from here of any kind? Is there anything we can do for you? Did you see Yasar? Be sure to do so some time and give him my love. I sort of miss Turkey. I felt terribly at home there—good reasons.

The book's going well. It's going to be number ten on the N.Y. Times best seller list the day before publication. I'm prostituting myself by going on every radio show and TV show I can get on and pushing it. The New York Times and the WJT assigned some bound-to-be-unfriendly reviewers to it. I checked the guys out—I know who they are. I'm not paranoid believe me. Did you hear the story about the man who went to the psychiatrist and said, Dr. what's the name of that disease when you think everybody is persecuting you and they are?

But the book is going well. My son, Nick, is the one who thinks I'm prostituting myself. He would like me to stay home and just be confident. But I don't like the sight of my own blood. Playboy half murdered, half scorned the book. It really got my temperature up. Book Week was extremely sniffy about the style and so forth—that got me burned up too. There will be more of that I know, but we've also gotten some excellent notices and my fighter puss is on the cover of the Saturday Review. I'm glad about this mostly for my mother. She reads the Saturday Review.

Eileen tells me I told you some of this in yesterday's letter, but you don't mind reading it again. I told my mother that you were in Bebek. She used to summer there long, long ago.

Love,

[William Redfield joined other critics in dismissing such inferior roles as Marlon Brando played in the World War Two film *Morituri* (1965). The actor and former intimate friend of Brando's deplored the transformation of a brilliant theatrical talent into "a commodity, a product on a shelf—which is all a movie star can ever be" (*NYT*, January 15, 1967).

Sol Stein's promotion of *The Arrangement* began with a reception aboard the *France* (berthed at Forty-eighth Street) followed by a buffet dinner at Brentano's for an intimate gathering of four hundred. Neither glib criticism in the popular press—"celluloid simplicity," "old wine in old bottles," a "muddled, massive mistake"—nor condescending reviews in the *New York Times* could dent the popularity of *The Arrangement,* which held first or second place on the best-seller list for thirty weeks. Stein exploited library censorship in Mount Pleasant, Iowa, by offering a free copy to every head of household. Eight hundred accepted. Kazan sold film rights to Warner Bros. in June for a reported $500,000.

James Baldwin reviewed *The Arrangement* while finishing a difficult autobiographical novel—*Tell Me How Long the Train's Been Gone* (1968)—in which Kazan appears as the director Konstantine "Connie" Rafaeleto. Baldwin's fictional counterpart regards him as a man who "tried to live by his convictions." Far from being "sniffy" about style, Baldwin found the "tone" of *The Arrangement* "extremely striking." The book does "not seem to depend on anything that we think of as a literary tradition, but on something older than that: the tale being told by a member of the tribe to the tribe. It has the urgency of a confession and the stammering authority of a plea." He placed Eddie Anderson's relationship with his Greek father at the center of the novel's moral argument. His "gallant" wife is treated without "hostility," but her "limits are subtle and deadly" and very much a product of the culture that surrounds her (*New York Review of Books,* May 23, 1967).] *TL, 2 pp., Wesleyan*

TO MARLON BRANDO

[New York]
[July 12, 1967]

Dear Marlon:

I first wrote this note to myself. But after I read it over I thought I should send it to you—without deleting anything. It says what's on my mind more clearly than I could hope to in a face to face conversation. I also believe we are close enough for me to do this. Even if we weren't, I'd have to—in this situation— lay out everything I've been thinking for you to look at. Obviously this is no ordinary picture for me. I want to talk to you at length. But I think it's better if you read this letter first.

When I went to Warner Brothers with my novel, I had chosen them over Fox and Paramount because I'd had good experiences with them as far as my freedoms went. They didn't supervise or press; they didn't even see the rushes. And I have always had, with them, complete say on casting. They wouldn't give me that right on this picture. They insisted on approval of the leading man. It soon became obvious that I would have to agree to this if I went elsewhere too; it was the deal everywhere.

With Warners, at least, it had something to do with you. They anticipated— correctly—that I would probably turn to you first. They had resistance to this—in fact resistance to a degree that shocked me. I hadn't been around film-making for four years, so I was totally unprepared for the way Warners felt.

Now I can deal with this. I'm not going to make this picture, or any other, with a cast NOT of my choosing. But here's the rest of the story. I think when you have been in good form, you have been the best actor we have. Now I want to go into the "buts". These—"buts"—first came up in my mind consciously when we talked at the St. Regis bar. You said to me then that you'd lost a lot of your feeling for acting, that there were now other things you preferred doing. I asked you to read my book. You did quickly and called me and said some warm things. I asked if you might be interested in doing it, and you sort of hesitated and said that you weren't sure you were right for it, but that you might "take a stab at it." This reaction upset me.

I remembered <u>On the Waterfront</u> where you told me repeatedly while we were shooting the picture that you weren't enthusiastic about it and were only making the picture "because your psychoanalyst was in New York" and that you wanted to make enough to pay his bills while still remaining in that city. I told my wife, Barbara, about this and she said just about what I was thinking, she said, "Oh, that's the way actors are, don't pay any attention to that—" and then she said, "Especially sensitive people."—which is what I thought more or less.

But then I read a bit in a newspaper and—well, I differ from more rational men in that I always believe columns. Someone said—whatever it is that is being dramatized or exaggerated in the column—there is some element of truth—she probably IS fucking him, he probably IS fucking her—you know? Anyway, you or your press agent or your agent must have said something that made this writer say that Mr. Brando didn't think that he was really right for the part.

I was meeting with Warners all the time in those days going into the "fine print" aspects of our deal, and they kept bringing up the question of the leading man choice. They made many of the sort of absolute statements that traders make and I didn't pay too much attention. But they asked me to "convince" myself and see <u>Countess from Hong Kong</u> and <u>Reflections in a Golden Eye</u>. Their point was not about your talent, but two other things, first, that you'd become terribly heavy, and second, that you were just "going through the motions" now. The big man there kept saying, "He's not the same fellow you're thinking of. He's another man."

Well, I saw the Chaplin film and all I could say was that they were right, that you were terribly overweight, in fact to the point where you did not seem to be "the same fellow". And they were right about your indifference—that's the word I'd choose to describe your performance in that film. You had told me the story behind the Chaplin film, so I was prepared to a degree for what I saw. But it affected me anyway. I thought, "Christ, I'm too damned old and this particular picture is too important for me to PUSH anyone into it or through it." . . .

In the years since <u>Waterfront</u> I found out one thing—it is that I'm a mediocrity—even worse—except when I'm stirred in some basic respect with enthusiasm. I also found out—at the Lincoln Centre Repertory Theatre—how corrosive on me the lack of enthusiasm in the people I'm working with can be. You said to me on the phone, "Well, I might take a stab at it." Well, I thought to myself, I'm too damned old now to <u>pump up</u> an actor I'm working with. I need ALL of that energy for the main things, the real problems, which are enormous here.

Of course, I thought, enthusiasm is often more professed than felt, and I'm by nature quite suspicious of euphoric gargle, but still—I thought—on this one, which is so damned hard, and which I hope will say so much, I'm damned well going to give myself something: an actor that comes to work each morning eagerly, full of desire, like a young man coming up, not someone tired of his trade or disillusioned, or wishing he was something else not an actor. As they say in the fight racket, I promised myself that this time I'd get me some one who "came to fight."

I began to think—well, if Marlon says he's not right for this, think a minute, he may <u>not</u> be right. I thought about that. And true, the first part of this story is different than anything I've seen you do. Eddie, at the beginning of the film comes on strong, sells, sells himself even more than the product, has an eager aggressive, pushy front. He doesn't lie back and react, etc. Even the rest of the part wouldn't be dead easy for you. But I concluded as before—at the top of your form, the absolute top, you'd be the best guy I knew for it, if, that is, you'd be willing and eager to break down some old habits and go some directions that were new for you, in effect enlarge yourself. "But a man would have to like acting to do that," I thought, "He says he doesn't anymore."

I'm not holding any brief for acting. I'm not sure it's the thing that would give you the greatest sense of fulfillment and dignity and worth in your life. What you're doing for the UN seems more that sort of thing. But that's abstract thinking—after all, what I care about—underline <u>I</u>—is this film. This means a lot to me thematically, no matter what it means to anyone else.

Then I saw <u>Reflections in a Golden Eye</u>. And I admired you. Without any real help from Huston (he seems to direct to make everybody "characters," thus, in a subtle way, patronizing them) you were bold and daring, and made a most difficult part moving and human. I know it was tough to do so I admired you more. But what I said about your looks in <u>Countess from Hong Kong</u> was even more true here. You looked like "a different person." Physically, I see Eddie like this: Some people when they are troubled, anxious and full of self disgust, eat a lot. Others get thin. Eddie is of the second group.

Now I don't really know whether you want to go back to the way you were—as far as weight goes. It's very tough after forty as I know from my own experience. And except for a kind of vanity, there isn't much point to it. It means cutting out a lot of the more enjoyable things in life. Christ, I won't urge it on you. But I don't want Eddie plump. Also since so much of his pain is brought out through sex, there is something about the hefty or plump image that goes against this. I can't afford to deceive myself about this.

I kept remembering that you said in the St. Regis bar that you didn't really want to act any more. Well, if you don't, who can blame you? Not me. It's a loss to the films, a big one, but a man has to choose his own way. But at the same time, part of really being an actor is to keep in training, to keep in shape, to stay "a certain way," you might say, proud of the image you present. And especially in a part like this. So you see, I'm not trifling with this picture. That's why there is a chance that it might be a good one. I care about it.

But just as I'm not kidding you in this letter, don't kid me now. I'll like you just as much personally (I have some love for you, which is deeper than I understand; the word "like" doesn't cover it) if you tell me: "I don't really want to break my balls anymore." I'll admire you for saying this if it's true.

But I'm speaking my piece now, not yours, and I only want to do this film with you if you really like the book, if it really means something to you, if you are genuinely enthusiastic about it, if it is in effect your story, if you'll hazard ALL on it, and finally if you will be available some ten months from now back at the weight you used to be in during On the Waterfront. Don't kid me—be a true friend and don't kid me in either respect.

When I saw that Chaplin film—and the other too, where I admired you—I said to myself—if I didn't know you, if I didn't know a LOT about you, I'd never consider you for my part. But I know from our conversation in the St. Regis, that you are still very living, that if you really want to, you can be a blazing actor again. The wanting is the hard part.

Love,

[Warner Bros. probably arranged a preview of *Reflections in a Golden Eye* (released later in 1967) to " 'convince' " Kazan of Marlon Brando's liability. Nonetheless he continued to recruit Brando with an appeal based on the professional challenge of playing Eddie Anderson, who passes through submissive and rebellious phases to realize his identity. Brando's wavering interest in *The Arrangement* ended with the assassination of Martin Luther King on April 4, 1968. A final meeting between actor and director occurred in Los Angeles: "King had been shot, and this had made Marlon fear for our future. I agreed that it was a terrible tragedy. We went on talking, standing in the parking area. He was so intense and so convincing that I didn't realize he'd walked me back to my car and opened the door to help me in. Before I got behind the wheel, he informed me that he simply couldn't do the part in my movie. At which he kissed me and looked so sorry I didn't ask any questions but drove away" (*A Life*, p. 752).

With Brando's refusal, Barbara Loden no longer "fit" the role of Gwen Ward and it was given to Faye Dunaway, her former understudy in *After the Fall*. Resentment prevailed, or so Kazan claimed.] *TL, 6 pp., Wesleyan*

TO JAMES BALDWIN

[New York]
November 29, 1967

For chrissake Jimmy, what the hell has it got to do with your place in my heart or my place in yours? Sure I love you, I truly do! I will always have a feeling of love for you. But that doesn't prevent me from hollering like hell when you do something I think wrong, or telling you about it as I feel it. And it's not a matter of believing what I read in the papers either.

Fitelson was the first. He talked to your agent, Lantz, and Lantz told him that the book and your services had been sold to films (Stuart Rosenberg) and to forget it. Then Abe Lastfogel called me from California and said did I know that it was about to be sold (About to be. Lastfogel is not a liar; Lantz is. Lastfogel, who incidentally represents Stuart Rosenberg but is my friend, was telling me to move fast to protect the "property" if I wanted it. Lantz was jockeying the book and you into the biggest commission he could get for himself.) To Lastfogel I said, "Don't worry, I have been meeting with Baldwin and Haley, we had a weekend conference in Long Island and nothing was said about a movie negotiation. That rumor is without foundation." Then, however, Fitelson got me and said, "You've been taken! I heard from Lantz again," he said, "and it's over. Forget it!"

That was when I called you and got your "how-can-you-doubt-me" over the phone. I believed you. I relaxed. And you went to California. I asked you, do you remember, "What the hell are you going to California for, why don't you start writing, time is short." 'You had to see some people' you said. And you did see some people.

Next thing was Ted Mann. He came in and said he wanted to be in on the play. I said there were others interested, but for him to talk to you and then you and I would consult. I was sizing him up. He cut that adventure in psychological research short, coming back with the word from (That Liar) Lantz to the effect that it had been really and truly and finally sold to films, and you had gone with it, in fact, received a certain amount of money and Betty some, and that it was for the good of the children. (Who couldn't sympathize with that?) So then I began to wonder, maybe I'm in for the Blues For Mr. Charlie Treatment again, there will be some good reason for it all, and I will bow my Anatolian head in resignation and smile, and in my heart say, "Write your own material, buster, so you don't have to play anti-room to these authors ever again."

The clincher came through Hal Prince. When you originally told me to find a producer who could give you an advance, I contacted Prince. It took him a while to read it, but when he did he went for the project altogether. He thought it was ridiculous that you were fooling with the motion picture studios; he said he could give you and Betty an advance himself (not on movie scale, but good for New York). Well by now, as I said, the message from T.L. Lantz had beaten me down and I had to begin to believe it. Prince said he'd speak to Lantz. Lantz (T.L.) told him to forget it, the Autobiography of MX was no longer available for stage adaptation and production. (This is your agent talking, kiddo, not the N.Y. Times, not a gossip columnist, and he's talking to one of the best producers currently on the street, and to me.) So Prince talked to me and we decided, for the hell of it, <u>not</u> to give up. We asked Lantz to find out if Columbia was interested in a play to be done <u>before their</u> movie. The answer came back—in a note that I saw from T.L.—No!! They were in no way interested in any kind of stage production. Period. P.S. from Lantz, unspoken: Will you forget it, for chrissake?!

Jimmy, I thought, may have sold the movie rights without knowing it. Technically, that's impossible because Alex and Betty would have to sign. Yes. Right! But perhaps Big Bobby made what's known as a "handshake deal" for his client, Baldwin. For chrissake—<u>something</u> has happened! Then I got your letter and I figured it out.

You propose to sell the movie rights now, right, and then make a play—do the play script, then do the movie script. Is that it? If that is it, let me disillusion you. No stage producer will put up the cash necessary to produce the play IF THERE ARE NO MOVIE RIGHTS FOR THE PLAY PRODUCER. Why should they? It's an expensive production on a "ticklish" subject. Furthermore, there is another movie on the subject being written now by Louis Lomax and about to be produced by Fox. That doesn't help the play production either. Anyway, Prince is not interested, and I'm not if there is going to be a movie contracted for, at the same time, or earlier, and if the producer is therefore going to be excluded from his share of the movie rights. That's your right to do—but forget me and forget Prince. This is a case of you can't have both, my friend.

And now my personal opinion. With love. I think you will be happiest, finally, in the long run, if you don't get involved with agents, studios and movie people on this yet. In my opinion there is no way any big movie company, no matter what they tell you, can put on the screen what you and your conscience—not to mention the pressures of the times and Negro America—must needs put on the screen. What's the use of fooling yourself? Sit down and write a work of literature in play form. You're going to do this just once in your life. Stop worrying about how long it will take to write, too. Do it with all your energy and all your talent and with as much time as this project needs. You went to England to get quiet—and cab courtesy—and to write this. It's not a job, not an assignment, not a "property," not a wrangle. It's not someone else's anything. It's yours, your big challenge—a subject so big and so important that any artist can only ask: Am I good enough? Can I do it justice? What you are going to make is a work of art—not Warners', not Columbia's, not Richard Brooks', not Stuart Rosenberg's, not mine—but James Baldwin's statement (through Malcolm) of what he feels now about the most important subject in the world now. How good this play is depends not on the subject—but on how good <u>you</u> can be. You may make false starts and go back, you may louse it up and have to start over. A play is not an easy thing to write. So forget about time. Forget about doing it this spring (It should be done in the early fall anyway.) Just write the best play you are capable of writing. Then put it away for a couple of weeks, maybe show it to whoever you want to direct it (this would be the case in re a movie, too) and whoever you trust—outside show business—and get a few reactions. Then go over it again. You're only going to do this subject once in your life. Do it so you'll be proud of it the rest of your life. Then—if you do a successful play, watch them come for it, the movie people. They'll kill themselves to get it, and fork up much more money, too.

As for the rest, I wish, simply, that you'd keep me informed. I don't want to hear news of your doings on a project in which I have not only a strong interest but also a considerable investment of time and thought, through an agent or to read it in the papers. I think we ought to treat the people we love better, not worse, than other people. I mean we all get into difficulties and make mistakes and—as in this case—don't realize what's involved. But communicate, man. If you had told me, "Betty needs the dough, we've got to take it from Warners' or Columbia," hell, I'd understand that. And now, if you truly want to make it as a movie—or with another director on stage, I'll be disappointed, but I'll truly understand. But just tell me. Trust me to still be your friend.

With love,

EK/vml

[James Baldwin conferred with Alex Haley and Kazan in the preceding August and quickly drafted a dramatic outline of the Malcolm project entitled "One Day, When I Was Lost." Kazan's view of Baldwin as "a slippery fish" was soon confirmed by a press report (speculative, it turned out) that he was writing "a film biography of Malcolm X" for Stuart Rosenberg. Plans for a dramatic production were abandoned when Marvin Worth, an independent producer, acquired rights to *The Autobiography* and hired Baldwin to write the screenplay. He denied any role in the sale of the book and had reluctantly set aside "grave doubts and fears about Hollywood" to keep faith with Malcolm: "He had trusted me in life and I believed he trusted me in death, and that trust, as far as I was concerned, was my obligation" (Baldwin, p. 99). The assassination of Martin Luther King deepened Baldwin's commitment to an uncompromising treatment of Malcolm, as well as the determination of Columbia Pictures to avoid inflammatory rhetoric. Before abandoning the project and leaving California in 1969, Baldwin reflected on the "strange and dangerous" position of the black artist in America, especially in Hollywood, where films are "geared" to an audience imbued with "the doctrine of white supremacy" (*NYT*, February 2, 1969).

Marvin Worth produced *Malcolm X* (1972) in a documentary format with narration by James Earl Jones and extensive use of archival and interview material. Baldwin did not participate, nor was his screenplay used (Leeming, pp. 287–302). It remained for Spike Lee to draw on the earlier Baldwin-Perl script in filming *Malcolm X* (1992).] *TL, 4 pp., Wesleyan*

TO ROBERT WISE

Dear Bob:

I'm sorry this is so goddamn late. You've probably guessed what happened. On the one hand I keep going over <u>The Arrangement</u>. Last chance, I think, people say it's long, I say, you end the picture too often, I say, well, do something about it! But I don't do much. I like it the way it is, and I take an obdurate stance. I know the damned thing is long for a lot of people and I have a suspicion that in a few years I'll think it long myself. But I take out three minutes only and scowl at imaginary critics and that's the way it goes. But that all takes time. I'm beginning to wish the damned thing would open and so be taken away from me.

I'm writing you all because I know you're familiar if not with the ridiculous psychology at least with the particular moment of time that I'm in. I've been with Schulberg in Puerto Rico and if the phrasing of that reminds you of the phrase: With Livingston in deepest Africa—well it's something like. That island seems to be on the verge of a revolution, and not at all a place to make a film in. However, we're going to try. But I'm not going into that.

I thought you and Jewison and Sturgis all made sense in the meeting, and I think you three are well qualified to figure out what practical and immediate tactics we should use. I simply want to say that I think it has <u>also</u> to be approached "from the top," as it were. And with a long view.

I don't see how we can do too much contractually about the past. Maybe Sturgis knows a way. I hope so. Maybe good legal advice can find a way. I hope so. But in any larger view, their indiscriminate chopping up of our films misrepresents our work publicly and degrades our "images." It seems to me—now I'm being anything but legalistic—that when they buy a film, they buy a film. When they chop it up, they make it <u>not</u> our film, but something else. It's no longer our film.

I'm going to make a wild suggestion, one that you'll all three think a bit "cracked." I think the Directors Guild should sue the producers and sue the networks. I think we should take the lawsuit as far as the Supreme Court. I think the higher up in the courts we go with a case of this kind, the more chance we'll have to win it.

On what basis? Sooner or later someone has to maintain that there are other rights besides property rights. That, I believe is the stand we should take. All we have is our talents, our past, our films. Our present employment depends upon these factors being in good order. In short, when they hurt our public face, they hurt us. We have no more valuable property than our reputations. That is what we have, and when they demean these, they are doing us great harm. This is the reason I agreed that we should engage someone who is of sufficient standing and prestige, sufficiently broad in his vision and FINE enough so that he can present THIS kind of position.

I testified some years ago for Otto Preminger against the TV networks. Otto did pretty well. But he had two things against him. His own lawyer was a rather ordinary person—not a bad person, simply an ordinary lawyer. Sometimes he seemed almost apologetic in presenting Otto's case. I sensed that deep down, instinctively, so to speak, by his basic training too, he shared the position of most legal men that property rights are the pre-eminent rights and all others subordinate. The other thing that Otto had against him was the judge. He also wasn't a bad person. He was an ordinary man too, and without much vision. He behaved in a kindly way towards us "artists"—but in this smiling, patient attitude there was something extremely patronizing. I don't know if Otto felt it! I did.

But now several things have changed. Above all the public view towards films has changed. The public is much readier to be sympathetic towards an idealistically-based case. Public Opinion in 1970 is much readier to consider films an art, not just the "neighborhood movie." As a matter of fact, a legal fight of the kind I suggest—even if we lost it the first time around—will raise our position in the public eye to where it should be.

While our agents take our talents seriously enough when it comes down to money negotiations with the producers, studios and financiers, we directors still do not occupy the public position we should. We're getting there, but ever so slowly. Compare the position of directors in Europe! I think we should fight now to have our worth recognized. It's about time. And this issue—the mauling we get on TV, the indiscriminate, insulting, destructive mauling is the issue we should make it on.

Even at the meeting we had at the Guild that night, I felt among our own members an uncertainty, a wavering, an embarrassment to fight on any grounds except legalistic grounds. In other words, I don't think we value ourselves sufficiently! We have to begin to.

As for pictures in the future—that is a simpler fight. We've discussed that. It needs the threat of a strike action by an elite. That's just a matter of getting as many fellows as we can to go along with us. Incidentally, I checked out one more of the Eastern contingent. Otto, of course, is completely with us.

I hope the above doesn't seem too visionary—or "lofty." Or just plain silly. Actually I think it is the final practicality.

Yours,

EK/vml

[Robert Wise won Academy Awards for *West Side Story* (1961) and *The Sound of Music* (1965) and in 1971 became president of the Directors Guild of America.

Later he and Kazan collaborated in founding the Special Projects Department of the Guild.

The Arrangement was "taken away" from Kazan for a benefit performance at the Actors Studio in mid-November, but not before he reportedly cut "daring footage" of genitalia to gain at least an "R" rating by the Motion Picture Association of America.

In October Kazan and Budd Schulberg marched with students protesting ROTC activities at the University of Puerto Rico. The press quoted Kazan as being "'anti-imperialist'" and "'in sympathy'" with the protestors, although his recent arrival in San Juan gave him little understanding of local politics. He and Schulberg were conducting research and cultivating support for their collaboration on a Puerto Rican film project.

Kazan rejected a bid of $675,000 for three telecasts of *Baby Doll* in reaction to the "mauling" of *Viva Zapata!* and *Suddenly Last Summer*. CBS officials insisted on "'normal editing privileges'" and rejected Kazan's "conditions" that the film be aired uncut with commercials limited to the beginning, end, and a middle point (*Variety*, October 29 and November 26, 1969). Film rights to *Baby Doll* had reverted to Kazan in 1966.] *TL, 3 pp., Wesleyan*

With Arthur Miller and Budd Schulberg at Elia's seventieth birthday celebration

Part VII

Later Years

1970–1988

TO JAY LEYDA

PM: New York, NY, January 6, 1970

Dear Jay:

I guess that was one reason. I made the picture to disturb people, and it sure as hell did. The little biddie on NEW YORK MAG said it "embarrassed" her. Poor dear thing! The student going down on John Voight in the men's room of the movie theatre didn't embarrass her even though the cocksucker kept his glasses on during the entertainment. But that's low life, riff raff, forty-second street, derelicts! You know how depraved (still colorful) they are! But when it gets into the good old solid middle class and familiar Penates like D. Kerr and K. Douglas, its embarrassing. Well shit on my tea service! I also think they resent me for my general independence. They tried to kill the book—two terrible reviews in the NY Times. But failed. So back to the kill with all the ferocity of the intellectual-predator who's missed a kill. Oh, shit, Jay, they're all a kind of jelly. Just look at their faces sometimes. Its embarrassing, that's what it is, to be praised by them.

I'm going away for three weeks. Vacation. Also research, on the side. I dont ever really stop. That's the fun of it. But I'll be here in Feb., and will be glad to come up if only to see AEROGRAD (right!) again. I'll wait on Sembene's films. There's an excellent chance I'll be living some forty five min. from New Haven in the spring, so I imagine I might well make one of the two showings of these films you're planning.

Dont worry about not remembering as well as you used to. I have four children, which shouldn't be a problem. But I sometimes call them by the wrong name. Oh well, they're used to it now. Best to Si-lan.

As ever, yrs. etc. Elia

[The problem with Kirk Douglas, as Kazan soon realized, was an aura of invincibility either overlooked or underestimated in casting the part of an advertising executive bent on self-destruction. The scale of *The Arrangement* permitted "no exit" from such a "dreadful mistake" and reinforced Kazan's desire to film more simply (*A Life*, p. 754).

"Little biddie" Judith Crist reviewed *Midnight Cowboy* (1969) without flinching at oral sex but found "the chronicle of male menopause" in *The Arrangement* "just as embarrassing on film as it was in print" (*New York Magazine*, November 24, 1969). Her counterpart at the *New Yorker* wondered "how Kazan can talk to us about spiritual renewal" and make such "a big, cliché-riddled, false-eyelashes-in-bed, star-stoned movie?" Pauline Kael surmised that he "may be destroying his talents by the intensity of his wish for greater moral stature. To an outsider, it appears that, far from finding himself, he has been losing his way ever since he tried to become the whole show" (November 22, 1969). Vincent Canby replaced Bosley Crowther as lead reviewer for the *Times* and instituted an annual list of "The Ten

557

With Marco, Barbara Loden, and Leo

Worst Films," which included *The Arrangement* in 1969. The film had a solid opening run in New York but faded thereafter. Originally conceived as a sequel to *America America* in a projected trilogy of films, *The Arrangement* held special importance for Kazan: "I haven't gotten over being rejected so thoroughly on that one and don't think I will for a long time" (to Leyda, February 8, 1970, NYU).

Kazan visited Florida and Mexico in January and Arizona in February with attention to his forthcoming novel *The Assassins* (1972). In the Southwest he smoked pot with dropouts living in communes and began to form impressions of characters soon to be involved in a murder trial.

Leyda held a faculty position at Yale in the early 1970s and introduced Kazan to *Aerograd* (1935), a classic Soviet film directed by Alexander Dovzhenko. Ousmane Sembène, a contemporary African film director, was also of interest.] *TLS, 1 p., NYU*

TO EDWARD ALBEE

[New York]
March 11, 1970

Dear Edward:
I wish I'd never read it. It's so powerful! And it makes what I'm now writing seem inferior. I was particularly impressed with the terror and power of the ending. That will be tremendous on the screen. And those terrible years recalled—that's good to do for many reasons. What troubled me was: 1. Sometimes I felt that confrontation, vituperation and just plain put-down were

replacing story. And, 2. That the ugliness, meanness and viciousness was unrelieved. I don't see things quite that way. It's like a circle of hell, your script. But terrible people are more terrible because usually their intentions are "good" and often they are defending values they desperately prize. All evil is somehow done in the name of good. Lebensraum, even. I can see why you liked Visconti's film so much. And sometimes the high-powered furious bickering got on my nerves, so that the effect of the whole—up to the marvelous end— was fitful. But that is the main thing in a film—to have that one overwhelming thing at the end. And I loved your way-out bits. They made what you called my "occasional excesses" seem modest indeed. I'm for excesses.

At any rate, the point is that on Saturday Budd Schulberg is coming to town with the draft of our Puerto Rican movie and I fully expect to do that and it will take nine months—the way I do films now-a-days, which is doing it all. And I am still—though a bit deflated—writing on my book. So I can't take on anything at the moment. But I admire you. And wish you all luck.

I was late getting back to you because I wanted to read it in the country over the weekend in the quiet. Then I wanted to read it again, which is why the telegram yesterday.

Affectionately,

PS. I'm mailing the script back to you.

[Edward Albee based *The Death of Bessie Smith* on a widespread rumor that the blues singer was barred from segregated hospitals in Memphis and bled to death. Smith in fact was taken directly to Clarksdale, Mississippi, and admitted to a black hospital, where she died on September 26, 1937, from injuries suffered in a car accident (Albertson, pp. 215–26). Kazan loosely associated the nurse's racist views in *Bessie Smith* with Lebensraum, the desire for "living space" that informed Hitler's policy of territorial expansion and assault on Jewry. Luchino Visconti's film *The Damned* (1969) depicts the corruption of an industrial family during the rise of Nazism and may have prompted Kazan's allusion. Stage and televised productions of Albee's one-act preceded the screenplay, which apparently has not been filmed.

The "Puerto Rican movie" planned by Kazan and Budd Schulberg was based on Piri Thomas's autobiography *Down These Mean Streets* (1967). A surviving draft of the screenplay (June 15, 1972, Wesleyan) begins with the passage of the Lopez family from a life in the countryside to the crowded tenements of San Juan and New York. Their ensuing story, however grim and discouraging, was not to be "a dour, gray, unrelieved tale like ON THE WATERFRONT." The family's "humanity" and "humor" must be preserved, Kazan emphasized in correspondence with Budd Schulberg (July 6, 1973, Wesleyan). Puerto Rican groups in San Juan and New York were reluctant to support the project and lack of studio funding killed it. The collaborators courted Sam Spiegel in 1973, the "last gas pump before a thousand miles of desert," as Schulberg put it, to no avail. Kazan attributed the film's demise to controversial subject matter, "brown poverty," although he continued to clip "stuff" in hopes that he and Schulberg would "do it" one day.] *TL, 1 p., Wesleyan*

[New York]
July 15, 1970

Dear Tenn:

Eddie Kook gave me <u>The Two Character Play</u> to read and I admired you. Again. You are the truest writer I've worked with. But this play is <u>too</u> clear, too explicit. The characters keep telling us how desperate and frightened and hopeless they are till I got sick of hearing it. The facts of their condition—fantastic and symbolic—are clear enough. Members of a Company that has disappeared, abandoned, with no place to stay, no hope ahead, constantly forgetting what they're supposed to say and do and even be—we understand. I continuously wished that you weren't so intent on making us appreciate their condition in terms of absolutes. I wished the play were more confused.

Which gets me to the single basic suggestion I will make. I wish the two characters did not know their situation at the beginning of the play—or only a part of it. I wish they'd learn what their situation is as they progress through the play, bit by bit. Why can't they just come to the theatre to play a performance? Tonight The Two Character Play is scheduled. So they prepare themselves and finally start to play it. Slowly, as they go along they notice a series of alarming developments. These accumulate. Finally, at the end and only at the end, they have learned what their situation is. Leave the broader significances to us.

I like the basic set up of the play. No one writes as well as you do, I mean nobody. But I'm concerned that you might be facing another unhappy experience in the theatre if you proceed with this as it is. Please do consider my suggestion for rewriting this play in this way. Let the two actors be physically tired at the beginning, cold, discouraged, emotionally near exhaustion, their nerves on edge, etc., the way any pair of leading actors might be at the end of a long and rather unsuccessful tour through the provinces, the "bus and truck route." Gradually, as they prepare and go into that night's show, they learn the true extent of their condition.

That is what we all do, isn't it? We learn what desperate straits we're in as we go along. We're actually in trouble from the beginning, but don't know it. It takes time before we can admit to ourselves what our condition is. We keep it from each other. It is too painful to face, so we behave "gallantly", live in secrecy.

There is one final fact that even your two people have not found out: that at the end they will be <u>alone</u> in their misery. That, I think, is the worst of all.

I don't know where you are. But, through Kook, I am sending this out like Wordsworth's arrow. I hope it reaches you. With my love.

Gadg

[Tennessee Williams left an earlier meeting with Eddie Kook (owner of Century Lighting in Manhattan and associate of the producer Joel Schenker) doubtful of his interest in backing *The Two Character Play*. Kook's indelicate question had also offended Williams: "'Do writers lose their talent, or just their rhythm?'" The London premiere (1967) raised similar questions concerning the ordeal of a brother and sister, whose only alternative to silence is to perform an obscure private play after being abandoned by their touring company. Reviewers found the interplay of Felice and Clare "repetitive" and their dramatic situation in the cold, empty theater unconvincing. Much the same criticism would resurface in Chicago (1971), where "square houses" and "a bad set of newspaper notices," as Williams put it, ruined the American premiere and suspended plans for a Broadway production.] *TLS, 2 pp., HRC*

TO CHRIS KAZAN AND NICK PROFERES

June 2, 1971

Dear Chris and Nick:
One of the advantages of being the director of a film and not its producer or co-producer is that its o.k. to write notes like this one.

Your next important job is to see that this film is marketed right. There is no sense in having made as good a film as you've made, having worked as hard as you've worked and then not seeing to it that the film reaches the people for whom it was made. What I'm saying is that you cannot relax—you producers—until the film is completely and satisfactorily launched and doing as well as it can do. That, in my opinion, is very well. But this film needs very special handling. And that is up to you—its producers.

It is critically important how HOME FREE is shown to distributors, even how it is shown to UA, Picker and the others. Here are my very strong feelings. This is a very powerful picture. It is not an "entertainment", it is an experience. It seems to have overwhelmed Bill when he saw it. He saw it alone and he thought about it afterwards a great deal; it got to him. It did because it is—can become—part of the conscience of the day.

I think it would be a disaster to project this film as if it were an entertainment. It should be shown, in this initial stage of its exposure, to a person or two at a time. To be corny—the person should be alone in the projection room with the film and his conscience. I know that everytime I myself saw it, HOME FREE stayed with me. I did not shake off its effect quickly or easily.

Now that Bill has seen it, I dont think anyone else should until the music and the complete soundtrack are present. I dont think anyone should see it until the scene with the Viet Namese girl is IN. I think Picker should be the first one to see the completed picture—and we should complete it as soon as we possibly can—but Picker should not see it until then.

When it comes time to show the film to the critics, I think you should show it to the important critics one at a time. And in a quiet projection room—I mean by "quiet" a room not full of the phony bustle of PR people. Canby should see it with whomever else he wants to bring from the Times, but see it only with them, at a showing especially set up for them. The film, Canby and his conscience. The same with the other important critics.

The public should not ever see the film until the reviews are OUT. If there ever was a film to which the public has to be brought by the critics, this is it. The critics have to tell (instruct!) the public that this is an exceptional film, an experience they must not miss, the film of the day. I think they will.

If it is shown without this kind of intellectual sponsorship, the public will merely see it as entertainment-manque. They have to be prepared in order to take the film on its proper level. So I urge you, think of it that way. It is your job to protect what we have made. Dont just throw it out for people to take as they will. Handle it with care. And persist to the end.

Bill is your friend and a most valuable advisor. He is quite correctly intent on getting you the best possible deal, especially with respect to "money up front." But money up front is not the most important thing now—not on this one. What is most important is that the film be given its every chance. And I am convinced that the way to do this is to proceed as I have sketched above.

That is what you owe to the work you've done. As the man said, your task is just beginning.

E.K.

[*The Visitors* (initially "Home Free") was filmed in seven weeks on the Kazan property in Sandy Hook, with unknown actors, a small nonunion crew, and novice producers, at a cost of $175,000. Chris Kazan's first professional screenplay was photographed and edited by Nick Proferes, who had collaborated with Barbara Loden on the film *Wanda* (1971). "I'm out in the snow and the extreme cold a lot," Kazan wrote to Budd Schulberg, but "its great, like beginning all over again and I'm enjoying the shit out of it" (n.d., Dartmouth). *The Visitors* made common cause with other low-budget independent films that portrayed Vietnam veterans as unwelcome, embittered, and prone to carry on the violence of an unpopular war. Two drifters released from Leavenworth on a technicality seek revenge on a former GI, whose testimony convicted them of raping and killing a Vietnamese girl. The informer, now a pacifist, is beaten and his girlfriend, oddly attracted to one of the visitors, raped. They leave as suddenly as they arrived. Chris Kazan claimed special relevance for the film in light of atrocities in Vietnam, especially the My Lai massacre and court martial of Lieutenant William Calley. To Kazan's surprise, a part of the audience booed the film's New York premiere in 1972. Vincent Canby proved an exception to the strong majority of reviewers and found *The Visitors* "extremely moving," if only "because everything—from the physical production to the melodrama—is kept in small scale" (*NYT*, February 3, 1972).

Elia funded the project with a bank loan (reimbursed by the film's distributor, United Artists) and was "proud" to have worked with his son. Joseph Losey reportedly used his influence as a judge to sabotage the film at Cannes. He had chosen exile in England rather than answering a subpoena of the House Committee on Un-American Activities in 1951.] *TLS, 2 pp., Wesleyan*

TO TENNESSEE WILLIAMS

[New York]
October 19, 1971

Dear Tenn:

Just a short note to thank you for your beautiful letter. I am dictating it hurriedly and sending it to Maria who I know will get it to you. Why I put "Important" on the envelope is I am going to do a damn fool thing and not only advise you but urge you not to sell your little house in Key West. Just keep it. Let a friend live in it, rent free, somebody retiring and quiet who will take care of it for you. Stay in Europe as long as you want. For the rest of your life if you want. But don't give up your house there. There is something very disorientating about giving up a place you have lived in for a long time. It is not a matter if you are happy there or unhappy—it has just become part of you and don't give it away. Certainly not for money, which is worthless. The only thing of value I have in the world—I mean I am talking about material things aside from some books and stuff—is houses and pieces of land. And they give more to me than anything else I own, the stocks I have are garbage. I've had three

With Tennessee Williams

goddamn financial advisors and all I've ever done in the market, be it stocks or be it bonds, is lose, lose, lose.

The money you got from Key West somebody would lose for you. They would see to that sure as hell. But you put a lot into that place down there so hold on to it.

About splitting, I have and am happy over here on this side. Will write you someday soon or maybe not soon but someday. That's all for now. With much love.

As ever, E.

[Tennessee Williams praised Kazan as "a poet," perhaps "the greatest" he had known, and advised that scornful critics be defied: "We've paid our dues, as Lenny [Bruce] would say. We paid them in the forties, fifties and sixties. I think we have every right and reason to tell them to fuck off in the seventies if they put us down." Williams deplored American intolerance and was "planning to emigrate to Europe," although it would be "a wrenching experience" to sell the "little house in Key West" (October 10, 1971, Wesleyan). He retained the Bahama-style cottage purchased in 1950 and often used it as winter quarters until his death in 1983. As for "splitting" the United States, Kazan declined.] *TLS, 1 p., Columbia*

TO VICTOR S. NAVASKY

[New York]
March 26, 1973

Dear Mr. Navasky:

Been out of town so this answer is late. Sure we can talk. A little. I am going to do that scene myself and dont intend to undercut my book. Another thing: I prefer to describe my stands outside the envelope of some one else's comments. After transit through another person what I said doesn't come out as I said it. I usually regret the interview which provided material for the—as I see it—distortion.

I liked the third paragraph of your letter. It is candid and self-questioning. But, to be equally candid, I still believe you incapable of being objective about what I did 21 years ago. In your TIMES piece yesterday I found gentle distortions and some errors of omission that come from where your sympathies are. Nothing wrong with that, its human. But why intimate that I was rationalizing? Perhaps someone on the "wrong" side was sincere even if mistaken. Perhaps the son of a bitch believed in what he did. And what is a difficult decision except one which causes pain either way one goes.

I have never forgiven you, Mr. Navasky for using the word "peddling" with reference to me in a previous piece you wrote for the TIMES. I wont until you publicly withdraw that slur. Did you read THE ASSASSINS? Perhaps if you had you'd understand the urge I felt to get as many people as possible to read it. Perhaps that urge wasn't altogether concerned with dollars.

Another reason I'm reluctant to talk: I have no intention of attacking any of my old friends. I have never NOT liked Art Miller. I sort of admire old Ramrod Lil, who wouldn't?

We can meet but I have to warn you as per above. You are welcome to come sit with me. I work in room #405 every morning I'm in NYC, usually starting around eight and going till about twelve. After that, Tuesday, Wednesday? I'll be here.

Sincerely, Elia Kazan

P.S. I dont give you this for the Letter Section of the NY TIMES MAG—or for quotation by you later. I trust you for that.

[Kazan reserved comment on the HUAC hearings for his own "book," an autobiography already planned but nearly a decade away from concentrated research and writing. Victor Navasky had recently criticized Kazan and other "friendly" witnesses, who "rationalized" HUAC tactics as no worse than the party's and refused to "sacrifice their careers for something in which they no longer believed." The claim did not fall to the level of "slur" in Kazan's estimation, as had an earlier reference to *The Assassins*. Navasky reported that the novel "has just been peddled as a paperback for the record-breaking sum of $425,000," and went on to predict that Kazan "wouldn't take more than that for the reprint rights to his statement of 1952 in which he named more names than a Leonard Lyons column on a good day" (*NYT,* March 25, 1973, and December 12, 1971). Divisions of race, gender, and politics arise in *The Assassins* during the trial of a Mexican American sergeant who has killed his daughter's hippie lover. Kazan suggested that moral issues surrounding the war in Vietnam rather than "dollars" may have motivated the author and justified the novel's circulation.

Kazan met Navasky on March 28 and refused to open his papers at Wesleyan University or to cooperate with plans for an article in *Esquire*. A Yale Law graduate, Navasky published *Kennedy Justice* in 1971 and in 1978 became editor of the *Nation*. Articles and reviews in the press would culminate in *Naming Names* (1980), an influential exposé of antidemocratic House Committee tactics and the cooperation of informers such as Kazan and Budd Schulberg.] *TLS, 1 p., Wesleyan*

TO NORMAN MAILER

[New York]

August 14, 1973

Dear Norman:

Somebody close to me snatched your book out of my hand the minute they saw it. Now they've finished and I'll be at it soon. I wouldn't worry about Miller.

We'll talk about him sometime. He is not what you would call a "straight", quite a tangle in fact. For one thing he's as vain as anyone I've ever met including all the actors. I'm sure nothing would satisfy him except his own version of the events. By the way, in "After The Fall" he quotes Marilyn as reviling him with: "You judge"! This is really an admirable piece of self-revelation—and rare for him. Art's in the business of being right, which is the same business lawyers are in and politicians. I mean what the hell is a lawyer if he's not right. Miller's never confessed to any dark side or unflattering aspects of himself. A fault we don't have. That's what I mean by "bond". Among other things.

e.k.

[Kazan was among those interviewed in "modest depth" for Norman Mailer's biography *Marilyn* (1973). He is represented in the text by a single quoted reference to the Hollywood agent Johnny Hyde, an early benefactor of Marilyn Monroe's. It is inconceivable that Mailer, steeped in gossip, rumor, and innuendo, and tutored by Budd Schulberg in the workings of Hollywood, was unaware of Kazan's intimacy with Monroe in the early 1950s. Kazan may have spoken off the record with the understanding that he was reserving this material for his autobiography.

In several cases Arthur Miller appears in Mailer's biography as a figure of caricature: "grave poet of the middle-class mind," "the first Jewish Pope [who] puffed upon his pipe as if it were the bowl of the Beyond." His marriage with Marilyn Monroe is viewed in less pontifical terms. She has "the most talented slave in the world," while Miller is "ambitious, limited, and small-minded, an intellectual who is often scorned by critics outside the theatre for his intellectual lacks." Mailer quotes several passages from *After the Fall* as commentary on episodes reported in the biography. With reference to "bond," Kazan excused himself and Mailer from pretention or hypocrisy.] *TLS, 1 p., Wesleyan*

TO TENNESSEE WILLIAMS

[New York]
December 6, 1973

Dear Tenn:

Sorry this is so late. I've been trying frantically to complete a piece of rewriting on my new book which Stein is going to publish. When? As soon as I get it redone. I've a lot of work and I'm not sure I can do it well. But I've been struggling and still am and will be for a long time. Directing is a cinch compared to writing. Anyway, that is why you may have been waiting.

I read your play twice, as soon as I got it. I wrote you two long letters of suggestions. Then I tore them up. I thought them presumptuous and off base. I'm not sure its a good idea to give another writer concrete suggestions. Personally

I prefer destructive criticism. I used to be gung ho for structural outlines and all that. But now, no. I'm afraid we all have to struggle on our own and for as long as it takes.

First. Good news. For the first time in years, you've got hold of a theme, an emotion, a set-up of your own size. This will be one of your very good plays. You know the rest of it. You've not found a final shape.

Here is all the advice I can give you. Stop offering (presumption coming back a bit, I'm afraid) the play to stars, stop playing that 'Who's the best director?' game. You aren't ready for that yet. Its a bit of a head trip now. Get your ass down to P. Vallarta or wherever. Faye Dunaway aint going nowhere, she'll still be around when you get the play ready. And be riper too. Ditto Keach. And directors? What plays are there for them to do? They're all starving to death. Man, they'll fight over your play, all of them, when you get it right. They wont talk about 'whose play it is' and all that, what commitments they have and all the rest of it.

You have only one obligation now and that is to yourself. That is your size. Let them wait. Imagine Eugene O'Neill running after Faye Dunaway? And I am very fond of her. You're the same as O'Neill—only richer. What the fuck is your hurry? You'll get the thing on and spend the next five years of your life rewriting it. Do the rewriting before it hits Broadway.

Molly used to say of me that when I felt something was not right, she could always tell because I'd cover it with direction. I think you've done some of that here, covered the faults with poetry and brio, with beautifully written stage directions, "presentational theatre" and with a lot of moment to moment theatrical heat applied equally and sometimes repetitiously. Well, baby, you can blow the fast ball by them once or twice or ten times but you cant do it all night.

What you need is a shape, a story line, a continuous flow of emotion and energy going in one direction—well, you've heard it all before and you've said it to others no doubt.

This play is going to be the real T.W. but now it flounders around amid the firework of characterization and the machine-gun crackle of incident and everywhere there is the huge talent of the author. But all these elements are in search of a vessel with a shape. When you get that, some of your stuff will fit and some will have to shift and some will have to be forgotten.

That's the one thing the bloody old Greeks did. They'd get an elemental, straightline of story, MEDEA, Jesus! Who could stop the movement of that thing? The story in a poetic work, which this is, should have the clarity of a legend.

You haven't done that yet. But you can this time. I think its your day coming around again. That is what I truly think. Just stop pissing away your time and energy playing casting games. They gratify the ego and are dangerous. And now too early. You've a ways to go alone. Go it alone. For a few months still BE THAT BOY AGAIN, sit, sit and think, thinking is a lot harder than writing, I know that too. Get at the bone of this thing, the single damn bone up and down its middle. Fuck Stacey Keach for now. He may have a point as it is now. Emotionally he is wrong, construction-wise maybe. When you get the play as it will be, he wont complain 'its the woman's play' etc. Its too early for any director to write you detailed suggestions and show off how knowledgeable he is.

I'll make two other remarks. I think King may be the centre of the action of this play. Maybe his basic situation should be laid down earlier? She (WDT) is the emotional centre. But he's got the stuff to DO. He's torn this way and that. He has the ambivalences. She is more or less doing the same thing. You might work on KING first and maybe let him shove WDT a little off the centre.

One other thing. There is a tendency since the 2-Character Play for people to say things about themselves that people only say about other people. But not about themselves. NC? What I mean is that we make observations about other people but they dont proclaim these things about themselves. Once in a while, O.K. But like half of WDT's part is that. And it tends to make her— what?—self-conscious? I got tired of hearing her tell how hungry her pussy was. I didn't have to be told that all the time. Let her just DO things to satisfy that mouth down there and stop telling about it so much.

But what I am herewith sending you is simple encouragement. And an invitation to solitary confinement. Your own pause. For your own sake. No director, including the man writing you, can do what is needed for this play as it now stands. Only you can do that. And that is the truth.

With everlasting love,

[Kazan's report was delayed by pressing work on *The Understudy*—current novel in progress. Tennessee Williams completed a first revised draft of *The Red Devil Battery Sign* in mid-1973: "'I was in Tangiers, without air-conditioning, with an all-night garage nearby. The hammering kept me awake. I wrote with a kind of fury that got into the play. . . . The theme is the moral decay of our country in 1963—and our disengagement. Moral corruption started to surface with the first Kennedy assassination and continued with other political assassinations and the war in Indochina'" (*NYT*, July 15, 1975). King Del Ray, a mariachi bandleader, falls in love with the Woman Downtown, whose political secrets make her a target of insidious figures in the conspiratorial world of Dallas after President Kennedy's death. Williams did "pause" to think and revise the play, as Kazan recommended, but it was offered unsuccessfully in Boston in 1975. Asked if it was closing for "good" after an exceptionally brief run, the producer David Merrick replied that "'it is not closing for good; it's closing for bad.'" Since the Boston premiere, *Red Devil* has been performed internationally and in the United States—although not on Broadway.] *TL, 2 pp., Wesleyan*

TO SOL STEIN

[New York]
December 18, 1973

Dear Sol:

I appreciate that you did not do a paste job on my first nine pages. I would not have cared for that. I prefer negative criticism. "Watching two simultaneous ping-pong games" is good criticism. Everything else increases your emotional stake in a particular solution and puts a burden on the author. It also precludes any other solution—since we would be discussing only one particular solution.

You raise certain questions. I comment. The "I" says the book is about Sidney. Of course this is an intentional false lead by E.K. The book is about the narrator. The narrator does not know this. But I believe if we start with what a great and colorful star Sidney was, it would start the book wrong.

The situation of the central figure of the book (the "I") is that he is between two ways of living. One is the ordered way, which is represented by Ellie. The other is the romantic way, represented by Sidney. The function of the first pages, those before we get into the scene dramatizing Sidney's colorful past, is to introduce the real story and to set up, quickly, the basic situation. Sidney's views are contrasted to Ellie's. Which way will the "I" go?

The stuff about the other two wives does not belong, it is ridiculous there and extremely distracting. I believe it is those other wives ("Jesus, do I have to remember about all these characters?" the reader might well be asking) their presence in the opening which makes it seem like simultaneous ping-pong games. Hopefully, everything the "I" says about Sidney's view of him is contrasted to what Ellie feels, thinks and IS in his life. I've now tried to do this as quickly as possible. The "I" is shown between two strong forces. We have a "Triangle".

Why the RAVE bit? Because the hero is not entirely on Ellie's side—though he seems to say he is. The "I" is terribly troubled by the fact that he has not become a real star, a true artist, a bold "up-front" man. At the end of the book he breaks loose and becomes—what? A neo-Sidney. Thus, at the end, while he seems to be living in a way that Ellie approves, he is reserving a part of himself to live in a way that Sidney would approve.

To start in a direct-time-sequence narration is the way someone else would do the opening of the book. It might very well be better for this someone else. It is not for me. You have offered a solution, true, but it's not the one I'd choose. In what's attached, I've tried to overcome your justified criticism.

E.K.

P.S. I will come to you tomorrow. Please let me know when is good for you.

[*The Understudy* (1975) sold well in paperback but failed to approach the success of Kazan's earlier novels—nor did it improve the author's literary standing in New York. The title indicates a reversal of fortune for Sidney Castleman (né Schlossberg), a flamboyant star of the 1940s reduced to understudying a popular actor whom he once befriended and now torments with demands of loyalty. Kazan admitted in a dust jacket statement that Castleman was "plucked from a garland of friends" but was "most like" Clifford Odets. In all likelihood the character of Sonny, the long-suffering narrator, was "plucked" from Kazan's own career as a stage actor with more technique than raw talent. Ellie, who reprises the abrasive role of Gwen Ward in *The Arrangement,* abhors Castleman's dependency on her husband and flees the chaos of New York City for the relative safety of Florida. Kazan derived the novel's social psychology, curtly dismissed by reviewers, from the naturalistic drama of predators and prey he observed on safari. Sonny's own African safari is recorded in a long, digressive middle section intended to mirror his relationship with Sidney and the urban jungle of New York in the 1970s. The perennial issue of informing arises when Sonny, usually reserved in performance, testifies before a grand jury investigating mob-related activity. His "rave act" transforms him into a passionate actor and leads to the death of a racketeer, who has implausibly become a theatrical "angel." Castleman dies from cancer, as did Clifford Odets.] *TLS, 2 pp., Columbia*

TO NORA SAYRE

[New York]
December 5, 1974

Dear Miss Sayre:
A new Hollywood? Plus ca change, etc. Money speaks the language it knows. There is one difference. The old monsters, Goldwyn, Harry Cohn, Zanuck, Jack Warner had more vanity. Which is sometimes a creative force. When these old buggers planned to put "a personal production of" on a film, it meant no expense, no effort was to be spared. Their egos demanded it. Sometimes the result was shit but it was never budget-minded. Darryl at the rushes: "I didn't like the way that scene came off today." Me: "Can I shoot it over again tomorrow?" "Go ahead." A word to the back lot and it was all mine.

Coppola's spirit is that of the old Hollywood. And Friedkin's. But the others? Lawyers, accountants and agents run the place now. I detest it.

For the hell of it I'm sending you my book. Your newspaper will hack its guts out, twice, but read it anyway. You may enjoy it.

Write the social stuff again sometime. I clipped out some of your old pieces, they were good.

Elia Kazan

[Nora Sayre wrote features on art, politics, and the New York scene before taking a post reviewing films for the *Times*. Many of her articles, including the "social stuff" noted by Kazan, were collected in *Sixties Going on Seventies* (1973). *On the Waterfront* is treated extensively in Sayre's second book, *Running Time: Films of the Cold War* (1982). Kazan and Schulberg freely discussed "their movies and their opinions" with Sayre but placed the congressional testimony off-limits, as though "surrounded with barbed wire." Kazan sent a copy of *The Understudy* to Sayre and accurately predicted its reception in the *Times:* "Oddly enough, for someone who has spent so much time so successfully in film and theater, Kazan seems to have no reflective feeling for character at all. Personal psychology, for his characters, consists almost wholly of mammoth self-contradiction and inexplicable motivation" (*NYTBR*, January 12, 1975).] *TLS, 1 p., Wesleyan*

TO ROBERT DE NIRO

PM: New York, N.Y., April 15, 1975

Dear Bobby:

You like my letters? Here's another. Something very important that I forgot to tell you or put in the notes I gave you. Stahr has a sense of mission. A mission that he has to carry out single-handedly. Which is a romantic way of living your life, isn't it?

How many people do you know who have a sense of mission? In olden times, princes and young kings had a sense of mission. They are the subjects of romantic novels and poems. Stahr is determined to single-handedly and against the tide of all those money-fuckers around him, carry out his mission.

What is it? To make the Motion Picture be recognized as an art. Thalberg actually made a speech about this and it's in the book that I gave you. But I think his mission was an even deeper and more human one. He wanted to give the work he was engaged in respect and thereby give his own life dignity. To that end he was a controlled, quietly determined, unshakeable visionary. Even a revolutionary.

He changed Pictures. And, mind you, he did this single-handed. No one on the lot is with him except the technicians, the cutters, the grips, the electricians, the property men. Some very powerful, ruthless and violent men are against him. Some of these men, Brady, Fleishacker, are shown in our film. Brady is out to get him. To, in effect, kill him. While always pretending to like him. Even more deadly because of that.

Stahr is a terrific part, something you have never attempted. I know you can do it. But nothing of that much size and meaning is easy. It will take a lot

of work, good happy work. And thought and care and experiment—and work.
So don't come to it tired. Not for my sake, Bobby, as much as FOR YOUR
SAKE.

Much affection. E.K.

[Kazan agreed to direct *The Last Tycoon* (1976) after Mike Nichols reportedly
withdrew rather than tolerate Sam Spiegel's interference. Al Pacino, Dustin Hoffman, and Jack Nicholson either considered or were offered the role of Monroe
Stahr, based loosely on the career of Irving Thalberg, "Boy Wonder of Hollywood," who headed MGM production in the 1920s and '30s. The scenarist Harold
Pinter derived his leading character and the film's romantic story line from *The
Last Tycoon* (1941), F. Scott Fitzgerald's unfinished novel. Louis B. Mayer, studio
chief and former mentor of Thalberg's, became the "deadly" enemy Pat Brady in
novel and film. Kazan played a typical hunch in casting Robert De Niro against
type to play an ambivalent artist-tycoon, at once inspiring and aloof, gentle and
commanding, beset, as were Thalberg and Fitzgerald, by conflicting artistic and
commercial desires. Spiegel's repeated criticism of De Niro's personal and professional shortcomings and threat to replace him added to the irritants of a production that wore Kazan down to "a stub" (*A Life*, pp. 765–81).] *TLS, 2 pp., HRC*

TO ROBERT DE NIRO

SH: Tycoon Service Co.
5451 Marathon St., Hollywood, Calif.
September 18, 1975

Bobby:
Here is something you might start making very clear and precise for yourself:
MINNA. What she was when you met her. How she changed (became "too
professional"). Her death and how and why he liked her best then. His guilt
in relationship to her, etc. She has to be very real for you. Her presence is all
through the film, references and photographs, etc. And the house he is living
in is her house, the bedroom, the one they shared, etc. He thinks of her, for
example, when we see him enter the bedroom for the first time. Pinter says
that he pauses in the doorway. His sex life since she died which might be taken
as nothing—even though it's three years. But that is up to you. He certainly is
a hungry man when he meets Kathleen. But that hunger can't be assuaged in
the way men usually do, not for Stahr, the romanticist.

And if you meet a doctor or talk to one, you might begin to find out about
his heart problem, what it does for him, how his strength suddenly seems to
go, how he pumps it up when he has to function professionally or appear publicly. What he feels about the coming course of his illness, etc.

Just something to make your vacation more of a vacation. (ha, ha). Have a great time.

Gadg.

EK:fs

[F. Scott Fitzgerald departed from Irving Thalberg's biography by adding a deceased wife and a vague romance with Kathleen Moore. (Norma Shearer married Thalberg in 1927 and outlived him by nearly fifty years. The marriage, a first for each, produced two children and by all accounts was secure and happy.) He hoped *The Last Tycoon* would be "something new, arouse new emotions, perhaps even a new way of looking at certain phenomena." The Hollywood setting also promised "an escape into a lavish, romantic past" made all the more appealing as war edged closer to the States before Fitzgerald's death in 1940. Presumably the "new emotions" would be aroused by the blurring of past and present, film and reality, and especially the ambivalence of Monroe Stahr, whose affair with Kathleen is clouded by haunting images of his deceased wife, Minna. Harold Pinter seems to have taken the author's musing seriously, especially in regard to the love affair of Monroe Stahr and Kathleen Moore, which Fitzgerald implausibly described as "the meat of the book" (Fitzgerald, pp. 162–68). Filming their romantic interludes, staged plein air in Thalberg's unfinished oceanside house, challenged Kazan's ability to represent layers of memory and desire that mark the romance.

Irving Thalberg was born with a congenital heart defect and learned as an adolescent that his expected life-span would probably be brief. A sense of urgency and periodic depletion of energy ensued as Thalberg faced all-powerful directors, the scandalous death of a close friend and colleague, and a power struggle with Louis B. Mayer. In 1925 he suffered the first of several heart attacks (he was twenty-six at the time) and died eleven years later. A writer who visited Thalberg shortly before his death was stunned by his frailty: " 'He looked like a little figure made of white ashes' " (Vieira, p. 328).] *TLS, 1 p., Wesleyan*

TO MARIA KALKANIS AND STELLIO YEREMIA

[Los Angeles]
November 24, 1975

Dear Maria and Stellio:
Your aunt Athena died last Friday morning. Of cancer. Her illness was comparatively brief and her period of pain much less arduous than it might have been. She slipped into death and my wife Barbara and I were at her bedside when she went. She was eighty-seven years old and had had a good life, eventful and I think satisfying. All anyone could ask for, I believe. I mourn her but I also rejoice that her life was as worthy as it was. She never did anything of

which she might have been ashamed. She was a fine example of how to live and how to die to everyone who knew her. She will be venerated by her children and her grandchildren and remembered by many, many people with the greatest respect and affection. Her life was her memorial.

I send you my love. Remember me to everyone there.

Elia

[Elia's note to his Greek cousins was more customary than candid. Athena Kazan began an independent life in Rye, New York, after her husband's death in 1960. Her immediate care fell to Elia, who brought his family to Los Angeles in October and removed Athena from familiar surroundings during her final illness. The nearness of death, he thought, released "hidden feelings" of resentment for a life "squandered" in the service of others. "I'd like to think that she'd died happy, praising me as a good son. But when I tried to tell myself the truth, it was that she'd died in bitterness, alone and far from home." Elia returned to the set of *The Last Tycoon,* and in the absence of energy or vital interest decided to "just finish the job" (*A Life,* p. 778).] *TLS, 1 p., JKMP*

TO SAM SPIEGEL

[5451 Marathon Street, Hollywood, California]
January 7, 1976

My dear Sam:

I want some personal advice from you. Friend to friend. It's about my feet— and a certain psychological problem I have. I am working for this excellent producer, making a film that has been difficult but on the whole, rewarding. Now we are getting towards the end of the work schedule but into what is perhaps the most difficult kind of filming—night work.

Last night we were out somewhere in this faceless city, about a half hour from the studio, the kind of place you know you could never find on your own. It was dark and it was cold and there were technical problems that took a long time for the crew to handle. I had to wait long waits between each shot and I had no where to sit down, no shelter from the cold, no place where I could perhaps study my script.

Robert DeNiro had a nice bungalow on wheels and Angelica Huston an even nicer one. They certainly deserve these accommodations for they are both excellent people. Besides they have to be kept in good shape for the filming when it came around to the filming.

The property people had a large truck with a heater and refreshments on hand. The Sound truck was especially nice, I know because I sought refuge

With Robert De Niro and Sam Spiegel on the set of *The Last Tycoon*

there for a bit. The electric truck was there, handy to the shooting, full of men who were discussing world and personal problems, a pleasant hum of conversation.

But I had no place to go. I was on the pavement. On my feet. Someone opened his personal car for me, I stayed there a few moments, but it was clammy and there was no light for me to study by. Then my feet began to get cold. I went and got some coffee and an apple turnover and sat on the curb eating the pastry and drinking the coffee and that would have been a pleasant interlude between the times of pacing around except it was very damp there. And I was contracting a chill.

About ten o'clock, Sam, I must confess that despite my fondness for the producer and my respect for the film he was making, I began to lose interest. In fact, I began to want to go home. I didn't because that would have been a breach of discipline and a bad example to all. But I began to wish for the night's work to be over. That is the first time on this picture that I felt that way.

The irony of the situation is that I thought the entire production situation ridiculous. Here we are, filming a tiny scene in a car between two people, just a small intimate talk and a little psychological play between the eyes perhaps, and we had one of the largest caravans of equipment since World War II. We looked like an invading army, what with the cops everywhere and the red lights and flares.

And I could appreciate my producer's wish—obviously that was it for I doubt that he has anything against me personally. I mean I can't believe for instance that he prefers DeNiro to me—to not further increase the size of the caravan. But I kept asking myself, how come DeNiro has a place to rest and concentrate and I, the director of the film, do not. No one seems to have thought of it.

I confess to you, Sam, that I had moments when I wished that I was Mike

Nichols or John Frankenheimer. They would have solved the problems without the complication of sympathy for the producer's problem. Or Otto Preminger, an old friend of my producer—my God, he would have solved the problem with scowl and a yell.

That is where my psychological problem comes in. It has to do with my wife. She has told me again and again that when you are too nice and too obliging, people take advantage of you. That is why she—as well as Mrs. DeNiro—drives a Mercedes, not a Ford. Barbara, a great realist, says that I don't act my size and that people take advantage of my agreeability.

I told her that my producer has said that everyone around the production is scared to death of me. But she poo-pood that. She says I would gain much more respect if I really throw my weight around, not a little, a lot. Well Sam, you remember, that is the way I used to be. Now I have controlled my bad temper, behave agreeably, cooperate and make the best of things. I don't want to go back psychologically.

Still, here I am, this morning, my feet still a little cold and a bit sore. Here I am, not having slept well again, the second night in a row, with a sore throat coming on, and a lot of night shooting ahead. And feeling some way uncared for, abused, unsheltered, demeaned, taken advantage of.

And all this at the hands of a producer who is an internationally famous host, a man famous for his social generosity and open hand. And a man I like. Who is saddled with an awesome problem: the Hollywood method of production, a piling on of personnel and equipment so overwhelming that it's ludicrous.

On the other hand—well, it has been on my mind what to do. I thought about it last night and again this morning and became very angry. But I talked myself out of it, decided instead to turn to you, a wise man, for advice. What should I do?

I decided, instead of blowing off, to write you this letter. But I shouldn't be taking time off for even that, should I? I should be on the back lot figuring out the Wylie Walk and the Flood and all the rest of the thorny problems of production. Well—you tell me what to do.

Affectionately,

EK:fs

[Daily warfare recorded in Kazan's diary surprised neither director nor producer and left no aspect of *The Last Tycoon* without conflict or unstable resolution, including the film's "ridiculous" scale of production. A budget approaching $7.5 million and a "star-stoned" cast featuring Dana Andrews, John Carradine, Tony Curtis, Ray Milland, Robert Mitchum, Jeanne Moreau, and Jack Nicholson, in addition to De Niro, surpassed many times over the modest scale of *The Visitors*. Kazan claimed in *A Life*—and repeated for Sam Spiegel's biographer—that financial need caused by his mother's illness led him to accept the commission. The prestige of Fitzgerald, Thalberg, and the scenarist Harold Pinter may also have attracted Kazan with the prospect of lifting a film career in decline.

With filming complete in February, Spiegel and Kazan declared a truce and expressed confidence in the forthcoming production. As editing began, Elia was more cautious in a letter to Katie Kazan: "Many of the pieces seem good but film is tricky. All the pieces can be good and the film can come out uncertain. And the pieces can seem mediocre and the film come out stirring. It all goes back to the basic story, the legend itself. If that has some heat and weight, all will be o.k." (February 25, 1976, KKP).] *TL, 3 pp., Wesleyan*

TO SAM SPIEGEL

[New York]
August 3, 1976

My dear Sam:

I must say I was surprised by what you said over the phone from Monte Carlo. How can you talk about any part of WATERFRONT and LAST TYCOON in the same sweat? Whatever else you say about WATERFRONT, it is basically an action melodrama. The love scenes there have great tension not primarily because they follow scenes of violent action, as you said, but because Terry Malloy is stuck on the sister of the man he killed which is a hell of a melodramatic situation. There is no comparable situation under our K-S scenes. Our love story is narrative more than drama and is in all ways ambivalent, dealing with wisps of memory and half-truths. The basic issue is never quite dealt with up front, never altogether confronted. That is Harold's way.

Did you expect the distributor mentality to take to that? Man, they yearn to see the giant ape falling off the Merchandise Mart towers. Again! Nor can you reasonably hope that people who go to films for kicks and charges will scramble over each other to get to THE LAST TYCOON. They will ask where a Sergio Leone is playing.

"The distributor crowd was not excited about the film!" Indeed! Did they like your cigars? Sam, they will be excited about our film when critics tell people to go see it—if they do. And if people do go see it, which may or may not happen. I think we are at the mercy of "intelligent opinion" Goddamn it! You must have known that when you took on the project. I never expected a blockbuster. A decent success I believe we will have.

Unless we betray ourselves. What we would never forgive ourselves for— and what will not work—is if we adjust the film to the reactions of people whom we don't respect. As soon as we begin to swerve in the direction the distributors' noses point, we will end up with neither our thing nor theirs. Our hope is to maintain the integrity of what we have. There is no half way point this time. You can't have both. . . .

Our love scenes are "slow?" That is their nature, isn't it, Sam? They are full of information we need to know. The story of Stahr's past is all through them and it is played, I believe, as it should be. If we hustled Stahr's story about his relationship with Minna, for instance, I promise you the scene would not seem faster but slower. The thing that has to be delivered there is not information but Stahr's emotion about his past with Minna. DeNiro does this brilliantly. If this moment is hurried, thereby minimized, the scenes will become more exposition. Ergo slower. Empty.

An audience senses very quickly when a nervous filmmaker begins to rush his film. It rattles them; nerves are infectious. Every picture has its own tone and pace. Ours is tender and introspective. And rather melancholy. It is rendered by indirections and half tones. This film cannot be "saved" by editing, it cannot be made into another film. You may wish now that Harold and you had chosen to set up scenes with more violence, more head to head conflict. But it's too late for that. And it cannot be done with the material we have. Not even in part.

I once criticized the script to Harold, saying, "It's like it was all happening under water." Harold's answer was, "Isn't that where it all happens?" In life, he meant. That, Sam, is what we're "stuck with," that kind of film. I like THE LAST TYCOON the way I do a couple of my close friends, appreciating that they are quite different from most people I know. Our film is like no other. It is packed with duplex meanings, one piled on another. And it has its own beauty. I'm proud I made it.

But it is not what you might hope for squatting in a projection room with a gang of jolly film salesmen, hoping to raise their enthusiasm. That will not be forthcoming, old boy. There will be no full page reproductions of "Dear Sam" telegrams on the pages of the weekly VARIETY this time. Unless you pay for them yourself.

A couple of months ago, you repeatedly said to me that under no circumstances would you pay attention to anyone's opinion but our own. Say it to yourself now. Don't lose your nerve. Be what you are, a strong man.

Forgive the tone of this letter if you find it excessively preachy. But I think we may be at a dangerous moment, I think we can hurt the film now by making little "insignificant" trims and cuts, here and there. I've worked a long time on THE LAST TYCOON and I cannot stand by quietly and see it reduced. By all of which I mean: let's leave the film as it is.

As usual, with much affection,

P.S. I would like to send a copy of this letter to Harold. I have, from the beginning, sent him copies of my communications to you when I thought them important. I think this is. Harold has, as have you and I, spent a long time on the film. But I'd prefer it if you would send him my letter. I haven't had his reaction to the completed work and would like to have it.

e.k.

[Kazan's uncertainty about the "heat and weight" of the script was set aside until June, when a preview of *The Last Tycoon* failed to excite an audience of friends and colleagues. It remained for the "distributor crowd" to unnerve Spiegel and produce an outcry from his yacht in Monte Carlo. As Kazan knew, "It all goes back to the basic story."

Ingrid Boulting, a disappointing Kathleen, complained that delivering Harold Pinter's dialogue was like "blowing air into yeast when making bread." The effect of writing and filming "under water," as Kazan put it, was felt in long romantic sequences lacking intensity or resolution. Kazan claimed in *A Life* that Spiegel and Pinter had provided him with "nothing" to use as an ending, a disturbing indication that "something is very wrong earlier in the story" (p. 781). He directed Robert De Niro to walk down an empty studio street and enter a dark unused sound stage only to disappear in a fade-out.

The *Atlantic* reviewer put the case more sympathetically than several other critics: "*The Last Tycoon* is lifeless, not because anybody had a profound insight into the novel, but because it's the victim of a series of accidents—Fitzgerald's death, which left us with only a draft, a screenplay that takes no risks with the material, and poor choices in casting. The resentment aroused by such bad luck keeps breaking out in curious ways. Sometimes the actors seem just plain irritable, as if they too thought it was going to be a different kind of movie" (February 1977).] *TLS, 3 pp., Wesleyan*

TO KATHARINE KAZAN

[New York]
[March 1977]

AMANDA: Happy Birthday. Are you walking? Talking? Laughing? Well, I know you're laughing. I've got pictures all over to prove it. Much love, Grandfather.

KK, dear

Are you allright? Write me. How do you like it there? What are your plans? Haven't heard from you and wishing I had. I dont really quite know where you are. I know its on the big island but just exactly where? Send me a true picture, written or photographic. I'm going to California tomorrow. I'm going to get an agent for my new book. Its called THE VANISHING ACT and because of the divorce and something called Alimony (Does Women's Lib approve of unlimited, open end alimony? / Should there be a Men's Lib to demonstrate with signs saying, Get to work, divorced Girls!!) I was saying, because of alimony etc. I'm going to try to get as much cash out of this book as I can. So I've got a guy named Irving Lazar, nickname: "Swifty" reading the book this week end. He is a big shot in Hollywood, the kind of man who has famous-name paintings all over his place. If he likes it, I am going to take him on. Floria says that's the "most lucrative way to go." And its also the end of Sol Stein, for the time being. Sol, for one thing, cant give me the kind of advance I want. For another thing, I dont want him to edit it. I want a woman editor, this time. After which (the assignment of an agent) I will leave it in his hands till I have to start editing and cutting with whoever is going to be the publisher and the agent we choose. After which—or in between—I will go to Europe to do publicity for THE LAST TYCOON but mainly just to get a nice free trip. France, Germany, England and Greece. Then back in Sandy Hook for the spring—I wouldn't miss that—and make a garden and start work on the follow up to America America. The LTycoon, by the way, is a big critical and popular (!) success in Italy. A disaster in US. They think it can go in France and in Germany and think I can help. Well, I think I can. I'm "big" (as they say) in France. Partly because of my books. In California I will see Nick. He sounded a little depressed last time I talked to him. But he should feel good because his play was good. He's simply in a tough field. Chris's back is much better and he goes to a shrink. Leo is terrific, got a bplus, Aminus average in four subjects but not so good marks in Gym. . . . Judy I'm going to see on the way back from California. And will give her your love. Now, there's my news. Give me yours. Oh, the divorce settlement is going or coming (depending how you look at it) but slowly. Its not going to be cheap. But naturally she is anxious about her future. I haven't gotten an apartment yet. But will one of these months. I'm still in the same office. And like it here, in the middle of the city. Been up to Sandy Hook a number of times and Montauk once. Very very cold. By the way Montauk is not part of the settlement but I am giving her the house at 22 West 68th. st. What do you want me to do with your furniture, bureau, desk etc.?? Shall I reserve a room in the house there and put all your stuff into it? Or do you want it at all, or what do you want? The books for sure. Well, write me already. Much much love to all of you from Grandfather.

[Katie Kazan and family celebrated daughter Amanda's first birthday while living in Hawaii.

"Swifty" Lazar, former provocateur and "cute little bug," negotiated a contract with Alfred A. Knopf to publish Kazan's latest novel, *Acts of Love* (formerly "The Vanishing Act").

Kazan now envisioned the "follow up" to *America America* as a screenplay and novel recounting the involvement of Stavros in the Greco-Turkish War of Independence (1919–22). Evidence of the screenplay appears in 1979 as a four-page document entitled "The Greeks Redeem Smyrna" (Wesleyan). Publication of *Beyond the Aegean*, the novel, was delayed until 1994. Still to be addressed in

The Anatolian (1982) were the intervening years of the Stavros chronicle in New York City.

The Last Tycoon was released in the preceding November and proved a financial "disaster" at home and abroad. Nonetheless it was nominated for several prestigious awards, including the New York Film Critics Circle Award for best screenwriting.

The divorce proceeding was a mutual decision reached after years of estrangement. Barbara Loden's diagnosis of breast cancer in early 1978 precluded separation from Elia or further plans for divorce.] *TL, 1 p., KKP*

TO RICHARD BURTON

[New York]
May 3, 1978

Dear Richard:
You didn't call again as you said you would, so this letter. I became very fond of you and of Susan. It is for that reason that I think it's only right that I tell you, before the big silence, exactly what I think about what happened.

I had a bad taste in my mouth when LEAR collapsed. I had worked on it for two months as hard as I've ever worked on anything, making a "version," studying the text so I could write a long note to the scene designer, meeting and auditioning about a hundred actors, taking a trip to a town I don't favor, Beverly Hills, to talk to you, reading many books I would not ordinarily have read and so on, all very educational and even exciting.

Then, suddenly, on the basis of an issue which should have been settled before I ever came into the picture, the project collapsed. It was a shock to me. I felt taken. I was angry and still am.

One reason I quit show business and took up writing novels is that I didn't want the control of my time and energies in the hands of others. Of all waste, I hate the waste of my own efforts most. So when you tell my secretary on the phone that the project is still on as far as you're concerned, I have to tell you my side. For many days I didn't have the heart to do this—or the inclination.

But now I can look back at the whole incident. LEAR most certainly is an exhausting part. A man has every right to hesitate before he undertakes it. But I seem to remember what Cohen does, that you agreed to seven a week in Beverly Hills. And you certainly agreed to seven a week (after Chicago) over the phone from England to me. I put it to you as clearly as I could, I put it to you twice, Richard. When we were in California together would have been a good time to tell me that you couldn't do it. It would have saved me a month of very hard work and some embarrassing backtracking.

I can't help thinking that Cohen is right about another thing. Actually he took the possibility of six performances a week up with the Shuberts from whom he was getting a theatre. They said nothing doing. They wouldn't even talk about giving him a theatre on a basis where the star would not guarantee seven performances a week. You have no understudy, remember.

I don't see how any producer could present a contract to backers who are being asked to put up seven hundred thousand dollars for a production starring an actor who is going to play—if he thinks it necessary for his health—no more than six times. And that for only 24 weeks. Now, Richard, who could make you play—or want you to play—to a point that threatened your health? It was a matter of the contract, the good faith agreement. That is all.

I do not understand your side of it. I have often wished we had been together those days. I got your ultimatum from Valerie whom I don't know by way of Cohen's manager as I was auditioning actors at the Lyceum Theatre. You said something about having a producer who was ready to undertake the production on a seven if I can, six when I can't, basis. But talk is easy, Richard, particularly seduction talk. You know that from another of life's activities in another arena. But when it gets down to numbers, to the hard dollars and cents talk, when the accountants and the managers and lawyers get into it, it has been my experience that all producers talk exactly alike. They have to talk truth.

There is also this: I could not do LEAR with another producer. Since Cohen brought me into this project, I cannot shift. If he had done something horrible, well then—. But he has behaved perfectly with me in every respect. He was ready to undertake a very expensive production of a very difficult play, a play of which another production was playing at the time of the breakdown of negotiations (and to good notices) and with a star that would give him only 24 weeks. What the hell more could we ask? Fairly?

So what was left for me that day when the negotiating stopped except to do what I did: turn my back, walk away and keep walking. Which is what I've done.

I think it's a goddamn shame and so do a lot of other people in the theatre here. So many have called me or spoken to me. I agree with them. We had a chance—and that's all you ever have, isn't it?—to do a Lear that people might look back on and remember. So I thought, so you thought or we wouldn't have bothered.

But now I am deep into a book I like and that's that. Which is why I don't like show business. The shit a director has to go through to get three and a half weeks of rehearsal that he might enjoy!

So you are making a movie and in England, now that spring is here. I am fond of you and of Susan and want you to be happy and hope you are. So let's forget it, that's the sensible thing to do, forget all about it and enjoy whatever comes.

Work well and good luck always,

P.S. I have not told Cohen that you called me.

e.k.

[Kazan invested considerable time and energy in developing a revised version of *King Lear*—briefer, dramatically streamlined, verbally simplified, and with Cordelia's character developed along more informal lines—for a limited Broadway engagement starring Richard Burton. Announced by Alexander Cohen in February, the project "collapsed" when Burton apparently wavered on a verbal commitment and demanded a flexible schedule of weekly performances—"seven if I can, six when I can't"—that Cohen found untenable. Burton went on to film *The Medusa Touch* in England, while Kazan awaited publication of *Acts of Love* in July.] *TLS, 3 pp., Wesleyan*

TO ROBERT GOTTLIEB

[New York]
September 20, 1978

Dear Bob:
I try, with each book or film, after it's quieted down inside me, to try to analyze why it didn't turn out to be what I would have liked and when, as with "Acts of Love," people are generally disappointed, this is so.

I've written myself a note and enclose it. If you care to give me a reaction, I'll be happy to have it.

Fondly, E.

I think I've figured out what's wrong with A of L. I start the story by introducing a pair of Greeks, father and son. Neither is too bright, witty, engaging or even attractive. The son is devoted and dutiful, anxious above all to please his old man whom he respects in a traditional old-world style, one which is akin to fear. The father is a throw-back to an older tradition, one that is strong and honest even if it is pig-headed, somewhat bigoted and even destructive. They are equally loyal to the family; for them family is all. These are not modern people still you have to like them, even despite yourself.

Enter the girl, a neurotic and unsettled person, full of secrets, who is manipulative and keeps her true nature (if she has one) masked. She dresses to arouse lust and this feeling in men is the reassurance she constantly needs.

She succeeds in winning over the father, rather against his better judgment, to the marriage with his son. Then she goes home to obtain her own father's permission, an approval the boy's father insists on and to which she is indifferent.

The first thing she does in her own environment is get into bed with her old boy friend whom, it appears, she earlier betrayed. We soon learn that she has been promiscuous since adolescence. She seems to be making a last-stand effort to be decent. Is it too late?

What is the story I am telling? What "track" have I put my reader on? Here: this "good" pair, father and son, are in danger of being "taken" by a girl who is without a moral sense. We want them not to be "taken," or hurt. That is the story I've set up and which the reader looks forward to reading.

Then, it appears, I switch horses. The reader has been prepared to expect what Lazar described: the story of a bad girl breaking up a good family. I turn around and try to lead the reader in an opposite direction: a story of irony which is that this girl whom everyone in the community of the book condemns has, in the end, done nothing but good to everyone with whom she's been involved. It's stated in the last chapter, a final irony.

Question: is it too late? Can you start your reader going one way, then abruptly, without explanation, turn him around one hundred and eighty degrees and expect him to follow? I don't think so.

If I wanted to tell the story suggested by my final irony, perhaps I should have started with the girl, gaining the reader's understanding and interest and, in the broadest sense of a bad word, his sympathy for the girl by telling about her infancy, her adoption, and her childhood history in a family without love. I would show how the doubts about her own worth built up during her adolescence, how this made her extreme promiscuity understandable and how her lack of a real home and the support it might have given her, left her vulnerable and frantic in every other way.

I might then have built up, not sympathy but concern for Ethel. Only after this kind of start should I have introduced my rigid old Greek and his good-looking son, the lady-killer NC officer. In this way I might have had a book where the reader's interest, even his involvement would have been assured. I might have put the reader INSIDE Ethel instead of asking him to watch a parade of objectively stated "facts" which purport to be an account of her life but are never her inner experiences, truly felt through.

As it is now when I try to turn the audience around, it is too late. It can't be done. The concrete of my first two, three, four chapters has set, it cannot be remolded into another shape, the reader is firmly and finally pointed in the direction I've tried to describe above.

The book leaves the reader outside. There is no emotion. Everybody has observed this; it is the near-universal reaction even among those people who, otherwise, admire the book. No one is involved by it. The reader doesn't even know what I want him to feel.

Compare <u>America America</u>. There the reader is inside Stavros and wants him to get to his goal and so fulfill his pledge to his parents. The reader is happy when the boy does. Result: An experience shared. Love for the book.

[Robert Gottlieb was appointed executive vice president and editor in chief of Alfred A. Knopf in 1968 and president in 1973. A self-described "personal publisher," he was responsible for diversifying the firm's list of writers, including Kazan, whose novels and autobiography he edited with astute moderation. Kazan based the setting and argument of his latest novel on the Greek community of Tarpon Springs on Florida's Gulf Coast. Thirty years earlier he explored the local sponge fishing industry for a film project that was delayed and then completed by another director. In *Acts of Love* the same community harbors a figure of traditional European male culture, who is seduced by the aimless modernity of Ethel Laffey. Her "last-stand effort to be decent," to renounce the "excitement" of casual lovers, is formally invested in marriage to the son of Costa Avaliotis but more deeply and dangerously in the father-in-law, a moral guardian whose desire proves fatal. "He wasn't strangling her; he was holding her so she couldn't get away. It was an act of love." Kazan's play on the title expands into "a final irony" posthumously borne by Ethel. Her disruption of the insular community has freed and elevated the surviving characters and made a local "legend" of Costa, who is exonerated on a technicality and restored to the "proper" Greek way.

John Leonard anticipated Kazan's analysis: "There's enough material here for several novels, and I'm not sure which one Elia Kazan wanted to write" (*NYT,* July 21, 1978). Sales in the East were initially strong but reviews uniformly negative.]
TLS, 4 pp., Wesleyan

TO AVRAAM KAZAN

[New York]
March 19, 1979

My dear sweet good brother
First I want to thank you again and again for your solicitude and kindness and damned good advice when I was in Sarasota. The doctors I encountered were certainly first-class and took great pains with me and I'm sure that was because of you. The fact that they didn't find the cause of the red blood corpuscles being minus well, what the hell. Maybe it's just because I stopped eating as much rich stuff, no red meat, no ice cream, no booze. Yes, it's probably booze that makes red corpuscles so I will go back to some heavy drinking. I know I shouldn't have stopped.

Now about your advice. Christ, do you really want me to find some more aggressive postures? That's how I used to get into trouble all the time. I spent years trying to subdue those more aggressive postures. Maybe now they're hitting back at me. And who should be the objects of these aggressions? Since I started writing (not directing) I have no playmates, no sparring partners, no victims. Maybe I should give up sitting on my tail as I do (today from 8 to 4) and get out and mess up a few acting careers. No. Tennis. Swimming. Yes! But the tennis I am able to play now is NON aggressive. And I can't swim good enough to race anybody. Besides, I don't feel competitive. My psychoanalyses have relieved me of aggression and competitiveness. I am calm. I am good natured. I am sweet tempered, gentle spirited. Even when I go to Turkey I am ready to be shot. What the hell will I do? Well, I will find something I am sure. But regard this hen egg irony. Maybe when I am feeling good and have my full complement of red corpuscles, that's when I get aggressive and when I'm thin on the red ones is when I'm so damned sweet. Advise please.

Much love from Elia.

[Avraam Kazan, MD, second born of the four Kazan sons, directed the Mental Hygiene Division of the Westchester County Department of Health before entering private practice as a psychoanalyst in White Plains, New York. In 1970 he moved to Sarasota, Florida, and continued in private practice. Elia soon reported that his anemia had "suddenly, for no reason," disappeared.] *TLS, 1 p., JKMP*

TO JESSICA TANDY AND HUME CRONYN

[New York]
September 12, 1979

Dear Jess and Hume:
Well the fact is that you missed one hell of a party. I am enclosing a copy of the guest list to make you even more homesick. I would say, after reading your letter, Hume, that your schedule is too heavy. Where is the time for excursions to the Bahamas and to the savannahs of East Africa? I don't see that specified. My, God, you're both famous and successful and, I do believe, rich enough. Why don't you do less and do more. Well—I'm talking to you like I used to talk to myself not so long ago. The thing I look forward to most is your play, Hume. No, more than that to seeing you again.

I was going to come over to England and France this fall but I don't think that's possible now because B. isn't feeling perfectly well. But if I do I will cable and I will tell you what news there is.

Our friend, Joe Mank wrote me a rather sad telegram telling me he couldn't come to the party. Billy Friedkin, just out of his movie, didn't show out of general exhaustion, I imagine. But everyone else was there and B. made it the event of the fall. I made one bad mistake. You know my perverse streak. Well, I invited John Simon. I'd gotten to know the rather maudlin side of the man (yes, I said maudlin) and I forgot the rest, exercised my perverse rights of host and invited him. This upset a few people. If I had remembered that Bob and Zoe were going to be there—I knew they were but I forgot that Simon had insulted her in print—I wouldn't have invited Simon. And old H. Clurman said, "What the hell did you invite him for?" But it gave the dash of distemper that any perfect party needs to show up that it's perfect. I felt much younger than seventy, like sixty-nine. All the food was Greek and there was only wine, also Greek.

Other news—Bobby DeNiro bought the place on Long Island just down the hill from our dune and he'll be a welcome neighbor not only because I like him a lot but also because he has a swimming pool. The kids are back in school and both matured. Leo spent the summer on a freighter, eight weeks from port to port around the Mediterranean and up to Odessa. I'm writing—which is no news—another long novel. Teresa Wright gave me a box of typewriter paper for my birthday and said, five hundred sheets so you will write a short book, emphasizing <u>short</u>. And so on. The fall is beautiful here and I love you both.

E.

P.S. The wine? Delicious—many fond thanks. e.

[Jessica Tandy and Hume Cronyn enjoyed a huge success in *The Gin Game* (1977) and looked forward to the opening of *Foxfire* in 1982—a modest Broadway hit.

Among the guests who celebrated Kazan's seventieth birthday were the Arthur Millers, Bobby De Niro, Betsy and Budd Schulberg, Bob Fosse, the Arthur Penns, Irene Selznick, Audrey Wood, William Inge, and Zoe and Robert Whitehead. Harold Clurman deplored the presence of John Simon, renowned for harsh reviews and personal attacks.

Barbara Loden began chemotherapy at the Cleveland Clinic in July after considerable resistance and delay. Although not "feeling perfectly well," as Elia wrote discreetly, she "could still rise to an occasion, and she did," in planning the celebration. Elia assured Barbara that none of the guests knew of her illness and "whispered in her ear that she was never going to die." The prognosis received at the Cleveland Clinic had encouraged no such hope (*A Life*, p. 803).

Beyond the Aegean is probably the "long novel" in progress.] *TLS with enclosure, 3 pp., private collection*

Dear Tenn:

I was saddened to hear about your mother's going. You've immortalized her, of course, but gave her so much more, loyalty and love and care—I saw it. So I can imagine what a loss this must be for you.

You've been in my thoughts as you always are, with love,

Elia

[Edwina Dakin Williams was "immortalized" as Amanda Wingfield in *The Glass Menagerie* (1945). Her distinctive southern speech was embedded in her son's memory and constitutes much of the domestic poetry of the play. Edwina also contributed unwittingly to the lore of *The Glass Menagerie* in a backstage meeting with Laurette Taylor, who originated the role of Amanda. "'Well, Mrs. Williams,'" said Laurette, "'how did you like yourself?'" To which she replied, "'Myself?'" Tennessee Williams later described Laurette Taylor as instinctively kind but unable to resist such an opportunity. "'You notice these bangs I wear? I have to wear them playing this part because it's the part of a fool and I have a high, intellectual forehead'" (Williams/*Memoirs*, p. 85). Edwina reportedly missed the humor. In fact she was an educated gentlewoman who counseled and encouraged Tom Williams in the early stages of his career. He was a loving, if often exasperated, son who cared for his mother until her death on June 1, 1980, in St. Louis.] *TLS, 1 p., Columbia*

TO JOSHUA LOGAN

Dear Josh:

I care for you too, did from the first time I met you. Thanks for your fine letter. Yes, you have it right: the heart of the tragedy here is that Barbara had so many plans, so much appetite, so much spirit, so much she wanted to do. She was the opposite of defeated. Her room is full of scripts she'd been working on and notes she'd made. It's grating, it eats me out to think of her being killed off. Frankly, I look at the other people walking the street, most of them, and I distrust life, its fairness.

Well—what else can I say. Thanks. Best to Nedda. Hope I see you sometime soon and hope that you are well always.

E.

[Barbara Loden, forty-eight years old, died on September 5, 1980, at Mount Sinai Hospital. The talent and determination she brought to New York from her native North Carolina produced two substantial achievements: the award-winning performance in *After the Fall* (1964) and the production of *Wanda* (1971), an independent, small-budget film that Loden wrote and directed and in which she played the title role of a drifter without personal resources or hope of success. "'I've been like that myself. I came from a rural region, where people have a hard time. They don't have time for wittily observing the things around them. They're not concerned about anything more than existing from day to day.'" She described Hollywood in the same interview as a leaden ship that "'won't float anymore'" (*NYT*, March 11, 1971). *Wanda* was originally shown at the Venice Film Festival in 1970 and opened the following year in New York to strong reviews. Sons Leo Kazan and Marco Joachim survived Barbara.] *TLS, 1 p., Library of Congress*

TO LEHMAN ENGEL

SH: The Harold Clurman Professorship of Theatre
Hunter College of the City University of New York
April 17, 1981

Dear Lehman,
A group of actors and theatre people in New York City are eager to raise a memorial for Harold Clurman. We think our generation of performers, directors and teachers are, in all essentials, his children. He is not only important to us, he is dear to us. We want him remembered.

Hunter College, where he taught for ten years, has made a proposal to us: they would set up a Harold Clurman chair or visiting professorship in cooperation with us. The funds necessary to set this up are two hundred thousand dollars, half of which they would provide to match the hundred thousand we would raise.

We've been stirred up by this proposal and are appealing to women and to men in our profession who've been influenced and, we believed, shaped by Harold's ideas, personality and feelings. We believe you are one of these and that you'd be as anxious to participate as we are in what seems to us like a just and fitting cause. The way of our world is to forget the dead as quickly as possible. We don't want this to happen to Harold.

Sincerely, Elia Kazan
Stella Adler
Robert Whitehead

[The signatories led a fund-raising drive to honor Harold Clurman—mentor, former husband, theatre colleague—who died on September 9, 1980. Elia remembered him as a prophet who changed American theater: "We'd come through a great deal together—and survived as friends. The thirties were a time for prophets, and Harold was ours. He came out of the wilderness of the Lower East Side to change his world, that of the theatre. Speaking with a fervor just short of hysteria to young actors hungry for an artistic faith, he brought them together into a Group Theatre and gave them the possibility of a life in art worth living. He made the Group a cause, and it became, for eight long years, *my* cause. . . . To the extent that I became an artist, I had Harold to thank first" (*A Life,* p. 811). The Harold Clurman Professorship continues to support visiting playwrights and other theater professionals at Hunter College.

Lehman Engel composed, arranged, or supervised the music for innumerable Broadway shows. Among the earliest was a Group Theatre production of *Johnny Johnson* in 1936.] *TLS, 1 p., Yale Music Library*

TO ROBERT GOTTLIEB

[New York]
February 2, 1982

Dear Robert:

Here it is. I must tell you again, despite your distaste for praise, what a brilliant job you've given me. You did more than edit my manuscript, in many places you rewrote it—to my great advantage. I am most grateful.

I've been over the text twice, the first time to examine your cuts (red checks) and the second time looking for more cuts (green checks) There is one short rewrite (half a yellow page) Some passages you will find with a question mark alongside which means that I was unsure and will, generally, take your decision, cut or retain. Where I felt strongly, you will know it. Stay cool, kid! I changed my mind in a few places and those passages are messy and smudgy. Sorry. You're so light fingered, so neat. I think you will be able to figure out what I intended.

I have accepted more than 95% of the cuts, rearrangements and rewrites you have suggested—isn't that some kind of record—and most happily. I did disagree with you here and there but only once seriously, even violently. That is in what you asked me to do in the Mr. Fernand town house scene where I believed that if I agreed to your deletions, I would be hurting my (your) book. I did not sympathize with your concern there (balance, etc.). As you recognized from the beginning, although the book is plotted, even structured, it will never be a literary athlete, cant ever have a trim figure, be well-proportioned and graceful in movement. There will always be lumps and bulges. Its merits lie in what you once called texture and even, here and there, in its excursions. And, hopefully, in its originality. This particular hunk of our society has never been dragged into light before. I think the scene in Mr. Fernand's townhouse is one of the most unusual and original in the book and I'm passionately devoted to it, want it to go as I've left it please. I have felt during our last talks that you were gently pushing me to hurry. But considering the length of the book, I haven't taken too long, have I? . . .

The title. THE HAMAL (or something related) seemed inevitable to me as I went through the book again. That is what the book is about, this fellow's hamalness, his character, indigestible in the USA's belly. The word is strange, yes, but if the book is accepted, it will soon begin to arouse curiosity and even wonder. People will ask each other what it means and will talk about it. A dust jacket suggesting how Stavros looked before he arrived here (as a hamal) and showing him clearly all dressed up in his Mr. Fernand clothes, might help. I firmly believe we are in the right area with this title.

For reasons like these, I'd very much like one more clear-headed go through. I'll be back here on the 20th of February. That would give us time to have the manuscript retyped. I'd look at immediately when I get back and return it to you on the first of March. Finished.

My secretary, Eileen, fell and broke her arm in three places and fractured her pelvis. Explaining the lousy typing. Again, Bob, thanks. People who say there is no one like you are right.

Affectionately, Elia

[*The Anatolian* was represented by "Swifty" Lazar and accepted for publication by Robert Gottlieb in mid-1981. Kazan takes up the story of *America America* in 1909 with Stavros Topouzoglou established in the rug trade and awaiting his family's arrival from Smyrna. Seven years of labor to provide passage and fulfill a promise to his father have passed without marriage or issue. Vasso, his mother, finds New York cold and forbidding, while his brothers and sisters quarrel incessantly and reject the authority of the eldest son. Life apart from the family is centered in an affair with Althea Perry—blond, beautiful, promiscuous, American, unattainable by Stavros—and association with Sarrafinian Brothers, a prosperous concern in Persian carpets.

The "town house scene" in *The Anatolian* reveals a "hunk" of society unknown to readers and "passionately" defended by Kazan. The wealth of Fernand Sarrafinian, an Armenian voluptuary, is derived from oil rather than carpets and displayed in a town house on West Sixty-eighth Street "'arranged for pleasure'" and run by a Japanese majordomo who directs the traffic in prostitutes. Fine food, drink, and especially "'the art of hospitality'" abound. Aged and nearly impotent, Fernand represents the extreme refinement of wealth and cynicism, while Stavros, intrigued and hopeful of an endowment, is gross ambition (*The Anatolian*, pp. 292–311). The long, densely textured scene contains at least two personal notes: Kazan owned a town house on West Sixty-eighth Street in New York, and his portrait of Fernand Sarrafinian probably owes much to Sam Spiegel.

The "hamalness" of Stavros amounts to a philosophy of survival hardened by several years as a porter on the docks of Constantinople. Silence, suspicion, cunning, rancor, and brutality—Stavros carries a knife he learned to use in *America*

America—produce a life "'lived entirely on one emotion,'" which Althea Perry identifies as anger. Stavros explains himself in terms Kazan adopted as artist: "Remember what offends people is what's keeping your soul alive" (*The Anatolian*, p. 370).] *TLS, 2 pp., Wesleyan*

TO ROBERT GOTTLIEB

[New York]
February 20, 1982

Dear Robert:

I got the manuscript. It must have been typed by some one who gets paid by the page because despite the ample cuts we made it is longer. I've read 90 pages and it read well. I have found some tiny trims that will make it trip along faster. And I am going to Connecticut (203,426,4542) to keep at it intensely until I get it done.

Last night I passed a book store and in the window was displayed a novel, published by Harper and Row, KAMAL. The dust jacket was handsome and had a picture of the hero, a young terrorist, chock full of violence, in a dramatic posture. Too close for comfort, all of it. But I had already turned against this title when I saw it in the retype. The sight of the new novel clinched a disaffection. HAMAL wont do for us.

I do have a strong feeling as to what we should call the book. I threw this title at you once and you threw it over your shoulder and out the window. No, not THE UNREDEEMED. I want the book to be called THE ANATOLIAN. Look at the first four words of the text. The title, THE ANATOLIAN and these first words would point quickly and directly to whom the book is about and (very soon) what its about, a character, the character of a man.

I like this title very much. It is straight forward, plain and honest. Its a Dreiser title, a Balzac title, a Dickens title. It doesn't try to dazzle, it leaves that to the book. But it will be remembered. Trying to attract purchasers by a title doesn't seem to work. The book in time clothes a title. THE HAMAL is kind of arch— "Oh, we know something you dont know." Who responded favorably to the title, Mme. BOVARY, THE TITAN, BABBITT, SISTER CARRIE? THE ANATOLIAN is embracing, it embraces the book. Its a true title. I've tried it in the last hours on a number of people and they responded, if not enthusiastically, favorably.

Bob, please. THE ANATOLIAN.

From one such, Elia

[The title of Kazan's current novel was debated for several months by author and publisher. Robert Gottlieb dismissed "The Unredeemed" as "pretentious" and suggested "The Family" or "The Homeland" instead. "The Unredeemed," Kazan answered, "is specifically what my book is about, about a whole people separated from their homeland" (November 19, 1981, Wesleyan). In arguing for *The Anatolian,* a title Gottlieb also disliked, Kazan pointed to "the first four words of the text": "Stavros Topouzoglou, the Anatolian." He preserved the earlier title as a dedication: "To the Unredeemed."] *TLS, 1 p., Wesleyan*

TO BUDD SCHULBERG

[New York]
April 9, 1982

Dear Budd:

Thanks for sending me a copy of your letter to Georgakas. Of course I agree. But after I read it I kept wondering if there was something seriously wrong with me for not getting quite as exercised as you about what Navasky says or Biskind or John Simon? Is there? I know John Simon fairly well and have broken bread with him twice when he was distraught because the girl he wanted was going with the fellow (Danish?) who was just convicted of killing his wife by injecting her with insulin. Poor old John Simon was pathetic. I can't take him seriously after those conversations. As for Navasky, you know what I think of him—a political-culture racketeer. No one has ever behaved differently towards me openly since the testimony. Of course I don't see most of them face to face and I'm sure they knock hell out of me behind my back. But, hell, Budd, if one of my close friends, you say, turned against me I'd be very upset. But what the hell do I care about Simon, Navasky, et al. As for my rep.—well it seems to be o.k. except in a very narrow, repeat VERY narrow, circle. People respect artists. Navasky was cheer-leading. And he's so goddamn ugly you can't take him seriously. And Hellman looks like Navasky in drag. What does Biskind look like?

Well, shit, I'm not going to worry about them. I'm glad that you tell them off and I'm now proceeding to work on my autobiography and that should draw plenty of blood but I'm not going to get into the ring with a club fighter. You are a big man, Budd, you've written some classics. And at least two of your films are classics. People know that. They've forgotten the shit in NAMING NAMES—at least to judge by how they come on with me. I'm pressed about once every two months to reply and I tell them I will (and I will) but in my own time. I'm too ornery-proud to rush to battle with that ilk. Well, that's probably all wrong, as an attitude, and perhaps shameless but shit, baby, that's my attitude. God help me. . . .

Yesterday I handed my edited galleys into Gottlieb and that's that. I just ran out of things to do on the book and although Chris said I should have put it away for some more months and that it needs more work, looking after and so forth, I simply did all that I could and gave it to Knopf. I don't think anybody in that high-class firm is wildly excited about the book nor do they think it will be a success. That's all I miss about Stein, the goddamn hype and his way with promotion. But I would still rather work with Bob—much.

So I'll be back end of April, the very end, and if you want me to look at something, anything, I'll be very glad to, as always. I still have my godson's present. Can Betsy drop by sometime and pick it up? Otherwise, he may outgrow it. Well, meantime much love.

E.K.

P.S. I forgot to tell you—where I'll be back from is France and Greece. e.k.

[Dan Georgakas's interview of Budd Schulberg (*Cineaste*, winter 1981–1982) included rebuttal of Victor Navasky and Peter Biskind, critics of Schulberg's HUAC testimony and alleged defense of informing in *On the Waterfront*. In correspondence with Georgakas, copied to Kazan, Schulberg repeated his criticism of Navasky's "McCarthy tactics" and rebuked film critics who "rush to judgment" in ignorance of the compositional history of *Waterfront* (April 3, 1982, Dartmouth).

In March a Rhode Island jury convicted Claus von Bülow of attempting to murder his wife with injections of insulin. His attorney doubted "'if we will ever know how large a part his love affair with another woman took in this case, or his aristocratic background and Danish citizenship.'" Alexandra Isles, a former actress, testified for the prosecution that she met von Bülow in New York in 1978 and rejected an unnamed suitor in anticipation of marrying her lover.

Victor Navasky's summary of HUAC hearings in *Naming Names* is comprehensive, garnished with scholarship, and only superficially balanced in characterizing the informers. Navasky treated Budd Schulberg passively at first by reprinting passages from interviews in which he attributed his testimony to "'guilt'" for having "'contributed unwittingly to intellectual and artistic as well as racial oppression.'" Navasky countered that "resentment against the Party's brutally imposed proletarian aesthetic seems a poor excuse for dignifying the Committee's comic-book aesthetic, and no excuse at all for acceding to its ritualistic requirement of names" (Navasky, pp. 242, 302). Schulberg regretted his cooperation and later branded Navasky's tactics and position "a kind of neo-Stalinism." Navasky began a lengthy treatment of Kazan with reference to Arthur Miller's withdrawing *A View from the Bridge* as a lesson to "'stool pigeons.'" He did not report Miller's explicit public denial of the incident, nor did he question Tony Traber's allegation that Kazan signed a lucrative film contract shortly after naming former communists in the Group Theatre. Kazan considered legal action and continued to reserve discussion of his testimony for *A Life*—currently under way.

Alfred A. Knopf published *The Anatolian* in July.] TLS, 2 pp., Dartmouth

TO BUDD SCHULBERG

[New York]
May 26, 1982

Dear Budd:

You're a smart guy and know me better than most anybody so you must have sensed that something was going wrong with me and your project. I'm not going to do it. The fact is that I'm not "Gadge," the hard-throwing director anymore. I don't even believe I can now work on a script I didn't write. I keep having the thought in re your script—and it's a very good script—that I would have written it differently. Not better, different. With respect to the character of Rhodes, for instance. As it is, despite the fact that it reaches so much further, it is essentially a remake. I feel I have directed some of the scenes before and couldn't do them as well now.

There is something else happening to me. I've arrived at the point where I don't believe life will go on forever. I used to believe I'd never die, that I had all the time I'd need to do everything I wanted to do. But these last two years and all the deaths have shaken me up. I'll be 73 in September and there are certain things I must do before I cash in. As I get older it will be more and more difficult, if not impossible, for me to do these things in the time I have left. So I feel a need to hurry.

There are several books I want to write and must write before my memory fades. First there is my autobiography. I made a start on it last year, about 120 pages. They turned out locally o.k. but not in the style or proportion I wanted. So much has happened to me. A comparatively minor element for me, but present, concerns the issues about which I've remained silent. It's time to speak out on them. So many others have had their say, now I'll have mine. So last week I went up to Wesleyan, where my papers have been collected, and made a fresh start on this book. And I don't want to stop.

Another book I want to do and must do now is the one to follow THE ANATOLIAN (at the moment a 750 page screen play). After that novel is published, I intend to make a film of it to go with AMERICA AMERICA. Surely you will understand how much that means to me. A film such as yours would have taken me at least a year and three months before I could turn to something else. Feeling as I do now, that's a lot of time.

There is also the novel I want to write and must about my mother when she first came to this country in 1913. I keep stressing want and must because while I think your script should certainly make an excellent film, I have been sort of backing into it slowly, week by week, never really all the way in, then slowly, privately, backing out. A good deal of what involved me was my feeling of intense friendship for you. I didn't want to let you down and don't now. But finally I know the projects I want most to do and I'm going to set about doing them.

Perhaps if we had started from the beginning on FACE 2, working out the movement of the story as we did on the first two films, I wouldn't have felt I was playing catch-up ball when I made a suggestion to you the other day. When I first read your script in Florida I said to you that Rhodes, this time, should be a "hero." After your strong negative response to the suggestion I made the other day, I'm not at all sure I'm right. I see that your attack on L.R. is deeply felt and organic, fixed, yours! And, of course, the man should be as you feel him, not what any director might twist him into. I would have this L.R. more engaged. As many guitar-totters are today. Which is wrong. Right? You see, Budd, I'm thinking like a writer, for better or worse. And it's late to change. Twenty-five years have passed since we made FACE.

I don't believe I could work for anyone now; I couldn't stomach a boss. You know that the person who signs the checks has the say. I'm way past consulting with the two K's and Miss Lansing and paying respect to their wishes. I haven't even been made to feel that they really want me. You must have had conversations with them about a director which you didn't tell me about. Betsy said to me, when you returned from one of your trips west, "Budd still wants you to direct it." Still! The implication could only be that you wanted me and they did not.

I don't blame them. You know how long I'd last in that atmosphere. I have no intention of ever again putting myself in the power of anyone like those people. I'd ask for final cut, for a change of HQ, a lot of dough, and complete say about casting, art people, cameraman and crew. I'd do everything possible to make myself invulnerable and them impotent. They know they'd have nothing but trouble with me.

As I said to you over the phone, these people don't behave like the NEW Hollywood, more like the old MGM where a producer gathered a team, writer, director, cameraman, art people and some stars (fait accompli to the director) and proceeded to make the film with these specialists. My stance, and yours, is different: we believe a picture should be made by a partnership of writer and director and these two artists should pick everybody, above all the actors, who they believe will make their vision of the film come true. Did the K's and pretty Miss Lansing tell you before they talked to Redford? Did they tell you before one of them slipped the script to Warren? What a fantastic way to work, limit the casting possibilities to two actors both of whom are wrong for the role! Not for me, kid.

So I'm backing out as I backed in. Get yourself a hungry, hard-hitting young director who has in mind ONLY your story and sees it exactly as you do, one who doesn't want to "open up" the script again and can work in the system out there. You won't have any trouble finding a good man—Scorsese? Mark Rydell? How many fine scripts are there around?

And don't be too mad at me. It's what happens as you grow older and per-haps—I hope—grow. Anyway, change. I feel I must lean on my own stuff now. I can. And will. You know that I will always root for you and always love you.

E.K.

[Lost in addition to Barbara Loden and Harold Clurman were actors Kazan had directed in theater and film: Michael Strong, Richard Boone, and Natalie Wood. Lee Strasberg's unexpected death on February 17, 1982, completed the disturb-ing necrology of the last two years.

Robert Gottlieb doubted the commercial appeal of *Beyond the Aegean*, the "750 page" draft submitted to him in the spring of 1981, and was also uncertain of its form: "What is it," he asked Kazan, "a screenplay or a novel?"

Apparently Lonesome Rhodes was to be recast as a Vietnam veteran in an updated version of *A Face in the Crowd*. Kazan advised Budd Schulberg that Rhodes share his wartime experience with the sinister general of the original film, arousing his painful memories of an earlier war and disgust with the "pillow-faced business men who sit around the table with Ronald" in the 1980s (November 24, 1981, Dartmouth). Kazan's withdrawal did not prevent his reading later drafts of the screenplay or prodding Lawrence Kasha in 1984 to reach an agreement "with dispatch" so filming could begin. Kasha was busy producing *Knots Landing* for CBS and declined. Nothing more came of the project.

As Kazan was "backing out" of collaboration with Schulberg, he was "very deep" into a new relationship with Nicholas Gage, whose investigation of his mother's execution by communist guerrillas in the Greek civil war (1946–49) awaited pub-lication by Random House (*Eleni*, 1983) and filming by Kazan. The initial plan called for author and producer-director to scout locations in Greece and for Chris Kazan to write the screenplay.

Cutting the Chain, a "crazy play" written by Kazan and developed at the Actors Studio, also claimed attention in 1982.] *TLS, 3 pp., Dartmouth*

TO JESSICA TANDY AND HUME CRONYN

[New York]
June 29, 1982

Dear Jessica and Hume:
The damned old fool has gone and done it again.

Love, E.

[Elia and Frances Rudge married in New York on June 28, 1982. She is the author of three novels to date: *Good Night, Little Sister* (1986), *Halide's Gift* (2001), and *The Dervish* (2013). The latter two reflect Mrs. Kazan's study of Turkish history and culture at New York University, her wide travel in the Middle East, and the ability of a gifted novelist to find compelling personal stories within vast cultural movements. Mrs. Kazan is also a lecturer, producer, and supporter of the arts in New York.] *TLS, 1 p., private collection*

TO AVRAAM KAZAN

[New York]
March 28, 1983

Dear Avraam:

Thank you for that fine, concerned and thoughtful letter. My reaction to it was: WHAT A WONDERFUL BROTHER I HAVE and I WISH I SAW HIM MORE OFTEN. As for the book, it's way back in time for me now. I'm writing an autobiography or a confessions. Eileen, who is one of two people who've read it, says I won't have a friend left when it's out. That, of course, is not my purpose in writing it. On the other hand, if I'm going to do it, there's no point in pulling punches or not saying what I think plainly even if it's not to my credit. I've lived a human life and that means not without fault. But partly because of the people I've been with and partly because of what work I've done, I believe it is interesting and even worthy of attention. But my main purpose is personal. I simply want to—now nearing the end—take a good look at the whole thing and how I became what I became and so on. It's been very interesting but stretches on and on. I'm up to the year 1932–3 and I've already got a little over 200 pages. And I don't think I'll shorten up, rather go on as I am and worry about the length when I've got it all together. I'm not even sure anyone will publish it because it is a bit nasty and extremely personal. But Gottlieb, the man who published my last two books, is interested and reads each chapter as it comes off Eileen's typewriter.

Much of what you said about THE ANATOLIAN is true—although I wasn't altogether aware of the points you make as I wrote the book. I suppose the process is largely or partially unconscious. One thing worried me in what you said, that there was no love in my family. But when I thought it over, I doubt that there was much love in Evanthia's family or between A.E. and Evanthia's family. Only between Mary and A.E. By the time I got the wind of what was happening between A.E. and father, there was tremendous resentment there about something or other. I didn't feel love in the family except from mother. She had love for all her children and for everything good in the world; she was an angelic person. And I think she loved father too because whenever I said the slightest thing against him, she'd correct me. Only after he died did she make some harsh remarks about him. Once she even said, "Your father was a stupid man." And once she said, "The last years since he died were the best years of my life." And, actually, she did live a better life after he died, she read and she watched Huntley/Brinkley and she sat quietly and thought and she translated some small items for me—sayings, mottos, something of that kind. Once, in payment, I gave her a check for fifty dollars and instead of cashing it, she had it framed and hung it on her wall. She said it was the only money she'd ever earned in her life. But she was full of love, for her sons and for her grandchildren, all of them and for people she hadn't seen for years and years and years with whom she corresponded, writing to the old world. But otherwise, God, Abe, I hung around Evanthia's house and I never felt any love there except Evanthia for her dog, the one she called KNOXIE. Do you remember? And, I suppose in a back-country way, she loved her sons and daughters. But I'm not sure that word (love) describes what she felt. It was what animals feel for their progeny, she guarded them, she argued with them, she fed them, she watched over them SO WHEN IT CAME TIME TO WRITE THE ANATO-LIAN, I wasn't full of a conviction that there was love in the family. And as for A.E (yes, Stavros, is supposed to be something like him, something like, not exactly) I don't think that man loved anyone—except the pleasure of living as A.E. Kazan, world traveller and successful rug merchant. So, you're right, that quality is missing from the family in the book. But what can I do about that?

Your analyses, insights and so on are good and they are accurate and interesting. The best thing is to talk about the book this summer, if you are still interested. It's coming out simultaneously in France and England so I'm going over with Frances (free trip) and do publicity so I'll be thinking about it. But mostly now it's the autobiography. As for slowing down, I don't want to.

Much love from, E.

[Elia remembered Evanthia, his step-grandmother, as a source of Old World history and family lore. "When I was five or six, my parents would leave me with this old woman when they went visiting or took a trip out of the city. An Anatolian Greek of near-peasant stock, she spoke no Greek, only Turkish, the language of the oppressor. She used to take me into her bed and tell me stories of life in Turkey and how we'd managed to escape and come to America. I'd never forgotten that old woman's stories" (A Life, pp. 546–47). She was loosely recast in The Anatolian as Vasso, a misplaced person whose complaint resonates with her son Stavros: "'Why you put me here this country?'" An acrimonious parting scene in which Stavros disavows his quarrelsome brothers and sisters and relinquishes the family rug trade, which cleared the way for his return to Greece at the close of World War I. Family love, if it ever existed, was replaced by patriotism and a mission to "redeem" Greek Anatolia from Turkish control. "Stavros was an Anatolian again" (The Anatolian, p. 357). Athena Kazan, "full of love" for her family, made no appearance in the novel. Judy Kazan Morris has corrected Elia's memory of Athena's sole employment. The check was cashed and then framed.

Chris Kazan praised The Anatolian as very nearly "a work of literature, something that will live," but wished for a richer, less hurried ending. Reviewers agreed that although Kazan's formal control had matured, the novel lacked restraint and proportion in the last eighty-odd pages. In closing Kazan seemed intent on setting his hero on "the road to success" and perhaps laying groundwork for a sequel. The earlier authentic dialogue, memorable characterization, and vivid dramatic scenes were replaced by "mechanical contrivance." *The Anatolian* fell short of the *Times* best-seller list, although it was selected as a "notable" book of 1982.] *TLS, 2 pp., JKMP*

TO AMANDA JANE GORAY

[New York]
March 11, 1984

My dear dear Amanda:

Eight years old. My God! And how wonderful. I wish I was there to hug you and eat some of the cake and see your presents. I also wish you were here.

In the old days, before our family came to America and before there were airplanes and even many trains—only between the very biggest cities—our family used to live—live in the same city or community (that's more like it, because it wasn't the size of a city) and everybody was there, grandfathers and grandmothers, fathers and mothers, aunts and uncles, and children of all ages and they used to see each other always. What do I mean by always? I mean always. When they had nothing to do on a warm spring evening since there was no television or even radio, and no magazines or newspapers (you see one part of you comes from a very primitive society) they'd walk to see each other. And the place they'd usually congregate on such evenings and on Sundays after church was where your great-great grandfather lived. Because they had to comfort him and his wife, to go there and kiss him and listen to his corny jokes and his dubious wisdom and tell him he didn't look so bad when of course he didn't look quite as well as the last time they'd seen him. And they'd always bring him something they'd cooked and sometimes some flowers not that they'd bought but from their gardens because in that country everybody had a garden. And so there would be this community of family and even a few friends and they'd sit around and drink tea and have different kinds of cookies and then some hor d'ouevre—Katie will tell you what that is—and laugh at even the simplest stories not so much because they were funny as because the people telling them and the people listening to them were glad to be together. That was reason enough.

And that is what I wish were the situation now, that KK and you and all the rest of your uncles and aunts and cousins lived nearby and close enough to get together. Well, it won't be because now we have civilization and everybody

With Willa, Amanda, and Zoe (in front), and his children:
Chris, Nick, Judy, Leo, and Katie

is independent which is better for sure and has different interests which is
better—still I can't help, on your birthday, wishing for the old ways. I'd like
that now.

Much love to you, Miss Eight-year-old, and your dear mother.

From grandfather.

[Spread over New York, New Jersey, Connecticut, Delaware, Washington, Florida, Wisconsin, and California, as well as Greece and Turkey, "the clan" gathered
at Sandy Hook in 1981 and was photographed in their several generations.] *TLS,
1 p., KKP*

TO KATHARINE KAZAN

[New York]
[c. April 1984]

Katie, my darling daughter. Thanks for the letter and for sending me Mike's
piece which I liked; it was well written and very "felt" and just a little beyond
me. He did, for the first time ever, say something that no one else has had
the guts to say, that my movies only started to be good after I testified. What
an irony!!! One that those fellows on the left have never figured out. Their
bewilderment is a source of amusement to yr dear old daddy. All I ever truly

feel about all the attacks is that I hope none of you, Chris, Judy, Nick and Leo will be hurt by some slurring bastard. You must have all heard shit you've never spoken to me about and I'm sorry you've had to listen to that. But, what the hell; pain makes the man. I'm in excellent health and have no conscience problems. I think people who supported the USSR after the Stalin Hitler pact, after Khrushchev's speech denouncing Stalin, they, not I should have bad consciences. Otherwise? I'm writing my autobiog and have close to 550 pages and am up to 1945. My problem is that I have collected too much research and have to plow through too much before I can write. NOW, about August. I am planning to go to Turkey then. I mean to finish my book, the one called BEYOND THE AEGEAN and still hope to make a film of it, so I need to take a good hard look around there once more. But something strange has happened; I've written three friends there, asking if they think its a good idea for me to come visiting now (they got mad at America America and at my article praising Guney) and I have not had an answer from any of the three. So, I'm thinking it over and writing again. I'll let you know. If I do I'll get more soap for Amanda. . . . BIT OF NEWS. Chris seems fine and is working on something he doesn't tell me about. Nick I saw and he has a nice home, wife and lovely, lively vigorous little daughter. Judy has written me and she sounds fine. Willa may go to Vassar (MDT) or Williams (EK). Are you still going to school. Kiss Amanda for me. She has a lot of love in the bank here.

Yrs, forever, Daddy

[Mike Wilmington's claim ("The Informer," *Isthmus*, April 20, 1984) was restated by Kazan in *A Life:* "The only genuinely good and original films I've made, I made after my testimony. The ones before were professionally adept, not sufficient praise—that word 'adept'—for a man as hungry for excellence in achievement as I was. The films after April 1, 1952, were personal, they came out of me. . . . They're films I still respect" (p. 485). Wilmington became lead film reviewer for the *Chicago Tribune* in 1993.

The historical scale of *Beyond the Aegean* required filming in Greece, Turkey, and France. In the following years Kazan estimated production costs in the range of $15 million to $24 million to potential backers.

The silent "friends" in Turkey were probably wary of Kazan's association with the director Yilmaz Güney. Kazan praised his filmmaking in 1975 and urged the Turkish government to grant amnesty for the director, who was accused of harboring subversive figures. Several years later he visited Güney in prison after his conviction for murdering a judge and reported the experience in the *New York Times* with a minimum of political commentary (February 4, 1979). After his escape in 1981, Güney continued to work abroad, to the embarrassment of the Turkish government.

Elia's "vigorous" granddaughter Zoe was born to screenwriters Nick Kazan and Robin Swicord in 1983. She studied at Yale and has acted prominently in theater and film. Her play *We Live Here* opened at the Manhattan Theater Club in 2011, and her movie *Ruby Sparks* was released in 2012. Her sister, Maya, an actress and director, was born in 1985. Willa Day Morris, her cousin, chose Williams College "'in no small part because Elia had gone there.'"] TLS, 1 p., KKP

TO KATHARINE KAZAN

PM: New York, NY, October 24, 1985

Katie dear

They are—I don't know what. Some very sad, some very happy-looking where we all look very happy. I suppose basically we are. The rest is life, painful and meaningless in its pain—so I believe. I'm having some of them framed. I already have up on the wall the one you made earlier and gave to Jeneene and she gave me of Nick and the older man. Nick, I observe, had a very strong face and I am convinced he was developing very well. Chris put a life's work into that kid and I was convinced it was going to show up.

My own great regret is that I didn't make some violent speeches to him about the dangers of the highways. But then I did. I don't think he used drugs. But with kids you never know. He was, I believe, too open to peer pressure. But then most of them are. Shit! It's a mystery. We had some talks but you know they were probably not enough; I am rather close-mouthed.

I told Chris and Nick that I was giving them the VW November 1 (which I have just done) and that I wished he'd use it instead of that car he had. But this gift came too late.

I believe Chris and Jeneene are doing better than could be reasonably expected of them. Chris is a terrific man and I admire him very much.

Love, Yr. father.

[Elia's grandson and two classmates died on the morning of August 4, 1985. Speed, revelry, and a narrow country road near Southbury, Connecticut, contributed to the accident. Nicholas Kazan, the driver, had recently graduated from high school and planned to attend Western Connecticut State University in the fall. Later Elia wrote to Katie of the parents' grief: "I spent most of this past week in Sandy Hook and saw a lot of Jeneene and Chris and I think they are noble, wonderful, extraordinary and the finest there is."] *TLS, 1 p., KKP*

TO ROBERT GOTTLIEB

[New York]
January 10, 1986

Dear Bob:

Recall that you were concerned about how Leo would come off in the book. I think what follows (an insert) will help.

* * * *

When he was about eight years old Leo began to look like me; people noticed and made comments. I knew the falsehood could no longer be maintained and should never have been allowed to go on as it had.

We were on vacation in Florida when I took Leo for a walk on the beach and broke the lie. I told him that the man he believed to be his father was not; I was. I expected a strong reaction; just what it would be, I couldn't imagine. What I got was nothing. He didn't say a word. His expression didn't change. He'd raised the mask I used when I was a kid. I tried to say a little more but couldn't think of what. We walked home in silence.

When I was alone with Barbara, I told her what I'd done. She was furious with me. "Now that you've taken his father away," she said, "it's up to you to fill the gap, not only by what you say—talk is cheap—but by what you do. I wash my hands of it all; it's your problem."

Now I was furious with her. Had she wanted the lie to continue? I was ashamed I'd let it go on as long as I had. I remained angry with her for many weeks and, deep down, permanently.

But what happened was what she'd expected. I was too busy, too involved in too much, too often absent from home to give Leo what a father should have. I didn't allow a space for the small, intimate, human things I should have done for him.

Leo was left with no father. His mother became everything for the boy. Unhappily, children have to pay for their parents' misdeeds.

It took me fourteen years to heal the wound I'd left. I believe I have now and he believes I have. In the past year and a half, I devoted myself to this. I found relief and pleasure in it. Now at last—so he told me—we are friends.

[Leo Kazan was born on January 2, 1962, in New York City, the son of Elia and Barbara Loden. The "insert" written by his father in response to an editorial concern was not included in *A Life*.] *TL, 2 pp., Wesleyan*

TO NICHOLAS GAGE

[New York]
February 17, 1987

Dear Nick:

I got your letter. My alienation from you had nothing to do with not being involved in filming your book. It had to do with the hurt my son suffered because of the way he was dismissed. You are also a Greek father and you will understand that feeling. I love my son, Chris, as much as any living human and

I couldn't bear to see him hurt—or bear to see the person who hurt him. Chris is better now and when he gets over it, I'll be over it.

I can well realize the kind of wrangle you fell into with that gang making a film of your excellent book. I can't believe that at that time you knew enough about what a screen play should be to reject Chris's. But you had a right—and unfortunately for Chris, the power—to drop him and acquiesce to another screen writer. I have never seen ELENI, the film, and have no idea what the outcome was. But I must believe you submitted a poor choice. I don't know Cohn, Tesich or Yates. I'm sure you're smarter and tougher now.

I read that you've rewritten your book on Greece and call it HELLAS. Years ago when I read the book as it was then, I thought it the best book on Greece available. My autobiog? Hard sledding but it's going to be o.k. Comes out in the fall.

My very best to your excellent wife. And we'll see each other in time to come.

Yours,

[*Eleni* commanded $850,000 in film rights and was acquired by independent producers in association with CBS Entertainment. Nick Gage stated at the time of the sale that *Eleni* was not a "property" but his "life." Chris Kazan's progress on the script before dismissal is unclear. Peter Yates and Steve Tesich, director and screenwriter, repeated their award-winning collaboration on *Breaking Away* (1979). Gage initiated contact with Kazan earlier in February and answered the present letter with reference to Chris: "I fought like hell and even offered to give back the money but they wouldn't yield" (February 24, 1987, Wesleyan). Kazan and Gage resumed friendship "in time to come." *Eleni* was released by Warner Bros. in 1985 with disappointing results.] *TL, 1 p., Wesleyan*

TO THE ACTORS STUDIO BOARD

[New York]
June 1987

Last week Arthur Penn and I had an unplanned and unanticipated phone conversation about the Studio. Ellen had sent me a notice to come to a Board meeting to be concerned with our principles and plans for the future. I'd not been able to go there—or anywhere else at that time. Arthur did attend and felt that nothing had been satisfactorily resolved. So we talked.

Before going on, Arthur and I want to at last express our gratitude to Ellen for taking on the management and artistic direction of the Studio after Lee's death when it might have fallen apart and to Paul for time after time saving the Studio's life. We owe the fact that the place is still going—and debating its course—to them. We both hope that nothing we say or anyone else does, shakes their commitment to the Actors Studio.

It is now over forty years since the Studio started. It is certainly time for a reexamination of our purpose, of our work and its worth, which means its future. In that spirit we urge that you study our suggestions which will seem drastic but perhaps it's time now, if ever, to consider if any fundamental changes, or even any serious reevaluation is possible. Many of us, besides Arthur and I, feel that the Studio is in a crisis and that something bold needs to be done to shake it up. We call for a self-confrontation which would be salutary and stimulating.

We both feel that despite Lee's work of so many devoted years—but to an extent also <u>because</u> of that work—many of our actors are not usefully trained for the Theatre as it is now. Both of us have found this to be true in productions we've done where we worked with Studio people. We believe that our program of work needs reexamination. Whatever we were in the past, we must now ask, are we on a correct and useful path.

Not to go into a theoretical discussion of the techniques of acting, we must say only this, that there seems to us to be an excessive concern now with the techniques of arousing emotion within the actor and that these techniques often result in excessive self-absorption. We feel that the root question in our work should not be how can an actor be made to feel more intensely, but a simpler, older question: how can the circumstances of the play be made real to him, then on to: what does the actor in the role want and how will he best go about getting it. The critical words, it seems to us, along with truth, are want and do, not feel.

We must also now, regretfully, ask if there aren't a number of actors who've been in the Studio for a long time, perhaps too long, who have gained whatever they could gain from the work there and will not ever progress and reward the attention they're getting with artistic results.

We both believe that our young actors, those who want to do the work and are capable of developing, need another kind of training emphasis, not in the processes of their psychological experiences but in the impetus provided by answering the question, what do you want and how, in the given circumstances, do you propose to get it. The emphasis thereby goes not to the actor's inner experience but to the relationships in the scene and to the circumstances, physical and otherwise, within which the scenes will be played. This emphasis will turn the actor out, to the other people and the circumstance in the scene.

Furthermore, all our people need training—however belated—in the other aspects of our profession: voice, speech, dance, movement, mimicry, external and internal character creations—all those old classics of our trade. This training must be made mandatory. We have neglected many of the most important areas of an actor's talent because of our concern with our psyches. Notice that more and more plays that are being written for the Theatre now call for those oldtime "theatric" capabilities and talent. It seems to us that a new group of young actors, not the oldtimers who may have reached their limits and stopped developing but those who are capable of an about-face in their work and wish to make it, should be grouped and trained in these fundamentals.

None of this was emphasized by Lee. His work seemed to go deeper and more obsessively into the actor's concern with his own experience and resulted in certain arcane techniques which came close to self-hypnosis, techniques which during rehearsals often held the director at arm's length. One result was that some of our actors "talked a good game" but often didn't produce anything more than a glassy-eyed psychological posturing.

We urge that a group of young actors be brought together to be, in effect, re-trained, particularly in those aspects of acting which would prepare them not for the Theatre of the Forties and the Fifties, the psychologically based theatre, but for our Theatre of today. We urge that you consider making this re-training group with all its various activities dealing with the body and the voice and the mimetic qualities and, etc., etc., etc., one of the two basic activities of the Studio and every support and emphasis be provided it. We might then have created at the end of the Eighties, a new cadre of young actor, broadly trained to fulfill the requirements of OUR Theatre. . . .

We believe we should now fearlessly reexamine the worth of our traditional Tuesday/Friday sessions. They were uniquely suited to Lee as a springboard to what he had to say. They also created a body of actors devoted to psychological self-examination, to judging themselves and judging others. They have often seemed to both of us to be meetings of an elite club, actors coming together twice a week to socialize as Theatre people do, less to work than to judge each other's work. We both feel that in Lee's time, year after year, the same fundamentals were droned on again and again for the benefit of the very same actors.

These Tuesday/Friday sessions have always been the main activity of the Studio; we suggest that they now be set aside and in their place an alternative central activity, an extended continuous program of Studio productions based on plays that the Playwright's group turns out, be set up, that is to say, work on new plays dealing with current life or plays revived because they had a meaning for our time or were of special concern to one of our directors. There should be, we believe, an extensive, on-going program of such producing and that these productions should be seen through to the end, offered to an audience completed just as our Actors Studio evenings are now.

We believe that a program replanned along such lines would result in a "new" Actors Studio with a lively rebirth of its life, one suited to our day and our Theatre and the problems which our playwrights are now setting up for us all, actors, directors, producers. Ask yourselves, wouldn't it be stimulating, all-in-all creative and fun as well, to replace the sameness of what's become our habitual life with a new and livelier program? Don't you all feel that for one reason or another, we have been running in a rut that began in the early Sixties and has endured unchallenged, a quarter century until now? You all know it's time for a fresh look at ourselves, at who we are and why we've come together and are still miraculously together and above all what our purpose is. To not change is one definition of death.

Elia Kazan

[A "troika" consisting of Elia Kazan, Arthur Penn, and Al Pacino assumed interim leadership of the Actors Studio following Lee Strasberg's death in early 1982. Later in the year Ellen Burstyn and Al Pacino were named codirectors. In a cover letter Burstyn encouraged "the entire Board of Directors [to] join Elia in putting their thoughts in writing as to the future direction, management and operation of The Studio."

In large part, Kazan based his criticism of the Studio on Lee Strasberg's legacy of actors unprepared for the contemporary stage. At issue was a charge of misguided instruction as old as Group Theatre debates of the 1930s. Kazan echoed Stella Adler's criticism of Strasberg by recommending that the actor's personal experience be subordinated to "the circumstances of the play." The "psychologically based theatre" of the postwar years, theorized by Strasberg *and* staged by Kazan, had been superseded by plays requiring "oldtime 'theatric' capabilities and talent." With reference to a "continuous program" of production based on indigenous projects, Kazan evoked the dismal history of the Studio Theatre and the repeated failure of the Playwrights Unit to sustain interest and bring projects to fruition. The East and West Coast Institutes founded by Lee Strasberg claimed more of his attention and by the late 1970s had reportedly limited the standard "Tuesday/Friday sessions" at the Studio to a single two-hour exercise.

Kazan's foray into the "Theatre of today" reinforced criticism of the Studio for neglecting the fundamentals of acting. *The Chain* was written and directed by Kazan and featured young actors drawn from the Studio rehearsing a presentational version of the *Oresteia*—in contemporary dress, minus author, amid confusion over their motivation and the play's meaning. Kazan appreciated their energy, devotion, and attractiveness but was shocked by the overall "poor speech" (*A Life*, p. 145). A reviewer deemed the cast incompetent and the playwright incoherent when *The Chain* premiered at the Hartman Theater, Stamford, Connecticut, in 1983.] *TLS, 5 pp., Herrick*

TO ROBERT GOTTLIEB

[New York]
July 23, 1987

Dear Bob:

Concerning the chapter in question: I gathered from Kathy that you hoped I'd find a middle ground between seeming arrogant and being a "wimp." You know that in my field, to seek such a middle ground is a disaster. I was astonished to hear that. The fact is that in a quiet way I am arrogant. The very act of writing what I have written, is an act of supreme arrogance. I'm content to have it so judged.

In my time, I've taken a fearsome amount of insult and punishment and am not about to plead for that understanding which is a pardon. I have no hope that our body of think-alike New York intellectuals will ever approve of me. I believe they can't help liking much of this book, but me—that's another matter. I'm a popular target for literary critics and other bright boys. I've written seven books, all I believe of value; they have rarely received a welcome. Even THE ARRANGEMENT which endures in the memory of many women and men, was put down as a sex book, semi-trash, by intellectuals. My best book, THE ANATOLIAN, was a marketplace failure.

Perhaps this general judgment is deserved but I don't think so and it has not made me more agreeable. I've had to find my own place outside our literary society. I am not welcome in the book world here nor do I hope I ever will be. I have no recourse except to live by my own evaluation of my worth which is (please destroy this letter) considerable. I believe that my books tell a great deal about our time, more than, for example, those of highly praised fellows like William Styron.

My testimony brought me general shame in my own circle. But in a difficult, personal and political situation, I believe I did well. I did not lie, as many others did. In the end, I was not ashamed. Why should I be humble about how I behaved. Let my enemies be humble. I do not hope to ease my reputation completely, not ever. To tell the truth (the necessary standard for an autobiographer) I am presently still defiant, will remain so and ask for nothing in the way of respect from anyone except for what's on the screen and what's on paper. In the end, I am proud of myself. If I appear, from time to time, to be arrogant, that is inevitable and should even be encouraged. You know me by now and whatever I am, whatever angry feelings I have, they are based on experience, which is a hard thing. I do not fear to give the impression that I am arrogant. What I do fear and can't do, is to appear to be what I am not. What is "wimpy?" And I certainly don't want to be in between. I believe that in my field, people's respect can come only when a writer or a filmmaker is plain, blunt, honest, absolute, UN-reasonable and defiant, proud of what he is and paying only the most cautious respect to the opinion of others.

You know how much I respect your advice and how grateful I am for your continuous concern and for Kathy's. But finally this book, particularly the part of this book that seems to worry you, has to speak for me, not for you. I have to like it. To please New York's liberal literary community—fuck that; I don't expect it. It's not one of my goals.

So be content to think of me as peculiarly arrogant, a man who's gotten along well enough without pleasing everyone. That, dear Bob, pleasing more people, is what your hope that I should find a middle ground between the arrogant and the "wimpy" seems to me to come down to.

About this section. Up until 1952, up until that ugly crisis, I'd tried to get along by staying in the middle and, at whatever cost, making accommodations to both sides, so keeping everyone a friend. Then that became impossible. I had no choice except to think and choose and find my own way. I had to stand up for what I believed, however unpopular that would be, state it when challenged, let come what may. This was a new experience for me.

I began to ask myself certain questions and come to answers which in the world where I moved were anathema. I would be totally against the tide and generally despised; I knew that. But to have continued to be both-ways understanding and all-ways a "good guy" was now impossible. Furthermore, that idea—and my past behavior—now offended me. I needed to make enemies and while that still made me uncomfortable, once I'd taken the plunge, anger and defiance saved me. I experienced a new kind of exhilaration, that of not bending and standing alone. That was the end of my "Both" life.

E.K.

[Robert Gottlieb began to read "Confessions of an Outsider" in 1982, well before Kazan rejected the original working title of his autobiography and suggested *A Life* instead: "It sounds like I'm a con or feel guilty about something or want to relieve my soul of the burden of some mistake. It's exactly what some small percentage of the population expect of me and I don't want to do it" (to Gottlieb, December 23, 1985, Wesleyan). The long-delayed explanation of how Kazan became an informer was of prime concern to Gottlieb and his coeditor Katherine Hourigan. It was feared that readers would turn to this chapter first and be disaffected by Kazan's seeming arrogance.

Kazan's decision to recreate the "ambivalence" and the "sudden shifts of mood" was vital to preserving the fateful, entangling nature of his congressional testimony without recourse to "polemic" or "apology" (to Hourigan, August 30, 1987, Wesleyan). The strategy did not preclude naming committee members who had leaked Kazan's initial testimony, or respecting friends who preferred the " 'decent alternative' " of revealing one's political history without implicating others. Kazan reconsidered the same option in a later diary note: "Why didn't I do it that way. I would have been a great hero today" (Wesleyan). At the time his "scrupulous" wife answered the question by upholding the civic " 'duty' " to inform Congress of subversive activities. It remained for the analyst Bela Mittelmann to ask Kazan if the situation were reversed, would former friends and Group Theatre members protect him by " 'endangering their careers' "? Darryl Zanuck put the case bluntly, urging Kazan to " 'Name the names, for Chrissake. Who the hell are you going to jail for?' " (*A Life*, p. 455). Unspoken but understood by Kazan was the readiness of Fox executives to use the blacklist. Kazan partially deflected responsibility for his revised testimony by placing himself within the range of influential advisers. Where he stood alone and confident—and accurate, as historical scholarship has confirmed—was in acknowledging the party's conspiratorial tactics and plan to infiltrate American institutions. The "anger and defiance" that "saved" Kazan in the immediate aftermath of his testimony did not relieve the residual effects of informing: "Here I am, thirty-five years later, still worrying over it" (*A Life*, pp. 444–65).

As it turned out, the HUAC chapter drew little rancor, save in die-hard leftist quarters such as the *Village Voice*. Kazan's stated motives in naming former communists did not, however, prevent reviewers from supplying their own interpretation of events: "emotional needs" rather than political principles were at work; betrayal in matters social, sexual, and political "held a fatal fascination" for Kazan; as an immigrant American, he decided "to truckle to a committee which invigilated 'un-Americanism.'" A writer for *Commentary* wished to have it both ways. Kazan had justly "exposed the fans" of a murderous regime but now "affects qualms of conscience" for injuring the betrayers of democratic ideals.

A cover note typed and dated 7/23/87 by Eileen Shanahan indicates that the present letter was filed and not mailed to Gottlieb: "EK had phone conversation with Kathy Hourigan; asked me to file letter. Do Not Send."] *TLS, 3 pp., Wesleyan*

Elia and Frances

TO KATHARINE KAZAN

PM: New York, NY, January 22, 1988

KK dear:

Thank you for that swell, two-part letter. First of all I want to say that I am glad as well as you are glad that Dan is not like me. I was—and am no longer, I so believe—a pretty neurotic man. I think I am o.k. now but I am not quite reliable, not in ways I used to be but always ambivalent and "a spy" and not quite saying what I think etc. (But who does.) But Frances seems to be at ease with me and I'm glad of that.

I didn't mean to burden you with a big secret, namely this book but I had been cautioned by the publisher people not to let it fall into the hands of anyone who might let it fall into the hands of media people. And I felt that too. So "Please dont talk about it." But as soon as the bound galleys came into existence, there was no need for secrets. Everybody now seems to be stealing or borrowing copies and gabbing about the book.

I agree about more editing time. But I did get fed up, worn out, sated with the damned book and am now. I've had it, as they say. But I also wish I'd made that part near the end about the Actors Studio Theatre simpler and shorter. At the same time I enjoyed writing that. I do have a vengeful streak no matter how well I hide it. I got to thoroughly dislike Strasberg and the bunch of actors who had their tongues up his ass all the time. So I lashed back.

As for adjustments in marriage, Christ, Katharine, I made a hell of a lot of those and of different kinds, to Molly first of all—I was not like her or she like me and I, at least, was adjusting until I couldn't anymore. And you must have guessed that I made a lot of adjustments to Barbara. I adjusted and I adjusted until I couldn't anymore. And so did Molly. And so did Barbara. Since I am not an easy person, not to live with that is. And you can go just so far with that—well—

I do feel that I deserve your compliment at the end, the one about being an honest father. But it was not always thus and I had to work hard for it and I did hurt some people, some very good people. But I still dont know if you can get through life without hurting people.

As for Mandy, tell her about the part where I put down "womanizing", say that its a despicable word, that I did whatever I did as a continuation of work and of a development of friendship. So there is that dreadful word, "Womanizing" that demeans both sexes. I believe that Mandy will have a wonderful life but its going to be a complex one because she is a very curious girl and full of beans and has a wonderful, smiling [way] of looking at her grandfather which that man loves.

And, here's the last word. I dont believe that any man worth his shit stays with a woman because she is Spring. Men stay with a woman like the story books say—this being one place where they tell the truth—because the woman is wonderful, takes care of them, produces good children, makes them laugh, is a good driver, saves a little money, is smart, therefore interesting, inventive, surprising and is a hell of a good companion. And if I sound like all those "How to save your marriage" magazines, I dont care. That is what I've found to be true. With the cutey girls, as you come you wonder, "How the hell can I get them out of here, how can I be alone again. And with the real good girls, what follows is as good as any of the rest of it.

Your father truly loves you and I hope I never give you, or Judy or Nick or Chris or Leo anymore pain. O.K.?

[Katie Kazan received a set of galleys in late 1987 with a wish that she "read them before anyone else." Elia hoped that the candor of his autobiography would not "upset" her and that she would "like it." Her "two-part letter" has not been preserved.

Kazan recounted the failure of the Actors Studio Theatre and his resignation from the directorate, but the more telling emphasis in *A Life* fell on Lee Strasberg as potentate, who assumed the role of "a judge, not an artistic collaborator." The director of East and West Coast Institutes who emerged in the 1970s further insulated himself from the "dangers" of production. "Was the success he'd won the success he'd wanted? Of course not. In the end, you do the best you can" (pp. 707–14). Kazan agreed to modify his original treatment of Strasberg, which Robert Gottlieb thought obsessive.

Elia admitted in *A Life* that Molly Kazan's death, while "a tragedy," was also "a blessing" that allowed "a truer self" to appear—not "the prettiest thing in the world," as his analyst observed, but a necessary departure from the expeditious "Gadg." He rejected "womanizing" as "a prim, stuffy, fightened, middle-class word," claiming that his affairs with actresses formed a "strong bond of interest" and did not "endanger other, more lasting, human bonds" (*A Life*, pp. 719–22). Such candor, brandished like an "open blade," aroused more critical ire than Kazan's informing and led a critic to remark, "How can all this frankness stay so unaware and feel so sly?"

Kazan received an advance of $825,000 with payments spread over seven years. Released in 1988, *A Life* sold well, although it did not approach the success of *The Arrangement* or reach the best-seller list. A promotional statement by Norman Mailer closed the book, as it were, with an inadvertent echo of the original title: "*A Life* has that candor of confession which is possible only when the deepest wounds have healed and honesty can achieve what honesty so rarely arrives at—a rich and hearty flavor. By such means, a famous director has written a book that offers the kind of human wealth we find in a major novel."] *TL, 1 p., KKP*

CHRONOLOGY

Biography

1909	Elia Kazanjioglou born September 7 in Constantinople (Istanbul), Turkey, to George and Athena Kazanjioglou.
1913	Moves with his family to New York.
1920–26	Attends Mayfair School and New Rochelle High School. Enters Williams College in the fall of 1926.
1930	Graduates B.A. cum laude in English from Williams. The Group Theatre is founded by Harold Clurman, Cheryl Crawford, and Lee Strasberg. The first meeting occurs in November. Among the original members are Franchot Tone, Morris Carnovsky, Sanford Meisner, J. Edward Bromberg, Ruth Nelson, Margaret Barker, and Stella Adler.
1932	Marries Molly Day Thacher. Attends the Yale School of Fine Arts, Drama Department. Attends Group Theatre summer camp at Sterling Farms, Dover Furnace, New York, as an apprentice. Theatrical debut as stage manager and understudy for the Theatre Guild production *The Pure in Heart* in Baltimore.
1933	Broadway acting debut in Sidney Kingsley's *Men in White* for the Group Theatre. Accepted as a full member of the Group Theatre.
1934–36	Member of the Communist Party. Active in workers' theaters: Theatre Collective, Theatre Union, and Theatre of Action. Teaches acting and directing at the New Theatre League.
1935	Appears in Clifford Odets's *Waiting for Lefty*.
1936	Daughter Judy born.
1937	Lee Strasberg and Cheryl Crawford resign from the Group Theatre, leaving Harold Clurman as sole director, with an advisory council consisting of Kazan, Roman Bohnen, and Luther Adler. Appears in Clifford Odets's *Golden Boy*. Assistant director on the documentary film *People of the Cumberland*. Spends some months in Hollywood, assisting director Lewis Milestone.
1938	Son Chris born. Broadway directing debut, *Casey Jones*, for the Group Theatre.
1939	Directs plays: *Quiet City* and *Thunder Rock*.
1940	Appears in the film *City for Conquest*, starring James Cagney.
1941	Appears in the film *Blues in the Night*. The Group Theatre disbands.
1942	Directs plays: *The Strings, My Lord, Are False; Café Crown;* and *The Skin of Our Teeth*, for which he receives New York Drama Critics' Circle Award for best director.
1943	Directs plays: *Harriet* and *One Touch of Venus* (musical).
1944	Directs plays: *Jacobowsky and the Colonel* and *Sing Out, Sweet Land* (musical).

1945	Son Nick born. Directs film: *A Tree Grows in Brooklyn*. Directs plays: *Dunnigan's Daughter* and *Deep Are the Roots*.
1947	Films: *The Sea of Grass, Boomerang!, Gentleman's Agreement*. Plays: *All My Sons, A Streetcar Named Desire*. Wins Tony Award for direction of *All My Sons*. Receives Oscar, Golden Globe, and New York Film Critics awards for his direction of *Gentleman's Agreement*. Receives National Board of Review award for his direction of *Gentleman's Agreement* and *Boomerang!* Receives New York Drama Critics' and Donaldson awards for direction of *Streetcar*. Cofounds the Actors Studio with Robert Lewis and Cheryl Crawford. Lewis leaves after the first year. Three years later Kazan invites Lee Strasberg to direct the Studio's acting program.
1948	Daughter Katie born. Play: *Love Life* (musical). Film: *Pinky*.
1949	Play: *Death of a Salesman*. Receives Tony Award for direction.
1950	Forms the motion picture company Newtown Productions. Film: *Panic in the Streets*. Lee Strasberg becomes artistic director of the Actors Studio.
1951	Film: *A Streetcar Named Desire,* for which he receives an Oscar nomination and receives New York Film Critics Circle Award for direction.
1952	Appears before an executive session of a subcommittee of the House Committee on Un-American Activities on January 14. Admits to his former membership in the Communist Party but refuses to give the names of his associates. On April 10, he appears voluntarily and gives the names of former fellow Communist Party members, including eight members of his Group Theatre unit, among them Clifford Odets, Morris Carnovsky, Tony Kraber, Art Smith, and Paula Strasberg. Offers a lengthy self-exculpatory notice in the *New York Times* explaining the reasons for his testimony. Film: *Viva Zapata!* Play: *Flight into Egypt*.
1953	Film: *Man on a Tightrope*. Plays: *Camino Real* and *Tea and Sympathy,* for which he wins a Donaldson Award as best director.
1954	Forms a second motion-picture producing company, Athena Enterprises. Film: *On the Waterfront,* for which he receives an Academy Award, the New York Film Critics Circle Award, and a Golden Globe. Receives honorary doctorate from Wesleyan University.
1955	Play: *Cat on a Hot Tin Roof,* for which he wins a Donaldson Award for best director. Film: *East of Eden*.
1956	Film: *Baby Doll*.
1957	Play: *The Dark at the Top of the Stairs*. Film: *A Face in the Crowd*.
1958	Play: *J.B.* Receives Tony Award for direction.
1959	Receives honorary Master of Arts degree from Yale University. Play: *Sweet Bird of Youth*.
1960	Appointed codirector with Robert Whitehead of the Repertory Theatre of Lincoln Center. Film: *Wild River*.

Best Director for *Gentleman's
Agreement*, at the Academy Awards,
1948

1961	Film: *Splendor in the Grass.*
1962	Son Leo born to Barbara Loden. Alters status at Actors Studio from active to inactive member. Book: *America America.* Receives honorary doctorate from Carnegie Institute of Technology.
1963	Molly Day Thacher Kazan dies. Film: *America America,* for which he receives a Golden Globe for his direction.
1964	Stages for the Repertory Theatre of Lincoln Center: *After the Fall, But for Whom Charlie,* and *The Changeling.* Receives honorary doctorate from Williams College. Resigns from the Repertory Theatre of Lincoln Center.
1966	Discusses with Oscar Lewis a film of Lewis's *La Vida.*
1967	Marries second wife, Barbara Loden. Meets with James Baldwin and Alex Haley to discuss a film about Malcolm X. Book: *The Arrangement.*
1969	Film: *The Arrangement.*
1972	Receives New York City's Handel Medallion. Book: *The Assassins.* Film: *The Visitors.*
1975	Book: *The Understudy.*
1976	Film: *The Last Tycoon.*
1978	Discusses with Richard Burton a production of *King Lear.* Book: *Acts of Love.* Receives honorary doctorate from Katholieke Universiteit, Leuven, Belgium.
1980	Second wife, Barbara Loden, dies.

1982	Marries third wife, Frances Rudge. Book: *The Anatolian*.
1983	Receives Kennedy Center Honors Lifetime Achievement Award. Becomes Special Honorary Life Member of Directors Guild of America. Play: *The Chain*.
1986	Receives D. W. Griffith Special Lifetime Achievement Award from Directors Guild of America.
1987	Honoree, American Museum of the Living Image.
1988	Autobiography: *A Life*.
1989	American Film Institute refuses to honor Kazan: "He named names and we just can't honor someone who did that."
1991	Son Chris dies.
1994	Book: *Beyond the Aegean*.
1996	Receives Honorary Golden Bear Award from Berlin Film Festival.
1999	Receives Lifetime Achievement Award from Motion Picture Academy of Arts and Sciences.
2003	Dies September 28, aged ninety-four.

Directing

STAGE

1931	*The Second Man* by S. N. Behrman. Toy Theatre, Atlantic City.
1934	*Dimitroff, a Play of Mass Pressure,* by Elia Kazan and Art Smith, codirected with Art Smith for the Group Theatre.
1935	*The Young Go First* by Peter Martin, George Scudder, and Charles Friedman. Codirected with Alfred Saxe for the Theatre of Action.
1936	*The Crime* by Michael Blankfort. Codirected with Alfred Saxe for the Theatre of Action. Cast: Martin Ritt, Nicholas Ray, Norman Lloyd.
1938	*Casey Jones* by Robert Ardrey. Set design: Mordecai Gorelik. Cast: Van Heflin, Charles Bickford, Peggy Conklin. Kazan's Broadway debut. Group Theatre.
1939	*Quiet City* by Irwin Shaw. Score: Aaron Copland. Set design: Mordecai Gorelik. Cast: Morris Carnovsky, Luther Adler, Frances Farmer. Two private performances only. Group Theatre.
	Thunder Rock by Robert Ardrey. Set design: Mordecai Gorelik. Cast: Luther Adler, Morris Carnovsky, and Frances Farmer. Group Theatre.
1942	*Café Crown* by H. S. Kraft. Produced by Carly Wharton and Martin Gabel. Set design: Boris Aronson. Cast: Sam Jaffe, Morris Carnovsky.
	The Strings, My Lord, Are False by Paul Vincent Carroll. Cast: Art Smith, Walter Hampden, Constance Dowling, Will Lee, Ruth Gordon, Hurd Hatfield. Theatre Guild. Set in Scotland in 1941.

He was fired before the opening but remained the director of record.

The Skin of Our Teeth by Thornton Wilder. Produced by Michael Myerberg. Set design: Albert Johnson. Costumes: Mary Percy Schenck. Cast: Tallulah Bankhead, Fredric March, Florence Eldridge, Montgomery Clift, E. G. Marshall, Florence Reed, Dick Van Patten, Morton da Costa. New York premiere: Plymouth Theatre, November 18, 1942. New York Drama Critics' Circle Award for best director. Pulitzer Prize for Drama.

1943   *Harriet* by Florence Ryerson and Colin Clements. Produced by Gilbert Miller. Set design: Lemuel Ayers. Costumes: Aline Bernstein. Cast: Helen Hayes, Rhys Williams, Joan Tetzel.

It's Up to You by Arthur Arent. Department of Agriculture.

One Touch of Venus by S. J. Perelman and Ogden Nash. Music by Kurt Weill. Lyrics by Ogden Nash. Produced by Cheryl Crawford. Choreography: Agnes De Mille. Set design: Howard Bay. Cast: Mary Martin, John Boles, Kenny Baker, Sono Osato, Pearl Lang.

1944   *Jacobowsky and the Colonel* by S. N. Behrman, adapted from a play by Franz Werfel. Produced by the Theatre Guild. Music: Paul Bowles. Set design: Stewart Chaney. Cast: Oscar Karlweis, Annabella, Louis Calhern. New York Drama Critics' Circle Award for best foreign play.

Sing Out, Sweet Land! Uncredited. A salute to American folk and popular music. Conceived and written by Walter Kerr. Staging attributed to Leon Leonidoff and Walter Kerr. Produced by the Theatre Guild. Cast: Alfred Drake, Burl Ives.

1945   *Deep Are the Roots* by Arnaud d'Usseau and James Gow. Produced by Kermit Bloomgarden and George Heller. Cast: Barbara Bel Geddes, Gordon Heath.

Dunnigan's Daughter by S. N. Behrman. Produced by the Theatre Guild. Set design: Stewart Chaney. Costumes: Mainbocher. Cast: Dennis King, June Havoc, Luther Adler, Richard Widmark, Jan Sterling. John Golden Theatre, December 26, 1945–January 26, 1946.

1946   *Truckline Cafe* by Maxwell Anderson. Directed by Harold Clurman. Coproduced by Elia Kazan in association with Harold Clurman and the Playwrights' Company (Maxwell Anderson, S. N. Behrman, Elmer Rice, Robert E. Sherwood, Sidney Howard). Set design: Boris Aronson. Costumes: Millia Davenport. Cast: Kevin McCarthy, June Walker, Virginia Gilmore, Karl Malden, Marlon Brando, Lou Gilbert, Richard Waring. Belasco Theatre, February 27, 1946–March 9, 1946.

1947   *All My Sons* by Arthur Miller. Produced by Elia Kazan, Harold Clurman, and Walter Fried in association with Herbert H. Harris. Set design: Mordecai Gorelik. Cast: Arthur Kennedy, Karl Malden, Beth Merrill, Ed Begley, Lois Wheeler. New York premiere: Coronet Theatre, January 29, 1947. Tony Awards for best author, best director. New York Drama Critics' Circle Award for best American play. Donaldson Award for best play.

A Streetcar Named Desire by Tennessee Williams. Produced by Irene Mayer Selznick. Scenery and lighting: Jo Mielziner. Costumes: Lucinda Ballard. Cast: Jessica Tandy, Marlon Brando, Kim Hunter, Karl Malden. New York premiere: Ethel Barrymore Theatre, December 3, 1947. Pulitzer Prize for drama. New York Drama Critics' Circle Award for best American play, best director. Donaldson Award for best director. Tony Award for best actress (Jessica Tandy).

1948 *Sundown Beach* by Bessie Breuer. An Actors Studio Production. Set design: Ben Edwards. Cast: Phyllis Thaxter, Julie Harris, Cloris Leachman.

Love Life, a musical by Alan Jay Lerner and Kurt Weill. Produced by Cheryl Crawford. Choreography: Michael Kidd. Set design: Boris Aronson. Cast: Nanette Fabray, Ray Middleton.

1949 *Death of a Salesman* by Arthur Miller. Produced by Kermit Bloomgarden and Walter Fried. Set design: Jo Mielziner. Costumes: Julia Sze. Music: Alex North. Cast: Lee J. Cobb, Mildred Dunnock, Arthur Kennedy, Cameron Mitchell, Tom Pedi, Howard Smith. New York premiere: Morosco Theatre, February 10, 1949. New York Drama Critics' Circle Award for best American play. Tony Award for best play, best director. Donaldson Award for best play. Pulitzer Prize for drama.

1952 *Flight into Egypt* by George Tabori. Produced by Irene Mayer Selznick. Set design: Jo Mielziner. Costumes: Anna Hill Johnstone. Cast: Paul Lukas, Gusti Huber, Zero Mostel, Joseph Anthony, Jo Van Fleet.

1953 *Camino Real* by Tennessee Williams. Directed with the assistance of Anna Sokolow. Produced by Cheryl Crawford and Ethel Reiner, in association with Walter Chrysler, Jr. Set design: Lemuel Ayers. Costumes: Lemuel Ayres. Cast: Eli Wallach, Frank Silvera, Jo Van Fleet, Joseph Anthony, Hurd Hatfield, Jennie Goldstein, Barbara Baxley, Salem Ludwig, Martin Balsam, Gluck Sandor, Michael Gazzo. New York premiere: National Theatre, March 17, 1953.

Tea and Sympathy by Robert Anderson. Produced by the Playwrights' Company with Mary K. Frank. Set design: Jo Mielziner. Costumes: Anna Hill Johnstone. Cast: Deborah Kerr, John Kerr, Leif Erickson. Donaldson Award for best director, best first play.

1955 *Cat on a Hot Tin Roof* by Tennessee Williams. Produced by the Playwrights' Company. Set design: Jo Mielziner. Costumes: Lucinda Ballard. Cast: Barbara Bel Geddes, Ben Gazzara, Burl Ives, Mildred Dunnock, Pat Hingle, Madeleine Sherwood. New York premiere: Morosco Theatre, March 24, 1955. Pulitzer Prize for drama. New York Drama Critics' Circle Award for best American play.

1957	*The Dark at the Top of the Stairs* by William Inge. Produced by Arnold Saint-Subber and Elia Kazan. Set design: Ben Edwards. Costumes: Lucinda Ballard. Cast: Teresa Wright, Pat Hingle, Eileen Heckart, Evans Evans, Timmy Everett.
1958	*J.B.* by Archibald MacLeish. Produced by Alfred de Liagre, Jr. Set design: Boris Aronson. Costumes: Lucinda Ballard. Cast: Pat Hingle, Raymond Massey, Christopher Plummer, Nan Martin, Bert Conway, Ivor Francis, Andreas Voutsinas. New York premiere: ANTA Theatre, December 11, 1958. Tony Award for best director, best play. Pulitzer Prize for drama.
1959	*Sweet Bird of Youth* by Tennessee Williams. Produced by Cheryl Crawford. Set and lighting design: Jo Mielziner. Costumes: Anna Hill Johnstone. Cast: Paul Newman, Geraldine Page, Sidney Blackmer, Rip Torn, Diana Hyland, Bruce Dern, Madeleine Sherwood, Martine Bartlett. New York premiere: Martin Beck Theatre, March 10, 1959.
1964	*After the Fall* by Arthur Miller. Produced by the Repertory Theatre of Lincoln Center. Set design: Jo Mielziner. Costumes: Anna Hill Johnstone. Cast: Jason Robards, Zohra Lampert, Faye Dunaway, Barbara Loden, Salome Jens, Ralph Meeker, David Wayne, Hal Holbrook.
	But for Whom Charlie by S. N. Behrman. Produced by the Repertory Theatre of Lincoln Center. Set design: Jo Mielziner. Costumes: Theoni V. Aldredge. Cast: Jason Robards, Ralph Meekev, Faye Dunaway, David Wayne, Salome Jens.
	The Changeling by Thomas Middleton and William Rowley. Produced by the Repertory Theatre of Lincoln Center. Set design: David Hays. Costumes: Ben Edwards. Cast: Barbara Loden, Faye Dunaway, John Phillip Law, Clinton Kimbrough.
1983	*The Chain* by Elia Kazan. An adaptation of Aeschylus' *Oresteia*. Cast: Joseph Ragno, Salem Ludwig, Corinne Neuchateu. Stamford, Conn.

FILM

1935	*Pie in the Sky.* Codirected with Ralph Steiner and Molly Thacher Kazan, for Nykino, a branch of Theatre of Action/Shocked Troupe, an agitprop theater group. A satire on organized religion.
1937	*People of the Cumberland.* Assistant director. Directed by Sidney Meyers (Robert Stebbins) and Jay Leyda (Eugene Hill). Cinematography: Ralph Steiner. Frontier Films, a progressive film cooperative.
1941	*It's Up to You.* Screenplay: Arthur Arent. Music: Earl Robinson. Cast: Helen Tamiris. Department of Agriculture. A stage play with film material.
1945	*A Tree Grows in Brooklyn.* Produced by Louis D. Lighton.

Screenplay by Tess Slesinger and Frank Davis, with additional dialogue by Anita Loos. Adapted from the novel by Betty Smith. Cinematography: Leon Shamroy. Editing: Dorothy Spencer. Art decoration: Lyle Wheeler. Cast: Dorothy McGuire, Joan Blondell, James Dunn, Peggy Ann Garner, Lloyd Nolan, Ted Donaldson, James Gleason. Twentieth Century-Fox. Academy Award for best supporting actor (James Dunn); Special Award to Peggy Ann Garner as outstanding child performer.

1947   *The Sea of Grass.* Produced by Pandro S. Berman. Screenplay by Marguerite Roberts and Vincent Lawrence, based on the novel by Conrad Richter. Cinematography: Harry Stradling. Editing: Robert J. Kern. Cast: Spencer Tracy, Katharine Hepburn, Robert Walker, Melvyn Douglas. Metro-Goldwyn-Mayer.

Boomerang! Produced by Louis de Rochemont, for Darryl F. Zanuck. Screenplay by Richard Murphy, from the article "The Perfect Case" by Anthony Abbot (Fulton Oursler). Cinematography: Norbert Brodine. Cast: Dana Andrews, Jane Wyatt, Arthur Kennedy, Lee J. Cobb, Sam Levene, Karl Malden, Ed Begley, Joe Kazan. Twentieth Century-Fox. National Board of Review Award for best director. New York Film Critics Circle Award for best director.

Gentleman's Agreement. Produced by Darryl F. Zanuck. Screenplay by Moss Hart, from the novel by Laura Z. Hobson. Cinematography: Arthur Miller. Editing: Harmon Jones. Cast: Gregory Peck, Dorothy McGuire, John Garfield, Celeste Holm, Anne Revere, June Havoc, Dean Stockwell. Twentieth Century-Fox. Academy Awards for best supporting actress (Celeste Holm), best director, best picture. National Board of Review Award for best director. New York Film Critics Circle Award for best film; best director. Golden Globe for best director.

1949   *Pinky.* Produced by Darryl F. Zanuck. Screenplay by Philip Dunne and Dudley Nichols, from the novel *Quality* by Cid Ricketts Sumner. Cinematography: Joe MacDonald. Editing: Harmon Jones. Cast: Jeanne Crain, Ethel Barrymore, Ethel Waters.

1950   *Panic in the Streets.* Produced by Sol C. Siegel. Screenplay by Richard Murphy, with contributions from Daniel Fuchs, based on a story by Edward and Edna Anhalt. Cinematography: Joe MacDonald. Editing: Harmon Jones. Cast: Richard Widmark, Paul Douglas, Barbara Bel Geddes, Jack Palance, Zero Mostel. Twentieth Century-Fox. Academy Award for best screenplay. Venice Film Festival: International Prize.

1951   *A Streetcar Named Desire.* Produced by Charles K. Feldman. Screenplay by Tennessee Williams, adapted by Oscar Saul. Cinematography: Harry Stradling. Editing: David Weisbert. Cast: Vivien Leigh, Marlon Brando, Kim Hunter, Karl Malden. Warner Bros. Academy Awards for best actress (Vivien Leigh), best supporting actress (Kim Hunter), best supporting actor (Karl

Malden), best art direction. New York Film Critics Circle Awards for best film, best director. Venice Film Festival: Special Prize, Elia Kazan.

1952   *Viva Zapata!* Produced by Darryl F. Zanuck. Screenplay by John Steinbeck. Cinematography: Joe MacDonald. Editing: Barbara McLean. Cast: Marlon Brando, Jean Peters, Anthony Quinn, Joseph Wiseman, Margo, Mildred Dunnock, Arnold Moss. Twentieth Century-Fox. Academy Award for best supporting actor (Anthony Quinn).

1953   *Man on a Tightrope.* Produced by Robert L. Jacks. Screenplay by Robert Sherwood, based on the story "International Incident" by Neil Paterson. Cinematography: Georg Krause. Cast: Fredric March, Gloria Grahame, Terry Moore, Adolphe Menjou. Twentieth Century-Fox. Berlin Film Festival International Delegate: Jury Prize of the Berlin Senate.

1954   *On the Waterfront.* Produced by Sam Spiegel for Horizon Pictures. Screenplay by Budd Schulberg, based on articles by Malcolm Johnson. Cinematography: Boris Kaufman. Editing: Gene Milford. Score: Leonard Bernstein. Cast: Marlon Brando, Karl Malden, Lee J. Cobb, Rod Steiger, Eva Marie Saint. Columbia. Academy Award for best picture, best director, best actor (Marlon Brando), best supporting actress (Eva Marie Saint), best writing, best art direction, best cinematography, best editing. New York Film Critics Circle Award for best film, best director, best actor (Marlon Brando). Golden Globe for best director. Venice Film Festival: International Prize, Elia Kazan.

1955   *East of Eden.* Produced by Elia Kazan. Screenplay by Paul Osborn, from the novel by John Steinbeck. Cinematography: Ted D. McCord. Editing: Owen Marks. Art direction: James Basevi. Cast: James Dean, Julie Harris, Raymond Massey, Jo Van Fleet, Lois Smith, Burl Ives, Richard Davalos. Warner Bros. Academy Award for Best Supporting Actress (Jo Van Fleet). Golden Globe Award for Best Motion Picture (Drama). Cannes Film Festival: Best Dramatic Film Award.

1956   *Baby Doll.* Produced by Elia Kazan. Screenplay by Tennessee Williams, based on his plays 27 *Wagons Full of Cotton* and *The Unsatisfactory Supper.* Cinematography: Boris Kaufman. Editing: Gene Milford. Cast: Karl Malden, Carroll Baker, Eli Wallach, Mildred Dunnock, Madeleine Sherwood, Rip Torn. Newtown Productions for Warner Bros.

1957   *A Face in the Crowd.* Produced by Elia Kazan. Screenplay and story by Budd Schulberg, from his book *Some Faces in the Crowd.* Cinematography: Harry Stradling, Gayne Rescher. Editing: Gene Milford. Cast: Andy Griffith, Patricia Neal, Anthony Franciosa, Walter Matthau, Lee Remick. Newtown Productions, Warner Bros.

1960   *Wild River.* Produced by Elia Kazan. Screenplay by Paul Osborn, based on the novels *Mud on the Stars* by William Bradford Huie and *Dunbar's Cove* by Borden Deal. Cinematography: Ellsworth Fredricks. Editing: William Reynolds. Cast: Montgomery Clift, Lee Remick, Jo Van Fleet, Albert Salmi, Barbara Loden, Bruce Dern, Pat Hingle. Twentieth Century-Fox.

1961 *Splendor in the Grass.* Produced by Elia Kazan. Screenplay by William Inge. Cinematography: Boris Kaufman. Editing: Gene Milford. Costumes: Anna Hill Johnstone. Sets: Gene Callahan. Production design: Richard Sylbert. Cast: Natalie Wood, Audrey Christie, Warren Beatty, Pat Hingle, Barbara Loden, Zohra Lampert, Fred Stewart, Sandy Dennis, Phyllis Diller, William Inge. Warner Bros. Academy Award for Best Screenplay.

1963 *America America.* Produced by Elia Kazan. Screenplay by Elia Kazan, based on his novel of the same name. Cinematography: Haskell Wexler. Editing: Dede Allen. Score: Manos Hadjidakis. Production design: Gene Callahan. Costumes: Anna Hill Johnstone. Cast: Stathis Giallelis, Frank Wolff, Elena Karam, John Marley, Katharine Balfour, Paul Mann. Athena Enterprises, Warner Bros. Golden Globe for Best Director.

1969 *The Arrangement.* Produced by Elia Kazan. Screenplay by Elia Kazan, adapted from his novel. Cinematography: Robert Surtees. Editing: Stephan Amsten. Production design: Gene Callahan. Cast: Kirk Douglas, Faye Dunaway, Deborah Kerr, Richard Boone, Hume Cronyn. Athena Enterprises, Warner Bros.–Seven Arts Production.

1972 *The Visitors.* Produced by Chris Kazan and Nick Proferes. Screenplay by Chris Kazan. Cinematography: Nick Proferes. Cast: Patrick McVey, Patricia Joyce, James Woods, Steve Railsback, Chico Martinez. United Artists.

1976 *The Last Tycoon.* Produced by Sam Spiegel. Screenplay by Harold Pinter, based on the novel by F. Scott Fitzgerald. Cinematography: Victor Kemper. Cast: Robert De Niro, Tony Curtis, Robert Mitchum, Jeanne Moreau, Jack Nicholson, Ingrid Boulting, Dana Andrews, Theresa Russell. A Sam Spiegel–Elia Kazan Film. Paramount.

Acting

STAGE

1932 "Louis, a bartender" in *Chrysalis* by Rose Albert Porter; also stage manager. Directed by Theresa Helburn. Theatre Guild.

1933 "An orderly" in *Men in White* by Sidney Kingsley. Directed by Lee Strasberg.

Stage manager for *Gentlewoman,* by John Howard Lawson. Group Theatre.

1934   "Polyziodes" in *Gold Eagle Guy* by Melvin Levy; also stage manager. Directed by Lee Strasberg.

Stage manager for *Awake and Sing!* by Clifford Odets. Group Theatre.

1935   "Agate Keller" and "Clancy" in *Waiting for Lefty* by Clifford Odets. Directed by Clifford Odets and Sanford Meisner.

"Baum" in *Till the Day I Die* by Clifford Odets. Directed by Cheryl Crawford. Group Theatre.

"Kewpie" in *Paradise Lost* by Clifford Odets. Directed by Harold Clurman. Group Theatre.

1936   "Private Kearns" in *Johnny Johnson* by Paul Green and Kurt Weill. Directed by Lee Strasberg. Group Theatre.

1937   "Eddie Fuselli" in *Golden Boy* by Clifford Odets. Directed by Harold Clurman. Group Theatre.

1938–39   "Joe Bonaparte" the lead role, tour of *Golden Boy.* Group Theatre.

1939   "Eli Lieber" in *The Gentle People* by Irwin Shaw. Directed by Harold Clurman. Group Theatre.

1940   "Ficzur, the Sparrow" in *Liliom* by Ferenc Molnár. Directed by Benno Schneider. This production starred Burgess Meredith and Ingrid Bergman. Produced by Vinton Freedley.

"Steve Takis" in *Night Music* by Clifford Odets. Directed by Harold Clurman. Group Theatre.

1941   "Adam Boguris" in *Five Alarm Waltz* by Lucille S. Prumbs. Directed by Robert Lewis. Produced by Everett Wile. Character based on writer William Saroyan.

FILM

1934   Shorts *Café Universal* and *Pie in the Sky,* both directed by Ralph Steiner.

1940   "Googi Zucco" in *City for Conquest,* directed by Anatole Litvak. Warner Bros.

1941   "Nickie Haroyen, a clarinet player" in *Blues in the Night,* directed by Anatole Litvak. Warner Bros. Also, uncredited contribution to the script.

1950   "Mortuary assistant" in *Panic in the Streets.* Uncredited.

1988   "Old man in coffee shop" in *Le Brouillard,* directed by Omer Zulfi Livanelli.

Writing

1934 *Dmitroff: A Play of Mass Pressure*. One-act play by Kazan and Art
     Smith, as benefit for *New Theatre* magazine. League of Workers
     Theatre.

1983 *The Chain*.

NOVELS

1961 *America America*. New York: Stein & Day.

1967 *The Arrangement*. New York: Stein & Day.

1972 *The Assassins*. New York: Stein & Day.

1975 *The Understudy*. New York: Stein & Day.

1978 *Acts of Love*. New York: Alfred A. Knopf.

1982 *The Anatolian*. New York: Alfred A. Knopf.

1994 *Beyond the Aegean*. New York: Alfred A. Knopf.

AUTOBIOGRAPHY

1988 *Elia Kazan: A Life*. New York: Alfred A. Knopf.

ACKNOWLEDGMENTS

Editing *The Selected Letters of Elia Kazan* would not have been possible without the permission and support of Frances Kazan, widow of Elia and executor of the estate. A talented novelist in her own right, Mrs. Kazan knew the importance of "letters" in further elucidating her husband's distinguished career. Her timely support in the early stages of the project is especially appreciated.

Katherine Hourigan, managing editor of Alfred A. Knopf, played a vital role in guiding the project from inception to publication. Her persistence and editorial skill are greatly valued—as is the assistance of general counsel Anke Steinecke, and the talents of Kevin Bourke, Iris Weinstein, Roméo Enriquez, Carol Devine Carson, and Sean Picone.

Exchanges with Judy Kazan Morris, Katharine Kazan, and Nick Kazan, children from Elia's marriage to Molly Day Thacher, saved the editor many factual errors and added a friendly note to research. Judy and Katie, avid collectors like their father, contributed important letters and photographs for which the editor is grateful.

Andrea McCarty, curator of Wesleyan University Cinema Archives, joined the Film Studies Department in 2012 and graciously welcomed the editor in a subsequent visit to the campus. Joan Miller, head archivist, has organized the vast Kazan collection held by Wesleyan with skill and unusual perseverance. Her knowledge of the holdings and readiness to answer questions with attention to detail and nuance helped to make the project feasible. She is the proverbial gem.

The Research Council of the University of Missouri gave generous support in the form of research leaves enhanced by funding for travel to collections, research assistants, and manuscript preparation. Patricia Okker, former chairperson of the English Department, and Michael J. O'Brien, dean of the College of Arts and Science, were especially understanding during the later stages of the project.

Once basic legal and procedural issues have been settled, the work of a correspondence editor turns to collection. No one could be more fortunate than to have such a talented colleague as Rachel Harper. She designed and executed a far-ranging search for Kazan letters and other pertinent documents that set the project on a solid foundation. The Ellis Library staff at the University of Missouri gave invaluable help throughout. Delores Fisher found obscure material through Interlibrary Loan, while Anne Barker, liaison librarian for the humanities faculty, tutored the editor in searching databases and retrieving information that he would not have found otherwise. Her support went beyond any reasonable expectation and is greatly appreciated. Louise Allen, Alison Gabel, Amanda Hoffman, Christine Horsford, Katherine Kerans, and Stefanie Wortman proved valuable research assistants and colleagues. Mikayla Hahn Dimov transcribed the letters with astonishing speed, accuracy, and infectious enthusiasm. She kept the project on schedule and is also a gem.

A rich scholarly and critical literature has confirmed the collaborative nature of research and equipped the editor to annotate Kazan's correspondence: Jackson Benson (John Steinbeck), Christopher Bigsby (Arthur Miller), Margaret Brenman-Gibson (Clifford Odets), Michel Ciment (Kazan), Robert Collins (American history), Robert Cornfield (Kazan), William Demastes (Clifford Odets), Thomas Doherty (Joseph

Breen and the PCA), Scott Donaldson (Archibald MacLeish), Anne Edwards (Vivien Leigh), Scott Eyman (John Ford), Natasha Fraser-Cavassoni (Sam Spiegel), David Garfield (Actors Studio), Arthur and Barbara Gelb (Eugene O'Neill), Drewey Wayne Gunn (Tennessee Williams), Gilbert Harrison (Thornton Wilder), Mary Henderson (Jo Mielziner), Sarah Johns (Tennessee Williams), David Leeming (James Baldwin), Lyle Leverich (Tennessee Williams), Manning Marable (Malcolm X), Lloyd Michaels (Kazan), Brian Neve (Kazan), Penelope Niven (Thornton Wilder), Thomas Pauly (Kazan), Frank Rich and Lisa Aronson (Boris Aronson), Richard Schickel (Kazan), Wendy Smith (Group Theatre), Margaret Thornton (Tennessee Williams), Mark Vieira (Irving Thalberg), Ralph Voss (William Inge), Frank Walsh (film censorship), and Edgar Young (Lincoln Center). The only indispensable source was Elia Kazan's autobiography—*A Life* (1988).

Librarians and other research specialists replied to editorial queries and photocopied documents with unfailing promptness. John Mead of Lovett Memorial Library, Pampa, Texas, exemplifies their generosity. He searched obscure newspaper files to document Kazan's foray to the Texas Panhandle in the late 1930s and clarified the dating of an important letter.

Curators and archivists associated with research institutions formed the backbone of the project. Haden Guest, former curator and acting director of the Warner Bros. collection at the University of Southern California, kindly invited the editor to lunch and taught him to turn delicate manuscript pages with an ivory paddle. He opened the large collection for efficient analysis and made an indispensable contribution to the project. He currently directs the Harvard Film Archive. Additional West Coast research at the Doheny Library, University of Southern California, the Young Research Library, UCLA, and the Margaret Herrick Library revealed correspondence and documents pertinent to Kazan's association with Warner Bros., Twentieth Century-Fox, and the Production Code Administration. Special thanks are due Ned Comstock (USC), Julie Graham and Peggy Alexander (UCLA), and Barbara Hall and Peggy Romero (Herrick).

The identification and copying of correspondence was facilitated by special collections personnel at Boston University (Ryan Hendrickson), Dartmouth College (Sarah Hartwell and Ilana Grallert), Harry Ransom Center, University of Texas at Austin (Patrice Fox, Elizabeth Garver, Richard Oram, Steve Wilson, and Richard Workman), Harvard University (Mike Mellor), Indiana University (Becky Cape), Kent State University (Craig Simpson), Library of Congress (Barbara Moore), Morgan Library & Museum (Leslie Fields), New York University (Gail Malmgreen), Stanford University (Ronald Bulatoff), State Historical Society of Wisconsin (Harry Miller), University of Houston (Amelia Abreu), Williams College (James Kolesar), and Yale University (Christine Weideman). Richard Kramer, a most zealous proxy, identified Kazan letters held by Columbia University, New York University, and New York Public Library for the Performing Arts, Lincoln Center. John Nondorf performed the same valuable service at the State Historical Society in Madison, Wisconsin.

For Marlene Devlin the highest praise and thanks are reserved—not for the usual wifely sufferance of a lengthy project or for passive support. Her astute reading of Kazan's correspondence and letter-by-letter criticism of the editor's annotations made her a true collaborator. Whatever readable virtues the collection may possess are evidence of her critical skills and good taste.

KEY TO CITATIONS

Albertson	Chris Albertson, *Bessie*. Stein & Day, 1972.
A Life	Elia Kazan, *Elia Kazan: A Life*. Alfred A. Knopf, 1988.
Anderson	*Dramatist in America: Letters of Maxwell Anderson, 1912–1958*. Ed. Laurence G. Avery. University of North Carolina Press, 1977.
Baer	*Elia Kazan: Interviews*. Ed. William Baer. University Press of Mississippi, 2000.
Baldwin	James Baldwin, *No Name in the Street*. Dial Press, 1972.
Bankhead	Tallulah Bankhead, *Tallulah: My Autobiography*. Harper & Brothers, 1952.
Benson	Jackson J. Benson, *John Steinbeck, Writer*. Penguin Books, 1990.
Bentley	Eric Bentley, *The Dramatic Event: An American Chronicle*. Horizon Press, 1954.
Brando	Marlon Brando (with Robert Lindsey), *Brando: Songs My Mother Taught Me*. Random House, 1994.
Chambers	Whittaker Chambers, *Witness*. Random House, 1952.
Ciment	*Elia Kazan: An American Odyssey*. Ed. Michel Ciment. Bloomsbury Publishing Ltd., 1988.
Clurman	Harold Clurman, *The Fervent Years: The Story of the Group Theatre and the Thirties*. Alfred A. Knopf, 1945.
Crawford	Cheryl Crawford, *One Naked Individual: My Fifty Years in the Theatre*. Bobbs-Merrill, 1977.
Doherty	Thomas Doherty, *Hollywood's Censor: Joseph I. Breen & the Production Code Administration*. Columbia University Press, 2007.
Donaldson	Scott Donaldson (in collaboration with R. H. Winnick), *Archibald MacLeish: An American Life*. Houghton Mifflin, 1992.
Finstad	Suzanne Finstad, *Warren Beatty: A Private Man*. Harmony Books, 2005.
Fisher	James T. Fisher, "John M. Corridan, S.J., and the Battle for the Soul of the Waterfront, 1948–1954." *U.S. Catholic Historian* 16 (1998): 71–87.
Fitzgerald	F. Scott Fitzgerald, *The Last Tycoon*. Ed. Edmund Wilson. Charles Scribner's Sons, 1941.
Fraser-Cavassoni	Natasha Fraser-Cavassoni, *Sam Spiegel*. Simon & Schuster, 2003.
Fromm	Erich Fromm, *Escape from Freedom*. Rinehart & Company, 1941.
Garfield	David Garfield, *The Actors Studio: A Player's Place*. Collier Books, 1984.
Gelb	Arthur and Barbara Gelb, *O'Neill: Life with Monte Cristo*. Applause Books, 2000.
Gray	Paul Gray, "Stanislavsky and America: A Critical Chronology." *Tulane Drama Review* 9 (1964): 21–60.
Hellman	Lillian Hellman, *Scoundrel Time*. Little, Brown, 1976.

Hook	Sidney Hook, *Out of Step: An Unquiet Life in the 20th Century*. Harper & Row, 1987.
Isherwood	*Christopher Isherwood Diaries*, vol. 1, 1939–1960. Ed. Katherine Bucknell. HarperCollins, 1996.
Johns	Sarah Boyd Johns, "Williams' Journey to Streetcar." University Microfilms International, 1980.
Kolin	Philip C. Kolin, "The First Critical Assessments of *A Streetcar Named Desire.*" *Journal of Dramatic Theory and Criticism* 2 (1991): 45–67.
Kirstein	Lincoln Kirstein, "Lincoln Shelter." *New York Review of Books*, April 13, 1981.
Leeming	David Leeming, *James Baldwin: A Biography*. Alfred A. Knopf, 1994.
Lewis	Robert Lewis, *Slings and Arrows: Theater in My Life*. Stein & Day, 1984.
Martin	Olga J. Martin, *Hollywood's Movie Commandments*. Arno Press, 1970.
Mielziner	Jo Mielziner, *Designing for the Theatre: A Memoir and a Portfolio*. Atheneum, 1965.
Miller	Arthur Miller, *Timebends: A Life*. Grove Press, 1987.
Navasky	Victor S. Navasky, *Naming Names*. Viking Press, 1980.
Neve	Brian Neve, *Elia Kazan: The Cinema of an American Outsider*. I. B. Tauris, 2009.
Niven	Penelope Niven, *Thornton Wilder: A Life*. HarperCollins, 2012.
Odets	*The Time Is Ripe: The 1940 Journal of Clifford Odets*. Grove Press, 1988.
On Directing	Elia Kazan, *Kazan on Directing*. Ed. Robert Cornfield. Alfred A. Knopf, 2009.
Pelkonen	*Eero Saarinen: Shaping the Future*. Eds. Eeva-Liisa Pelkonen and Donald Albrecht. Yale University Press, 2006.
Raymond	Allen Raymond, *Waterfront Priest*. Henry Holt and Company, 1955.
Rich	Frank Rich (with Lisa Aronson), *The Theatre Art of Boris Aronson*. Alfred A. Knopf, 1987.
Rose	Frank Rose, *The Agency: The William Morris Agency and the Hidden History of Show Business*. HarperCollins, 1995.
Saint-Denis	Michel Saint-Denis, *Theatre: The Rediscovery of Style*. Theatre Arts Books, 1960.
Schulberg	Budd Schulberg, *On the Waterfront: A Screenplay by Budd Schulberg*. Southern Illinois University Press, 1980.
Selznick	Irene M. Selznick, *A Private View*. Alfred A. Knopf, 1983.
Singer	Arthur J. Singer, *Arthur Godfrey: The Adventures of an American Broadcaster*. McFarland & Company, 2000.
Smith	Wendy Smith, *Real Life Drama: The Group Theatre and America, 1931–1940*. Alfred A. Knopf, 1990.
"Staging a Play"	Elia Kazan, et al., "The Staging of a Play." *Esquire*, May 1959.

Steinbeck/ Journal	*Journal of a Novel: The East of Eden Letters of John Steinbeck.* Viking Press, 1969.
Steinbeck/ Letters	*Steinbeck: A Life in Letters.* Ed. Elaine Steinbeck and Robert Wallsten. Viking Press, 1975.
Strasberg	*Strasberg at the Actors Studio: Tape-Recorded Sessions.* Ed. Robert H. Hethmon. Theatre Communications Group, 1965.
Vieira	Mark A. Vieira, *Irving Thalberg: Boy Wonder to Producer Prince.* University of California Press, 2010.
Walsh	Frank Walsh, *Sin and Censorship: The Catholic Church and the Motion Picture Industry.* Yale University Press, 1996.
West	E. J. West, "G.B.S. and the Rival Queens: Duse and Bernhardt." *Quarterly Journal of Speech* 43 (1957): 365–73.
Wilder	*The Journals of Thornton Wilder, 1939–1961.* Ed. Donald C. Gallup. Yale University Press, 1985.
Williams/ Conversations	Tennessee Williams, *Conversations with Tennessee Williams.* Ed. Albert J. Devlin. University Press of Mississippi, 1985.
Williams/ Memoirs	Tennessee Williams, *Memoirs.* Doubleday & Company, 1975.
Williams/ Notebooks	*Notebooks: Tennessee Williams.* Ed. Margaret Bradham Thornton. Yale University Press, 2006.
Young	Edgar B. Young, *Lincoln Center: The Building of an Institution.* New York University Press, 1980.
Zanuck	*Memo from Darryl F. Zanuck: The Golden Years at Twentieth Century-Fox.* Ed. Rudy Behlmer. Grove Press, 1993.

KEY TO COLLECTIONS

Beinecke — Beinecke Rare Book and Manuscript Library, Yale University

Brenman-Gibson — Margaret Brenman-Gibson, *Clifford Odets: American Playwright*. Atheneum, 1981.

BRTC — Billy Rose Theatre Collection, New York Public Library for the Performing Arts, Lincoln Center

BU — Howard Gotlieb Archival Research Center, Boston University

Columbia — Rare Book and Manuscript Library, Columbia University

Dartmouth — Rauner Special Collections Library, Dartmouth College

Harvard — Houghton Library, Harvard University

Herrick — Margaret Herrick Library, Center for Motion Picture Study, Academy of Motion Picture Arts and Sciences, Beverly Hills, California

Hoover — Hoover Institution Archives, Stanford University Libraries

Houston — Special Collections, University of Houston Libraries

HRC — Harry Ransom Center, University of Texas at Austin

HTC — Harvard Theatre Collection, Houghton Library, Harvard University

Huntington — Department of Manuscripts, Huntington Library, San Marino, California

Indiana — Lilly Library, Indiana University

JKMP — Judy Kazan Morris Papers

Kent State — Department of Special Collections and Archives, Kent State University

KKP — Katharine Kazan Papers

Library of Congress — Manuscript Division, Library of Congress, Washington, D.C.

NYPL — Manuscripts and Archives Division, New York Public Library

NYU — Bobst Library, New York University Libraries

Pierpont Morgan — Pierpont Morgan Library and Museum, New York

UCLA — Arts Library Special Collections, Young Research Library, University of California, Los Angeles

USC — Cinema-Television Library, Doheny Memorial Library, University of Southern California

WB Archives — Warner Bros. Archives, University of Southern California

Wesleyan — Wesleyan University Cinema Archives, Middletown, Connecticut

WHS — State Historical Society of Wisconsin, Madison

Yale Music Library — Yale Music Library, Yale University

INDEX

Page numbers in *italics* refer to illustrations.

Hall, Peter, 433
Hammerstein, Oscar, 261
Hanley, Tommy, 244
Harlem Globetrotters, The (film), 542
Harris, Jed, 57, 70, 290
Harris, Julie, 117, 125, 254, 259, 260, 263, 266, 267, 324, 416, 420
Harris, Leonard Barron, **letter to,** 4–5
Harrity, Richard, 68–9
Hart, Kitty Carlisle, 270–1
Hart, Moss, 115, 205, 456, 459; **letter to,** 270–2
Harvey, Laurence, 439
Hatfield, Hurd, 116
Hatful of Rain, A (Gazzo), 302, 327
Hayes, George "Gabby," 48
Hayes, Helen, ix
Hayward, Leland, 225, 230
Hearst, William, 223
Heimat (Sudermann), 377
Heindorf, Ray, 264, 265
Hekimoglou, Meserref, **letter to,** 473–5
Helburn, Teresa, 6, 72; **letters to,** 76–7, 82–3, 88–9, 100–2
Hellas (Gage), 605
Hellman, Lillian, 74, 89, 197, 328–9, 445, 593
Henning, Pat, 251
Henry Miller Theatre, 538–9
Henry VIII, King of England, 461
Hepburn, Katharine, 104
"Herakles," 531–2
Heresy, Yes—Conspiracy, No! (Hook), 183, 336
Hersey, John, 410
Hewes, Henry, 423, 426
Hill, George Roy, 426
Hill, Gladys, 530
Hingle, Pat, 380, 398, 453, 504
Hiss, Alger, 197
Hitler, Adolf, 37, 601
Hobson, Laura, 180
Hoffa, Jimmy, 489
Hoffman, Dustin, 572
Hoffman, Ted, 468
Holden, Bill, 268
Home Free (*The Visitors*; film), 561, 562
Hook, Sidney, **letter to,** 183
"Hook, The," 161, 221–2
Hostage, The (Behan), 435, 436
Hourigan, Katherine, 610

House Committee on Un-American Activities, vii, ix, 123, 173, 174, 176, 188–9, 197, 240, 253–4, 328–9, 563, 565, 608–11; **letter to,** 181–2
Houseman, John, 81, 82, 116
House of Atreus, see Oresteia
House of Connelly, The (Green), 7, 32
Huie, William Bradford, 314, 343; **letter to,** 316–17
Hunter, Kim, 154, 170, *171*
Huston, John, 128, 129, 138, 232, 530, 546
Hyams, Joe, 450, 452
Hyde, Johnny, 566
Hyder, Bob, 9
Hyder, Margery, 9

I Am a Camera (Van Druten), 260
Iceman Cometh, The (O'Neill), 335
Idiot's Delight (Sherwood), 184
Inge, William, 225, 363, 381, 422, 433, 435, 442, 445, 455, 476, 587; **letters to,** 364–6, 470–1, 498–501, 504–5
International Photographers, Local 644, Executive Board, **letter to,** 333–4
In the Summer House (Bowles), 253, 254
Irving, Jules, 532
Isherwood, Christopher, **letter to,** 299
Island in the Sun (film), 357
Isles, Alexandra, 594
Ives, Burl, 300, 302, 309, 312

Jacobowsky and the Colonel, 76–9, 83, 89
Jacobs, Moe, 81
J.B., x, 377–80, 383–6, *386*, 392–4, 396–9, 403, 425, 480
Jerome, V. J., 184
Johnny Belinda (film), 151
Johnny Johnson (Green and Weill), 36, 510–12
Johnson, Edwin C., 165, 166
Johnson, Malcolm, 189
Johnston, Johnny, 482, 483
Jones, Harmon, 325
Jones, James, 258, 502
Jones, James Earl, 550
Jones, Jennifer, 251
Jones, Margo, 113, 133
Joyce, James, 6
Judgment at Nuremburg (film), 453
Juilliard Foundation, 407

Stalin, Joseph, 601
Stanislavsky Method, xiii, 7, 42–3, 117, 350, 437, 438
Stapleton, Maureen, 117, 330, 351
Star is Born, A (film), 263–4, 271, 272
Steele, Wilbur Daniel, 66, 68
Steffens, Lincoln, 205, 207
Steiger, Rod, 254
Stein, Julie, 296, 383
Stein, Sol, **letters to,** 528, 569–70
Steinbeck, Elaine, 232, 258, 295, 308, 530, 533
Steinbeck, John, xi, 15, 52–4, 61, 120–1, 122, 123, 147–8, 177–8, 179, 183, 191, 225, 232, 261, 263, 268–9, 295, 494–6, 533; **letters to,** 214–16, 226–8, 228–30, 258–60, 305–8, 426–7,
Steiner, Ralph, 11, 74, *117*
Stevens, Ann, 90
Stevens, Loretto, 82, 90, 91
Stevens, Molly, 90
Stevens, Nancy, 90
Stevens, Roger, 295, 444
Stevens, Susan, 90, 91
Stevenson, Adlai, 205
Stoddard, Eunice, 9, 31
Stoddard, Julian, 9
Stone, Carol, 116
Story on Page One, The (film), 399
Stradling, Harry, 192, 203, 333–4, 419
Strange Interlude (O'Neill), 504
Strasberg, Lee, viii, 6, 7, *11*, 31, 34, 40, 42, 57, 59, 66, 68, 73, 103, 104, 116, 190, 325, 358, 430, 605, 608; **letters to,** 11–15, 28–29, 133–5, 321–4, 334–5, 449–52, 467–70, 475–8
on Lincoln Square project, 336, 347, 348, 367, 368, 411, 412, 431–2, 433, 449–52, 467–70, 475–7, 501
Strasberg, Paula, 449, 452, 467
Streetcar Named Desire, A (film), 129–30, 135–6, 137, 145, 148–53, 155, 159–60, 161, 162–3, 167–8, 215, 241, 253, 254, 257, 264–5, 327, 333–4, 391, 426
cuts to, 171, 174
moral complaints about, 164–9, 174–5, 216–17, 356
rape scene in, 137, 149–50, 151, 154–60
rewriting of, 145
score of, 265

Streetcar Named Desire, A (Williams), viii, xi, xiii, 105, 107–9, *108*, 112, 117–20, 131, 132, 145, 281, 297–8, 346, 430, 444
Kazan's alleged co-authorship of, 287–90, 303
Strings, My Lord, Are False, The (Carroll), 68
Strong, Michael, 597
Success Story (Lawson), 10
Suddenly, Last Summer (Williams), 401, 553
Summer and Smoke (Williams), 133, 298, 400
Sundown Beach (Breuer), 124–5, 132, 153–4, 260
Sweet Birth of Youth (Williams), 133, 371–4, 380–3, 387–91, 400, 401, *404*, 423, 424–5, 426, 438
opening of, 402–6
Sweet Smell of Success (film), 359
Sweet Thursday (Steinbeck), 261
Swicord, Robin, 602
Swimmer, The (film), 540
Sykes, Gerald, 6, 8, 9
Symphony (March), 70

Tamiris, Helen, 8
Tandy, Jessica, ix, 113, 137, 536; **letters to,** 586–7, 597–8
Taubman, Howard, 462, 532
Taylor, Elizabeth, 439, 441
Taylor, Laurette, 588
Tea and Sympathy (Anderson), 231, 364
Teahouse of the August Moon (film), 310, 312
Tell Me How Long the Train's Been Gone (Baldwin), 543
Ten Commandments, The (film), 357
Tennessee Valley Authority, 316–17, 342, 369, 409
Tesich, Steve, 605
Thacher, Alfred B., 253
Thacher, Molly Day, *see* Kazan, Molly Day Thacher
Thacher, Mrs. Alfred B., 251, 253
Thalberg, Irving, 572, 573, 577
"Thanksgiving, 1963," 512–14
Theatre Guild, 6, 22, 89, 101, 102, 106–7, 120, 123, 335
Theatre of Action, 22

Elia Kazan was born in 1909 in Istanbul. He graduated from Williams College and attended the Yale School of Drama before joining the Group Theatre. He was the founder of the Actors Studio, and he won three Tony Awards for direction (for *All My Sons, Death of a Salesman,* and *J.B.*) and two Academy Awards (for *Gentleman's Agreement* and *On the Waterfront*), as well as an honorary Oscar in 1999 for lifetime achievement. He was the author of seven novels and a landmark autobiography. He died in September 2003.

Albert J. Devlin, professor emeritus of English at the University of Missouri, has written and edited books on Eudora Welty and Tennessee Williams. He received a senior fellowship from the National Endowment for the Humanities for editorial work on volume 1 of *The Selected Letters of Tennessee Williams,* which the Modern Language Association recognized as a "model edition" of letters and on which it bestowed its annual Cohen Award.

Marlene J. Devlin graduated from the University of Kansas. She taught at the University of Missouri and Columbia Public Schools.